Fundamentals
of Money, Banking,
and Financial Institutions

Fundamentals of Money, Banking, and Financial Institutions

JONAS PRAGER
New York University

HARPER & ROW, PUBLISHERS, New York
Cambridge, Philadelphia, San Francisco,
London, Mexico City, São Paulo, Sydney

1817

Sponsoring Editor: *John Greenman*
Project Editor: *Jo-Ann Goldfarb*
Designer: *Frances Torbert Tilley*
Senior Production Manager: *Kewal K. Sharma*
Production Assistant: *Jacqui Brownstein*
Compositor: *Black Dot, Inc.*
Printer and Binder: *R. R. Donnelley & Sons Company*
Art Studio: *Fine Line Illustrations*

Fundamentals of Money, Banking, and Financial Institutions

Library of Congress Cataloging in Publication Data
Prager, Jonas.
  Fundamentals of money, banking, and financial institutions.
  Includes index.
  1. Money. 2. Banks and banking. 3. Financial institutions. I. Title.
HG221.P9195   332.1   82-887
ᵀSBN 0-06-045253-6   AACR2

TO HELEN

She opens her mouth with wisdom,
And the teaching of kindness is on her tongue.

PROVERBS 31:26

Jonas Prager is currently Associate Professor of Economics at New York University, where he regularly teaches money and banking courses at both the undergraduate and graduate levels. Professor Prager received his Ph.D. from Columbia University and served as Director of Graduate Studies in the Economics Department of New York University from 1977 to 1981. He has been the recipient of a Fulbright-Hays Faculty Fellowship and an American Philosophical Society grant, and has written a number of articles on monetary economics and Middle Eastern affairs for such scholarly journals as the *Journal of Finance* and the *Quarterly Banking Review* and such popular publications as *The Wall Street Journal* and *The New York Times*. Professor Prager edited *Monetary Economics: Controversies in Theory and Policy* (1971). In addition, he has served as a consultant for government and private industry.

CONTENTS

"You a regular doctor? Reason I ask, I got a nephew that's a doctor, but he isn't worth a damn if you got a bellyache, because he's a doctor of economics." He laughed heavily. *"And he ain't much good on the stock market either."*

Character in a Harry Kemelman mystery

These days economists suffer doubly. Not only do they feel agony when faced with the economic illiteracy of the general public, but they grind their teeth as people continually misunderstand their role. The character just quoted is not a fictional being to the economist. He is all too real.

These remarks have greater cogency for those who specialize in monetary economics. Its very popularity in an age of inflation means that more people are interested in economics. They follow the economic news in the daily papers and weekly magazines, and on the ubiquitous tube. But while they are exposed to a constant flow of information, most people lack the background to understand what's happening. They experience economic upset, but do not have either a historical awareness or a conceptual framework to relate it to current events. They often end up with half-baked notions and simplistic formulations with which they torture their economist friends.

I do not mean to castigate the American public, but like common sense, economic literacy is not common. Students in a money and banking course have the opportunity to break out of this pattern, to develop a sense of history and methods of analysis that will place the present in its proper perspective. A textbook should serve as a guide that, along with the professor's direction, should both broaden and deepen the student's comprehension of the financial system and monetary policy.

This book is a traditional money and banking textbook. Its claim to uniqueness lies in its being designed for an audience that has heretofore been neglected. Most of the students enrolled in a typical money and banking course will not become professional economists. Indeed, the largest percentage will not continue the study of economics beyond the college level. Their need is not for technical detail but for a more general appreciation of the role of money and the financial system in the overall economy. The institutional environment in which the system functions, the historical background that provides the foundation for our present financial structure, the theoretical explanation of the working of the entire monetary system, and the issues that remain to be resolved all deserve a hearing. But inundating students with a wealth of detail serves only to impress them with the erudition of the author. Few students will retain a lasting impression of a detailed money and banking course; not only will the chaff be lost, but so will the kernel.

Quality material can be transmitted to the student even if the amount of detail is reduced. Basic concepts deserve—and in this book receive—elaboration; technical details can be—and are—relegated to appendixes. For example, students must master the concept of the money multiplier, for without it they will fail to comprehend not only how the modern banking system can create deposits but also how the monetary authorities control the supply of money. Nevertheless, the formulation of complex multiplier fractions can safely be placed in an appendix. Most instructors will feel amply rewarded if their students clearly comprehend the basic concepts.

Two exceptions to the policy just set forth must be noted. First, a chapter on the national income accounts is included in this book. While many students will have already been exposed to these terms and their uses, all too often this material has been forgotten by the time they study money and banking (an example of the lasting effect of forcing students to memorize detail in elementary courses). *GNP, disposable personal income,* and *saving* are terms that need to be deeply ingrained in students of macroeconomics, so they are repeated here.

Second, a chapter is devoted to IS–LM analysis because of the popularity of this topic among teachers of money and banking. To facilitate learning, IS–LM is explained through arithmetic as well as geometric examples. Rest assured, however, that continuity is not lost, nor will any other chapter be less meaningful if Chapter 18 is omitted.

A word about the order of the chapters. Instructors who prefer to teach deposit creation in the introductory section can move Chapter 10 forward. And while the quantity theory of money is presented in Chapter 14 and monetarism in Chapter 20 (the reason being that monetarism is the intellectual offspring of Keynesian analysis and can best be understood after having mastered traditional macroeconomic theory), one can easily shift the section on quantity theory in Chapter 10 to the beginning of Chapter 20.

While students' calls for "relevance" in their courses have receded, the quest for relevance can be seen in their choices of majors, courses, and instructors. Economics, especially money and finance, has benefited from the more practical orientation of today's students. Any student with some awareness must be convinced of the importance of a course of this nature. In order to maintain student interest, this book stresses the recent past more than most, for without the appropriate background, today's events dangle helplessly in a void. Yet, because students comprehend events that occur in their lifetime more readily than events in what they view as the distant past, the present is the primary focus of this book. This is one reason that government regulation of banking is explored in depth, not only in the two chapters devoted to it but throughout. The monetary history of the 1970s is treated as more important than that of the 1920s. However, the Great Depression is surveyed in detail because it had such a lasting impact on economic life in general and macroeconomic thought and policy in particular.

A number of study aids are included in this book. Each chapter begins with a list of highlights that notes some of the more important aspects of the chapter. Questions and exercises are provided at the end of each chapter. They are designed to stimulate thought and further activity instead of merely requiring students to repeat the material covered in the chapter. A definition appears in the margin of the page the first time a key term or phrase is used. And each chapter contains a variety of digressions in the belief that a biographical note, cartoon, or sidelight will stimulate students to stay with it. I often advise students suffering from insomnia to take an economics book to bed; it's a guaranteed soporific. The digressions have been added lest this book share a similar fate. Moreover, they introduce an element of humanity and lightness to what might otherwise degenerate into grist for the cram mill.

Many people read part or all of the manuscript or helped in other ways, and I am indebted to all of them. I am grateful to Peter I. Berman, Bank of America; Donald T. Buck, Southern Connecticut State College; John J. Harrington, Seton Hall University; Duane G. Harris, Iowa State University; Richard H. Hoenig, Federal Reserve Bank of New York; Mark L. Ladenson, Michigan State University; Stephen McCafferty, Ohio State University; Robert P. Muir, West Texas State University; Gerald O'Driscoll, New York University; Benedict J. Pedrotti, California State University, Northridge; M. Ray Perryman, Baylor University; Robert S. Rippey, Central Connecticut State College; the late Joachim O. Ronall, Federal Reserve Bank of New York; Geoffrey H. Segebarth, Missouri Western State College; Don Schilling, University of Missouri, Columbia; Charles Siegman, Board of Governors of the Federal Reserve System; Edward Steinberg, U.S. Department of Commerce; M. Dudley Stewart, Jr., Stephen F. Austin State University; Roger C. Trenary, Kansas State University; Bernard Wasow, New York University; and Henry F. Werling, Concordia College. These reviewers deserve a great deal of credit; the book is immeasurably better as a result of their perceptive comments. I would be equally happy to blame them collectively for any remaining deficiencies. But I can't. Responsibility comes with the exercise of discretion. Since the final decision to accept or reject suggestions was mine, so, too, is the ultimate blame mine alone. *Mea culpa.*

I should also express my gratitude to the graduate assistants at New York University who were intimately involved in the research underlying this book: May Ling Wu, Bill Alexander, Debbie Mustell, Maureen Hayes, and Ted Joyce. Students in my money and banking classes were kind enough to comment on the book in its various manuscript stages; their remarks were most encouraging and often provided a needed uplift. John Greenman, the sponsoring editor, was a strong booster from the start, an ever-available adviser, and a source of tactful reminders that kept me on course. The painstaking editorial work and cheery demeanor of Jo-Ann Goldfarb contributed much to the accuracy and consistency of the text. Finally, without my children, whose financial needs provided a motive for completing the book, and my wife, who shouldered more than her share of family responsibilities during its writing, the book would never have been completed. My warm thanks to them all.

Jonas Prager

Fundamentals
of Money, Banking,
and Financial Institutions

PART ONE

INTRODUCTION

One for the Money: An Introduction

Money is not everything. And, everything's not money.

Groucho Marx, comedian (1925)

Money is a matter of functioning four, a medium, a measure, a standard, a store.

Norman Angell, British author (1929)

CONTENTS

The Nature of This Book

The Functions of Money

Money as a Unit of Account
Money as a Medium of Exchange
Money as a Store of Value
Money as a Standard of
   Deferred Payments

Summary

Some Useful Information

CHAPTER HIGHLIGHTS

1. The decade of the 1970s as represented in a series of charts.
2. The two primary and two subsidiary functions of money.
3. The importance of acceptability in establishing and maintaining a medium of exchange.

The period we are living in is an exciting and frustrating one for monetary economists. Even the most lethargic student must be energized by contemporary economic conditions, which affect each of us daily and surely shape our future. The study of money is no longer a desiccated, theoretical pursuit left to the inhabitants of academe. Now it's the real thing; it's where the action is.

Who has remained unaware of or unaffected by the inflationary spiral of the last few years? Who doesn't know what's happened to the price of gold and silver? Even people who are unfamiliar with concepts like the prime rate are worried when a TV news reporter notes that the prime is reaching one historic high after another. You will soon discover that many of today's economic problems are directly related to the contents of the course you are now enrolled in.

To borrow a phrase from Dickens' *Tale of Two Cities*, this is "the best of times" and "the worst of times" for economists. On the one hand, never have so many people—political leaders, heads of industrial and commercial giants, and the general public—turned to economists for an explanation of what's been happening and for advice to protect their interests. On the other, rarely have economists been so unsure of the true explanation for the high rate of inflation, for unacceptable levels of unemployment, for an unstable, frequently weak dollar at home and abroad, and for the unwillingness of the economic system to respond to efforts to control it. True, theories are propounded in abundance; what is missing is a generally accepted one. Thus, along with the strong interest in economic matters comes frustration.

Perhaps some charts will lend perspective to our current chagrin. Figure 1.1 (a–j) presents some general indicators of economic activity in the past decade. Figures 1.1 (a) and 1.1 (b) plot the real gross national product[1] and industrial production, which measures the output of the goods-producing sectors of the economy. Both were clearly rising except for a brief recession in 1974–1975 and an even shorter slowdown in 1980. The unemployment rate in Figure 1.1 (c) shows a wavelike movement,

---

[1]Gross national product is the nation's total production. "Real" indicates that the data have been adjusted for inflation. GNP is discussed more fully in Chapter 15, while adjustments for price changes are dealt with in Chapter 14.

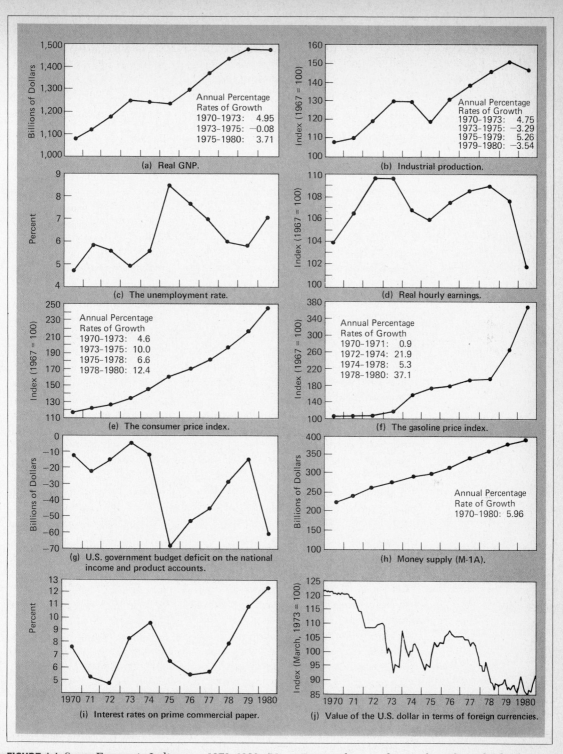

FIGURE 1.1 Some Economic Indicators, 1970–1980. (Note: Dots on lines in figures throughout this book denote annual data. Monthly or quarterly data are depicted without any dots.)

Sources: *Economic Report of the President, 1981*; U.S. Department of Commerce, *Survey of Current Business*; Board of Governors of the Federal Reserve System, *Bulletin*.

fluctuating between 4.9 and 7.1 percent but interrupted by a sharp rise in 1974–1975. In the second half of the decade unemployment was clearly falling until the 1980 recession. In general, these figures suggest the economy was moving forward.

Take a look now at Figure 1.1 (d), which plots hourly earnings in private, nonagricultural industries, adjusted for inflation. Adjusted wages rose until 1972, remained steady in the next year, fell steadily during the recession years of 1974–1975, recovered until 1978, and then fell again in 1979 and 1980. The erratic movement was not due to falling wages; inflation was the culprit as it ate away the fruits of higher earnings.

Figure 1.1 (e) plots the consumer price index, one of the best-known measures of inflation. Prices rose in every year of the decade; only the rate of growth changed. Part of the explanation for this inflation is supply shortages, either natural or contrived. Figure 1.1 (f) charts the price of gasoline. Can you relate the sharp increase in the cost of this source of energy in 1974 to the general inflation that occurred in that year despite the recession?[2]

Supply factors alone cannot explain the spiraling inflation of the 1970s. The role of general spending as reflected by one component, the budgetary deficit of the U.S. government, appears in Figure 1.1 (g). In every year the federal government's demand for goods and services exceeded its income. That the budgetary deficit declined between 1975 and 1980 does not necessarily indicate aggressive utilization of the budget as an antiinflation instrument. To a large extent the numbers reflect inflation's impact—price rises boosted incomes, leading automatically to higher tax payments to the federal government. Inflation redistributed income from the public to the government and added to the consumer's feeling that the sailing was not smooth. Many Americans object to "double taxation," that is, first by inflation and then by the tax collector.

Inflation is a monetary phenomenon, and much of this book deals with how the money supply affects the economy and how the growth of money can be controlled. Figures 1.1 (h) and 1.1 (i) illustrate two monetary elements—the growth of the money supply and interest rate levels. It is evident that the annual rates of money growth have been high; they averaged 6 percent in the 1970s compared to 3.8 percent in the previous decade. Interest rates show a saw-toothed pattern; they reached the first peak in 1974 and the second one shown for 1980. In both years the rate of inflation also reached historic peacetime highs.

The interaction between interest rates and inflation is another of those subjects that are of concern to you beyond your role as a student. Most of us are both borrowers and savers. Can you, as a saver, use high interest

---

[2]The growing concern with supply deficiencies has given rise to what is called supply-side economics, which relegates demand to second-class status. While it is not the intent of this book to ignore the supply element, the focus of the text leans more heavily on the traditional demand side. This is done for two reasons: (1) The demand side *is* important, and (2) the impact of monetary policies is primarily demand oriented.

rates to protect yourself from the erosion of purchasing power by inflation? As a debtor, can you benefit from inflation even if you have to pay substantial finance charges? And what's the relationship between the two? Do high rates of inflation cause high interest rates, or do high interest rates bring in their wake substantial price increases?

Here's another "which came first, the chicken or the egg?" question. The value of the U.S. dollar has been declining relative to that of foreign currencies, as is shown in Figure 1.1 (j). A dollar buys less abroad now than it did at the beginning of the decade. Is the decline a consequence of the high rate of inflation in the United States, or is inflation due, at least in part, to the falling value of the dollar?

As noted earlier, no economist has really answered these questions so authoritatively that all of his or her colleagues will agree. And disagreements in theory lead to conflicting policy recommendations. Not surprisingly, economists find a place to roost in the most conservative camps and in the most liberal—and everywhere along the political spectrum.

□ The Nature of This Book

Obviously, a balanced textbook cannot offer solutions in the absence of a professional consensus. It can, however, point out where consensus does exist and suggest the source of the difference where disagreement prevails. This book, like most money and banking textbooks, explains how the monetary system has evolved (Part One), the role played by banks and other financial institutions in it (Part Two), and the role played by the Federal Reserve System (Part Three). These fundamental chapters focus on basically noncontroversial issues. Here and there questions do arise, but they are tangential to the body of accepted knowledge.

Part Four is the theoretical centerpiece of the book, focusing on the now-traditional theory of John Maynard Keynes and the less familiar quantity theory of money. In this part the conceptual distinctions that underlie policy analysis are developed. Just as two physicians examining the same patient may arrive at different diagnoses and hence prescribe incompatible remedies, so, too, doctors of economics who disagree on the theoretical cause will differ on the cure. In fact, even economists whose diagnoses are similar may advocate contradictory restorative policies. Part Four also analyzes the two major contemporary schools of macroeconomic thought, the neo-Keynesians and the monetarists. Part Five, which deals with monetary goals, policies, and history, is the culmination of the course in money and banking—you've learned about the evolution of the banking system and how the monetary system works in order to understand how the economy is supposed to work. You surely are going to wonder why it's not working better, especially if economists know so much.

Part Six deals with the international sector. The prominence of the U.S.

economy in the total world picture has been eroding; the idea that we can go it alone is much less true today than ever in this century. The economies of the world are linked together in a variety of ways, and our economy, which in the past was a major factor in the well-being of the rest of the world, is now subject to multidimensional influences. (It used to be said that when the United States sneezes, Europe catches pneumonia. Nowadays each can infect the other.) How the United States and the dollar fit into the world picture is discussed in this final part of the book.

By the time the semester is over, you will be better prepared to cope with today's macroeconomic problems. Not only will you be able to make more intelligent decisions as a citizen, but your own financial decisions will be more thoroughly grounded. Of course, this assumes that you master the material. It also helps to start off with a Ph.D.—"Poppa has Dough"!

It surely is appropriate for a money and banking textbook to begin with a discussion of what money is. The functions of money are the subject of the remainder of this chapter; the next chapter deals with the evolution of money and the present situation in the United States.

☐ The Functions of Money

Money is one of those concepts that are known to all and understood by very few. Virtually all income recipients in the United States receive their income in the form of money.[3] Certainly all of us use money to purchase the necessities of life and the luxuries that contribute so much to life's many pleasures. And yet, while we spend a good part of our lives dealing with money, few of us have given much thought to the nature of money. Think about it—you have paid over $15 for this textbook, and in exchange the seller has been satisfied with a couple of pieces of rather unattractive green-and-white paper. Why? What makes a piece of paper worth a textbook? Another question: In recent years, as we all know, the value of the dollar has declined in terms of its power to purchase goods and services. Yet does the general public truly comprehend what makes money change in value?

The number of objects that have served and still are used as money is enormous. Despite what many of us were told as children, money has grown on trees—almonds served as money in India during the sixteenth and seventeenth centuries, and cocoa was used as money in pre-Columbian America. About cocoa money Petrus Martyr, an early observer of the Indians, wrote, "Oh blessed money which not only gives the human race a useful and delightful drink, but also prevents its possessors

---

[3]There are exceptions, of course. Some people receive partial payment in kind: the baker who takes home some bread and cake or the waiter who eats lunch at the restaurant. But these instances are insignificant in the overall picture.

from yielding to infernal avarice, for it cannot be piled up or hoarded for a long time."[4]

Money has been animal, vegetable, and mineral; even slaves served as money in ancient Ireland as well as in Africa. Stones, shells, and precious metals have all played a role in the history of money. Box 1.1 reproduces part of the table of contents of one of the better-known works on early money, Paul Einzig's *Primitive Money*, just to give you a taste of the variety of commodities that have served as money in the past.

The moneys listed here share a number of characteristics. Two of them, the unit-of-account function and the medium-of-exchange function, are essential to the nature of money. The other purposes served by money, alluded to in the second quotation at the beginning of this chapter, are subsidiary ones. They are derived in large measure from the two primary functions.

---

[4]Quoted in D. Taxay, *Money of the American Indians and Other Primitive Currencies of the Americas* (New York: Nummus Press, 1970), p. 47. Taxay notes that avarice did not entirely disappear: Some people substituted dirt for the cocoa kernel to produce a counterfeit cocoa bean.

BOX 1.1 Portion of Table of Contents from Paul Einzig's *Primitive Money*

Part I. Oceania
1. Mat and Bark Cloth Money in Samoa
2. Whales' Teeth Currency of Fiji
3. Other Currencies of the Eastern Pacific
4. The Stone Money of Yap
5. The Bead Currency of Pelew
6. Other Micronesian Currencies
7. Pig Exchanges on the New Hebrides
8. The Feather Money of Santa Cruz
9. Shell Loans on the Banks Islands
10. Shell and Teeth Currencies on the Solomon Islands
11. The Intricate Currency of Rossel Island
12. Debts in Dogs' Teeth on the Admiralty Islands
13. Shell and Yam Currencies of the Trobriand Islands
14. The "Sacred" Money of New Britain
15. New Guinea's Boar Tusk and Shell Currencies

Part II. Asia
16. Rice Standard in the Philippines
17. The Drum Currency of Alor
18. Bronze Guns, Bees' Wax, and Buffaloes as Money in Borneo
19. Other Moneys of the Indonesian Archipelago
20. "Homeric" Currencies in Cambodia
21. Gambling Counters as Money in Siam

(continued)

BOX 1.1 (continued)

22. Tin Ingots and Gold Dust in Malaya
23. Weighed Silver and Lead Currency in Burma
24. Tea Brick Currency in Mongolia
25. Coconut Standard on the Nicobars
26. Grain Medium of Exchange in India
27. Reindeer and Cattle Standard in Asiatic Russia
28. Currencies at the Persian Gulf

Part III. Africa
29. Iron Currency in Sudan
30. Salt Money of Ethiopia
31. Livestock Standard in Kenya
32. Bead Money of Tanzania
33. Cowries as Currency in Uganda
34. Other East African Currencies
35. Calico Currency in Zambia
36. Cloth, Metals, and Slaves as Currency in Equatorial Africa
37. Cowrie Crises in the Former French Sudan
38. Cowries, Slaves, Cloth, and Gin Money of Nigeria
39. Gold Dust Currency of Ghana
40. Other Moneys of the Guinea Bay
41. Debased Brass Rod Currency of the Congo
42. Shell Money of Angola
43. Cattle and Bead Money of South-West Africa
44. Cattle Currency in South Africa

Part IV. America
45. Fur Currency in Alaska
46. Shell, Fur, and Blanket Currency of Canada
47. Wampum and Other Shell Currencies in the United States
48. Cocoa Bean Currency of Mexico
49. Maize Money of Guatemala
50. Cattle Standard in Colombia

Source: Paul Einzig, *Primitive Money in Its Ethnological, Historical, and Economic Aspects* (Elmsford, NY: Pergamon Press, 1976).

Money as a unit of account

Distance is measured in miles or kilometers, weight in pounds or kilograms, volume in cubic yards or meters. How is value measured? The market value of an article, be it a pair of Bill Blass pants or a Kawasaki motor cycle, is essentially a relative value that depends on the quantity of other articles that can be obtained or exchanged for it. A midfield seat at a National Football League game can have the following values: 2 shirts, ½ pair of glasses, 4 hair styling sessions, 6 cartons of cigarettes, 400 telephone calls, ⅕ air coach fare from New York to San Francisco, and so on. Of course, a similar list could be prepared for each item produced and traded in the economy. Running even a small-scale shop and certainly an entire economic system would be difficult, to say the least; innummerable tables of relative values would have to be maintained by each buyer and seller. Would it not be more convenient to single out one specific item and relate all values to that object?

In early colonial times the trading companies that provided the indigenous Indians with goods in exchange for furs set up the beaver pelt as the **unit of account**. A facsimile of a trading list is reproduced in Figure 1.2. The single purpose of the beaver unit of account is to permit all values to be stated in terms of the value of a pelt and thus to make clear their relationships to one another.

When one commodity is chosen to provide the unit against which all other goods, services, and debts are valued, that commodity becomes the **unit of account.**

July 14th. 1703.
Prices of Goods

Supplyed to the
Eastern Indians,

By the several Truckmasters ; and of the Peltry received by the Truckmasters of the said *Indians.*

ONe yard Broad Cloth, *three* Beaver skins, *in season.*
One yard & half Gingerline, *one* Beaver skin, *in season*
One yard Red or Blew Kersey, *two* Beaver skins, *in season*
One yard good Duffels, *one* Beaver skin, *in season.*
One yard & half broad fine Cotton, *one* Beaver skin, *in season*
Two yards of Cotton, *one* Beaver skin, *in season.*
One yard & half of half thicks, *one* Beaver skin, *in season.*
Five Pecks Indian Corn, *one* Beaver skin, *in season*
Five Pecks Indian Meal, *one* Beaver skin, *in season.*
Four Pecks Pease, *one* Beaver skin, *in season.*
Two Pints of Powder, *one* Beaver skin, *in season.*
One Pint of Shot, *one* Beaver skin, *in season.*
Six Fathom of Tobacco, *one* Beaver skin, *in season.*
Forty Biskets, *one* Beaver skin, *in season.*
Ten Pound of Pork, *one* Beaver skin, *in season.*
Six Knives, *one* Beaver skin, *in season.*
Six Combes, *one* Beaver skin, *in season.*
Twenty Scaines Thread, *one* Beaver skin, *in season.*
One Hat, *two* Beaver skins, *in season.*
One Hat with Hatband, *three* Beaver skins, *in season.*
Two Pound of large Kettles, *one* Beaver skin, *in season.*
One Pound & half of small Kettles, *one* Beaver skin, *in season*
One Shirt, *one* Beaver skin, *in season.*
One Shirt with Ruffels, *two* Beaver skins, *in season.*
Two Small Axes, *one* Beaver skin, *in season.*
Two Small Hoes, *one* Beaver skin, *in season.*
Three Dozen middling Hooks, *one* Beaver skin, *in season.*
One Sword Blade, *one & half* Beaver skin, *in season.*

What shall be accounted in Value equal One Beaver in season : Viz.

ONe Otter skin in season, is one Beaver
One Bear skin in season, is one Beaver,
Two Half skins in season, is one Beaver
Four Pappcote skins in season, is one Beaver
Two Foxes in season, is one Beaver.
Two Woodchocks in season, is one Beaver.
Four Martins in season, is one Beaver.
Eight Mincks in season, is one Beaver.
Five Pounds of Feathers, is one Beaver.
Four Raccoones in season, is one Beaver.
Four Seil skins large, is one Beaver.
One Moose Hide, is two Beavers.
One Pound of Castorum, is one Beaver.

FIGURE 1.2 The beaver skin as a unit of account.

The unit of account is simply the measuring rod of value. Over time this measuring rod ceased to be identified with a particular commodity, such as beaver pelts or shells or even gold. In the United States today, as in most countries in the contemporary world, the unit of account has become an abstract, intangible measure. In the United States the unit of account is the dollar; in England it is the pound and in Switzerland it is the franc. But all this means is that economic values are expressed in dollar or pound or franc prices. This evolution surely is no different from that of the foot, which originally represented a physical, actual measure and now, instead of being the average length of the feet of the first sixteen people leaving church, is simply a certain distance in space.

One of the principal functions of money, then, is to serve as this unit of account, this measuring rod of value, permitting all relative values to be expressed in absolute money terms. No longer need we compare football seats to a long list of goods and services. When we say that the seat is worth $40, we've said it all.

Money as a medium of exchange

The function of money as a unit of account is compatible with a barter economy. In a barter system goods and services are traded directly for other goods and services. Trade, of course, will take place only if both parties to the transaction are satisfied with the arrangement. A common unit of account facilitates trades, for if a horse is worth ten strings of beads and a goat is valued at two strings, then it is clear to both parties that a horse is worth, and tradable for, five goats.

It is possible to conduct an efficient barter system. As an economy increases in complexity, however, barter transactions become ever more difficult to accomplish. In a primitive economy the surplus fish hooked by a fisherman could be traded for the surplus meat caught by a hunter. In a highly specialized economy like ours, in which the range of goods produced and consumed is so vast and each worker often contributes only a small share of the final product, barter is the exception, hardly the rule.[5] It would be exceedingly difficult, if not impossible, for a professor to find a group of students who wish to learn about money and banking, and, in exchange, can provide the goods and services desired by the professor.

The problem of finding trading partners is frequently referred to as the absence of a **double coincidence of wants**—one trader must be willing to give up precisely that commodity or service which is desired by the trading partner, while the latter must be similarly inclined. More generally, it might be said that the time spent in finding a trading partner involves an opportunity cost, that is, the cost of the goods and services

A **double coincidence of wants** exists when each trading partner is satisfied with the exchange offered by the other.

---

[5]Trade-ins are an example of barter. So, too, are player trades in professional sports leagues and the exchange of baby-sitting services. One also finds barter in international trade; Egypt has exchanged its cotton for Soviet armaments.

Double coincidence of wants.
Drawing by B. Tobey; © 1975 The New Yorker Magazine, Inc.

that could have been produced in the interim. These **search costs** increase as the economy becomes more complex. Indeed, an economy is not likely to develop to any great extent if time that might have been available for production is devoted instead to searching for trading partners. It is not a coincidence that there is a strong correlation between a nation's level of economic development and the degree of monetization of its economy.

Suppose one commodity—say, cattle—is generally desired by the community's inhabitants. One can imagine a situation evolving in which a party to a trade is willing to take cattle that are equivalent in value to the article given up—say, a sack of corn—even though the recipient of the cattle has no immediate use for them. The latter understands that if he wished to purchase some slaves, he could trade the cattle for slaves. As the realization that cattle can be exchanged for other goods and services spreads, and as more and more people take cows not for their intrinsic value but simply to facilitate trade, in time cattle become the **medium of exchange**.

The medium of exchange (the cows) is money. Now, it is quite plausible for the article used as the unit of account to also be the medium of

Search costs are the expenses, including time and effort, involved in obtaining information.

A **medium of exchange** is any asset that is generally accepted not for its intrinsic value but in order to facilitate further payments.

exchange. Not only are prices expressed in terms of cows or gold, but cows or gold bars actually change hands in the buying and selling process. In fact, like the chicken and the egg, social scientists are not certain which came first, the unit of account or the medium of exchange. But that there is a historical relationship between these two functions seems clear.[6]

The importance of the *general acceptability* of the medium of exchange cannot be stressed sufficiently, for this feature, which depends basically on faith, is clearly the critical characteristic of money. Much of monetary history is concerned with the methods used by governments to instill this quality of general acceptability into government-issued money. The **legal tender** quality of most currency—the fact that, for example, U.S. coinage and paper money are lawful money—represents an attempt to convince people that such money is generally acceptable and, hence, should be accepted by any individual. More important in ensuring acceptability than the words *lawful money*, however, is the fact that normally the government itself will accept legal tender in payment of taxes. Thus, a significant outlet for any paper money that we wish to get rid of is close at hand; we can return the paper to its source and settle our debts to the government with it. At times this feature has not sufficed to make a currency acceptable, and some governments have had to use other means to get their currency accepted: In France after the Revolution the death penalty was decreed for anyone who was unwilling to accept the new national money. We might imagine that the *assignats*, as the paper was called, became generally acceptable in a short time, but they did not.

More surprising, and not well understood, is the natural evolution of some commodities, such as precious metals, as money. No one selected gold to become money, yet somehow it became widely used for that purpose. Similarly, such nongovernmental money as checking account funds, which are only intangible book entries, are money because they are generally accepted. A checking account is money because most people are willing to accept a credit on their checking account in payment for services rendered, goods sold, or debts paid. (Note that it is *not* the check that is money; the check is simply an order to transfer funds out of the payer's account into the payee's account. The funds recorded on the bank's books are the money.) Thus, the U.S. medium of exchange consists of government-issued currency—coins and bills—and privately created checking deposit accounts.

What about gold? Since people generally do not accept gold in payment—you do not walk into a ski shop and purchase a pair of boots with some grains of gold—it is not money in the United States. (See Box 1.2.) This point should be intriguing rather than confusing. It is not the

Legal tender is any item offered (or "tendered") in payment that has been so declared by the law.

---

[6]It should be noted, however, that the two functions can be performed by different items. In early colonial times Spanish dollars circulated as a medium of exchange, but all prices were expressed in English pounds. In certain Latin American countries the U.S. dollar served as the unit of account during periods of severe inflation. Prices were denominated in dollars, but actual payments were made in domestic currency.

BOX 1.2 Gold as Money in the United States

Gold as a Circulating Medium

For most of the nineteenth century, gold was money. Gold coins circulated freely, and even paper money was for the most part at least theoretically redeemable in gold. Of course, the discovery of the yellow metal at Sutter's Mill in California in 1848 led to a sizeable increase in the amount of gold in this country, thereby facilitating its circulation. By the end of the century, despite the lobbying of the silver bloc, gold reigned supreme.

The Gold Standard Act of 1900 recognized in law the situation that existed in fact. The U.S. dollar was defined in terms of gold—23.22 grains of gold nine-tenths fine, to be precise. At that rate, an ounce of gold was worth $20.67. Anyone could purchase gold from or sell it to the Mint at that price (plus a slight service charge).

The glitter disappeared from gold in the years of the Great Depression. Its role as money in the United States has receded ever since, until today gold is not money either domestically or internationally. The initial inroad was made by President Franklin D. Roosevelt in April 1933, when he made it illegal to own gold coins, bullion, or gold certificates (paper money redeemable in gold) except for certain industrial or collecting purposes. The Gold Reserve Act of 1934 made Roosevelt's executive order the law of the land. That law was not reversed until 1976 when it once again became legal for Americans to own gold.

Gold as "Backing"

Under the Federal Reserve Act, issues of Federal Reserve notes were to be backed by a gold reserve of at least 40 percent while the Reserve banks' deposit liabilities were to be backed by at least 35 percent of their value in gold. When gold was recalled in 1934, the Federal Reserve received gold certificates in exchange for the gold it turned over to the Treasury, and those gold certificates provided the backing. In 1945 fears of inadequate flexibility to expand the money supply led Congress to reduce the gold reserve against both deposits and notes to 25 percent. Fears of gold losses to other countries led to further reductions in the gold backing. In 1965 gold was no longer required to back Federal Reserve deposits, and in 1968 it was dropped as a reserve against notes.

Thus, by 1968 the bulk of the money in the hands of the public was not backed by any commodity at all. All Federal Reserve liabilities—notes and deposits—were backed by Federal Reserve assets, primarily Treasury securities. Our paper money is backed by paper promises—government securities—promises that are payable in paper money. A neat circularity!

The International Role of Gold

While gold was barred from circulating domestically in 1933, it still backed the dollar internationally. Foreign treasuries and central banks

(continued)

intrinsic value of an object that determines its "moneyness"; rather, the critical characteristic is its general acceptability in transactions. And of course, what is acceptable in one place and at one time need not be acceptable at another place at the same time or even in the same place at another time.

Money, *then, is the word used to describe the unit of account and the circulating medium of exchange.* These two functions of money give rise to two subsidiary functions: money as a store of value and money as a standard of deferred payments.

Money as a store of value

People accumulate assets for many reasons: for future consumption, for the proverbial rainy day, to leave an inheritance to a group of contented and probably unappreciative heirs, and so on. The types of assets held vary widely, ranging from real estate to consumer durables to securities to cash. Different assets serve different purposes: A Duncan Phyfe antique table not only provides aesthetic pleasure to the collector during her lifetime but may be sold at a profit either while the owner is alive or by her estate. Securities pay dividends or interest, can be sold relatively easily, and may also appreciate in value. But for the value of any of these assets to be realized, they must be converted into money, into the medium of exchange. It is possible, and in fact usual, to hold onto the medium of exchange directly; its one advantage lies in the fact that it need not be converted and thus is immune from capital loss. True, in the United States the medium of exchange for the most part does not pay any interest today, while corporate bonds do. (Demand deposit accounts at commercial banks do not pay interest; checking accounts other than demand accounts do.) But the price of bonds is not guaranteed in terms of money, and a holder who wishes to part with them prior to maturity risks selling at a price that would entail a capital loss. Moreover, even at maturity there is some risk of nonrepayment. Money, however, is money. Consequently, people hold some of their wealth in money form. Money performs its store-of-value function when wealth is held in monetary form.

In an advanced economy, money substitutes are readily available. Numerous **liquid assets** that are riskless can be obtained; savings accounts are just one example. Indeed, now that telephonic transfers of deposits are permissible, you could maintain all your funds in a savings account in the same bank that holds your checking account. Then, when your checks arrive for collection against your account, a single phone call will transfer your savings funds to your checking account.

A **liquid asset** is any asset that is quickly convertible to money at little or no capital loss.

In fact, more and more householders and many corporate financial managers aim at zero demand deposit balances, a result of the high interest rates of the past decade and a half. Since demand deposits yield no return and alternative liquid assets were yielding historically high rates, these other assets were used instead of money to perform the store-of-value function.

For money to act effectively as a store of value, another condition must be met. The holder must be confident that the medium of exchange will maintain its purchasing power over time. If the value of money is expected to decline, however, then assets that maintain their value during periods of inflation become more attractive. Fewer people will wish to hold money, whose value declines during inflationary periods. The demand for money will fall, although it will not disappear entirely; even though money will no longer be desired as a store of value, it will still be used for transaction purposes. Only in severe **hyperinflations,** in which money loses its value at an extremely rapid pace, will the demand for the medium of exchange shrink to the point of disappearance.

The accepted definition of **hyperinflation** is a price increase in excess of 50 percent monthly.

Money as a standard of deferred payments

Not only are current values expressed in money terms as money serves its unit-of-account function, but contracts involving future payments are also denominated in money. The mortgage contract of the typical American homeowner obligates the payer to amortize the loan over a period of time. The homeowner borrowed dollars; the contract requires that dollars be repaid.

Perhaps the use of the monetary unit as a standard of deferred payments can best be understood by considering a case in which a future contract is not denominated in the unit of account. In recent years many countries have sold bonds that are not denominated in their national currency, their unit of account. Since the risks of currency depreciation were high, the risk of market rejection of the bonds was also great. To protect the lenders, the bonds are denominated in more stable currencies like the U.S. dollar, the Swiss franc, or the German mark. The standard of deferred payment, then, is the foreign currency in which the bonds are denominated; for domestic payments, of course, the unit of account is expressed in terms of the domestic currency.

But these are exceptions. Normally, the domestic unit of account serves as the standard of deferred payment. Protection against loss of purchasing power is provided not by switching to another standard but by adjusting the terms of the loan contract. Higher interest rates or linking the principal and interest to some price index are means of protecting the lender without modifying the standard of deferred payment.

The U.S. dollar serves all four of the functions of money. Prices are denominated in dollars, as are all future contracts. The public uses dollars in the form of currency and checking deposits to transact its daily business, and hoards these assets as a store of value. To answer the question raised earlier in this chapter, "Why are vendors willing to accept pieces of paper in exchange for goods and services?" the answer is obvious. As long as those vendors can obtain goods and services by passing on the slips of paper, why should they not accept them? It is certainly more convenient to accept pieces of paper than it is to barter for one's needs, especially since those needs will be met by passing the paper on. General acceptability is the key concept.

While this answer might suffice to explain why any individual is willing to accept paper, it is still unclear why the community as a whole finds paper and, in the case of checking deposits, book entries, acceptable. In trying to answer this broader question, it will be useful to examine the historical development of money, which is the task of Chapter 2.

☐ Summary

The quotation by Marx (Groucho, not Karl) that opens the chapter sums up its contents rather cryptically. A more modern philosopher, W. Allen, has elaborated somewhat on the initial phrase of the quotation. Woody writes,

> Money is not everything, but it is better than having one's health. After all,

one cannot go into a butcher shop and tell the butcher, "Look at my great suntan, and besides I never catch colds," and expect him to hand over any merchandise. . . . Money is better than poverty if only for financial reasons.[7]

When the monetary system functions smoothly, the economy rolls along; when the monetary system malfunctions, with either too little or too much money circulating, the economy is derailed. The 1970s cannot be singled out as one of the more prosperous decades in our history. While the country succumbed neither to a deep and prolonged economic depression nor to a stultifying, runaway inflation, neither did it avoid a sharp recession or an inflation. These circumstances are directly related to monetary actions. One major purpose of this book is to explain how the monetary system operates and why malfunctions generate general macro-economic pathology.

As Groucho declared, "Everything's not money." This introduction has distinguished assets that are money from those that are not by defining money in functional terms. Specifically, any asset that serves the community as a medium of exchange and as a unit of account is money. Dollar bills are money, and so are the balances held by the public in checking accounts, because each is used as a medium of exchange. Prices in the United States are *dollar* prices; the dollar is the unit of account by which the economic value of all goods and services, credits and debts is expressed. The essence of a medium of exchange is its property of *general acceptability*. Only if the public is generally willing to accept an asset in exchange transactions can that asset be considered money. Thus, money need not be government endorsed or a precious metal; checking accounts have neither of these properties. Nor is a government imprimatur or extreme scarcity sufficient to endow an asset with the quality of being money; history is replete with examples of government-sanctioned money that the public refused to accept. And while diamonds may be a girl's best friend, they're not money either.

Two subsidiary functions of money were noted—as a store of value and as a standard of deferred payments. Wealth is often held in money form, and contracts involving future payments are denominated in the unit of account.

In an interesting and oft-cited article written by a British officer concerning his experience in a German prisoner-of-war camp, R. A. Radford relates how cigarettes, which were sent to the prisoners periodically by the Red Cross, became money in the camps. The prices of other commodities and even of services performed by one prisoner for another were expressed in terms of cigarettes, so the cigarette served as the unit of account. Transactions were conducted in cigarettes, so cigarettes served as the medium of exchange. They were hoarded for later use, so they served as a store of value. And although Radford does not mention it,

---

[7]Woody Allen, *Without Feathers* (New York: Warner Books, 1975), p. 109.

we can assume that the cigarette also served as the standard of deferred payment.[8]

Obviously, money serves a highly useful purpose; it *had* to be invented at some stage of social and economic development. Indeed, it is virtually impossible to imagine any modern society functioning without money. The evolution of money is traced in Chapter 2.

☐ Some Useful Information

A serious student of economics needs more than a textbook and a professor. Economics as a field is in continual motion, and its dynamism is clearly evident in the money and banking area. Keeping current is not a luxury, it's a necessity. The following sources have been chosen to help you to stay abreast of the latest developments in the monetary sphere. The listing is far from comprehensive, but it's a start.

1. *Newspapers and general magazines.* So much happens every day that it's a good habit to accustom yourself to read at least one newspaper or magazine that offers comprehensive coverage of economic and financial news. *The Wall Street Journal* and *The New York Times* are among the most distinguished newspapers in terms of economic and especially financial coverage, with interpretations by nationally respected columnists to supplement their wide-ranging news stories. Weeklies like *Business Week* and biweeklies like *Fortune* provide supplementary and often more comprehensive information on a specific topic. (*Business Week*, for example, annually devotes a special feature story to banking.) If you can afford it or can read it at the library, don't neglect England's *The Economist*. This weekly is not limited to Great Britain; its "American Survey" is a journalistic treasure.

2. *Popular periodicals.* The best sources of specialized information in the monetary area, written for the educated public rather than the technically sophisticated, are the publications of the Federal Reserve and the nation's larger banks. That they are available free is an additional bonus; a letter to the appropriate Federal Reserve or bank office requesting that you be placed on its mailing list for a specific publication is all that's necessary. The following are of particular interest:

   Federal Reserve Literature
   a. *Quarterly Review*, published four times a year by the Federal Reserve Bank of New York. This bank prides itself on housing one of the largest research departments in the United States. And because it is located in one of the world's major financial centers,

---

[8]For a fuller account see R. A. Radford, "The Economic Organization of a P.O.W. Camp," *Economica* 12 (November 1945). This article has often been reprinted in books of readings.

the bank has been delegated special responsibilities by the Federal Reserve in both domestic and international operations. As a result, its journal reports on a broad range of topics. The articles tend to be pragmatic rather than ideological.

b. *Business Conditions*, published monthly by the Federal Reserve Bank of Chicago. Features frequent discussions of banking system issues.

c. The *Review* of the Federal Reserve Bank of St. Louis, published monthly. This is the organ of the Fed's ideologues of monetarism, a concept that will become familiar to you if it's not so already.

d. The Federal Reserve *Bulletin*. Contains informative articles, the testimony of Reserve officials before congressional committees, current actions by the Board, summaries of Open Market Committee decisions, and most important, a wealth of data. The articles tend to be somewhat technical and will not always be appreciated by the beginning student. But the data are extensive and provide raw material for anyone who wishes to do empirical work in money and banking. (Extensive international data may be obtained from the monthy *International Financial Statistics*, published by the International Monetary Fund, Washington, D. C.)

e. In addition to general articles on money and banking, the various Federal Reserve banks feature articles dealing with their specific region and its special interests. Thus, the Kansas City bank often publishes pieces on agriculture, the Atlanta bank publishes material on the Caribbean Basin, and the San Francisco bank reports about the Pacific region.

Bank Publications

Most of the larger banks publish monthly bulletins that are available to the public for the asking. The *Survey* of New York's Morgan Guaranty Bank is one of the best-written ones; its occasional "Mouseville" articles are amusing as well as informative. Citibank has taken a monetarist approach, and its monthly bulletins reflect this. Forecasts are a regular feature of Manufacturers Hanover's.

3. *Semitechnical annuals.* Perhaps the best review of the economy over the past year is the *Report* of the President's Council of Economic Advisors, which is issued every January in conjunction with the President's annual *Economic Report.* Some Federal Reserve banks also issue annual publications based on conferences that they sponsor. The Chicago Fed releases *Bank Structure and Competition*, while the Boston Federal Reserve Bank's conference report deals with a different topic each year.

4. *Technical journals.* The growth of the economics profession has led to a plethora of specialist journals in the monetary area that supplement

such general journals as the *American Economic Review*, the *Journal of Political Economy*, and the *Review of Economics and Statistics*. A serious student should be familiar with the *Journal of Money, Credit, and Banking*, the *Brookings Papers on Economic Activity*, the *Journal of Monetary Economics*, the *Journal of Bank Research*, and the *International Monetary Fund Staff Papers*.

A person who reads everything written in the money and banking field will have little time for anything else. The other extreme—reading nothing—leaves one with lots of time but poorly informed. You'll have to find your own happy medium.

☐ Questions and Exercises

1. Some commentators have argued that the American citizen is better off today than he or she ever was. They point to the ever-increasing gross national product as proof of their claim. Do you accept this contention? Explain.
2. Explain Mr. Angell's ditty (to be found at the beginning of the chapter) as to the nature of money.
3. Barter networks have sprung up in various parts of the United States. A carpenter may repair a dentist's furniture and receive in exchange a specified number of points. The carpenter may use these points to acquire goods and services from another member of the barter club, say a painter or a cab driver or even the dentist himself. Can you find a reasonable explanation for the unwillingness to use money, reverting to barter instead?
4. Now that gold may be legally owned and used for transaction purposes, can we anticipate the restoration of gold coin circulation? Why not?
5. Why will the public wish to own less money (as opposed to other assets) when inflation is anticipated?

CHAPTER 2

Cows, Tobacco, Coins, and Green Paper

And Abraham weighed to Ephron . . . four hundred shekels of silver, current money with the merchant.

Genesis 23, 16

CONTENTS

A Short History of Money

Money in the Ancient World
Money in the American Colonies
Money in Eighteenth- and Nineteenth-Century America
U.S. Government-Issued Money Today
A Brief Review
Bank Money
Another Glance Back

A Current Issue: M-1 versus M-2

M-1, M-1A, and M-1B
Near-Money
M-2: An Alternative Definition of Money
M-2: The Federal Reserve Definition
Growth in M-1 and M-2, 1969–1980
The Need for a Definition

Summary

Convenience is a key theme in the development of money. We have already discovered that it is easier to function in an economic system that uses a monetary unit of value than in a system without a monetary unit. Similarly, the difficulties of barter are obviated by a monetary medium of exchange. But what does this medium of exchange consist of? The answer can be provided by the economic historian. This chapter opens with a survey of money in the ancient world, then moves on to the prerevolutionary North American colonies of Great Britain. Monetary evolution in the United States during the eighteenth, nineteenth, and twentieth centuries traces the ascendancy of paper money and, ultimately, checkbook money. As you look back from the vantage point of the 1980s, you will realize how much our monetary system has changed.

The evolution of money continues. The issue of which assets ought to be considered money in the contemporary United States is one that remains controversial. Chapter 2 concludes with a juxtaposition of the two leading contenders for the title of best definition. What must be stressed even in this introduction is the practical importance of this apparently semantic debate. Monetary policy, with its impact on prices and employment, is inextricably linked with the appropriate definition of money. If the monetary authorities track and control the wrong variable, all of us will bear the consequences—inflation or deflation.

☐ A Short History of Money

Money in the ancient world

The development of Chinese knife money is illustrative of the stages of monetary evolution. At the earliest stage, the medium of exchange

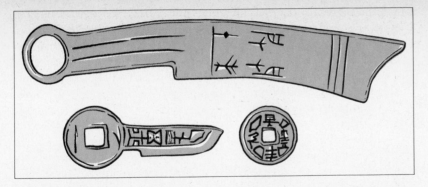

FIGURE 2.1 The evolution of modern Chinese "cash" from early "knife money." The large knife money dates from 1122 to 255 B.C. and the small knife money from 7 to 22 A.D.

Source: Adapted from R. A. Lester, *Monetary Experiments: Early American and Recent Scandinavian* (Princeton: Princeton University Press, 1939), p. 10.

appears to have been actual knives, as shown at the top of Figure 2.1. People sold goods and services and received full-sized, functional knives in exchange. Presumably, those knives were not held primarily for use; after all, how many knives can one person or family use? Instead, they were desired so that the owner could exchange them for other goods and services. As time passed, the Chinese must have come to realize the inconvenience of storing and transfering knives, even though the knives were not particularly bulky or heavy. Moreover, it must be imagined that a substantial amount of real resources—raw materials and labor—was tied up in these knives, which circulated from hand to hand rather than being used for cutting. Why, then, not use a symbolic representation of a knife, one that was shaped like the real article and indeed could be exchanged for a real knife but was smaller? Thus, the representative knife, shown in the lower left hand of Figure 2.1, came into being. At a later stage the same underlying reasons led to the disappearance of the blade and handle, leaving only the end of the handle, that is, the round coin. (The hole in the middle of the coin enabled the owner to pull a string through a series of coins and wear the chain. Similarly, American Indians strung wampum, or hollowed shells, and wore wampum belts.) We are told that coins are circular because "money which is meant to roll around the world should itself be round."[1]

The evolution of precious metals for monetary purposes in the early Mediterranean civilizations must have come about in similar stages. Cattle were both the medium of exchange and the unit of account. But the inconvenience of holding indivisible cattle of heterogeneous quality led to the substitution of symbolic cattle—metal ingots in the shape of a hide. At some early stage the weight and fineness of the precious metal deter-

---

[1] N. Angell, *The Story of Money* (Garden City, N.Y.: Garden City Publishing, 1929), p. 81.

mined the monetary value of the metal; presumably, for a given amount of metal one could acquire a cow or any other commodity. But again, as time passed, the gold and silver proved more convenient to use than the cattle, eventually replacing cattle entirely. Indeed, the major innovation in the development of metallic money was this transformation of the value of the original commodity money into metal.

The next stage appears to be the movement away from assaying and weighing metals at each transaction; each metal bar or coin was marked to assure its purity and weight. In the centuries following the development of the first coins, coinage spread. These early coins were **full-bodied;** their weight and quality was the same as that of the commodity they represented. (A dollar bill is not full-bodied, since the value of the paper and ink is only a fraction of a cent, while the monetary value of the dollar is, of course, a dollar.) The relationship of the early coins to the commodity they represented was not only one of equivalent value. Plutarch refers to Athenian coins bearing the head of an ox, thereby linking the coins to the cattle medium of exchange.

At some point the issuers of the coins—the minting of coins probably began as private enterprise but soon became a government monopoly—realized that the coins were being accepted for their own sake and were not even being examined for quality. The temptation to reduce the coin's precious-metal content, either by substituting a less valuable metal or simply by reducing the weight of the coin, was hard to resist. The full-bodied coin became a **token** coin. Over a period of two and a half centuries, for example, the silver content of the Roman *denarius* fell from approximately 100 percent silver to almost no silver at all. In the end, only a silver surface covered a bronze coin. Similarly, all U.S. coins circulating today are token money.

Money in the American colonies

Early English settlers in North America brought with them their native coins. However, other coins circulated in even greater volume. The paucity of English coins stemmed at least in part from the legislative policy of the mother country. The British government, laboring under the misconceptions of **mercantilism,** banned the export of gold and silver to the colonies. In the absence of gold and silver mines, the colonists were forced to find substitutes. And they did. Strings of wampum served as means of payment, first in colonial New England and later throughout the colonies. Spanish pieces-of-eight, many of which found their way to these shores in the holds of pirate ships, circulated too. (The colonists split the pieces-of-eight into quarters to provide smaller coinage. Each eighth was a "bit," and thus "two bits" became synonymous with a quarter.) The word *dollar* derives from the Spanish dollar, which circulated abundantly prior to the American Revolution. In early Virginia, tobacco served as the medium of exchange. An account of that colony in 1620 describes young

When the monetary value of a medium of exchange equals its commodity value, this money is considered **full-bodied.**

When the purchasing power of a money is greater than its value as a commodity, it is called **token** money.

Mercantilism was an eighteenth-century economic doctrine that preached that a nation's wealth was increased by exporting, so that gold and other precious metals were accumulated by the exporting nation.

Virginians running dockside, "each carrying a bundle of the best tobacco under his arm and taking back with him a beautiful and virtuous wife" who had been imported by the Virginia Company for the woman-starved settlers.[2] The problems of using tobacco money, like the drawbacks of using cattle as money, were numerous: (1) It was difficult to control quality; (2) its value fluctuated with supply: (3) tobacco was expensive to transport; and (4) it deteriorated over time. Let's examine each in turn.

Quality control. The best-quality tobacco was either consumed at home or exported to England, while the worst-quality tobacco circulated as money. The reason was simple.

Because the better-grade tobacco commanded more as a commodity than it did as money, the growers sold it for consumption purposes either in the other colonies or in England. On the other hand, the low-grade tobacco was priced below its monetary value, inducing people to use this poorer-quality tobacco as the medium of exchange. The result was that only poor-quality tobacco circulated as money.

This very natural reaction is a perfect demonstration of **Gresham's law,** named after a sixteenth-century British financier, diplomat, and financial agent of the Crown. (Bad money refers to money that is worth less in alternative uses than as money, like the poor-quality tobacco just mentioned.)

In simple terms, **Gresham's law** proclaims that "bad" money drives "good" money out of circulation.

A similar situation occurred not too many years ago in the United States with respect to silver-backed paper money and coins. The "silver certificates" that circulated differed from our present Federal Reserve notes by offering the holder silver in exchange for the certificate. By the mid-1960s, the market price of silver had risen to a point at which it became profitable to convert the paper certificates into actual silver. So many people did so that the Treasury announced its unwillingness to redeem certificates after June 30, 1968. Not too much later, as the price of silver continued to rise, it became profitable to melt down silver coins, even though it was illegal to do so. The market value of the metal embodied in the coin, which was 90 percent silver, was worth more than the monetary value of the coin. (These token coins became full-bodied.) Thus, this "good" money—the silver certificates and the silver coinage—just about disappeared from circulation. Congress reacted by permitting coinage of the now-prevalent "sandwich" quarters and dimes, which consist of a copper core with a copper-nickel amalgam on the surface. Interestingly enough, the American economy has not suffered from the elimination of silver coinage; no one feels that the sandwich quarters are worth any less than the silver quarters.

Supply-induced fluctuations in value. Tobacco money suffered from another defect: Its value depended on the supply of tobacco, which in

---

[2]R. A. Lester, *Monetary Experiments: Early American and Recent Scandinavian* (Princeton, N.J.: Princeton University Press, 1939), p. 11.

turn depended on its production costs. As long as tobacco's monetary value exceeded its cost of production, an incentive to increase supply was at hand. But as the supply increased, its price fell. Attempts to stabilize the price took various forms—restrictions on who could grow tobacco, destruction of low-quality and some high-quality crops, and even an outright moratorium agreed to in 1666 by Virginia, Maryland, and Carolina, which ceased all production for a year. As the impact of these measures was short-lived, Virginians took the matter into their own hands by uprooting tobacco plants wherever they found them. This destruction reached such proportions that the Virginia Assembly decreed the death penalty for treasonous groups of tobacco destroyers.

Transportation costs. Tobacco was bulky and, hence, expensive to ship. At one time a Virginian who paid his taxes in tobacco at the tax office rather than having it collected at home received an 8 percent discount just for saving the tax collector the cost of haulage.

Deterioration. Finally, tobacco money lost value over time as it rotted. While Petrus Martyr found this a moral virtue in cocoa money, lack of durability certainly is a disadvantage for a money that is to serve as a store of value as well as a circulating medium.

Some means had to be found to retain the virtues of a medium of exchange while minimizing the deficiencies of commodity money. Or, to use contemporary terminology, a method was sought to reduce the costs associated with money while maintaining the benefits. Virginians ultimately introduced **representative** paper **money.** Tobacco was brought to government warehouses, where it was inspected and graded, after which a warehouse receipt was delivered to the owner. This paper, which entitled the holder to a barrel of tobacco of a specified grade, now circulated instead of the tobacco. Since the warehouse receipts were fully backed and fully exchangeable for tobacco, the public was willing to accept the paper. Indeed, the public must have been more willing to use the paper than the tobacco, since it was more convenient in many ways.

Once representative paper money circulates, it is but a short step to the issuing of paper backed by commodities that had not previously served as money. The impetus for issuing paper money in the colonies was the shortage of specie, or "hard" coinage, mentioned earlier. Since money greases the wheels of commerce, the colonies, finding themselves with insufficient grease, improvised. By financing an expedition against the French at the end of the seventeenth century, Massachusetts became the first, but not the last, of the colonies to print paper money. One after another of the colonies solved the shortage of circulating money by issuing paper (see Figure 2.2). Some paper was backed by land, although it is hard to believe that the holders of the money ever felt that they could obtain an equivalent value of land in exchange for the paper money. For example, in 1723 the Pennsylvania Assembly acted to issue paper money

Representative money is money that is fully convertible into full-bodied or token money.

FIGURE 2.2 Facsimile example of Pennsylvania paper money, 1773, (Left: front. Right: back.)

in exchange for mortgages on real estate, which provided the collateral for the notes. The rate of interest charged was 5 percent, and the loans were to be paid off in eight years, so that the issue would self-destruct at the end of the period.

On the other hand, in the early eighteenth century New York issued a series of notes without any real backing. This **fiat money** was to be redeemed from tax revenues over a twenty-year period. Both the New York and Pennsylvania issues—one backed and the other unbacked by any physical substance—proved successful. The money circulated and was generally accepted.

Not all the paper issues of the colonies fared as well. In general, the New England issuers overdid a good thing, which led to a decline in the value of their paper. Massachusetts, which issued notes totaling only £7,000 in 1690, had increased the issue to £160,000 by 1710. By the fourth decade of the century, owing to continual issues of paper money, the purchasing power of each unit of money had declined to one-tenth of its original value. Rhode Island, whose population numbered some 20,000 in 1743, had a paper note issue of £400,000; the value of each unit of money declined almost to zero.

Fiat money is unbacked by and not convertible into any commodity. It circulates on faith alone.

Money in eighteenth- and nineteenth-century America

The note issues of the colonies set the precedent for financing the American Revolution. Since "taxation without representation" loomed so large as a cause of the revolt, and taxation with representation pleased the public little more, the weak Continental Congress was not empowered to impose new taxes; all contributions by the states were voluntary. Unfortunately, voluntarism did not extend very far; of the $66 million that the Treasury took in as income between 1775 and 1783, only $6 million (9%) was derived from taxes. The remainder was financed by loans and mostly by money creation. Supplies for waging the war and payments to the army were made with paper promissory notes (see Figure 2.3). The first issue, in June 1775, was a modest $2 million; just four years later, the note issue amounted to $242 million. One noticeable result of this voluminous issue of "continentals" was a decline in their value, as in the case of the overissued Massachusetts and Rhode Island money mentioned earlier. At the beginning of 1779, for example, a gold dollar could buy eight continental dollars; by the end of the year, it took forty paper dollars to buy a dollar's worth of gold. By the next year, the value of the continental dollar had fallen 100 percent; it now took eighty continental dollars to acquire a gold dollar. As Gresham's law would lead us to expect, gold virtually disappeared. And soon, because of the ever-falling value of the paper, the public became unwilling to accept continentals. This occurred despite the revolutionary fervor of the times and despite severe penalties, such as branding the vendor or creditor who refused to accept paper as a traitor and, in some states, cancellation of the debt if continental currency was refused.

FIGURE 2.3 Facsimile of paper half-dollar.
Courtesy of Chase Manhattan Archives.

While the issuing of paper money could be defended as a necessary adjunct to waging a war, the consequences of overissue taught the framers of the Constitution a lesson. They wrote a document that came down strongly on the side of gold and silver as legal tender— "No state shall . . . make anything but gold and silver coin a tender in payment of debts" [Article I, Section 10(a)]. Indeed, the currency of the new nation was both gold and silver coinage. Paper was not issued.

This planned **bimetallic standard** never really worked, but it set the stage for much of the nation's monetary history and legislation for more than a century thereafter. For a bimetallic standard to operate successfully, the value of the two metals backing, and exchangeable for, the currency must equal their value in the marketplace. Otherwise, Gresham's law operates to drive one or the other of the metals out of circulation. Under the Mint Act of 1792 Congress set the value of a gold eagle ($10) at 247.5 grains of pure gold, while the silver dollar was to contain 371.25 grains of silver. The mint ratio of the two metals thus was set at $1 of gold to $15 of silver. The law permitted free coinage, so that anyone with gold or silver bullion could present it to the Mint and receive an equivalent value in gold or silver coins. While this 15:1 ratio was consistent with the market value of the metals in 1792, those market values soon changed. By 1799 the bullion markets valued one ounce of gold as equivalent to more than 15 ounces of silver, 15.75 ounces to be precise. Silver was overvalued at the Mint. No one would be so foolish as to turn in gold in order to obtain 15 units of silver per unit of gold when the gold could be sold on the market for the equivalent of 15.75 units of silver. The result, of course, was that gold was no longer sold to the Mint and silver coinage flourished. The overvalued silver, in accordance with Gresham's statement, drove gold into other, nonmonetary uses.

Congress reacted with its usual speed. Three decades later, in 1834, a new ratio of 16:1 was substituted for the old one. Unfortunately, the new ratio overvalued gold, an ounce of which was now worth less than 16 ounces of silver in the free market. So, in a reversal of the trend of earlier decades, gold drove silver out of circulation. During the remainder of the nineteenth century numerous attempts were made to reestablish silver coinage. Among the more memorable of these was the passage of the Bland-Allison Act of 1878, which required the Treasury to purchase vast sums of silver for coinage purposes, and the presidential election of 1896, which culminated in a famous declaration by Democratic candidate William Jennings Bryant: "You shall not press down upon the brow of labor this crown of thorns, you shall not crucify mankind upon a cross of gold." (He lost the election despite this noble sentiment.)

Although silver interests agitated and the 1896 election was fought on the basis of gold versus silver, gold remained supreme as the coinage of the United States until 1933. In that year, in the midst of the greatest depression ever experienced by the United States, President Roosevelt took the country off the **gold standard**. Not only would gold

When each of two metals provides the basis for the money in circulation and the issuer stands ready to buy or sell either of the two metals at stated prices, the monetary system is called a **bimetallic standard**.

Under a **gold standard** the monetary unit is defined in terms of a specific quantity and quality of gold and is freely exchanged for it.

coins no longer circulate, but Americans would not even be able to own gold for monetary purposes, a situation that was not reversed until 1976.[3]

For almost all of the time that gold and silver coins circulated, so too did paper money. The Constitution prohibited states from circulating paper money, but it was silent about the right of private bodies, such as banks, or the federal government itself to do so. More will be written about banks in Chapter 4; here it will suffice to note that banks printed paper money from the earliest days of this nation's history. The federal government exercised a truly amazing degree of restraint; it refrained from issuing paper until another major war—the Civil War—and the accompanying and irresistible requirements of military expenditures. In 1861 Lincoln's Treasury consisted of an empty coffer. Early in 1862, to pay for what was expected to be a short war, Congress permitted the Secretary of the Treasury to print $150 million in paper money called United States notes. The notes were legal tender but were not redeemable into gold or silver coins. The initial issue of these "greenbacks," as the paper was quickly dubbed, was followed by a second issue of the same magnitude in July 1862. In March 1863 President Lincoln signed an act authorizing an additional $150 million worth of greenbacks. But this turned out to be the last issue of paper money to finance the Civil War. For as the war progressed and new taxes were imposed—including the first income tax—the need to issue additional greenbacks was curtailed. While in fiscal 1862 United States notes accounted for 20 percent of the federal government's net receipts and in 1863 they accounted for 41 percent, this figure fell drastically, to only 5 percent in 1864. The supply of notes actually decreased in 1865. By the war's end in 1865, $431 million of the authorized $450 million remained in circulation.

Nevertheless, the issue of such a large amount of money in a brief period did have lasting results. The outcome of this rapid expansion in the money supply is not hard to guess: a rapid decline in the value of the greenback and the virtual disappearance of gold and even silver coinage. From a rough parity with gold in early 1862, the value of the greenback fell to less than 60¢ in gold value by early 1863. After a short-lived increase in value in the middle of 1863, it fell further, reaching a low of 35¢ in July 1864.

Of course, Gresham's law came into effect as the value of gold and silver rose above the coins' monetary value. Wesley C. Mitchell, whose *A*

---

[3]The reason for the abolition of gold ownership is rather interesting. One of the plans that were implemented to end the Depression involved raising the level of prices, a plan that was itself of dubious merit. But higher prices would inevitably lead to a gold outflow, for the public would increase its demand for low-priced imports. The gold outflow would decrease the gold-based money supply and, according to the tenets of the quantity theory of money (see Chapter 14), would induce a fall in prices, thus offsetting the initial action. So the link between money and gold had to be severed, and was.

History of the Greenbacks[4] is the leading monograph on this monetary episode, lists the prewar gold coin circulation in 1861 at $245.3 million, of which only $22 million remained in 1862. This $22 million, however, circulated in the Far West, which was relatively immune from the war. Silver coinage shows a similar pattern: From $42.2 million in 1861, the amount of silver in circulation fell to $3.0 million the next year. In other words, in the East and the central United States, gold and silver coins had ceased circulating.

Incidentally, the constitutional right of Congress to declare paper money "legal tender" was not clear; it was the subject of a number of court cases in the post-Civil War period. Only in 1884 did the United States Supreme Court finally resolve the issue: Congress indeed has the prerogative to declare paper money to be legal tender.

Paper money was issued by the federal government in various forms over the postwar decades. The major change that occurred in federally authorized paper money, however, did not come until the formation of the Federal Reserve System in 1913. The Federal Reserve Act essentially set the pattern for the monetary system as it stands today.

U.S. government-issued money today

Today 91 percent of government-issued money is in the form of irredeemable, unbacked Federal Reserve notes. The remainder consists of various forms of U.S. Treasury paper and coin. All coins are liabilities of the Treasury, and some Treasury paper money still circulates today. The obligations of both the Federal Reserve and the Treasury are token money. Neither is worth as much in intrinsic value—metal or paper—as it is in terms of its purchasing power as money. Table 2.1 lists U.S. government-issued money as of December 31, 1980.

Silver and minor coins. The silver dollars that are currently in circulation are included here. "Minor coins" are all other coins. As noted earlier, quarters and dimes no longer contain silver, while nickels are made primarily of and pennies wholly of copper.

TABLE 2.1 U.S. Currency, December 31, 1980 (millions of dollars)

Coins	
Silver and minor	12,418
Treasury paper	
U.S. notes	309
Silver certificates	206
Other[a]	67
Federal Reserve notes	124,239
Total	137,179

[a]This category includes national bank notes and Federal Reserve bank notes (p. 34).

Source: U.S. Treasury, *Bulletin*, April, 1981.

---

[4]Chicago: University of Chicago Press, 1923.

The coin shortage that developed in the last decade remains something of a puzzle. Among the explanations presented are the proliferation of coin-eating vending machines, the rise in coin collection as a hobby, and in the case of pennies, the melting down of the coins as the price of copper rose. Congress has authorized a reduced copper penny, containing only 2.4% copper and 97.6% zinc, to be minted beginning in 1982.

United States notes. These are the greenbacks of Civil War times. They still circulate today; although they were supposed to be removed from public use, Congress decided against further redemption in 1878. Since the total has remained constant, the Treasury simply replaces old, worn-out notes with new ones. They remain an historic relic.

Other. At various times the Treasury has issued paper money for different purposes. Also included here are the notes issued by national banks, a subject that is discussed more fully in Chapter 4. The Treasury took over the banks' liability for these notes in 1935. Finally, three emergency issues of Federal Reserve bank notes complete this category. There is no logical reason for any of these issues to circulate; they could be safely withdrawn from circulation and replaced by Federal Reserve notes and no one—except numismatists—would be aware of the change. However, like so many other issues in the money and banking area, the logical answer is not necessarily the most practical course.

Federal Reserve notes. These are the familiar bills that circulate today. The denominations of these notes run the gamut from the $1 bill to the new $2 bill first printed in 1976 to the largest circulating paper bill, a $10,000 note (see Figure 2.4). (One wonders whether such bills are "money" in the sense in which the term was used in the last chapter. Would such a note be "generally acceptable"? In fact, only 361 of them exist, and they do not circulate.)

FIGURE 2.4 Facsimile of a $10,000 bill.
Courtesy of Chase Manhattan Archives.

A brief review

The vast majority of circulating currency today is fiat money, backed by nothing and convertible only into other fiat money. U.S. coinage is token money that, if it were melted down, would be worth only a fraction of the coins' monetary value. Yet we, the people, have no qualms about accepting this intrinsically valueless money. Why? Have we lost our senses?

The answer appears to lie in the historical evolution traced in the last few pages. Money, as we have seen, originally was a commodity that circulated as a medium of exchange. The coins that first replaced a commodity money were convertible directly into that commodity. Over time, metallic coins seemed to take on a life of their own; they proved useful in transactions and did possess intrinsic value in themselves. As history continued to unfold, the utility of coins as a medium of exchange transcended their intrinsic value. The stage was set for the next development: representative money, nonmetallic money convertible into metal, or token money containing less metal than the full-bodied coin with which it was presumed to be identical. Ultimately, paper money took on the aura associated with metallic money, and because it proved more convenient for large transactions, it became accepted for its own sake. Commodity money simply evolved into paper money over time without conscious design. It could not have been foreseen, and it probably required all the stages in the evolutionary process so that people could adjust to a new type of money at each point along the way.

For those who like to draw lessons from history, the evolution of money from commodity to paper has its moral. A paper-money system can function tolerably well; paper money can maintain its value as long as it is issued in modest amounts. It is cheaper to produce than metals, so it economizes on the resources necessary for the production of money. (This statement must be qualified, however. Can you explain why we use coins for small change, rather than the cheaper paper?) Of course, metallic money can be overissued as well, but nature and economics limit the exploitation of metallic money more than they do that of paper money. There are fewer gold mines than trees! So while it is not necessarily rational to use paper backed by confidence, the system has evolved in that way and most of us are satisfied with it.

Bank money

The system continues to evolve. Remember that the medium of exchange in the United States and most other economies today consists not only of currency but of checking deposits as well. These deposits possess no tangible form, nor are they backed by currency, not to mention precious metals. True, each of us could write a check for "Cash" and receive currency in exchange for our deposit balances. It's not obvious, however, how we'd all be paid—the commercial banks held just over $20 billion in cash at the end of 1980, while they owed the nonbank public $335 billion on checking balances alone.

What are checking deposits? Two types can be distinguished: demand deposits and other checkable deposits. Most significant in terms of their volume are **demand deposit** accounts. (At the end of 1980 they constituted 94 percent of all checking deposits.) Almost all the nation's demand deposits are to be found on the books of commercial banks.

The second category of checking deposits consists of accounts that the bank need not honor legally on demand. In fact, however, the banks have treated these deposits, which go by names like **NOW** (negotiable order of withdrawal) **accounts**, as demand accounts.

In either case, the deposit itself is no more than an entry on a ledger or a computer tape at the bank. It indicates the bank's obligation to the depositor.[5]

The depositor's checkbook records a credit corresponding to the bank's entry. This is the sum owed to the depositor by the bank. Aside from checks written by the depositor and deducted from the checkbook balance but not yet cleared at the bank, the liabilities owed by the bank to the depositor should equal the assets claimed by the depositor from the bank.

Thus, the monetary system has evolved to the point where money has no tangible form, a system based entirely on faith. Credits are transferred by one person or corporation to another by sending orders—checks— through the mail, if not by personal delivery. And of course, the check as a means of transfering funds has substantial advantages over cash: (1) It is safer; (2) a single piece of paper can be tailor-made to the amount required; and (3) when endorsed, the check provides a receipt of payment.

In recent years, however, the amount of paper work associated with the tens of billions of checks has led the banks to search for cheaper means of transfering deposits. Since these deposits are claims on one bank that are being transfered to another bank, and since these claims are, for large numbers of banks, electronic impressions on magnetic computer tape, computer-to-computer transfer has become possible. This eliminates the need for a paper-check intermediary. A number of computer-based schemes to avoid using checks have been experimented with. The Social Security Administration, for example, pays recipients who so desire, not by check, but by delivering a computer tape containing the benefits due each person to the recipient's bank. At the bank the beneficiary is

A **demand deposit** is an account that must be transfered immediately upon the request of the depositor.

A **NOW** (negotiable order of withdrawal) **account** is a savings account against which checks may be written.

---

[5]The check itself is a "negotiable instrument," which means that it is an unconditional order, written and signed by the drawer, ordering some bank to pay the drawee a specific sum at a specific time (i.e., on presentation). Negotiability is a legal quality that protects the holder of an instrument acquired in good faith against legal liability. Thus, if a retailer has accepted a check from Joel Jones that was written by Sharon Smith to Joel, and Sharon later claims that Joel obtained the check from her under fraudulent pretenses, Sharon can sue Joel but has no recourse to the retailer, who accepted her check from Joel in good faith.

credited with the appropriate amount. The recipient can write checks against the account, or withdraw cash, just as if a check had been deposited there physically. The Treasury saves all the costs of writing and shipping a large number of checks, and the banks cut down substantially on their processing costs. Finally, the client does not have to worry about loss or theft of the check.

It is highly unlikely that checks will disappear in the near future. But it is most probable that banks will make increasing use of the cost-saving features of computer technology. Cash machines, which enable the bank's customers to withdraw cash by inserting a magnetic bank card into the machine, are appearing with increasing frequency in major urban centers. They provide bank customers with 24-hour access to cash, and the bank saves processing costs as well as other labor costs.

Despite all this new banking technology, the nature of money has not changed. The "money" is not the card, just as the check itself is not money. The money is the checking account; it is simply being transfered in a new manner.

Another glance back

The human race has come a long way since primitive times. Nowhere is this more evident than in its degree of financial sophistication. Can you imagine yourself trying to explain to the members of a tribe recently discovered in the Amazon rain forest that part of your wealth consists of invisible impressions on a piece of computer tape? One can visualize a ludicrous confrontation between a native, whose total wealth consists of some cattle, a grass hut, and a few utensils and tools, and a modern American who wants to buy some implements and pay by check. She could try to convince the Amazonian that the check is convertible into a large variety of goods and services, but could you blame him for thinking the American is a megalomaniac?

Perhaps we are all megalomanics for thinking our bank accounts represent our individual wealth. But it is comforting to realize that we all share the same syndrome, which is precisely why the system functions as well as it does. The owner of a checking account can make payments anywhere in the world relatively easily and costlessly. A check sent in the mail by an America importer of Danish furniture will be accepted as payment by the Dane. No commodities, no precious metals entailing expensive freight and insurance costs, not to speak of transport time, have to be sent in payment. Certainly it's easier and safer to go on vacation with a sound bank balance and a few checks in your pocket (and some acceptable identification!) than to take along a pile of paper bills, let alone full-bodied coins or commodities. Convenience and reduced costs dictated the evolution of credit money. And, having evolved, it appears well entrenched and not likely to disappear within our lifetime.

□ A Current Issue: M-1 versus M-2

The Federal Reserve provides two alternative definitions of the assets that can be considered to be the medium of exchange in the United States. Both are subsets of M-1. But not all economists accept the medium-of-exchange definition of money. They prefer to include a broader group of assets, M-2. Each of these definitions, and its implications, will be discussed in this part of the chapter.

M-1, M-1A, and M-1B

M-1A consists of currency, demand deposits adjusted, and nonbank traveler's checks.
M-1B equals M-1A plus other checkable deposits.

M-1, the narrow definition of money, comes in two versions, **M-1A** and **M-1B**. Included in M-1A are government-issued paper and coin and the adjusted demand deposits held at commercial banks. The term *adjusted* refers to four exclusions: (1) deposits of government, both the federal government and official foreign institutions, on the ground that the motivations of the owners of these deposits differ radically from those of private individuals and firms; (2) deposits of foreign banks, for the same reason; (3) interbank deposits, because these are held mainly as reserves against private deposits and thus are not independently available for spending; and (4) transit items, whose inclusion would lead to the overstatement of total deposits.[6] Since 1981, with improved reporting procedures, traveler's checks issued by firms other than banks (such as American Express) are also included. No one argues against considering currency, demand deposits and travelers checks as media of exchange.

In the last decade a variety of assets have surfaced that also perform a medium-of-exchange function. Among them are NOW deposits, **ATS accounts, share draft balances in credit unions,** and demand deposits at mutual savings banks (MSBs are discussed in Chapter 11).

An **ATS** (automatic transfer from savings) account is a savings account that permits, on the basis of a preauthorized order, the transfer of funds out of the account into a checking account.
Share draft balances in credit unions are deposit accounts in a type of bank (see Chapter 11) against which checklike drafts can be written.

In the 1970s the desire of thrift institutions (or "thrifts") to offer their customers a greater variety of services led them to introduce a series of new financial instruments. Commercial bankers responded in kind in order to protect themselves against the competitive threat. The bank regulators, and to some extent Congress, rather hesitantly approved these innovations. NOW accounts were opened first in New England in 1972; New York was added in 1978; and with the passage of the Depository Institutions Deregulation and Monetary Control Act of 1980, NOW accounts were permitted throughout the nation. Demand deposit accounts in mutual savings banks were sanctioned in 1976, while ATS accounts and share drafts were first approved in 1978. These regulatory actions were confirmed by Congress in the 1980 Act.

The element that is common to all these accounts is ready availability; depositors can, and do, use them as media of exchange. In recognition of

---

[6]If a $1000 check has been added to the depositor's balance before it has been subtracted from the check drawer's account (and that is frequently the case), the combined records of the two banks would show deposits of $2000 when clearly only $1000 should be recorded.

the growing importance of these new financial instruments, the Federal Reserve has included them in M-1B, its expanded definition of the assets that serve as a medium of exchange. Consequently, M-1 has two components, M-1A and M-1B.[7]

Near-money

In a modern economy liquidity is a property that is shared by a large number of assets. Assets like U.S. government savings bonds are similar to money in that they are easily and risklessly convertible into the medium of exchange. The same is true of the cash surrender value of a life insurance policy and a variety of marketable U.S. government securities, such as Treasury bills.[8] All of these assets serve the store-of-value function of money. However, if they are to be used to finance transactions or settle debts, they must be converted into money, the medium of exchange. consequently, these assets are called **near-moneys.**

What distinguishes money from near-money is whether the asset functions as a medium of exchange or not. Most economists still subscribe to this distinction and define money rather narrowly as M-1.

Assets that are highly liquid, but are not used as a medium of exchange are called **near-moneys.**

M-2: an alternative definition of money

A large and growing number of economists are not satisfied with the narrow definition of money. These economists, disciples of Professor Milton Friedman (see Box 2.1), believe that the public's spending decisions are not based solely on ownership of the medium of exchange. Their empirical studies have led them to focus on a broader conception of money. Friedman and his associates have defined money to include not only currency and commercial bank demand deposits (M-1A) but also **time** and savings **deposits** in commercial banks. However, also for empirical reasons, large ($100,000 or more) **certificates of deposits (CDs)** are excluded from **Friedman's M-2.**

Of course, singling out two particular types of near-moneys— commercial bank time deposits of less than $100,000 and savings deposits —opens up Pandora's box. Why not include savings deposits in institu-

A **time deposit** is an interest-paying deposit that cannot normally be withdrawn prior to its maturity.
A **certificate of deposit** (CD) is a document attesting to ownership of a time deposit.
Friedman's M-2 consists of currency and all commercial bank deposits except CDs of over $100,000.

---

[7]Why two—why not use only M-1B, since all of its components are exchange media? Federal Reserve economists believe that the extension of NOW accounts nationally will cause some temporary problems. A large portion of the funds that will flow into NOW accounts will be held for long-term saving purposes rather than medium-of-exchange spending motives. Thus, during a period of transition M-1B will overstate the actual growth in medium-of-exchange balances, while M-1A will understate true growth. Having both sets of numbers brings an improved perspective. In January, 1982, M-1B became the official definition. For further information on the new definitions and their rationale, see the February 1980 issue of the Federal Reserve *Bulletin*.

[8]Savings bonds are redeemable but are not marketable; they cannot be sold to another individual. Most Treasury securities, such as the bills mentioned here, are marketable; that is, they can be bought from or sold to third parties. The bills themselves bear an original maturity of one year or less, which makes them highly liquid.

Courtesy of the Hoover Institution.

BOX 2.1 Milton Friedman

If nothing else, this short, balding, animated Nobel prize laureate is a controversial figure in the world of economics, a status that he seems to enjoy. Professor Friedman does not shirk challenges; he is a skilled and persuasive debater who relishes public discussion. In fact, Friedman's basic works are challenges to the thoughts that have become the conventional wisdom of the economics profession.

This was not always so. Friedman was a bright but ideologically orthodox student. At Rutgers University, where he arrived as a 16-year-old in 1928 for his undergraduate education, he met and was influenced by Arthur F. Burns, the conservative economist who headed the Federal Reserve System from 1970 to 1978. At the urging of another of his professors, Friedman chose the University of Chicago for his graduate studies in economics. There he came under the tutelage of some of the most highly respected names in economics at the time. Their impact on Friedman was so considerable that he views his ideas and policy recommendations as continuing the tradition of the "Chicago School." Friedman returned to Chicago as a professor after the end of World War II and in 1963, in recognition of his work, was appointed Paul Snowden Russell Distinguished Service Professor of Economics. It was only in his second exposure to Chicago that Friedman became the iconoclastic economist who is so admired by many people.

As the winner of the $160,000 Nobel Prize in Economics in 1976, Professor Friedman was cited for a number of outstanding contributions to economic science, each of which was aimed at correcting an aspect of economics that he thought to be wrong. First, Friedman was lauded for his brilliant revision of consumption theory; he is the originator of the "permanent income hypothesis" of consumer behavior (see Chapter 16, Appendix A).

Second, the award came for his major contributions to monetary economics. Friedman's revitalization of the quantity theory of money (see Chapters 14 and 20) and his recognition of the critical importance of the money supply came at a time when money's causal role in the economy had been severely downgraded. Since Friedman's initial exposition of his views on the subject in the late 1950s, monetarism not only has become respectable but has captured a substantial following in the economics profession. Friedman's seminar at Chicago has given birth to more high-quality monetary economists in recent decades than any other course at any institution.

As a corollary to Friedman's studies in monetary economics, he elected to use a broader definition of money, M-2, rather than the conventional M-1. The fact that the Federal Reserve now presents monthly data on M-2 and pays attention to that variable in setting its policy is another indication of Friedman's influence.

Friedman's third outstanding contribution is stabilization policy. Since Keynes's time, economists have believed that the economy could be controlled relatively easily and, by the mid-1960s, relatively precisely by using fiscal and monetary policy. In fact, however, macroeconomic control is neither simple nor exact, a point that is important in money and banking courses in particular, as Chapters 19 and 23 will indicate. Friedman rightly deserves much of the credit for emphasizing the complexity of stabilization policies.

Friedman considers himself a liberal in the nineteenth-century meaning of the term. Indeed, some wags have suggested that Friedman would feel more at home in the nineteenth century than in the twentieth. His political economics are very conservative, and it is no surprise that the professor could serve as an economic adviser to President Reagan in 1976 and 1980. Friedman would like to see far less government intervention in the economy, reserving to the government only such functions as the maintenance of peace and the assurance of a stable currency. In *Capitalism and Freedom* Friedman argues that the government should not regulate monopoly, nor should it license professionals, nor should it redistribute income via the tax system, nor should it run the post office, and so on. His views on current economic practice can be found regularly in the pages of *Newsweek*, where they present to the general public the views of a highly articulate conservative thinker.

Friedman's TV programs for the Public Broadcasting System reiterate these views. Economists who disagree with Friedman, and many do, differ less with the plausibility of his basic conceptions than with his often extreme conclusions. Thus, today's economists no longer downgrade the causal role of money, but they are hardly ready to concede that money supply control à la Friedman will solve most of economy's ills. Obviously, economic liberals reject Friedman's arguments for almost absolute *laissez faire*.

Friedman himself continues to be energized by these controversies. His is a name that will be repeated frequently in this book; no one can doubt that his impact on monetary economics is pervasive, if not always persuasive.

---

tions other than commercial banks? After all, is the owner of a savings deposit in a commercial bank likely to act any differently than the owner of a deposit of equal size in a savings bank?

M-2: the Federal Reserve definition

What about other, newly developed instruments? You have already read that the Federal Reserve responded to the recent evolution of money by expanding M-1 to include all assets that perform the medium-of-exchange function. At the same time, it redefined M-2. In addition to M-1B, the new M-2 includes (1) **overnight repurchase agreements** (RPs) issued by commercial banks, (2) certain overnight **Eurodollar deposits,** (3) **money market mutual fund** shares, and (4) savings and small time deposits (less than $100,000) at all depository institutions that are not

In an **overnight repurchase agreement** (RP), a bank customer purchases from the bank a part of the bank's asset portfolio, paying with a debit on the customer's deposit account with the bank. The bank buys back its assets the next day at an agreed upon price that includes principal plus one day's interest.

A **Eurodollar deposit** is a dollar deposit held in a bank outside of the United States.

Money market mutual funds sell shares to the general public and buy highly liquid assets (primarily large-denomination CDs) with the proceeds.

already included in M-1B. Each of these instruments requires a brief explanation.

When interest rates are high, it is expensive to maintain large cash balances that earn no interest. A $1 million demand deposit engenders a daily opportunity cost of over $400 when the annual interest rate is 15 percent. (If that doesn't seem large, consider that it comes to $4,000 in ten days and $40,000 in just over three months.) Corporate treasurers have discovered numerous ways to minimize the amount of cash lying idle, even if that money will be inactive for only a day. Overnight RPs and Eurodollar deposits are two such devices. In the former, the banker sells assets from the bank's own portfolio to the depositor, simultaneously agreeing to repurchase the assets the next day for principal plus interest. The whole process, of course, is a subterfuge intended to circumvent the congressional prohibition against paying interest on demand deposits. (What is not so obvious is the banker's gain from this procedure. The banker's acquiescence seems to be grounded in the fear of losing the customer, who otherwise would take the firm's banking business to a competitor.)

Depositor involvement in the Eurodollar market, where an overnight deposit also earns income, can be explained in a similar way. American banks have opened branches all over the world. In the late 1960s and early 1970s they showed a special preference for the Caribbean. With negligible or even zero tax rates and virtually zero governmental supervision, a branch that was little more than a mailbox for recording transactions with the home office could prove highly profitable. By booking dollar deposits at the Caribbean branch, the bank was able to accommodate its larger, more highly sophisticated customers. From the depositor's viewpoint, the interest earned on the demand deposit is a decided advantage. The depositor's risk is minimal, since the deposits are denominated in U.S. dollars. Again, the overnight Eurodollar deposit negates the prohibition of interest payments on demand deposits.

Both of these vehicles—overnight RPs and Eurodollar deposits—permit deposit holders to give up deposits for a night and have them available the next day. Thus, they are readily available funds with extremely high liquidity. Indeed, they are so liquid that the Federal Reserve can be criticized for including them in M-2 rather than M-1B. The owners of these deposits never really lose control over their accounts; they're here today, gone overnight, and back the next day. In fact, the Federal Reserve has not taken a rigid stance on this matter. To accommodate those who would like to include these assets in M-1B, it publishes their weekly volume in its release entitled "Money Stock and Liquid Assets" (H-6). Roll your own money supply numbers!

The same applies, although with less force, to the third of the new M-2 components: shares of money market mutual funds. The primary impetus for the development of these assets was the low interest rates that savers were earning on their deposits in commercial and savings banks. For example, in 1980, commercial banks were limited to offering 5¼ percent on regular savings accounts, while savings banks could not exceed 5½ percent. Savers soon realized that the value of their money was declining faster than the interest was accumulating. They searched for alternate assets that were liquid and secure and offered high yields, such as Treasury bills. But the $10,000 minimum bid for direct purchases from the Treasury (thereby avoiding brokerage fees) deterred many potential buyers. Moreover, even savers who could afford a T-bill could not purchase a higher-yielding large-denomination CD; how many had the requisite $100,000?

Money market funds provided a solution for the public. By pooling their funds—typically one needs at least $2,500 to open an account, although some funds accept as little as $1,000—savers could participate in the CD market, earning the market interest rate less a fee to the fund's management. (Table 2.2 lists a typical portfolio of a money market fund. Note the proportion of its investment in CDs. Also note the rate earned—a whopping 14.85 percent!)

The reason for including money market funds in M-2 lies in another feature of those funds. Most of the funds permit their shareholders to withdraw from the fund by writing a check. In theory, this implies that money market funds should be included in M-1B, and again the Federal Reserve provides the data on a weekly basis. Nevertheless, the Federal Reserve believes that few of these accounts are held for medium-of-exchange purposes; the data suggest that they serve primarily as savings accounts. Thus, de facto, the accounts are included in M-2.

Growth in M-1 and M-2, 1969–1980

Table 2.3 (p. 46) provides some data on the growth trends of M-1A, M-1B, M-2, and their components. M-1A and M-1B grew at comparable rates. Despite the spectacular growth rate of other checkable deposits, their absolute magnitude is small, so their contribution to M-1B's growth is small. M-2 grew at the more rapid rate of 9.9 percent over the period, the primary contribution coming from the higher growth rate of small-denomination time deposits and all savings deposits. Within this group, the deposits at credit unions grew most rapidly.[9]

The need for a definition

In light of these divergent rates of growth, which increase the complexity of conducting an active monetary policy, the authorities must discover an operative definition of money. This issue is certainly not a new one. In the early nineteenth century famous British economists debated the question of whether specie and bank notes alone were to be

---

[9]Friedman's M-2, which omits deposits not at commercial banks, did not grow as rapidly; its rate was 8.2 percent.

TABLE 2.2 Holdings of a Typical Liquid Asset Fund, March 18, 1980

Principal amount			Annualized yield on date of purchase	Market value
Negotiable bank certificates of deposit (51.9% of total)				
$	10,000,000	Bank of America[a] 4/1/80	15.00%	$ 9,981,547
	25,000,000	4/2/80	14.75	24,979,644
	5,000,000	4/9/80	14.43	4,988,550
	10,000,000	4/28/80	14.51	9,961,117
	5,000,000	5/8/80	14.15	4,974,027
	10,000,000	5/12/80	14.13	9,940,804
	10,000,000	5/21/80	13.55	9,924,167
	5,000,000	6/2/80	13.37	4,945,524
	5,000,000	6/4/80	14.15	4,947,014
	5,000,000	7/9/80	13.43	4,922,650
	25,000,000	7/15/80	14.10	24,603,270
	10,000,000	1/29/81	15.11	9,997,425
	15,000,000	1/30/81	15.20	14,991,315
	10,000,000	2/6/81	17.58	10,004,440
$	150,000,000			
$	85,000,000	Bankers Trust Co.		
$	205,000,000	Chase Manhattan Bank		
$	104,000,000	Chemical Bank		
$	103,000,000	Citibank		
$	128,000,000	Continental Illinois National Bank and Trust Co. of Chicago		
$	15,000,000	Crocker National Bank		
$	10,000,000	First City National Bank of Houston		
$	30,000,000	First National Bank in Dallas		
$	15,000,000	First National Bank of Boston		
$	5,000,000	First National Bank of Chicago		
$	10,000,000	First National Bank of Oregon		
$	15,000,000	Harris Trust & Savings Bank		
$	4,000,000	Irving Trust Co.		
$	168,000,000	Manufacturers Hanover Trust Co.		
$	90,000,000	Mellon Bank		
$	132,000,000	Morgan Guaranty Trust Co.		
$	15,000,000	Northern Trust Co. of Chicago		
$	5,000,000	Philadelphia National Bank		
$	38,500,000	Republic National Bank of Dallas		
$	27,000,000	Seattle First National Bank		
$	125,000,000	Security Pacific National Bank		
$	10,000,000	Texas Commerce Bank		
$	22,000,000	United California Bank		
$	15,000,000	Wells Fargo		
$1,526,500,000	Total			

Average annualized yield on all CDs: 14.82%

Bankers' acceptances (10.7% of total)

$ 66,000,000	Bank of America
$ 22,500,000	Bankers Trust Co.
$ 10,000,000	Chase Manhatten Bank
$ 6,000,000	Chemical Bank
$ 5,000,000	Chemical Bank (San Francisco)
$ 60,000,000	Citibank
$ 9,499,000	Citibank International (San Francisco)
$ 18,000,000	Continental Illinois National Bank and Trust Co. of Chicago
$ 10,000,000	First National Bank in Dallas
$ 20,000,000	First National Bank of Boston
$ 15,000,000	First National Bank of Chicago
$ 23,000,000	Manufacturers Hanover Trust Co.
$ 7,000,000	Mellon Bank
$ 8,000,000	Morgan Guaranty Trust Co.
$ 8,000,000	National Bank of Detroit
$ 9,080,431	Republic National Bank of Dallas
$ 8,000,000	Security Pacific National Bank
$ 13,500,000	United California Bank
$ 318,480,431	

Average annualized yield on all BAs: 14.68%

Commercial paper (20.3% of total)

$ 40,000,000	Bank of America Corp.
$ 55,700,000	Bankers Trust New York Corp.
$ 20,000,000	Chase Manhattan Corp.
$ 15,000,000	Chemical New York Corp.
$ 125,000,000	Citicorp
$ 32,000,000	Commonwealth Edison Co.
$ 10,000,000	Engelhard Minerals & Chemicals Corp.
$ 15,000,000	General Electric Credit Corp.
$ 48,470,000	General Motors Acceptance Corp.
$ 110,000,000	Manufacturers Hanover Corp.
$ 15,000,000	Mellon National Corp.
$ 70,000,000	Security Pacific Corp.
$ 45,000,000	Wells Fargo & Co.
$601,170,000	

Average annualized yield on all commercial paper: 15.47%

U.S. Treasury bills (4.8% of total)
$143,000,000

Average annualized yield on all Treasury bills: 15.12%

Other (11.1% of total)
$325,000,000

Average annualized yield on all other: 13.89%

Total Investments	98.8%
Cash and Receivables (Net)	1.2%
Net Assets	100.0%

Average annualized yield on all investments: 14.85%

aOnly the holdings of Bank of America CDs are decomposed into subtotals and maturities. A similar breakdown for the other entries would also have been possible.

TABLE 2.3 Components of M-1 and M-2, 1969–1980 (billions of dollars)

December	Currency	Demand deposits at commercial banks	M-1A[a]	Other checkable deposits At commercial banks	At thrift institutions	M-1B
	(1)	(2)	(3)(=1+2)	(4)	(5)	(6)(=3+4+5)
1969	46.9	163.5	210.4	0	0.1	210.5
1970	50.0	171.2	221.2	0	0.1	221.3
1971	53.5	182.1	235.7	0	0.1	235.8
1972	57.9	199.5	257.5	0	0.1	257.6
1973	62.7	208.8	271.5	0	0.3	271.8
1974	69.0	213.9	282.9	0	0.4	283.4
1975	75.1	220.8	295.9	0.4	0.7	296.9
1976	82.1	231.3	313.5	1.3	1.4	316.1
1977	90.3	247.0	337.2	1.9	2.2	341.3
1978	99.4	261.5	360.9	5.3	3.1	369.3
1979	108.3	271.1	379.4	12.8	4.2	396.4
1980	118.5	276.2	394.7	21.0	6.1	421.8
Compounded annual rate of growth, 1969–1980	8.8	4.9	5.9	120.8[b]	45.3	6.5

December	Overnight RPs	Overnight Eurodollars	Money market funds	Small-denomination time deposits and all savings deposits At commercial banks	At savings and loan associations	At mutual savings banks	At credit unions	M-2[e]
	(7)	(8)	(9)	(10)	(11)	(12)	(13)	(14)(=6+7+8 +9+10+11 +12+13)
1969	2.5	0	0	163.9	135.0	66.5	13.5	590.7
1970	1.4	0	0	175.7	144.4	70.6	15.2	627.3
1971	2.5	0	0	204.9	171.4	80.3	17.9	711.3
1972	3.1	0	0	230.2	203.1	90.2	21.0	803.5
1973	6.8	0	0.1	242.0	222.5	94.8	24.0	860.1
1974	7.2	0	2.3	257.1	236.8	96.7	26.9	908.5
1975	7.5	0	3.6	300.9	278.0	107.5	32.1	1024.5
1976	13.6	0	3.4	355.1	325.8	119.7	37.7	1169.1
1977	17.6	1.0	3.8	384.8	374.8	130.2	44.7	1295.9
1978	21.0	2.0	10.3	399.3	413.5	137.7	51.2	1402.9
1979	21.7	3.6	43.6	431.6	440.5	139.6	53.7	1527.7
1980	25.5	4.6	75.8	475.4	467.1	146.1	59.9	1674.7
Compounded annual rate of growth, 1969–1980	23.5	66.3[c]	129.1[d]	10.2	11.9	7.4	14.5	9.9

[a]Unadjusted for nonbank travelers checks. In 1980 travelers checks equaled $3 billion.
[b]Compounded from 1975.
[c]Compounded from 1977.
[d]Compounded from 1973.
[e]Total is slightly less than sum of components primarily because it excludes some double-counting.
Source: Board of Governors of the Federal Reserve System, Statistical Release H. 6.

considered money or whether demand deposit accounts, which were not nearly as extensively used then as they are now, were also to be included. Today the inclusion of checking accounts is taken for granted. Still up for clarification and resolution is the matter of where to draw the dividing line: Should we stop at checking-type deposits, also include other types of deposit accounts, or range even further and include other near-moneys too?

M-1 and M-2 draw the line distinguishing near-money from money in different places. Because the liquidity of each of the assets listed differs, the decision on where to draw the line is bound to be somewhat arbitrary. Consequently, economists who are interested in the monetary scene monitor not only M-1A, M-1B, and M-2 but also M-3 and L and their components. (See Box 2.2.) One (though hardly the only) reason why so many economists disagree on policy recommendations derives from the monetary variable they emphasize the most.

This question of definition may be interesting for historical reasons or semantic purposes. It is vital to contemporary policy: There are critical issues at stake. Today, as we all know, a central bank like the Federal Reserve System possesses the power and authority to mold the money supply in line with stated economic goals. While a discussion of the methods used by the System and the goals sought by it is best left for later chapters, it is clear even at this juncture that controlling the money supply is one of the major means of achieving the Federal Reserve's goals. But if one is unclear as to precisely what constitutes the money supply and how the money supply is changing over time, then monetary policy becomes an enigma not only to the public but to the central bankers as well.

Consider the two instances portrayed in Table 2.4. In the first period, the authorities believed that a growth rate of 4–8 percent in M-1A and between 6 and 10 percent in M-2 was consistent with their policy goals.

TABLE 2.4 Alternative Money Supply Definitions, Growth Targets, and Actual Growth

	M-1A		M-2	
	Target	Actual	Target	Actual
Period I	4–8%	7.9%	6–10%	9.8%
Period II	5–7.5%	3.2%	8.5–10.5%	9.0%

These were the monetary targets. As a matter of fact, the actual growth rate for each of these definitions lay within the target ranges. No problem of conflicting interpretation occurred; no complex analysis was called for.

Now consider the second period. Here the respective targets for M-1A and M-2 were as given. M-2 hit its target range, but M-1A undershot its range. Thus, on the basis of the broader aggregate, the Federal Reserve's policy was on track and no changes were required. On the other hand, if policy was to be predicated on the narrow, M-1A definition of money, then actual policy was too tight and should be loosened to permit more rapid growth in the money supply. If you were a member of the Board of Governors of the Federal Reserve System, how would you have voted—to leave well enough alone or to ease up? Lest you think these numbers do not portray real cases, be assured that they do. Period I covers the third quarter of 1978; period II covers the time from the second quarter of 1975 to March 1976.[10]

The debate still goes on. Neither the Chicago school nor those who favor the M-1 definition have brought forth incontrovertible proof, either theoretical or empirical, to convince the other side. True, the debate demonstrates the vitality of monetary economics, but it leaves little room for complacency, not for the observer of the economic scene and certainly not for the directors of monetary actions.

☐ Summary

Chapter 2 began with the initial stage of money's long evolution. At that stage the value of money consisted not only of the goods and services for which a monetary unit could be exchanged but also of its own intrinsic value (e.g., knives, cattle). As time marched on, money's value came to depend less and less on the commodity value of the money substance and more and more on what it could buy. Thus, the full-bodied Chinese knife money gave way to the more convenient token knife, and Virginian representative tobacco money was substituted for the bulky tobacco leaves. It was but a short step to issue money whose value was dependent solely on its purchasing power, as the first issues of colonial fiat money

---

[10]Thus, the M-2 used here is Friedman's definition, the one actually used by the Federal Reserve prior to its 1980 revision.

demonstrated. Today, money's value, in most circumstances, depends entirely on its exchange value.

Of course, there are exceptions. Commodity moneys are still found in some contemporary primitive societies and, in special circumstances, even in modern economies. For example, the cigarette is used as money in U.S. penal institutions today as it was used in German prisoner-of-war camps during World War II. Barring these few exceptions, the bulk of the money in virtually all economies today consists of intangible book entries on the ledgers and computer tapes of the nation's banks. This is true even in planned economies. In the USSR, for example, all interbusiness transactions are conducted by means of transfers of funds at the State Bank, which not only provides for payment but, more important, keeps a running check on the consistency of firms' expenditures with the national plan.

The chapter also highlighted the workings of Gresham's law, especially as it rendered inoperative the planned bimetallic standard of the United States and caused the disappearance of gold and silver during the American Civil War.[11]

In the contemporary United States money consists of government-issued paper and coin, the largest component of which is Federal Reserve notes. But the amount of government-issued money is dwarfed when it is compared to the amount of money issued by the nation's banks. All in all, this system of faith money has worked amazingly well, although, of course, there have been interruptions and problems. Nevertheless, we cannot claim to have resolved all outstanding issues, or that the monetary system will never falter in the future.

In this chapter we explored one major current issue: Will the true money supply please stand up! The development of new financial assets with medium-of-exchange properties—NOW and ATS accounts, share draft balances at credit unions, and demand balances at thrift institutions —has forced the coining of a new definition of money, M-1B. M-1B adds these balances to M-1A, which consists of currency and demand deposits (adjusted) at commercial banks. Moreover, other assets, now excluded by the Federal Reserve from the M-1 definition but included in the new M-2 definition, are certainly near-moneys and perhaps ought to be included in M-1B as well. Precisely where to draw the dividing line between money and near-money remains an open question. Since proper economic policy hinges on correct understanding of the monetary concepts, it is important that this conflict over what money really is be resolved.

Before proceeding to a more intensive examination of the U.S. banking system, it will be useful to conclude this introductory section of the book with some remarks about interest rates. While economists often simplify by talking about "the" interest rate, the task of Chapter 3 will be to

---

[11]Gresham's law worked even in the P.O.W. camps. Since some cigarettes give better-tasting smokes than others, the best brands were literally consumed and the poorer-quality brands circulated as money. Shades of colonial Virginia!

explore more deeply the variety of interest rates found in the financial markets.

☐ Questions and Exercises

1. Although you realize that paper money is intrinsically worth very little and also understand that it has no tangible backing, you would be unwilling to dispose of your own green bills in the wastebasket. Why not? Would you feel differently about throwing away blank checks? Why treat them differently?

2. How did Gresham's law work in early Virginia, and how did it make unworkable the bimetallic monetary standard of the early United States? Why does Gresham's law not drive the paper dollar out of circulation?

3. Some have argued that only gold can give money value and that fiat money is doomed to depreciate into worthlessness. Can you find some historical examples that demonstrate the truth or falsity of this assertion?

4. How does M-1A differ from M-1B and M-1B from the Federal Reserve's definition of M-2? Are there any components of M-2 that should be included in M-1B?

5. Take a back issue of the Federal Reserve *Bulletin* and jot down the growth rates of M-1A, M-1B, and M-2 for the last quarter-year. Then take a more recent issue of the *Bulletin* and find the "Record of Policy Actions of the Open Market Committee," which details the objectives of the Open Market Committee for that quarter. How good was the Committee's marksmanship?

☐ For Further Study

The two classic works on early money are Arthur R. Burns, *Money and Monetary Policy in Early Times* (New York: A. M. Kelley, 1965, from original 1927 edition), and Paul Einzig, *Primitive Money in Its Ethnological, Historical and Economic Aspects* (Elmsford, N.Y.: Pergamon Press, 1976). An interesting conceptual tracing of money's evolution, focusing on the search for ever cheaper forms of money, is found in Chapter 2 of M. J. Flannery and D. H. Jaffee, *Economic Implications of an Electronic Money Transfer System* (Lexington, Mass.: D. C. Heath, 1973). An abstract, highly advanced treatment is that of Karl Brunner and Allan H. Meltzer, "The Uses of Money: Money in a Theory of an Exchange Economy," *American Economic Review* 61 (December 1971): 784–805.

Milton Friedman and Anna J. Schwartz provide a survey of money definitions and their rationale in Chapters 2 to 4 of their monumental *Monetary Statistics of the United States: Estimates, Sources, and Methods* (New York: National Bureau of Economic Research, 1970), while the Federal Reserve's reasons for its definitions are presented in "The Redefined Monetary Aggregates," Federal Reserve *Bulletin* 66 (February 1980): 97–114. A careful survey of the empirical evidence on the appropriate definition of money is provided by E. L. Feige and D. K. Pierce, "The Substitutability of Money and Near-Monies: A Survey of the

Time-Series Evidence," *Journal of Economic Literature* 15 (June 1977): 439–469. The bibliography attached to this article is encyclopedic.

C. Dunhamb's "The Growth of Money Market Funds," Federal Reserve Bank of Boston, *Economic Review* (September-October 1980): 20–34, provides a useful survey of this remarkable new financial vehicle.

CHAPTER 3

Interest Rates in the Money, Capital, and Futures Markets

Old economists never die, they just lose interest.

Anonymous

CONTENTS

Despite a history of diatribes by Western religious and philosophical ideologies against the taking and receiving of interest, it would be difficult to visualize a modern commercial economy operating without interest rates. Interest is a universal phenomenon. It is charged not only in capitalist economies but in socialist ones also; not only in developed economies but in less developed ones as well. Interest rates are prices and, as such, send signals to savers and investors, to borrowers and lenders, to private individuals and firms, and to public policy makers. Interest rates influence both microeconomic and macroeconomic behavior, and obviously are central to the study of money and banking.

This introductory chapter on interest rates begins by defining some terms, proceeds to discuss money and capital markets, considers the impact of risk and maturity on interest rates, and concludes by examining a recently introduced but fast-growing new institution—the interest rate futures market. When you've mastered this chapter you will have gained a fringe benefit—a working grasp of the financial pages of a good newspaper.

☐ Kinds of Interest Rates

For the typical consumer who owns a savings deposit in a commercial or savings bank, the question of interest rates never arises. The consumer knows from the big sign in the window that the Thrifty Savings Bank pays each depositor 5.25 percent a year on a savings account. Moreover, when the depositor leaves the interest in the account, compounding will turn the $5.25 into $5.47 for each $100 deposited.

In a sense, the same is true for the purchaser of a bond issued by a corporation. When someone buys a bond that has just been issued by, say, the American Telephone and Telegraph Company, whose face value is $1000 and maturity date is 2001, the buyer receives the 7 percent

The **coupon** interest **rate** is the interest rate that the issuer is obliged to pay, as stated on the bond document.

interest rate stated on the bond certificate itself. This interest rate is called the **coupon rate.** The coupon rate defines the obligation of AT&T to its bondholders: For a 7 percent coupon rate, AT&T will have to pay $70 in interest each year for every $1000 in bonds outstanding.

Yet there is a critical difference between the AT&T bond and the savings account. The former is marketable—it can be sold by the bondholder, usually through an organized security market—while the latter, though redeemable for cash or check, cannot be sold to someone else. (Note: the bond issuer, AT&T, is under no obligation to purchase the bond; its only obligation is to pay interest and redeem the bond at maturity in the twenty-first century). The marketability of a bond, be it corporate, private, or government, gives rise to an important concept, that of **current yield.**

The **current yield** equals the dollar interest payment divided by the market price of the bond.

No one can assure the bondholder that the bond, if sold prior to maturity, will sell at its face value. Because of conditions in the bond market, the $1000 bond may sell at a price of $950. Looked at from the new purchaser's perspective, a bond paying $70 annually has been acquired for $950, for an interest return of

$$\frac{\$70}{\$950} = 7.37\%$$

The purchaser of a bond at a price below its face value not only gains a market-determined interest rate that exceeds the coupon rate but also stands to obtain a capital gain. At maturity the bondholder will receive the full $1000 owed by the corporation, even though the bond's purchase price was only $950. This element of gain gives rise to a third interest rate concept, that of **yield to maturity.** If someone purchased the AT&T bond at $950 in the year 2000, held onto it for a year, and then redeemed it in 2001, the bondholder's return would be $70 in interest plus a $50 capital gain. On the initial expenditure of $950, this yield to maturity equals

The **yield to maturity** of a bond includes both the interest payment and the capital gain (or loss).

$$\frac{\$70 + \$50}{\$950} = 12.63\%$$

Of course, capital losses are also possible. The price of the bond may rise. If the coupon rate on a $1000 bond is 7 percent per annum and the market price rises to $1050, then with one year left before maturity the yield to the purchaser will be

$$\frac{\$70 - \$50}{\$1050} = 1.90\%$$

While the bond owner gains the $70 interest payment, he or she receives only $1000 from the paying corporation, for a loss of $50 in capital value.

When the time to maturity exceeds one year, the capital gain or loss is divided by the number of years remaining. Thus, had the maturity date of the bond just described been five years hence, the yield to maturity would have been calculated as

$$\frac{\$70 - (\$50/5)}{\$1050} = \frac{\$60}{\$1050} = 5.71\%$$

Economists prefer to use the yield to maturity definition, since it is the most comprehensive concept and we will follow this convention, using the terms *interest rate* and *yield* as synonymous with *yield to maturity*.

The yield, then, is variable; it fluctuates with bond prices. *If bond prices rise, yields fall; if bond prices fall, interest rates rise.* (Be sure you understand this important relationship.)

☐ Nominal versus Real Yields

Interest rates are quoted in the newspapers in **nominal** terms. Economists and the public in general are also interested in **real** interest rates. The distinction between the two is crucial when the prices of goods and service are changing.

Nominal interest rates are current market rates unadjusted for price changes, while **real** interest rates are nominal rates adjusted for inflation or deflation.

An individual who lent out $1000 for a year at a nominal rate of 20 percent may end up earning considerably less if the inflation rate was 15 percent. True, at the end of the year the lender would receive $1200 from the borrower. Yet because prices have risen, the value of the $1000 principal would be only $850. In terms of purchasing power, the lender would receive only $850 + $200 = $1050.

An alternative method of reaching this conclusion is in terms of real interest rates. Equation 3.1 states that i_r, the real interest rate, equals i_n, the nominal rate, *minus p*, the rate of inflation.

$$i_r = i_n - p \tag{3.1}$$

In our case, $i_r = 20\% - 15\%$, or 5%. When multiplied by the $1000 principal, the real return is only $50 on the initial principal. The lender gets back $1000 + $50 in inflation-adjusted dollars.

The calculation of the real rate of interest from the nominal rate is a simple matter *ex post facto*, that is, once the appropriate numbers are in hand. It is not so easy to calculate the real rate of interest when considering the present or the future. In these circumstances the real rate must be understood to be the difference between the nominal rate of interest and the *expected* rate of inflation, the latter being most difficult to pin down. To be sure, the beliefs of borrowers and lenders about future inflation will be reflected in the financial marketplace. But it is nearly impossible to disentangle the components of a rise in interest rates during an inflationary period. We just do not know how much of the increase is due to changes in inflationary expectations and how much is a result of fundamental supply and demand shifts.

Failure to comprehend the difference between nominal and real interest rates is a frequent source of confusion. For example, in Part Four you will read that when the money supply rises, interest rates fall. This appears to conflict with real-world observations that a rise in money supply is often followed by a rise in interest rates rather than by the predicted fall. One response to this paradox is that while nominal interest rates rise, real rates fall. It is the decline in real interest rates that is the expected consequence of an increase in money supply.

Similarly, observers who track interest rates to discern the thrust of monetary policy often fail to distinguish between real and nominal rates, which leads to faulty conclusions. Thus, a rise in nominal interest rates may suggest that the Federal Reserve authorities have tightened the money supply. However, if real rates fall simultaneously—if the increase in nominal rates is less than the expected increase in the price level— then the actual tendency of monetary policy is toward looseness, not tightness.

On a practical level, the annual 5¼ percent nominal interest rate that you may have received on your saving account in recent years turns out to be a negative real rate. Considering that prices have risen at a double-digit rate, you are not even breaking even on your savings. In fact, your principal is being eaten away. (This explains the popularity of money market funds, which pay low but positive real yields.)

Thus, no one can afford to neglect real interest rates nor to be fooled by high nominal rates in an inflationary environment. And in Part Four, when we deal with the impact of interest rates on the economy, remember that the relevant rates are in real terms.

☐ Money and Capital Markets

The **over-the-counter** market deals in securities that are not listed on security exchanges, normally because the corporation issuing the stocks or bonds does not meet the exchanges' conditions for listing. Trading is over the telephone rather than at some physical location.
Private placement occurs when a security issuer sells directly to the purchaser, bypassing the organized and over-the-counter markets.

Securities are sold and bought either on organized stock and bond markets, on **over-the-counter** markets, or by **private placement**. In the latter, the borrower, usually a major industrial or commercial enterprise, sells the entire issue to the lender, which is often a financial institution such as an insurance company or a pension fund. The types of securities involved, and their terms, are tailored to the specific needs of both parties. The volume of private placements in total financial flows is rather limited. Most of the trading in securities takes place on the various regional or telephone markets, with brokers bringing buyers and sellers together.

The best-known organized markets are the various stock exchanges: the New York Stock Exchange and the American Stock Exchange, both located in New York City; the Midwest Stock Exchange in Chicago; and the Pacific Stock Exchange in San Francisco. The bulk of the trading on these exchanges is in the common stocks of the nation's leading corporations.

Similar to the stock markets but accounting for a substantially larger dollar volume and the bond markets. In 1980, for example, total trading in just the U.S. government securities segment of the bond market came to \$4,568 billion compared with the \$522 billion for all the nation's stock markets. This chapter is concerned with these fixed-income securities rather than with equities.

Economists and financial writers often find it useful to distinguish between two types of fixed-income securities markets: the **money market** and the **capital market**. Although both types of market deal with financial instruments that share a common characteristic—namely, the commitment of the issuer to pay a fixed rate of interest and to redeem the principal upon maturity—nevertheless, the instruments do differ in degree of liquidity. Because of their short maturity, money market instruments are highly liquid. On the other hand, capital market securities are relatively less liquid.

The **money market** trades in securities whose initial maturity is one year or less.
The **capital market** is concerned with securities whose time to maturity at issue exceeded one year.

The money market

Money market trade occurs in both private and government securities. Table 3.1 lists quotations for a variety of money market assets as they actually appeared on the financial pages of a major newspaper.

Begin with the first line of the table, **Federal funds**. During the day the Federal funds rate ranged from a low of 8¾ percent to a high of 10½ percent; it closed at 10½ percent. (Note that all rates are expressed on an annual yield basis.) The daily range was very small, to be sure—only 1¾ percentage points per year during the day. But when billions of dollars are involved, even small differentials work out to large sums. The trader who managed to purchase \$100 million in Federal funds for her bank at

Federal funds are reserves held by banks at Federal Reserve banks. These funds can be lent, usually for a day at a time.

TABLE 3.1 Selected Money Market Rates, July 2, 1980

Private securities

Federal funds	*High:* 10½%	*Low:* 8¾%	*Close:* 10½%

Bankers' acceptances	**Bid**	**Asked**	
30–89 days	8.80%	8.70%	
90–119 days	8.65	8.55	
180–270 days	8.60	8.50	

Eurodollars	Bid	Asked	
1 month	9⁵⁄₁₆	9⁷⁄₁₆	
3 month	9⁷⁄₁₆	9⁹⁄₁₆	
6 month	9¹¹⁄₁₆	9¹³⁄₁₆	

Certificates of Deposit		**Yield**
30–59 days		8.0%
90–119 days		8.1
180–239 days		8.25

Government securities

Treasury bills (in basis points[a])	Bid	Asked	
Due Aug. 19, 1980	7.5	7.14	7.30
Due Oct. 2, 1980	7.94	7.88	8.14
Due Jan. 29, 1981	8.05	7.85	8.29

[a]Basis points are 1/100 of a percentage point. Thus, a 7.5 bid means willingness to purchase for an annual rate of 0.0750.

Source: *New York Times*, July 3, 1980.

8¾ percent instead of 10½ percent saved the bank $4,861.11 on that deal alone.

Bankers' acceptances are promissory notes that have been guaranteed by a bank, substituting the bank's credit for the less well-known reputation and, hence, lower credit rating of the note's originator. The **bid** represents the buy offer of a securities dealer, while the **asked** quotation is the sell offer. The **spread** is the difference between the bid and the asked yield.

Bankers' acceptances are listed next. Only three of a series of maturities, with a range from one to two months to one-half to two-thirds of a year, are included in the table. Two rates are quoted for each maturity, a **bid** and an **asked** yield. Since yield varies inversely with price, the higher bid yield represents a lower price offer than the lower asked yield. The difference between the two, the **spread**, is the dealer's margin. A 0.1 percentage-point spread on a $100 million transaction comes to $100,000. Of course, not all of this sum is profit; the dealer's expenses must be subtracted before the net return is calculated.

Next the table lists Eurodollar rates, with yields higher than those on bankers' acceptances, and rates on certificates of deposit, with the lowest yields of the private securities group.

U.S. government securities with an initial maturity of one year or less are known as **Treasury (or T-) bills**.

The last set of yields in the table are those attached to three **Treasury bills**. For any given maturity, T-bill rates are the lowest; since they are backed by the credit of the U.S. government, they are virtually riskless.

Risk is one element that determines the interest rate. Another is the time element—time to maturity. While these aspects will be discussed shortly, it should be pointed out that two different configurations are discernible here. The rates on acceptances fall as time to maturity increases, while the yields on Eurodollars, CDs, and T-bills rise as maturity lengthens, the more usual pattern.

The capital market

The securities traded on the capital market can also be classified as government or private issues. Selected bonds, taken from the financial tables of a daily newspaper, are listed in Table 3.2.

TABLE 3.2 Selected Capital Market Issues Traded on the New York Stock Exchange Bond Market, July 2, 1980

Private bonds

Name	Coupon rate (%)	Maturity	Current yield (%)	Sales ($000s)	High	Low	Last	Net change
AT&T	4⅜	1985	5.3	77	82½	80½	82½	+½
AT&T	8¾	2000	10.3	129	86	85⅛	85⅛	−¼
Phila Elect	11	2000	12.0	19	92½	92	92	−2⅞
Shell Oil	8½	2000	10.2	1	83	83	83	−1
Standard Ohio	8½	2000	10.5	5	81¼	81¼	81¼	—

U.S. government bonds

	Coupon rate (%)	Bid[a]	Asked[a]	Net change	Current yield[b] (%)
May, 2000-05	8¼	82.13	82.29	−0.4	10.14
Feb., 2005-10	11¾	112.2	113.6	+0.1	10.27

[a]Prices are in 32nds of a point. Thus, the bid of 82.13 is 82¹³/₃₂, which equals $824.0625 per $1000 face value.
[b]Yields are in basis points based on asked quotations.
Source: *New York Times*, July 3, 1980.

The first line of the table lists a bond issued by AT&T, American Telephone and Telegraph, the most widely owned corporation in the United States. After listing the corporate name, the table lists the coupon rate, that is, the rate the company is obliged to pay in interest to the bondholders. A rate of 4⅜ percent on a $1000 bond means, of course, that AT&T must pay the owner of the bond $43.75 a year. The maturity date is given next; this particular security will be redeemed by AT&T in 1985. Both the coupon rate and the maturity date are listed to identify the issue, since many large corporations have a number of bond series outstanding at any time. The next column lists the current yield; the purchaser who bought on July 2, 1980, will be earning 5.3 percent per annum. (Can you explain the difference between the coupon rate and the current yield? If not, check back to page 54.) The next column lists the sales volume; $77,000 worth of this issue changed hands. The bond's price varied during the day, and the next three columns summarize the day's action by recording the highest, lowest, and final prices for that day. The high of 82½ is to be read as $825.00 and the low as $805.00 per $1000 of face value. This high also happened to be the final price. The final column, which lists the change in the closing price from the previous day, indicates that the price rose by $5.00 per $1000. This particular issue is selling at a **discount**, since it costs less than $1000 to acquire a bond whose redemption value is $1000. (Bonds may also sell at a **premium**.)

A bond that is selling at a **discount** is selling below par or face value.
A bond that is selling at a **premium** is selling above par.

AT&T issues a variety of bonds, and the data on the series maturing in the year 2000 appear in the second line. It traded rather actively, $129,000 worth. The $851.25 final price represented a loss of $2.50 per $1000 since the day before.

Three other bonds are listed, all maturing in the year 2000. They are issued by the Philadelphia Electric Company, Shell Oil, and Standard Oil of Ohio. All were selling at a discount, and all but Shell Oil yielded more than the AT&T, 8¾, 2000. (Note again the relationship between the coupon rate and the yield, on the one hand, and the price relative to par, on the other. Think of this in connection with the association between yields and bond prices discussed earlier in this chapter.)

Government securities are listed somewhat differently and in a more concise format. In the lower portion of Table 3.2, the first column lists the maturity date while the second records the coupon rate. Note that both issues bear a dual date, 2000 and 2005 and 2005 and 2010, respectively. This kind of bond is known as a **callable** bond, since the issuer may redeem the security any time after the first date. However, should the Treasury not exercise its option, it nevertheless must redeem the bond by the second date. (Thus, the first bond may be called at any time after May 2000, but must be redeemed by May 2005.) Corporate securities also may be issued with a call option, giving the issuer greater flexibility.

A security that is **callable** may be redeemed by the issuer any time after the call date.

The 8¼ percent U.S. Treasury bond due in 2000–05 was being solicited from the bondholding public by a bond dealer at 82.13, or $824.06 per $1000 face value; the .13 stands for ¹³⁄₃₂, or $4.06 per $1000. The same bond was being offered to the public by the dealer at 82.29, or $829.06. Since the day before, the bond price had declined by $\frac{4}{32}$ of a percentage point. The yield of the bond, based on the asked price, was 10.14 percent, lower than that available from all the private issues of equal maturities listed in the upper part of the table.

The 11¾ issue of 2005–10 was selling at a premium; a seller on July 2 would have received $1126.875 for each $1000 of face value. Consequently, the 10.27 percent yield to the purchaser was less than the coupon rate.

Two basic conclusions may be derived from Table 3.2. First, interest rates vary with the riskiness of the asset. Second, yields differ with maturity. Each of these elements will be addressed in turn.

Risk. Professional credit-rating agencies assess the creditworthiness of borrowers. Among the most famous are Moody and Standard & Poor, both private companies with well-established reputations. Both estimate the ability of the borrower to pay interest and principal on time, and they rank borrowers on that basis, using a letter system. Top-rated bonds receive an Aaa on the Moody scale and an A+ on the Standard and Poor scale, while the lowest, most risky issues are ranked C by Moody and D by Standard and Poor. Other things being equal, the lower the rating, the higher the interest rate lenders will demand and borrowers will be forced to pay. The following are the ratings given by Standard and Poor to the corporate bonds listed in Table 3.2:

Name	S&P Rating
AT&T	A+
Phila Elect	B+
Shell Oil	A+
Standard Ohio	A

It is possible to infer from Table 3.2 that risk and yield are related. In general, the higher the risk, the higher the yield. However, many elements besides risk enter into the pricing of a security. We should not be surprised to notice similarly rated bonds yielding different rates, as indeed can be seen in the table. Compare, for example, the current yield on A+-rated AT&T with that on A+-rated Shell Oil. (Might the oil crisis have had anything to do with the yields?) Again, lest you think 0.1 percent to be meaningless, consider that it's worth $100,000 on a $100 million transaction.

Maturity. Just as risk differentials lead to disparate interest returns, so, too, does variety in maturity dates. Economists not only seek to observe the historic pattern of the **term structure of interest rates**, but also search for the causes underlying the various patterns. Figure 3.1 depicts two **yield curves**, demonstrating two frequent term structures. Both happen to relate to government securities. Equally graphic pictures could have been presented for corporate bonds, and whatever is said here about Treasury bonds can be applied to private securities as well.

The relationship between interest rates and time remaining to maturity is called the **term structure of interest rates**. When plotted, this relationship is known as the **yield curve**.

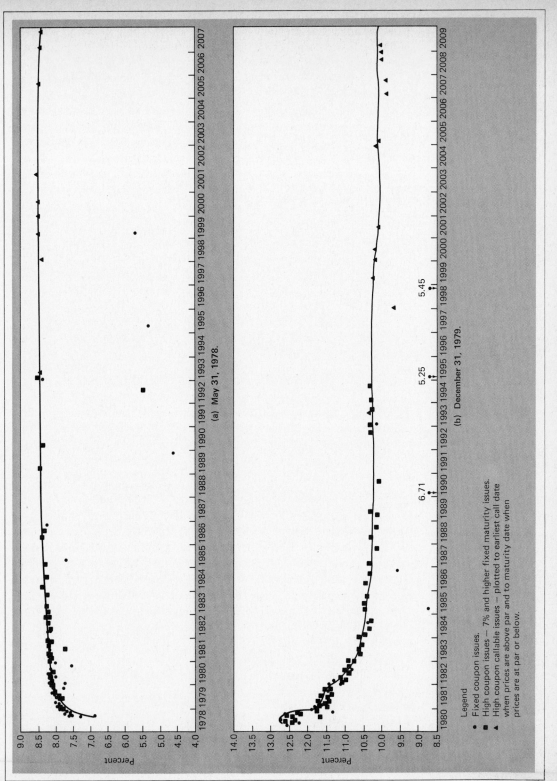

FIGURE 3.1 Yields of Treasury securities, May 31, 1978, and December 31, 1979; based on closing bid quotations. (Note: The curve is fitted by eye and based only on the most actively traded issues. Markets yields on coupon issues due in less than 3 months are excluded.)
Source: U.S. Treasury: *Bulletin*, June 1978 and January 1980.

Before analyzing the two panels separately, some common features should be pointed out. First, both curves represent market yields as of a single date. Tomorrow the picture could be modified drastically. Indeed, the quotations used are closing bid yields, so that the curves really represent the way the U.S. government securities looked at *one* moment of a single day. Second, there are a limited number of Treasury bonds, noted by the dots and squares of the charts. Notice the frequent gaps, especially for the years after 1983. The yield curve does not connect the issues; instead, a curve representing the general pattern is drawn in.

Now observe the rising yield curve of Figure 3.1 (a), which shows interest rates rising the further away the bond's maturity date is. Thus, a Treasury bill due near the end of 1978 yields about 7.6 percent, while a bond maturing in early 2007 brings in a return of 8.5 percent. This curve, incidentally, has been the most common one since the 1930s. Historically less frequent, although not uncommon during the 1970s, is the yield curve of panel Figure 3.1 (b), which shows a falling structure. In this pattern, shorter-term issues bring the investor a higher yield than those maturing later—the bond due in mid-1980 yields about 12.6 percent, which is to be contrasted to the 10.0 percent interest rate of the bond maturing in early 2009.

☐ Relations Between the Money and Capital Markets

How can these diverse patterns be explained? What is the relationship between long-term interest rates and short-term yields, between the capital and money markets, if indeed there is a connection at all? Two basic theories have been advanced to answer these questions, the "segmented-markets" hypothesis and the "expectations" theory.

The segmented-markets explanation

The segmented-markets thesis claims that in fact there is *no* relationship between issues with different maturities. Not only is the money market separate from the capital market, but the capital market itself is divided into distinct segments. The yield curve, which connects the markets, is a purely artificial construct that is meaningless at best and confusing and misleading at worst. The segmented-markets theory claims that the yield of each bond issue, or each maturity segment, is determined by the supply and demand for that maturity. Moreover, the prices of any one maturity are unlikely to affect the prices of any other. This is true because participants in one area of the securities market are not usually active in another segment.

Proponents of this view find its underlying rationale in institutional factors. The fact that commercial banks, which are heavily committed to short-term liabilities, are required by both prudence and regulation to hold relatively liquid assets means that they continuously buy and sell in the short-maturity end of the market, that is, the money market. But they do not engage actively in long-term trading. Life insurance companies, on the other hand, being blessed with a regular inflow of funds and limited short-term liabilities, pursue the reverse policy: They buy or sell long-term maturities while eschewing the short-term market. Thus, when commercial banks obtain funds in excess of their lending needs, they invest them in money market instruments. This demand for short-term securities drives prices upward on the money market, lowers short-term yields, and, since no other part of the yield curve is affected, generates a rising term structure. On the other hand, if insurance companies benefit from consumers' heightened awareness of the value of life insurance and find their inflows increasing in consequence, then, by demanding long-term bonds, they will bid up long-term prices, lower long-term yields, and induce the yield curve to fall. In short, the money market and the capital market are independent of each other, and what happens in one segment of the market has no impact on other portions of the securities market.

The expectations theory

Not so, claim proponents of the expectations hypothesis. Securities markets are interdependent. Any institution that desires a steady return over time can achieve this objective in a variety of ways. One alternative would be to purchase a long-term bond. A second would be to acquire a series of bonds with short maturities. For example, if a financial corporation is interested in earning some given income from 1982 to 1992, acquiring a ten-year bond with a 1992 maturity date would be one way of achieving its goal. But the purchaser could just as well buy a bond maturing in 1983, one year hence, and then, with the proceeds of that security, buy another one maturing in 1984, and so on continuously until 1991. A moment's thought should convince you that in a perfect market these two alternatives must yield equal returns.

Consider the following example. Assume that a two-year bond maturing at the end of 1984 yields 10 percent per annum. Assume, too, that a one-year bond yields 11 percent in 1983 and people expect interest rates to be 11 percent in 1984 as well. Given the choice between buying the two-year 10 percent bond or two one-year bonds at 11 percent, which alternative would you select? If all people elect, as you surely would, to buy the one-year bond now, what must happen to its yield? Moreover, will those who own the two-year bond continue to hold it at 10 percent when they can expect to earn 11 percent on two one-year bonds? And if they sell the two-year bond, what must happen to its yield? In short, as long as profitable opportunities appear somewhere in the securities market, some market participants will shift there. Markets are interrelated.

Critical to this analysis is the expected yield in the future. If the future yield for the one-year bond maturing in 1984 is expected to be 8 percent instead of 11 percent, the two-year bond is the better buy. After all, the average two-year yield of two one-year bonds yielding 11 percent for one year and 8 percent for a second year is only about 9½ percent. Thus, expectations play a critical role in determining the demand for bonds.

How does the expectations theory explain the yield curve? The answer, already implied in the preceding paragraph, is that expected future events influence current actions. When yields in the future are expected to be low—so that bond prices are anticipated to be high—the knowledgeable bond-trading public will demand more long-term securities now. By buying now, before the price rises, they stand to profit through a capital gain. Moreover, they will sell short-term securities in order to finance their purchases of long-term bonds. What happens then is that demand pressure in the long end of the market drives prices up and yields down, while sales pressure forces short-term prices down and yields up. The result is a falling yield curve, as shown in Figure 3.1(b). [You should be able to work out the logic underlying the yield curve of Figure 3.1(a). Show how expectations regarding future interest rates lead to a rising term structure.] In summary, the yield curve reveals what market participants believe about the future.

One interesting implication of the expectations theory is that the supply of securities does not determine interest rates. Yields are purely a result of the anticipations of market participants. On the other hand, the segmented-market theory considers the supply of securities as important as the demand for them.

Term structure and liquidity

It is appropriate to note two adjustments in the expectations theory. The first concerns liquidity preference; the second, inflation. Liquidity preference enters into the term structure in the following way. If people prefer to be more liquid rather than less liquid—a rather plausible assumption—they will have to be bribed by an interest premium to forsake liquidity and acquire longer-term securities. If an investor can earn 10 percent annually on a short-term (say, one-year) bond and 10 percent each year on a longer (say, five-year) bond, most people would prefer to hold the one-year bond. It gives them greater flexibility. Moreover, as Table 3.3 demonstrates, for any given interest rate the change in the price of a bond varies directly with the years remaining to maturity. A bond with one year remaining to maturity, with a coupon rate of 7 percent, will sell for $972.10 when market interest rates are 10 percent. If interest rates rise to 15 percent, the price falls to $928.20, a loss of $43.90. But if the same conditions are applied to a bond that matures five years hence, the loss is $158.80 as the price falls from $884.20 to $725.40. And if the bond has twenty years left before

TABLE 3.3 Bond Prices and Yields Related to Years to Maturity (for a $1000 Bond with a 7 Percent Annual Coupon Rate)

Years to maturity	Market interest rates (%)		
	7	10	15
1	$1000.00	$972.10	$928.20
5	1000.00	884.20	725.40
10	1000.00	813.10	592.20
20	1000.00	742.60	496.20

redemption, the loss is considerably greater, equalling $246.40.[1] Consequently, shorter maturities are preferred; the opportunities for capital loss are smaller. This preference for more liquid assets might well explain the previously noted historical frequency of the rising yield curve: Normally, investors will have to earn more to be induced to acquire longer-term issues.

Term structure and inflation

The second point refers to inflation. When commodity prices are expected to rise, the real value of the bondholder's fixed-interest return, being constant, declines. Creditors will have to be compensated by an inflation premium. Indeed, in many countries long-term loan contracts include a purchasing power protection clause whereby the principal and interest are linked to some price index. Thus, if the bond calls for an 11 percent interest payment and the cost of living rises by 10 percent during the year, the borrower will be required to pay 21 percent. In the United States such linkage is not uncommon for wage contracts, in which workers' pay is adjusted for inflation through an escalator clause. Only in the late 1970s, with continuing high inflation rates, have some long-term lenders insisted on linked bonds. Even when interest rates are not formally linked, however, the market mechanism will establish the appropriate relationship. When interest rates are expected to be 8 percent and a 10 percent annual rate of inflation is expected, the creditor will demand 18 percent per annum and the borrower, who expects to sell the product in an inflationary market, will be willing to pay 18 percent per year.

Not only will inflation be reflected in interest rates; so, too, will changing expectations about future inflation rates. Assume that, in the absence of inflation, interest rates are expected to be as follows:

Year 1—8 percent
Year 2—9 percent
Year 3—10 percent

If the rate of inflation is expected to be 10 percent in each of the three years, market rates of interest will rise to 18 percent, 19 percent, and 20

[1]The derivation of this relationship may be found in the appendix to this chapter.

percent, respectively. In this case the yield curve retains the same shape but is shifted upward by ten percentage points. But if inflation is expected to accelerate, to rise from 10 percent in year 1 to 11 percent in year 2 and 12 percent in the final year, the market rates will be 18 percent, 20 percent, and 22 percent, respectively. The yield curve itself will rise more steeply.

How, then, can one explain the declining yield curves that characterized recent years? One common explanation focuses on the relationship among inflation, liquidity preference, and uncertainty. In an inflationary environment, when neither borrowers nor lenders are confident about the future rate of inflation, both may shy away from long-term commitments. An especially strong liquidity preference characterizes the uncertain public, since rising rates of inflation, leading to higher interest rates, entail substantial capital losses on long-term debt holdings. (The AT&T bond maturing in 2000 had a market value of 15 percent below par in early July of 1980.) Consequently, lenders prefer shorter-term maturities over long-term bonds. Borrowers demonstrate similar preferences, being unwilling to commit themselves to high-cost long-term liabilities in the face of an uncertain future. To be sure, if borrowers were confident that inflation would persist at high and even rising rates, they might borrow long at high nominal rates because they understand that real interest rates would be significantly lower. The problem is the uncertainty that characterizes the future, making borrowers reluctant to undertake long-term commitments.

Borrowers' strong demand for short-term finance have driven short-term interest rates up. Simultaneously, their withdrawal from the long end of the market has driven interest rates at the far end of the capital market down. The end result is the falling yield curve.

A concluding thought on the yield curve

The two theories offer conflicting explanations of how the yield curve is derived. The segmented-market hypothesis relies on the rules of supply and demand to determine the yields of bonds, but also claims that the various market segments bear little relationship to each other. The expectations hypothesis believes the security markets to be interrelated, and further claims that market prices in the various maturity areas are arrived at by investors acting on the basis of their expectations of future market yields. As can well be imagined, proponents of the various views have attempted to confirm the appropriateness of their theories. While academic economists have leaned toward the expectations hypothesis, no one has yet shown conclusively that only expectations matter. Some evidence has been advanced in favor of the segmented-markets explanation as well. Moreover, substantial methodological questions remain in all of the empirical studies. At this point it is perhaps best to suggest that both theories, rather than being contradictory, are complementary.

Expectations are likely to affect yields, as the expectations theorists suggest, but so does the supply of securities, as is implied by the segmented-markets hypothesis. Indeed, perhaps the supply of securities affects the formation of expectations, so that a broader view of the two theories would lead to a single theory of the yield curve.

☐ Interest Rate Futures

While most transactions in financial markets involve exchanging securities for money, in recent years these **spot market** trades have been supplemented by a rapidly growing **futures market**. The prices listed in Tables 3.1 and 3.2 were spot prices, and were representative of a whole array of money and capital market security prices. In contrast, only a few types of securities are currently traded in the financial futures markets. The purpose of this section is to survey the background, structure, and strategies of financial futures markets and **futures contracts.**

Background

Commodity futures in the United States can be traced back to conditions in the midwestern grain and southern cotton trades during the second half of the nineteenth century. Farmers and merchants, subject to substantial price fluctuations caused by the impact of the weather both on crops and on the transportation system, sought to replace price uncertainty with some degree of stability. The concept of price commitments in advance of delivery suited both sellers and buyers, for by agreeing upon a fixed price months prior to delivery both parties minimized the risk of volatile prices. Planning was made easier. As the utility of futures markets became evident to more commodity producers and traders, the number of markets expanded accordingly. Today active markets exist in a variety of grains, livestock and meat, foods and fibers, and metals, woods, and oil. Their prices are listed daily in the financial pages of major newspapers.

Financial futures trading began quite recently, in 1975, when the Chicago Board of Trade established a market for Ginnie Mae certificates. (GNMA, the Government National Mortgage Association, is briefly discussed on page 261.) Since then, futures markets have been organized in **U.S. Treasury bonds, notes,** and bills, and in **commercial paper** and CDs. Trading has moved beyond Chicago as trading floors have been opened in New York City and, owing to the increasing volatility of interest rates, may open elsewhere.

Financial futures exchanges and contracts

In many ways the futures exchanges replicate the early days of the stock market. Trading on all the exchanges takes place in a trading room, where

Transactions on **spot markets** are at current prices for immediate delivery, while **futures markets** deal in futures contracts.

A **futures contract** is a standardized agreement to deliver or receive a specified commodity or financial instrument(s) at a particular date in the future.

U.S. Treasury bonds mature in ten or more years from the issue date, while **U.S. Treasury notes** mature in one to ten years.
Commercial paper consists of unsecured short-term promissory notes.

traders meet daily to execute buy-sell orders. The men and women on the trading floor act either for themselves or for brokers whose clients' orders are relayed to the market. Margins are low, so that substantial profits can be amassed with a minimal capital outlay. On the other hand, it's not difficult to be wiped out.

Financial futures are traded at the Chicago Board of Trade (CBT), the International Money Market (IMM), at the Chicago Mercantile Exchange, New York City's Commodity Exchange (COMEX), and the New York Futures Exchange (NYFE). The Chicago exchanges, being the oldest, are by far the most active.

All of the six types of financial futures (excluding only foreign currency for which futures markets also exist) are traded on at least one exchange (obviously) but none on all the exchanges. Moreover, even when a type of security is traded on more than one exchange, contract terms may differ in one or more respects. For example, while Treasury bill contracts are traded on both the IMM and COMEX in $1 million denominations, the IMM requires that the bills have 90 days to maturity while COMEX permits the bills underlying the contracts to contain maturities that vary between 90 and 92 days. And while the contracts on the IMM are deliverable in March, June, September, or December, the COMEX contracts mature in February, May, August, or November. Despite differences in detail, however, all existing financial futures contracts have some broad similarities.

1. All specify a face value for the securities underlying the contracts, as follows:

Contract	Face Value
90-day Treasury bills	$1 million
1-year Treasury bills	250,000
3–6-year Treasury notes	100,000
15+-year Treasury bonds	100,000
GNMA certificates	100,000
90-day commercial paper	1 million
6-month or less CDs	1 million

2. All specify a delivery date, one month per quarter.
3. All specify an initial deposit. The amount of the purchaser's own funds that must be provided varies by type of contract and exchange; some representative ones are the following:

Contract	Exchange	Face value	Deposit	Deposit as percent of face value
90-day Treasury bills	IMM	$1 million	$1,500	0.15
4-year Treasury notes	CBT	100,000	900	0.9
15-year Treasury bonds	CBT	100,000	2,500	2.5
GNMA certificates	COMEX	100,000	2,000	2.0
30-day commercial paper	CBT	3 million	1,500	0.05
6-month CDs	NYFE	1 million	1,500	0.15

4. The federal government regulates these exchanges through the five-member Commodity Futures Trading Commission (CFTC). All traders doing business with the public must register with the CFTC. The CFTC also approves the exchanges, as well as the contracts that may be traded on each exchange.

Strategies

Traders on futures markets can be classified as either **hedgers** or **speculators**. Hedgers avoid risk; speculators thrive on it.

Speculation. Speculative strategy is easy to explain. Assume that a speculator expects interest rates to fall (and, therefore, bond prices to rise) in the future. The speculator could buy long-term bonds now and hold onto them for six months. If the speculator predicted correctly, the bonds would be sold at a higher price for a capital gain.

Consider a Treasury bond with a face value of $100,000, a coupon rate of 10 percent, and 20 years remaining to maturity. If the bond is currently selling at par but the speculator expects the 20-year interest rate to decline to 9.5 percent in six months, then its price will rise to $104,440.00. Of course, if that happens, the speculator will have gained $4,440 on $100,000 in six months, which comes to an annual return of almost 9 percent. (Remember, the gain is made after holding the bond for only half a year.) Had the investor purchased the bond on a 50 percent margin, the rate of return on the speculator's own capital would have doubled. ($4,440 ÷ $50,000 = 8.88% for six months, or approximately 18% for the annual rate.)

The financial futures market offers even greater speculative opportunities. For the same $50,000 investment, the speculator could have acquired twenty Treasury bond contracts on the CBT, each with a face value of $100,000, for a total speculative stake of $2 million. The same interest rate decline, reflected by a similar change in the future market price, would have meant a profit of $88,000 on a $50,000 investment, or an annual return in excess of 350 percent!

Of course, this tremendous profit opportunity could just as easily have turned into spectacular losses. Had the speculator guessed wrong, had interest rates risen by as little as ³⁄₁₀ of 1 percent, the speculator's margin would have been eradicated. The rewards for being lucky (and perhaps skilled) at futures market speculation are phenomenal, but the costs of being wrong are sky-high, too.

Hedging. The hedger's concern is defensive; hedgers wish to protect themselves against adverse price (= interest rate) movements. They sacrifice the opportunity for phenomenal gain in order to avoid the chance of substantial loss.

Consider the following two cases, each representing a different hedging action.

Hedgers use the futures markets to protect themselves against adverse price movements.
Speculators seek to profit from correctly forecasting price changes.

1. *An investor desires to lock in high interest rates.* You (or your bank's portfolio manager or a corporate treasurer) own Treasury bills that mature in December, three months hence. You expect interest rates to decline between now and December, and thus anticipate an increase in the price of fixed-income securities. If you were to wait until December and reinvest then, you would be forced to accept the lower rate that you predict. Of course, you could be wrong; you might be able to reinvest at a higher yield. You have decided, however, that you are willing to trade off that possible gain in order to minimize the risk of the low interest rate.

You act. You buy a December Treasury bill futures contract, which will oblige you to purchase T-bills in December. (The minimum contract is $1 million, so you are committing yourself to purchase in December T-bills with a face value of $1 million.) You will pay the current price of that contract—say, $980,000—although you will not put up more than the required margin now.

Come December, your prediction turns out to be either right or wrong. If you are right and interest rates have indeed declined, the value of your futures contract will have risen. Typically, futures contracts are liquidated by reversing the initial transaction, so you now sell your contract for, say, $990,000, a $10,000 gain. You now renew your Treasury bill, and although you do so at the lower current yield, you now have the additional $10,000 earned in the futures market to supplement your interest return.

On the other hand, had interest rates gone up, you would have lost on the futures contract. The $980,000 contract now sells for $970,000, and you take a $10,000 loss when you reverse your initial transaction. But because you can now reinvest the proceeds of the maturing T-bill at a higher yield, your loss on the futures market is compensated for.

In a **long hedge** a futures contract is acquired for protective purposes.

This type of transaction is known as a **long hedge**, since a futures contract was bought and later offset by a sale.

2. *An investor wishes to be protected against rising interest rates.* You (or a banker or a business financial officer) believe interest rates are going to rise. Since you intend to borrow funds some months from now, you would like to avoid this expected added cost. You could borrow now, but that would entail paying interest even though you do not need the money immediately. Again the futures market provides an option. Your strategy is to **hedge short**. By doing so, you will be able to defend yourself against anticipated higher interest charges.

A **short hedge** entails the selling of a futures contract now and a reversal of that transaction later.

Here's what you do. You sell T-bill futures short, promising to deliver T-bills (which you do not own) at a later delivery date and at a stated price. Thus, you might commit yourself to deliver $1 million T-bills in six months at a price of $980,000. If interest rates do rise, the price of your $1 million futures contract will decline to, say, $970,000. Now you buy a $1 million T-bill futures contract to reverse your short sale, for a $10,000 gain. With this profit in your pocket, you can offset the higher interest costs of your loan. The net impact of the futures transaction and your current borrowing is a reduced total interest expenditure.

Again, had you predicted wrong, you would have been forced to reverse your futures transaction at a loss. (The futures contract may have risen from $980,000 to $990,000, forcing you to take a $10,000 loss.) But your borrowing costs at the later date would also have fallen, so that the futures market loss would have been offset.

In both of these cases the hedge strategy was used to reduce the uncertainty associated with interest rate volatility. Hedging, however, is not without its own risks. If futures and spot rates do not move precisely in conformity with each other, offsets in the spot and futures markets will be less than perfect. Net gains and losses may occur. Thus, an owner of $100,000 in Treasury bonds in early October 1979, anticipating a rise in interest rates, could have hedged by a short sale of a single Treasury bond futures contract. Interest rates did rise, and the actual gain made by reversing the transaction in November would have been $7,500. But in the same period the value of the $100,000 in bonds declined by $9,000. A wiser course would have been to sell the bonds in October and buy them back in November.

Of course, had the bondholder been prescient, that course could have been adopted. On the other hand, the bondholder could have simply held the bond and not hedged at all, in which case the loss would have been $9,000. The hedging operation represents the middle option. With good fortune, the hedging operation leads to avoidance of a net loss; with a little less luck, it leads to partial compensation, reducing the loss below what it would have been otherwise.

☐ Summary

It is important to distinguish among coupon interest rates, current yields, and yields to maturity. While the coupon rate is fixed for any fixed-income security once it has been issued, the yields fluctuate *inversely* with the market value of the bond. A second critical difference, especially in an era of inflation, is the contrast between nominal and inflation-adjusted real interest rates.

Interest rates on short-term money market issues typically differ from those available on long-term capital market securities. Money market instruments are highly liquid, a fact that is normally reflected in their yields. Even within the short-term market, however, yields differ, since some issues are shorter and others longer, some are more risky and others less so.

These distinctions hold with even greater force in the capital market, since any given change in interest rates induces far larger movements in the prices of long-term securities than in those of short-term issues. (The appendix to this chapter explains why this happens.) In general, too, the longer the maturity of the bond and the greater the risk, the higher the yield will be.

Interest rates on issues of the same type of security differing only in maturity date can be plotted to obtain a yield curve. While historically a rising yield curve has been more common, a falling yield curve has occurred with increasing frequency in recent years. Two theories that explain the term structure of interest rates are discussed in this chapter: the segmented-markets hypothesis and the expectations theory. The segmented-markets explanation views interest rates as determined by supply and demand relationships in specific market segments, each portion of the market spectrum reflecting the underlying preferences of borrowers and lenders. In contrast, the expectations theory views all maturity segments as unified; at least some market participants will take advantage of profitable trading opportunities irrespective of the portion of the market in which they crop up. Market expectations about future yields lead to profit-oriented transactions that shape the yield curve. Thus, if yields are expected to fall some years from now (and their prices rise), demand for these issues will rise now, leading immediately to rising prices and falling yields.

Both the segmented-markets theory and the expectations hypothesis can be supplemented by considerations of liquidity, inflation, and uncertainty. The liquidity desires of lenders suggest that an inducement in the form of higher interest rates will be needed to convince lenders to acquire long-term bonds. Inflationary expectations would reduce the desirability of holding securities with distant maturity dates, and again would require compensation in the form of higher interest rates. Uncertainty, on the other hand, may well lead to a declining yield curve as borrowers gather at the short end of the maturity range to finance their projects with short-term funds.

In the last few years financial futures markets have flourished, with trade taking place in a variety of issues and maturities. Speculators have been attracted to these markets by the low margin requirements. Those who are skilled and lucky can parlay a small stake into a considerable nest egg. Those who fail to predict interest rate movements correctly can forfeit vast sums. Hedgers use these markets defensively, to protect themselves against adverse interest rate fluctuations. They eschew large gains and avoid substantial losses by choosing strategies that reduce interest rate volatility.

☐ Questions and Exercises

1. What happens to (a) the coupon interest rate, (b) the current yield, and (c) the yield to maturity when the bond market experiences a strong upsurge in demand? Why?
2. In 1980 interest rates exceeded 20 percent for many borrowers, leading many businesses to complain about high interest rates. At the same time, economists felt that interest rates were not high at all. Could the differences in

perceptions stem from the distinction between nominal and real interest rates?

3. In general, the riskier an asset, the higher the interest rate that must be paid by the borrower. Yet, although both U.S. Treasury securities and U.S. government agency securities are backed by the full faith and credit of the federal government, their yields differ. Look in the financial pages of a daily newspaper under the headings "U.S. Treasury Issues" and "Government Agency Securities" (or similar headings) and study the yields of some representative issues to verify this statement. How can these differences be explained?

4. What does a falling yield curve indicate about investors' perceptions of future interest rates? Could recent falling yield curves suggest something about the market participants' concern about inflation?

5. Devise the futures strategies you would employ if (a) you were a speculator and expected interest rates to rise three months from today, and if (b) you wished to hedge against an expected fall in interest rates three months hence, when you expected to lend a substantial sum. Could the speculator and the hedger conclude a transaction with each other?

□ For Further Study

"Interest Rates and Inflation," Federal Reserve Bank of Chicago, *Economic Perspectives* 5 (May-June 1981): 3–12, reviews the theoretical and empirical relationships between interest and inflation, but does require some basic econometric knowledge or enthusiasm. A somewhat easier article that examines real and nominal interest rates is G. J. Santoni and C. S. Stone, "What Really Happened to Interest Rates?: A Longer-Run Analysis," Federal Reserve Bank of St. Louis, *Review* 63 (November 1981): 3–14.

The Federal Reserve Bank of Richmond has just released its *Instruments of the Money Market,* which contains a wealth of institutional detail. The capital market is examined in a number of books, including H. E. Dougall and J. E. Gaumnitz, *Capital Markets and Institutions* (Englewood Cliffs, N.J.: Prentice-Hall, 1980). Two brief, readable explanations of the term and risk structure of interest rates are published by the General Learning Corporation of Morristown, N.J.: Burton Malkiel, *The Term Structure of Interest Rates: Theory, Empirical Evidence, and Applications* (1970), and A. B. Cohan, *The Risk Structure of Interest Rates* (1973). A concise yet lucid description of the financial futures market is M. Arak and C. J. McCurdy, "Interest Rate Futures," Federal Reserve Bank of New York, *Quarterly Review* 4 (Winter 1979–1980): 33–48.

APPENDIX Some Mathematics of Finance

Chapter 3 distinguished between coupon rates and yields on fixed-income securities. The former is the constant dollar amount that the bond's issuer is obligated to pay in interest each period to the current holder of the security. Variations in the bond's price on the bond market do not affect the coupon rate. Yields, however, do vary with bond prices. The lower the price of the bond, the higher the yields, and vice versa. The basic arithmetic reason, as demonstrated at the beginning of Chapter 3, is that the yield equals the fixed interest payment divided by the varying market price.

Table 3.3 (p. 65) depicted another relationship, the relationship among bond prices, yields, and years to maturity. The table and the accompanying text asserted that the further away the maturity date is, the greater will be the impact of a yield change on the price of a bond. (A small tail can wag a big dog!) The purpose of this appendix is to explain why this occurs. But in order to understand that phenomenon it will be necessary to review the concepts of compound interest and discounting.

Compounding and discounting

Receiving interest on principal over time increases the principal in two ways. First, the interest itself adds to the principal. Second, because last year's interest is added onto the principal, interest this year will be paid not only on the old principal but also on last year's interest. In other words, interest is paid on interest, or interest is **compounded.** To calculate how much a given principal is worth at some future date, the simple compounding formula is as follows:

Compounding occurs when interest is paid on interest.

$$P_n = P_o (1 + i)^n \tag{3A.1}$$

where P_n is the principal at the later date, n; P_o is the original principal; and i is the interest rate at which compounding takes place. For example, if interest is paid annually at a 10 percent rate, $1000 today will be worth $1610.51 in five years:

$$\$1000 (1 + 0.10)^5 = \$1610.51$$

This equation is a shortened equivalent of a more complex derivation, which could be worked out as follows:

Year	Principal at beginning of year	Interest (at 10% per year)	Principal + interest (= principal at beginning of next year)
1	$1000.00	$100.00	$1100.00
2	1100.00	110.00	1210.00
3	1210.00	121.00	1331.00
4	1331.00	133.10	1464.10
5	1464.10	146.41	1610.51

If interest is compounded more frequently, such as every six months or every three months, the formula can be adjusted accordingly. The more frequent the compounding, the greater will be the actual interest paid. Thus, banks that pay 5¼ percent annually, compounded daily, in effect pay an interest rate of 5.47 percent on funds left for the entire year.

The upshot of this discussion is that an individual who can earn a 10 percent real interest rate compounded over a five-year period will be unlikely to lend out $10,000 today for a guaranteed $10,000 five years hence or even for $15,000 [= $10,000 + 5(.10) $10,000]. The lender would have to be paid at least $16,105.10 in five years' time in order to be induced to lend out $10,000 today.

A variation of this formula can be used to answer a slightly different question. Let us say that you were guaranteed a certain real return in the future. How much would you have to be paid today by someone who is willing to acquire this future return? Specifically, how much is a stipulated, inflation-adjusted payment of $1610.51 to be received in five years worth today, assuming that the interest rate today is 10 percent annually? The answer is clear: $1000. You would be unwilling to part with the right to the future return unless you received at least $1000, for you could relend the $1000 now received and, at the 10 percent interest rate, receive $1610.51. (From a practical standpoint, you might want to receive somewhat more than $1000 to make it worth the effort.) What is involved is calculating the **present value** of a future return, a process that is known as **discounting.** (Do not confuse this process with the process of borrowing from the Federal Reserve banks, which is also called discounting.)

The formula for present value is

$$P_o = \frac{P_n}{(1 + i)^n} \tag{3A.2}$$

Present value is the value today of a future payment, calculated by discounting the future return. When the values of future returns are divided by a compound interest factor, the procedure is called **discounting.**

In terms of the earlier problem,

$$\frac{\$1610.51}{(1.10)^5} = \$1000$$

Payment flows

Securities, of course, do not return their payouts in just one period. They yield a flow of receipts over time. The discounting formula developed in equation 3A.2 can be modified to compute the present value of such a flow.

Consider a $1000 bond maturing in two years and paying a coupon rate of 10 percent when yields in the market today equal 15 percent. How much is the bond worth today? It will be easiest to proceed by distinguishing between the interest payments and the repayment of principal.

The present value of the $100 return due next year is derived from the discount formula in equation 3A.2:

$$PV \text{ (first year's interest return)} = \frac{\$100}{1 + 0.15}$$

Similarly, the $100 return due two years is calculated as follows:

$$PV \text{ (second year's interest return)} = \frac{\$100}{(1 + 0.15)^2}$$

Next, the principal will be repaid two years hence, so that

$$PV \text{ (repayment of principal at end of second year)} = \frac{\$1000}{(1 + 0.15)^2}$$

Now total these three fractions to derive the present value of the bond:

$$PV = \frac{\$100}{1 + 0.15} + \frac{\$100}{(1 + 0.15)^2} + \frac{\$1000}{(1 + 0.15)^2} = \$86.957 + \$75.614 +$$

$\$756.143 = \$918.71$

In other words, a bond buyer should be unwilling to pay more for this particular $1000 bond than $918.71. Otherwise the yield would be less than the 15 percent that could be earned from alternative investments.

The present-value formula can be generalized as follows:

$$PV = \frac{R_1}{1 + i} + \frac{R_2}{(1 + i)^2} + \frac{R_3}{(1 + i)^3} + \ldots + \frac{R_n}{(1 + i)^n} + \frac{P}{(1 + i)^n} \quad (3A.3)$$

where the R's stand for the annual dollar interest returns: the subscripts refer to the years in which payment is received, from the first to the nth; i is the yield that can be obtained from alternative investments; and P is the principal. Thus, the present value of a $10,000 bond paying $500 a year with ten years to maturity can easily be computed. Indeed, some pocket calculators will do the work for you if you just enter the values of R, n, i, and P.

Interest rates changes, bond prices, and maturity

It is now a simple matter to verify the results of Table 3.3. Assume that interest rates rise from 10 percent to 11 percent. Consider the impact on a two-year bond and a twelve-year security, both with coupon rates of 10 percent and a face value of $1000. At 10 percent, the present value of both securities is $1000. (Are you surprised? You can work it out. Alternatively, you can think it through.) But when interest rates rise to 11 percent, the two-year bond is now worth

$$PV = \frac{\$100}{1.11} + \frac{\$100}{(1.11)^2} + \frac{\$1000}{(1.11)^2} = \$982.83$$

The twelve-year bond is worth

$$PV = \frac{\$100}{1.11} + \frac{\$100}{(1.11)^2} + \frac{\$100}{(1.11)^3} + \ldots + \frac{\$100}{(1.11)^{12}} + \frac{\$1000}{(1.11)^{12}} = \$906.85$$

What happened, of course, is that in the latter case the discounting process reached further into the future. Each year the denominator grew larger, partly because of the compounding feature (it's 1.21 in two years, but 2.839 after ten years), thereby reducing the value of each subsequent fraction.

We will conclude this appendix by calling your attention to a market phenomenon that is directly connected with the relationship between yield changes and maturity: Short-term interest rates are far more volatile than long-term yields.

A large variation in the commercial paper rate, for example, has a relatively small impact on its price. (In the last example, a 10 percent change in interest rates— from 10 percent to 11 percent—affected the two-year bond's price by $17.17 on $1000, or 1.72 percent.) Thus, potential purchasers of such paper are not likely to be dissuaded from acquiring it even if they anticipate marked fluctuations in interest rates. Similar variations at the long end of the market, however, would entail substantial price movements, scaring away potential bond buyers. (The same 10 percent interest rate change entailed a 9.3 percent change in the price of the twelve-year bond.) Thus, the market mechanism itself serves to moderate fluctuations in long-term bond prices.

PART TWO

COMMERCIAL BANKS AND OTHER FINANCIAL INSTITUTIONS

CHAPTER 4

Commercial Banking Through the Centuries: Abroad and at Home

Finance: n. The art or science of managing revenues and resources for the best advantage of the manager. The pronunciation of this word with the i long and the accent on the first syllable is one of America's most precious discoveries and possessions.

Ambrose Bierce, Satirist (1911)

The process by which banks create money is so simple that the mind is repelled. Where something so important is involved, a deeper mystery seems only decent.

John Kenneth Galbraith, Economist (1975)

CONTENTS

The development of money is intimately connected with another phenomenon, the rise of banking. In primitive economies operating under a barter system of exchange, neither money nor banks are needed. On the other hand, one cannot imagine a modern, functioning economy existing without an extensive network of banking institutions.

A central theme weaves through this chapter's history of banking. Modern banking starts with the process of money creation; how this was accomplished is examined by sketching out the role of the goldsmiths, truly the first of the modern bankers. The unifying theme is not money creation per se but how much money is to be issued. In Chapter 2 you became aware that governments are occasionally tempted to overexpand the supply of money. The exigencies of the moment overwhelm the policy makers, who may very well be aware of the undesirable longer-run consequences. With private bankers enjoying a similar privilege of money creation, a similar conflict arises: The interests of individual bankers may lead them to indulge the public's demands for financing, but the national interest might be better served by restraint. A fallacy of composition is present—what is beneficial for each individual may be damaging for all. Throughout the chapter you will be faced with instances in American history in which the desire of some people to expand the money supply clashes with the more restrained views of others. You will see the pendulum swinging one way and the other, with actions taken by Congress and the executive branch to legislate sound money or loose money. No single attitude ever prevailed; the controversy remains alive to this day.

Before we examine the historical record, some prefatory concepts will prove useful.

Banks are part of a broader category of institutions, known as "financial institutions," which includes not only commercial and savings banks but also life insurance companies, consumer finance agencies, and numerous other organizations concerned with borrowing and lending. In this and the next few chapters, our attention will be focused primarily on commercial banking. Not only are commercial banks the most important of the financial firms that characterize the economy of the United States; they are the primary sources and transfer agents of money. The other financial institutions will not be neglected entirely; Chapter 11 is devoted to the creators of near-money. But commercial banks, because of their quantitative importance and because of their role in the money creation process, deserve to be singled out.

Nevertheless, there is a thread that binds all financial institutions together, and it is proper to begin this section of the book by discussing this common feature. All financial institutions are **financial intermediaries.** Perhaps the best way to describe the function of financial intermediaries is to distinguish between "direct" and "indirect" finance.

> A **financial intermediary** is an institution that transforms assets of surplus units into the liabilities of deficit units.[1]

☐ Direct and Indirect Finance

Figure 4.1(a) on page 84 schematically portrays a situation that is known as **direct finance.** In this case, B is a deficit unit whose spending exceeds its current income. B's budget is in deficit, so B must borrow to finance its excess spending. L, on the other hand, is a surplus unit. Because L's income is greater than its present outlays, L has funds available to lend to B. If L and B transact together, with L lending funds to B without going through a financial intermediary, then direct finance has occurred.

> **Direct finance** occurs when the ultimate borrower obtains funds directly from the ultimate lender.

Examples of direct finance abound. A personal loan between friends is perhaps the simplest case. One friend, learning about the financial shortfall of his friend, digs into his pocket to help out; no third party is involved at all. However, personal relationships are not a necessary condition for direct finance. In fact, personal knowledge may well be a reason for avoiding financial dealings with a friend. Belief that the borrower is reputable, possesses a sound financial record, and will be able to repay the loan at maturity may be sufficient for lenders to transfer their funds to borrowers directly. Many large, well-established firms issue

---

[1]If this definition is less than enlightening, be patient. It is explained in the next few pages.

No precise, generally accepted definition of a financial intermediary exists. A broader definition than the one used in this book is "an enterprise whose assets and liabilities consist almost exclusively of financial instruments" [H. E. Krooss and M. R. Blyn, *A History of Financial Intermediaries* (New York: Random House, 1971), p. 8). Not only would this definition encompass commercial and savings banks; it would also include institutions like investment banks. The function of the latter is to assist corporations that are selling stock or bonds to find buyers. Under the narrower definition used here, the investment bank is excluded for two reasons. First, the investment banker does not issue any assets to the "lender" or liabilities to the "borrower"; it simply transfers the securities issued by one party to another. Second, insofar as the transaction involves stocks, which represent shares of ownership, no lender-borrower relationship has been established between the intermediary and the ultimate borrower and lender.

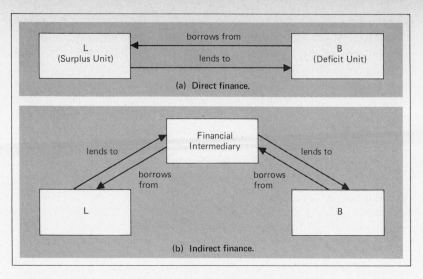

FIGURE 4.1 Direct and indirect finance: a schematic portrayal.

A **debenture** is a long-term bond that is not secured by any specific asset.

commercial paper or **debentures** that are sold directly to the public. The solid reputation of a General Motors or Dupont gives it direct access to public markets. Similarly, the Treasury of the United States is continuously involved in direct finance. To cover federal government deficits the Treasury issues a variety of securities—short-term bills (up to one year), intermediate-term notes (1–10 years), and long-term bonds (which mature in more than ten years), as well as the more commonly recognized series of savings bonds—many of which are purchased directly by the public.

Direct finance may involve lower borrowing costs for the issuer of the debt and higher returns for the lender; the middleman's charges can be retained by the principals. Nevertheless, the number of borrowers who have access to direct finance in the volume they desire is limited. First, personal friendships rarely suffice to provide borrowers with more then modest sums. Second, the number of major corporate names that inspire market confidence is circumscribed. Moreover, even prime corporations do not always wish to engage in direct finance. Funding for individuals and firms with limited access to direct finance is provided by the process known as **indirect finance.**

Indirect finance exists when the borrower and lender engage in transactions with a third party rather than directly with each other.

In indirect finance, the ultimate lender and the ultimate borrower are separated by a financial intermediary, such as a bank. The process is portrayed in Figure 4.1 (b). The borrower, B, turns to a financial intermediary—say, a savings bank—for a loan. The bank obtains its funds from the public and lends them to the borrower. While this process appears to be more complex, involving two sets of transactions rather than one, surprisingly the cost of indirect finance often is lower than that of direct finance. A lender dealing with a relatively unknown firm may find that the costs of obtaining and processing credit information loom so large as to preclude direct financing. If it costs $200 to obtain a comprehensive credit check on a potential borrower who wishes to obtain $5000 for six months at an annual interest rate of 10%, the $250 earned in interest leaves a net of only $50 or an annualized return of 2 percent.[2] The lender almost certainly could do better by depositing the funds in a savings account. On the other hand, a financial institution that regularly investigates clients and potential clients is likely to find its information costs much lower. Moreover, since the institution is interested in a continuing relationship with its clients, the cost of the investigation may be spread over a much larger dollar volume than the initial loan, thus reducing the per-dollar cost of the credit check. Specialization does have its economic advantages, as Adam Smith pointed out over two centuries ago.

Even more important than the cost-reducing role of financial intermediaries may be the transformation function that they perform. Financial intermediaries are able to reconcile different, indeed conflicting, demands on the part of borrowers and lenders. The typical lender wants not only profit but liquidity; the asset acquired in the lending process should be capable of being converted into money quickly without significant capital loss. The borrower, on the other hand, prefers to obtain use of the borrowed funds for a specific period; he or she normally would not be willing to pay back the debt prior to the expiration date of the loan. The borrower, in other words, desires a liability to the lender that is illiquid. The ability of the financial intermediary to reconcile these disparate interests may well be the rationale for the existence of financial intermediation.

Consider a savings bank in its role as a financial intermediary. On the one hand, the depositors—the ultimate lenders—are willing to supply funds to the bank not only for safekeeping but also because they can in fact obtain cash for their deposits whenever they wish. On the other hand, savings banks lend primarily to homeowners in the form of 20- to 30-year mortgages, very long-term loans. The lender is assured liquidity, while the borrower is assured an illiquid liability. The financial intermediary has transformed the liquid asset of the lender into the borrower's illiquid liability.

The same process can be applied to other financial intermediaries. Commercial banks provide demand depositors (read lenders) with an immediate claim on funds. Bank borrowers, on the other hand, are granted loans with maturities ranging from a few days to many years. Life insurance companies also gather funds and lend them out for long

---

[2]The total interest paid will be 5000×10 percent $\times \frac{1}{2}$ (year), which equals $250. Taking away the $200 cost of the investigation leaves $50, which on an investment of $5000 is 1 percent ($50/5000 = .01$). Since this return is earned in half a year, however, the annual rate of return is double the 1 percent.

periods. Nevertheless, their clients are able to borrow readily against the premiums they have paid to the insurance company.

Of course, the question that must have occurred to you is, How can a financial intermediary satisfy these two contradictory impulses—liquidity for the lender and illiquidity for the borrower? The answer hinges on the large number of depositors doing business with the financial institution. At any moment some depositors may be removing funds from the financial intermediary. But at the same time others are depositing money. The money you withdraw when you reach the teller's window consists essentially of funds deposited by someone else earlier in the day. The net change of funds at the bank may well be zero, the day's withdrawals being balanced by the day's inflows.

Normally a financial institution commands control over a permanent pool of funds. The pool may be drawn down temporarily, but it will be replenished soon. Consequently, the financial intermediary's demand for liquidity is dependent on its expected *net* losses of funds, not on its total potential losses, which, of course, equal the total amount of its deposit liabilities. To be sure, net losses depend on a variety of influences. A bank that is located in a declining community may expect continuous outflows, while one in a thriving neighborhood will experience a long-term deposit inflow. And certainly, if the bank's customers panic, the entire pool may disappear. But on the whole, the existence of this permanent pool of funds is the cornerstone of financial intermediation. The intermediary can guarantee liquidity to its depositors by paying them from the inflows plus a small reserve. At the same time, the intermediary guarantees longer-term lending by relying on the permanence of the bulk of the deposits.

Commercial banks pay a leading role in indirect finance. Table 4.1 lists the deposits or liabilities of the major financial intermediaries in the U.S. economy, as well as the loans outstanding in 1980. As can be seen, commercial banks, with 55 percent of all liabilities and 53 percent of all loans, overshadow all the rest.

The preeminence of commercial banking, and of financial intermediation in general, is a relatively recent phenomenon. In colonial times modern banks or similar institutions were unknown. Direct finance predominated, virtually to the exclusion of indirect finance. Friends lent

TABLE 4.1 Liabilities and Loans of Major Financial Intermediaries, December 31, 1980 (billions of dollars)

Intermediary	Liabilities	Loans
Commercial banks	$1,585.8	$ 932.5
Savings and loan associations	596.5	502.8
Mutual savings banks	171.9	111.5
Credit unions	71.7	47.8
Life insurance companies	476.3	172.5
Total	$2,902.1	$1,767.1
Percentage held by commercial banks	54.6%	52.8%

Source: Federal Reserve *Bulletin.*

to each other and businesses borrowed from other businesses. Typically, a colonial retailer granted credit to customers and took credit from suppliers. Since a good share of manufactured goods in prerevolutionary times were imported from England, the colonial merchant financed imports by borrowing from English suppliers. This chain of credit, of course, was held together by links of direct finance based on personal relationships between lenders and borrowers. Financial institutions as we know them today, including commercial banks, did not come to the American continent—with few exceptions—prior to the nineteenth century. Before considering the development of banking in the United States, it might be worthwhile to explore the history of banking in earlier times in Europe.

☐ A Short History of Commercial Banking

Two primary features characterize commercial banking today: (1) the transfering of liabilities at the command of the owner-depositor and (2) lending to deficit units. The overriding distinction of commercial banking in contemporary times as well as in the past, however, lies in neither of these qualities but in the fact that *commercial banks create money.* (How banks create deposits and the volume that can be created are discussed in greater detail in Chapter 10.)

Banking during the Middle Ages, which is truly the first period in which some modern banking functions can be identified, was associated with international trade. The transfer of money over great distances involved substantial costs and inconveniences, not to speak of the dangers of highwaymen. **Bills of exchange** were used to reduce the magnitude of the problem: The exporter drew a bill of exchange on the importer, who, by endorsing it, obligated himself to its terms. Now an Italian exporter of oranges to Belgium could take the endorsed bill of exchange and sell it to an Italian on his way to Belgium. The exporter received immediate payment in Italy, in Italian currency; at the maturity of the bill the importer paid the new owner of the bill in Belgium in the domestic currency, and the purchaser of the bill carried the claim, rather than gold, on his journey northward.

A **bill of exchange** is a negotiable instrument requiring the borrower to pay the lender a specified sum on a specified date.

The Knights Templar, initially a military order of churchmen, developed this practice to a rather sophisticated level. Because of the order's international network of temples, a bill could be drawn by a temple in one country payable by a temple in a second country. The Knights Templar also performed a warehousing function—the storing of valuables, including gold—and played a role in lending. In a very real sense these church nobles established the basis for many of the functions of modern banking. Although the order lasted only two centuries—it was destroyed in the fourteenth century—it served as a model for the great financial merchants of the Renaissance, the Fuggers and the Medicis.

Neither the Templars nor the Renaissance merchants created money: They lent funds and facilitated the transfer of funds, but they used existing, not created, money. The bills of exchange that were used were not money; they were not generally accepted, and they had to be converted into money.

The goldsmiths of England

The discovery of money creation is generally attributed to English goldsmiths. In 1640 Charles I confiscated privately owned gold, which had been held for safekeeping in the Tower of London. Confidence in the British monarch fell, and nobles and merchants who still retained some gold began to store it with goldsmiths, who, by virtue of their trade, kept their premises well protected and secure. At first the goldsmiths performed simple storage functions, providing a receipt as evidence of ownership. When payments had to be made, the owner of the gold took physical possession of the gold and transfered it to the person who had to be paid. At this point goldsmiths functioned like a modern bank's safe-deposit section; if someone holds cash in a safe-deposit box and wants to transfer it to another person, the money has to be removed from the box and physically turned over to the other party. However, it must have occurred to someone that ownership could be transfered more easily than by the physical movement of gold. Couldn't a letter be written to the goldsmith requesting that he transfer the funds to a second party? If that party was willing to retain the gold in place, a paper transfer of ownership could replace the movement of specie. Thus, the first checks were used to transfer ownership of gold.

In time the goldsmiths issued evidence of ownership in common denominations rather than writing out a receipt for a deposit of a specific sum. Instead of giving the depositor of £100 a statement saying that Lord Lancelot had £100 on account with Goldsmith Guy, Guy would give the lord twenty £5 pieces of paper that affirmed that each piece could be redeemed in gold on demand. These notes were paper money, fully backed by gold and fully exchangeable into specie. At this point (the second half of the seventeenth century), the goldsmiths had not yet moved beyond their initial storage function in any meaningful way. True, they had been innovative, substituting a convenient paper note for the bulkier gold coin—representative money had replaced full-bodied money —thereby facilitating money transfers. But they had not created money; the value of the notes issued by the goldsmiths did not exceed the value of the gold held in their coffers. Gold backed the notes 100 percent.

But money creation entered the picture in due course. The goldsmiths must have realized that it was rare for all depositors to demand their gold simultaneously. The smiths found that they could issue notes to individuals who needed this paper money and, in exchange for the immediate purchasing power it represented, were willing to add interest to the principal when they repaid it. The net result of this transaction was money creation: The goldsmith paid out notes whose total value was greater than that of the gold backing the note issue. Money creation, the distinguishing feature of commercial banking, had been discovered.

Today, as then, money creation is based on the concept of **fractional-reserve banking**. The goldsmith's evolution from storage to money creation is traced schematically in Table 4.2. As can be seen from section A, prior to any money-creating or lending activity by the smith, the notes issued precisely equal the gold backing; the gold reserve amounts to 100 percent of liabilities. When the first loan is made without gold backing (section B), the goldsmith issues £200 in notes in exchange for the loan, that is, the promise of the borrower to pay £200 (plus interest, which is omitted here). The smith now has £25,200 in notes outstanding backed by only £25,000 in actual gold, or a reserve ratio of 99.2, not 100 percent.

How large is the volume of new notes or loans that the goldsmith can make? Essentially, only the expected demand for actual gold limits the amount of notes that the goldsmith can issue. As long as confidence in each smith's ability to redeem his notes in specie held fast, no effective constraint on the amount of lending existed, nor was there any limit to the volume of notes that could be issued. Thus, a situation with a gold reserve of only 10 percent, as depicted in section C of Table 4.2, is certainly conceivable. Here the smith has lent out considerably more than he holds in gold, and has printed notes whose total value is ten times the value of his gold reserve.

It should be pointed out that there are finite limits to note issuance.

> **Fractional reserve banking** occurs when the reserves of a bank amount to less than 100 percent of total deposit liabilities.

TABLE 4.2 Money Creation by the Goldsmiths

A. Balance Sheet, Warehousing Function Only

Assets		Liabilities	
Gold	£25,000	Notes	£25,000

(Ratio of gold to notes: 100%)

B. Balance Sheet, Money Creation, I

Assets		Liabilities	
Gold	£25,000	Notes	£25,200
Loans	200		
Total	£25,200	Total	£25,200

(Ratio of gold to notes: 99.2%)

C. Balance Sheet, Money Creation, II

Assets		Liabilities	
Gold	£ 25,000	Notes	£250,000
Loans	225,000		
Total	£250,000	Total	£250,000

(Ratio of gold to notes: 10%)

First, the goldsmith's solidity was itself a function of his note issue. The lower the ratio of gold to notes, the less was the smith's ability to withstand a substantial demand for specie. Prudence thus dictated some limit to note issuance. Second, the larger the volume of notes circulating, the more suspicious the public might become regarding the smith's financial condition. Thus, if note owners wanted £50,000 in specie, a goldsmith with a balance sheet like section C of Table 4.2 would have to go into default.

We do not know whether such defaults actually occurred, but in any case the days of the goldsmith were short-lived. In 1672 Charles I, having borrowed more than £1⅓ million from the goldsmiths, decided not to repay his debt, a prerogative that few of us share today. Understandably, many goldsmiths went bankrupt, taking along with them thousands of London depositors. Nevertheless, the lesson of the goldsmiths—that money could be created—was not lost to future generations.

The Bank of England

From a small land and population base, Britannia ruled the waves for many centuries. As the saying went, "The sun never sets on the British empire"; its colonies stretched from one end of the world to the other. Not only was Britain the predominant political and military world power for many decades; it was the leading industrial nation as well. After all, the industrial revolution started in England. Even before that event, however, England had become the center of world finance, a tendency that was strengthened as British manufacturers conquered the international scene. British investment and finance supported and advanced the trade that provided England with its riches.

At the center of English finance stood the "Old Lady of Threadneedle Street," the Bank of England. The Bank of England is not the oldest of the world's banks—that honor is held by the Bank of Sweden—but, like England itself, it possessed unrivaled prestige. Although today its reputation and power must be shared with American and other Western financial institutions, the Bank of England remains an important institution. It was the Bank of England that provided the model for early North American banking.

Under **limited liability**, a stockholder can lose no more than the purchase price of the shares owned should the corporation fail.

The Bank of England was founded in 1694, almost a century before commercial banks were established in the United States. The bank was a corporation, having been granted the privilege of **limited liability**, a novelty in those days. Furthermore, in addition to being able to receive deposits from and make loans to the public, it was the bank of the government. Indeed, the impetus that spurred the bank's founding was the need to finance an impoverished, credit-poor monarchy. In return for a £1.2 million loan, the King granted a royal charter to the bank's promoters. The bank was given the right to print notes, and by the middle of the eighteenth century those notes had become the exclusive paper money of England. (That our own colonial leaders were familiar with banking in England is evident not only from the writings and speeches made in connection with the passage of the Constitution but also from the fact that some of those men, including George Washington, were stockholders in the Bank of England.) In addition to the concepts of chartering, limited liability, note issue, and lending to the government, the practice of restricting bank liabilities on the basis of bank capital—the precursor of reserve ratios—comes from the Bank of England. In one way or another, these ideas found their way across the Atlantic, and soon after independence they were implemented in the fledgling American banking system.

In England, as in other European countries, banking did not always function smoothly. Occasional panics caused the Bank of England to suspend conversion of its notes into gold. (Incidentally, this lesson too was learned by American bankers.) These "runs" would have destroyed the bank, for it lacked sufficient specie reserves to cover its notes in full. By temporarily reneging on its promise to convert notes into gold, the bank was able to remain in existence.

John Law and the "Mississippi Bubble"

Perhaps the clearest example of overexuberant banking, unfortunately followed by bankruptcy, is found in early eighteenth-century France and the episode known as the "Mississippi Bubble." In 1708 John Law, the son of a Scottish goldsmith, proposed to his fellow Scotsmen that prosperity could be brought to their poverty-stricken land through the expedient of money creation. The money was to be supported and backed by the value of Scotland's land, an idea that may have derived from Law's visit to the American colonies. Although Law's proposals fell on deaf ears in his native land, they were received enthusiastically some years later by the Duke of Orleans, then regent of France. Law's General Bank opened in 1716 with the power to receive deposits and issue notes redeemable in coin. The bank proved an immediate success, issued notes in moderation, and apparently stimulated the French economy. By December 1718, in recognition of its solidity and its contribution to economic expansion, the bank was reorganized into a state institution, the Royal Bank.

Law now saw an opportunity to reform and revitalize the entire French financial and economic system, and being a man of imagination and enterprise, he acted on it. He devised a scheme to exploit the Louisiana Territory, that sparsely settled but potentially rich French property in the New World. Law proposed to colonize the land; in addition to farming, the settlers were to mine gold and silver. His Mississippi Company sold shares that could be paid in depreciated state notes at full face value as well as in coin. In return for thus restoring the credibility of France's worthless paper money, the Mississippi Company was granted additional powers, including the power to issue coins and collect taxes. To this control over coinage and taxes Law added the national debt, offering to redeem it for stocks in the Mississippi Company.

A wave of speculative fever gripped the French, who thought they saw an opportunity to make vast profits. This natural avarice was encouraged by Law through some ingenious merchandising techniques, including the payment of dividends despite the absence of earnings. The result was a continuous increase in the price of the company's shares. The bubble's growth is vividly demonstrated by that rapid increase: A share of the Mississippi Company that sold at its par price of 500 livres in June 1719 rose to 1,000 livres in July and to 5,000 livres by September. In November 1719 the price of a share reached 10,000 livres, a 2,000 percent increase in just six months. In the eight months following the initial issue, the price of a share rose an average of more than 10 points a day! The term *millionaire* was first applied to owners of Mississippi Company shares.

The demand for shares was accompanied by a demand for money, a demand that Law's bank accommodated by simply printing notes. While 100 million livres in bank notes was circulating in the spring of 1719, the amount had increased twelvefold, to 1.2 *billion* livres, by the end of the year.

The beginning of 1720 found Law at the pinnacle of success. In January of that year he was appointed controller general of France. He was a respected nobleman who traveled in the circles of royalty, a genius whose advice was eagerly sought internationally. At the year's end Law escaped from Paris, lucky to leave with his head still attached to his body. He died, penniless and forgotten, in Venice in 1729.

What happened, of course, is that the bubble burst. When, in November 1719, some people began taking profits by selling shares instead of buying, the Royal Bank helped maintain share prices by printing fresh bank notes. In the spring of the following year, the Royal Bank agreed to buy or sell shares at 9,000 livres per share, virtually turning the stocks of the Mississippi Company into money. The bank's offer was accepted readily; company stock was converted into paper in vast sums, and the bank printed over 2 billion livres in just a few months. With the Royal Bank churning out new issues of money, prices in general rose rapidly. By the late summer of 1720 merchants refused to accept notes, demanding specie, whose value had shot upward, instead. A royal decree in October marked the formal end of Law's experiment. Payments were henceforth to be paid in gold or silver; Royal Bank notes were no longer legal tender.

The lessons of this episode are enlightening. First, a moderate expansion of bank money can stimulate economic activity, as Law had predicted and discovered to be true in his first few years in France. Second, overexpansion of the money supply can lead to massive bankruptcy and economic dislocations. When the bubble burst, it become evident that the Royal Bank had supported an artificial expansion. Third, a banking system based tenuously on real assets like gold can be manipulated both for the good and for the bad. Discretion and flexibility, as opposed to adherence to a fixed set of directions, are a direct consequence of a created-money system. In fact, much of banking theory is concerned with devising a framework for ensuring that bank-created money does not get out of hand, for maintaining flexibility without succumbing to the temptation of overissue. Precisely how to define "getting out of hand," however, is another matter; that question remains as much in dispute today as it was then.

☐ Commercial Banking in the United States

The history of banking in the United States can be seen as an interplay between "loose" and "tight" money concepts of banking. The more liberal, loose-money school argued, as Law did, that a larger volume of money accompanying a substantial expansion of bank lending would stimulate economic activity and bring boom times to the nation. Adherents of the more conservative tight-money attitude felt that only a sound, solid banking system—one that could bounce back after troubled times as well as serve its constituents during periods of prosperity—could bring true and continuous benefits to the economy. In truth, both schools had the same objective: a thriving, growing economic system. They differed only in their conception of the means required to achieve that end. Was it to be easy credit, liberal lending policies, or a more careful husbanding and distribution of financial resources?

The colonies that would later merge to form the United States functioned without commercial banks, although, as noted in Chapter 2, the lack of banks did not prevent the states from issuing their own paper money. The first bank on the American continent was the Bank of North America, located in Philadelphia. Chartered in 1781 by the Continental Congress, and then chartered by a number of individual states in 1782, the Bank was granted the right to issue bank notes. These notes differed in one substantial respect from earlier issues of state paper money: Bank of North America notes were freely convertible into specie. That is, anyone could exchange a bank note for its equivalent value in gold or silver coin.

The Bank soon proved a success and received the ultimate accolade— emulation. Banks patterned on the Bank of North America opened in New York and Boston in the 1780s and in a number of other cities prior to 1800. However, because the Bank followed a conservative money-issuing course, strong opposition was aroused among agrarian and speculative interests, who sought less constricting lending policies. Because of political pressure, the Bank's Pennsylvania charter, the one that permitted it to engage in business in its home state, was revoked in 1885. A new charter was granted two years later after much political bickering, and thereafter the bank survived with continual charter renewals. In fact, the Bank of North America still exists today, albeit under a different name, having been merged into the contemporary First Pennsylvania Bank of Philadelphia.

The first Bank of the United States

Since the 1890s the Bank of North America has had a rather uneventful history. The same cannot be written about the first Bank of the United States, which was born in controversy and died in strife. This first federally chartered institution opened for business in 1791, a brainchild of Alexander Hamilton, the first Secretary of the Treasury. Hamilton perceived a need for an institution that would become the banker for the government, a bank that would not only hold and disburse government deposits but also provide the federal treasury with a source of finance. In concept and in many details, the institution conceived by Hamilton was modeled on the Bank of England, for, as noted earlier, that bank too was set up to provide credit to a penurious government. In one important detail, however, the Bank of the United States differed from its English predecessor: It was formed as a quasi-public institution, owned partly by the government but mostly by the public. Hamilton's reason for this deviation was consistent with his objectives. Since the Bank's private stockholders were permitted to pay part of their contribution with Treasury bonds, Hamilton hoped thereby to increase the price—and, thus, the creditworthiness—of U.S. government bonds. (Shades of John Law—except that Hamilton's hopes were realized.) In other respects, however, the Bank of England did serve as the pattern setter. The notes of the Bank of the United States would be legal tender during the exclusive twenty-year charter granted to the bank. Similarly, the Bank of the United States would receive deposits from the public as well as the government.[3] Perhaps the most lasting import from the Bank of England was the precursor of the reserve ratio. In the practice of the time, a ratio of liabilities to specie holdings was set; for the Bank of the United States, an implicit ratio of 20 percent was imposed, so that total liabilities could not be more than five times the Bank's gold and silver holdings.

The Bank opened its office in Philadelphia, which at the time was the capital of the United States, in late 1791. During the next year branches were established in Boston, New York, Baltimore, and Charleston, and by 1805 additional branches had begun operations in Norfolk, Washington, Savannah, and New Orleans. The network of branches proved most beneficial to the Treasury, probably even exceeding Hamilton's expectations. Import duties collected in Savannah did not have to be transfered physically to Boston to pay for government purchases there. The Bank, by

---

[3]The distinction made today between a central bank (discussed in Chapter 12), which does not provide services to individuals, and a commercial bank, which does, was not made either in early nineteenth-century Britain or in America.

TABLE 4.3 Balance Sheet, Bank of the United States, March 3, 1809 (millions of dollars)

Assets		Liabilities and capital	
Specie in vault	$ 5.0	Deposits (gov't. and individual)	$ 8.5
Government securities	2.2	Bank notes in circulation	4.5
Loans to individuals (chiefly maturing within 60 days)	15.0	Capital	10.0
Due from state banks	5.0		

Source: Adapted from B. Hammond, *Banks and Politics in America from the Revolution to the Civil War* (Princeton, N.J.: Princeton University Press, 1957), p. 208. Because of the incomplete nature of the original accounting records, the two sides are not balanced.

virtue of its unified set of records, paid out from its Boston branch and offset that payment with the Treasury's receipt recorded in Savannah.

Another consequence of the Bank's operations was not only less foreseen but also less subject to universal approval. Because the Bank held the deposits of the federal government, to which payment was often made in state notes, the Bank of the United States became a major creditor of the state-chartered commercial banks. By demanding specie in exchange for their bank notes, the Bank of the United States threatened the profitability of the state banks. The state banks would have to maintain sufficient specie reserve to cover potential demands from the Bank of the United States. True, the result was a stable paper currency that was national in scope, but this virtue was disregarded in light of the inconvenience caused by the Bank's policy. The state banks resented the restraint on their freedom of manuever and on their profitability, which resulted from the need to hold high specie reserves. On the other hand, the Bank of the United States did lend to state banks, fulfilling the important function of lender of last resort.[4] Consistent with this lending function, the Bank held an unusually large proportion of specie. A typical balance sheet for the Bank, showing a ratio of specie reserves to liabilities of 38 percent—almost double the 20 percent implicit in the Bank's charter—is presented in Table 4.3.

The constitutionality of the Bank, a question that had already been broached at the time of the Bank's initial chartering, presumably had been answered affirmatively by the granting of the federal charter. Nevertheless, the issue arose again as the charter was about to expire in 1811: Did the federal government have the power to charter banks, since no such provision was to be found in the Constitution? Most students of the battle over charter renewal view this argument as a mere smokescreen concealing the true motives of the opponents of recharter. More substantial economic interests lay behind the opposition's position. Business and banking concerns preferred more liberal lending policies, which were

---

[4]For a more complete exposition of central banking and the lender-of-last-resort function, see Chapters 12 and 13.

made difficult by the conservative banking principles adhered to by the Bank of the United States. Moreover, the government's fiscal affairs, which were monopolized by the Bank of the United States, could have been a lucrative source of revenue for the state banks. For the number of banks had mushroomed. The banking system, which comprised only three banks in 1791, had grown to 88 in 1811; the only federally chartered institution was the Bank of the United States. By the narrowest of margins—one vote in the House of Representatives and a tie-breaking vote cast by Vice-President Clinton in the Senate—the bill for renewal of the charter was defeated. The Bank was dissolved in 1811, although its building and a portion of its assets were converted into a noncorporate private bank by a Philadelphia financier, Stephen Girard.

Aside from serving the Treasury well, the virtue of the Bank of the United States lay in its providing a stable, national currency. Both these advantages were lost with the termination of the Bank's charter. The Treasury used numerous state banks to receive and disburse payments, and consequently it became difficult to transfer funds from one part of the nation to another. And with the demise of centralized control over bank-issued money, the number of banks and the volume of money increased rapidly. Between 1811 and 1816 the number of banks almost tripled, from 88 to 246, while the stock of money is estimated to have more than doubled, from $28 million to $68 million. Surprisingly, the value of the dollar declined by only 16 percent; it was worth 79¢ in 1811 and 66¢ in 1816.[5] Needless to say, not all of these banks were established on solid grounds, with sufficient specie held in reserve against their liabilities. In fact, the dual problems of government finance and monetary diversity and instability were highlighted during the War of 1812, and led to demands for a new, second Bank of the United States.

The second Bank of the United States

The second Bank of the United States was clearly a child of its defunct forerunner; it was larger in terms of both capital and number of branches, but it bore the unmistakable imprint of its parent. And of course, the name was identical. The Bank was to serve as the government's banker; its notes were to be convertible into specie; and they were to be accepted in payment of government debts. The Bank was to be jointly owned by the government and the public, and its charter, too, was of twenty years' duration. Moreover, the 5:1 ratio of specie to liabilities was preserved.

The second Bank, chartered in 1816, began operations at its main office, also in Philadelphia, in January 1817. The Bank's formative years proved troublesome; poor management led to an oversupply of its bank

---

[5]Price indexes for this period are hardly reliable. Moreover, these and other monetary data in this chapter, unless otherwise noted, are based on prices in the eastern United States, where the banking system was more stable. Presumably, the increase in the money supply was smaller in the East than in the West.

notes, and even outright fraud was discovered during the first few years.[6] The reaction saw the pendulum swing the other way, with a sharp reduction in note supply and a deflation that was the consequence of this policy. By 1823 the Bank had passed through its childhood and adolescence and reached maturity. In that year Nicholas Biddle, a man of contrasts—intelligent but with limited business acumen, understanding but politically naive—ascended to the presidency of the Bank. At the age of 37, this man headed the largest corporation in the United States.

Biddle understood that the public responsibilities of the Bank of the United States ranked higher than the quest for profit that motivated many of the Bank's private shareholders. One concrete way in which these public responsibilities were met was in the area of governmental finance. The Bank received and made payments for the federal government, transfered its funds, and managed the national debt, all without charge to the U.S. Treasury. Perhaps even more important were Biddle's actions to provide the nation with a uniform currency. In the absence of abundant specie reserves and a uniform national currency, the nation's money consisted primarily of state bank notes. Some of the banks issuing those notes were stable, well-established institutions; others were not. As a result, the value of bank notes differed, depending on which and where the issuing bank was. Thus, a New Yorker buying an article priced at $5 might be able to pay with a $5 note of a well-known Connecticut bank. Should the customer wish to pay with the notes of a less well-known Ohio bank, however, the vendor might require $6 worth of notes. The merchant would know that the latter were circulating at a discount, and would value them accordingly. The reason for the discount was the cost of transporting the note back to the bank of issue for conversion into specie, as well as the risk of being unable to redeem the note in gold at all. The less well known the bank and the larger its circulation, the greater, of course, was the risk taken by the recipient of the banknote. (The vast number of bank notes, both legal and counterfeit, gave rise to publications like the *Bank Note Reporter and Counterfeit Detector*. Even by 1830, fourteen years after the formation of the second Bank, this publication listed discounts for 500 banks and about 1000 counterfeit notes.)

The very existence of Bank of the United States' notes that were redeemable in specie acted to bring some degree of uniformity to currency throughout the country, wherever the notes circulated. Biddle went one step further. Each week, bank notes that were issued by state banks and received at the Bank of the United States and its branches were returned to the issuing office for collection in specie. This policy ensured prudent action by the state banks. Each bank was forced to limit its note

---

[6] The broad interpretation of the Constitution—that anything that is not prohibited by the Constitution is permitted—was proclaimed by Chief Justice John Marshall in the famous case of *McCulloch* v. *Maryland*. The case centered on the right of Maryland to tax the Baltimore branch of the second Bank of the United States.

issue; it had to maintain sufficient specie reserves to cover demands for gold by the Bank of the United States. The result was an improvement in the value of all bank notes. For example, notes that had circulated in Tennessee at a 25 percent discount before the Bank's policy was implemented were afterward received at the substantially reduced discount of about 5 percent. Finally, the Bank attempted to moderate the impact on the economy of changes in the supply of money, especially when such changes resulted from external forces. Biddle claimed that the Bank mitigated the sharpness of the contraction of 1825 when it eased the credit tightening that had been caused by an outflow of gold.

Historians believe that the Bank achieved its two purposes—acting as the government's fiscal agent and serving as a source of a more stable currency—and certainly it did so after 1823. There is less agreement, however, on whether the Bank was able to stabilize the economy and mitigate deflations and inflations. Money supply data are not available for the entire twenty years of the Bank's existence, but estimates do exist for the period during which Biddle was in office. Between 1823 and 1834 (the terminal date is chosen because the Bank's powers declined considerably even prior to the expiration of its charter in 1836) the money supply rose from $88 million to $172 million, an increase of almost 100 percent in eleven years. But prices remained remarkably stable over the period; if anything, they declined a bit. Wholesale prices, for example, fell from an index level of 103 in 1823 to 95 in 1834. Yet, tempting as it may be to conclude that the Bank exerted a slight restraining effect on the economy, such an appraisal must be tempered for a number of reasons. First, while the second Bank of the United States did exert an influence, it is difficult to assert that it alone was responsible for whatever happened in the economy during the years of its existence. Moreover, the trend over the eleven-year period hides crosscurrents of stability, deflation, and even inflation. Prices fell by 13 percent between 1825 and 1830, remained stable between 1831 and 1833, and rose by 5 percent in 1835. Recall, too, that these statistics are, at best, good guesses rather than hard facts, so that any conclusions drawn from them must be treated with skepticism.[7] In short, it is difficult to evaluate the Bank's quantitative impact on the nation. It seems clear, however, that the Bank was, and was viewed as, a conservative, constricting force and to some observers seemed quite out of step with the demands of an expanding nation.

History often repeats itself. The demise of the second Bank of the United States was not unlike that of the first Bank. In 1832 Biddle believed the time was right to request Congressional renewal of the Bank's charter. Congress agreed. President Jackson vetoed the bill,

---

[7]For example, in *The Jacksonian Economy* (New York: W. W. Norton, 1967) Peter Temin cites data that show deflation between 1828 and 1830 and inflation, not stability, between 1830 and 1833 (p. 69).

however, and the "bank war" between Jackson and the Bank's supporters swung into the public eye.

Once again, economic historians have not agreed on the reasons underlying nonrenewal of this charter. Some claim that the agrarian, antibanking views expressed by Jackson were able to defeat the business-oriented eastern interests. Others see the more conservative businessmen, who cherished progress, but at a moderate pace, defeated by the new industrial and speculative entrepreneurs. Still others find the state bankers marshaling their armies against centralized control. Some see the issue as primarily political—Jackson versus Clay and Webster—rather than economic in origin. Be as it may, Congress failed to override the Jackson veto, and as 1837 rolled around, the United States again found itself without a federal bank. It was as if nothing had been learned since 1816.

The period from 1836 to 1864

The period between the Jackson-Biddle bank war and the Civil War was characterized by the absence of centralized control over the monetary system. Banking responded the way a stallion does to a loosening of the reins. Since the demise of centralized control came at a time when money and credit were being demanded to finance the early steps of American industrialization, not only was the stallion free to run, but he had ample room to do so. The free-enterprise spirit that underlay industrialization pervaded banking as well. From a total of 713 in 1836, the last year of the second bank's federal charter, the number of banks grew to 1556 in 1864. Indeed, this more than doubling of the number of banks understates the number of bank formations, since not all of the banks that were founded during the period survived to its end. Moreover, the net increase of 843 banks over the three decades conceals the ebb and flow of the intervening years.

The years between 1836 and 1864 were not all prosperous. At least two major "busts" occurred and left their imprint on the banking system through bank closings and failures. So, although the number of banks in the prosperous years of 1852–1854 increased by one-third, the net increase between 1857 and 1858, the years of the panic of 1857, was only six.

Spurring on, or at least permitting, rapid bank growth was the concept of **free banking.** All of the banks that were chartered prior to free-banking legislation were created by individual legislative acts; each bank charter required special legislative approval. This method of chartering banks not only fostered the corruption of public officials but also encouraged banking monopolies. Established banks would fight tenaciously to prevent the legislature from chartering a rival. Under free banking, any institution meeting preestablished legislative requirements would obtain

Free banking meant that any group that met preestablished legal conditions could operate a banking corporation without obtaining special legislative approval.

a charter automatically. Although Michigan passed the first free-banking law in 1837, it was a year later in New York that the law with the most lasting impact made its way through the legislative process.[8] Among the most important provisions of the New York free-banking legislation were the following:

1. Banks were required to deposit federal or state bonds with the state comptroller.
2. In exchange for assets deposited, the comptroller would issue an amount of bank notes equivalent in value to the face value of the securities deposited.
3. Banks were required to redeem in specie and on demand all bank notes with a face value of less than $1000.
4. In the event that the bank refused to redeem the bank notes, the comptroller could sell the deposited securities and so redeem the notes.
5. Specie reserves of 12½ percent had to be maintained against outstanding bank notes. (Although this provision was repealed in 1840, it was the forerunner of the practice of requiring reserves to be held in some proportion of liabilities.)

The New York legislation was copied, albeit with variations, in a number of states, although it would be wrong to state that free banking spread like wildfire. By 1860, however, eighteen states, or more than half of the nation, had passed free-banking laws. The expected consequence—more banks—followed; in New York, the number of banks nearly doubled before the law was three years old. Unfortunately, not all of those banks were solid, and the protection to noteholders implicit in the deposit of securities proved illusory.

At its worst, free banking encouraged outright fraud. Some promoters would deposit with the comptroller bonds whose market value was well below their face value. They would obtain notes equal to the face value and, after distributing those notes, could well disappear with their profit. When the notes were presented for redemption and the comptroller finally sold the securities, the value received was significantly below that of the outstanding bank notes. Other promoters opened banks without the required specie, either deluding the bank inspectors or bribing them. Some filled chests with nails and glass, placing a few rolls of gold coin on top. A story is told of a "banker" who came to a midwestern banking commissioner with two suitcases full of gold coins. While the commissioner was counting the coins in the second case, the banker took the first case out of the office, where a confederate repacked the coins in another case. The third case was then brought in to be counted, and this procedure was repeated until the requisite specie had been counted out.

_____

[8]The Michigan act was repealed in 1839, after the more than forty banks established subsequent to its passage had all failed.

The record of failures is perhaps exaggerated; while many banks failed, most did not. And even those that failed did provide a medium of exchange in a specie-deficient country.

The Civil War and the National Bank Act

The absence of a centralized banking system complicated federal finance. The Treasury, having withdrawn its funds from the Bank of the United States, initially used the services of the state banks, the so-called pet banks run by Jacksonian supporters. Dissatisfaction with this method soon induced the Treasury to set up its own local offices for the receipt and disbursement of government funds, a network that was called the Independent Treasury System. But the existing machinery could not cope with the demands forced upon it by the Civil War. Moreover, wartime expenditures mandated substantial amounts of borrowing, yet the Treasury had few facilities to float large public issues. Combined with these fiscal difficulties were those caused by the multitude of bank notes in circulation.

An innovative proposal was desperately needed. The Lincoln administration came through with an ingenious idea designed to resolve all of these problems simultaneously. State banking would be replaced by a system of national banks, that is, federally chartered institutions. These banks would buy U.S. government securities from the Treasury and would be permitted to issue national bank notes, which would become the uniform currency throughout the nation. An ideal solution, apparently. The national banks would lend the North the funds it required by purchasing federal bonds; the public would be assured a single, uniform national currency; and the Treasury, which had refused to accept state bank notes in payment of taxes and debts due it, would accept the national currency at its local offices. Moreover, the national banks would be permitted to maintain government deposits and thus could facilitate Treasury payments throughout the country. Accordingly, Congress passed the National Bank Act of 1864, and Lincoln signed it. (The original title of this piece of legislation was the National Currency Act of 1863. It was thoroughly revised in 1864.)

The National Bank Act remains one of the foundations of American banking practice, and it is worthwhile to detail some of its major clauses. Among the provisions of the Act were the following:

1. Any group could obtain a twenty-year national charter, a free-banking feature, provided that certain capital requirements were met. These requirements varied with the size of the community in which the bank was located, ranging from $50,000 in a city of 6,000 to $200,000 for cities with populations of over 50,000.
2. An office of the comptroller of the currency was established within the Treasury to charter national banks and issue currency.
3. National bank notes were obtained from the comptroller of the

currency in exchange for Treasury securities. In the initial Act, each bank's note circulation was limited to 90 percent of the lower of the current market price or par value of the bonds tendered. (This figure was raised to 100 percent in 1900.)

4. A three-tiered pyramid of national banks was constructed, with "central reserve city" (initially New York City) banks at the peak, banks in sixteen "reserve cities" in the middle, and "country banks," or all the remaining banks, at the base.

5. Reserve ratios were imposed against liabilities: 15 percent for country banks and 25 percent for reserve city and central reserve city banks. However, country banks could maintain a portion of their required reserves with reserve city or New York City banks. Reserve city banks, too, could hold deposits with New York City banks.

6. The Treasury could use the national banks as depositories.

Congress anticipated that state banks would readily convert from their existing charters to federal charters. However, few banks elected to do so, the constraints imposed, especially with respect to capitalization, being too onerous. By October of 1864 only 508 banks, with a note circulation of $45 million—constituting only one-third of the total number of banks and approximately one-quarter of the bank notes in circulation—had opted for national charters.

In 1865, to spur on the national banking system, Congress passed an act imposing a 10 percent tax on the notes of state banks. This tax effectively eliminated state bank notes, for their issuance was no longer profitable. By 1866 the number of national banks had grown to 1644, with a combined note circulation of $171 million. Fewer than 300 banks retained their original state charters.

But although the tax eliminated state bank notes, it failed to achieve a second objective—the dismantling of the state banking system. State banks survived, and they retain their strength to this day. The secret of their survival lies in the growth of deposit banking rather than reliance on note circulation as a major source of bank revenue.

Deposit banking

Because much of the preceding discussion has focused on currency and bank notes, you might have gained the impression that the deposit function of banks played only a minor role in banking history. Such an impression would certainly be incorrect: Recall that the goldsmiths held funds for depositors. And their earliest transactions involved transfering these accounts from one owner to another, usually through a written order, or check. Similarly, early American banks not only issued their own notes but also held depositors' accounts and transfered them on demand. Take another look at the balance sheet of the Bank of the United States on page 95: note that deposits accounted for almost twice the value of bank notes in circulation. For even the earliest American banks'

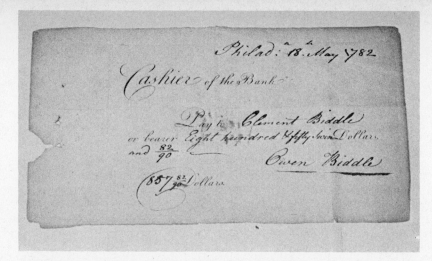

FIGURE 4.2 The oldest known check in the Western Hemisphere, drawn on the Bank of North America. (Note: The cents notation is 82/90, rather than 91/100, because the accounts were kept in Mexican dollars, which were valued at 90 cents in silver.)

Courtesy of the First Pennsylvania Corp.

deposits could be transferred by check, as Figure 4.2 indicates. (Why does the face of the check omit the name of the bank, the Bank of North America? Could it be related to the fact that in 1782 there were no other banks around?)

Although no reliable data on deposits in this country in the early nineteenth century are available, there is no doubt that deposits already constituted a large proportion of bank liabilities at the start of American banking history. In fact, early New York City banks, catering primarily to business customers, most likely held larger sums in deposit accounts than as note liabilities. How modern is the following description of banking, written by Alexander Hamilton in 1790:

> Every loan which a bank makes is in its first shape a credit given to the borrower on its books, the amount of which it stands ready to pay either in its own notes or in gold or silver, at his option. But in a great number of cases no actual payment is made in either. The borrower frequently, by a check or order, transfers his credit to some other person, to whom he has a payment to make; who in his turn is as often content with a similar credit, because he is satisfied that he can, whenever he pleases, either convert it into cash or pass it to some other hand as an equivalent for it.[9]

Throughout the pre-Civil War era, the public maintained a strong interest in deposit holdings, and at least by 1834, if not earlier, these

---

[9]B. Hammond, *Banks and Politics in America from the Revolution to the Civil War* (Princeton, N.J.: Princeton University Press, 1957), p. 81.

accounts at banks exceeded bank liabilities in the form of notes. Just prior to the beginning of the Civil War, at the end of 1860, deposits totaled 50 percent more than notes. (Data on deposits prior to 1914 do not distinguish between demand and time deposits. Consequently, the proportion of money in the form of demand deposits listed here is overestimated. Nevertheless, the increasing importance of demand deposits as opposed to currency is a trend that cannot be denied.)

Thus, when the tax on state bank notes was imposed, only one aspect of state banking operations was infringed upon. State banks that had minimal note issues were hardly affected. Furthermore, state banks that maintained substantial amounts of currency in circulation could still retain their state charter, provided that their customers could be persuaded to substitute checking accounts for note withdrawals. Of course, as indicated earlier, the majority of state banks did convert to national status. But as the second half of the century unfolded, more of the newly founded banks chose state rather than national charters.

In sum, through oversight—because the importance of the deposit function of banks had not been appreciated—and certainly not by plan, the United States has been saddled with a **dual banking system** in which state-chartered and federally chartered commercial banks operate side by side. This banking network, which is unique to the United States, has been a source of concern to bank regulators, and will be covered in Chapters 8 and 12.

When the Civil War ended, the legislative foundation had been set for a banking system whose characteristics remain basically the same today. Some features proved worthy of preserving; others were disposed of in the legislation that led to the formation of the Federal Reserve System in 1913. But all left their imprint on the American banking structure.

Because a bank can be chartered by either state or federal authorities, the U.S. banking pattern is called a **dual banking system**.

The second half of the nineteenth century

The pulsating industrial giant that is today's United States achieved its greatest degree of dynamism during the second half of the last century. In Rostow's terminology, the United States completed its "take-off and drive to maturity."[10] By the end of the century the divisiveness that had culminated in the Civil War had been repaired, if not fully healed; the nation was unified politically. The states were united in other ways, too—the far ends of the continent had been linked and then crisscrossed by railroads; the colorful frontier had been closed. Manufacturing had replaced agriculture as the predominant form of economic activity. While in 1869 manufacturing accounted for 33 percent of the nation's commodity output as opposed to 53 percent for agriculture, these percentages were exactly reversed by 1899. The labor force reflected these changes as

---

[10]W. W. Rostow, *The Stages of Economic Growth: A Non-Communist Manifesto* (Cambridge: Cambridge University Press, 1960).

the economy became ever more organized. American business no longer could be characterized as ruled by atomistic competition; the railroad, sugar, and oil trusts had made sufficient impact on economic and political life to warrant antitrust legislation during the last decade of the century. The economy's pace was rapid; between 1865 and 1900 the average annual rise in the output of goods and services exceeded 3.5 percent, or, for the entire thirty-five years, more than tripled. In per capita terms— for the population also increased markedly—a still significant rate of annual real output growth, 1½ percent, was achieved. That implies an increase in the standard of living of 67 percent by the end of the century.

Growth was not steady, however. Years of plenty were followed by years of famine. Although the economy surged forward, frequent down-turns occurred. Indeed, the longest economic contraction recorded in the United States, a 5½-year period between late 1873 and early 1879, occurred during this half-century.

Commercial banking shared both the upward trend and the shorter, cyclical ups and downs. The number of banks, which in 1865 was less than 2,000, had exceeded 12,000 by 1900. The initial predominance of national banks was reversed as state banks forged ahead. At the close of the century, not quite 4,000 national banks and almost 9,000 state banks supplied the nation with banking services. The amount of currency (consisting of greenbacks, national bank notes, specie, and subsidiary coins) doubled, rising from $0.6 billion in 1866 to $1.2 billion in 1900, while total deposits increased more than sevenfold, growing from $0.7 billion to $5.2 billion.

The growth of banking was sporadic; this industry, like many others, had high points and ebbs. The nation's economic booms affected and were affected by the health of the banking industry, and this was even more true of busts. Banking panics, which are unfamiliar today, were hardly unknown to Americans one hundred years ago, even if they were not frequent. Major runs on the banks and resulting waves of bank failures occurred in 1873 and 1893. These episodes, which rent the smooth fabric of the financial system, overshadowed the fundamental soundness of the banks as a whole. They were disturbing interludes, and as such led to demands for reform. The proverbial straw that broke the camel's back was the Panic of 1907. The economy turned down in the middle of that year, but after a few New York City banks failed and others refused to convert deposits into specie, the contraction turned into a full-fledged panic. Runs on the banks resulted in additional bank failures. Congress acted by setting up a National Monetary Commission to investigate the banking system and recommend ways to improve its performance so that panics would be remembered only in history books.

The ultimate consequence of this event was the creation of the Federal Reserve System, about which much of this book revolves. The formation of the system resulted from the commission's diagnosis of the basic structural faults of the banking industry. Understanding this diagnosis is important, for it not only enhances our comprehension of banking in the late nineteenth century but also underlies the restructuring that followed.

The prelude to the Federal Reserve Act

Perhaps the overriding weakness displayed by the monetary system was its inability to respond to changing economic circumstances. This rigidity may well have been a source of banking panics, and it certainly did nothing to dissipate the crises. Central to the system's inflexibility were two problems: (1) the "inelasticity" of the money supply and (2) the illiquidity of the monetary system.

The inelasticity problem. U.S. currency consisted primarily of gold and silver coins. Only one-third of the total currency consisted of paper money even as late as the first decade of the twentieth century. The supply of specie did not respond to the needs of the economy, nor could it be made to do so quickly. The availability of gold and silver depended heavily on serendipitous events like the discovery of new ore deposits and on economic forces like the balance of payments. (When domestic prices rose relative to prices in foreign markets, Americans would be induced to buy abroad, paying for those imports by exporting gold.) Thus, there could be no guarantee that the supply of specie would be adequate to meet the current demands of the economy.

The note supply was also encased in a rather rigid mold. The Civil War greenbacks were issued in a fixed amount that could not be increased without congressional action. While the number of national bank notes could be expanded, it was linked to bank ownership of Treasury securities. Frequently market forces worked in directions opposite to the path desired. During economic downturns bond prices rose, leading banks to sell their bonds in order to reap the resulting capital gains. But this decrease in bank bond holdings meant that the note issue would decline. And when business required additional currency, the banks, lacking sufficient Treasury securities, were unable to meet all the legitimate demands of borrowers.

The illiquidity problem. The pyramiding of reserves that was sanctioned by the National Bank Act shared a great deal of the responsibility for the tendency of the banking system to succumb to panics. When country banks called for the deposits they held on reserve with their reserve city or New York City correspondents, as they frequently did to meet seasonal demands at home, the reserve city banks experienced tightness. They would be forced to liquidate assets, which at that time generally meant calling in loans. Thus, the tightness was transmitted further. When the called loans had supported speculation in the securities markets, sales of stocks and bonds to pay off the bank debt meant falling prices in a highly visible segment of the economy. The system worked poorly; instead of expanding total credit to meet temporary needs, it merely shifted funds from one part of the country to another. Although the arithmetic effect might have been zero, a canceling out on a nationwide reckoning, the seasonal tightness did mean unnecessary disruption of the national financial mechanism.

Yet, while this seasonal inflexibility was a nuisance, it was not itself sufficient to lead to reform. After all, the seasonal pattern was naturally self-reversing. More disturbing were the actions of country banks during cyclical contractions. When these banks felt that their city correspondents might be in trouble, they demanded their deposits back in the form of specie. A prudent action, to be sure, for each one, but unfortunately it was unhealthy for the banking community as a whole. Such actions engendered a vicious cycle. Recall that banks operate on a fractional reserve basis, with liabilities greatly exceeding their reserves. So when many banks simultaneously demanded specie from the reserve city and New York City banks, the city banks could not meet the total desired. They simply did not possess sufficient specie on hand. True, they could call in some loans and liquidate some assets, and indeed they did so. But this exacerbated what might have already been tough times for bank borrowers, while asset sales *en masse* would only force their prices downward. *There was no way in which the entire banking system could supplement its stock of reserves at short notice.* The result, of course, was a greater clamor for currency on the part of banks and the general public as well, further declines in asset values, and ultimately, insolvency and the ruination of many banks. Essentially, this generalized picture outlines what happened during the Panic of 1907. The pyramiding of reserves may be seen as the root cause of the problem, but the absence of any degree of flexibility in providing reserves and currency permitted this structural weakness to be translated into a banking crisis.

The Federal Reserve Act of 1913 provided the resiliency that was absent in earlier banking legislation. It legislated an elastic currency by enabling the Federal Reserve to issue its own notes in response to economic needs, and also provided a method for increasing bank liquidity when circumstances warranted it. With the passage of that Act and the creation of the Federal Reserve System, the nation's basic banking structure was completed. Banking in the twentieth century takes place against the background of the National Bank and Federal Reserve Acts and their various amendments, as well as the institutions to which they gave rise.

The banking structure has undergone few substantial changes since 1913. National banks still coexist and compete with state banks, as they have for over one hundred years. To be sure, banks have grown larger, new corporate forms have been applied to banking, and the banking system has become more internationally oriented. New economic and legislative challenges have brought innovative responses, and they are important to our understanding of today's banking system. The current banking scene is the subject of Chapters 8 and 9, in which you will be encouraged to explore some of the more pressing issues affecting twentieth-century banking.

□ Summary

Commercial banks are financial intermediaries, participants in the process of indirect finance. They acquire funds from lenders (depositors) and pass them along to borrowers. Yet financial intermediaries are not mere transfer agents. They engage in *transformation*, whereby the short-term liabilities that they issue (e.g., deposits) are turned into longer-term debts (e.g., mortgages) that are acquired by the intermediary itself. Commercial banks are just one of an array of financial intermediaries; other types of banks and nonbanks perform similar functions. The uniqueness of commercial banks stems from the fact that their demand liabilities are the major component of money in modern economies. Of course, this money-creating ability itself is dependent on the ability of commercial banks to operate on a *fractional reserve* basis.

This chapter traced the evolution of the banks' money-creating ability. You will have realized that money creation is a two-edged sword: It can be used to stimulate the economy, but it can also drive the economic system to the extremes of inflation and deflation. Much banking history is centered on the tension between "hard money" supporters, who were concerned about economic instability arising from overissue, and "soft money" advocates, who were more growth oriented and less worried about instability. Galbraith, in his usual pithy and less forgiving manner, interprets this struggle as follows:

> It was to the pecuniary interest of some to have restraint, stable money and prices, and a lender and savior of last resort. It was to the pecuniary interest of others to have no restraint either on what could be gained by lending or what could be made by borrowing. The consequences, however disastrous, were not as bad as control.[11]

The controversy surrounding rechartering both Banks of the United States is a good example of this tension.

One of the underlying motives of national banking legislation of 1863 and 1864 was to ensure a more stable supply of bank notes, since the multiplicity of private issues had needlessly complicated the flow of money in the economy of the United States during the mid-nineteenth century. The aim of these laws was ultimately achieved by a tax on state bank notes, but as is often the case, unforseen side effects soon followed legislative action. One such unanticipated consequence was the expansion of deposit banking (as opposed to bank issues of notes), which kept alive state chartering of banks and is responsible for the present dual

---

[11]J. K. Galbraith, *Money: Whence It Came, Where It Went* (Boston: Houghton Mifflin, 1975), p. 71

banking system. The second unexpected consequence of the legislation stemmed from the new system of pyramiding reserves. With fractional-reserve banking, the banking mechanism becomes vulnerable to runs, which bring down solid as well as poorly managed banks in the turbulent avalanche of panic. The National Bank Act locked the banking system into a rigid structure that virtually ensured that a panic, once underway, would not be stopped until it had worn itself out.

By the beginning of the twentieth century, it was evident that the economy required a banking system that could react flexibly to business expansion by creating money when it was needed, but would also be protected from liquidity crises. To achieve both flexibility and liquidity in a privately owned banking system that had the power to create money and yet would not succumb to panic—these were the hopes that stimulated the formation of the Federal Reserve System.

At this juncture we take leave of banking history, having brought it forward to the present century, and turn to an examination of contemporary banking and current issues.

□ Questions and Exercises

1. Direct and indirect finance need not be viewed as conflicting ways of obtaining funds. Firms frequently engage in both. Under what circumstances might one alternative be preferred over the other?
2. "Transformation" is inherently risky. After explaining why this is so, you might think of ways that the banker might devise to minimize the risks.
3. For money creation to take place, the public must be willing to allow the banker to maintain fractional reserves. Demonstrate the truth of this statement by explaining what would happen to money creation if the public insisted that reserves always equal deposits.
4. Like many things, money creation can be beneficial or detrimental to the health of the economy. What lessons can be learned from the monetary experiments of the American colonies and John Law, as well as from the controversies surrounding rechartering of the first and second Banks of the United States, insofar as the impact of money creation is concerned?
5. The National Bank Act was passed to remedy some problems but, like much legislation, created some unforeseen difficulties of its own. On balance, do you believe the Act to have been more useful than detrimental? Support your contention.

□ For Further Study

One wonders whether John Kenneth Galbraith enjoyed writing *Money: Whence It Came, Where It Went* (Boston: Houghton Mifflin, 1975) as much as many people have enjoyed reading this best seller. Its early, historical chapters are both informative and entertaining. For a picture of banking in the fifteenth century, R. de Roover, *The Rise and Decline of the Medici Bank, 1397–1494* (Cambridge, Mass.: Harvard University Press, 1963), is marvelous. Ripping off the Bank of England by using forged bills of exchange is the topic of a novel by Stephen Sheppard, *The Four Hundred* (New York: Summit Books, 1979; paper, New York: Berkley Books, 1980).

Early American banking is nowhere better surveyed than in Bray Hammond's Pultizer Prize-winning study, *Banks and Politics in America from the Revolution to the Civil War* (Princeton, N.J.: Princeton University Press, 1957).

Benjamin Klebaner, *Commercial Banking in the United States: A History* (Hinsdale, Ill.: Dryden Press, 1974), offers an extraordinary wealth of detail in under 200 pages.

CHAPTER 5

Commercial Banking in the United States: An Overview

Banks are by far the most important of all our commercial establishments. They are the foundations of our currency, the depositories of our capital, and at once the wheels and pillars of our trade. Business to any great extent could not be carried on without them.

Thomas Joplin, British banker (1821)

CONTENTS

The nature of the American commercial banking system today differs radically from its configuration in the early years of this century. The contrast is so vast that the modern system would be virtually unrecognizable to a contemporary Rip van Winkle. True, Rip would notice that banks[1] today, as in 1900 or 1920, still accept deposits, transfer funds to third parties, and lend money. But he would soon discern that their deposit and lending activities are far more varied than they were in the earlier, and perhaps simpler, era. At the same time, Rip would discover that modern-day banks perform functions that were considered inappropriate for banks in earlier years.

This chapter surveys contemporary American banking, touching on the type of loans banks make, the kinds of services they provide to both consumers and businesses, the structure of the banking industry, and competition in banking. The sources of bank income and expenditures and bank profits are also examined. Some of the problems of contemporary bankers are mentioned, but the details are left for the remaining chapters in this part of the book.

☐ Bank Lending, Then and Now

Bankers should lend only for short-term, self-liquidating, commercial purposes, according to the **commercial loan theory** of banking or **real-bills doctrine.**

The typical bank in the early years of this century was run on the basis of the **commercial loan theory** of banking, also known as the **real-bills doctrine.** According to this view, the safety of banks from failure and illiquidity would be ensured only if the loans granted matured soon and were secured by tangible goods. When the goods were sold, the proceeds would be used to repay the loan. Loans granted to producers to pay for raw materials or to wholesalers and retailers for acquiring inventory were considered appropriate, since in the normal course of business the raw materials or inventory would be sold in a matter of months, whereupon the loan would be repaid.

This view of banking limited the types of bank customers as well as the

---

[1] Unless otherwise noted, the unmodified term *bank* refers to a commercial bank.

kinds of loans bankers would make. A consumer who wished to borrow in order to finance a new horseless carriage would not qualify for two reasons. First, since no income would be earned from the pleasure vehicle, the loan was not self-liquidating. Second, the proud owner would be unlikely to pay off the loan within a year. Long-term or even intermediate-term loans to business fared no better. A loan to finance a truck was unacceptable. True, the truck was an earning asset. But because the profit flow to pay off the loan would require years, not months, such a loan was inappropriate. Certainly, speculative loans of any sort were out of the question. Lending to finance the acquisition of stocks or bonds would not be undertaken, since no tangible goods were represented by those paper assets and since the risk of a falling market would leave the banker unprotected.

As a matter of fact, the real-bills doctrine was illusory; it worked well during years of prosperity, but it failed to guarantee the banks either liquidity or protection against default should the borrower fail or the economy plunge into recession. An inventory of car parts could well remain unsold if the automobile market declined. And even if they were salable, the parts might not bring in a sufficiently high price to repay the loan.

Partly out of necessity, partly out of the realization of the inherent illogic of the commercial loan theory, and partly because of new sources of bank liquidity, the banking community shifted gears as the twentieth century rolled on. In the mid-1930s, the Great Depression era, the banks were faced with sluggish loan demand. Moreover, reliance on the commercial loan theory had hardly prevented thousands of banks from failing and had not relieved the liquidity problems of others. (In truth, banks had already departed from the straight and narrow path of the real-bills doctrine by financing speculation in the soaring stock market of the late 1920s, and had even speculated on their own account.) Banks began to issue **term loans**. The real-bills doctrine gave way to the **anticipated-income theory** of bank lending, with the result that bankers began to lend for longer periods and to new types of customers. The truck financed by an intermediate-term loan of five years became legitimate. So, too, did the twenty-year mortgage on a warehouse. Consumer lending now became acceptable—provided, of course, that the repayment prospects of the borrower appeared certain. Take a look at Table 5.1 for the various types of loans and the varied maturities of bank loans outstanding on December 31, 1980. In fact, while commercial and industrial loans remain the single largest category of bank lending, they constituted only one third of the total.

It is truly an anachronism to call contemporary banks "commercial." They are more clearly seen as department or variety stores of finance— the British call them universal banks—providing a broad range of borrowers with a vast array of services.

A **term loan** carries an initial maturity of more than one year.

The borrower's expected capacity to pay the principal and interest of the loan on time is the critical element in the loan decision, according to the **anticipated-income theory** of bank lending.

TABLE 5.1 Loans of All Commercial Banks in the United States, December 31, 1980
(billions of dollars and percentages)

Type of loan	Billions of dollars	Percent
Real Estate Loans—total	$263.6	31.3
Construction and land development	36.8	4.4
Secured by farmland	8.7	1.0
Secured by 1–4 family residential properties	147.6	17.5
Secured by multifamily (5 or more) residential properties	6.6	1.0
Secured by nonfarm nonresidential properties	63.9	7.6
Loans to financial institutions	46.7	5.6
Loans for purchasing or carrying securities	12.5	1.5
Loans to finance agricultural production and other loans to farmers	31.6	3.8
Commercial and industrial loans	283.3	33.7
Loans to individuals—total	181.7	21.6
To purchase private passenger automobiles on installment basis	62.0	7.4
Credit cards and related plans	29.9	3.6
To purchase mobile homes	10.4	1.2
All other installment loans	46.2	5.5
Single payment personal loans	33.2	4.0
All other loans	22.1	2.6
Total loans	841.5	100.0[a]

[a]Total does not sum up due to rounding.

Source: Federal Deposit Insurance Corporation, *Annual Report, 1980 (Washington, D.C., 1981).*

☐ Bank Services

Consumer banking

The range of services offered by contemporary banks extends far beyond accepting and transfering deposits and granting loans. Most of us are consumers of bank services, and we know about the various types of checking and savings accounts available. We're also familiar with the various types of consumer loans: loans activated by credit card purchases or an **overdraft**, personal loans backed by collateral, education loans, and home mortgage loans. Modern banks also provide a host of services that are ancillary to their deposit and lending functions. Many banks offer safe deposit facilities and issue travelers checks, money orders, and U.S. savings bonds. Banks also provide a range of international services, exchanging domestic currency for foreign money and transfering funds abroad. They also act as trustees, executing wills and administering estates. In general, this type of banking, which deals with consumers, is called **retail banking**. Virtually all domestic banks engage in retail banking, but not exclusively.

In passing, mention must be made of the revolution in computerization that has affected the technical aspects of consumer banking. Banking, like most service industries, is labor intensive. Tellers are needed to accept deposits and loan payments; they must be ready to make change and pay out cash. Banking machines, which are spreading throughout the country,

When a bank permits a depositor to withdraw funds in excess of the depositor's balance, this automatic loan is called an **overdraft**. Usually overdrafts are activated by check, but they are always limited to a specific amount negotiated by the depositor and the bank.

Retail banking deals with private individuals rather than businesses.

perform these simple functions. Moreover, their 24-hours-a-day, 7-days-a-week availability makes them exceptionally convenient. But this is only the beginning. Consumer banking will change more radically in the next decade, with computer terminals providing banking services in nontraditional settings. Many new problems will arise, but so, too, will new opportunities; Chapter 8 takes a peek at some of these issues.

Wholesale banking

Wholesale banking is the alter ego of retail banking. Some wholesale banks cater almost exclusively to the financial needs of the business community; among them are New York's Morgan Guaranty and almost all the foreign banks that have offices in the United States. Most banks, however, combine wholesale banking with retail banking.

Wholesale banking involves the provision of banking services to the business community.

The range of services provided by banks to the business community encompasses those available to the retail market but extends far beyond them. The variety of loans is broader, as is that of deposit collection and transfer accounts. It would take many pages to list and explain each of these functions; a concise listing is provided in Box 5.1.

☐ The Structure of the Banking Industry

Banks are constrained by law from expanding their branches beyond specified geographic limits (see Chapter 8). This affects their retail activities far more than their wholesale efforts. Consumers tend to bank in their immediate neighborhood; businesses are more flexible, and the

---

BOX 5.1 Commercial Bank Services to Business

Deposit and Money Transfer Services
Checking and time deposits
Payroll accounts
Treasury tax and loan accounts (see p. 139)
Escrow accounts
Post office box plans

Loans	*Trust and Agency Services*
Commercial loans	Trustee for pension and profit-sharing plans
Accounts receivable loans	Trustee for employee stock purchase plans
Inventory loans	Transfer and dividend-disbursing agent
Term loans	Paying agent
Construction loans	
Leasing	
Factoring	

---

larger the business, the more geographically diverse its banking connections are likely to be.

Large corporations deal with large banks. Only the largest financial institutions can meet the variegated needs of the nation's industrial and commercial giants. Only they possess the capital base to lend immense sums of money and the expertise to provide sophisticated money transfer services. They also have the national and international links to arrange for speedy transfer of funds and for short-term investment, and the skilled personnel who can be consulted by clients for assistance and advice on financial issues. In the age of the telephone, the airplane, and microwave message transmission, state boundaries and even national borders pose no barrier to the wholesale banker.

The result of this wholesale-retail, national-local division is a highly-skewed distribution of banks. By far the largest group of banks consists of small, local ones. As Table 5.2 indicates, commercial banks with deposits of less than $50 million constituted 75 percent of the nation's banks in 1980, but accounted for only 14½ percent of the nation's deposits. At the opposite end of the size spectrum lie the behemoths of American banking. These giants, constituting only two-tenths of one percent of the banks in terms of number, account for almost one-third of the country's deposits.[2] (The largest thirty, ranked by asset size in 1980, are listed in Box 5.2).

The **regional banks** fit into the spectrum just below the giants. Although they are large compared to the rest of America's banks, they are not in the class of the giants. But many of these banks are aggressive, and it is from the ranks of the regionals that the new giants will spring.

A **regional bank** is one that is large in its own section of the country but is not sufficiently strong to compete effectively with the giants of banking.

TABLE 5.2 Size Distribution of All Commercial Banks, December 31, 1980

Deposit category	Number of banks	Percent of total	Deposits (millions of dollars)	Percent of total
Less than $5 million	874	5.9	2,673	0.2
$5.0–9.9 million	1,937	13.2	14,688	1.0
$10.0–24.9 million	4,662	31.7	78,072	5.1
$25.0–49.9 million	3,556	24.2	126,053	8.2
$50.0–99.9 million	1,972	13.4	135,735	8.8
$100.0–299.9 million	1,159	7.9	183,950	12.0
$300.0–499.9 million	197	1.4	76,961	5.0
$500.0–999.9 million	161	1.1	109,140	7.1
$1.0–4.9 billion	160	1.1	334,976	21.8
$5.0 billion or more	29	0.2	476,790	31.0
Total	14,704	100.0[a]	1,539,038	100.0[a]

[a]Totals may not sum up due to rounding.

Source: Federal Deposit Insurance Corporation, *Annual Report, 1980* (Washington, D.C., 1981).

[2]Does this mean that bankers exert monopoly control over American industry? To anticipate Chapter 8, the answer appears to be negative. There are too many large banks to believe that any one or even a few of them can impose their will either on other bankers or on major industrialists.

☐ Commercial Bank Charters

Most of the giant banks are **national banks**, which are chartered according to the provisions of the National Bank Act of 1864 (see p. 101). Of the thirty bank companies listed in Box 5.2, the flagship banks of only ten are not nationally chartered. On the other hand, most small banks are chartered by the states and are termed **state banks.** One reason for choosing a state charter stems from the fact that national banks must join the Federal Reserve System while state-chartered banks are not so mandated. The advantages and disadvantages of Federal Reserve membership are discussed in a later chapter (pp. 297–299), but it must be noted that since the passage of the Depository Institutions Deregulation and Monetary Control Act in 1980, the major reason for staying out of the Federal Reserve System no longer applies. All depository institutions—members and nonmembers alike—are now required to maintain non-

National banks receive their charter from the federal government, while **state banks** are chartered by the states.

interest-earning reserves with the regional Federal Reserve banks. Another reason for obtaining a state charter stems from the perception that the supervisory staffs of the comptroller of the currency and the Federal Reserve are more demanding than those of many state regulatory commissions. As a consequence, the dual banking system mentioned in Chapter 4 remains in existence. Whether the new Act will induce more banks to join the Federal Reserve System and thus weaken the hold of state regulators over state-chartered banks is a question that bears watching.

☐ Bank Profits

The larger the bank, the more varied the services it provides to its customers. Yet for even the largest banks the major source of bank income is the interest collected on loans. Table 5.3 summarizes data on income and expenses for 1980 for all insured banks in the United States. Interest income accounted for more than nine-tenths of all bank income and covered all bank operating expenses. Within the income category, interest on bank loans far overshadowed interest earned from various kinds of security holdings. Banks as a group earned $19.5 billion on operating profits, a pretax return of 18 percent on capital. However, 1980 was an exceptionally good year for the banks; the return on capital for the 1970s averaged only 15 percent.

TABLE 5.3 Commercial Bank Income and Expenses, 1980[a]

	Billions of dollars	Percent
Operating income		
Interest	173.8	91.1
Loans	127.0	66.6
Interbank balances	16.3	8.5
U.S. government securities	13.5	7.1
State and local securities	8.2	4.3
Income on Federal funds sold and		
repurchase agreements	8.8	4.6
Service charges	7.5	3.9
Other income	9.5	5.0
Total income	190.8	100.0
Operating expenses		
Employee expenses	24.7	14.4
Interest on deposits and borrowed money	103.4	60.4
Expenses on Federal funds purchased and		
repurchase agreements	16.8	9.8
Occupancy and equipment expenses	7.4	4.3
Other	19.1	11.2
Total expenses	171.3	100.0
Operating income before taxes	19.5	

[a]This table refers only to insured banks.

Source: Federal Deposit Insurance Corporation, *Annual Report, 1980* (Washington, D.C., 1981).

☐ Loans and Interest Rates

Loans are the bread and butter of the banking business. How thickly the butter is spread depends not only on the volume of lending but also on the rate of interest charged. Both cost and demand elements affect the rate of interest that bankers can charge any particular borrower. On the cost side, the banker must cover the direct costs involved in initiating and servicing the loan and, in the long run, overhead costs as well. While overhead costs do not vary with the size of the loan, direct costs per dollar lent decline as the size of the loan increases. This is so because not much more paper work and time is needed to process and service a $100,000 loan than for a loan one-tenth that size. And because loans are risky—borrowers sometimes fail to pay on time and sometimes fail to pay at all—the banker's charges must cover this risk.

Demand, too, plays an important role in the determination of an interest rate. Obviously, the strength of loan demand will be reflected in the interest rate charged. But aside from the overall strength of loan demand in the economy, specific demand considerations will affect the interest rate charged a particular borrower. The banker must consider whether the client could turn to other banks in the community or is large enough to consider direct finance as an alternative to bank borrowing. The banker will program into the lending decision such elements as the bank-customer relationship: Is the borrower a customer of long standing? Does the borrower maintain a large demand deposit? Has the customer been a source of income to the bank by using its services?

The banker must not forget the need to comply with government regulations, specifically, state-imposed **usury laws**. Usury laws are directed primarily at consumer loans, and in many states establish a ceiling to the rates bankers may charge their customers. (The impact of usury laws on bank lending is discussed in Chapter 9.)

A **usury law** specifies the maximum interest rate that borrowers may be charged on specific types of loans.

Finally, an important influence on the interest rate that can be charged is the general availability of funds. The monetary authorities can enhance or reduce the ability of the nation's bankers to respond to loan demands. When the central bankers impose a policy of monetary tightness on the banking system, interest rates in general will rise. They will fall if the authorities follow a policy of monetary ease.

Thus, the interest rate charged to any particular borrower at any moment depends on general economic and financial conditions—the general supply of and demand for funds—and also on the circumstances of the individual borrower in comparison to other customers seeking loans from the bank. Consequently, different interest rates will be paid by different classes of borrowers and, not infrequently, by different borrowers within each group.

The cornerstone of the interest rate structure of wholesale banking for the past fifty years has been the **prime rate**. Only the largest and most financially solid corporations qualify for the prime rate. Interest charges

The **prime rate** is the interest rate charged to the most creditworthy group of business borrowers.

to borrowers that either are smaller or are deemed to pose greater risk are higher than the prime, the differential depending on the loan officer's perception of the considerations outlined earlier. Thus, small businesses pay more than large businesses, both because bank expenses are relatively larger per dollar lent and because the failure rate for small business tends to exceed that for large business. (There are, of course, exceptions to this generalization. Many small businesses have served their community for many years and are financially solid. Also, the federal Small Business Administration's loan guarantee program offers banks protection against default.) As Table 5.4 shows, for both short- and long-term loans, the larger the loan, the lower the interest rate charged. Similarly, the more speculative a venture, the greater the differential over the prime. And the longer the term of the loan, the greater the differential.

The interest rate, however, is only one element of a loan contract. Other aspects of the contract affect profitability as well. The term of the loan is one such element; risk varies directly with maturity. Therefore, other things being equal, a higher rate accompanies longer maturity, as the contrasting rates on short- and long-term loans in Table 5.4 indicate. Collateral is another factor. Banks lend to government bond dealers and stock market brokerage firms, but maintain adequate collateral to protect their investment. A less obvious term in the loan contract is the **compensating balance** requirement. Bankers expect that the borrower will maintain a certain minimum demand deposit balance, usually a negotiated percentage of the loan. This balance is supposed to "compensate" for bank services to the borrower, but in reality it is an indirect means of increasing the bank's return. If, for example, a $1 million loan carries a 15 percent rate of interest and a compensating balance requirement of 10 percent, the cost to the borrower is $150,000 ÷ $900,000 = 16⅔ percent. (The former number is 15 percent of $1 million and the latter is $1 million minus the 10 percent compensating balance; it is the amount the borrower can actually use.) By changing the percentage required as a compensating balance, the banker can vary the effective cost of borrowing for certain borrowers.

The prime rate has both increased and decreased in importance over the last few decades. This paradoxical result stems from two innovations: **floating rates** and **superprime rates**. Until the mid-1960s, the interest rates negotiated by borrowers with their bankers tended to remain fixed

A **compensating balance** is a deposit maintained by the borrower with the lending bank.

Floating rates are loan interest rates that vary with changes in the prime rate.
Superprime rates are interest rates that are below the prime rate.

TABLE 5.4 Average Bank Interest Rates on Business Loans by Loan Size and Maturity, November 1976 (percent per annum)

Loan size	Short-term loans	Long-term loans
$ 1,000–9,000	8.83	9.39
$ 10,000–99,000	8.18	8.88
$ 100,000–499,000	7.66	8.14
$ 500,000–999,000	7.31	8.13
$1,000,000 and over	7.02	7.24

Source: Board of Governors of the Federal Reserve System, *Annual Statistical Digest, 1972–1976* (Washington, D.C., 1977), pp. 102, 104.

during the term of the loan. Thus, a two-year, $500,000 loan at 5 percent per annum meant that the borrower had to pay $555,000 at maturity. But in the last fifteen years, as interest rates increased and became more volatile as well, bankers began to feel that they were losing out by committing themselves to interest rates that remained constant during the life of the loan. Their response was the floating rate. The interest rate on outstanding loans was periodically revised; as the prime rate moved, so did the floating rate. By early 1980 over half of commercial and industrial loans were committed at floating rates.

While the advent of floating rates increased the importance of the prime rate, since it made the prime the cornerstone not only of new loans but of outstanding contracts as well, use of the superprime has reduced the importance of the prime. The advent of the superprime is closely related to major corporations' increasing use of the commercial paper market as a substitute for short-term bank financing. In 1978 these corporate giants discovered that commercial paper could be sold at a cost that was lower than the prime rate available to them from their bankers. As a result, more and more corporations became active in the commercial paper market, so that its volume increased from just over $30 billion in 1970 to more than $83 billion in 1978 and $125 billion at the end of 1980. The larger wholesale bankers reacted by offering these borrowers a special rate, the superprime.

A second reason for the declining importance of the prime rate stems from the pricing methods of foreign banks, which are becoming an even more significant element in the wholesale market. (This "foreign invasion" is discussed in Chapter 9.) Prime rate pricing is a phenomenon that is unique to U.S. bankers. In Europe, loans to businesses, as well as to governments, are priced in terms of points over the **London interbank offer rate,** or **LIBOR.** LIBOR is viewed as the cost of funds to the banks, and the added points over LIBOR are designed to cover the other costs as well as profits. This method is now being used in the United States, and frequently leads to interest rates lower than the prime.

The **London interbank offer rate (LIBOR)** is the interest rate that banks in London charge each other.

A final innovation in interest rate setting is the **formula prime.** In most American banks the prime rate is set by top-level management and is based on their perceptions of supply and demand for the next week or month. Some of the nation's largest banks have eschewed this approach and rely instead on a formula that relates the prime rate to the cost of funds to the bank. This method enables the bankers to escape public criticism for raising interest rates, since any increase in rates charged is attributed to prior cost increases.

When the prime rate is set in terms of a mechanistic relationship instead of at the full discretion of bankers, it is called a **formula prime.**

☐ Competition

Not only are domestic banks facing competition from foreign banks in the wholesale market but their position in the retail market is also coming under increasing pressure from aggressive nonbank financial intermediaries. While checking accounts were the exclusive domain of commercial banking until the advent of NOW accounts in 1972, the Depository Institution Deregulation and Monetary Control Act of 1980 permits all federally chartered thrift institutions to offer such checking accounts. The extent of this competition is still relatively insignificant, since the thrifts held only 10 percent of all checking accounts in December, 1980. But the indication is that interest-paying checking accounts will spread nationally, forcing commercial banks to respond. Undoubtedly, the cost of their deposits will rise.

The Act also liberalized the types of loans that thrifts could make, again encroaching on the terrain of the commercial banks. Similarly, the thrifts have adopted electronic banking techniques, providing their customers with full-time service.

Recent banking legislation has not been one-sided. Commercial banks have been permitted to engage in financial activities that are not strictly banking activities in the old sense. Moreover, banks have diversified their operations by forming holding companies and acquiring financial affiliates (see Chapter 8). The end result of all this legislation is a narrowing of the differentiation between commercial banks and nonbank financial intermediaries. Yet sharp distinctions still exist, and each group has its own particular structure and problems.

The next four chapters focus on the commercial banks. Because the asset-liability portfolio of the banks is so important, the next chapter describes this portfolio, tracing its evolution over the last two decades. The theory of portfolio management is the subject of Chapter 7, while contemporary issues are the focus of Chapters 8 and 9.

☐ Summary

In the early years of this century, bankers subscribed to the commercial loan theory of banking, also called the real-bills doctrine. Only short-term, self-liquidating commercial loans were to be made. This doctrine was replaced in the 1930s by the anticipated-income theory; as long as the borrower's ability to repay the loan and interest was assured, the loan should be undertaken. The result is that today commercial banks lend to all the sectors of the economy; lend for short, intermediate, and long terms; and lend to consumers and businesses alike. They are not "commercial" banks but department stores of finance.

Banks cater to both the retail and the wholesale segments of the banking market. They offer a variety of services to consumers and businesses. Yet, despite the fact that there are almost fifteen thousand banks in the United States, the banking industry is segmented. A handful of giant banks account for almost a third of bank deposits, while the smallest 75 percent account for less than 15 percent. Most of the large banks are national banks, while the vast majority of the small banks are chartered by the states.

Bank profits are generated primarily by their lending operations. The interest rates that banks can charge on loans depend on overall economic conditions, such as the demand for loans and the supply of loanable funds. The availability of funds is conditioned by the general stance of the monetary authorities. But aside from these overall conditions, individual loan rates vary from one customer to another. The best customers—the most creditworthy as well as those that are capable of obtaining finance elsewhere at competitive rates—will be able to borrow at the prime rate, perhaps even at the superprime rate. Borrowers whose record with the lending bank is poorer, whose business is less desired, or whose alternatives are more limited will be charged a premium over the prime. Similarly, the longer the term of the loan, the more speculative it is, or the smaller its size, the greater will be the premium over the prime.

In recent years, because of the rising trend of interest rates and their increasing volatility, the fixed prime has given way to the floating prime. Other changes include the introduction of the superprime in response to the increasing use of the commercial paper market by major corporations, and the introduction of LIBOR pricing by foreign banks seeking to increase their share of American wholesale banking.

Competition comes not only from these foreign banks but also from the thrift institutions, which are offering retail customers many of the services that previously were provided almost exclusively by commercial banks. The most notable example is the checking account, which may be offered by mutual savings bank, savings and loan associations, and credit unions throughout the country. But while there has been some narrowing of the gap between the specialized savings institutions and the broader commercial banks, the commercial banks remain the dominant force in American finance today.

☐ Questions and Exercises

1. Is the commercial bank that you (or your parents) do business with (a) state or federally chartered and (b) primarily retail or wholesale? Does either of these bits of information make a difference to you? Might they be important to a small business in your community? How about a large industrial firm with sizable borrowing needs?
2. Check the annual income statement of your neighborhood commercial bank and contrast it with the national percentages given in Table 5.3. If you spot significant discrepancies in the percentages, you might be interested in investigating the reasons for those differences.
3. As interest rates rise, bank profits should rise, too. You might wish to correlate interest rates and bank profits to see whether the relationship holds. This might aid in answering the following question: When bankers object to

rising interest rates, are they motivated by the desire for profits or are they posturing for public-relations benefits?

4. Why has the inflation that pervaded the United States during the 1970s induced an increasingly large percentage of bankers to favor floating interest rates?

□ For Further Study

The most interesting description of American banking you might ever encounter was written with a profound understanding of banking and a writer's flair for the smooth flow of language: Martin Mayer, *The Bankers* (New York: Weybright and Talley, 1974; paper, New York: Ballantine, 1976). For a comprehensive and authoritative guide to many of the intracacies of contemporary banking, consult the book the bankers use: W. H. Baughn and C. E. Walker, eds., *The Bankers' Handbook* (Homewood, Ill.: Dow Jones-Irwin, 1978). E. N. Compton, *Principles of Banking* (Washington, D.C.: American Bankers Association, 1979), covers much of the same ground but less extensively.

Bank lending is examined in detail in Douglas A. Hayes, *Bank Lending Policies: Domestic and International* (Ann Arbor: University of Michigan Press, 1977). In "Business Loans at Large Commercial Banks: Policies and Practices," Federal Reserve Bank of Chicago, *Economic Perspectives* 3 (November-December 1979): 15–23, R. C. Merris skillfully condenses a good deal of useful information on bank credit activities.

CHAPTER 6

Commercial Banks in the United States: Balance Sheet Developments, 1960–1979

Old bankers never die; they just lose their balance.

Anonymous

"I'm a banker," said Gore, "and one man's money is the same as another['s]."

Character in a Harry Kemelman mystery (1978)

CONTENTS

CHAPTER HIGHLIGHTS

1. The trends of major balance sheet entries.
2. The major asset components—loans, investments, cash—and their changing proportions in the balance sheet.
3. The primary liability categories—demand and time deposits and borrowings—and shifts between them over time.
4. The implications of the banks' declining capital: total assets ratios.

The preceding chapter presented an overview of contemporary banking in the United States. The next chapter focuses on the art of portfolio management. But before one can proceed to such thought-provoking questions as, What induces bankers to hold such a large proportion of their assets in loans? Why do they devote a decided share of their portfolio to various types of securities? What role has the CD played in the formation of a desired portfolio? it is necessary to do as Jack Webb used to say on "Dragnet": "Just give us the facts, Ma'am." This chapter is descriptive, the next one analytical.

The bottom line in banking stems primarily from interest income, interest received for lending and investing. But banks cannot put all their funds into loans and investments; they must maintain reserves and have sufficient liquid assets either at hand or readily available. Thus, cash assets, loans, and investments constitute the primary entries on the asset side of the balance sheet of any particular bank. The liability side of the balance sheet reflects the fund-gathering function of a financial intermediary. Banks obtain funds from depositors, from nondeposit liability sources, and from contributors of capital, that is, stockholders.

This skeletal list will be fleshed out in the present chapter. Not only will you examine in detail many of the items that appear on the balance sheet of the banking system, but you will also trace developments in banking as they are reflected in the balance sheets over time. Thus, the purpose of this chapter is a triple one: (1) to examine the balance sheet of the banking system, (2) to follow its development over the past two decades, and (3) to set the stage for the analysis of portfolio management, the subject of the next chapter.

☐ The Balance Sheet of the Commercial Banking System

Before turning to a detailed examination of balance sheets, a few introductory comments will prove useful. Note that three years—1960,

1968, and 1979—have been singled out for inspection. The first of these was a year of economic contraction. This downturn was extremely short-lived, more so than most downturns in the post-World War II period. The recession began in May 1960 and ended in February of the next year. The 1960–1961 contraction set the stage for the longest period of economic expansion recorded in the United States, an upturn that lasted just two months short of nine years. Since November 1969 was the terminal month of the expansion, December 1968—the second of the three chosen dates—was the final December of the expansion. It should be illuminating to contrast the condition of the banking system near the end of a contraction with its position near the termination of an expansion; this is achieved by comparing the Decembers of 1960 and 1968.

The 1970s, on the other hand, presented bankers with an experience that differed markedly from that of the go-go years of the 1960s. True, the business cycle pattern of earlier times appears to have returned. The decade began with a three-year upturn that was followed by a downturn lasting from late 1973 to early 1975. A second expansion began immediately and continued úntil early 1980. The distinguishing features of the eighth decade of the twentieth century were the continuing high levels of inflation coupled with high and sticky rates of unemployment, rates that did not fall back to the lower levels of the 1950s and 1960s. 1979 was selected to complement 1968; both were years of economic strength and were soon followed by the end of an economic expansion. A study of these two periods will highlight the balance sheet shifts over the decade. Choosing years of prosperity permits us to assume that any changes that were recorded in the balance sheets resulted from fundamental trends in the economy and basic structural changes in the banking system, rather than from merely cyclical forces.

□ An Overview of the Balance Sheets

Take a look at Table 6.1(b). It is clear that the major category on the asset side of the balance sheet is loans. In 1979 loans constituted 59 percent of total assets. Investments[1] ranked next; they contributed only 20 percent of total assets and were only one-third as large as the loan

---

[1]For economists, the difference between a loan and an investment is often imprecise. In general, a loan implies a tailor-made agreement between a lender (the banker) and a borrower. The terms (interest rate, maturity, collateral, penalty clauses, etc.) are agreed to by both parties. Frequently loans cannot be sold on a secondary market. An investment, on the other hand, tends to be a more generalized arrangement whose terms are decided upon in advance by the borrower. Often it is marketable and is sold on an organized security market. The lender-banker chooses to either accept the terms and acquire the investment or reject the terms and not purchase the security. A home mortgage is an example of a loan; a U.S. Treasury bond is an investment.

For portfolio management, these technical distinctions are less germane than the profitability and liquidity characteristics of loans and investments, as will become clear in Chapter 7.

TABLE 6.1 Balance Sheet of All Commercial Banks in the United States, December 31, 1960, 1968, and 1979

a. Amounts (billions of dollars)

Assets	12/31/60	12/31/68	12/31/79	Liabilities and net worth	12/31/60	12/31/68	12/31/79
Cash assets	53.1	85.0	198.9	*Total deposits*	266.9	502.4	1108.4
Reserves with Federal Reserve banks	16.7	21.2	32.2	*Demand deposits*	156.9	231.0	435.0
Currency and coin	3.5	7.4	18.6	Individuals, partnerships, and corporations[a]	122.0	183.2	351.9
Balances with domestic banks	14.4	19.7	57.3	Interbank	17.1	25.6	61.7[b]
Balances with foreign banks	0.2	0.5	8.3	State and local government	11.8	17.0	19.0
Cash items in the process of collection	18.3	36.2	82.2	U.S. government	6.0	5.0	2.4
				Time deposits	110.0	271.4	673.4
Loans	145.3	322.9	848.1	Individuals, partnerships, and corporations	103.4	245.7	589.0
Investments	94.0	150.6	287.8	Interbank	1.8	6.1	18.7
U.S. government securities	67.3	80.2	138.3	State and local government	4.6	19.2	64.7
State and local securities	18.3	58.9	133.3	U.S. government	0.3	0.4	1.0
Other	8.4	11.4	16.2				
				Borrowings	0.2	9.0	148.0
Other assets	6.6	17.3	102.9				
				Other liabilities	7.3	22.0	76.8
				Total liabilities	274.3	533.4	1333.9
				Net worth	24.6	42.4	103.8
Totals[c]	298.9	575.8	1437.7	*Totals[c]*	298.9	575.8	1437.7

b. Percentages

Assets	12/31/60	12/31/68	12/31/79	Liabilities and Net worth	12/31/60	12/31/68	12/31/79
Cash assets	17.7	14.7	13.8	*Total deposits*	89.2	87.2	77.1
Reserves with Federal Reserve banks	5.6	3.7	2.2	*Demand deposits*	52.4	40.1	30.2
Currency and coin	1.1	1.2	1.2	Individuals, partnerships, and corporations[a]	40.8	31.8	24.4
Balances with domestic banks	4.8	3.4	4.0	Interbank	5.7	4.4	4.2[b]
Balances with foreign banks	[d]	[d]	0.6	State and local government	3.9	2.9	1.3
Cash items in the process of collection	6.1	6.3	5.7	U.S. government	2.0	0.8	0.1
				Time Deposits	36.8	47.1	46.8
Loans	48.6	56.1	58.9	Individuals, partnerships, and corporations	34.6	42.8	40.9
Investments	31.4	26.1	20.0	Interbank	0.6	1.0	1.3
U.S. government securities	22.5	13.9	9.6	State and local government	1.5	3.3	4.5
State and local securities	6.1	10.2	9.2	U.S. government	0.1	0.1	0.1
Other	2.8	1.9	1.1				
				Borrowings	0.1	1.5	10.2
Other assets	2.2	3.0	7.1				
				Other liabilities	2.4	3.8	5.3
				Total Liabilities	91.8	92.6	92.7
				Net worth	8.2	7.4	7.3
Totals[c]	100.0	100.0	100.0	*Totals[c]*	100.0	100.0	100.0

NOTES:

Actual reserve ratio (reserves + currency and coin ÷ total deposits)	7.6	5.7	4.6
Loan:deposit ratio	54.4	64.2	76.5
Time deposits:demand deposits ratio	70.0	117.0	155.0

[a] Includes certified checks.
[b] Includes foreign government deposits.
[c] Totals may not sum up due to rounding.
[d] Less than 1/10 of 1 percent.

Source: Federal Deposit Insurance Corporation, *Annual Report* (Washington, D.C., 1961, 1969, 1980).

entry. Smaller still is the contribution of cash assets, while that of other assets is negligible. On the liability side, the table shows that time deposits loomed larger than demand deposits; the former constituted 47 percent of total liabilities and net worth (= total assets) against 30 percent for the latter. The third-largest category on the right-hand side of the balance sheet was borrowing, 10 percent of the total. The capital account registered only 7 percent and was dwarfed by deposits, which constituted more than three-quarters of total assets.

☐ Balance Sheet Growth, 1960–1979

Now consider balance sheet movements over time as portrayed in Table 6.1(a). Between 1960 and 1968 total assets grew by 92 percent while between 1968 and 1979 the increase came to 150 percent. The annual rates of increase were 8.5 percent and 8.7 percent, respectively.

The similarity in the annual rates of growth over the two periods is surprising. Normally, as the economy expands, moving from the depths of a recession to a business cycle peak, the economy rises relatively sharply. A much more moderate expansion characterizes a peak-to-peak movement. For example, industrial production, charted in Figure 6.1(a),

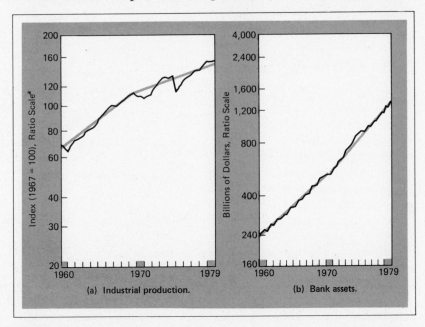

(a) Industrial production.　　(b) Bank assets.

FIGURE 6.1 Industrial production, 1960–1979; and total assets, all commercial banks, 1960–1979.

[a]In each graph within Figures 6.1(a) and 6.1(b), time is plotted horizontally on the usual arithmetic scale, but the corresponding values of industrial production and bank assets are plotted on a logarithmic (ratio) scale. The scale has the useful property of visibly demonstrating rates of growth. A constant rate of growth of a series—say, 10, 20, 40, 80—will appear as a straight line with a constant slope.
Source: Board of Governors of the Federal Reserve System.

grew faster between 1960 and 1968 than it did between 1968 and 1979. Yet the growth rate of bank assets, plotted in Figure 6.1(b), fails to portray this distinction.

The obvious explanation lies in the relatively rapid rate of inflation that characterized the decade of the 1970s. While prices grew by 20 percent during the first period (a 2.3% annual average), the eleven years between 1968 and 1979 saw prices *double*, for an average annual increase of 6.5 percent. Thus, if bank balance sheet totals had only doubled, the inflation-adjusted position of the banking system in 1979 would have been identical to its position in 1968. In fact, bank assets more than doubled; real growth had occurred. Inflation had simply distorted the underlying rates of increase.

Adjust, then, the data in each period for the respective rate of inflation. The expected pattern of growth emerges as the first period shows a faster rate of increase (72% for the eight years, or 7% yearly) when compared to the 1968–1979 period (50% for the eleven years, or 3.8% per year).

In addition to observing the growth of the banking system by studying balance sheet movements, it is important to understand the shifts that took place in the composition of the banks' portfolios. The remainder of this chapter focuses on the entries that make up the totals and how they changed over the two decades in question.

☐ The Asset Side of the Balance Sheet

Loans

Loans are the most important bank asset, a fact that was mentioned a few paragraphs ago. The loan category predominated in each of the years covered in Table 6.1; as part (b) of the table clearly indicates, bankers always held approximately half of their assets in loans.

The loan entries in Table 6.1(b) lead to a reasonable question: Is there any explanation for the increase in the ratio of loans to total assets that occurred over the past two decades? (Stop a moment and think of some reasons.)

Actually, two complementary answers may be advanced. The first explains the rise between 1960 and 1968, and is related to the economic expansion that took place during those years. During a recession, as in 1960, loan demand tends to be weak. Moreover, bankers become reluctant to lend. They scrutinize loan applications more carefully, wondering whether borrowers will be able to pay on time or whether they'll be able to repay at all. As a result, loans as a proportion of total assets fall. Bankers devote a larger share of their portfolios to other, less risky assets. As the economy expands, however, the reverse happens. Loan demand strengthens and bankers view borrowers in a more favorable light. A rise in the proportion of bank funds devoted to loans follows, with a corresponding decline in the other categories. This relationship is reflected by another ratio, found at the bottom of Table 6.1(b)—the loan:deposit ratio. A longstanding banking convention has it that loans should amount to around 60 percent of deposits in good times and less in periods of uncertainty. During the 1960 recession the ratio was a substantially lower 54 percent; it rose somewhat beyond the conventional level in 1968. The key to understanding the further rise of the loan:deposit ratio in 1979 to 76.5 percent, well beyond the old limit of banker prudence, is a shift in banking theory, a full explanation of which must await the next chapter. At this point it suffices to note that the rising interest rates that characterized the 1970s made it more profitable to lend. Bankers responded to this profit incentive by increasing their loans, both in absolute terms (from $322.9 billion to $848.1 billion, or 163 percent) and in percentage terms.

Arithmetic dictates that if one component of a fixed sum (in this case, 100%) rises, one or more of the remaining components must decline. The share of both investments and cash assets in the balance sheet fell. (See Figure 6.2.) One might say that the increase in loans was financed by the decrease in these other categories of bank assets. But the decline in investments and cash assets was not an across-the-board trend; there

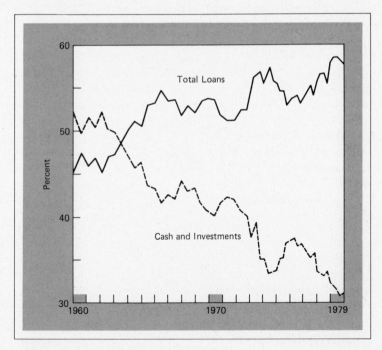

FIGURE 6.2 Loans and cash and investments as a percentage of total assets, all commercial banks, 1960–1979.
Source: Board of Governors of the Federal Reserve System.

were distinctive variations within each category. Consider investments first.

Investments

Bank investments are almost exclusively government securities of one kind or another. Of the almost $300 billion recorded in the investment category for 1979, 48 percent were obligations of the United States, 46 percent those of states or local authorities, and only 6 percent nongovernment debt.

Bankers prefer government debt for a variety of reasons:

1. *To back government deposits.* Insofar as banks hold government deposits, bank portfolios are expected to contain an equivalent amount of government debt, referred to as **pledged securities.**

2. *As reserves.* Some states permit banks to satisfy reserve requirements by holding government securities.

3. *Liquidity.* Short-term government securities provide bankers with assets that are easily liquidated. (Of the holdings of banks responding to the Treasury Department's survey of ownership of government securities, 29 percent matured in less than one year.)

4. *Income.* Government securities do provide bankers with income. In fact, federal securities are exempt from state and local taxes, while municipal securities are free from federal taxes, thanks to an 1894 Supreme Court interpretation of the U.S. Constitution.

5. *Legal constraints.* While bank portfolios may contain corporate debt, they are prohibited by the provisions of the Glass-Steagall Act from owning corporate stock. This Congressional legislation (also known as the Banking Act of 1933) stemmed from the collapse of many banks during the early years of the Great Depression. One reason for these widespread bankruptcies was bank ownership of stocks, whose value had plummeted with the stock market crash of 1929. The Act also prohibited depository banks from acting as investment bankers (see p. 83, footnote), a provision that some aggressive bankers are working to dilute.

Pledged securities, backing government deposits, may not be sold by the banks to finance their other activities.

Table 6.1(b) clearly demonstrates a shift in the composition of bank portfolios of government securities between 1960 and 1968. Holdings of federal securities dropped 8.6 percentage points, while the share of state and local bonds rose by 4.1 percentage points. Accordingly, while the latter constituted approximately one-quarter of federal security holdings of banks in 1960, by 1968 this proportion had grown to almost three-quarters.

The best explanation for the shift in these components of bank investments is directly related to conditions on the supply side of the securities market: The supply of local government securities rose relative to the supply of federal government issues. Both the federal government and local governments ran continuous budget deficits during the 1960s.

However, the growth of nonfederal debt was four times as great as the increase in federal government debt. A combination of larger growth in local expenditures and a relatively rigid tax structure underlies the rapid growth in nonfederal debt. As expenditures rose so much more rapidly than taxes, heavy reliance on borrowing to cover the resulting budgetary gap led to substantial security issues. Since this state and municipal debt was considered to be of the high quality sought by banks, bankers purchased it. No doubt the desire of many bankers to accommodate their state and local financing authorities also contributed to banks' absorption of such securities. For the most part, these investments in state and local debt consisted of intermediate- and long-term maturities, which were financed by reducing bank acquisitions of Treasury securities.

The yields earned on these state and municipal issues cannot be ignored. When comparing the after-tax yield of state and local securities to that obtainable from similar Treasury issues, bankers found a differential that increasingly favored municipal securities. A bank paying the full corporate tax rate received, in 1960, a return that was, on the average, 0.6 percentage points higher from an investment in nonfederal government debt than from an investment in federal securities. By 1968 that differential was up to one percentage point. (The difference in comparative yields between 1960 and 1968 comes to $4 million in extra tax-free income for each $1 billion invested in nonfederal as opposed to federal government debt.) Increased supply and more attractive rates, therefore, induced the bankers to acquire a larger share of municipal debt.

The narrowing of the trend between the two types of government debt continued during the next decade. By 1979 banks' holdings of municipal debt were almost equal to their holdings of U.S. government issues. Nevertheless, one change in the state and local securities row is thought-provoking: The ratio of this type of debt to total assets had declined. Indeed, this decrease had been continuous since 1974. (The annual rate of growth of bank holdings of nonfederal government debt between 1968 and 1974 was 9 percent; it fell to less than 6 percent between 1974 and 1979). While a number of plausible explanations have been advanced, the most convincing of them concerns the shock received by the municipal bond market in 1974 with the threat of default on New York State and City bonds. Furthermore, bankers and other investors came to realize that the financial difficulties facing New York were widespread; other cities, especially in the northeastern and north central regions, functioned on equally shaky financial grounds. Is it surprising that bankers took a more cautious stance toward municipal securities?

Cash assets

Turn now to cash assets, which also fell as a percentage of total assets as banks responded to an increased demand for loans. The major percentage decreases occurred in *reserves with Federal Reserve banks* and, according to the table, in balances with domestic banks during the earlier period.

The decline in the reserve holdings, which is also reflected in the fall in the actual reserve ratio [see the note at the bottom of Table 6.1(b)], was not to any significant extent attributable to a decline in Federal Reserve reserve requirement ratios. Indeed, for demand deposits the required ratio was unchanged from 1960 until it was increased in 1968. There were increases in 1969 and 1973 and a substantial reduction for small banks in 1972 and modest decreases for all banks in 1975 and 1976. For time deposits, required ratios were reduced for some deposits and raised for others. Despite all these changes, the trend of declining ratios of reserves to total assets cannot be attributed to Federal Reserve policy.

The primary explanation of this trend is intimately connected with another balance sheet development, the drastic change in the ratio of time to demand deposits. [These ratios may be found in the note to Table 6.1(b). Figure 6.3 plots demand and time deposits for the entire period.] It is quite clear that the share of deposits consisting of demand deposits fell continuously, while the share of time deposits increased steadily.

In order to comprehend how these conflicting trends affected the ratio of reserves to deposits, an additional fact must be supplied—the reserve ratios that member banks were required to hold against demand and time deposits. Invariably, the required reserve ratio maintained against time deposits is considerably lower than that held against demand deposits. In December 1968, for example, the *minimum* ratio against demand deposits was 12½ percent, while the *maximum* ratio on time deposits was 6 percent. In December 1979 the minimum ratio on demand deposits was 7 percent while on time deposits it could average as low as 3 percent.

The shift in public preferences toward deposit types meant a redistribution of deposits from the category that mandated a high reserve requirement to the kind that required a smaller reserve ratio. Arithmetic dictates that in such a case the average reserve ratio must decline.[2]

Three additional influences that reinforced the shift in deposit composition were the erosion of Federal Reserve membership, the decline in the importance of deposits, and the reduction in **excess reserves.** During the 1960s and 1970s some commercial banks withdrew from the Federal Reserve System. At the same time, many newly chartered banks never joined. Since nonmember banks did not maintain reserves in Federal Reserve banks, the decrease in System membership also reduced the proportion of bank assets held as reserves with the Federal Reserve. (The reasons for this attrition are discussed in Chapter 12.)

Second, deposits constituted almost 90 percent of total assets in 1960 but only 77 percent in 1979. Most of the decline is offset by an increase in

Reserves held in excess of the required amount are called **excess reserves.**

---

[2]If each of 50 percent of the people in a room weighed precisely 180 pounds and the remaining half weighed exactly 120 pounds each, then the average person's weight would be calculated as (50% × 180 lbs.) + (50% × 120 lbs.), or 150 pounds. Now, if the proportion of heavy to less heavy people changed as some people left and others entered the room, so that the first group now constituted only 25 percent and the second 75 percent, the average weight would fall to (25% × 180 lbs.) + (75% × 120 lbs.) = 135 pounds.

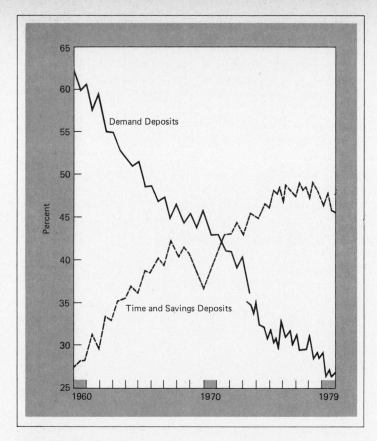

FIGURE 6.3 Demand and time deposits as a percentage of total assets, all commercial banks, 1960–1979.
Source: Board of Governors of the Federal Reserve System.

bank borrowings. Since borrowings had either no or rather small reserve requirements, the shift reduced the average reserve ratio, analogously to the shift from demand to time deposits. Finally, bank holdings of excess reserves declined over the period. During contractions, when lending opportunities are more circumscribed, banks are less reluctant to hold excess reserves. When the economy turns up and loans are provided more generously, banks scrutinize their reserve position more carefully in order to economize on excess reserve holdings. The total impact of this reduction in excess reserves is quite minimal, however, since even in periods of contraction banks are not prone to hold large percentages of idle excess reserves that pay no interest. At a minimum, bankers can lend their excess reserves on the Federal funds market. So even in December of 1960 excess reserves constituted only three-tenths of one percent of total assets. (In December 1979, excess reserves accounted for three one-hundredths of one percent of total assets.)

Balances with domestic banks are kept by **respondents** in **correspondent** banks for a variety of reasons:

1. *Reserve requirements.* For most of the present century, banks that were not members of the Federal Reserve System were permitted by state banking authorities to count as reserves deposits that they maintained at correspondents. Since 1981, however, even nonmember banks must hold deposits with their regional Federal Reserve bank, so that this motive has lost operative significance.[3]

2. *Check collection.* Checks drawn on distant banks can be cleared through the Federal Reserve (see Chapter 12). Often, however, it is more convenient to use the correspondent network. When the respondent sends checks for collection to the correspondent, the latter credits the respondent's balance. The correspondent collects the check either through the Federal Reserve, through another correspondent, or from the originating bank itself.

3. *Other banking services.* Correspondents typically (though not always) are larger than their respondents, and thus are equipped to offer their customers, be they nonfinancial corporations, individuals, or banks, a broad range of services. Moreover, they can often provide the same services more effectively. The correspondent banks, for example, are almost certainly linked to banks abroad and hence can supply the foreign exchange and documentation needed by respondents' customers. Similarly, the officer in charge of the respondent's investment portfolio may consult regularly with the skilled, specialized staff of the correspondent.

4. *Loan participation.* In cases in which the respondent is unable or unwilling to commit large sums needed by a particular borrower, the correspondent may be asked to participate and share the loan.

What does the correspondent gain from this relationship? Profits is the obvious answer. Some correspondents charge explicit fees for the services they provide. More common, however, is the convention that respondents maintain interest-free deposits with their correspondents. (These deposits appear on the liability side as "interbank demand deposits."[4]) The earnings generated by these interest-free funds are used to offset the

---

[3]Technically, the deposits still may be held at correspondent banks but the correspondent must maintain an identical sum at the district Reserve bank.

[4]You might wonder why "balances with domestic banks" do not equal "interbank deposits," since presumably both entries represent the same deposits, the former from the viewpoint of the respondents, the latter as accounted for by the correspondents. Most of the difference stems from the time lag in check clearing. Suppose a respondent sends a $100 check to its city correspondent for clearing. If the respondent is not granted credit immediately upon the city bank's receipt of the check, the respondent will record the $100 as a cash item in the process of collection, not as a balance with a domestic bank. Meanwhile, the correspondent of the originating bank, which has not yet received the check, cannot reduce the deposit balance of the respondent on which the check was drawn. Thus, during transit, interbank balances exceed balances with domestic banks by $100.

cost of servicing the respondents as well as to provide a margin of profit.

Balances with domestic banks as a percentage of total assets fell between 1960 and 1968 but were higher in 1979. The decline in the ratio of these balances to total assets once again stems from bankers' greater willingness to lend, which necessitated the drawing down of other balance sheet entries. Correspondent bankers, however, reacted by calculating more carefully the costs of servicing respondent accounts. In many cases they requested the respondents to increase their balances, leading to a higher ratio in 1979.

Balances with foreign banks, which came to less than $1 billion in 1960 and 1968, exceeded $8 billion by 1979. While the internationalization of banking (to be discussed in Chapter 9) may explain this increase, it should be noted that its importance in percentage terms is negligible.

Currency and coin have maintained a stable share in the balance sheet; bankers have long kept no more on hand than the minimum needed to meet customers' needs. The desire to minimize is also present in the *cash items in the process of collection* category, which refers to financial instruments, primarily checks, that have been deposited and are being processed and collected from other banks. Essentially, this item is a very short-term account receivable; as soon as the bank receives credit for the check, either as a credit in its Federal Reserve account or as an addition to its deposits with a correspondent, an equivalent sum will be subtracted from the "cash items" entry. The actual volume of cash items being processed at any one time is dependent on the amount of checks written, the speed of the transportation system that carries the cash items from one bank to another, and the processing efficiency of individual banks. Aside from the latter, individual banks cannot greatly influence the size of this component of the balance sheet.

□ Liabilities and Net Worth

The sum of liabilities and net worth must be equal to total assets.[5] Thus, the growth rates of the right-hand side of the balance sheet must be identical to those of the left-hand side. This section of the chapter will focus on the two major components of the right-hand side, liabilities and net worth, and on the categories of liabilities.

Deposits

Deposits are the primary source of bank funds. In 1979 they constituted over three-quarters of total assets. Quite noticeable from Table 6.1(b), however, is the declining importance of deposits, which fell from close to 90 percent of the total in 1960 to their 1979 level. Both banker and

---

[5]By definition, net worth equals assets minus liabilities. Symbolically, $NW = A - L$. Adding L to both sides results in $L + NW = A$ or $A = L + NW$, the balance sheet equation.

depositor initiatives account for the erosion of the deposit base. Bankers have discovered supplementary means of acquiring funds, as you will read shortly when bank borrowing is discussed. And depositors have taken advantage of available opportunities to reshape their own asset portfolios.

The shift from a low time deposit:demand deposit ratio to a high one was noted earlier in this chapter; it is now appropriate to explain the reasons underlying that switch. First, however, note that virtually all the deposit categories participated in this shift. The redistribution was especially strong in the "Individuals, Partnerships, and Corporations" entry, as the proportion of demand deposits in the total declined by 16.4 percentage points between 1960 and 1979 and the share of time deposits rose by 6.3 percentage points. Still, interbank and state and local government deposits manifested the change as well.

From the depositor's point of view, the primary motives were the following:

1. The rising interest rates that accompanied the economic expansion of 1960. They continued to rise during the 1970s, reaching historic highs.
2. The increased liquidity of time deposits with the introduction and widespread usage of certificates of deposit (defined on p. 39).

You know that while a demand deposit pays no explicit interest, it offers immediate liquidity to the depositor. A time deposit is somewhat less liquid, but it compensates by offering interest income. A calculating consumer or a corporate treasurer responsible for a firm's cash position weighs the convenience of maintaining a larger demand deposit on hand against the income that could be earned by depositing the funds in a time deposit account. When time deposit accounts pay only 2½ percent annually, the maximum permitted on a 3–6-month deposit in 1960, then maintaining an extra $100,000 in demand deposit form entails a loss of $2,500 over the year. But when interest rates rise, so that the 3–6-month time deposit can earn over 13 percent, as was the case near the end of 1979, then the opportunity cost of tying up an extra $100,000 in a non-interest-earning account exceeds $13,000. Is it really any surprise that the deposit shifts took place? Indeed, had they not occurred, one would have wondered whether corporate treasurers and financial advisers were really worth their high salaries.

One factor that might restrain responsible corporate money managers from acquiring a time deposit is the time deposit's comparative lack of liquidity. While depositors who maintain savings accounts are almost always able to withdraw their deposits on demand, this had not generally been true for owners of time deposits. They were expected to wait until the maturity date before cashing in their deposits. Consequently, the owner of the time deposit sacrificed some flexibility in order to earn the interest. (Incidentally, corporations have been permitted to open consumer-style savings accounts only since 1976. Business firms, corporate or otherwise, may not deposit more than $150,000 in such accounts.) But while the options on time deposit accounts were limited before 1961, the situation changed dramatically in subsequent years. In 1961 New York's Citibank introduced the negotiable CD, and a brokerage firm simultaneously agreed to manage a secondary or resale market in CDs. As a result, the owner of a 90-day CD with 60 days remaining to maturity could sell the CD to obtain immediate cash.

The existence of this new instrument and its easy marketability turned the time deposit into an earning asset that was highly liquid as well. Today all major banks in the United States issue their own CDs, and sophisticated money managers take full advantage of this flexible option to reduce their demand deposit accounts. A push-pull action was at work: The high yield on alternatives pushed funds out of demand deposits, and the presence of a liquid asset offering competitive yields pulled funds into the time deposit category. The shift was further strengthened as the new deposit innovations mentioned in Chapter 2 turned saving accounts into checking accounts. An interest-paying checking account was certainly more attractive than one that did not earn income.

In short, higher interest rates and the greater liquidity available in time deposits attracted funds into time deposits and out of demand deposits. It made little difference whether the depositors were businesses or consumers, private companies or state and local governments, nonfinancial corporations or banks. The only exception was the U.S. government.

The 1.9-percentage-point decline in *U.S. government-owned deposits* that took place during the two decades being surveyed derived from a different source. Unlike municipal governments, the federal government does not use commercial banks to arrange payments; this function is performed by the Federal Reserve banks. Until 1977 government deposits in commercial banks were kept partly to compensate the banks for services performed without charge to the government. Thus, commercial banks issue and redeem U.S. savings bonds and collect tax revenues for the federal government. (Since 1977 the Treasury has paid the banks for these services, but it also collects interest on its deposits.)

A more important motive for maintaining deposits in the commercial banking system is the stabilization function performed by those deposits. In essence, by keeping the deposits, called **Treasury Tax and Loan Accounts,** the banking system functions more smoothly.

Aside from a minimum balance kept by the Treasury in its Federal Reserve account, all of the federal government's deposits are kept in the banks in order to ease potential financial strains. The amount maintained varies with the Treasury's financial needs, based on its tax collections and expenditures, and is not really subject to banker discretion. (See Box 6.1.)

So, except for the federal government's account with the banking system, depositors found it profitable to increase the proportion of their deposits held in time accounts and to reduce the percentage held in

Deposits maintained in commercial banks on behalf of the U.S. government, into which payments for taxes and for purchases of various government loans can be made, are known as **Treasury Tax and Loan Accounts.**

BOX 6.1. U.S. Government Accounts in Commercial Banks: The Treasury Tax & Loan (TT&L) Accounts

The deposits of the federal government with domestic banks arise from two sources: (1) The proceeds of checks written to the order of the U.S. government for the payment of taxes are deposited with the originating banks, subject to their being above a minimum amount as determined by the Treasury. (2) When the Treasury markets securities it often grants the banks the privilege of paying for the securities they purchase by crediting the Treasury's accounts with them. As stated in the text, the Treasury does not write checks on these accounts, transfering them instead to the Federal Reserve banks for this purpose. The primary function served by the TT&L accounts is to enable the banking system to function more smoothly. The accompanying tables demonstrate what would happen in the absence of the TT&L accounts, and what does happen at present.

Payments to the Government in the Absence of TT&L Accounts

Assume that the JBP Corp. had to pay $40,000 in income taxes to the Internal Revenue Service. JBP would send a check to the IRS, which would clear it through the Federal Reserve Bank of Atlanta, the district Reserve bank for the Sharon bank, where JBP Corp. keeps its account. The balance sheet adjustments would be recorded as in the following T-account:

Federal Reserve Bank of Atlanta	First National Bank of Sharon	
Treasury: + $40,000 Bank deposits (reserves), First National Bank of Sharon: − $40,000	Reserves: − $40,000	Demand deposits, JBP Corp: − $40,000

Upon receiving the check, the Federal Reserve Bank of Atlanta would credit the Treasury's account by $40,000 and simultaneously subtract that sum from the account of the First National Bank of Sharon. When the check was returned to the Sharon Bank, that bank would deduct $40,000 from its liabilities to JBP Corp., thereby offsetting its reductions in reserves.

The initial consequences of this action would be a $40,000 reduction in demand deposits and, hence, in money supply. But the final impact would be more extensive. You may recall that deposits are always some multiple of the amount of reserves, so that when reserves decline, deposits decline by an even larger amount. (The details of this process are discussed in Chapter 10.) Less money circulates, placing contractionary pressure on the economic system. Since the Treasury periodically collects tax income from individuals and firms—withholding taxes as frequently as biweekly, corporate income taxes four times a year, and individual income taxes on that day of judgment, April 15—the economy would undergo equally periodic bouts of monetary stringency. This belt tightening would be imposed by the Treasury's collection pattern; it would not be a result of economic conditions that warranted tighter money. Only as the Treasury paid its bills would the reserves flow back to the banking system, reversing the contractionary impulse. A less disruptive alternative, which would not periodically upset the monetary system, would certainly be preferable.

Payments to the Government Using TT&L Accounts

The TT&L accounts provide this alternative. As the accompanying T-account demonstrates, no reserve loss occurs. When the Treasury receives the $40,000 check from the JBP Corp., it sends it back to the First National Bank of Sharon to be credited to its TT&L account. The entire change takes place in the liability side of the bank's own balance sheet. Reserves—the asset side of the balance sheet—are unaffected, and the balance sheet of the Federal Reserve Bank of Atlanta remains unchanged.* To be sure, the banks transfer the funds to the Federal Reserve according to a predetermined schedule (which varies for individual banks and can range from a day to a week), and this leads to a loss of bank reserves. However, these Treasury deposits at the Federal Reserve are spent almost immediately, so that the net loss of reserves is speedily reversed and no contractionary impact is felt by the monetary system.

Federal Reserve Bank of Atlanta		First National Bank of Sharon	
	Member bank deposits: no change	Reserves: no change	Demand deposits: JBP Corp.: − $40,000 TT&L account: + $40,000

*Technically, this statement is not entirely correct. Total reserves do not change as a result of the shift, but excess reserves do rise. Treasury deposits are exempt from the Federal Reserve reserve requirement. Thus, if the ratio required against demand deposits was 10 percent, the shift would free $4,000 in the reserve account of The First National Bank of Sharon. On the other hand, U.S. government deposits must be secured by the bank's holding an equal value in approved securities (primarily Treasury), so the freed reserves cannot be used for lending to the general public.

demand form. Bankers made the choice possible; the response is evident in the data.

Competition for deposits was strong in the past two decades, forcing the bankers to pay ever higher interest rates. The response of the banking community was to seek alternative sources of funding. One such nontraditional source was borrowing.

Borrowings

The increase in borrowings was dramatic. From $200 million in 1960, borrowed funds reached $148 billion in 1979. In percentage terms, the proportion moved from one-tenth of one percent of total assets to over 10 percent.

The sources of bank borrowing include the following:

1. *Federal Reserve banks.* All depository institutions that maintain re-

BOX 6.2. Trading in the Federal Funds Market

It was not a particularly busy day, Bill Duffy was saying. But as he spoke, brokers around his long desk at the Wall Street firm of Mabon, Nugent & Company began shouting at each other. A major bank wanted to borrow $200 million just for the day.

Up from their seats, the brokers, with telephone cords trailing and receivers wedged between chin and shoulder, were huddling over long lists of potential buyers and sellers. It took about a minute to piece together the $200 million from 10 banks around the country with extra funds on hand.

"It's just like buying and selling a car," Mr. Duffy said of the dickering that goes on between banks, either directly or through brokers. In this case, though, the bargaining is over the interest rate on borrowings, usually just for overnight, that come in multiples of $5 million. According to a Federal Reserve study, the volume of these borrowings averages between $45 billion and $50 billion a day, which is vastly more than the amount changing hands in the stock and bond markets.

This enormous money market, known technically as the Federal funds or Fed funds market, is more than simply a huge pool of funds for banks. The interest rate established by the banks' shifting desires to lend or borrow temporary funds is the economy's most sensitive interest rate. The pressures on interest rates, which work their way into the rates charged on business loans, mortgages, and eventually to consumer loans, show up first in the Fed funds market.

The Fed funds market has no central marketplace, no counterpart to the floor of a stock exchange. It consists instead of a web of telephone lines among banks and between brokers and banks. The telephone turret on Mr. Fieldhouse's [president of Garvin Guy Butler, a Federal funds broker] desk has 120 buttons, direct lines to traders at many of the 200 United States banks he deals with.

Mr. Fieldhouse also counts among his customers the United States subsidiaries or offices of 100 foreign banks. Although commercial banks dominate the Fed funds market, other participants include savings banks, savings and loan associations, and agencies of the Federal Government.

Mr. Fieldhouse and the dozen other brokers sitting at an I-shaped desk match up buyers and sellers, but the banks arrange the actual transfer of funds between themselves.

"We give up the names," he says meaning he reveals who the participants are to each other. "And then we disappear." Buyer and seller each pay Garvin Guy Butler or Mabon, Nugent a fee of 50 cents per $1 million.

The "name" is important because banks, after previously assessing the credit quality of potential buyers, have limits on how much they will sell to specific banks. A bank may have reached its limit because of other sales that day and may have to turn down a transaction.

The need for Federal funds originally arose—it is still highly important, of course—because banks that belong to the Federal Reserve can use them to meet their weekly "reserve requirements." The Fed requires its member banks to set aside specific percentages of their deposits. Banks with more serves with the Federal Reserve may request loans from their district Reserve bank.

2. *Other domestic banks.* Through the Federal funds market, banks in need of reserves can acquire them from other banks. (See Box 6.2.)

3. *Foreign banks.* Both foreign branches of domestic banking corporations and banks owned by foreigners and situated abroad channel funds to banks in the United States.

4. *The nonbank public.* The general public lends to banks, which issue a variety of debt instruments. Banks issue **finance paper**, which is purchased by the public. They also engage in repurchase agreements, selling securities for a specific maturity date and promising to buy them back at a price that includes the principal plus interest at the expiration of the agreed-upon time.

> **Finance paper** consists of short-term, unsecured promissory notes issued by banks.

In the last two decades, borrowing from all sources increased. That the bankers intensified their borrowing from the Federal Reserve is not surprising; expansions in economic activity are normally accompanied by a larger volume of loans from the Federal Reserve. During periods of business slack, banks are usually flush with reserves; bankers seek a greater degree of liquidity during recessions as an extra measure of protection, a fact pointed out earlier in this chapter. Also, with weak loan demand and generally poor business conditions, banks' funds outflows tend to be less severe. Thus, they need less of the protection offered to their balance sheets by their borrowing potential. But both of these reasons evaporate as expansion proceeds. The extra protective cushion seems less necessary in a dynamically growing economy. And as more activity is generated, the chance of being caught with insufficient reserves increases. Thus, bankers find themselves in debt to the Federal Reserve banks more often, and the amounts borrowed tend to be larger. For instance, borrowings from Federal Reserve banks in December 1960 amounted to only $87 million, while the banking system simultaneously held $769 million in excess reserves. In other words, **net free reserves** equaled $682 million. By December 1968, net free reserves were minus $310 million. They were minus $1.7 billion in December 1979.

> **Net free reserves** are the excess reserves that banks maintain at the Federal Reserve less the amount of bank borrowings from the Federal Reserve.

The Federal Reserve banks limit the frequency and volume of bank borrowing from this source, thereby inducing bankers to turn to alternatives. The Federal funds market provides individual banks with substantial amount of reserves and, indeed, has overshadowed the Federal

Reserve as a provider of borrowed funds. While in December, 1960 such borrowing amounted to a meager $184.4 million, by December 1968 the volume had risen to $7.5 billion. By the end of the 1970s the amount of Federal funds outstanding reached many tens of billions of dollars.

Similarly, banks in the United States have borrowed from the Eurodollar market and from the public. By the end of 1979 the banking system had borrowed over $100 billion dollars from nondeposit sources. As Table 6.1 indicates, borrowings have become a significant source of bank funds.

The final entry on the liability side is *other liabilities,* which includes the remaining debt of the banking community, such as accounts receivable.

Net worth

The obverse of the slight increase in the proportion of total liabilities to total assets is the modest decline in the banks' capital ratio, from 8.2 percent in 1960 to 7.3 percent in 1979. The decline was not continuous, as Figure 6.4 shows. Nevertheless, the trend is unambiguously negative.

Bank capital merits special consideration, for one of the issues that troubled (and continues to bother) bank regulators is the adequacy of bank capital. The regulators must grapple with the question of whether individual banks maintain sufficient net worth to meet their needs. Of course, underlying this question is another: How much capital is "sufficient"?

Net worth represents the stake of the owners of the banks in their institutions. When any corporation is formed, capital equals the amount contributed by the owners. As the firm develops and accumulates profits,

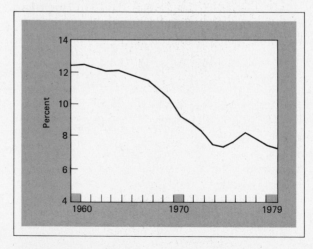

FIGURE 6.4 Capital accounts as a percentage of total assets, all commercial banks, 1960–1979.

Source: Board of Governors of the Federal Reserve System.

the profits plowed back into the firm and not distributed as dividends are added to its capital. Capital, together with the firm's indebtedness, enables the business to acquire assets and operate as a going concern.

Take a look at a manufacturing firm's balance sheet; you may find one in an accounting or economics textbook. Net worth as a percentage of total assets is rarely below 50 percent and typically is well above that level. The reason is obvious. While many owners of businesses would be happy to borrow as much as 100 percent of total assets—then, if the firm fails, the owners have risked none of their own assets—financiers are unwilling to lend under those conditons. Creditors insist on a serious commitment of borrowers' funds in their own businesses so that should the firm run into difficulties, the lenders are guaranteed some margin of protection. Thus, if assets total $100 million and liabilities equal $50 million, the lenders of the $50 million are protected, at least on paper, by $2 in assets for every $1 they have lent the firm. If the firm is forced to liquidate and the assets bring only $70 million, the lenders can be repaid fully. The remaining $20 million reverts to the owners, who will have to absorb the $30 million loss.

The capital ratios of banks bear little resemblance to those of nonfinancial institutions. As the 1979 percentage demonstrates, the ratio of capital to total assets was only 7.3 percent. In other words, for every dollar's worth of assets, liability holders supplied 92.7¢ worth while the stockholders provided only 7.3¢. Why are the "lenders" so willing to risk their funds? What distinguishes banking from a manufacturing operation insofar as the capital:total assets ratio is concerned? Four reasons suggest themselves:

1. A substantial group of creditors—namely, all depositors with $100,000 or less in any individual bank—are protected by deposit insurance. Since the advent of deposit insurance in 1935, losses to holders of deposits in insured banks have been insignificant. No depositor lost funds that were within the insurance limits if the bank was covered by the Federal Deposit Insurance Corporation (FDIC).
2. Bank assets are highly liquid, far more so than those of nonfinancial firms. For any bank that is in trouble, a substantial percentage of its cash, investment, and even loan assets can be disposed of with little or no loss. This situation does not hold true for nonfinancial firms, which tie up a large share of their assets in plant and equipment. Indeed, the relatively liquid position of banks has enabled the FDIC to recover its payments to depositors in most instances.
3. Banks' ability to borrow from the Federal Reserve also provides a degree of protection.
4. Few banks fail, so that the need to worry about deposit loss is negligible.

In short, the issue of capital adequacy does not concern bank depositors directly. They are amply protected.

However, the bank regulatory authorities cannot share this benign neglect. Insofar as they are ultimately responsible for the health of the banking system and must be prepared to bail out financially troubled banks, the authorities have a stake in ensuring the smooth and uninterrupted working of the system. No agreed-upon measure of adequate capital has been found, but historical precedent suggests that 10 percent is an appropriate ratio of capital to total assets. Federal Reserve and FDIC officials were concerned as the capital ratio declined in the 1960s and fell still further in the 1970s. They attempted to reverse the decline. The trend of the capital ratio shown in Figure 6.4 does not indicate success.

☐ Summary

Chapter 6 has dealt with numbers, the raw material of portfolio analysis. The balance sheets recorded in this chapter summarize the history of banking in the United States, its successes and failures, over the past two decades. The salient points of that history are as follows:

1. The value of commercial banking assets expanded more rapidly than the rate of inflation as demand for loans was accommodated by the nation's commercial bankers. The growth of bank assets was uneven; when adjusted for inflation, the increase was faster during the 1960–1968 expansion than during the peak-to-peak trend of 1969–1979.
2. Loans continued to be the major asset of the nation's banks, while deposits remained preeminent among the sources of bank funds.
3. Loan growth can be explained by the uninterrupted expansion of the 1960s and the additional years of prosperity in the 1970s. As the proportion of loans recorded on the balance sheets increased, the percentage of cash assets and investments declined.
4. A noticeable shift of bank investments toward state and local securities and away from U.S. government issues can be explained by the greater abundance of the municipal securities as well as the improved after-tax return they offered. However, this trend was reversed after 1974 owing to the public's markedly diminished confidence in nonfederal government debt.
5. The ratio of reserves held by banks with the Federal Reserve declined, primarily because depositors' preferences shifted in favor of time rather than demand deposits.
6. The redistribution of private and government deposits from demand to time deposits itself reflected the increasing yields on time deposits paid by the banks as the years marched on. The availability of highly liquid certificates of deposit after 1961 intensified the deposit shift.
7. Despite the predominant role played by deposits as a source of funds, the two decades witnessed a decline in their importance. Nondeposit

sources—borrowings from domestic and foreign banks, from Federal Reserve banks, and from the nonbank public—were increasingly used to supplement deposit inflows.

8. Bank capital ratios continued their declining trend, despite the concern voiced by the banking industry regulators. Depositors paid little attention to the decline, relying for protection on deposit insurance, the high liquidity of banking assets, bankers' ability to borrow from the Federal Reserve, and the insignificant number of bank failures in recent decades.

Numbers alone, even with the explanations suggested in this chapter, cannot tell the whole story. They need to be interpreted within a coherent framework. The question "What happened?" has been answered. How the bankers responded to the challenges of the past two decades, how portfolios were managed to achieve the goals set by bankers for their institutions, is the subject of the next chapter.

☐ Questions and Exercises

1. The Annual Reports of the FDIC provide more recent balance sheet data than those found in this text. Examine the newer data to ascertain whether major changes have occurred in balance sheet composition. Try to explain these modifications, using your knowledge of general economic conditions as well as specific alterations in the climate of the banking system.

2. How would the spread of floating-rate loans affect bank loan portfolios? What about changes in tax legislation that would reduce the tax-free exemption of certain types of municipal securities that are favored by commercial banks?

3. The Federal Reserve now charges for its check-clearing services, a practice that began in 1981. How is this likely to affect correspondent balances?

4. Why might a large corporate depositor be interested in a bank's capital ratio while the typical depositor couldn't care less?

5. As a banker, would you prefer a low, intermediate, or high capital ratio? Explain.

☐ For Further Study

The postwar experience in financial markets, which sets this chapter into a broader perspective, is surveyed and analyzed by B. J. Friedman, "Postwar Changes in Financial Markets," in M. Feldstein, ed., *The American Economy in Transition* (Chicago: University of Chicago Press, 1980), pp. 9–78.

A good examination of the correspondent relationship and its profitability for correspondent banks may be found in a series of articles by Robert E. Knight that appeared over the years in the *Monthly Review* of the Federal Reserve Bank of Kansas City. Look for the two-part "Correspondent Banking" (November and December 1970), "Account Analysis" (December 1971), "Customer Profitability

Analysis" (April and September-October 1975), and "Account Analysis in Correspondent Banking" (March 1976).

The changes in Treasury tax and loan account procedures are explained in R. W. Lang, "TTL Note Account and the Money Supply Process," Federal Reserve Bank of St. Louis, *Review* 61 (October 1979): 3–14. However, defer pages 7–14 until after you've mastered Chapter 10.

Yair E. Orgler and Benjamin Wolkowitz, *Bank Capital* (New York: Van Nostrand Reinhold, 1976), explore the bank capital controversy from the points of view of bankers, economists, and regulators. It's worth reviewing.

CHAPTER 7

Portfolio Management: Playing the Banking Game

The business of banking ought to be simple; if it is hard, *it is* wrong.

Walter Bagehot, British economic journalist (1873)

The state was set for the second revolution, which is still in progress: the switch from demand to time deposits as the central source of funds, from "asset management" to "liability management" as the central skill of banking, from good connections to good brains as the requirement for bank leadership.

Martin Mayer, author (1974)

CONTENTS

Asset management is shaping the asset side of the balance sheet.

Liability management is determining the liability components of the balance sheet.

Discretionary funds management is the use of funds over which the banker has control to achieve management goals.

The balance sheet of a commercial bank contains a variety of entries, many of which were examined in some detail in the last chapter. The balance sheet structure and the relative importance of the components do not occur in a random manner, nor are they merely a result of bankers' passive responses to external events. Bankers can and do consciously determine the percentages of total assets, liabilities, and net worth in each category, although their control is not absolute. This process of shaping the portfolio, known as *portfolio management*, is the focal point of this chapter.

Portfolio management has undergone significant changes during the past century. Until the early 1960s the banker practiced **asset management**; the 1960s and early 1970s saw the advent of **liability management**. In more recent years a generalized concept known as **discretionary funds management** has evolved. This chapter reviews each of these in turn, looks at two approaches to asset management, and traces the evolution of current practices.

First, however, it is necessary to spell out the fundamental need to which portfolio management is the response.

☐ The Banker's Dilemma

The underlying demand for portfolio management stems from the conflicting bank needs for liquidity on the one hand and profitability on the other. Banks must keep sufficient funds on hand not only to meet banking regulatory requirements—most checking deposits, as we all know, must be paid on demand—but also for continued operation of the business. Obviously, a note from bank executives to depositors requesting the latter to refrain from drawing on their funds will in short order lead to a loss of customers, who will take their business to a competitor that guarantees immediate payment.

One way of assuring sufficient liquidity is to maintain very high cash reserves. To take the extreme case, a bank that stays 100 percent liquid by holding all of its assets in the form of reserves with its district Reserve bank will always be able to pay each depositor fully and immediately. Unfortunately, this fully solvent bank will not survive long. Cash assets earn no income, and bankruptcy is inevitable.

The other extreme is equally unacceptable. A bank that grasps all profitable lending opportunities, that devotes its entire asset portfolio to earning income, will find itself insolvent. It will be unable to meet its obligations to depositors because loans are rather illiquid. They cannot be easily converted to cover immediate demands for funds.

Portfolio management, then, involves reconciling these conflicting demands. It is essentially an optimizing problem that seeks to resolve two opposing objectives, liquidity and profitability, by selecting a combination of balance sheet components that will, in some sense, be the best. Figure 7.1 outlines the issue schematically. On the one hand, as the right side of the sketch shows, management must attract deposits and other liabilities, the raw materials of banking, without which no bank could earn income. On the other hand, as the left side indicates, management must decide how much of the inflow must be allocated to each asset category. Each alternative has costs and benefits associated with it. Thus, demand deposits are costless insofar as no interest is paid to the depositor. But because demand deposits tend to be less stable than savings deposits, bankers experience greater operational outlays and must maintain a stronger liquidity position. Loans, to take another example, tend to be the least liquid of all assets, but they compensate for that drawback by contributing the highest earnings. One method of resolving the portfolio dilemma is asset management, to which we now turn.

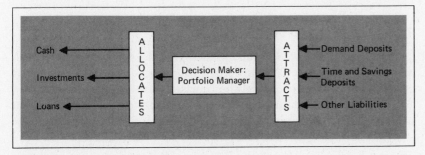

FIGURE 7.1 The portfolio management problem.

☐ Asset Management

Assume that the bank's balance sheet contains $10 million in liabilities, of which $8 million consists of demand deposits and the remaining $2 million of time deposits. The problem facing the asset portfolio manager is to allocate these funds in the optimal way. The manager operates under general constraints: the amount of liabilities as well as the need for sufficient liquidity to meet anticipated withdrawals. And, not to be forgotten, sufficient income must be generated to cover the expenses of the operation and have something left over for the stockholders in the form of profit. The manager's asset choices, to simplify greatly, are limited to three: cash assets, investments, and loans. Were these three categories to be arranged in order of liquidity, they would be arrayed as follows:

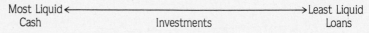

Most Liquid ←————————————————————————→ Least Liquid
Cash   Investments   Loans

The profitability scale, however, would reverse this order:

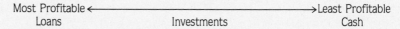

Most Profitable ←————————————————————————→ Least Profitable
Loans   Investments   Cash

How much of the $10 million available should be allocated to each category? That is the key issue.

Two basic approaches have evolved to solve the problem. The first method allocates assets by relying on a number of rules of thumb. This approach tends to be conservative, involving adherence to the rules rather than to independent decision making. It is not an entirely unreasonable approach, and it does offer certain advantages, simplicity being an important one. This method of operation will be explored first. A more complicated approach, which is essentially an "economic" method, will be examined next. Economic analysis involves investigating the costs and benefits of alternative decisions and then selecting the best one. The two approaches may well recommend similar asset portfolios, but that is hardly likely. The differences in practice will be discussed after the two methods have been described.

The conservative approach[1]

Of the two goals, liquidity and profitability, the conservative approach takes it for granted that the former is preeminent. A banker's first responsibility is to take care of the bank's depositors, for both legal and business reasons. Consequently, the manager must make sure that an adequate reserve exists to meet anticipated demands. Bagehot, in another

---

[1]This section depends heavily on Roland I. Robinson, *The Management of Bank Funds* (New York: McGraw-Hill, 1962). A summary is contained in J. Prager, ed. *Monetary Economics: Controversies in Theory and Policy* (New York: Random House, 1971), pp. 24–27.

context, puts it succinctly: "Adventure is the life of commerce, but caution, I had almost said timidity, is the life of banking."[2]

The volume of reserves required depends not only on the expected volume of funds demanded but also on the timing of these demands. Some outflows might occur within the next few days, others only in subsequent months. Moreover, virtually all banks must maintain reserves to meet regulatory requirements. Depository institutions, for example, must keep reserves in the form of vault cash or demand deposits at their district Federal Reserve banks. Consequently, some reserves must be in highly liquid form and are called **primary reserves**. Others must be liquid, but to a lesser degree, and are referred to as **secondary reserves**.

Primary reserves. Primary reserves serve two purposes: They comply with regulatory mandates and they enable the bank to meet immediate needs. Such immediate needs arise in the normal course of business. People enter the bank to withdraw cash; it had better be ready for them. Deposit drains, of course, account for a larger share of total withdrawals. Checks written by depositors work their way through the clearing process and end up as a demand for payment from the depositor's bank. These checks must be honored; they are debited to the bank's reserve account. If the bank's management expects to lose $50,000 today, having already considered the inflow of reserves that it anticipates receiving from other banks, then it would maintain sufficient funds in its reserve account to cover this outflow.[3]

The form in which primary reserves are held is dictated by the underlying need for the reserves. To meet reserve requirements, primary reserves must be held either in vault cash or in demand deposits at the Federal Reserve. For banks that are also subject to state-determined reserve requirements, most states accept correspondent deposits in addition to cash, and some accept holdings of U.S. government securities. Banks will also hold some excess reserves to meet their projected needs. (However, if the bank's managers estimated their reserve needs accurately, these excess reserves will disappear from the balance sheet by the day's end. Can you explain why?)

Consequently, if the reserve requirement to be held against demand deposits is 10 percent and that to be held against time deposits is 5

Primary reserves are cash assets held to meet legal reserve requirements and for immediate liquidity needs.
Secondary reserves are assets held for imminent but not immediate liquidity needs.

---

[2]*Lombard Street: A Description of the Money Market* [Homewood, Ill.: Richard D. Irwin, 1962 (from the 1873 edition)], p. 113. On the same page Bagehot writes, "There is a cardinal difference between banking and other kinds of commerce; you can afford to run much less risk in banking than in commerce, and you must take greater precautions."
[3]In reality, the process is somewhat more complicated. According to present Federal Reserve regulations, a bank need not maintain the required reserve on a daily basis. An averaging procedure is used, as will be noted in Chapter 13. Thus, the asset manager could do nothing, let the bank's reserve account fall, and hope that during the remainder of the period sufficient funds would accrue to the bank's account to compensate for the present deficiency. Should that not occur, the manager could borrow reserves temporarily. However, the conservative approach to portfolio management abjures any technique that relies on borrowing to bail the bank out.

percent, the required reserve for our sample bank would equal (10% × $8 million) + (5% × $2 million) = $800,000 + $100,000 = $900,000. But primary reserves could be greater than that sum. If the bank's executives had expected to lose $50,000 in the check-clearing process, the bank's beginning-of-the-day reserve holdings would have to be $945,000 in primary reserves: $900,000 as stated plus $45,000 to meet the anticipated outflow. ("Why $45,000 and not $50,000?" you might ask. Because when the checks written by the bank's depositors are honored, the bank's demand deposit liabilities fall by $50,000. As a result, the required reserve falls by $5,000, or 10 percent of $50,000. This $5,000 can be used in addition to the excess reserve of $45,000 to cover the $50,000 outflow.)

The overriding disadvantage of holding primary reserves, especially in cash and at the Federal Reserve banks, is their singular lack of earning power. Obviously, vault cash earns no income. But neither does a demand deposit with the Federal Reserve, even for reserves held in excess of the requirement. Thus, even though the liquidity of primary reserves is higher than that of any other asset category, holding only the amount needed certainly makes good business sense.

Secondary reserves. When the bank's officers still require liquidity but their needs are of a less immediate nature, they will consider alternatives to primary reserves. Picture the following situation: A scheduled payday leads to a withdrawal of $250,000 every Friday. The bank must have these funds in the form of primary reserves on Friday. The bank's officers would be foolish to engage in, say, consumer installment lending in this amount during the week; that would jeopardize the bank's weekend liquidity position. But the bank would be forfeiting income if a quarter of a million dollars were held in nonearning form during the week. A suitable vehicle that would be highly liquid and yet would provide some income should be found. In fact, a number of assets meet these criteria. Two examples of such assets are Federal funds and **dealer loans**.

Bank one-day loans to government security dealers are called **dealer loans**.

You have already learned that banks lend to other banks. These loans of Federal funds are typically one-day loans and, thus, are highly liquid; they are repaid on the very next day. And they do earn some income— whatever the particular Federal funds rate is at the moment of lending. (At a Federal funds rate of 20 percent per annum, lending $250,000 brings in $138.80 daily, which is not much. But it is certainly greater than the cost of a phone call and a moment of a bank officer's time. And while funds transactions tend to be in units of $1 million, loans for as little as $25,000 have been arranged in the past.)

Dealer loans to U.S. government securities dealers are made to that handful of firms that regularly stand ready to buy and sell government securities. Those firms maintain voluminous inventories of such securities, but provide only a small proportion of their own capital. They finance the bulk of the inventory by borrowing, both from banks and from large firms that temporarily hold surplus funds. The dealers borrow on a day-by-day basis, and it is not unusual for a dealer to scrape together hundreds of millions of dollars each day from a myriad of sources. Of course, on the opposite side of this operation stands the lender, who receives interest for the use of the funds for the day. Thus, the lender earns some income and maintains the high degree of liquidity required. Federal funds and dealer loans serve well as secondary reserves.

Other assets can be used as secondary reserves, too, but they are more desirable under slightly different conditions. Take the case of a bank operating in a locality that is characterized by a marked seasonal business pattern, such as an agricultural region or a tourist center. The nature of the seasonal activity obviously affects the community's loan demands. When, for instance, crops are sold, deposit balances are large and loan demand is weak. But as the year progresses, the balances are drawn down, and when planting time rolls around loans for seed, fertilizer, and equipment are needed. The bank must respond to these loan demands, and must be prepared for them. It must have funds on hand when they are needed, having husbanded its resources from the earlier season of slack demand.

It would be the height of folly to hold the funds that have been set aside in nonearning primary reserves. Putting them up for borrowing on the Federal funds market or to dealers is a possible alternative. But since these loans would be renewed daily and interest rates might fall over the period, an asset whose maturity is somewhat longer—say, three to six months—might be preferable. Such an asset would still have to be highly liquid, but it would offer a more secure return over the entire period. A Treasury bill would be a perfect vehicle for use as a secondary reserve. Since Treasury bills are issued in three-, six-, and twelve-month maturities and since they are auctioned off by the Treasury each week, a banker can tailor a portfolio of Treasury bills to the bank's expected needs. The same result can be achieved by acquiring CDs issued by a large commercial bank. The original depositor may have intended to maintain the time deposit for nine months but been forced to sell it after two months. The banker could purchase the CD for all or part of the remaining period to maturity. Both Treasury bills and CDs are bought and sold in an active secondary market, guaranteeing the acquiring bank that a further sale could be easily and profitably arranged.

To continue with the example at hand, assume that imminent liquidity needs amount to $2,055,000. Then the bank's managers would elect to acquire secondary reserves in this sum.

Again, a disadvantage of secondary reserves—relatively low yields— should be noted. In 1976, for example, the average yield on a three-month Treasury bill was 4.98 percent on an annual basis; on a CD with a similar maturity, the rate was 5.26 percent annually.[4] (Incidentally, can

---

[4] This is not always true. Sometimes short-term assets yield more than their longer-term brethren. Recall the discussion of yield curves in Chapter 3.

"I don't know. I was just in a borrowing mood."

Drawing by Vietor; © 1977 The New Yorker Magazine, Inc.

you explain the difference between the two interest rates? Might it be related to the degree of risk inherent in each asset?)

Loans. Once liquidity has been assured through adequate primary and secondary reserve holdings, bank management can concentrate their efforts on pursuing profits. And to most bankers profits means lending. Recall the balance sheets of the commercial banking system in Table 6.1; it is no coincidence that the largest category of bank assets is the loan group. Of course, the banker must decide which type of loans to undertake and what share of the bank's resources should be devoted to each category of loan—agricultural, industrial, commercial, real estate, consumer, and so on. The relative return to be gained from each loan group will be a critical variable in the banker's decision. But that decision will be made after considering the division of bank resources between liquid and nonliquid assets.

True, loans tend to be the least liquid of all assets. However, this need not disturb our banker; the bank's liquidity needs have already been taken care of through the allocation of funds to primary and secondary reserves. Consequently, it would not be improper for the banker to devote $7 million to loans. The asset side of the balance sheet would then look like this:

Primary reserves	$ 945,000
Secondary reserves	2,055,000
Loans	7,000,000
Total assets	$10,000,000

Investments. Not always will the banker be willing or able to commit all available funds for loans. It may very well turn out that fewer applicants come forward with requests for loans. Perhaps the banker overestimated the dollar amount desired by the public. Alternatively, loan demand might be strong, but the banker estimates the risk of loss to be too high to warrant taking a chance with some of the potential borrowers. When the banker perceives this situation as likely to continue for some time, alternatives to loans will be sought. Once again, liquidity is not important; income is. Consequently, the banker will be attracted to intermediate- and long-term investments of high quality, such as those issued by the U.S. or municipal governments or the debentures of highly rated corporations. In general, the yields of longer-term securities are higher than those of short-term investments; the reverse is true of the liquidity of the assets.

In sum, the conservative view of bank asset portfolio allocation suggests a rigid set of priorities— primary reserves, secondary reserves, loans, and investments. Only when liquidity is assured is profitability to be pursued. Table 7.1 summarizes this conservative view of bank asset management.

The "economic" approach

Rules tend to be inflexible; by their very nature they do not permit exceptional situations to be handled through judgmental decisions. The economic view of asset management is not rigid at all; it handles each circumstance—the normal and the exceptional—by finding the best outcome for the individual case. The concept is simple; it requires

TABLE 7.1 The Conservative View of Asset Management

Category	Purpose	Type of asset
1. Primary reserves	a. Legal requirements	a. Vault cash, reserves with Federal Reserve banks, interbank deposits
	b. Immediate needs	b. Vault cash, reserves with Federal Reserve banks, interbank deposits, excess reserves
2. Secondary reserves	Imminent needs a. Very near future	a. Federal funds and dealer loans
	b. Not quite so near	b. Treasury bills, CDs
3. Loans	Income	All types of loans (other than Federal funds and dealer loans)
4. Investments	Income (when loans are unavailable or undesirable)	U.S. government notes and bonds, state and local securities, high-quality corporate issues

This table should provide a useful review. Be sure you understand the concepts involved and why the priorities are ordered the way they are.

ascertaining the possible courses of action, evaluating the alternatives, and selecting the most desirable one.

An example with a two-asset model will illustrate the approach. Though simplified, it does not neglect any critical concepts or analysis. Once again, the sample bank maintains a deposit base of $10 million that its managers must allocate between two asset categories—liquid assets and earning assets. For every dollar held as cash (liquid assets), the banker forfeits a certain amount of income. This opportunity cost reflects the current income that could have been earned—both as interest and as an increase in the capital value of the acquired earning asset—had the banker decided to purchase an earning asset rather than stay liquid. It must be stressed, however, that these potential gains, and therefore the opportunity costs, cannot be calculated with certainty. The loan (earning asset) may turn sour; interest payments may be delayed for months and possibly for years; and the hoped-for capital gain might turn out to be a capital loss. Nevertheless, it is possible to estimate the potential gain, taking into account such objective elements as the financial condition and reputation of the borrower and the general condition of the economy, as well as such subjective evaluations of the likelihood of default, delay, or adverse market reaction. The most likely gain, then, represents the opportunity cost of holding liquid assets rather than earning assets.

On the other hand, the benefit of maintaining a substantial degree of liquidity must be reckoned. Essentially, the benefit results from possessing liquid assets on hand when they are needed. When checks debited against the bank exceed checks collected from other banks, the adverse clearing balance must be settled. If sufficient liquid assets are not at hand, they will have to be obtained, either by selling assets or by borrowing. Each of these alternatives involves a cost in the form of interest, and when assets have to be sold, the possibility of capital loss cannot be ignored. Not having to incur such costs, as would be the case when sufficient cash assets are held, is thus a gain. But again it must be stressed that the banker operates in an uncertain world; it cannot be taken for granted that liquid assets will be required. After all, fund inflows might exceed outflows. And even if that doesn't happen, the magnitude of the need for liquidity is unknown. Thus, neither the costs nor the benefits of liquid asset holdings can be calculated with certainty. The calculations, however, can and must be made even if they are only guesstimates.

Follow this concrete example. The banker estimates that the bank requires $900,000 to meet its reserve requirement. The portfolio manager further anticipates that the bank's demand deposit accounts will be reduced by $1 million during the next week. The question is, Should cash assets equal to $1,800,000[5] be maintained or should a chance be taken and should some, if not all of these liquid assets be devoted to earning assets? The manager might come up with the following calculations:

---

[5]Here again the reduction in deposits by $1 million frees reserves of $100,000, so that the manager must supply an additional $900,000, not $1 million.

Alternative	Acquire earning asset	Opportunity cost of remaining liquid	Benefit from remaining liquid (11.1%)	Net gain from lending (cost−benefit)
A	$900,000	$90,000	$100,000	−$10,000
B	550,000	80,000	61,050	18,950
C	450,000	67,500	49,950	17,550

If the banker selects option A and ties up the $900,000 in loans and investments, the expected return is 10 percent of $900,000. Thus, the $90,000 will represent the opportunity cost of remaining fully liquid; it stands for the amount that the banker will *not* earn. But should the need for the funds materialize according to the manager's expectations, and should the funds have been tied up in earning assets that cannot be liquidated easily, the banker would have to borrow the entire $900,000 at an assumed interest rate of 11.1 percent. The benefit of keeping the entire sum liquid is avoiding this payment of $100,000. On the basis of this calculation, the banker should reject lending the entire sum, since the $90,000 that would be earned would be more than offset by the anticipated $100,000 cost of borrowing, as the final column indicates.

Take a look now at option C. If the banker decides to lend only $450,000 and maintain the remainder in the form of liquid assets, the benefit-cost picture is modified significantly. Because the banker is lending out a smaller sum, the loan officer can be more selective in the choice of customers to service. Consequently, the net rate of return should be higher; here it is assumed to be 15 percent. Should the banker's estimation of deposit outflow prove correct, only $450,000 would have to be borrowed at 11.1 percent. Now, the borrowing cost of $49,950 is less than the gain from lending $67,500. It would be more profitable, then, to acquire the $450,000 in earning assets and borrow the funds, should the need arise. A net gain of $17,550 would result.

What about acquiring earning assets for another $100,000? The desirability of such a move depends on relative rates of return. As long as the expected rate earned on these additional funds exceeds 11.1 percent, additional lending would pay. At worst, the bank portfolio manager would have to borrow $100,000 more, but at a cost of 11.1 percent. Alternative B describes this situation, which turns out to be optimal. Here the banker decides to lend or invest $550,000. The bank earns 11.1 percent on the marginal dollar lent, bringing the total amount that would be earned to $80,000. The costs avoided by holding liquid assets rather than borrowing $550,000 come to $61,050. Selecting alternative B and retaining only $1,250,000 instead of the entire $1,800,000 in liquid assets adds to the profits of the bank.

Of course, this example of the economic analysis of assets is simple to the point of naiveté. More assets have to be introduced into the model, and the time dimension—days, weeks, and months—must be included explicitly. Nevertheless, while such models will be more inclusive and more sophisticated, the essential considerations remain the same. The benefits of alternative courses of actions are weighed against their costs, and the alternative ultimately chosen will be one in which the cost-benefit differential is the greatest.

Can you think of some instances in which the conservative and economic theories of portfolio management will recommend different strategies?

Conservative versus economic theories of asset management

The two theories of asset portfolio management both accept the need for a diversified asset portfolio. Normally, no profit-oriented banker will maintain a large share of the bank's total assets in liquid form. Similarly, no banker will commit the bank to a loan portfolio that threatens the bank's liquidity position. The two theories nevertheless lead to different conclusions, specifically, in the degree of liquidity that should be maintained for a given liability portfolio.

Three cases will serve to illustrate both the similarities and the contrasts between the two approaches.

Case 1: A deposit in a CD account

The First National Bank of Sharon accepts a $500,000 90-days-to-maturity certificate of deposit account from the JBP Corporation and sets aside $15,000 to meet the assumed reserve requirement of 3 percent. The bank's managers must decide how to allocate the remaining $485,000.

Think first about the nature of the account. Because it is a CD account with a 90-day maturity, the Sharon banker can be certain that the deposit will remain for the full three-month period. Should the JBP Corp require funds in the interim, it can sell off the CD to a second party, which will then obtain ownership of the CD. But the deposit itself will remain untouched. On the other hand, the banker cannot be sure that the deposit will be renewed for a second three-month period. Consequently, the bank does not need additional primary or secondary reserves to serve as a liquidity buffer, but in seeking out a profitable lending opportunity, attention would have to be paid to the short-term tenure of the deposit.

The banker might undertake lending to an automobile dealer who requires a few months' financing to maintain his inventory in preparation for the late-spring sales surge. Or, if loan demand is weak or too risky, the banker might consider investing in a three-month Treasury bill.

Both theories of asset management would subscribe to this analysis and decision. The parameters of the decision are well defined, and the outcome follows clearly from the conditions surrounding the deposit.

Case 2: An increase in demand deposits

How would the management of the First National Bank have reacted to the $100,000 deposit if it were placed in the JBP Corporation's checking account? After the presumed 10 percent is set aside to meet the reserve requirement, the remaining 90 percent must be allocated under less certain circumstances. JBP's check-writing pattern leads to irregular, and surely less predictable, demands on the bank's funds than a CD account does. A significant portion of the account might be drawn upon within a week, leaving a small remainder for a longer period, or the bulk of the deposit might remain for several weeks and then be diminished substantially.

The conservative theory's reaction to this case is to emphasize liquidity. Prepare for the worst likely eventuality: Maintain a high porportion of the deposit in secondary reserves that could be liquidated speedily should the need arise. Plan on lending only a small share. To be sure, an experienced banker will examine the past history of the JBP account and know something about the company's financial flows. Nevertheless, the uncertain nature of the deposit leads to an emphasis on liquidity.

The economic approach would weigh the risks and costs of being caught with inadequate liquid assets should JBP draw down its account beyond the banker's guesstimate against the gains to be made in utilizing the funds in more lucrative, though less liquid, ventures. Other things being equal, the economic approach is likely to lead to less emphasis on secondary reserves and greater stress on profit-earning assets. This approach does not treasure liquidity for its own sake. By its very nature, it is more risk oriented.

Case 3: A rise in loan rates

Finally, consider the reactions suggested to the portfolio manager by each type of approach when the rates that bankers charge their customers move upward. If the liability side of the balance sheet remains unchanged, with both the totals and the distribution among liabilities staying as before, the conservative approach would recommend that the asset portfolio manager not react. After all, the bank's liquidity needs, which are predicated on its liability structure, have not been modified, and hence there is no reason for adjusting the asset structure. Of course, changes will occur over time. Old loans and investments will mature, and the funds will be re-lent at the new, higher rates. But the proportion of liquid assets to earning assets depends on the unchanged liability structure.

The advice tendered by the economic approach differs markedly. Since loan rates have risen, the opportunity cost of remaining liquid has also increased. The balance has shifted in favor of additional lending. Consequently, the loan segment of the portfolio should be increased, while the liquid asset share should decline. The higher earnings from loans warrant taking a greater chance on not having adequate liquidity. If the additional liquidity is required, additional costs will be incurred, but they will be offset by the additional profits earned from the loan expansion. And if additional liquidity is not required, the increase in lending will clearly be translated into increased revenue for the bank.

An evaluation of the two approaches

Which approach is correct? The answer, as is often the case in economics, is, "It depends." For a capable and lucky banker, revenue from the asset portfolio should be higher under the economic approach than under the conservative method. In general, the former will recommend that a smaller proportion of total assets be held in low-earning liquid assets and a larger proportion in higher-earning loans and investments. But consideration must be given to the costs of running each type of approach as well. Not only does the economic approach require additional information, but it requires staff and equipment to gather and process the information. The financial markets have to be monitored continuously, and a computer would process the resulting input, working with a complex model that has been fed into its memory. In short, the economic approach, being more complex, is also more expensive. It is likely to be profitable only for larger banking organizations. Indeed, it will surprise no one to learn that the giant commercial banks, with their massive portfolios running into the billions of dollars, their heavy capital investments, and their specialized staffs, are devotees of the economic approach.

For a smaller bank, the expense of running this operation is likely to overshadow the revenue to be earned. The cost looms so large that the less sophisticated, rule-of-thumb method turns out to be better. The less specialized staff of a small bank has neither the time nor the experience to watch carefully over modest portfolios. The manager of a small bank uses the bank's scarce resources more efficiently by devoting them to other, more profitable aspects of banking.

Summary

Asset portfolios are not shaped accidentally; conscious management decisions account for their basic contours. For large banks with a volume of operations that warrants employing specialized staff and equipment, the cash assets, loan, and investment portfolios are monitored continuously and carefully. Decisions concerning the optimal portfolio are made at the highest management levels, but the top executives rely on input from the staff, which provides statistical projections and interpretations. An "economic" model, weighing and quantifying the costs and benefits of alternative courses of action, plays a critical role in the final decision.

Optimal decision-making procedures for smaller banks, in which the income to be derived from paying careful attention to the asset portfolio will not cover its cost, involve the more conservative approach. Small banks tends to husband their liquid assets, keeping extra funds on hand to meet the unexpected. Even modest-sized banks, however, will minimize their primary reserve holdings; the Federal funds market has become a fruitful avenue for increased profits even for smaller banks. The two approaches to asset management lead to different portfolio allocations and to different reactions to changes in market conditions, but the contrasts should not be exaggerated. All bankers realize the importance of both liquidity and profitability.

☐ Liability Management

The years since 1961 have directed increasing attention to the management of the liability side of commercial banks' portfolios. The large volume of liquid assets acquired by the commercial banking system during the 1940s through the massive debt issues of the federal government had enabled them to finance the loan demand of the 1950s. They were able to sell these superfluous liquid assets and bring their portfolio ratios closer to their historical levels. Thus, in 1947 the loan:deposit ratio was only 26.5 percent; by 1960 it had jumped to 54.4 percent. Correspondingly, the ratio of investments to deposits fell from 54.1 percent in 1947 to 35.2 percent in 1960.

By the early 1960s commercial bankers were finding it increasingly difficult to respond positively to profitable loan opportunities. Further adjustment of their asset portfolios was limited by their reduced liquidity. An innovative response was needed. It came, initially, with liability management in two manifestations: (1) the renaissance of the Federal funds market and (2) the development of the negotiable CD.

The Federal funds market

Looked at from the point of view of the lending bank, the Federal funds market provides a high-quality secondary reserve asset. The combined features of high liquidity and some income meets the needs of bank managers and, as was noted a few pages ago serves handsomely to meet imminent outflows of funds.

From the viewpoint of the borrowing bank, the existence of the Federal funds market enables its managers to obtain reserves—albeit at a price—even when the bank's own primary reserve holdings prove inadequate. Consequently, the banker can expand the bank's lending operations with reduced concern about adequate liquidity. Should the bank's executives discover that reserves are insufficient in light of the expanded loan portfolio, they can turn to the Federal funds market to plug up the hole. It was this kind of thinking that underlay the significant growth of the Federal funds market during the 1960s. In 1961 major bank net purchases of Federal funds totaled less than $1 billion. A decade later they had grown more than tenfold. By the end of 1979 net purchases exceeded $20 billion.

The CD in liability management

During the fifteen years that followed the end of World War II, bankers reacted passively to time deposits. The interest payable on time deposits made them less profitable than demand deposits. Time deposits were tolerated, but hardly welcomed. Nor were treasurers of nonfinancial enterprises enamoured with them, since they lacked the high liquidity offered by Treasury bills.

With the advent of the negotiable CD in 1961 and the establishment of a secondary market in which they could be purchased or sold, commercial bankers were able to offer an instrument that rivaled the liquidity of the Treasury bill. Moreover, bankers could adjust the rates on CDs to ensure its competitiveness with the Treasury bill interest rate. Commercial bankers now possessed a flexible instrument to attract deposits and, perhaps more important to the individual bank officers, keep corporate treasurers from pulling out their deposits.

The 1960s saw interest rates rising steadily. From an average of slightly over 2 percent in 1961 the three-month Treasury bill rate rose to 5½ percent by 1966. By 1969 it had risen to 6⅔ percent. Other market interest rates, such as those on commercial paper, followed a similar rising trend. The nonearning demand deposit became increasingly less attractive to depositors. Commercial bankers had to protect themselves against deposit outflows, so they raised the interest they were willing to pay on CDs. As a result, from a low of 2½ percent paid on a three- to six-month CD in 1961, the rate rose to 6 percent by late 1969. And, as noted in the previous chapter, the response of business and the public was strong; the ratio of time deposits to demand deposits rose during the entire decade.

By adjusting the rates that a commercial bank was willing to pay for CDs, the liability manager could attract deposits should the bank require additional funds. And by lowering them, even only marginally, the manager could ensure that profit-seeking funds owners would turn elsewhere. Thus, the rate that a banker offered on CDs became a means of controlling the inflow of liabilities, thereby assuring closer management of the bank's liability portfolio.

One major reversal in the growth of CDs occurred in 1969. This turnaround is interesting for two reasons. First, it yields insight into the relationship between the bank regulators and commercial bank management. Second, the episode provided the impetus for the development or expansion of additional instruments for liability management purposes.

The maximum interest rates that commercial banks may pay on savings and time deposits are fixed by the Federal Reserve's **Regulation Q**.

Fundamental to understanding liability developments in 1969 is **Regulation Q**. In 1969 the interest rate ceiling on large CDs with an initial maturity of 90–179 days was 6 percent. As the year unfolded, interest rates on comparable assets rose higher, creating a significant margin between CD rates and other interest rates. Figure 7.2 (b), which plots the CD ceiling rates against comparable prime commercial paper rates, illustrates this differential. Businesses that were sensitive to this differential permitted their outstanding CDs to mature and, rather than renewing them, bought Treasury bills and commercial paper. The result was a loss of over $10 billion in CDs at the larger commercial banks in less than a year's time, as is seen in the upper panel of the chart.

The Federal Reserve's purpose in maintaining the unrealistically low ceiling was to try to restrain bank lending. The reasoning was direct and simple: If commercial banks could not compete effectively for funds, they

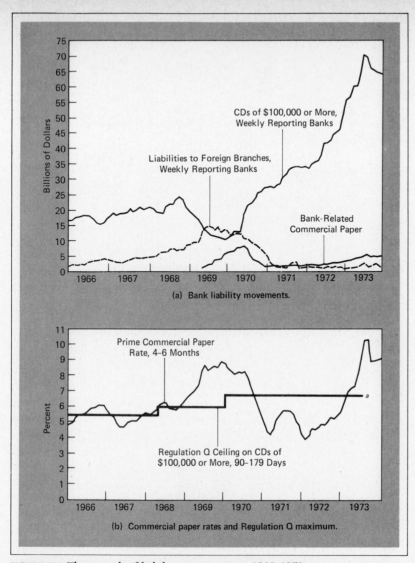

FIGURE 7.2 The growth of liability management, 1966–1973.

[a]Ceiling suspended May 16, 1973.

Source: Federal Reserve Bank of Boston, *New England Economic Review*, May–June 1974.

would not attract them. And if the banks could not obtain funds, they couldn't lend them out. What Federal Reserve officials failed to anticipate was the banking community's action to replace the declining deposit totals. Bankers reacted imaginatively to find substitutes for the lost deposits. Among the most notable of their responses was expansion of Eurodollar deposits and the development of bank-related commercial paper.

The Eurodollar deposit

Eurodollars, you will recall, is the generic term for dollar deposits held outside of the United States. Acquisition of Eurodollars by U.S. commercial banks certainly did not begin in 1969, but in that year the Eurodollar account expanded so substantially that it largely offset the decline in CDs.

To see how this technique worked, refer to Figure 7.3. The U.S. parent bank expects to lose the depositor's $200,000 CD because its terms are no longer competitive. The banker suggests to the depositor that a higher rate of return could be earned if the funds were placed in a Eurodollar account—thus avoiding any exchange rate risk—at the bank's foreign branch. When this suggestion is accepted, the CD at the parent bank is transfered to the foreign branch, as step 1 demonstrates. The next step is internal to the bank, as the branch lends the parent $200,000, denoted by step 2. The net result is to leave the parent's liabilities unchanged and, hence, maintain the asset total of the parent as well. The foreign branch, however, has gained $200,000 in both liabilities and assets.[6] If the balance sheets were consolidated, the internal borrowing and lending would cancel out; the balance sheet remains unchanged. But the bank has successfully protected itself against a decline due to a loss of CD liabilities. Ultimately, the Federal Reserve Board imposed conditions that in effect closed this avenue of escape. However, by that time the commercial bankers had discovered a new, unregulated loophole in the form of bank-related commercial paper.

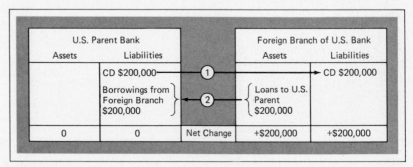

FIGURE 7.3 Liability management and Eurodollars.

---

[6]Until the fall of 1969, when reserve requirements were levied against borrowings from foreign branches, the parent bank actually gained excess reserves from the transaction outlined here. With a 6 percent reserve requirement against CDs, the bank in the example would have had to maintain reserves of $12,000. When the form of the liability was transformed from "deposit" into "borrowing," this $12,000 could be loaned out. (What would the reserve gain have been if the initial withdrawal had come from a demand deposit account, with its 16½ percent reserve requirement?) The new regulations imposed a 10 percent reserve requirement on any increase in Eurodollar borrowing exceeding the total outstanding on May 28, 1969. The effect was to reduce (and, for some, to eliminate) this aspect of the gain.

Bank-related commercial paper

With commercial bankers committed to finding sources of funds so that the asset portfolio, and especially the bank's loans, could be supported, any interference by the regulatory authorities clashed with the basic interests of the banking community. In the late 1960s the largest commercial banks found that the holding-company form of organization offered them numerous advantages, which are spelled out in greater detail in Chapter 8. One of the side effects of this structural change was a new means of maintaining liabilities at desired levels.

The interest rate limitations of Regulation Q apply only to banks; other subsidiaries of bank holding companies, such as a consumer finance company or the holding company itself, are not subject to Regulation Q. Thus, the nonbank subsidiary could issue commercial paper in its own name and, with the proceeds, acquire the loans issued by the commercial bank affiliate. Now, if the bank's depositor acquired the commercial paper issued by the affiliate, the pattern depicted in Figure 7.4 would be complete. In step 1 the depositor allows the CD to mature and with the proceeds buys the higher-yielding commercial paper issued by the consumer finance affiliate. Step 2 finds the finance company purchasing the loans from the commercial bank affiliate and adding them to its asset portfolio. The net effect is a $200,000 reduction in the balance sheet of the commercial bank, a corresponding increase in the balance sheet of the consumer finance company, and for the holding company as a whole, no net change at all. The liabilities of the entire holding-company operation come to rescue the bank from the restraints imposed by the regulators. And the formal loss of the deposit, which forces the bank to reduce its assets, has been a loss only on paper; the holding company has neither gained nor lost.

Other types of instruments were utilized by commercial banks during the 1960s to circumvent restrictive regulations and maintain their lending operations at a high level. But the scope of commercial banks' maneuver-

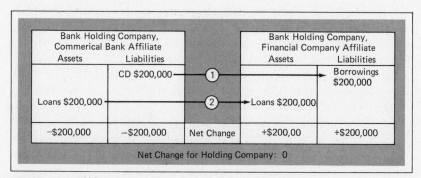

FIGURE 7.4 Liability management and bank holding companies.

ability was continually limited by new Federal Reserve regulations, and it became ever more difficult to uncover further means of circumventing them.

The game played by the two protagonists, the Federal Reserve and the commercial banks, ended in a stalemate in the early 1970s. In 1970 the Federal Reserve suspended the ceiling on 31–89-day large CDs, and 1973 it similarly rescinded the ceiling on 90–179-day CDs. The CD, unleashed from its interest rate fetters, soon became (and remains) the predominant instrument of bank liability management.

In short, in liability management the banking system found a method of protecting itself against deposit runoffs and, thus, against reductions in income-generating assets. It's been a new game ever since.

The problems of liability management

The benefits of liability management to individual banks must be weighed against the disadvantages to the banks themselves and to the economy as a whole. The constant devotion of resources to circumventing the rules rather than to improving services offered to the public or bringing down the costs of bank operations means that bank resources are being used inefficiently. Ultimately, it is the borrowers and depositors who will end up paying for the increased burden, a burden caused to a large extent by the onerous regulations imposed on the banks by the monetary authorities.

But aside from the general costs of the cat-and-mouse game being played by the bankers and the regulators, liability management has resulted in bankers placing themselves in more exposed positions. A less liquid asset structure, with a heavy commitment to loans, is predicated on a more flighty, less stable liability structure. Funds are very mobile and will leave any bank that fails to offer competitive terms. And such terms include not only interest rates but the depositors' perceptions of the risk involved in leaving funds with the bank. This **confidence-sensitive** money may lead to a flight of funds from the bank, threatening its entire asset holdings. Of course, banks have always faced the possibility of runs, as past panics have vividly demonstrated. Rarely, however, have bank executives purposely engineered such a fragile liability structure. Some major banks have painted themselves into a corner without leaving themselves a clear way out.

Confidence-sensitive money will leave a bank when depositors' confidence in its management deteriorates.

The case of the now-defunct Franklin National Bank of New York illustrates well what can happen when confidence is eroded and confidence-sensitive funds depart. In 1973 the bank ranked within the top twenty-five banking corporations in the United States; its assets exceeded $5 billion. By the end of the next year it had ceased to exist. Certain officers of the bank had overextended the institution's foreign-exchange obligations, taking substantial risks that turned out to be disastrous. A multimillion-dollar loss set the stage for the exodus of funds, beginning with some suppliers of Federal funds who discontinued their dealings with Franklin National. Subsequently, large depositors began to withdraw, and ultimately, as the presumed shakiness of the bank became general knowledge among the public, even small depositors began to remove their funds. In just half a year the bank's deposit liabilities declined from $2.6 billion to $1.6 billion. Without massive aid from the Federal Reserve Bank of New York, Franklin National would have collapsed. As it was, it was forced out of business by the FDIC, and some of its executives now are guests in penal institutions. The remaining depositors were spared any loss, because the bank's operations were taken over by another New York bank. While it is true that liability management cannot be considered the cause of the collapse, it is equally true that once the snowball started rolling, the bank's liability structure, which was heavily dependent on confidence-sensitive funds, ensured that an avalanche would follow; the bank's dissolution was almost inevitable.

☐ Discretionary Funds Management

The 1970s saw bank portfolio managers combine asset and liability management into a more sophisticated technique—discretionary funds management. The vertical division of the balance sheet into assets and liabilities was discarded for a new dichotomy: **discretionary** and **nondiscretionary** funds. While these categories are not watertight, the distinction revolves around the ability of banks to influence the volume of these assets or liabilities in the short run. Among the nondiscretionary liabilities are demand deposits and small time and savings deposits; bankers' short-run control over these deposit flows is rather limited. Similarly, bank capital is a nondiscretionary item. Legal reserves and cash items in the process of collection are examples of nondiscretionary assets. So, too, to a large degree are loans, since the amount outstanding at any moment is derived from decisions made months or even years earlier. Moreover, the banker's discretion over new loans is often circumscribed. Frequently, prior loan commitments have been made, and the banker can hardly fail to accommodate them.

Discretionary items are also found on both the asset and liability sides of the balance sheet. The secondary reserve group of assets is an example of the former; short-term Treasury securities can certainly be sold at the banker's discretion. On the liability side, the whole array of borrowed funds—Federal funds, Eurodollars, finance paper, and borrowings from the Federal Reserve—must be included, as must large CDs.

The essential problem of discretionary funds management can now be formulated: How can a change in the net volume of nondiscretionary funds be accommodated? Consider the following example: The banker increases loans by $100 million in September. Simultaneously, demand depositors write out checks for $50 million in September, and none of the

A **discretionary** asset or liability is one that is subject to short-term control by bank management When such control is limited, the balance sheet items are classified as **nondiscretionary**.

funds that are withdrawn find their way back to the bank. Thus, the banker's nondiscretionary assets have increased by $100 million while nondiscretionary liabilities have declined by $50 million. The bank has lost, or stands to lose, $150 million in September.

The portfolio manager's problem is to come up with that sum. Part of it will come from the bank's primary reserve: If the required reserve ratio is 10 percent, the $50 million deposit loss frees $5 million in primary reserves. The remaining $145 million will come from discretionary items.

The manager will now consider the costs involved in working with various discretionary items. If the Federal funds rate is 12 percent, the rate on CDs is 10 percent, and the discount rate is 8.5 percent, the banker may decide to approach the Federal Reserve. The Reserve bank is a reluctant lender, however, and limits its loans to days, not weeks. Thus, the initial approach to the Federal Reserve will be supplemented by efforts to use other sources of discretionary funds, in this instance the CD market. The banker will offer the going rate of 10 percent, perhaps a bit more, to attract CDs to the bank.

Of course, in the more complex real world the choice is never that obvious. Strategies must be devised for dealing with uncertainty and for costs other than interest rates. The percentage of reserves and their return, if any, must be programmed into the calculation. Maturity is important, as are anticipated movements in interest rates. Because of these other factors, the portfolio manager may make choices that seem poorer from the point of view of yield alone, but more optimal when all the elements are considered. (If interest rates are expected to rise in the near future, the banker facing the hypothetical case of the last few paragraphs may be wise not to borrow from the Federal Reserve at all. Borrowing $50 million for one week at 8.5 percent per annum from the Reserve bank costs $11,640. If the banker is then forced to refinance the $50 million in the CD market at an increased interest rate of 11 percent for another 25 weeks, that cost will come to $376,625, for a total half-year cost of $388,265. The alternative of 10 percent per annum, 26-week financing through CDs is only $356,070.)

Bankers who are engaged in discretionary funds management may be even more aggressive than has been suggested so far. Confidence that discretionary funds can always be obtained can lead to an active lending strategy. In an extension of the economic theory of asset management discussed at the beginning of this chapter, the economic theory of discretionary funds management may be advanced. A banker should consider the costs of discretionary funds and should acquire assets—loans —that yield more than they cost. Marginal analysis suggests that as long as marginal returns (adjusted for risk) exceed marginal costs (including all relevant costs), the banker's profits will increase.

Discretionary funds management, building as it does on liability management, suffers of course from the same defects as the latter. The underlying assumption that discretionary funds are always available at a price may prove to be a delusion. Bank managers may be taking unwarranted risks. Indeed, the regulatory authorities' concern about the declining capital ratio of the banks, a pattern that is evident in Table 6.1 (b) and Figure 6.4, was pointed out in the last chapter.[7]

The macroeconomic impact of discretionary funds management also troubled Federal Reserve officials. As inflation continued unabated in the late 1970s, the money supply rose more rapidly than they wanted it to, and banks continued to expand loans by acquiring more borrowed funds, the monetary authorities imposed reserve requirements on managed liabilities. In so doing, the Federal Reserve eschewed the piecemeal approach it had adopted in the 1960s, which had consisted of regulating each form of borrowing as it evolved. Instead, it adopted broader controls. In late 1979 all borrowed funds, as well as large time deposits, became subject to a reserve requirement. By limiting sources of discretionary funds, the monetary authorities aimed to constrain discretionary assets and thus tighten credit.

☐ Summary

This chapter has surveyed three methods of bank portfolio management: (1) asset management, (2) liability management, and (3) discretionary funds management. In each case the objective is to shape the bank's portfolio so as to maximize profits without impairing bank liquidity.

Asset management achieves its goal by using either the conservative or the economic technique. The former requires the portfolio manager to follow rules of thumb in allocating the bank's asset portfolio. A two-step method was described in this chapter: First assure the bank of sufficient liquidity and then lend and invest for profit. In contrast, the economic theory of asset management views liquidity and profitability as goals to be achieved through a cost-benefit analysis. As long as the cost of remaining liquid (in terms of profits forgone) exceeds expected benefits, liquidity should be reduced and profit-yielding assets should be acquired. Only when the cost-benefit scale balances will the asset portfolio be optimal.

Both theories of asset management assume bank liabilities to be passive entries on the balance sheet. The practice of liability management assumes instead that banks can be aggressive in their pursuit of liabilities. Profitability can be achieved through the asset portfolio, while liquidity is

---

[7]A corollary of both liability and discretionary funds management is the reduced significance of the loan:deposit ratio. As is clear from Table 6.1(b), the ratio already exceeded the long-accepted 60 percent by the end of the 1960s; it remained there during the 1970s, too. The new theories of bank portfolio management stress that liquidity can be obtained from the liability side of the balance sheet, so that a low secondary reserve:deposit ratio, implied by a high loan:deposit ratio, need not imply imprudent management. In lieu of the loan:deposit ratio, the ratio of confidence-sensitive money to loans might be observed. The higher this ratio, the more risky the bank's position.

obtained by acquiring sufficient liabilities, such as Federal funds, CDs, or other borrowed funds. During the 1960s the monetary authorities tried to turn liability management to their own purposes, using it as a fulcrum for their policy of monetary restraint by limiting bank access to CDs and imposing reserve requirements on various managed liabilities. This effort was abandoned by the early 1970s; it had proved unworkable.

More recently, the banking fraternity has practiced discretionary funds management. By distinguishing between funds that are subject to banker discretion and those toward which the banker is essentially a passive agent, portfolio managers carried liability management to its next stage. Discretionary funds are used to compensate for any undesired change in the portfolio due to shifts in nondiscretionary funds. Moreover, discretionary funds can be used to finance the acquisition of profitable nondiscretionary funds.

Liability management and discretionary funds management threaten the stability of individual banks and the banking system as a whole. Because both procedures require the use of confidence-sensitive funds, fears of bank soundness may lead to the demise of a bank that is fundamentally solvent. And because lenders to banks can easily turn to alternative assets (e.g., Treasury bills, gold, Eurodollar deposits in non-U.S. banks), a general crisis of confidence can threaten the entire banking system. While this fear appears groundless, the banking authorities are concerned; ultimately, it is they who bear the responsibility for a smoothly functioning financial system. The bank regulators are actively engaged in inducing banks to act more cautiously.

In truth, this concern applies to a small minority of American banks. Not all bankers want to or find it profitable to devote the necessary resources to managing a portfolio with the requisite care. Bank executives who run small operations are unlikely to be active managers of discretionary funds. Such bankers are asset managers, and in that role they are likely to adhere to the conservative, rule-of-thumb method. It is the managers of larger banks who have been the innovators in portfolio management. They continue to maintain a strong interest in carefully managing their institutions' massive portfolios. These executives operate in a highly profit-oriented environment and are paid to weigh alternatives, calculate opportunity costs, and select the best strategy for their bank.

☐ Questions and Exercises

1. Contrast the annual balance sheet of one of the nation's largest banks with that of a small local bank. Could you detect any evidence to indicate the type of portfolio management policies that each is pursuing? (Hint: Calculate some appropriate ratios.)

2. Study the data in a recent Federal Reserve *Bulletin* to determine the growth

of the various components of bank liabilities (CDs, Eurodollars, etc.). Are any different patterns discernible?

3. How would an increase in the cost of borrowed funds (e.g., the discount rate) affect a banker who pursues (a) a conservative asset management approach, (b) an economic approach, (c) liability management, or (d) discretionary funds management?

4. While both liability and discretionary funds management concepts increase the potential instability of the banking system, they also permit a larger volume of bank lending. On the whole, how would you weigh the benefits against the disadvantages?

5. At the end of 1980 the FDIC possessed $11 billion in assets, or slightly over 1 percent of the deposits it insured. It can obtain $3 billion in additional assistance by drawing on a line of credit from the U.S. Treasury. Are these sums adequate in light of the portfolio management techniques discussed in this chapter?

☐ For Further Study

See G. W. McKinney, Jr., W. J. Brown, and P. M. Hurvitz, *Management of Commercial Bank Funds* (Washington, D.C.: American Bankers Association, 1980), for an overview of management techniques and problems. A fine compilation of articles may be found in T. M. Havrilesky and J. T. Boorman, eds., *Current Perspectives in Banking: Operation, Management, and Legislation* (Arlington Heights, Ill.: AHM, 1980). Liquidity and discretionary funds management are nicely summarized in William L. Silber, *Commercial Bank Liability Management* (Chicago: Association of Reserve City Bankers, 1977), while D. G. Luckett, "Approaches to Bank Liquidity Management," Federal Reserve Bank of Kansas City, *Economic Review*, March 1980, pp. 11–27, not only provides an overview but also presents some actual cases.

A more technical (but only 30-page) treatment of portfolio analysis in general, which can be applied to individual and business asset holdings as well as to banking, is W. J. Baumol, *Portfolio Theory: The Selection of Asset Combinations* (Morristown, N.J.: General Learning Press, 1970).

CHAPTER 8

Banking Regulation: Chartering, Branching, Mergers, and Holding Companies

The biggest problem facing commercial banking today is not the new competition but the old regulations.

Walter B. Winston, Citicorp chairman (1979)

CONTENTS

CHAPTER HIGHLIGHTS

1. Overall, how regulation has shaped the banking industry.

2. Why a banker will elect a state or a federal charter, and whether such an option benefits the public.

3. Whether competition and efficiency are enhanced by limiting banker choices on expansion through branching.

4. How bankers have circumvented branching restrictions.

5. Legal constraints on bank mergers and holding companies, the underlying rationale, and circumvention of the restraints.

This chapter and the next one cover a variety of apparently unrelated issues that affect the banking industry, both its present and its future. But though the topics covered are to a large extent independent, a basic thread—the intervention of government in banking—is woven through most of them. The federal and state governments set the basic outlines for the operation of the banking industry through their chartering regulations, through legislation regarding the proper methods of bank expansion, the definition of appropriate assets for bank acquisition, the interest rates that may be charged and paid, and even through special tax provisions directed at banking. That the government should play a major role in banking is certainly not a novel idea; you read about the early development of banking in Chapter 4. Politics and banking have been bedfellows for a long time, sharing a tradition of both conflict and cooperation.

The focus of these next chapters is a dual one; you will explore a number of issues both from bankers' individual points of view and from society's more global viewpoint. Bankers have to work within the regulatory framework, trying to achieve their private goals in a manner that is compatible with, if limited by, legal constraints. Economists, on the other hand, can question the usefulness of the rules themselves. They can analyze the impact of regulations and suggest alternatives that might achieve the desired social goals more efficiently. True, in many, perhaps most, cases attempts at reform run into the roadblocks of inertia and past accommodation to circumstances. Bankers and legislators prefer walking down a well-trodden path to blazing new trails; successful reform requires that they be shown the advantages of forward motion. Moreover, the banking and political communities have accommodated to the regulations of the past. Change, bringing in its wake a new set of rules, involves an uncertain future with little guarantee that any individual banker will be better off after the change than before. The result is that the rules of the banking game are modified at a snail's pace. Even if new approaches to banking regulation are advocated, only infrequently are they put into practice. Occasionally progress has been achieved: Structural reforms have not only been advocated but actually legislated as well.

The present chapter deals with a number of current issues that owe their prominence to their status as anachronisms. First the spotlight is focused on the chartering process and the regulations that accompany it. The divided authority of the federal and state governments, a legacy of U.S. banking history, not only sets the stage for the chartering controversy but influences the structure of the banking system in a variety of ways. The focus then shifts to three related issues: bank branching, mergers, and conglomeration.

Banks, stymied to some extent by regulation at home, have shifted their operations abroad. The next chapter follows this trend by looking at multinational banking. Another result of the substantial degree of government intervention is an industry characterized by an extremely low failure rate. This is not surprising, given the protection that banking has received from the regulatory authorities. Nevertheless, banks have failed, and the next section of Chapter 9 is devoted to problem loans and bank failures.

The discussion of the next chapter proceeds with the regulation of charges on both loans and deposits. These regulations also have a long history, but they are under intense scrutiny today.

The 1980s may be a decade of emancipation for the commercial banking industry. An auspicious start came with passage of the Depository Institutions Deregulation and Monetary Control Act of 1980. Its major provisions are discussed in the penultimate section of Chapter 9.

The final section of Chapter 9 assesses the present situation in banking and concludes that the regulation of banking is too intense. It has confined the banks to a rigid structure, and its stifling impact has been alleviated only because bankers have found ways to circumvent it.

☐ Bank Chartering

Chapter 4 pointed out that commercial banks were generally chartered by state legislatures. Initially such charters required special legislative acts, but by the late nineteenth century the concept of free banking—granting charters as long as preestablished legislative conditions were fulfilled—became the norm. Furthermore, with the passage of the National Bank Act of 1864 the federal government acquired chartering power. You will recall that the federal government anticipated, indeed sought, the demise of state banks, but that this expectation was not realized. Today fifty states, the District of Columbia, and the federal government are in the bank-chartering business. Any group of promoters seeking to open a bank in any state has the option to file for a state charter or for a federal one. It should be obvious that the promoters will select the option that is most favorable to the implementation of their plans. What, then, are the advantages of state and national charters?

Three considerations that bear on the decision are: (1) membership in the Federal Reserve System, (2) the extent of banks' corporate powers, and (3) the attitude of the chartering authority. A federally chartered commercial bank must become a member of the Federal Reserve System. Until late 1980, only member banks were entitled to such advantages as the free supply of currency from the Federal Reserve and the privilege of borrowing reserves. At the same time, however, member banks had to maintain non-interest-earning deposits with their district Reserve banks. State-chartered banks *may* join the Federal Reserve System but are not required to do so. And while most states require banks chartered by them to hold reserves, often such reserves may earn income. (Since 1980 all banks that maintain checking accounts for their depositors must keep reserves with the regional Reserve bank and may borrow from it.) Thus, until recently, in deciding whether to opt for a state or a national charter one of the decisive considerations was whether membership in the Federal Reserve System constituted a net burden or a benefit.

An additional element to be considered in the selection of a chartering authority involves the range of corporate powers permitted to the bank. State banking laws bind only state-chartered banks. Nationally chartered banks are exempt from some restrictive conditions levied by the states, for in certain cases federal legislation supersedes state law.

The attitude of the chartering agency has often played a major role in the choice of a national or a state charter. While the initial approach to a chartering authority is made by the promoters of the bank, the final decision is made by the authority itself, working within legislative guidelines. Present statutes on the national level require that the comptroller of the currency consider the following elements in deciding whether to grant a charter to a new bank:

1. The adequacy of the bank's capital structure.
2. The bank's future earning prospects.
3. The general character of the bank's management.
4. The convenience and needs of the community to be served by the bank.
5. Whether or not the bank's corporate powers are consistent with the purposes of the law.

Since the last provision is a formality, the remaining factors blend into what have become known as "banking considerations" (1, 2, and 3) and "need" elements (4). However, federal law leaves to the discretion of the comptroller the decision as to whether an applicant bank meets these general, vague criteria. Room is left for a good deal of subjective evaluation. One example of an interpretation of item 4 is the following question, which must be considered by the government bureaucrat in approving a new bank charter:

Whether it would appear that his [i.e., the promoter's] desire to organize a new bank is primarily for personal reasons (borrowing opportunities, unjustified personal animosity toward existing banks, prestige, or immoderate personal gain), rather than as a sound investment opportunity which will result in fulfilling a community need.[1]

There are no hard-and-fast rules that can indicate to the promoters whether a charter will be approved or not. As a consequence, the attitudes of the regulators, both federal and state, as perceived by the banking community are critical in determining whether a national or federal charter will be sought.

James J. Saxon, who served as comptroller of the currency from 1961 to 1965, believed in relaxing constraints on national banks. One area in which his liberal attitude found expression was the chartering of new national banks. While only 335 national banks were chartered between 1936 and 1960, Saxon permitted the chartering of 513 national banks between 1962 and 1965. The consequence of the more lenient approach to national chartering is evident from Table 8.1. The ratio of state-chartered to federally chartered banks stood at 1.90 in 1960; by 1965 it had fallen to 1.87, despite the fact that new state banks had been formed. The ease of obtaining a charter was clearly a major element in explaining the growth of national banks.

Since then the tide has reversed itself, as can also be seen in Table 8.1. Two factors explain why the ratio has moved in the opposite direction: more restrictive attitudes in the comptroller's office and a rethinking of the value of Federal Reserve membership. With Saxon's resignation in 1965, the older, post-Depression thinking about bank chartering reasserted itself. Believing that more banks increased the instability of the banking system—more competition might lead to greater numbers of bank failures—subsequent comptrollers applied stricter interpretations than Saxon had. Moreover, many banks have reevaluated the cost-benefit ratio of Federal Reserve membership and concluded that the costs of

TABLE 8.1 Numbers and Classes of Commercial Banks, 1960, 1965, 1970, 1975, 1980

	1960	1965	1970	1975	1980
Chartering authority					
a. State	8,592	8,989	8,882	9,632	10,279
b. Federal	4,530	4,815	4,620	4,741	4,425
Ratio (a:b)	1.90	1.87	1.92	2.03	2.32
Membership status					
a. Member bank	6,174	6,221	5,767	5,788	5,422
b. Nonmember bank	6,948	7,583	7,735	8,585	9,282
Ratio (a:b)	0.89	0.82	0.75	0.67	0.58

Source: Federal Reserve *Bulletin.*

[1]U.S. Congress, House of Representatives, Committee on Banking and Currency, *Conflict of Federal and State Banking Laws* (Washington, D.C.: GPO, 1963), p. 304.

belonging to the System exceed the benefits derived therefrom. The latter reasoning is reflected in the continued decline in the ratio of member to nonmember banks. As Table 8.1 shows, the ratio stood at 89 percent in 1960. But as the number of nonmember banks increased by over one-fifth, the ratio of member to nonmember banks fell to 67 percent in 1975. By 1980 fewer than one out of every three banks were federally chartered and only one out of every three banks was a member bank.

In short, in considering a state versus a national charter the prospective banker calculates which alternative is best for the proposed bank and chooses accordingly. In recent years more and more bankers have selected state over national chartering. However, this trend may be reversed as a result of legislation passed in early 1980, a point that will be examined at the end of the next chapter.

The public interest in chartering

Where does the public interest in bank chartering lie? Do we need controls over the formation of new banks at all? And if such regulation is indeed necessary, is the present extent of regulation optimal?

It can be argued that in no other industry in the United States is entry as constrained as it is in commercial banking. Nowhere else is motivation examined, and rarely is potential profitability a source of government concern. In general, the American tradition is one of freedom of entry, based on the supposition that more firms imply greater competition. The resulting benefits to the consumer, as well as more efficient organization and operation, come only through competition. By that reasoning, bankers ought to be able to open up a bank with the same facility as a shoe manufacturer can begin to produce or a trucker can open a transportation firm. As long as the owners believe that profits are to be made, they ought to be given the opportunity to try. Should the business or bank fail, its stockholders would bear the loss.

In contrast to this laissez-faire attitude toward bank chartering, others view banking as a public good. The failure of a bank can cause damage not only to the owners but to the entire community. Even if the bank's depositors are insured, the loss of a lending institution and a monetary transfer agency could cause the residents a good deal of inconvenience. Moreover, even if the market provides sufficient scope so that penetration by an additional bank does not lead to bank failure, it might turn out that all existing banks will be forced into low and uneconomical operating rates. It may be more sound to have fewer strong banks than to have many weak ones.

Most economists feel that the regulators have been overly restrictive. Bank failure rates have been low, averaging only six banks per year out of over 14,000 banks for the period between 1950 and 1980. When failures have occurred, the cause has most often been fraud rather than poor performance. The easier chartering provisions of the Saxon era do not appear to have weakened the viability of the banking system. Moreover, while competition thrives in the larger cities, where many commercial banks operate side by side, the benefits of competition are lost to the residents of smaller communities. Indeed, some states still offer banks in less populated localities **home office protection**, in which only one bank is based in each town. Some easing of entry in order to break down the dominant position of these banks would appear to be warranted from the point of view of the residents of these communities as well as from that of the economy as a whole.

One further implication of the American style of commercial bank chartering ought to be mentioned. Bank offices are limited to the state in which their main office is located, a fact that is no less true of national banks than of state-chartered institutions. An Oregon bank cannot merge with an Arizona bank and maintain both an Oregon charter and an Arizona charter, or even maintain a single charter and operate the other office as a branch. The outcome is that American banking is substantially a local industry, with most customers coming from the immediate neighborhood. Of course, this statement should not be taken to mean that banks may not lend to or accept deposits from out-of-state residents. Nor does it imply that these legal restraints cannot be circumvented; they can be, as the discussion of bank holding companies later in this chapter will indicate. Nevertheless, this prohibition of multistate chartering is an important barrier to nationwide banking systems. In this respect U.S. banking differs markedly from banking elsewhere in the world. In other economies, both developed and developing, a few banks with extensive networks throughout the nation dominate the banking system. This is obviously not true of banking in the United States.

But what about expansion via branching? Cannot a Georgia bank open branch offices in South Carolina or Florida? The answer is negative; to understand why, read on.

□ Unit and Branch Banking

A concommitant of state chartering has been state regulation of branching. Control over branching, however, has had a shorter history than bank chartering; it is basically a twentieth-century phenomenon. As late as 1909, 60 percent of state laws were silent when it came to branching. Branching was simply not an issue; there was little need for restrictive legislation when there were few branch banking systems in the United States. And those few had hardly any branches. Indeed, until the early part of this century branching was seen as a means of bringing the benefits of banking to a nation composed of small, isolated communities. Remember that the complex network of roads and electronic communications that has truly unified the United States was still to be developed.

Home office protection laws prevent any bank from opening a banking office in a community where another bank maintains its main office.

Around the turn of the century, however, attitudes toward branching began to change. First, the number of banks in America had increased so rapidly—from fewer than 10,000 in the early 1890s to over 25,000 in the years preceding World War I—that the smaller communities were being served by their own local banks. Second, independent bankers saw in branching a threat to their own profits. When in 1909 California passed a very tolerant branch banking law, these bankers mobilized and successfully induced several state legislatures to limit the scope of branching. A second antibranching effort came in the early 1920s, when bankers began to fear federal passage of probranching legislation. Until that time successive comptrollers of the currency had interpreted the National Bank Act as prohibiting the establishment of branches by national banks. But many individuals, including the comptroller, began to advocate branching powers for national banks. Again opponents of branching mobilized state legislatures, the outcome being a substantial degree of success for the antibranching forces. In 1896, only 13 states prohibited branching; by 1924, 25 states did so. Indeed, by then only 8 states did not restrict branching in some form.

Today the scene remains basically the same as it was in 1924, although its contours have been modified somewhat. Federal law, in the form of the Banking Act of 1933 (the Glass-Steagall Act)[2] mandates that a national bank adhere to the branching laws of the state in which it is chartered.[3] This has effectively constrained nationwide branching systems, for state laws prohibit branching across their own borders.

Branching within states

Within the states themselves, three types of branching laws can be identified: **unit banking, limited branching,** and **statewide branching.**

In 1980 there were eleven unit banking states, most of which are found in the central part of the country. (See Figure 8.1.) In such states a bank is blocked from opening even a single branch. (One midwestern bank connected its headquarters with an adjacent building and thus was able to open a second office. After all, the two buildings were now one, and the bank was still operating in a single location.)

Unit banks do not have to be small banks. Substantial amounts of money can be amassed even when one is doing business from a single location. In fact, five of the largest banks in the United States are located in Chicago, even though Illinois is a unit banking state.

One noticeable difference between unit banking states and other states can be found in the number of banks in each type of state. In unit banking

Unit banking requires that any bank operate only from a single location; no branches are permitted.
Limited branching permits banks to open branches within geographic boundaries specified by state law.
Statewide branching means that branches can be opened anywhere within the state.

[2]This Act also mandated the separation of commercial banking from investment banking. The fact that these two functions were carried out by the same firm was thought to be a reason for the massive bank failures in the early 1930s.
[3]It has become common to refer to the federal constraints on national bank branching as the McFadden Act, the 1927 legislation that was reinforced by the 1933 Banking Act.

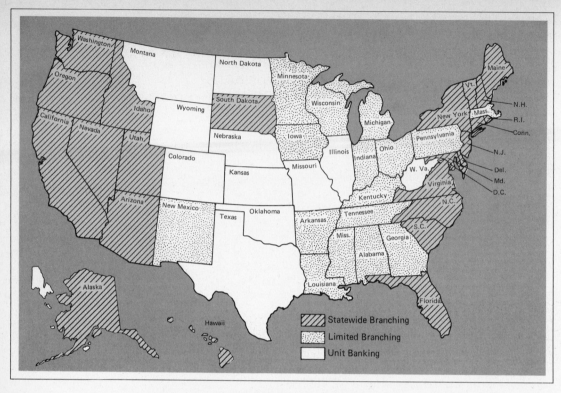

FIGURE 8.1 State branching laws, 1980.
Source: Board of Governors of the Federal Reserve System.

states the number of banks is relatively large: in 1980 there were 1.4 per 10,000 people, compared to 0.47 per 10,000 in non-unit-banking states.[4]

At the other extreme lie the states that permit statewide branching. In California (since 1909) and New York (since 1976), for example, banks are able to open branches anywhere in the state, although approval for the branch must be obtained from the appropriate regulatory authority. It is not surprising to learn that the largest bank in the United States, the Bank of America, with over 1000 branches, is a California institution. As Figure 8.1 shows, twenty-three states located in the western part of the country and some eastern-seaboard states (and the District of Columbia) are in the unlimited-branching category.

The remaining sixteen states impose some type of territorial constraint on branching powers. In some states, such as Arkansas, banks cannot branch beyond their home communities. In other states, such as Georgia,

---

[4]If banking offices (head office plus branches) are counted, the picture is changed. Per 10,000 population, banking offices in unit banking, limited-branching, and unlimited-branching states, respectively, were 19, 26, and 22.

banking regions encompassing the home county have been legislated. Intracounty branching is permitted; intercounty branching is not.

The rationale for branching restrictions

As noted earlier, local bankers who feared competition were the primary force leading to the restriction of branching. The protection of local monopolies represented a logical pursuit of self-interest. The rationale for branching limitations, however, was couched in more altruistic terms. Unit bankers argued that competition is enhanced by large numbers of banks in a state, so that bank depositors and borrowers are the primary beneficiaries. Similarly, a unit banker is said to be more involved in the community and, hence, more knowledgeable about local conditions and more sensitive to local needs.

How compelling are these arguments? Do unit banks really offer advantages, and as such, ought they to be encouraged by prohibitive legislation directed against alternative forms of bank structure?

In a survey of the pros and cons of branch banking, Professors Guttentag and Herman reviewed four areas:[5]

1. *Nonprice competition*—competition in quality and the marketing of bank services.
2. *Price competition*—the rates charged on loans and paid on time deposits.
3. *Operational efficiency*—the costs of providing bank services.
4. *Allocational efficiency*—general resource allocation from the point of view of the community, including responsiveness to community banking needs.

Guttentag and Herman concluded from their review of the literature that the claims of the opponents of branching are not supported. In each of the categories just listed, the evidence does not justify the conclusion that branch banks are less effective, less responsive, or less competitive than unit banks. Branch banking does not necessarily lead to reduced competition, nor does it bring in its wake less community-oriented lending activities. To be sure, the evidence does not suggest unequivocally that branch banking is superior to unit banking. But it clearly rejects the conclusion that unit banking is preferable to branch banking.

Perhaps the force of this type of evidence, along with the pressure of branch bankers, has been responsible for the liberalization of branching regulations in the past few years. In 1961, for example, the number of unit banking states stood at 16 while unlimited-branching states numbered 19; by 1980, these figures were 11 and 23 respectively. Moreover, in a number of limited-branching states the branching laws have been

[5]J. M. Guttentag and E. S. Herman, *Banking Structure and Performance* (New York: New York University, Institute of Finance of the Schools of Business, 1967).

liberalized to extend the branching powers of the banks beyond the earlier territorial constraints.

Branching liberalization

Will the next step be in the direction of still more liberalized branching? The new technology of computerized banking has brought this question to the fore. Many banking functions can now be performed by machines located outside of the traditional banking office. These banking machines, dubbed automated teller machines or ATMs, can accept deposits and dispense cash without the presence of a teller. Remote computer terminals (RCTs) located in retail outlets can perform similar functions and, also, by being linked to the bank's computer, can transfer funds from the buyer's account to that of the seller. (See Box 8.1.) And technology is already on line for the direct transfer of funds via the depositor's telephone. Are all of these three instances—banking machines outside of the bank, RCTs in retail stores, banking through home telephones—to be considered forms of branching? Are they subject to state restrictions on branching?

In a number of test cases involving ATMs and RCTs, state courts have ruled on both sides, some declaring that they are not branches and others finding them to be branches. Ultimately the Supreme Court will be faced with this issue, but for the present each bank is subject to the ruling of its state court.[6] Of course, it is obvious that in Illinois, where ATMs and RCTs were found to be branches, banks are barred from using these devices; recall that Illinois is a unit banking state. The question of funds transfer from the home via the telephone has not been a subject of litigation, presumably because it differs little from transfering funds via the mail. Neither the cashing of checks nor the depositing of checks or cash can be handled in this way, but these functions can be performed with ATMs and RCTs.

However, the potential for nationwide banking via the phone does exist. There is no reason why a depositor in Omaha, Nebraska, could not maintain a deposit relationship with a Dallas, Texas, bank, mimicking the actions of national corporations. The depositor would order her Omaha employer to deposit her wages—via the company's phone hookup—in her Dallas account. She would then make payments to her creditors by means of calls to an 800 phone number maintained by the Dallas bank. A good part of the banking activity of the typical consumer—namely, bill payments—could be performed through a bank located anywhere in the nation.

Other steps in the direction of branching liberalization come obliquely through holding-company operations. As will become evident in the next section, expansion within the state—and, in the past, between states as

---

[6]Under present law savings and loan associations and mutual savings banks may be granted regulatory permission to establish remote service units.

BOX 8.1 Banking by Remote Computer Terminal

How to Authorize a Deposit

1. Bring your check or cash to the seller's checkout counter or designated register.

2. Present the clerk with your bank card.

3. Punch your individual secret code into the terminal. The clerk will insert your card into the terminal. Upon verifying your identity through the computer linkup, the clerk will punch in the amount of the deposit.

4. Your deposit will be credited to your account immediately, and a receipt signed by you and the clerk will be handed to you.

How to Authorize a Withdrawal

1. Present your bank card to the checkout clerk and tell the clerk the amount of the withdrawal.

2. Punch your individual secret code into the terminal. The clerk will insert your card, enter the amount of the withdrawal, and verify the status of your account.

3. The clerk will give you the amount requested (provided, of course, that your account has sufficient funds in it to cover the withdrawal).

(continued)

BOX 8.1 (continued)

How to Pay for Purchases

1. Present your card to the checkout clerk.

2. Punch your secret code into the terminal. The clerk will insert your card into the terminal and enter the value of your purchases.

3. This sum will automatically be transfered from your account to the account of the seller.

4. You will be asked to sign a receipt, which will also be signed by the clerk, and a copy will be given to you.

---

well—is possible through use of the holding-company vehicle even when state laws prohibit branching in one form or another. Each bank of the holding company is legally independent, but a central management often sets general direction for all holding-company bank affiliates. Also, efforts are already underway to develop reciprocal banking privileges between states. In this case one state, such as Maine, would permit Illinois banks to establish branches in Maine under the proviso that Maine banks would be permitted to set up branches in Illinois. (Indeed, Maine has approved such legislation.) Naturally enough, bankers who view such agreements as a threat to their own survival are actively resisting them. Where the power lies is a question that cannot be answered at this point. But it is an interesting development to follow and may well portend momentous changes in the structure of U.S. banking.

Branching and bank size

Most branch banks are small. The average number of banking offices for branch banking systems is less than six. Of course, such small systems rarely meet the public's eye. Far more noticeable are the banking giants, most of which possess extensive branch networks. What would happen if the large banks were to expand nationally, open branches in other states, and gain control of many local markets? Would banking become an oligopoly in which a few huge branch banking systems are surrounded by a large fringe of small banks?

Perhaps the best way to answer this question is to explore two related issues: bank mergers and bank holding companies.

☐ Bank Mergers and Bank Holding Companies

Banks, like other businesses, can increase their size in a variety of ways: by reinvesting their earnings, by floating bond or stock issues, through the liability management techniques outlined in Chapter 7, or by consolidating their operations with those of other banks. In fact, all of these methods have been and continue to be used by commercial banks. Certainly the most dramatic and visible of all these procedures is the merger, in which two or more banks in a community become one. Often the name of the bank is changed; the signs and forms are reprinted. Mergers increase bank size more rapidly than any other means, since the assets of the merging banks are combined immediately.

In the United States mergers seem to run in cycles. Insofar as the banking system is concerned, periods of heavy merger activity occurred at the turn of the century, again during the 1920s and early 1930s, and most recently in the 1950s and early 1960s.

The Bank Merger Act (1960)

Bank mergers generated little formal resistance either from the banking regulatory agencies, who in the 1930s were granted limited statutory powers over mergers, or from the Justice Department, which monitors compliance with the antitrust laws. Congress, prodded by both the rising trend of mergers and fears of banking concentration and by the federal banking authorities themselves, finally strengthened the powers of the latter in the Bank Merger Act of 1960. The major provisions of the Act were two. First, virtually all bank mergers must have the explicit approval of some federal banking authority. (Permission of the comptroller was required if the resulting bank was a national bank, of the Board of Governors of the Federal Reserve System if the resulting bank was to be a state member bank, or of the FDIC if the resulting bank was to be a nonmember insured bank. The approving agency was required to consult with the other two agencies and with the Justice Department prior to acting on a merger request.) Second, the factors that were to be considered by the authorities in ruling on mergers were outlined in the Act. In addition to the general banking and need factors mentioned on page 177 in connection with new-bank charters, the agencies were to consider, in the words of the Act, "the effect of the transaction on competition (including any tendency toward monopoly)." Approv. merger could come only if "after considering all of such factors, it ne responsible agency] finds the transaction to be in the public interest."

With passage of the Bank Merger Act, the federal banking authorities were required to undertake a more active role in mergers. Fewer mergers were consummated in the years immediately following the Act; the annual average of 167 mergers between 1952 and 1960 fell by 13 percent to an average of 148 a year between 1960 and 1966. It is a moot question to ask whether the reduction was a direct consequence of the Bank Merger Act. On the one hand, it could be argued that since the regulatory authorities rejected very few of the proposals brought before them for approval, the Act hardly imposed severe constraints. The cyclical nature of mergers may be proposed as the reason for the decline in mergers after passage of the Act. In essence, it is a mere coincidence that the Bank Merger Act and the decline in the bank merger activity occurred at about the same time. On the other hand, it may well be that the numbers of mergers approved and rejected do not tell the entire story. How many mergers were discouraged informally, with the regulatory authorities responding to unofficial feelers by suggesting that an application for approval might not be appropriate just then? How many bankers did not pursue mergers, knowing that their proposals would be turned down? The questions that have to be answered in order to evaluate properly the effectiveness of the Bank Merger Act are truly unanswerable.

Competition and bank mergers

One conclusion, however, can be drawn: The competitive impact of a merger had risen from insignificance to prominence. The major role of competition is best illustrated by a 1963 Supreme Court ruling in the *Philadelphia National Bank* (PNB) case. PNB and the Girard Trust Corn Exchange Bank had obtained permission to merge from the comptroller of the currency. The Justice Department intervened, arguing that the combination would be sufficiently anticompetitive to violate the antitrust laws. The Supreme Court, deciding in favor of the Justice Department, in effect ruled that even when a bank merger is approved by the banking agencies because it is deemed beneficial on the basis of banking and need considerations, the merger can be blocked if the consolidation would lead to a violation of the antitrust laws. Competitive impact became the overriding criterion in approving or rejecting merger proposals.

The PNB decision, along with some other restrictive Court actions, led influential bankers to request that congress revise the 1960 Act. The application of the anticompetitive constraints of the antitrust laws to banking was thought to be too severe. Why should not community needs be granted equal weight in merger decisions? Why should a merger that was beneficial in all other ways be barred solely on the ground that it would stifle competition? Congress acceded to this appeal, and in 1966 it amended the law. The critical passage of the revised act reads as follows:

The responsible agency shall not approve . . . any proposed merger transaction . . . whose effect in any section of the country may be substantially to lessen competition, or to tend to create a monopoly, or which in any other manner would be in restraint of trade, unless it finds that the anticompetitive effects of the proposed transaction are clearly outweighed in the public interest by the probable effect of the transaction in meeting the convenience and needs of the community to be served.

In other words, congress mandated that the regulatory agencies perform a cost-benefit analysis when considering merger approvals. If the benefits of satisfying a need outweighed the costs of reduced competition, the merger could be approved.

The courts, however, have interpreted this amendment rather narrowly, and the change that was the intended outcome of the amendment has not materialized. In 1968, in the case of a Tennessee bank that was experiencing severe problems, although it was not quite on the verge of failing, the Supreme Court ruled that a merger with a large bank was illegal.[7] The regulatory agencies had felt that, despite the anticompetitive impact, the benefit to the community of preserving the bank outweighed the adverse competitive effect. The Court disagreed. True, said the Court, the community would benefit from the merger, which would preserve the bank. But, it ruled, other ways of salvaging the bank had not been explored. Bringing in new management, for example, might have maintained the smaller bank as a competitive element in the market. Thus, it was not clear that in a more comprehensive evaluation the benefits would have outweighed the costs. In other words, the fact that benefits outweigh anticompetitive costs does not provide sufficient ground for approving a bank merger. It must also be demonstrated that no other viable alternatives exist. This ruling has put a substantial damper on merger activity. Between 1968 and 1980 bank merger activity declined to an average of around 125 a year.

Mergers have also been constrained somewhat by the application to banking of the **potential competition** doctrine. When firm M does not compete with firm A, perhaps because the two are far from each other, a merger would not reduce competition—the two firms, after all, are not competing now. Or would it? If A maintains a policy of service to its customers at reasonable terms because it fears that otherwise M would penetrate its market, then even if A and M do not appear to be competing, the existence of M leads to competitive benefits in A's market. A merger between the two obviously would remove the threat of potential competition. Or consider the following possibility: R expects to enter I's territory. R can either acquire I through merger or open up a branch office of R. It is obvious that the latter alternative would lead to more competition than the former. Thus, even when two banks do not compete directly, mergers could lead to anticompetitive outcomes.

The potential-competition doctrine has been accepted by the courts.

When two (or more) firms do not compete in the same market, but ,at least one has the ability to penetrate the market of the other, their relationship is said to be **potentially competitive.**

---

[7]*United States* v. *Third National Bank of Nashville*, 88 Supreme Court 882 (1968).

However, the judiciary has not permitted the Justice Department to apply the potential-competition argument to banking as aggressively as it applies the actual-competition argument. Consequently, it is easier for banks to merge today if they do not compete in the same local market than if they have offices in the same city or town. Nevertheless, the threat of a potential-competition suit may well have deterred some banks from merging.

A national banking oligopoly?

To return to the question that anticipated the present discussion: Can we expect a highly concentrated national banking system if branching restrictions were liberalized? The answer would appear to be no, if the consolidation is to come via the merger route. As the federal courts have interpreted the law, it has become clear that mergers of large banks leading to substantial degrees of market control will be prohibited. The data on bank concentration support this assertion. Despite the liberalization of branching and the bank mergers that have occurred in the past two decades, the concentration of deposits among the largest banks has not increased. Indeed, the reverse is true. Between 1957 and 1973, for example, the share of total domestic deposits held by the largest 100 banks in the nation fell from 47 to 45 percent.

Concentration of economic power, however, can be discerned at levels other than the national one. Yet at both the statewide and the local level, the trend of bank concentration is downward, although this statement is not true for every state and city. In most areas not only can individuals and small businesses choose among competing banks, but the range of choice has widened somewhat over the years. (This statement is qualified by the existence of bank holding-company affiliates. As will be noted soon, competition is less intense than the data presented here indicate.)

Undoubtedly, legislative, regulatory, and judicial intervention has prevented the domination of the banking industry by a few giant banks. But the existence of markets in which banks of all sizes survive suggests that an economic explanation, too, can be advanced to explain the absence of oligopoly in banking. Economists believe that one precondition for oligopoly is an increase in the efficiency of the firm as the scale of its operations expands. When these economies of scale are substantial in comparison with market demand, the expected outcome is an industry dominated by a few large firms. Economies of scale do exist in banking. It takes some minimum scale of operations to warrant specialization of personnel and investment in modern but expensive technology. Most studies indicate, however, that such economies can be achieved by modest-sized banking corporations, ones with deposits in the neighborhood of $25–50 million. Since almost one-half of the nation's fifteen thousand banks held deposits in the $25–100 million range, the absence of oligopoly can be attributed partly to the fact that economies of scale can be achieved even by banks that do not qualify as multibillion-dollar giants. Thus, even in the absence of legal restraints on banking growth—other than the basic antitrust statutes—economic theory would hardly predict an industry composed of a small number of immense banks.

While half of the banks in the United States are large enough to attain optimum economic size, the other half is too small to take full advantage of economies of scale. By operating at a cost level that is above the optimum, the banks force their customers to endure extra charges, reduced services, and lower interest payments on deposits.

Mergers and public policy

Can any public policy conclusions be drawn from the preceding assessment of the condition of the banking system in the 1970s? What should public policy toward mergers be?

A consensus view appears to be as follows: When middle-sized and large-sized banks, those that are already taking advantage of economies of scale, wish to merge, an a priori case *against* such mergers exists. Since large efficiencies are not likely to result from such consolidation and harm may arise because of reduced competition, the case in favor of a merger must be strong indeed. In such instances economists and jurists are likely to reach a common decision—not to permit the merger. However, when small banks propose a merger the economist is wont to weigh the benefits derived from the greater efficiency gained by taking fuller advantage of the economies of larger size against the potential anticompetitive impact of the merger. No advance conclusion can be presented; each case must be evaluated on its own merits. The economist and the antitrust lawyer part company: The latter is forced to consider the competitive impact alone, whereas the economist can and does take a broader view.

Bank holding companies

Mergers have declined in importance for the reasons outlined earlier. But banks have consolidated and amassed greater power through a different avenue, namely, the **bank holding company**. The holding company is a legal device that enables a group of individuals to gain control over a number of banks without merging them. Each bank maintains a separate corporate charter, and formally is an independent entity. However, since a sufficient number of common stocks is held by the holding company, control over each bank is effectively in the hands of the umbrella company. The bank holding company may also own companies other than banks, thereby expanding its power beyond commercial banking itself. A brief history of the development of bank holding companies since the 1950s will lend some perspective to the problems that have surfaced in this area in recent years.

Much as was the case with antimerger regulations, only weak provisions against the spread of holding companies were enacted during the

A **bank holding company** is a corporation whose assets consist almost exclusively of equity shares of other companies, one or more of which are commercial banks.

1930s. Holding companies could control banks without federal authorization, nor were any constraints imposed on holding-company expansion. Moreover, bank holding companies could own not only banking firms but other businesses as well. The outcome was not cataclysmic at all: By 1950 twenty-eight bank holding companies controlling two or more banks held only 12 percent of all bank deposits. This very fact explains why little legislative action was taken to restrain bank holding-company growth for the next two decades. What apparently motivated congressional activity was the expansion of the Transamerica Corporation, the holding company that included the giant Bank of America. In 1952 Transamerica owned a majority interest in forty-seven commercial banks, and the Federal Reserve contended that it controlled 39 percent of all commercial bank deposits in five western states. Congress reacted to fears of bank expansion via the holding-company route by passing the *Bank Holding Company Act of 1956*. This law provided that any bank holding company that owned two or more banks must receive permission from the Board of Governors of the Federal Reserve System prior to acquiring additional banks.[8] (See Box 8.2.) Moreover, any group that proposed to form a new bank holding company must obtain prior approval from the Board. Finally, a bank holding company could not maintain ownership in nonbanking businesses, nor could it expand by acquiring banks in other states.

In anticipation of the 1956 legislation, the deposits of the largest bank holding companies increased rapidly. In the two years prior to 1956, the fifteen largest banks expanded their deposits at a rate that was double that of general bank growth. By 1956, however, they still loomed relatively small in terms of the percentage of total deposits; all holding companies together held only 8.3 percent of the total.

The holding-company movement in banking remained relatively quiescent throughout the remainder of the decade and a good part of the 1960s. Then, around 1967, the picture changed. Bankers found that growth through merger had become increasingly difficult, especially in light of the hard line taken by the courts. In addition, they perceived profitable opportunities in areas that were related to banking but legally were beyond the bankers' reach. While such activities were prohibited to commercial banks, bank holding companies could penetrate these markets through subsidiary corporations. The big bankers soon exploited a major loophole left open by congress: Bank holding companies that owned only a single bank were not subject to the constraints of the Bank Holding Company Act.[9] Between June 1966 and April 1970, one-bank

---

[8]The conditions under which the Federal Reserve may accept or reject a proposed expansion of a holding company are virtually identical to those spelled out in the Bank Merger Act, namely, banking, need, and competitive criteria.

[9]The reason for this exemption had to do with the legislators' perception that holding companies that owned only one bank were not really in the banking business and did not threaten to dominate the banking market.

BOX 8.2. A Holding Company Bank Acquisition Decision by the Board of Governors of the Federal Reserve System

Fidelity Union Bancorporation, Newark, New Jersey

Order denying acquisition of bank

Fidelity Union Bancorporation, Newark, New Jersey ("Applicant"), a bank holding company within the meaning of the Bank Holding Company Act (the "Act"), has applied for the Board's approval under section 3(a)(3) of the Bank Holding Company Act (12 U.S.C. § 1842(a)(3)) to acquire all the outstanding shares of Garden State National Bank, Paramus, New Jersey ("Bank").

Notice of the application, affording opportunity for interested persons to submit comments, has been given in accordance with section 3 of the Act. The time for filing comments has expired, and the Board has considered the application and all comments received, including those of the United States Department of Justice, in light of the factors set forth in section 3(c) of the Act (12 U.S.C. § 1842(c)).

Applicant, with five subsidiary banks, is the fourth largest banking organization in New Jersey.[1] It holds aggregate deposits of $1.7 billion, representing 6.2 percent of total commercial bank deposits in the state. Through its subsidiary banks, Applicant conducts its banking business at a total of eighty-six banking offices located in ten local banking markets in northeastern New Jersey.[2] Bank, the twelfth largest banking organization in New Jersey, holds deposits of $709.6 million, representing 2.6 percent of statewide deposits. Bank conducts its banking business through thirty-seven banking offices located in six local markets in northern New Jersey.

Section 3(c) of the Act provides, in part, that the Board may not approve any proposed acquisition, the effect of which, in any section of the country, may be substantially to lessen competition or to tend to create a monopoly, or which in any other manner would be in restraint of trade, unless the Board finds that the anticompetitive effects of the transaction are clearly outweighed in the public interest by the probable effect of the transaction in meeting the convenience and needs of the community to be served.

The Board has consistently expressed its concern regarding acquisitions that impact significantly on statewide structure and the concentration of banking resources within a state, and has indicated that there are limits as to what it regards as approvable under the standards of the Bank Holding Company Act. The Board has been particularly concerned where proposals involved banking organizations of relatively large absolute size.[3] In New Jersey the four largest banking organizations hold 28.9 percent of the total deposits in the state, and the ten largest banking organizations hold approximately 48 percent of statewide deposits. The acquisition of Bank by Applicant would increase the concentration of deposits held by the four largest banking organizations in New Jersey to over 31 percent. Further-

(continued)

BOX 8.2 (continued)

more, consummation of the proposed acquisition would have the immediate effect of increasing both Applicant's deposits and its number of banking offices by over 40 percent. It would also enable Applicant to move from its position as the fourth largest banking organization to become the largest banking organization in New Jersey. Finally, the Board is concerned that this proposal represents an undesirable trend of merger and acquisition activity that, if permitted by the Board, would result in further increases in concentration among New Jersey banking organizations.[4]

Under Section 3(c) of the Act, the Board is not required to permit the development of undue concentration among banking organizations in New Jersey before it is empowered to intervene. Indeed, the Clayton Act, which was incorporated into section 3(c) of the Act, provides authority for arresting mergers at a time when the trend to a lessening of competition is in its incipiency in order to break the force of a trend toward undue concentration before it gathers momentum. See *Brown Shoe Co.* v. *United States.* 370 U.S. 294, 317–18. Based on the facts of record, the Board views the proposed transaction as representing a trend toward concentration of resources in New Jersey, and the Board concludes that consummation of this proposal, which would combine the resources of two significant banking organizations and increase by 2.6 percent the amount of statewide deposits held by New Jersey's four largest banking organizations, would have substantially adverse effects on the concentration of banking resources in New Jersey.

In addition to the effects of the proposed acquisition on the concentration of banking resources in New Jersey, consummation of the proposed transaction would affect both existing and potential competition within thirteen local banking markets.[5] In particular, both Applicant and Bank compete in the Paterson, New Jersey banking market, where the combined market share of Applicant and Bank would be 4.4 percent. In addition, both Bank and Applicant compete in the metropolitan New York banking market, which includes portions of several northern New Jersey counties. While neither organization has a significant presence in that market, which is somewhat distorted because of the large New York City banks, Bank is the 20th largest of 126 banking organizations competing in New York and, what is more important, is the second largest New Jersey banking organization in the market. Accordingly, the Board concludes that the proposal would eliminate a slight amount of existing competition between the two organizations.[6]

With regard to potential competition, consummation of the proposal would foreclose the possibility of competition in the future between Applicant and Bank in eleven banking markets.[7] In particular, Applicant competes in eight New Jersey markets where Bank does not presently have offices. In the Freehold, Asbury Park, and Newark banking markets, where a large share of market deposits are concentrated in a few banking organizations, Applicant is regarded as one of these dominant organizations with market shares of 33, 17, and 14.1 percent, respectively. The Board views Bank as a likely entrant into these markets, in view of its size and resources, as well as its significant presence in adjacent banking markets.[8] Furthermore, Applicant also operates in five less concentrated markets where Bank does not compete; however, Bank may also be regarded as a likely entrant into those markets because of its overall size and resources and presence in adjacent markets. Conversely, Bank has offices in three markets where Applicant is not currently represented. In the Board's view, both Applicant and Bank have sufficient resources to enter into each other's markets in a less anticompetitive fashion than the present proposal. This conclusion is supported by the record of expansion of both organizations. For example, over the past five years, Applicant established 15 branches de novo, and in the same period Bank established three de novo branches and acquired four through mergers. Based on the record in this application, particularly the large number of local markets affected by this proposal, the Board concludes that the proposed acquisition would have substantially adverse effects on potential competition. Accordingly, the Board has determined that the overall effects of the proposal on competition and concentration of resources are so serious as to require denial of the application, unless such anticompetitive effects are outweighed by considerations relating to the convenience and needs of the communities to be served.

The financial and managerial resources of Applicant, its subsidiaries and Bank are considered to be satisfactory and their future prospects appear favorable. However, the Board notes that Applicant would incur a substantial amount of indebtedness in connection with this proposed transaction, which could reduce its financial flexibility. Accordingly, banking factors lend no weight toward approval of the application.

With respect to the convenience and needs of the communities to be served, Applicant has asserted that the acquisition of Bank will have two beneficial results. First, Applicant intends to raise the interest rates paid to Bank's customers on certain time deposit accounts, as well as to lower the interest rates charged on certain loans. While the Board favors such specific public benefits that have a direct impact on consumers, it notes that there appears to be no reason that an institution of Bank's size could not make the proposed rate adjustments absent the proposed acquisition. Applicant also states that it will assist Bank in increasing its commercial lending services through expertise to be provided by personnel of Applicant, as well as the availability of a greater lending capacity through the holding company system. It is the Board's view that the benefits to the public are not sufficient to outweigh the substantially adverse effects on competition and concentration of banking resources in New Jersey that would result from consummation of the proposed transaction. Accordingly, it is the Board's judgment that the proposed transaction would not be in the public interest and that the application should be denied. Based on the foregoing and other facts of record, the application is hereby denied.

(continued)

BOX 8.2 (continued)

By Order of the Board of Governors of the Federal Reserve System, effective November 16, 1979.

Voting for this action: Governors Wallich, Partee, Teeters, and Rice. Voting against this action: Chairman Volcker and Governors Schultz and Coldwell.

[SEAL]

(Signed) GRIFFITH L. GARWOOD,
Deputy Secretary of the Board

Dissenting Statement of Chairman Volcker and
Governors Schultz and Coldwell

We do not find that the application of Fidelity Union Bancorporation to acquire Garden State National Bank will have such serious adverse effects on competition as to warrant denial. Accordingly, we would approve the application for the following reasons.

First, as the Board emphasized in its Board Order, we too are concerned about the effects of certain proposed acquisitions on the banking structure and concentration of banking resources within a state. However, based upon our review of the facts of this case, unlike the majority of the Board, we do not find that the banking structure in the State of New Jersey is now overly concentrated. Moreover, we do not believe that the proposed acquisition, which will increase the deposits held by the four largest organizations in New Jersey by only 2.6 percent, evidences a trend in New Jersey of anticompetitive acquisitions and mergers that would result in any dramatic increase in the concentration of banking resources in New Jersey.

Second, while the proposed combination will eliminate some existing and potential competition, we do not view the effects of this proposal on such competition in any local market involved to be so significant as to warrant denial. Neither Applicant nor Bank may be regarded as dominant in any of the markets in which they compete. Indeed, neither is the largest organization in any local market in which it competes, and in ten of the thirteen markets involved, Applicant and Bank hold well under 10 percent of the total market deposits. Moreover, in the principal market of Garden State Bank it holds less than 1 percent of total market deposits. We would agree with the majority if a bank this size were located in a market where it held a sizeable share of market deposits.

Finally, the majority of the Board finds significant anticompetitive effects resulting from the combination of two such sizeable banking organizations. However, we believe that the combination may, in fact, have procompetitive effects in that it would result in a New Jersey-based banking organization that would be of sufficient size to be a more effective competitor for business in the New York banking market.

Based on the foregoing, we believe that the application should be approved.

1. All banking data are as of December 31, 1978.
2. In addition, Applicant's subsidiary, Suburban Finance Company, operates 15 consumer finance offices in New Jersey.

3. *E. g. Old Kent Financial Corporation.* 65 FEDERAL RESERVE BULLETIN 1010 (Order of November 2, 1979); *First City Bancorporation of Texas, Inc.* 65 FEDERAL RESERVE BULLETIN 862 (1979); and *First International Bancshares, Inc.,* 60 FEDERAL RESERVE BULLETIN 290 (1974).
4. In commenting adversely on the proposal, the United States Department of Justice maintains that this is the latest in a recent series of proposal acquisitions by the largest banking organizations in the state.
5. The local banking markets most seriously affected by this proposal are more fully described in the Appendix to this Order. (Not provided.)
6. The United States Department of Justice has indicated its view that the proposal would have much more serious effects on existing competition. Its conclusion is based upon a more inclusive definition of the Newark banking market, and the fact that within that market the combined market share of Applicant and Bank would be 14.3 percent. The Justice Department also relies on the fact that in that area 20 offices of Applicant are located within ten miles of an office of Bank.
7. Applicant urges that the effects of the proposal on competition in local banking markets are mitigated by the fact that Applicant is primarily a "wholesale" banking organization, whereas Bank serves the "retail" banking customer. However, the Board does not generally view such a distinction as meaningful, particularly where, as here, both organizations have the ability and resources to serve retail customers.
8. The Board notes that in general banks in New Jersey have authority to establish branches throughout the state.

Source: Federal Reserve *Bulletin*, November, 1979.

holding companies grew in number from 641 to 1116; in terms of ownership of deposits, they increased from a minuscule 4.7 percent to a significant 32.6 percent. Of the largest ten banks in the United States, only two were bank holding companies in 1966. By 1970, eight had adapted their corporate structure to the holding-company form. And with the new structure, bank expansion through subsidiary bodies forged rapidly ahead.

Legislative reaction was reasonably swift; in 1970 the Bank Holding Company Act was amended to bring one-bank holding companies under its aegis. However, while this Act reduced holding-company expansion options, bankers were granted some relief as another section of the Act was modified in their favor. The areas into which bank holding companies could expand were broadened, so that any subsidiary that could satisfy the Federal Reserve Board that its activities were "so closely related to banking or managing or controlling banks as to be a proper incident thereto" [Section 4 (c) (8)] would be permissible. The result is that bank holding companies have enabled their flagship banks to range well beyond traditional banking areas. They now engage in mortgage lending through specialized mortgage lending companies, real estate consulting, equity financing, **leasing** operations, **factoring**, financial computer technology, and so on. The outcome is national expansion by commercial bank subsidiaries—after all, they are not limited to the state in which the flagship bank is chartered—and diversification into new and growing sources of business. (See Box 8.3.)

In a **leasing** arrangement the bank buys business plant and equipment, such as factories and machines, and rents them to the user.
Factoring involves purchasing the accounts receivable of a firm at a discount. The factor collects the bills due.

Market power and holding companies

A number of questions arise with respect to the desirability of giant bank holding companies, both in terms of their own viability and in terms

BOX 8.3. Bank Holding Company Activities Permited and Denied by the Board of Governors of the Federal Reserve System.

Permitted (as of 1979)
Extension of credit
   Mortgage banking
   Finance companies: consumer, sales, and
      commercial
   Credit cards
   Factoring
Industrial bank, Morris Plan bank, industrial
   loan company
Servicing loans and other extensions of credit
Trust company
Investment or financial advising
Full-payout leasing of personal and real property
Investments in community welfare projects
Providing bookkeeping or data processing services
Acting as insurance agent or broker, primarily
   in connection with credit extensions
Underwriting credit life, accident, and health
   insurance
Providing courier services
Management consulting for unaffiliated banks
Buying and selling gold and silver bullion and
   coin
Issuing money orders and general-purpose variable
   denominated payment instruments
Futures commission merchant to cover gold and
   silver bullion and coins
Underwriting certain federal, state, and municipal
   securities
Consumer-oriented financial management courses
   and related instructional material
Check verification
Sale at retail of money orders with face value
   less than $1000 and travelers checks, and
   sale of savings bonds.

Denied
Insurance premium funding (combined sales of mutual
   funds and insurance)
Underwriting life insurance not related to credit
   extension
Real estate brokerage
Land development
Real estate syndication
General management consulting

Property management
Computer output microfilm services
Underwriting mortgage guaranty insurance
Operating a savings and loan association
Operating a travel agency

of their market power. The first issue will be addressed in a subsequent section. A comment on the question of market power is in order. Some observers have expressed the fear that bank holding companies give the banking barons a means of amassing further economic power. The merger route has been effectively blocked, but by modifying their legal structure banks achieve a similar result, one that enables them to exert excessive influence on America's economy. This view appears to be misdirected. While the influence of the nation's banking community cannot be shrugged aside, it is not clear that the holding-company structure has led to a major change in power relations. First, the degree of control central management exerts over holding-company affiliates varies greatly. In some instances, centralized direction is substantial; in others, each affiliate is virtually an independent entity. Consequently, giant bank holding companies do not necessarily imply massive power. What is perhaps even more illuminating and surprising is the fact that concentration ratios do not suggest increased power. Between 1968 and 1973 the domestic deposits of the 20 largest commercial banks grew less rapidly than those of the 80 next largest. And the concentration ratios for the 100 largest banks fell during those years. At the state level, it is true that concentration ratios did increase in some states, but virtually none of those states were ones in which concentration had already reached substantial levels. As Dr. Talley, one of the nation's leading observers of banking concentration, wrote, "However serious the banking concentration problem may be, the problem generally did not worsen between 1968–73 [the years of major bank holding company expansion]." Indeed, some contend that on the whole a positive impact has been generated by the bank holding-company movement. New capital and management skills have been infused into many moribund banks, with resulting economies to the banks themselves and improved services to their customers.

One thing is clear from all of this: The bank holding company is here to stay. Bank holding companies do provide a vehicle for expansion beyond traditional banking boundaries. Bank holding companies accommodate empire building by aggressive bank managements. And even if concentration ratios have not increased, the absolute amount of bank assets under the thumbs of holding-company managements has risen substantially. Nevertheless, the legislative safeguards, the bank regulatory mechanism, and the economies of large-scale banking all point to the fact that worries about oligopoly in banking, of domination by a few banking giants, appear groundless.

In fact, with the spread of international banking these fears become even less troublesome. For no longer does the borrower—especially the large business borrower but even, to a certain extent, the smaller bank customer—have to depend solely on U.S. banking institutions. Foreign banks have set up offices in the United States, and American banks have established their own network of offices on foreign shores. The next chapter begins by addressing itself to both of these phenomena: U.S. banks abroad and foreign banks in the United States.

☐ Summary

Four elements that determine the structure of banking today were explored in this chapter: chartering, branching, mergers, and holding companies. The imprint of the government is evident in all of these areas.

A bank charter is a legal privilege. The survival of the dual banking system has meant that chartering takes place on either the national or the state level. The statutes and, even more, the attitude of the chartering authorities have limited the entry of new banks into the U.S. banking industry, a policy that most economists view as anticompetitive.

Economists have voiced similar objections to restraints on branching. The McFadden Act prohibits branching across state lines, while most states have imposed some geographic restrictions on branching within their borders. The available evidence does not support the belief that unit banks are more effective in servicing their communities or more competitive in pricing their services than branch banks.

The impact of these restrictions may have been mitigated by the introduction of banking machines and the bank holding-company movement. The latter initially enabled banks to expand both outside and inside their home state by acquiring subsidiaries rather than branches. As a result of the Bank Holding Company Act of 1956 and its 1970 amendments, out-of-state expansion of bank subsidiaries is no longer possible (although nonbank affiliates may so expand). Today the formation of bank holding companies, as well as their expansion into new lines of activity, must receive prior approval from the Federal Reserve Board. While bank holding companies, by marshaling large amounts of financial resources, may threaten the competitive market, present evidence indicates that this fear is unlikely to be realized.

Banks have grown by merging, a process that also can limit competition. However, because of the Bank Merger Act of 1960, amended in 1966, and subsequent Supreme Court interpretations, the merger movement in banking has not made much headway. In general, the banking system of the United States remains far more competitive than the more obvious manufacturing industries, despite the presence of some giant banks. One of the reasons for the competition is the internationalization of banking, the subject that begins the next chapter.

☐ Questions and Exercises

1. Are bank charters necessary at all? If they are, does the dual banking system make economic sense?
2. Computer technology not only will affect the branching issue mentioned in the chapter but may well alter the very nature of banking. Develop a scenario that will turn a typical retail store into a vehicle for the maintenance and transfer of deposits.
3. Examine the distribution of banks in the local communities of your state— how many have only one commercial bank, how many towns have two or three offices of different banks, how many localities have as many as ten different banks. Use this information to evaluate the competitiveness of banking in your state.
4. Examine the distribution of banks in your state by considering the entire state as the relevant market. Have there been any significant changes in the number of banks in the state in recent years? Also, distinguish between banks that are independent and those that are subsidiaries of the same holding company. Comment on the likely competitiveness of banking in your state. (Does your answer depend on whether you examine the state as a whole or local markets within the state?)
5. Has the drastic rise in gasoline prices over the last decade affected banking competition?

☐ For Further Study

The best and most comprehensive review of branching, merger, and chartering issues is Gerald C. Fischer, *American Banking Structure* (New York: Columbia University Press, 1968). G. J. Benston, "The Optimal Banking Structure: Theory and Evidence," *Journal of Bank Research* 3 (Winter 1973): 220–237 [reproduced in U.S. Senate, Committee on Banking, Housing, and Finance, *Compendium of Issues Relating to Branching by Financial Institutions* (Washington, D.C.: GPO, 1976), pp. 455–473], surveys a great deal of the literature on the economics of bank industry structure.

Jack M. Guttentag, "Branch Banking: A Summary of the Issues and Evidence," also found in the aforementioned *Compendium*, pp. 99–112, and the 1981 U.S. Treasury report and supporting studies, *Geographic Restrictions on Commercial Banking in the United States*, are useful extensions of the issues discussed in the text.

E. S. Herman, "The Philadelphia Bank Merger Decision and Its Critics," *The National Banking Review* 3 (March 1964): 391–400, examines this landmark decision and provides some interesting insights into the legal and economic aspects of bank merger policy. It and a number of major articles on different aspects of commercial bank structure are reprinted in Office of the Comptroller of the Currency, *Studies in Banking Competition and the Banking Structure*

(Washington, D.C.: U.S. Treasury, 1966). Look for Peltzman's seminal piece on bank entry regulation. Potential merger cases are reviewed in W. S. Smith, "The History of Potential Competition in Bank Mergers and Acquisitions," Federal Reserve Bank of Chicago, *Economic Perspectives* 4 (July-August 1980): 15–23.

M. A. Jessee and S. A. Seelig, *Bank Holding Companies and the Public Interest* (Lexington, Mass.: Lexington, 1977), provide an up-to-date examination of the holding-company phenomenon in banking.

CHAPTER 9

Banking Regulation: Multinational Banking, Bank Failures, Interest Rate Ceilings, and Deregulation

We need a comprehensive plan to restructure financial institutions so that they can be more competitive and responsive to the technological, social, and marketplace changes they now face.

Alan Cranston, United States senator, D.,California (1979)

Banking must be brought out of the 1930s in order to prosper in the financial marketplace of today and to serve the legitimate needs and convenience of the American banking public in the 1980s and beyond.

John Tower, United States senator, R., Texas (1979)

Contents

CHAPTER HIGHLIGHTS

1. The reasons that American banks have established offices abroad and foreign bankers have begun banking operations in the United States.

2. The implications of the multinationalization of banking for banking regulation.

3. The causes of bank failures in recent years, and why more banks have not failed.

4. How constraints on interest rates affect the allocation of credit.

5. The major provisions of the Depository Institutions Deregulation Act.

6. What the banking scene might look like in the absence of extensive government regulation.

Four issues are covered in this chapter: (1) international banking, (2) bank failures (3) limits on interest rates, and (4) deregulation of banking. As noted in Chapter 8, the profit motive compelled commercial banks to diversify both functionally and geographically. The holding-company arrangement made it possible for commercial banks (via their subsidiaries) to provide new services and to expand their boundaries beyond the borders of their own states. The same impetus led to expansion abroad, the first topic to be explored in this chapter.

Expansion carries risks, but even risk-taking banks rarely fail, for reasons that are examined in the second section. Surely part of the low failure rate is due to the fact that banking competition is constrained by regulation.

Commercial banks and other depository institutions may have been aided by another set of regulations: those on interest rates. While banks are prohibited from exceeding certain maximum interest rates, especially to consumer-borrowers, they appear to also benefit from the ceilings imposed on the interest rates they pay to savers. The third section analyzes the impact of maximum interest rates on the economic system and on the banks themselves.

Deregulation has made headway, notably in federal legislation passed in 1980, which is explored next. The chapter concludes with a general evaluation of banking regulation.

☐ Multinational Banking

"The European Connection" might well be a title for a movie remake. In the present context, of course, the reference is to American banking relationships with foreign countries. Such international banking connections are hardly news. Foreign trade has played a critical role in America's growth, and still accounts for hundreds of billions of dollars' worth of business activity. And wherever foreign trade is found, financing of that trade makes its presence known.

The attention that has been focused on the international aspects of banking in the past decade, however, has little to do with the financing of exports and imports. Rather, it is concerned with the mushrooming of branches and affiliates of American banks abroad and the heavy loan commitments made to foreigners by American banks, both through their domestic headquarters and through their foreign offices. Similarly, some observers have been concerned about the growth of foreign banking outposts in the United States.

American banks abroad

Only a few American banks operated offices abroad in the early 1960s. In fact, in 1960 only eight American banks were established abroad. Most domestic banks handled their foreign business through correspondents on other continents, using their services as the need arose. After 1967, however, the picture changed considerably. In that year the number of banks with offices outside of the United States rose to 15. By 1968 the number had almost doubled again, rising to 26. The next year saw another doubling, to 53, and by 1972, 108 U.S. banks had opened offices outside the United States. The number of banking offices abroad rose from 131 in 1960 to over 600 by 1972, and the assets reported by those offices increased from $3.5 billion to $90 billion over the same period. By 1980, banking offices outside the United States held almost $400 billion. Corresponding to these changes, the percentage of total deposits of U.S. banks derived from foreign operations also rose drastically. Some large American banks had become heavily dependent on their foreign markets, earning 50 percent or more of their profits from their international activities.

The motives underlying this shift in emphasis are varied. First, they reflect the greater activity of U.S. businesses abroad. As the multinational business corporation grew in importance during the 1950s and 1960s, as more and more American firms expanded their manufacturing operations, especially in Europe, their banks followed them. Rather than lose established customers to foreign bankers, U.S. banks moved along with their clients to provide the needed credit facilities. And during the 1960s even the larger regional banks, those located outside the major money centers, followed their customers abroad. They feared losing not only international business but even their domestic business to the money market banks of New York, Boston, Chicago, and San Francisco.

A second and complementary reason has to do with the credit restraint program imposed on bank lending abroad. The Voluntary Credit Restraint Program, initiated in 1965 to slow the dollar outflow, limited U.S. bank lending to foreign customers, including foreign subsidiaries of

American corporations. However, bankers could lend to the same corporations through foreign branches. A third motive for the shift was the policy of monetary tightness imposed by the Federal Reserve in 1966 and again in 1969. As the earlier discussion of liability management indicated (p. 166), U.S. bankers found that CD nonrenewals could be compensated for to a large extent by borrowing from their offshore branches. The prerequisite, of course, was the existence of such foreign offices. It is interesting to note that with the imposition of reserve requirements on borrowing from foreign branches, which increased the cost of such funds transfers, and the termination of the Voluntary Credit Restraint Program, the growth of overseas branches slowed. In recent years an increasing proportion of the banks' international business has been transacted at the home office. Some banks have gone so far as to close down their operations abroad.

A number of voices in the banking community have expressed concern about the heavy dependence of certain large banks on their foreign operations. This worry surfaced in the years following the OPEC-decreed major oil price hikes in late 1973 and again in 1980. In the past few years a number of the fuel-poor, less developed countries have been caught in a squeeze—the prices of the commodities they export have not kept pace with their fuel bills. Their subsequent deficits were partly financed by public international bodies. Large American and European commercial banks shared in this financing effort. The fear expressed by some observers is that these bankers have overextended themselves.

At the same time, a substantial share of the surpluses of the oil-exporting nations were deposited in American banks. This, too, raised questions about the potential volatility of these foreign-owned dollars, with the possible threat to the viability of the U.S. banking system. The scenario that emerged ran along these lines: American bankers had accepted deposits from Arab oil sheiks, deposits that could be withdrawn on relatively short notice. The bankers had lent these funds to countries that were strapped for credit, with little likelihood of speedy repayment. Should significant numbers of depositors demand their funds, the banks would be hard pressed to deliver the liquid resources to pay off those demands. The end result would be bankruptcy. Of course, this scenario is dismal indeed, and represents the worst possible instance. But it does highlight the kinds of issues that have concerned some bankers and public officials who are responsible for the sound functioning of the banking system. Concern, however, need not lead to resolution of the problem.

The American banking authorities can exert control over the domestic activities of U.S. banks. They may indirectly influence, but hardly control, the policies of foreign branches and subsidiaries of U.S. financial institutions, which must abide by the rules of the countries in which they are domiciled. The banks are multinational; the regulators are only national. This leaves gaps in the regulatory mechanism, and allows for maneuvering on the part of bankers. It permits banks to perform in one country certain functions that might be inappropriate in a different nation. (The use of Eurodollar borrowing to offset the Federal Reserve's policy of credit stringency in 1966 and 1969 is but one example. Avoiding the limit on loans to a single customer, a provision of U.S. banking law, is another illustration.) While this situation is an uncomfortable one, it is not easily remedied. To be sure, the central bankers of the world do cooperate, but this voluntary coordination of policies is a weak substitute for control.

Foreign banks in the United States

The internationalization of banking has not been one-sided; foreign banks have expanded their operations in the United States, too. Whereas in 1960 few foreign commercial banks had opened offices in the United States, by mid-year 1980 150 foreign banks were operating 332 offices. Originally compelled by much the same motives as those that brought American banks overseas—servicing their globe-trotting customers— these banks began to offer banking services to domestic customers as well. For the most part, the U. S. offices of foreign banks have specialized in wholesale banking, concentrating on large business borrowers. And they have been successful. By 1980 foreign banks accounted for 20 percent of all the business loans made by large U.S. banks.

American bank managers have expressed mixed emotions about these foreign "invaders." Bankers running large domestic institutions are certainly not anxious to roll out the welcome mat; the presence of foreign banks, of course, means more competition. On the other hand, they see no way of preventing such market penetration without imperiling their own foreign operations.

In addition, both the banking community and the regulatory authorities were concerned for other reasons. Bankers were upset by the unfair advantage their foreign rivals received in this country. For example, the branching limits imposed on national banks were not applicable to foreign banks; the latter could open branches and have done so in several states. The Federal Reserve also expressed dissatisfaction with the status quo. Foreign banks, when they did not voluntarily join the Federal Reserve System, were beyond the controls and supervision both of the Federal Reserve and of the comptroller of the currency. And as they became increasingly important on the domestic scene, their freedom to operate without control proved disconcerting and potentially disruptive.

The passage of the International Banking Act of 1978 was aimed at resolving the absence of supervision and control of foreign banks as well as the competitive inequality. Foreign bank offices became subject to the reporting, examination, and reserve requirements of domestic banks. (They were also granted the privilege of borrowing from the Federal Reserve.) Foreign banks were also subjected to the restrictions on nonbank activities that are imposed on domestic bank holding companies.

Moreover, each foreign bank must select a "home state" and become subject to the branching limits imposed on national banks located in that state. In effect, this prohibits both domestic and foreign banks from opening deposit-collecting offices out of the state. Competitive inequality, if not eliminated, will certainly be reduced in the future.

The banking system itself weathered a period of substantial loan losses, with a number of larger banks finding themselves under scrutiny by the comptroller of the currency. The next section of this chapter is devoted to the quality of bank lending in recent years.

☐ Problem Loans and Bank Failures

Most of the fifteen years prior to 1975 were boom ones for the commercial banking system. Loans were pursued aggressively; in a thriving economy even marginal loans were viewed optimistically. Bankers had pushed the problems of the Great Depression and its massive loan failures into the far recesses of their minds. Indeed, the new breed of bankers had not even been born then; to them, depression banking was a historical quirk, an aberration that was in no way related to modern bank management. The possibility of wholesale loan defaults was thought to be remote.

The years 1974 and 1975 led to a reassessment of these attitudes. A look at bank failure statistics is enlightening. Figure 9.1(a) indicates a stable trend in the number of bank failures between 1961 and 1974, averaging six per year. But 1975 shows a drastic doubling in the rate of failures. Figure 9.1(b) plots the same basic information from a slightly different perspective. Instead of the numbers of bank failures, it shows the asset totals of the failed banks. The contrast between the years before 1973 and those after it is startling. Since 1973, a few of the nation's largest banks have succumbed. Of course, the FDIC stepped in, the behemoths were absorbed by other giants with FDIC approval, and continuity of bank operations was maintained. In these cases the depositors were fully protected. Nevertheless, when giants can fail, questions about smaller institutions are bound to arise.

Banks that are thought to have significant weaknesses, potentially requiring FDIC assistance, are considered **problem banks** by the FDIC.

Another indicator of banking system difficulty was the marked rise in the number of **problem banks**, banks that are listed by the FDIC for special and continued surveillance. All signals pointed downward; all was not well with the commercial banking system.

What has happened to make the banking system more vulnerable to failure in recent years? Undoubtedly, the recession of 1973–1975 was inopportune to the banking community. But rather than viewing the recession as the gale that caused the difficulty, one should perhaps think of it as the strong wind that blew away the façade hiding some basic problems of loan quality.

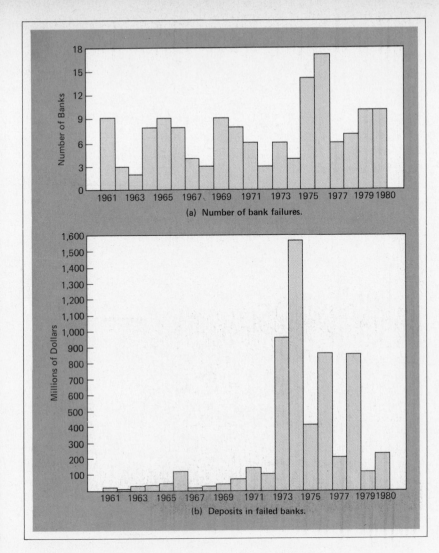

FIGURE 9.1 Bank failures, 1961–1980.

Source: Federal Deposit Insurance Corporation, *Annual Report 1980* (Washington, D.C., 1981).

The real estate boom and bust

A number of underlying problems can be identified. Perhaps the most glaring one was associated with **real estate investment trusts (REITs).** In 1960 Congress had enacted that REITs were to be exempt from corporate income tax, provided that 90 percent of their profits were distributed to the owners. In subsequent years, especially 1972 and early 1973, with construction booming, REITs not only acquired high-yielding mortgages but also lent money for the construction of commercial buildings,

A **real estate investment trust (REIT)** is a legal arrangement for pooling funds and investing in real estate.

shopping centers, and residential developments. To finance these projects, the REITs borrowed heavily from both commercial banks and the commercial paper market. Access to funding by some of the largest REITs was smoothed by their relationship to commercial banks; many of the giant bank holding companies had sponsored affiliated REITs to siphon off lucrative management and loan fees. Thus, Chase Manhattan Bank lent substantial sums to Chase Manhattan REIT.

As interest rates rose to historic heights in the mid-1970s, the REITs found themselves in a profit squeeze: The rates they were paying for borrowed funds was rising faster than the rates they were charging. And when the real estate market collapsed in 1973, many REITs found themselves owning large amounts of overvalued property. The problem was of such magnitude that in 1974 one-third of the entire REITs' holdings of short-term mortgages were not paying interest. To protect their loans to the REITs, the banks fed in additional funds, so that by the end of 1974 the REITs' total debt to the largest banks exceeded $5 billion. The banks were soon involved in real estate in a more direct way through foreclosures and takeovers of buildings. By 1976 the twenty largest banks held over $1 billion in property coming this way. Over 40 percent of their real estate loans were paying reduced interest charges or not paying any interest at all.

The turnaround in the real estate market since 1976 altered the picture somewhat. Much of the property became salable. But once burned, forever cautious (see Box 9.1).

The municipal bond market

While the banks were reeling from the battering they had received from the REIT storm, a second gale struck from a different quarter as the municipal bond market plunged. Commercial banks had increased their holdings of state and local bonds over the past decade, as you will recall from the discussion in Chapter 6. By 1974 commercial banks held $99.9 billion, or 11.3 percent of their total assets, in municipals. In fact, commercial banks were a major purchaser of municipal bond issues. These supposedly risk-free securities had acted as a source of tax-free income, and had been viewed by the bankers as quality paper.

Shock waves rippled through the financial community in early 1975 as the Urban Development Corporation, a New York State agency, defaulted on its bonds. By the time summer rolled around, the specter of default by New York City and New York State loomed as a real possibility. New York City's major banks, holding $4 billion in such bonds, watched unbelievingly as market prices plummeted.[1] At one point during the year

---

[1] The Federal Reserve reported that 236 banks held New York debt equal to more than 50 percent of their capital, and an additional 718 banks held 20–50 percent of their capital in New York-related debt. By far the largest holders were banks in New York State.

BOX 9.1 Once Burned, Twice Shy: The Experience of a Loan Officer

Thirty-three-year-old James Lientz heads a loan department of Atlanta's largest commercial bank. He is charged with providing lending and other bank services for REITs, utilities, and other specialty areas. Along with other loan officers at Citizens and Southern National Bank, Lientz aggressively pursued new customers during the promising years of the late 1960s and early 1970s, and the booming Atlanta real estate market spurred them on. At one point real estate loans constituted one-quarter of the bank's total loan portfolio, an unusual percentage for a commercial bank. The collapse of the real estate market in 1974 hit C&S hard, forcing it to write off more than $30 million in bad loans and setting another $35 million aside for possible loan losses. The bank's earnings fell by 60 percent in 1974, and the Federal Reserve included C&S on its list of problem bank holding companies.

The economy's recovery in 1975 left Lientz relieved but cautious. "I'm still out to make every loan I can," he says, "but I'm more conscious of quality now."

Before approving a loan, Mr. Lientz says he now gives a lot more attention to the quality of a company's managers. "We used to bet on people being able to do things they said they could do but hadn't done before," he says. "But now if a company wants money to expand or diversify, we look beyond the costs of building a plant or buying new equipment. We look at things like how well management handles its employees and how quickly it can adapt to changing market conditions. We try to get a lot closer to the people involved."

As a result, Mr. Lientz says he will probably make fewer loans in the future than he did in the past. "But they'll be better ones," he says emphatically.

In accordance with this new outlook, Lientz has rejected a $2.5 million loan application from a national retailer, despite the fact that C&S has had a long and profitable relationship with this client. Moreover, when it grants business loans the bank often demands guarantees, including personal guarantees by the borrowing firms' officers. If the personal assets of the officers are at stake, Lientz believes, the likelihood of timely and full payment is greater.

While Lientz remains committed to lending, not least because the size of his annual bonus hinges on the new business he brings in, he claims that the lesson of the 1974 recession has not been lost.

"We used to think we couldn't lose money in real estate," he says. "We never looked behind the numbers at the actual projects our money was building. That's a mistake I'll never make again, in real estate or any other area." He adds: "We got fat and happy, and we did some dumb things. Never again."

Source: Adapted from *The Wall Street Journal*, March 12, 1976.

these "risk-free" bonds turned out to be worth only one-half of their former value. And with severe doubts raised about New York's financial stability, similar qualms were expressed throughout the country about the financial viability of other municipalities and local government agencies.

Again, the threat passed. Neither New York City nor New York State defaulted as severe budgetary restraints were imposed. Nevertheless, these episodes will not be dismissed quickly by the financial community. In fact, holdings of municipals as a percentage of total bank asset portfolios declined from about 11 percent in 1974 to 10 percent by the end of 1979. Moreover, demands by bankers for more information from issuers of governmental bonds, enabling financial analysts to inspect the quality of such issues more closely, are now common.

The banks and OPEC

The Arab-inspired quadrupling of oil prices in 1973 was a third source of problems for commercial banks. The oil-exporting countries were the obvious beneficiaries of the price hike. The major industrial countries proved to be secondary beneficiaries as the oil exporters spent billions of dollars there to purchase consumer and industrial goods as well as military hardware. Their unspent funds ended up in Western banks, primarily as short-term deposits in the United States, West Germany, and Switzerland. The oil-importing less developed countries (LDCs) found that their revenues, which fell during the worldwide recession of 1974–1975, were insufficient to cover steeply higher fuel costs. Their need for external financing increased correspondingly. Some aid came from bilateral governmental loans and international lending agencies. But a good share—over 40 percent of the $68 billion needed in 1974 and 1975—came from the banking systems of the industrial nations.

U.S. banks and their European counterparts performed their intermediary function by channeling the OPEC surpluses into the non-oil-producing LDCs. This continuing intermediation has led to the fear that some banks have overextended themselves. Most of the funds have percolated to Latin America, and doubts were expressed in 1974 and again in 1980 concerning the ability of a few countries to service these loans and ultimately to repay them. Have the big banks put too many eggs in too few baskets?

Public policy toward bank failures

Despite all these problems, the U.S. banking system did not fare badly even during the worst of recent years. Profit rates fell sharply for some banks. But most of the big banks, which were most threatened, were able to absorb their losses with their accumulated reserves and still pay dividends to their stockholders. And despite the failure of a few large banks, the solidity of the banking system cannot seriously be questioned.

That impression of banking system stability can be confirmed in a variety of ways. First, the public continues to maintain confidence in the banks they do business with; obviously, there has been no panic in recent years. The banking authorities—who might well be blamed for not forestalling the failures—acted to permit smooth transitions, prevent depositor loss, and discourage a buildup of tension that might have led to panic. The FDIC's method of selling insolvent banks to solvent, well-managed ones has surely done much to keep losses down and faith up.

This FDIC policy is eminently sound. Indeed, the FDIC could hardly permit giant banks to close up and then pay off their depositors. The FDIC now holds assets in excess of $11 billion, which is hardly a substantial sum when contrasted with the liabilities of the U.S. National Bank of San Diego (insured deposits: $889.8 million; failed in October 1973), Franklin National Bank of New York (insured deposits: $3,730 million; failed in October 1974), and the Hamilton National Bank of Chattanooga, Tennessee (insured deposits: $470.1 million; failed in February 1976).

Second, despite the large sums involved in these failures, they must be seen in proper perspective. The deposits of all banks that failed between 1973 and 1980 totaled $5.1 billion but amounted to only 0.33 percent of all bank assets in 1980; the total number of banks that failed between 1973 and 1980 was equal to only one-half of one percent of all U.S. commercial banks existing in 1980. This is hardly a significant percentage, and could not possibly be indicative of a weak system.

Third, the bank failures that have occurred since the Great Depression have been due to specific problems in the failing banks rather than to general malaise in the banking system. In the case of San Diego's U.S. National Bank, self-serving loans by the bank's chief administrator to companies controlled by him led to the bank's demise. (That gentleman is currently serving a prison sentence for his misdeeds.) Poor management practices, including an abnormally large percentage of borrowings in the Federal funds market, high-risk loans, and foreign exchange speculation, as well as criminal offenses, ultimately led to Franklin's collapse. (Some of Franklin's chief executives are also incarcerated.)

Finally, the very anticompetitive aspects of commercial banking that are incorporated in law or implemented by the regulatory agencies protect the banks under their umbrella. By limiting the formation of new banks through restrictions on new charters and inhibiting branching both between and within states, the authorities can hold down the number of bank offices. This limits competition, thereby reducing the risk of bank failures.

The growth of bank holding companies and multinational banking also promotes banking system stability. The more diverse banks are, the larger and more geographically dispersed their loan and deposit accounts are, the less likely they are to fail. As Mark Twain responded when notices of his death appeared in newspapers, "The reports of my death are greatly exaggerated." So too, are current fears about the health of the banking system. Despite minor problems, the economic physician must report that the patient is in remarkably good health.

☐ Interest Rate Regulation

To constraints on bank formation and expansion must be added limits on the interest rates banks may pay and may charge. In 1933 Congress prohibited the payment of interest on demand deposit accounts and authorized the Federal Reserve (and soon thereafter the FDIC and in 1966 the Federal Home Loan Bank Board) to impose interest rate ceilings on savings and time deposits. In December 1980 a savings account of the day-of-deposit-to-day-of-withdrawal type earned a maximum compound interest rate of less than 6% per annum. On the other hand, various states have enacted usury laws, which impose interest rate ceilings on charges to noncorporate borrowers. So, while the cost of liabilities is constrained, so, too, are earnings from the asset portfiolio.

Economists raise two objections to these restraints: (1) They lead to allocational inefficiency (see p. 183 for definition) and (2) they impose undesired side effects.

The first criticism can be demonstrated by looking at the simple supply and demand curves of Figure 9.2. The downward-sloping demand curve reflects the fact that borrowers are less prone to borrow at higher interest rates than at lower ones. Conversely, lenders are more willing to lend at

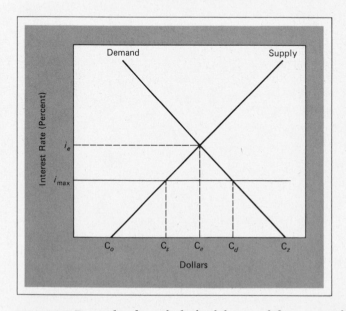

FIGURE 9.2 Demand and supply for bank loans and deposits: a schematic diagram.

higher rates than at lower ones. In a perfectly competitive market, the interest rate determined by market forces would be i_e, the rate at which quantity supplied and quantity demanded are equal. The amount of borrowing and lending equals C_e. The virtue of this competitive equilibrium is well known—the borrowers whose needs are most urgent, as expressed by their willingness to pay at least the market rate, obtain the funds, while those whose demands are less intense are closed out of the market. For instance, when housing demand is strong and the home builder is willing to pay a 15 percent interest rate on a construction loan, while the demand for recreational vehicles is weak and the RV distributor is able to pay only 8 percent, the market mechanism responds to the builder's needs before those of the RV dealer. More intense consumer needs are served before less urgent demands.

Consider now the imposition of an interest rate ceiling at i_{max}, lying below i_e. Lenders are told that they violate the law by charging more than i_{max}. The impact on law-abiding lenders will be to limit their lending to C_s; the costs of lending more than C_s are greater than i_{max}, so they cut down on loans. Borrowers, on the other hand, are willing to borrow more at the lower interest rate; they want C_d. The discrepancy between C_d and C_s is the excess demand, the amount of credit demanded that is in excess of what lenders wish to supply.

How will the reduced amount of credit be allocated? Which of the C_d potential borrowers get the C_s available credit? Since the price mechanism no longer functions, other allocating devices must be introduced. Perhaps "first come, first served" will be the practice (which in fact it is). If so, the RV distributor has as good an opportunity as the builder, despite their different market-determined needs. This leads to an inefficient allocation of credit resources.

The same conclusion can be reached for interest rates paid by banks. Use the same diagram, but let the suppliers be the people who supply credit to (i.e., deposit with) banks. The banks are the demanders in this case. In a market-determined situation the banks will pay the equilibrium rate, i_e, and obtain C_e quantity of funds. Similarly, depositors will earn i_e by providing C_e deposits. But set the interest rate at zero: Then bank demand for funds is much larger, reaching C_z, since the lower the cost of funds, the more readily banks will borrow and lend. But except for minimum checking needs, why should depositors maintain funds in zero-earning accounts? Once again, a discrepancy between the quantities supplied and demanded is created artificially. Banks now obtain fewer funds—C_o is less than C_z—and thus banks' loans will be artificially restricted. (The analogous process occurs when an interest rate ceiling is imposed on savings deposits. The ceiling is greater than zero but less than i_e—say, i_{max}. Can you explain why this also leads to an inefficient allocation of resources?)

In short, if banks are constrained in their quest for funds, the lending process is compromised. If, in addition, they are constrained from charging market rates, the efficiency of the economic system is reduced further.

But not only are these controls inefficient; they are also ineffective in achieving their goals. Like rent control on housing, the ceiling interest rate is designed to make credit cheaper to a certain class of customers. Rents are controlled to help the poor; interest ceilings are set to aid the consuming public and those who purchase houses for personal use. Yet controlled rents do not help the poor. The experience with rent control, especially in New York City, where it has been in effect since World War II, is that the supply of housing diminishes. It doesn't pay for landlords to maintain housing if the rents they collect are less than the costs they incur. Similarly, it doesn't make sense financially to lend to noncorporate customers who must be charged a lower interest rate than can be charged to equally creditworthy business customers.

The same is true for the depositor. Interest rates on savings were held down partly to help the savings banks. These institutions hold a large volume of low-earning mortgages and would not survive if they were forced to pay competitive interest rates. What happened is not surprising: Funds left these low-earning accounts, and so the threat of disaster came not from lack of profits but from severe liquidity pressures. Thus, controls on interest rates do not help those who are presumed to benefit, and such constraints are an inefficient means of allocating resources.

Interest rate limits have been imposed for macroeconomic purposes as well. Here, too, they do not work. In the examination of liquidity management in Chapter 7 (pp. 164–168), it was observed that Regulation Q had been used as an instrument of monetary restraint. The Federal Reserve restricted interest rates that banks could pay in order to slow down the flow of deposits into banks. The theory was that fewer deposits lead to fewer loans, ergo monetary tightness. It was further pointed out that the banks had successfully circumvented these monetary restrictions by developing new instruments, ones that were not subject to existing regulations. Thus, when interest rates in the United States exceeded the Regulation Q ceiling on CDs in 1969 and banks found their time deposit liabilities falling, the decline in CDs was largely offset by an increase in Eurodollar and other types of borrowing. And each time the Fed closed one loophole a new instrument was devised to get around the restraint. As you may recall, the end came when the monetary authorities abandoned Regulation Q as a means of monetary control and permitted the banks to issue large CDs at whatever rates the market demanded.

The abandonment of Regulation Q on all deposits and the granting of permission to banks to pay interest on demand deposits is a reform that is advanced not only by academic economists but also by economists in the government. It had the support of Presidents Johnson, Nixon, and Carter. As yet, Congress has been unable to muster sufficient votes to eliminate entirely these artificial restraints on interest rates. But clearly its day will come. The future is evident in the provisions of new major legislation.

☐ The Depository Institutions Deregulation and Monetary Control Act of 1980 (DIDAMCA)

The scope of DIDAMCA is broad indeed: the Act covers nine separate topics. Of special interest for this chapter are two sections, Title II, which deals with interest rate ceilings on deposits, and Title V, which deals with usury laws. According to Title II, Regulation Q will cease after a period of six years. Maximum interest rates on time and savings deposits will no longer be set by law; the competitive marketplace will determine the interest rates that depository institutions will pay to savers. Congress realized, however, that immediate freeing of the interest rate would cause severe problems for many banks. Consequently, DIDAMCA's Title II provides for a phase-in period. A Depository Institutions Deregulation Committee, with representatives from the Federal Reserve Board of Governors, the FDIC, the Federal Home Loan Bank Board (discussed in Chapter 11), the National Credit Union Administration Board (Chapter 11 also discusses credit unions), and the comptroller of the currency, was established to monitor the transition. The authority to set Regulation Q was transfered to the Committee until 1986, after which the Committee will be disbanded along with Regulation Q.

Title V substitutes a new, flexible maximum for any state usury laws applicable to any insured bank. The federal ceiling varies by one to five percentage points above the discount rate, depending on the purpose and size of the loan.

Other provisions of the Act affect reserve requirements and the powers of nonbank financial institutions. However, nowhere in the Act are the other issues addressed in this chapter and the last one examined. It surely is a move in the right direction, but it is a far cry from a thorough regulatory overhaul.

Yet the direction of the nation's lawmakers is clearly toward deregulation. In the International Banking Act of 1978, Congress requested that the President report to Congress on the appropriateness of the McFadden Act restrictions on branching. Similarly, the Glass-Steagall Act has come under repeated pressure from both bankers and investment firms, the former because they'd like to profit from underwriting, the latter to keep out the competition. Where deregulation will lead is a question you might think about.

☐ Deregulation in Banking

That banking has been singled out for special government attention should be obvious by now. Perhaps no other industry in the United States is so closely supervised and governed. To a degree, this regulatory environment stems from the key importance of commercial banks, whose operations penetrate every sector of the economic system. The importance of money was recognized by the framers of the Constitution, which reserves for Congress the exclusive right "to coin money, [and] regulate the value thereof."[2] As you know, government-issued money, or currency, constitutes only a small share of the total money supply. Private financial interests are the government's partner, even senior partner, in using the money-creation power. Hence derives the motive of regulation: All money-creating institutions must be forced to operate according to the national interest.

Other motives, too, account for regulation of commercial banking. As you recall banking's history in America, the awesome powers of eastern financial influences were often thought to—and not infrequently did—act against western pioneering interests. The balance was restored in part by turning to the political arena. Similarly, fears of banking monopoly led to constraints on banks' ability to grow. The experience of banking panics led to a search for a more stable banking system and, hence, more regulations. We should not forget, too, that the banking community often lent support to legislation designed to protect its own profits. And banking itself is not monolithic—some bankers sought laws to protect themselves against threats posed by members of their own community.

Finally, economists are partly responsible too. By explaining the role money plays in affecting prices and economic activity, they showed that monetary control is important, and indicated that commercial banking must be regulated if the economy is not to shatter on the rocks of inflation or depression.

In light of all these forces—historical, national, and personal—total deregulation of banking is unlikely, even if it is viewed as desirable. Yet we might try to imagine what the U.S. financial system would look like if some morning Congress and the state legislatures woke up and abolished all constraints specific to banking. Out go the chartering restrictions and the prohibitions on forming various kinds of associations; acquisitions are liberally permitted; reserve requirements disappear, as do deposit insurance and limitations on interest rates paid and charged.

Many competitive consequences would follow, and perhaps some anticompetitive effects as well. Interest rates paid on liabilities would fluctuate with the demand and supply of funds, and the small saver could benefit from high interest rates. On the other hand, banks would no longer subsidize borrowers by shortchanging small savers. Banks could be expected to expand to new territories and to acquire businesses outside of banking. This would increase competition as they opened branches in areas that were previously closed to them. On the other hand, banking concentration would increase as national bank holding companies were formed. Whether this would lead to serious national problems depends on one's faith in the efficacy of the antitrust laws, which, not being specific to banking, would not have been abolished. Similarly, banks' influence over nonfinancial concerns might decrease competition in some indus-

[2]Article I, Section 8. Section 10 prohibits states from coining money.

CHAPTER 10

Money Creation, or How to Make Money

Deposit (noun). A charitable contribution to the support of a bank.
Ambrose Bierce, satirist (1911)

Money is like muck, not good except it be spread.
Francis Bacon, essayist (1625[?])

CONTENTS

The last few chapters focused on the banking industry, its development, its present status, and some current issues facing both bankers and regulators. It is now time to turn to the distinguishing feature of commercial banking: the money-creating function of the commercial banking system. As you learned in earlier chapters, the uniqueness of commercial banking lies in the fact that its demand liabilities constitute the lion's share of the nation's money supply. (Of the total supply of M-1A outstanding on December 31, 1980, $275 billion, or 70 percent constituted demand deposits, while the remaining $118 billion consisted of currency liabilities of the U.S. Treasury and the Federal Reserve banks.)

This chapter will elaborate on the deposit-creating function of the commercial banking system. You already know that the banking system issues liabilities that circulate as the medium of exchange, that they are the equivalent of and in some ways superior to currency. Recall the example of the goldsmith, that early banker, and how goldsmiths were able to create money (pp. 88–90). The methods by which a modern banking system engages in deposit creation, as well as the limitations beyond which such creation is not feasible, differ little in principle from those that existed in the time of the goldsmith. They will be spelled out with greater care and depth in this chapter and its appendix.

Fundamental to money creation is the role played by fractional reserves. A banker who must keep a dollar on hand for each dollar deposited retains no room to maneuver. This 100 percent reserve ratio places bankers in a straitjacket; they cannot lend or invest or create new deposits. They are a passive factor on the economic and financial scene. But if a banker needs to keep only 50 cents on hand for each dollar deposited, then the other 50 cents can be passed on to someone else. The outcome is money creation. The recipient of the 50 cents owns that sum and can do with it as he or she pleases. At the same time, the original depositor still owns and can spend the dollar represented by the deposit. The amount of money that can be circulated has magically increased from $1.00 to $1.50. The exact mechanics of this process, detailing the method and its limits, follow. It will be easier to begin with a hypothetical example and develop some basic principles. Greater realism will be incorporated into the model at the second stage.

"Come on in, Dolores. Al got in twenty-five cords of firewood. I froze and canned a winter's supply of food. And now we're just putting the finishing touches on six months' worth of money."

Drawing by W. Miller; © 1981 The New Yorker Magazine, Inc.

☐ The Monopoly Bank Case

The earliest American banks were widely dispersed, with relatively little daily contact with banks in other cities and states. You will remember that these local banks could issue their own bank notes or paper promises to pay legal money. People brought specie to the bank largely because of the safekeeping facilities offered at the bank building, receiving the right to withdraw specie or its equivalent—notes—from the bank. The transaction of an individual who placed $100 in specie into this bank would be recorded on the bank's balance sheet as follows:

Mono Bank	
Assets	**Liabilities**
Reserves (= specie) +$100	Deposits +$100

(This type of balance sheet, which shows only changes rather than the total balance sheet, is called a T-account.) The bank owes the depositor $100, and its asset side indicates that it holds $100 in reserve in the form of the gold received. The depositor could withdraw the $100 either in paper bank notes or in gold coin, or transfer it to another person by means of a written order to the bank. In any case, the bank's liability to this depositor would then cease.

As a matter of fact, rarely would all of the bank's depositors withdraw all their funds at once. Normally, deposits would fluctuate in one direction or another but would center on some basic average. Some, perhaps many, depositors would withdraw funds, but others would replace them. As Figure 10.1 shows, the gold removed by Ilana to pay Rebecca ends up back in the Mono Bank. After all, this monopoly bank is the only such institution in the region, so that all the people who wish to use banking facilities have no alternative to the Mono Bank. The only result of the transaction described by Figure 10.1 is the recording of an internal transfer. The Mono Bank credits Rebecca with one sack of gold, simultaneously debiting Ilana for that sum.

But if the Mono Bankers did not have to worry about major fund outflows and could convince depositors who wish to pay bills by withdrawing specie to accept its own bank notes or transfer by check in lieu of specie, then the bank could increase the quantity of deposit liabilities well beyond the amount of specie on reserve.

Let's suppose that, for every $100 deposited in the bank, the banker believes that only $10, or 10 percent, is likely to be withdrawn in specie, never to be redeposited. It is destined for payments outside the region. In that case the banker could be satisfied with holding only $10 in specie for every $100 on deposit. If $1,000 in specie is deposited, the banker could permit the liabilities of Mono Bank—that is, its deposits—to rise to $10,000. Why? Because for this $10,000 in deposits the banker needs only 10 percent, or $1,000, in specie to "back" it. We encounter fractional reserves once again.

But how does the banker multiply the $1,000 initially deposited in the Mono Bank into the $10,000 in deposits? The answer derives from the lending-investing function of banking. In Chapter 5 you saw that bankers' earnings stem primarily from interest earned on loans and investments, rather than from service charges on deposits or safe-deposit fees. As borrowers approach the Mono Bank's officers for loans or the latter perceive profitable lending or investing opportunities, loans or investments will be undertaken. Say that the AB company needs a $4,000 loan. The banker and AB's management agree on terms, and a $4,000 loan—a bank asset—is signed by the principals. AB is granted a $4,000 addition to its deposit balance with the bank; this is a bank liability. The Mono Bank's T-account will reflect the transaction as follows, omitting only the capital account and the accruing interest:

Mono Bank

Specie	$1,000	Deposit of original depositor	$1,000
Loan to AB	4,000	Deposit of AB	4,000
Total assets	$5,000	Total liabilities	5,000

Soon afterward the local government seeks temporary finance and markets an interest-bearing three-month bond. The Mono Bank decides

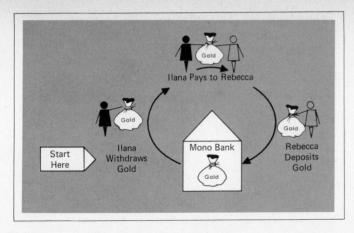

FIGURE 10.1 Clearing and the monopoly bank.

to buy $5,000 worth of the bond issue, crediting the government's account with it by the full sum. The T-account covering both transactions will now appear as follows:

Mono Bank

Specie	$ 1,000	Deposit of original depositor	$ 1,000
Loan to AB	4,000	Deposit of AB	4,000
Investment in		Deposit of government	5,000
government bond	5,000		
Total assets	$10,000	Total liabilities	$10,000

Through the lending-investing process, Mono Bank has raised its liabilities from the $1,000 owed the original depositor to the $10,000 of the final T-account. The bank maintains the 10 percent in specie desired by its decision makers, and has acquired $9,000 in earning assets.

This example is, of course, highly unrealistic. No longer do we have monopoly banks. Nor can banks decide entirely on their own the ratio of reserves (specie in this example) to deposits; minimum reserves are specified by bank regulators. Nevertheless, one important conclusion can be derived from this case: A banking system—in this instance consisting of one bank—can create deposits equal to a multiple of its reserves. In fact, a first approximation of the relationship between reserves and deposits can be obtained from the formula

$$DD = R \times (1/r_{DD}) \tag{10.1}$$

where DD = demand deposits, R = reserves, and r_{DD} = the ratio of reserves to demand deposits.[1] (This formula is basic to the entire chapter

---

[1] Uppercase letters are used to connote absolute values, while lowercase letters represent ratios.

and should be memorized as well as understood.) The fraction $1/r_{DD}$ is the simplest expression of the **deposit multiplier.**

The **deposit multiplier** refers to the number by which reserves are multiplied in order to calculate total demand deposits.

Substituting numbers for the letters, we have $\$10{,}000 = \$1{,}000 \times 1/.10$.[2]

In passing, it should be noted that it will often be convenient to deal with changes in the variables rather than with their absolute values. In that case equation 10.1 is modified so that the change in demand deposits ($\triangle DD$) is equal to the change in reserves ($\triangle R$) times the deposit multiplier. Thus,

$$\triangle DD = \triangle R \, (1/r_{DD}) \tag{10.2}$$

□ A Multiple-Bank Banking System

Now drop all the assumptions of specie reserves, a voluntary reserve ratio, and a monopoly bank that were maintained to keep the analysis simple. Instead, (1) realize that the reserves that banks maintain are primarily deposits with their regional Reserve banks; (2) the percentage that the banks are required to hold are set by the Federal Reserve Board within certain statutory limits; and (3) most banks, certainly the larger ones, cannot assume monopoly status. Their depositors, not only the large corporate accounts but even most consumers, can select from among a variety of banks.

The simplest, though still extreme, case involves an assumption that is nearly the reverse of the monopoly bank case. In that example, it was assumed that virtually no funds would leave the bank because no alternative depository institutions existed. Now it will be assumed that each bank works under the assumption that *all* created funds will leave the bank. (The truth, of course, lies at neither extreme.) Follow the implications of this set of assumptions.

Begin with an initial deposit of $\$1{,}000$ by Joel. The T-account of the First National Bank of Sharon will appear as follows:

First National Bank of Sharon

Reserves	$1,000	Demand deposit (J)	$1,000
Total assets	$1,000	Total liabilities	$1,000

---

[2]Using this formula, you can see why money creation cannot take place in the absence of fractional-reserve banking. If the bank kept backing on a dollar-for-dollar basis, r_{DD} would equal 100% or 1, and $1/r_{DD} = 1$, so that DD = R. You should also be able to work out the relationship between different r_{DD}'s and DD, a subject that is taken up in Chapter 13.

The steps used in calculating the solution are as follows:

$$\frac{1}{.1} = \frac{1}{1/10} = 1 \times \frac{10}{1} = 10$$

Assume that the bank must adhere to a 10 percent reserve requirement ratio (r_{DD}). Then the bank's portfolio manager must maintain only $100 as the required reserve against the demand deposit (R_r); the remaining $900 are excess reserves (R_x). The T-account can be rewritten, using the subcategories in lieu of the totals. Thus,

First National Bank of Sharon

Reserves, required	$ 100	Demand deposit (Joel)	$1,000
Reserves, excess	900		
Total assets	$1,000	Total liabilities	$1,000

If the bankers decide to invest $900 in school board bonds or to lend $900 to Andrea, deposit creation occurs. Suppose they make the loan. Andrea's account with First National is credited with $900, and the bank's assets rise correspondingly. The new T-account will look like this:

First National Bank of Sharon

Reserves, required[3]	$ 100	Demand deposit (Joel)	$1,000
Reserves, excess	900	Demand deposit (Andrea)	900
Earning assets	900		
Total assets	$1,900	Total liabilities	$1,900

From even a cursory glance at the last T-account, it is evident that the First National Bank of Sharon has created money. The bank began with deposits of $1,000; it now reports $1,900. The extra $900 is created money. Again, the fractional reserve system is at work.

What happens now? Borrowers like Andrea do not borrow and pay interest in order to let their funds sit idle. Andrea may have wanted the $900 to finance the vacation at Michael's Lodge that she has long been promising herself. She writes a check to Michael, who deposits it in his bank account, which may well be in the Second National Bank of Sharon. (Can you set up the T-account for the First National Bank if Michael maintains his account there too?) In Second National, Michael's account is credited with $900, and the check becomes a "cash item in the process of collection." It will be cleared in the course of the day, and the $900 will be credited to the bank's reserve account at the regional Federal Reserve bank. Simultaneously, the Federal Reserve bank clerks will debit First National for the $900. The entire process is sketched out in Figure 10.2. When the process is complete, Andrea is no longer the owner of a $900 checking balance—she has spent it—and First National no longer owns any excess reserves—it has used the reserves to honor Andrea's check. First National T-account is stripped down:

---

[3] Actually, required reserves should rise to $190 and excess reserves should be reduced to $810. Ignore this apparent error; it will prove to be self-correcting.

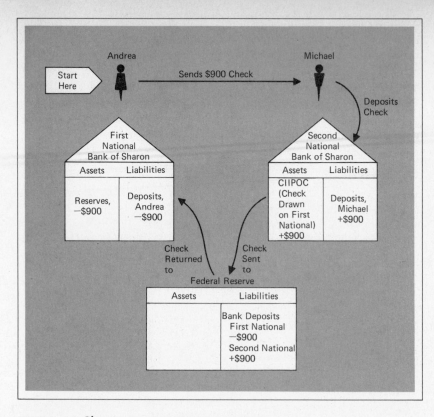

FIGURE 10.2 Clearing in a contemporary setting.

First National Bank of Sharon			
Reserves, required	$ 100	Demand deposit (Joel)	$1,000
Earning assets	900		
Total assets	$1,000	Total liabilities	$1,000

The reserve requirement ratio of 10 percent has been met and Andrea's loan still stands, to be paid when it is due. First National Bank cannot make any further loans or investments unless new deposits flow in or until Andrea pays her debt. The bank is "loaned up" for now.

What about the situation in the Second National Bank of Sharon? Its T-account will indicate that the bank has credited Michael with $900 and has in turn been credited by the Federal Reserve bank with $900 added to its reserve account. Given the 10 percent reserve requirement, only $90 must be maintained as required reserves. The remaining $810 is excess reserves. The Second National's T-account reads as follows:

Second National Bank of Sharon

Reserves, required	$ 90	Demand deposit (Michael)	$900
Reserves, excess	810		
Total assets	$900	Total liabilities	$900

The managers of Second National can now consider acquiring earning assets the same way First National did. So when Helen comes in and asks for an $810 loan to buy a very used car and her credit standing is good, the banker is able to grant the loan. Again, with the signing of the loan agreement a simultaneous set of obligations is created: Helen owes Second National $810 and interest, and Second National will honor up to $810 in checks written by Helen against her account. The T-account looks like this:

Second National Bank of Sharon

Reserves, required	$ 90	Demand deposit (Michael)	$ 900
Reserves, excess	810	Demand deposit (Helen)	810
Earning assets	810		
Total assets	$1,710	Total liabilities	$1,710

When this latest T-account is compared to the one immediately preceding it, it is apparent that $810 in new deposits, or new money, has been created.

The process does not end here. Helen buys the car for $810 and pays by check; the check is made out to Honest Julius, the used-car dealer. Honest Julius, who uses the Third National Bank of Sharon, deposits the check there, and the check is cleared back to Second National. Second National loses its excess reserves, which are now credited to Third National, and consequently no longer owes Helen $810. By honoring and paying Helen's check, Second National terminates its liability to Helen. The T-accounts of both banks now appear as follows:

Second National Bank of Sharon

Reserves, required	$ 90	Demand deposit (Michael)	$900
Earning assets	810		
Total assets	$900	Total liabilities	$900

Third National Bank of Sharon

| Reserves | $810 | Demand deposit (Honest Julius) | $810 |
| Total assets | $810 | Total liabilities | $810 |

Second National Bank is loaned up, while Third National is rarin' to go.

Third National also operates on fractional reserves, so it too will be able to divide its reserves into required and excess reserves. The bank will be able to create additional deposits and acquire new earning assets. On the basis of the two previous examples, you should now be able to fill in the two remaining T-accounts for Third National: (1) the position after new deposits have been created but prior to the borrower's spending the funds, and (2) the "loaned-up" position. Try it.

Of course, deposit creation does not end with the third bank. Table 10.1 works out a number of additional stages and then sums up the totals. Figure 10.3 presents the information in the form of a bar graph.

Study the table and the graph, and you'll notice the following:

1. New deposits in any bank (except the first) will always equal the earning assets of the previous bank. You have already learned that the earning assets of a bank are equal to its excess reserves, which are lost in the clearing process.
2. The amount of deposits created at each particular stage is less than the amount created in each earlier stage.
3. Banks are "loaned up" when all excess reserves disappear. Then all the reserves in the banks are required reserves.
4. When the deposits, reserves, and earning assets are totaled for all banks, the sums are identical with the totals for the monopoly bank case, when Mono Bank is "loaned up." In other words, *for the banking system as a whole, equation 10.1 holds true:*

$$DD = R \times (1/r_{DD})$$

Excess reserves are, as you have seen, the fundamental building blocks on which deposit creation rests. When a banker lends or invests, deposits

TABLE 10.1 The Expansion of Deposits in a Multibank Banking System: Summary Data[a]

Bank	Demand deposits	Required reserves	Earning assets	Cumulative deposits
First National	$1,000.00	$100.00	$900.00	$1,000.00
Second National	900.00	90.00	810.00	1,900.00
Third National	810.00	81.00	729.00	2,629.00
Fourth National	729.00	72.90	656.10	3,358.00
Fifth National	656.10	65.61	590.49	4,014.10
Sixth National	590.49	59.05	531.44	4,604.59
Seventh National	531.44	53.14	478.30	5,136.03
Eighth National	478.30	47.83	430.47	5,614.33
Ninth National	430.47	43.05	387.42	6,044.80
Tenth National	387.42	38.74	348.68	6,432.22
⋮	⋮	⋮	⋮	⋮
Totals	$10,000.00	$1,000.00	$9,000.00	

[a]Note: The numbers are predicated on the existence of $1,000 in reserves (= initial deposits) and a required reserve ratio of 10 percent.

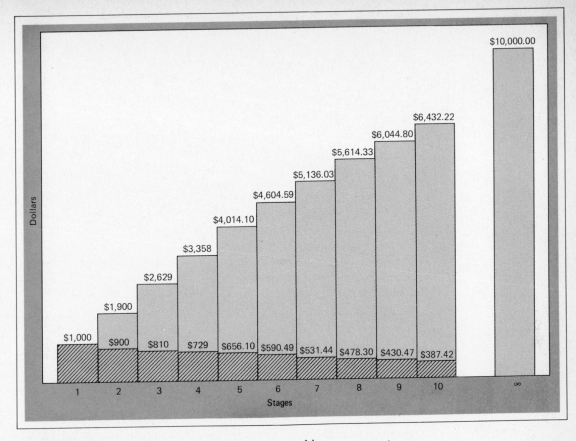

FIGURE 10.3 Deposit expansion, by stages. (Note: Striated boxes represent deposit creation by each bank; shaded boxes are added to show the cumulative totals.)

are created. Some of these deposits will flow out of the bank permanently; the borrowers write checks in payment for goods and services and the recipients of the checks bank elsewhere. The banker must be able to honor the demands for payment coming through the clearing process, and can do so with the excess reserves held in the bank's asset portfolio.[4] It follows that the greater the amount of excess reserves available, the greater the ability of the banker to create deposits. But as more deposits are created, the amount of reserves that is sterilized in the form of required reserves also rises. Given a finite amount of total reserves— $1,000 in the example—the greater the amount used up as required reserves, the smaller the amount available as excess reserves. Conse-

---

[4]In Chapter 7 it was pointed out that alternative means of meeting adverse clearing balances do exist; both asset and liability management strategies were reviewed. The discussion here obviously simplifies.

quently, fewer additional deposits will be created at each successive stage of the process. When excess reserves disappear—and that happens when all available reserves have become required reserves—then deposit creation must cease. In the example just used, when deposits reach $10,000, the entire $1,000 in reserves are required to meet the 10 percent legal requirement; the maximum amount of deposits that can be supported by the $1,000 in reserves has been reached.

You may wonder what might happen if a bank lent out or invested a sum greater than its excess reserves. If it can be assumed for the present that there is no resale market for the banker's assets and there is no way to borrow reserves, then the bank will end up in a state of insolvency. The banker will be unable to meet the legal obligation to pay off demand deposits at the will of the depositor.

Consider the following for instance. What would have happened if the First National Bank of Sharon's officers had decided to act as if their bank were a monopoly bank? Instead of lending out $900 upon the receipt of a $1,000 inflow, they might have decided to lend out $9,000. The T-account would then be as follows:

First National Bank of Sharon

Reserves, required	$ 1,000	Initial deposit	$ 1,000
Earning assets	9,000	New, created deposits	$ 9,000
Total assets	$10,000	Total liabilities	$10,000

Assume now that one of the borrowers paid $2,000 to Joseph, who banks at Second National. The check is deposited and cleared through to First National, which must pay the $2,000 from its reserve account. But the reserve account holds only $1,000!

Bankers try to avoid such situations. They try to estimate their reserve needs and keep a corresponding amount on hand. Consequently, the availability of excess reserves does serve as a constraint on the volume of deposit creation. True, banks can borrow and can sell secondary reserves to offset adverse clearing balances. This complicates but does not destroy the essential truth of the example.

While it is obvious that no single bank operating in a multibank banking system can act as if it were a monopoly, the banking system as a whole does possess monopoly features. Reserves flow from one bank to another, but they tend to remain within the banking system. Certainly this occurred in the case just examined. One bank's excess reserves provided the deposit-creating sustenance for a second bank. Is it really surprising, then, that when the banking system is viewed as a single entity, deposit creation is identical with the monopoly case? The formula $DD = R\,(1/r_{DD})$ serves equally well for the banking system as a whole as it does for the monopoly bank. The deposit-creating power of a single bank is limited by its excess reserves. For the banking system as a whole as for the monopoly bank, the limit is total reserves rather than excess reserves.

☐ The Destruction of Deposits

The obverse of the coin of deposit creation is deposit destruction. Just as new deposits and new reserves lead to the creation of additional deposits many times over, so, too, will the elimination of reserves and deposits lead to a multiplied reduction in deposits. The formula for deposit creation can take a negative sign as well as a positive one; $-\triangle R$ can be substituted for $\triangle R$ to yield:

$$-\triangle DD = -\triangle R \, (1/r_{DD}) \tag{10.3}$$

When loans are paid off, deposits are destroyed. Similarly, when investments mature and are redeemed by the issuer, somewhere in the system deposits are destroyed. Consider Andrea, who had borrowed $900 and paid for a vacation trip. Months have passed and the loan has matured; the day of reckoning has arrived. Andrea takes her paycheck, drawn by her employer, who banks at the Eleventh National Bank of Sharon, and endorses it to the First National Bank. The check is cleared; Eleventh National loses $900 in reserves while First National gains $900. At First National the loan obligation is canceled, leading to the following sets of T-accounts:

Before:

First National Bank of Sharon

Reserves, required	$ 100	Demand deposits	$1,000
Earning assets	900		
Total assets	$1,000	Total liabilities	$1,000

Eleventh National Bank of Sharon

Reserves, required	$ 90	Demand deposits	$900
Reserves, excess	810		
Total assets	$900	Total liabilities	$900

After:

First National Bank of Sharon

Reserves, required	$ 100	Demand deposits	$1,000
Reserves, excess	900		
Total assets	$1,000	Total liabilities	$1,000

Eleventh National Bank of Sharon

Reserves, required	$0	Demand deposits	$0
Reserves, excess	0		
Total assets	$0	Total liabilities	$0

Notice that, with the paying off of the loan of $900, the banking system loses $900 in deposits. What does *not* change is the total reserves of the banking system; the excess reserves are transfered, moving from Eleventh National to First National. Thus, First National can lend to someone else or purchase securities, and the deposit total will increase to its earlier level. Nevertheless—and this is the point—the reduction of the banking system's earning assets will be accompanied by a destruction of deposits.

The results would be different if the banking system experienced a net loss of reserves. Assume that somehow the initial $1,000 is removed from the banking system. (How this can occur is explained in Chapter 13.) Imagine that the initial deposit of $1,000 disappeared; the first depositor wrote a check, which now has to be honored by the First National. Refer back to the T-account on page 230. You will notice that the bank, being loaned up, held no excess reserves to honor the check. To be sure, the bank did maintain $100 in required reserves, which would no longer be necessary when the $1,000 deposit flowed out of the bank. But where would the remaining $900 come from?

You realize, of course, that it is in anticipation of such events that bank portfolios contain secondary reserves. The portfolio manager sells some of those secondary reserves—$900 worth, to be exact. This sale on the bond market will bring in the needed $900. First National Bank's deposit liabilities and its assets both decline by $1,000.

But where did the $900 received by First National come from? Presumably, some depositor in another bank—say, the Second National Bank of Sharon—thought the asset sold by First National was priced sufficiently low to warrant its acquisition. So that person wrote a check on his account at Second National, payable to First National. In other words, First National collects from Second National.

Now, how does Second National pay the check? Recall the T-account of Second National as it appeared on page 231; it contained $900 in deposits, balanced on the asset side by $90 in required reserves and $810 in earning assets. At this stage, then, First National will have seen its deposits fall by $1,000 and Second National's will have decreased by $900. This process will continue until $10,000 in deposits have been extinguished. At that point required reserves will have declined by $1,000, corresponding to the initial $1,000 loss in reserves. Or, in terms of equation 10.3: $-\$10,000 = -\$1,000(1/.10)$.

☐ Leakages

A number of simplifications were, of necessity, made in order to bring to the fore the essence of deposit creation and destruction. As you know, the real world rarely corresponds to the abstract, simplified world of theory. The time has come to drop some of the assumptions made earlier in order to better approximate reality.

In essence the complexity of deposit creation derives from a variety of sources. Deposits are not uniform. The example has been framed in terms of demand deposits, but commercial banks hold time deposit accounts too. Nor do banks adhere rigidly to a given reserve requirement; they can borrow reserves or willingly maintain excess reserves. Nor does the public necessarily hold all of its money in deposit form; cash is an acceptable, and in some cases superior substitute. Each of these variations gives rise to **leakages** from the maximum deposit formula specified earlier.

Leakages refer to elements that lead to a reduction in the value of the demand deposit multiplier.

Cash leakage

Deposit creation by any bank depends on obtaining excess reserves. Normally, the reserves will accrue to a commercial bank as the bank's customers deposit checks drawn on other banks. However, if the depositors fail to deposit the entire sum received and take out some cash instead, the receiving bank will obtain fewer dollars in deposits and, hence, fewer excess reserves. The chain of deposit creation will be forced to contract.

Thus, if Michael had cashed the entire $900 received from Andrea, the Second National Bank would not have obtained any new deposits or reserves. The chain of deposit creation would have ended right there. Had Michael deposited only half of the $900 received, then, obviously, additional deposits could have been created, but in a smaller volume. The critical variable turns out to be the relationship between currency held by the public and the public's demand deposits. *The higher the ratio of currency to demand deposits, the smaller the deposit multiplier.* (The proof will be found in the appendix to this chapter.)

The currency:deposit ratio is not constant. It varies with the season, the phase of the business cycle, and the stage of the economy's secular progress, and for other reasons as well. At the year-end holiday gift-buying time, the cash:deposit ratio increases, falling again after the new year begins. Table 10.2 lists some cash:deposit ratios for recent Decembers and Januarys.

Similarly, the cash:deposit ratio fluctuates with business activity. As sales boom, the public's demand for currency relative to demand deposits is likely to rise; the opposite tends to occur when the economy undergoes

TABLE 10.2 Cash:Deposit Ratios,
Selected Months and Years

December 1976	0.355
January 1977	0.349
December 1977	0.366
January 1978	0.358
December 1978	0.380
January 1979	0.379
December 1979	0.399
January 1980	0.393

a recession. And in general, as the economy grows secularly over long periods, the cash ratio can be expected to decline. Recent history, however, as depicted in Figure 10.4, appears to contradict these assertions.

The darkened-in areas in the diagram are business cycle recessions. In all three of the most recent recessions, the cash:deposit ratio rose, moving

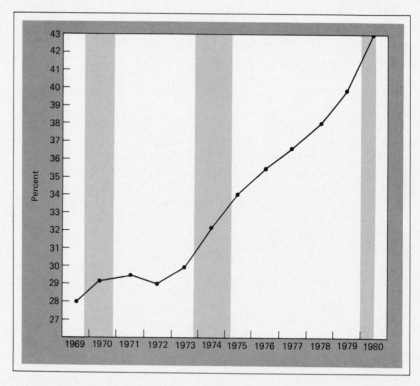

FIGURE 10.4 Cash: deposit ratios, Decembers 1969–1980. (Note: Shaded areas represent business cycle contractions as dated by the National Bureau of Economic Research.)

in the direction opposite to that predicted. During the expansion that ended the decade as well as the one that began in 1974, the ratio did rise as expected, but in the 1970–1972 expansion the ratio fell and then rose. Moreover, since 1967 the basic pattern has been an upward one, in contrast to the predicted downward movement.

It may be that the growth of illegal activities like gambling and the narcotics trade, in which transactions are not normally conducted by check, account for the rising trend. The expansion of the "underground" economy of unreported (for tax purposes) activities is another possible cause. The declining importance of demand deposits as account owners switched into time deposits (reducing the denominator of the cash:deposit ratio) must be reckoned with as well. No completely satisfactory answer has been provided as yet.

Nevertheless, it is evident that the currency:deposit ratio cannot be considered a constant; it varies for a number of reasons.

Leakages due to excess reserves; borrowed reserves

When banks maintain excess reserves voluntarily, not all of the excess reserves that flow into a bank will be available to acquire earning assets. If the bankers believe that secondary reserve protection in the form of excess reserves is required, then in addition to the reserves maintained by the bankers to meet the mandate of the Federal Reserve, the bank's portfolio will include these extra excess reserves. Returning to the example used earlier, the $900 in excess reserves of the First National enabled the bank to acquire $900 in new earning assets, for as the adverse clearing balance of $900 was experienced, the bank paid out its $900 from this excess reserve account. However, if the banker wished to maintain excess reserves of, say, $90, then she would be wise to lend or invest and thus create deposits of only $810. Then the demand for reserves arising from the deposit outflow would total only $810, leaving the banker with the $90 in excess reserves that she planned to hold. So, should the initial depositor wish to withdraw some of the initial deposit, the bank would have some excess reserves available to meet this demand. If many bankers acted in this manner, significantly fewer deposits would be created.

As a matter of fact, the percentage of excess reserves held by banks is not large. The Federal funds market provides such an attractive outlet for excess reserves that few bankers will willingly retain such zero-earning assets. In fact, the large trade in Federal funds suggests that many banks do not even maintain all their required reserves from their own funds. They may well use almost all of their available funds, including those in the required-reserve category, and if they are caught short, borrow the shortfall. Thus, the banker might very well lend out $950 instead of $900, counting on borrowed funds to meet any adverse outflow that might occur. Then, instead of a leakage, deposits will be created in larger amounts than calculated on the basis of the formula. (Excess reserves and borrowings are analyzed more formally in the appendix to this chapter.)

The time deposit leakage

As you know from your own experience, depositors do not place all the checks they receive into demand deposits. They do maintain time or savings deposits and, as the data in Chapter 6 indicated, have done so in ever-increasing proportions. Time deposits pay interest, demand deposits do not. But, of course, each dollar that is removed from a demand deposit account and placed in a time deposit account means fewer demand deposits. Thus, like the currency leakage, the time deposit leakage reduces the sum of demand deposits created. However, in one way the time deposit leakage differs from the cash leakage: Cash flows out of the banking system, whereas time deposit accounts remain in the system. True, M-1, which includes demand deposits and currency, will be reduced by a shift from demand to time deposits, but M-2, which adds time deposits to the M-1 total, will increase. (Consult the appendix for further elucidation.)

The presence of leakages makes multiplier calculation more difficult than the fraction $1/r_{DD}$ implies. As mentioned in connection with the cash leakage, the ratio of cash to deposits is not constant. But neither are ratios connected with excess reserves, borrowings, or time deposits. Each variable responds to economic forces like the stage of the business cycle and interest rates. Precision in multiplier forecasting requires substantial knowledge about a variety of relationships.

☐ Other Complications

Aside from the calculation of the aforementioned leakages, a number of other problems complicate the numerical derivation of the multiplier and, thus, the derivation of demand deposits and money supply. These problems are caused by the existence of differential reserve requirements and, in the past, by the presence of nonmember banks. As will be made more specific in Chapter 13, reserve requirements are levied on the basis of a bank's deposit size. The lowest requirement at the close of 1980 was 3 percent for a bank with checking deposits of $25 million or less. On the other hand, banks maintaining demand deposits in excess of $25 million were required to hold 12 percent of all deposits exceeding that sum in reserves. Thus, shifts in the deposit flow from smaller to larger banks or vice versa imprison or release excess reserves and thereby affect deposit creation. If, for example, a depositor in a giant bank paid a $100,000 invoice by a check that was deposited by the recipient company in a small bank, the large bank's required reserve would fall by $12,000 while the small bank's required reserve would increase by only $3,000. The net result of this deposit shift is a freeing of $9,000 in reserves—they become excess reserves—and, thus, potential for deposit creation.

The same thing occurred when funds flowed between member and nonmember banks. Before late 1980, nonmember banks were not required to adhere to Federal Reserve regulations; they were subject to the statutes of the state in which they were chartered. Some states, such as New York and Missouri, require relatively high reserve ratios; others, such as Ohio and West Virginia, maintain low reserve requirements. Illinois has no reserve requirement at all. And even in states where high requirements are imposed, the reserves may frequently be held in the form of investments. Thus, a shift of deposits from member to nonmember banks freed reserves, while a reverse shift tended to freeze reserves.

☐ Concluding Comments

In short, the multiplier fraction, $1/r_{DD}$, developed in this chapter is hardly more than a first approximation to a description of the relationship between reserves and demand deposits. The deposit multiplier indicates that commercial banks have the power to create and destroy demand deposits, the major component of the nation's money supply. This power, however, is shared with others. The multiplier's value depends on leakages, which themselves hinge on various forces that are not directly subject to banker control. How the public reacts to shifts in the economy, interest rates, changes in life style, and the like also affects the deposit multiplier. Furthermore, the supply of deposits depends on the reserves available to the banking system, and the creation of reserves is normally beyond the ability of the banking system.

A fitting conclusion to this chapter is to examine the deposit multiplier. More useful, however, is to scan movements of the *money multiplier*, which includes both demand deposits and currency and relates them to reserves.[5] Despite relatively infrequent changes in the required reserve ratio, the money multiplier has had its ups and downs (see Figure 10.5), averaging over a 3½ percent[6] change each year for the 1971–1980 period. The diagram indicates a declining trend and no cyclical pattern is discernible. Nevertheless, some economists have been able to devise

---

[5]The deposit multiplier discussed in this chapter is far too simple an approximation to warrant further investigation. Even the more complicated fractions presented in the appendix are less than optimal. The money multiplier is plotted indirectly by using a variation of DD/R, which equals $1/r_{DD}$. The specific formula used is $m^* = $ M-1A/(C + R), where C = currency in the hands of the public and all other letters stand for the appropriate variables mentioned in the body of the chapter.

[6]This average disregards signs. Only the absolute changes are considered.

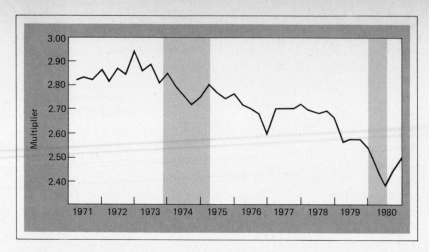

FIGURE 10.5 The Money Multiplier, 1971–1980. (Note: Shaded areas represent business cycle contractions as dated by the National Bureau of Economic Research.)

equations that predict movements in the money multiplier with a modest degree of success.[7] So, despite the inherent difficulty of calculating the multiplier, a factor that complicates the process of monetary control, some headway has already been made and surely will continue into the future.

☐ Summary

Deposit creation fundamentally depends on fractional reserve banking, which itself hinges on the belief that depositors will not withdraw all their deposits at once.

When a monopoly bank exists and when the banker need not be concerned about deposit losses to rival banks, but is subject to a reserve requirement, the monopoly banker's ability to expand deposits is limited by the bank's available reserves. The volume of deposits supported by the monopoly bank's reserves is derived by the formula $DD = R(1/r_{DD})$. The monopoly banker can create deposits in excess of the bank's reserve assets.

When many banks compete for deposits, each banker must assume that deposits will flow out to other banks. Consequently, each banker will limit the deposits created in the lending-investment process to an amount no greater than the bank's excess reserves. Deposit creation will take

[7]See A. B. Balback, "How Controllable is Money Growth?" Federal Reserve Bank of St. Louis, *Review* 63 (April, 1981): 3–13. A more advanced treatment may be found in J. M. Johannes and R. H. Rasche, "Predicting the Money Multiplier," *Journal of Monetary Economics* 5, (July, 1979): 301–325.

place, but in contrast to the monopoly banker, each individual banker will create deposits equal to a fraction of the bank's initial deposits.

Nevertheless, when the deposits created by each banker are totaled, the sum will be a positive multiple identical to that of the monopoly banker. For the banking system as a whole, $DD = R(1/r_{DD})$.

The addition of new reserves to the banking system will lead to the creation of new deposits through the multiplier process. Similarly, a reduction of reserves leads to the multiplier's working in reverse; a multiple volume of deposits will be destroyed.

Because of such leakages as public demands for cash and time deposits and bank demands for excess or borrowed reserves, the deposit multiplier will be a more complex fraction and, in fact, lower than the value of the reciprocal of the reserve ratio.

The unpredictability of the money multiplier (the deposit multiplier adjusted for public cash holdings) complicates monetary control. The Federal Reserve's ability to forecast the next period's money supply is compromised, and its power to maintain money supply growth within its target range is weakened. Nevertheless, monetary economists today understand the working of the money multiplier more clearly and are devoting a good deal of effort to increasing the forecasting accuracy of the Federal Reserve.

☐ Questions and Exercises

1. Assume that the required reserve ratio (r_{DD}) equals 5 percent of deposits and that banking system reserves (R) equal $200 million.
   a. Compute the deposit multiplier.
   b. Calculate the total volume of deposits that the banking system can support.
   c. What will be the value of the earning assets of the banking system?
2. Using the initial data given in question 1, calculate the values of (a), (b), and (c) if the banking system consisted of only one bank. What conclusions could you draw upon comparing these two sets of results?
3. It seems strange that if the public decides to increase its cash holdings, which, of course, means their holdings of money, the total money supply will decline. Explain this anomaly.
4. Bankers claim that they cannot create money; that is the prerogative of the government. How would you explain to a banker that in fact the banking community is a far more important element in the money creation process than the government?

☐ For Further Study

All of the research on the multiplier works with the equations developed in the appendix to this chapter. Notable among them are Albert E. Burger, *The Money Supply Process* (Belmont, Calif.: Wadsworth, 1971), and Jerry L. Jordan, "Elements of Money Stock Determination," Federal Reserve Bank of St. Louis, *Review* 51 (October, 1969). Whether multiplier changes offset actions of the monetary authorities is dealt with by W. R. Hosek, "Determinants of the Money Multiplier," *Quarterly Review of Economics and Business* 10 (Summer, 1970): 37–46. J. Prager uses indifference curve analysis in "Portfolio Analysis and the Money Multiplier," in J. Prager, ed., *Monetary Economics: Controversies in Theory and Policy* (New York: Random House, 1971), pp. 37–44.

While the Federal Reserve Bank of Chicago's *Modern Money Mechanics: A Workbook on Deposits, Currency, and Bank Reserves* (Chicago, 1975) is out of date, it is nevertheless a useful and detailed introduction, at an elementary level, to the material covered in this chapter as well as to some of the information discussed in Chapters 12 and 13.

APPENDIX Multiplier Fractions

The multiplier fraction found in the chapter was predicated on the assumption that the only leakage from the deposit-creating stream was the reserve requirement. And although other leakages were discussed in a qualitative manner, no attempt was made to modify the multiplier fraction appropriately. This appendix remedies that deficiency. The multiplier fractions are expanded, and their implications for deposit and money creation are discussed.

As an introduction to these expanded fractions, it will be fruitful to rewrite and explain the simple deposit-creation formula:

$$DD = R \ (1/r_{DD}) \tag{10A.1}$$

Multiplying both sides of the equation by r_{DD} leads to

$$r_{DD} \ DD = R \tag{10A.2}$$

When $r_{DD} = 10$ percent and $R = \$1,000$, then according to equation 10A.1, $DD = \$10,000$. Rewriting this per equation 10A.2, $(10\%)(\$10,000) = \$1,000$. This last equation can be interpreted to mean that all available reserves—the initial \$1,000—are utilized as required reserves, the product of the two terms on the left side. The 10 percent reserve requirement imposed against the \$10,000 in demand deposits means that \$1,000 will be needed as required reserves. Thus, deposit expansion ceases when all available reserves become required reserves.

Introducing currency

The public holds currency in addition to maintaining demand deposit accounts. Decisions to hold currency rather than demand deposits affect the amount of demand deposits that can be created from any given amount of reserves. In terms of equation 10A.1, the deposit multiplier is the variable that will be forced to adjust to changes in the public's desire to hold or not hold currency. How, precisely, does this happen?

Assume that the public wishes to hold a constant proportion of currency in relation to demand deposits, say, 10 percent. Define then:

$$c = C/DD = 10\% \tag{10A.3}$$

where C stands for currency and DD, as usual, for demand deposits.

One additional tidbit of information is still needed. Under the present banking system, currency can be converted into reserves by the commercial banks. Banks, when collecting cash in the normal course of business, often find themselves with surplus currency on their hands. They can ship this excess currency to the Federal Reserve bank in their region, whereupon the banks' reserve accounts will be credited with the full value of the currency deposit. Conversely, should member banks require currency to meet customer cash needs, the Federal Reserve will deliver the required amount to the banks and deduct an identical sum from the banks' reserve balance. Thus, currency and reserves are exchangeable on a dollar-for-dollar basis and, therefore, must be treated as analytically similar. It follows that R alone cannot fully represent the deposit-creating base of the banking system. C, too, has potential deposit-creating power.

Add, then, currency to reserves, and the result is a concept known as **high-powered money** or the **monetary base**:

High-powered money or the **monetary base** equals bank reserves plus currency in the hands of the public.

$$H = R + C \tag{10A.4}$$

where H is high-powered money, R is the reserves of the banking system, and C is the currency held by the public. A multiplier formula including cash can now be developed.

Deposits will have expanded to their maximum when, as equation 10A.2 showed, $R = r_{DD}$ DD. In addition, in stating that $c = C/DD$ equation 10A.3 implied that $C = cDD$ (10A.3'). Substituting both of the right-hand expressions into equation 10A.4 results in

$$H = r_{DD} \, DD + cDD \tag{10A.5}$$

Factoring out the DD term leads to

$$H = DD(r_{DD} + c) \tag{10A.6}$$

Solving for DD by multiplying both sides by $\dfrac{1}{r_{DD} + c}$ yields

$$DD = H\left(\frac{1}{r_{DD} + c}\right) \tag{10A.7}$$

The amount of deposits will increase to the point at which they equal high-powered money times the deposit multiplier, which in this instance equals

$$\mu = \frac{1}{r_{DD} + c} \tag{10A.7'}$$

To derive M-1 from this relationship, recall that M-1 = DD + C and, according to equation 10A.3', C = cDD. Consequently,

$$\text{M-1} = DD + cDD = DD(1 + c) \tag{10A.8}$$

Relate equation 10A.8 to equation 10A.7 to derive the following:

$$\text{M-1} = DD(1 + c) = H\left(\frac{1}{r_{DD} + c}\right)(1 + c) = H\frac{(1 + c)}{r_{DD} + c} \tag{10A.9}$$

Put these algebraic formulas to work by substituting some numbers for the symbols. Assume that $H = \$1000$, $r_{DD} = 10\%$, and $c = 10\%$. Then, the demand deposits supported by H, according to equation 10A.7, equal $\$1000 \, (1/.1 + .1) = \$1000 \, (1/.2) = \$1000(5) = \$5000$. Five thousand dollars can be created from a monetary base of $1000.

Now take a look at the banking system's T-account:

The Banking System

Reserves, required (R_r)	$ 500	Demand deposits	$5000
Earning assets (EA)	4500		
Total assets	$5000	Total liabilities	$5000

With deposits of $5000 and a 10 percent reserve requirement, the amount of required reserves equals $500, leaving the remainder of the asset side, $4500, to be employed as earning assets.

In addition to the $5000 held by the public in the form of demand deposits, the public also wished to hold 10 percent of its deposits in the form of currency. Ten percent of $5000 comes to $500, which will be held by the public outside of the banking system. All the high-powered money has now been accounted for: $500 is in the banking system as required reserves and the remaining $500 is currency held by the public.

What about M-1? Since DD = $5000 and C = $500, then M-1 = $5500. This can also be derived from equation 10A.9: M-1 = $1000 (1.1/.2) = $5500.

Compare this result with the example in the chapter. You'll notice that in the present case demand deposits are substantially lower than in the earlier case. The public's removal of funds from the banking system has prevented the system from creating still more deposits. Should the public decide to get rid of currency by depositing it in banking institutions, then C and c would fall to zero and the deposit-creating equation would revert to equation 10A.1: DD = $R(1/r_{DD})$. Then the $1000 in high-powered money would again support $10,000 in deposits.

Excess reserves or borrowed reserves

Assume that the portfolio managers of the banking system decide to keep 5 percent of their demand deposit liabilities in the form of desired excess reserves. Define:

$$e = R_x^d/DD = 5\% \tag{10A.10}$$

where R_x^d is the absolute amount of excess reserves that bankers wish to hold. Following the algebra used in the previous section, equation 10A.5 can be expanded to

$$H = r_{DD} \, DD + cDD + eDD \tag{10A.11}$$

Factoring out DD yields

$$H = DD \, (r_{DD} + c + e) \tag{10A.12}$$

Solving for DD gives

$$DD = H \left(\frac{1}{r_{DD} + c + e} \right) \tag{10A.13}$$

The demand deposit multiplier, the last term of the equation, is, of course,

$$\frac{1}{r_{DD} + c + e}$$

Employing the values for H, r_{DD}, and c that were used earlier,

$$DD = \$1000 \left(\frac{1}{.1 + .1 + .05}\right) = \$100 \, (1/.25) = \$4000$$

Solving now for the remainder of the balance sheet entries, where R_r is the dollar amount of required reserves, R_x^d is as defined above, EA is earning assets, and R is total reserves held by the banks:

$$R_r = (.1)(\$4000) = \$400$$

$$R_x^d = (.05)(\$4000) = \$200$$

$$EA = DD - R = \$4000 - \$600 = \$3,400$$

The balance sheet can then be set up as follows:

The Banking System

Reserves, required	$ 400	Demand deposits	$4000
Reserves, desired excess	200		
Earning assets	3400		
Total assets	$4000	Total liabilities	$4000

Held outside of the banking system is the public's currency, which equals (.1)(4000), or $400. M-1 will then equal $4400.

If bankers decide to act as net borrowers rather than as holders of excess reserves, then instead of the leakage just worked out, reserve balances will be inflated, leading to a larger volume of deposit and money supply. Let

$$b = B^d/DD = 5\% \qquad (10A.14)$$

where B^d stands for the absolute amount of desired borrowings. Then

$$H + B^d = r_{DD} \, DD + cDD \qquad (10A.15)$$

Borrowing reserves increases the high-powered money available to the banking system; it is added to H. Bringing B^d over to the right and substituting bDD, the outcome is

$$H = r_{DD} \, DD + cDD - bDD \qquad (10A.16)$$

Then

$$H = DD(r_{DD} + c - b) \qquad (10A.17)$$

and solving for DD leads to

$$DD = H\left(\frac{1}{r_{DD} + c - b}\right) \qquad (10A.18)$$

Borrowing has the precisely opposite effect of maintaining excess reserves. The latter decreases the multiplier; the former increases it.

Again using the same numbers as before,

$$DD = \$1000\left(\frac{1}{.1 + .1 - .05}\right) = \$1000\,(1/.15) = \$6666.67$$

As expected, deposits increase as compared to the immediately preceding case.

Completing the T-account results in the following:

The Banking System

Reserves, required	$ 666.67	Demand deposits	$6666.67
Earning assets	6333.33	Borrowings, desired	333.33
Total assets	$6700.00	Total liabilities	$6700.00

Although the banking system maintains reserves at the required percentage, the borrowing liability indicates that only half of the actual volume of reserves held is derived from the banks' own resources. The other half comes from funds borrowed outside the banking system.

What is M-1? Does $H - B^d = \$1000$? Try it yourself.

Time deposits and the multiplier

The final deposit multiplier fraction and deposit creation equation to be presented here deals with time as well as demand deposits. Time deposits keep reserves within the banking system, but they do represent a diversion away from demand deposits. By law and tradition, the reserve ratio for time deposits is lower than that for demand deposits. Thus, shifts from demand to time deposits free reserves, while shifts in the opposite direction, from time to demand deposits, reduce the banking system's capacity for deposit expansion. The multiplier fraction must reflect these facts.

The reserve ratio against time deposits, r_{TD}, is defined as

$$r_{TD} = R_{TD}/TD \qquad (10A.19)$$

or the absolute amount of reserves that must be held against time deposits divided by time deposit holdings. Set it to equal 5 percent. Further, let the public wish to maintain a ratio of time to demand deposits equal to 300 percent, or

$$t = TD/DD = 3.0 \qquad (10A.20)$$

In other words, for every dollar held in a demand deposit account, the public wishes to hold $3.00 in a time deposit account. Then, following the pattern that is by now familiar,

$$H = r_{DD} DD + r_{TD} TD + cDD + eDD \qquad (10A.21)$$

But since according to equation 10A.20, $TD = tDD$,

$$H = r_{DD} DD + r_{TD}tDD + cDD + eDD \qquad (10A.22)$$

Consolidating terms,

$$H = DD\, (r_{DD} + r_{TD}\, t + c + e) \qquad (10A.23)$$

And, consequently,

$$DD = H\, \left(\frac{1}{r_{DD} + tr_{TD} + c + e} \right) \qquad (10A.24)$$

The deposit multiplier, then, is

$$\mu = \left(\frac{1}{r_{DD} + tr_{TD} + c + e} \right) \qquad (10A.25)$$

This final multiplier fraction is the most inclusive; all the previous formulas can be derived from this fraction by valuing the appropriate terms at zero. And if you wish to memorize one multiplier fraction—it is hoped that you will understand it, too—this is the one.

Notice that in this formulation the second term in the denominator is a product—it equals $t \times r_{TD}$; therefore, special care should be taken in the computation.

Once again a T-account can be set up; the earlier numbers are preserved. With $H = \$1,000$ and $\mu = \dfrac{1}{.1 + (3.00)\,(.05) + .1 + .05}$ then $DD = \$1,000\,(1/.4) = \$1,000\,(2.5) = \$2,500.$

Now, since $TD = 300$ percent of DD, TD must equal \$7,500. The liabilities side of the T-account can then be drawn up:

The Banking System

Demand deposits	\$ 2,500
Time deposits	7,500
Total liabilities	\$10,000

Proceed now to the asset side of the account. Required and desired reserves can be computed from the appropriate relationships. According to equation 10A.2, $R_{DD} = r_{DD} DD = (.10)(\$2,500) = \$250$; according to equation 10A.19, $R_{TD} = r_{TD} TD = (.05)(\$7,500) = \$375$; equation 10A.10 implies that $R_x^d = eDD = (.05)(\$2,500) = \$125$. Total reserves held by the banking system equal $\$250 + \$375 + \$125 = \$750$. Subtracting these reserves from the previously calculated total liabilities leaves the banking system with earning assets of \$9,250. The T-account will then be as follows:

The Banking System

Reserves, required against demand deposits	\$ 250	Demand deposits	\$ 2,500
Reserves, required against time deposits	375	Time deposits	7,500
Reserves, desired excess	125		
Total reserves	\$ 750		
Earning assets	\$ 9,250		
Total assets	\$10,000	Total liabilities	\$10,000

Currency held by the public will equal $(.1)(\$2,500) = \$250$, and H = \$750 + \$250 = \$1,000, so all the high-powered money is accounted for.

In this expanded case, attention need not be limited to the narrow definition of the money supply, M-1. Since time deposits are included, M-2 can be calculated as well. Accordingly, M-1 = \$2,500 + \$250, or \$2,750, while M-2 = \$2,750 + \$7,500 = \$10,250.

Concluding remarks

You should not fall into the trap of memorizing a formula or equation and believing that it describes the real world accurately. As has been noted repeatedly, the value of the deposit multiplier is subject to a variety of economic and noneconomic forces. The assumption of constancy of r_{DD}, r_{TD}, t, c, and e served to facilitate algebraic manipulation. But these fractions are never constants; each is a variable. Thus, it would be more correct to formulate each term in the denominator as an intermediate product, itself related to other variables that underlie it. That, however, would be beyond the scope of this book.[8]

---

[8]If you are interested in exploring this idea further, you might survey John T. Boorman and Thomas M. Havrilesky, *Monetary Macroeconomics* (Arlington Heights, Ill.: AHM, 1978), chaps. 1, 2.

CHAPTER 11

Nonbank Financial Intermediaries

Continued inflation and unprecedented fluctuations in interest rates spelled difficult times for the savings and loan industry, times in which both the number of loans originated and the total earnings of the industry fell substantially. Though no immediate resolution of these problems is in sight, the Bank Board expects that its work in several key areas offers cause for optimism in the long run.

Richard T. Pratt, chairman, Federal Home Loan Bank Board (1981)

CONTENTS

Commercial banks dominate the financial intermediary industry in the United States. This is clearly evident from Table 4.1, which showed that 53 percent of all loans outstanding in 1980 were issued by commercial banks. These department stores of banking are active along a broad financial front, lending to all sectors of the economy. A variety of specialized lending institutions, the nonbank financial intermediaries or NFIs, compete with the commercial banks by concentrating on a narrower segment of the market. Savings banks and savings and loan associations specialize in mortgage loans to homeowners. Consumer finance companies and credit unions are active in the installment sales market. Businesses and government entities also find financing with NFIs. Life insurance companies and pension funds acquire corporate and government debt. Commercial factors lend to business firms against their accounts receivable, while business finance companies support the acquisition and maintenance of business inventory.

This chapter is devoted to an exploration of some of these financial intermediaries. The common thread binding all the NFIs together is the transformation process described at the outset of Chapter 4. NFIs gather funds from the public, providing the suppliers of funds with a relatively liquid asset. They transfer those funds to borrowers, who in exchange give the NFIs a claim for future payment, one that is relatively less liquid.

This transformation—taking a liquid liability and converting it into a less liquid asset—provides an essential service to the economy. The borrowers obtain the funds they need to carry out vital projects. Simultaneously, the ultimate lenders are provided with an instrument that overcomes their basic reluctance to part with control over their money.

In recent years some degree of public attention has been focused on NFIs and the role they play in the economy. Questions have been asked about the role of NFIs, especially the deposit-type ones, in contemporary American society. Do these NFIs continue to serve a unique role by performing highly specialized functions? Can they survive without adapting to the expected environment of the 1980s and thereafter? Related to these questions is another: What is to be the relationship between NFIs, on the one hand, and commercial banks, on the other? A second set of issues deals with the relationship between NFIs and monetary policy. Does monetary policy discriminate against NFIs, and if so, should modifications in policy be instituted? Do the NFIs complicate the job of the monetary authorities, and if so, should something be done to simplify that task?

The plan of the present chapter is to discuss a sample of NFIs, surveying their development and focusing on the issues raised in the previous paragraph. We begin with the familiar deposit-type NFIs.

□ Savings and Loan Associations (SLAs)

The American SLA traces its origins to British building societies. Indeed, SLAs were initially called building societies. These organizations, first formed in the late eighteenth century, were mutual loan societies whose sole purpose was to support homeownership among their members. Each member of the society purchased shares in it. When sufficient funds had been collected, loans would be made available to the members for the building of residences.

This idea of a home-financing institution spread to the United States in the 1830s, with the first one founded near Philadelphia in 1831 and the second established in Brooklyn, New York, in 1836. The societies filled a financial void, one that had been neglected by the commercial banks. The latter were primarily business oriented and concentrated on short-term lending. The rising worker class, consisting of potential homeowners but perennially short of cash, found commercial bankers unsympathetic to their long-term borrowing needs. Yet the workers did hold steady jobs at wages that enabled them to set aside some savings. The building societies provided a means by which workers could pool their savings, combine their financial resources, and eventually enable all members to obtain loans for home acquisition. By the 1880s, virtually every state was the home of at least one building society. By the turn of the century, their numbers had grown to 6000, with over 1¼ million members and about $475 million in combined assets.

The transition from a "building society," in which each member's savings were linked to that member's loan for housing purposes, to a "savings and loan association," in which the savers and borrowers often were different groups of people, was gradual. Over time, members felt the need or desire to withdraw their funds for reasons that were not connected with housing. And as the number of savers grew, it became possible to honor withdrawal requests on demand without jeopardizing the solvency of the institution. By the 1920s many of the more than ten thousand building societies then existing had adopted the more accurate name of "saving and loan association" to reflect the change in their function. They had become banks that collected savings from anyone who was willing to leave funds with them, receiving interest and liquidity in return. At the same time, borrowers no longer were required to have a longstanding relationship with the association.

What had not changed was the emphasis on lending for home purchases or building. As an official of the United States Saving and Loan League stated in 1961, "The fundamental reason for [the] existence [of SLAs] is to finance the purchase of existing homes and the construction of new homes with the funds accumulated."[1] Since 1900, excluding only the depression years of the 1930s and the war years of the 1940s, at least 65 percent of the assets of SLAs have consisted of mortgages on one- to four-family houses. Table 11.1 lists the balance sheet for the SLAs for 1980; as can be seen, 66.3 percent of SLA assets consisted of this type of loan. By contrast, less than 10 percent of commercial bank assets were in mortgage loans for one- to four-family houses.

The special attention paid by the government to SLAs is based to some extent on their historical evolution. This concern is reflected partly in the type of organizational structure used by SLAs and partly in the substance of government regulation.

While some SLAs have taken a corporate form, most are mutual organizations. That is, each SLA is owned by its depositors. Formally, then, the depositors are not creditors of the SLA as a depositor in a commercial bank is. Consequently, earnings on deposits paid out of profits are not "interest" but are technically "dividends." This mutuality, of course, derives from the SLAs' origins, when an initial bond of commonality held the owners = depositors = borrowers together. While this bond rarely exists today, the form of the relationship has not changed. One consequence is that the savers elect each SLA's management. As a matter of fact, most savers are not aware of this right, nor are they

TABLE 11.1 Assets and Liabilities of Savings and Loan Associations, December 31, 1980
(millions of dollars and percentages)

Assets			Liabilities and Net Worth		
Cash and liquid investments	$ 49.6	7.9%	Savings deposits	$511.0	81.1%
Mortgage loans	502.8	79.8	Federal Home Loan		
(of which, loans secured			Bank advances	47.0	7.5
by 1–4-family properties)	417.8	66.3	Other liabilities	38.5	6.1
Other loans	46.4	7.4			
Other assets	31.1	4.9	Total liabilities	596.5	94.7
			Net worth	33.3	5.3
			Total liabilities		
Total assets	$629.8	100.0%	and net worth	$629.8	100.0%

Source: United States League of Savings Associations, '81 Savings and Loan Sourcebook (Chicago, 1981).

[1]Leon T. Kendall, *The Savings and Loan Business: Its Purposes, Functions, and Economic Justification* (Englewood Cliffs, N.J.: Prentice-Hall, 1962), p. 1.

particularly interested. Even the IRS defines SLA dividends as interest for income tax purposes.

SLAs, like commercial banks, can obtain charters either from the state government or, since 1933, from the federal government. Most SLAs—57 percent in 1980, holding 46 percent of industry assets—are state chartered, but, again like commercial banks, virtually all of the SLAs come under federal regulation through the deposit insurance program. Eighty-seven percent of all SLAs, accounting for 98 percent of all assets, were insured by the Federal Saving and Loan Insurance Corporation. Like commercial bank depositors, each SLA depositor is insured up to $100,000.

Regulation of SLAs at both the state and federal levels entails general supervision of their activities to ensure compliance with the laws and regulations imposed on the industry. In addition, liquid asset ratios are set by the regulators. They also specify the type of assets that may be acquired by SLAs and the kinds of accounts that may be offered the public. For example, federally chartered SLAs may hold only limited percentages of corporate issues, such as bonds or commercial paper. In issuing mortgage loans, federally chartered SLAs until recently were restricted to buildings within a 100-mile radius of the main office.

The benefits of federal regulation are considerable. Deposit insurance speaks for itself; without it, it is difficult to conceive of an SLA competing effectively for customer deposits with insured commercial banks and other thrift institutions in the neighborhood. For federally chartered banks, additional advantages accrue. When Congress passed the Federal Home Loan Bank Act in 1932, it arranged for the establishment of a system of Federal Home Loan Banks (FHLBs) to provide loans to member SLAs. The twelve FHLBs are the conduit through which FHLB bonds are sold to the general public. The proceeds of these bond offerings are passed on to the member SLAs, which may borrow either to cover unusual deposit withdrawals or to use the funds for making additional loans to borrowers. (The Federal Home Loan Banks, thus, are government-sponsored financial intermediaries.) Thus, unlike the Federal Reserve loans to commercial banks referred in Chapter 6, which are activated primarily to help banks that face unexpected reserve losses, the FHLBs provide a source of funds for profitable mortgage lending operations. As Table 11.1 shows, 7½ percent of all SLA liabilities and net worth derived from Federal Home Loan Bank advances. The motive underlying this government aid to the SLA industry is, of course, the government's interest in stimulating home ownership, the *raison d'être* of SLAs.

The twelve Federal Home Loan Banks are not independent entities. Although they are owned by the member SLAs, they are subject to the control of the Federal Home Loan Bank Board (FHLBB), a three-member board appointed by the President with the advice and consent of the U.S. Senate. No more than two of the board members, who serve for staggered four-year terms, may be affiliated with the same political party. The FHLBB approves SLA applications for membership and raises the funds for the entire system. It also sets the guidelines under which the Federal Home Loan Banks operate. Thus, it is the FHLBB that determines the conditions concerning Federal Home Loan Bank advances, such as eligibility and terms. The FHLBB also holds the ultimate power to dissolve a Federal Home Loan Bank. In addition to setting Federal Home Loan Bank policy, the board is in charge of the Federal Savings & Loan Insurance Corporation, and the chair of the FHLBB is a member of the Depository Institutions Deregulation Committee, which is charged with gradually removing the maximum interest rates that may be paid on deposits by SLAs. The FHLBB also supervises the Federal Home Loan Mortgage Corporation ("Freddie Mac"), which provides SLAs with funds by acquiring mortgages from them. At the end of 1980, Freddie Mac held a portfolio in excess of $5 billion worth of mortgages.

□ Mutual Savings Banks (MSBs)

Nowadays a second group of deposit-type financial intermediaries performs virtually the same functions as SLAs. This category consists of the mutual savings banks. MSBs originally were designed to encourage thrift on the part of small savers, to provide a safe haven for savings, and through prudent investing of the amassed savings, to cover operating expenses and pay interest to the depositors. The term *mutual* in the title does not imply ownership by the depositors, as it does in the case of mutual SLAs. What it means is that in case of liquidation the depositors alone share in the value of the liquidated assets. (This is true for mutual SLAs, too. But in the latter group the depositors are the owners, which is not true for MSBs.) Nor do MSB savers have a voice in determining management. Each MSB is run by a group of trustees, who tend to perpetuate themselves in the office. Lest that seem odious, it must be pointed out immediately that being a trustee of an MSB is not remunerative. Trustees are prohibited from receiving salaries. They serve in a fiduciary nature, so that they share responsibility without sharing benefits. This is one of the reasons that MSBs have tended to lag behind SLAs in terms of growth: With the profit motive removed, few individuals are interested in sponsoring and operating MSBs.

MSBs are chartered in only seventeen states; since 1978 the federal government has chartered MSBs as well. They are strongest on the eastern seaboard, where the industrial revolution began and the need for them first surfaced. By the time industry moved westward, SLAs and commercial banks provided many of the services offered by MSBs, so they never gained a foothold in the West. Nevertheless, in the states that permit MSBs to operate, they are not noticeably different from SLAs to the typical saver or borrower.

TABLE 11.2 Assets and Liabilities of Mutual Savings Banks, December 31, 1980
(millions of dollars and percentages)

Assets			Liabilities and Net Worth		
Cash and due from banks	$ 4,334	2.5%	Total deposits	$153,501	89.5%
U.S. Treasury and federal agency obligations	8,949	5.2	Ordinary savings	53,971	31.5
			Time and other	97,445	56.8
Corporate bonds	17,333	10.1	Checking and other deposits	2,086	1.2
Mortgage backed bonds	13,849	8.1	Borrowing and mortgage warehousing	4,511	2.6
State and local obligations	2,390	1.4	Other liabilities	2,184	1.3
Other bonds, notes, and debentures	3,876	2.3	Total liabilities	160,196	93.4
Corporate stock	4,224	2.5	Net worth	11,368	6.6
Mortgage loans	99,865	58.2			
Other loans[a]	11,733	6.8			
Other assets	5,011	2.9	Total liabilities		
Total assets	$171,564	100.0%	and net worth	$171,564	100.0%

[a]Includes federal funds, passbook loans, and other nonmortgage loans.

Source: National Association of Mutual Savings Banks, *1980 Annual Report* (New York: 1981)

Table 11.2 records the status of the MSB industry at the end of 1980. As is evident from the table, while MSBs do not concentrate their assets in mortgages to the extent that SLAs do, nevertheless mortgages constitute by far their most substantial asset category.

Since most MSBs are chartered by state governments, they could be immune from federal control. Here again, insurance of deposits provides a pathway for federal government regulation. MSBs can obtain deposit insurance from the FDIC. In 1980, 70 percent of the MSBs, holding 91.5 percent of the industry's deposits, were insured by FDIC.

□ Credit Unions

A third type of depository NFI that has been receiving attention because of its rapid growth in recent years is the credit union. Most frequently formed among people who share a common bond at work—being employed at the same plant or with the same firm—credit unions are mutual-help associations. Although credit unions were latecomers to the United States—the first credit union law was passed in Massachusetts in 1909—the basic idea differed little from that underlying the building societies: a cooperative venture amassing the savings of members in order to lend to members. But while the early SLAs were designed to meet the homeowning goals of depositors, credit unions were and continue to be engaged primarily in consumer lending. The nature of their relationship to their depositors—the mutual-help, not-for-profit organization—has brought benefits but has also imposed restraints. Congress has exempted their retained earnings, their profits, from income taxes, for example. On the other hand, their asset holdings are circumscribed. Funds that are not lent to members must be held in government securities, bank deposits, or loans to other credit unions. Federal regulations also mandate the maximum interest rate charged borrowers by federally chartered credit unions, a rate now set at 21 percent.

In 1980, 21,922 credit unions were in operation, of which 12,440 were federally chartered and the remainder were chartered by the individual states. Federal legislation signed in 1977 extended the powers of credit unions, placing the nationally chartered unions on par with those chartered by most states. On the asset side, federally chartered unions can now engage in home financing and can issue credit cards with unsecured lines of credit. The typical credit union savings account has been augmented by the approval of savings certificate accounts.

Most controversial has been the permission to offer depositors "share draft" accounts, which are essentially interest-bearing checking accounts (they're included in M-1B). Over three thousand credit unions have made this service available to their customers, who maintained year end balances in 1980 of $2.6 billion. Of course, this sum hardly rivals the commercial banking industry's $270 billion total. And although commercial bankers are not overjoyed with this new source of competition, they must live with it since Congress approved share drafts in 1980.

The growth of credit unions has been astounding. In 1950, credit unions together held only $1 billion in assets, and by 1964 they held less than $10 billion. By 1980, the total had grown to some $71.7 billion. One consequence of this rapid development has been a call for government regulation. Today federally chartered credit unions come under the aegis of the National Credit Union Administration, which is responsible for their supervision. The Administration is also responsible for the Insurance Fund, which insures the deposits of credit union members much as the FDIC insures those of commercial bank depositors.

The credit union movement, despite its rapid growth, is still not quantitatively significant. The balance sheet of the nation's federal credit unions for 1980 appears in Table 11.3.

☐ Current Issues

Both SLAs and MSBs have faced serious financial difficulties in the years since the mid-1960s. As interest rates in the securities markets rose, depositors in thrift institutions realized the discrepancy between yields on their savings deposits and market rates. In 1974, for example, thrifts offered depositors 5¼ percent on regular savings deposits; three-month Treasury bills were offering their holders an average interest rate of over 7 percent. Money market mutual funds, which pooled small deposits and invested the proceeds in CDs, yielded their depositors rates exceeding 10

TABLE 11.3 Balance Sheet of Federally Chartered U.S. Credit Unions, December 31, 1980
(millions of dollars and percentages)

Assets			Liabilities and Net Worth		
Loans to members	$26,350.3	65.7%	Notes payable	$ 836.1	2.1%
Cash	683.7	1.7	Accounts payable		
Total investments	11,997.2	29.9	and other liabilities	786.4	2.0
Other assets	1,060.7	2.7	Shares	36,263.3	90.4
			Total liabilities	37,885.8	94.5
			Reserves	1,490.6	3.7
			Net worth	715.4	1.7
	$40,091.9	100.0%			
Total assets			Total liabilities and net worth[a]	$40,091.9	100.0%

[a]Totals do not sum due to rounding.

Source: National Credit Union Administration, *1980 Year End Statistics* (Washington, D.C., 1981).

Disintermediation refers to fund outflows from financial intermediaries, replacing indirect finance with direct finance.

percent. **Disintermediation** took place as savers found these higher-yielding alternatives far more attractive. This put a liquidity squeeze on the thrifts as they found withdrawals speeding up and inflows of deposits slowing down. During a number of months the net outflows of funds were negative; withdrawals exceeded inflows. Moreover, declining values of the assets held in the portfolios of the thrifts threatened their solvency. Aid by the Federal Home Loan Banks, which pumped $6.7 billion into the banks during 1974, proved critical for a number of SLAs. But such assistance served merely to highlight the problem: In the absence of government subsidization of the thrift industry, the continued existence of a viable deposit-type nonbank financial intermediary system was threatened.

Could a rise in interest rates paid to depositors by the thrifts have helped preserve their deposits? Undoubtedly so. Yet this solution leads to a problem that is no less pressing. If interest rates had been raised, then all deposits, new and old, would have earned the higher rates. But the bulk of the thrifts' earning assets, home mortgages, accrue interest at past, lower interest rates. The outcome would have been a severe earning squeeze for the entire industry. A 0.8 percent point increase in interest would have raised SLA and MSB costs by $2.7 billion in 1974 and wiped out industry profits. Indeed, it is for this very reason that the thrift industry has continuously supported the imposition of the maximum interest rates payable on deposit accounts. For the thrifts, higher interest rates is a recommendation of the "out of the frying pan into the fire" type, hardly one to be espoused. If the MSBs and SLAs are to survive in the future, the double threat of insolvency and illiquidity must be neutralized in some other manner.

One stopgap measure was enacted in June 1978, when Congress permitted financial institutions to offer money market certificates (MMCs) to the public. With the rates on MMCs linked to those on Treasury bills, the new instrument was designed to reduce disintermediation; savers could be offered competitive rates, and the banks' solvency would be preserved. On the other hand, the profit squeeze was mitigated by setting a minimum deposit size of $10,000 for MMCs. Smaller sums in savings accounts were still to be subject to the Regulation Q ceiling. (Between 1978 and 1980 regular savings deposits paid, even with the compounding, less than 6 percent while MMCs rose in yield from 7 percent in 1978 to 15 percent in 1980.)

In fact, the MMCs served at least one purpose: Disintermediation did slow down. The outflow of funds from thrifts in the years between 1978 and 1980 was significantly smaller than it was in the early 1970s. Nevertheless, Figure 11.1 shows the continued inverse relationship between interest rates and deposit flows.

A second source of support to the thrift industry stems from the federal government's commitment to nurture housing. As far back as 1938, Congress created the Federal National Mortgage Association ("Fannie Mae") to supply funds to the housing industry. When Fannie Mae became a privately owned, though government-sponsored, corporation in 1968,

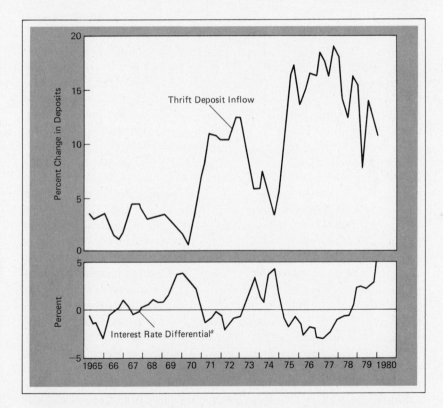

FIGURE 11.1 Savings and small time deposit inflows at thrift institutions and interest rates.
[a]The interest rate differential is the four- to six-month commercial paper rate minus the maximum rate payable on small, non-floating-rate time deposits at commercial banks.
Source: Federal Reserve Bank of Kansas City, *Economic Review*, April 1980, p. 13.

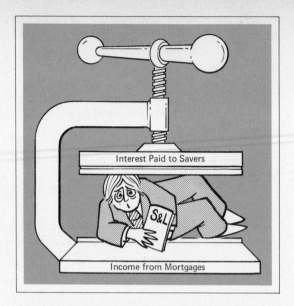

Courtesy of the Federal Reserve Bank of Philadelphia.

direct subsidization of housing was taken over by "Ginnie Mae," the Government National Mortgage Association, part of the Department of Housing and Urban Development. The subsidies offered by Fannie Mae and Ginnie Mae, of course, did not affect the thrift industry directly. But other activities of these two organizations do provide assistance.

An active secondary market in mortgages exists today, much of it due to the initiative of Fannie and Ginnie Mae. These two corporations purchase mortgages initiated by others. Thus, an SLA requiring additional liquid assets may sell mortgages in the secondary market, where Fannie Mae or Ginnie Mae or, for the matter, "Maggie Mae," the privately run MGIC Mortgage Corporation, or "Freddie Mac," a subsidiary of the FHLBB, or a private investor may acquire the mortgage.

An investor in a **pooled mortgage** purchases a share in a portfolio of mortgages. Each month the principal and interest paid by the mortgages are **passed through** to the shareholders of the pool.

An innovation of the thrift industry itself is the **pooled mortgage pass-through.** Banks sell to investors the right to participate in a specified group of mortgages, thereby sharing the risk as well as the returns. The thrifts can use the funds acquired from the sale to lend to new-home purchasers or other borrowers.

The sale of mortgages on the secondary market is an example of the thrifts practicing asset management, selling one asset (a mortgage) in order to acquire another (cash). The use of MMCs is an example of liability management, an area in which the savings bankers have followed the lead of commercial bankers. In fact, while the MMC symbolizes the most visible move into liability management, savings bankers have also emulated commercial bankers by issuing CDs and borrowing on the Eurodollar market. They have learned from nonbank financial intermediaries to sell commercial paper. Also, they have intelligently activated their illiquid mortgage portfolio by using it as backing for bond issues. In 1981, the Federal Reserve also announced its readiness to lend to thrifts facing severe liquidity pressures.

Yet resolving the problem of illiquidity has not led to resolution of the danger of bankruptcy. All of these new innovations require the thrifts to pay interest rates that are higher than the yields they earn on their assets. A more fundamental reform is needed.

Two approaches to this issue have come to the fore in recent years. The first attacks the rigid asset structure of the industry, while the second seeks to increase the flexibility of thrift income. One seeks a solution by proposing a major restructuring of thrift portfolios. Thrifts would be permitted to diversify their loan portfolios so that they would be less reliant on long-term mortgage loans. At the same time, the interest rate ceiling would be lifted, so that thrifts would be able to pay competitive interest rates to depositors. These more expensive liabilities would be invested in higher-earning assets, and thus the profitability of the industry would be preserved. At least two national commissions, the Commission on Money and Credit in 1961 and the Hunt Commission (formally, the President's Commission on Financial Structure and Regulation) in 1971, felt that greater diversity in both deposit liabilities and asset acquisitions would stabilize the thrift industry. The Hunt Commission went still further, recommending that the SLAs and MSBs be authorized to offer demand deposit accounts and other third-party payment accounts. In light of the new computer-based payments technology, the thrifts might find themselves without customers if they are not given a shot at the action. Of course, if the thrifts were to become virtually indistinguishable from commercial banks, the tax, reserve requirement, and other advantages enjoyed by the thrifts would have to be abandoned. A more equitable relationship among all types of depository institutions would have to be devised. Simply put, if the thrifts face insurmountable long-run problems, they should be given the opportunity to convert to commercial banks, with the accompanying benefits, but also subjected to the same legal and regulatory constraints as commercial banks.

Some initial experimentation occurred in the 1970s. In New England and New York State, thrift institutions offered checking deposit accounts. Unquestionably, this proved a success insofar as attracting deposits is concerned. It is less clear whether it has been profitable. Moreover, the experiment is really only partial, and is in no way comparable to the plan discussed earlier. For example, the rates paid by the thrifts on depositor accounts were still subject to the interest rate ceiling.

A major reform came into effect with the Depository Institution Deregulation and Monetary Control Act of 1980. This Act accepts in part the idea that the survival of the thrift industry requires that savings institutions be allowed greater diversity. On the one hand, thrifts are permitted to offer transaction accounts against which checks can be written. These accounts, which should be familiar from the definition of money (M-1B) in Chapter 2, are no longer limited to thrifts in the northeastern United States; any bank in the country may offer its depositors third-party transfer services. The thrifts' asset holdings, too, have been broadened since they have been permitted to enter the consumer loan market; the Act authorized SLAs to issue credit cards as well as to invest up to 20 percent of their assets in consumer loans. Federal MSBs are now allowed to allocate up to 5 percent of their total assets to business loans. These are obvious moves in the direction of generalized banking service.

But with the broadening of the portfolio come two constraints. First, nonearning reserves must be held against transaction accounts, with the required reserve ratio identical to that set by the Federal Reserve for commercial banks. Congress has clearly stated that insofar as transaction accounts are concerned, commercial banks and thrift institutions are to be treated equally. Second, the ability to compete with commercial banks in all phases of financial services has been withheld from the thrifts. Congress has been willing to protect the earning base of the thrifts by permitting greater diversity of income sources, but it has not wished to abandon the specialization that is the legacy of the thrift industry. The problem of financial survival requires further action by the federal legislature.

Other portions of the Depository Institution Deregulation Act are predicated on an alternative concept for saving the thrift industry. This second approach would involve maintaining the basic structure of the thrift industry and the portfolios of the savings banks but eliminating its rigid, unadaptable earnings flow. Virtue is seen in preserving the thrifts as institutions that finance housing. The logical solution, then, is not to increase asset options—which would have the undesired side effect of reducing the availability of loans for housing—but to increase bank earnings on existing assets. Permitting **variable-rate mortgages** (VRMs) is seen by some economists and bankers as one path to survival, if not glory. As market interest rates rise, forcing thrifts to pay higher rates on deposits, so, too, will the income thrifts earn from their mortgage loans. Mortgage borrowers will no longer pay a constant interest rate, but one that fluctuates with underlying financial market conditions. (This need not imply varying monthly payments as interest rates change. Alternatives have been proposed to minimize the variability of the mortgagee's periodic payment.)

A **variable-rate mortgage** (VRM) is a mortgage loan whose interest rate varies with market interest rates.

VRMs have been authorized for all nationally chartered SLAs and credit unions, and have already been marketed in a number of states. Similar mortgage arrangements can be found outside of the United States in such countries as Brazil, Canada, and Israel. In all cases lender initiative has been responsible for these innovations; the lenders have sought to protect themselves against erosion of their income in an inflationary environment. Consumers have acquiesced, often because they were able to find no alternative. When fixed-interest mortgages are offered as an alternative, however, borrowers seem to prefer them, even at an interest rate somewhat in excess of the initially lower-cost VRM.

The Depository Institution Deregulation Act does not go the VRM route, choosing limited deregulation of interest rates instead. The Act supersedes state usury ceilings on mortgage loans and small business and agricultural loans unless the states pass specific legislation to override the Act. In the case of mortgage loans, which became unprofitable when the rates thrifts paid to depositors neared the maximum that banks were permitted to charge borrowers, thrifts are now able to raise their lending rates in line with their cost of funds. The preemption of the ceiling on business and agricultural loans applies only to loans of $1,000 or more. Moreover, the ceiling is not revoked entirely but is made flexible—the banks may not charge more than five percentage points above the Federal Reserve discount rate. The idea behind both of these propositions is to enhance the earning ability of the thrifts. (Along the same lines, the FHLBB has already authorized federal SLAs to issue mortgage contracts with renegotiable interest rates.)

But in this instance as well, a *quid pro quo* is demanded. Along with the freeing of interest rates on loans, Congress also deregulated interest rate payments. Over a six-year transition period, the ceiling on rates paid by commercial banks and thrifts to non-demand depositors will be phased out. Regulation Q will be repealed.

It is far too early to evaluate the combined impact of these reforms. Some are directed at increasing bank profitability; others may well reduce profits. Congress intended the Act to revitalize the thrift industry. Whether this hope will be realized cannot yet be predicted.

☐ Finance Companies

Not all of the intermediaries that cater to consumers accept deposits. One type of financial institution that is heavily engaged in supplying credit to the public is the finance company. *Sales finance* companies are significant suppliers of installment credit to consumers, who use them to finance purchases of consumer durables like automobiles and home furnishings. *Consumer finance* companies offer straight cash loans to nonbusiness borrowers.

Sales finance companies normally deal with consumers only indirectly. When a purchaser of a new automobile, for instance, requests installment financing from a dealer, the latter will supply all the necessary forms and make all the financial arrangements. The dealer rarely provides the money itself; the funds come either from a commercial bank or from a sales finance company.[2] The bank or the finance company pays the dealer for the car, and the proud owner of the new automobile pays the

---

[2] At the end of 1980, of the $116.4 billion in automobile loans outstanding, commercial banks lent $61.0 billion (52.5%) while finance companies accounted for $34.2 billion (29.5%). Credit unions supplied $21.1 billion (18.2%).

installments to the ultimate lender. This type of financing is so profitable that sales finance companies often finance the inventories of dealers in order to establish a favored relationship with them. The dealers then will be more likely to steer customers their way. At the same time, the dealer earns a percentage from the finance company, an operation that often nets the dealer a greater profit than the sale of the automobile itself. You will not be surprised to learn that General Motors Acceptance Corporation and Ford Motor Credit Corporation are among the giants of the sales finance industry.

Consumer finance companies specialize in personal loans to consumers. While the interest rates charged by such companies normally exceed the rates on personal loans by commercial banks, this need not indicate excessively profitable operations. First of all, the relative cost of transacting many small-volume loans is high. Second, the clients of consumer finance companies tend to be high-risk customers. The interest rate must contain a premium for this added risk and for the expected larger percentage of loan defaults. For the borrower with a good credit history, however, the rates are higher than those obtainable elsewhere. One is reminded of the truth of an advertisement bidding us "Never borrow money needlessly," especially at a consumer finance company. Household Finance Corporation and Beneficial Finance Corporation are two of the best-known consumer finance companies.

Two characteristics are shared by both types of finance companies. First, while these firms are not immune to government regulation and are especially affected by the usury laws of many states, which limit the interest rates they can charge on loans, finance companies are not limited geographically, as deposit-type NFIs and commercial banks are. The largest of the sales and consumer finance companies crisscross the nation with an extensive network of offices in most major and many minor cities. Penetration of local markets is one of the primary factors that have made consumer finance companies attractive acquisition prospects for bank holding companies. With commercial bank subsidiaries of holding companies blocked from many lucrative lending markets by laws limiting branching, the consumer finance company affiliate can step in to fill in the gap.

A second characteristic of both types of finance companies is the source of financing. Both consumer and sales finance companies rely primarily on borrowed funds to provide the wherewithal to meet their lending needs. Since finance companies are not deposit-type intermediaries, their borrowing needs are met by reliance on the nation's securities markets. Long- and short-term debts are found in the portfolios of the finance companies, the latter in the form of either bank loans or commercial paper issued by the finance companies themselves. The larger finance companies can sell their unsecured promissory notes on the market, and will do so whenever the terms are more favorable than bank loan terms. Smaller finance companies are more dependent on commercial bank credit, since their access to the commercial paper market is limited.

Finance companies certainly must be included as financial intermediaries, for they do participate in the transformation process that defines FIs. When finance companies sell commercial paper to lenders, the surplus units, they are paid by checks drawn on commercial banks. The finance companies acquire these highly liquid assets in exchange for the short-term liabilities that they issue. These deposits are then transfered to the borrowers, the ultimate deficit units. The borrowers sign an installment contract with the finance company. The net result of this chain of events is that the finance company has created a liquid liability—the commercial paper it owes—and transformed it into a relatively less liquid asset—the installment loan owed to it. So, like all other financial intermediaries, finance companies play an important role in funding economic activity.

☐ NFIs and Monetary Policy

It is premature to discuss monetary policy in detail at this point. That is the subject of later chapters. Nevertheless, it would be senseless to ignore the impact of the thrift industry on monetary policy and, conversely, of monetary policy on SLAs and MSBs, in a chapter devoted to NFIs.

Begin with the latter, for part of the previous discussion can be brought to bear here. The impact of the interest rate ceilings imposed on thrifts by government regulators has already been mentioned. Disintermediation occurs, you will recall, when market rates rise above the fixed ceiling rate. A tight monetary policy, driving interest rates upward, directly threatens the thrift industry by causing disintermediation.

But the issue of monetary policy and the thrifts extends beyond that. There is convincing evidence that a tight monetary policy, accompanied by higher interest rates, imposes a disproportionately disturbing impact on the housing sector of the economy. As interest rates rise, lenders shy away from residential mortgage loans; the return on such loans—often subject to state-legislated usury laws—falls below the yields available in other sectors of the economy. Thus, even if the thrifts were permitted to offer higher depository interest rates, the constraints on interest rates charged to consumers may well inhibit profitable lending by SLAs and MSBs during periods of monetary stringency. The income squeeze might be unavoidable.

This imposes a dilemma on the monetary authorities. To preserve the viability of thrift institutions in the absence of some structural reforms, Federal Reserve officials might be forced to ease up, imposing less tightness than is thought desirable. But in so doing, they could be accused of neglecting their primary responsibility—ensuring macroeconomic stability. To let up on the degree of tightness that is deemed necessary might lead to an overheated economy; to forge ahead with no concern about possible side effects might imply wholesale difficulty for the thrift institutions. Neither alternative is palatable.

Sales and consumer finance companies are less threatened by monetary policy actions. Their ability to pay those who buy their commercial paper the going market rate implies that such firms will not experience any relative decline in borrowing ability. And while usury laws do limit the rates that finance companies can charge their nonbusiness customers, the ceiling appears to be high enough not to pose much of a constraint.

The other side of the coin involves the impact of NFIs on monetary policy. Recall the discussion in Chapter 2 on the issue of whether the nonchecking deposit liabilities of NFIs should be included in the definition of money or not. The resolution there was to accept the conventional definition of money, M-1. Consider, too, the asset side of the balance sheet. Loans made by NFIs would appear to be no less expansionary than those derived from commercial banks.

The argument runs as follows: Just as commercial banks create money by creating checking deposits, so, too, NFIs can create savings deposits. And just as commercial banks create loans through the lending process, so, too, do NFIs. When a saver deposits a sum of money in an SLA savings account, for example, the bank records the deposit as a liability, with cash or perhaps a cash item in the process of collection as the corresponding asset. A small percentage will be set aside as reserves, and the savings banker can lend or invest the remainder, acquiring earning assets for the bank. Thus, loans can expand even while the original saver maintains the liquidity of his or her deposit. It would seem that a "near-money multiplier" can be calculated along the lines of the money multiplier discussed in the last chapter. Now, since the Federal Reserve has no direct control over this near-money multiplier, the central bank's regulation of the volume of credit in the economy is weakened. And if funds shift away from commercial banks to NFIs in response to tight money conditions, then monetary control is weakened at the precise moment when strength is desired.

Actually, there is a flaw—indeed, a major one—in this argument. Recall the discussion in Chapter 10 of leakages and the deposit multiplier —the larger the leakages, the smaller the value of the multiplier. In the case of NFI deposits and loans, the leakages are thought to be substantial. The borrower from the SLA removes funds to pay for a newly purchased home. The chances are high that the seller will not redeposit these funds in a thrift institution savings deposit. The heavy weight of the commercial banks in the financial system suggests that the bulk of these funds will wend their way to the commercial banks rather than to the thrifts. If the leakage is as substantial as it appears to be, the near-money multiplier is small. Thus, there is little cause for concern over NFIs upsetting the monetary cart.

In addition to this conceptual evidence downplaying the role of NFIs as disruptors of effective monetary policy, it is difficult to uncover empirical evidence to support the contention that NFIs exacerbate problems of monetary control. When all is said and done, the conclusion that one must come to is that monetary policy causes difficulties for deposit-type NFIs; the opposite is simply not ture.

□ Summary

The focus of this chapter on nonbank financial intermediaries has been a selective one. Consumer-type financial institutions have been its primary interest. But there are other types of NFIs that cater to business and the government. Their basic features as NFIs do not differ, although obviously each has special characteristics of its own.

Each of these intermediaries is unique, yet they share a common characteristic: their role as financial middlemen in the transformation process.

Savings and loan associations were founded to enable workers to pool their funds in order to finance home purchases. To date, mortgages are still the major asset of SLAs, accounting for some 80 percent of their total assets. SLAs are regulated by the Federal Home Loan Bank Board and its district Federal Home Loan Banks, and their deposits are insured by the Federal Savings & Loan Insurance Corporation. In contrast to the Federal Reserve banks, the FHLBs play a significant role in financing SLAs. They borrow funds by selling securities and lend the money collected in this way to SLAs.

The original function of *mutual savings banks* was to serve as a repository for small savings. MSBs began and still are most prevalent on the eastern seaboard. Mortgages constitute their primary asset, but investments are important, too; in 1980 the percentage of total MSB assets devoted to mortgages was 58.2 percent and the percentage devoted to investments was 29.6 percent. Deposits at most MSBs are insured by the Federal Deposit Insurance Corporation.

Credit unions have grown rapidly in recent years. These mutual-help associations engage primarily in consumer lending, but their tens of billions of dollars in loans outstanding are insignificant in comparison to the amount of commercial bank loans.

Because of the nature of their assets as well as government regulation of interest rates, thrift institutions faced a dilemma in the early 1970s. The low interest rates paid to savers led to deposit losses when interest rates elsewhere were higher. But paying higher interest rates, as the thrifts did on money market certificates after 1978, produced a profit squeeze. Relief for the SLAs and MSBs will come through liberalization of the asset structure of thrifts as well as a lifting of the interest rate ceiling on mortgages, moves that have already been begun by the Depository Institution Deregulation and Monetary Control Act.

Finance companies are nondepository consumer financial intermediaries. They obtain funds by selling securities and lending the proceeds to finance installment sales (sales finance companies) or outright cash loans (consumer finance companies). Because finance companies can establish offices nationally, they have become prime targets for acquisition by bank holding companies.

NFIs frequently have borne the burden of tight monetary policies—rising interest rates cause either disintermediation or a profit squeeze.

This poses a dilemma for the monetary authorities, who must regulate the growth of the money supply in order to control inflation and at the same time preserve the banking industry. The measures taken by Congress to permit changes in the thrifts' asset structure and to liberalize interest rate ceilings on both borrowers and lenders may resolve this dilemma in the next few years.

On the other hand, NFIs have some impact on the expansion of money and bank credit. In periods of inflation, when the Federal Reserve is attempting to slow the growth of money and credit, the activity of NFIs may be inflationary. Most economists, however, view their impact on money creation as slight.

☐ Questions and Exercises

1. Some editorial writers have blamed the recent financial problems of the thrift industry on bank managers, citing their excessive willingness to innovate. Thrift bankers have countered by pointing to the rigid government regulations that surround their every move, as well as the inability of the authorities to keep inflation under control. Evaluate these arguments.

2. Legislation passed by Congress in 1981 established a new savings vehicle designed to help bail out the thrifts. With an interest rate keyed to 70 percent of the rate on government securities, its novelty lies in a limited income tax exemption for savers.

   a. How is this new instrument likely to help the savings banks?

   b. Is this device preferable to such alternatives as FSLIC loans to thrifts facing technical bankruptcy (liabilities exceed assets)?

3. Although the Federal Reserve Board has prohibited the acqusition of thrifts by commercial bank holding companies, their attitude is changing in the face of the continued problems faced by the thrift industry. In fact, the idea of interstate acquisition of failing thrifts is being considered most seriously.

   a. Why might a commercial bank be interested in acquiring failing savings banks?

   b. Can you anticipate any anticompetitive actions resulting from such a policy?

4. Why might a borrower be willing to approach a consumer finance company rather than a bank, when normally finance company terms are more onerous than those offered by banks?

☐ For Further Study

Doris E. Harless, *Nonbank Financial Institutions* (Richmond, Va.: Federal Reserve Bank of Richmond, 1975), though dated, is a brief, straightforward description of financial intermediaries. A more elaborate treatment may be found in B. E. Gup, *Financial Intermediaries: An Introduction* (Boston: Houghton Mifflin, 1980). H. E. Kroos and M. R. Blyn, *A History of Financial Intermediaries* (New York: Random House, 1971), take a historical approach, while Raymond

W. Goldsmith, *Financial Intermediaries in the American Economy* (Princeton, N.J.: Princeton University Press, 1958), the classic work in the field, takes a more empirical view.

The impact of nonbank financial intermediaries on monetary policy was extensively developed by John G. Gurley and Edward S. Shaw. Their book *Money in a Theory of Finance* (Washington, D.C.: Brookings Institution, 1960) presents their viewpoint most cogently.

Numerous books on particular aspects of financial intermediaries have appeared, but the structure of the industry is changing so rapidly that almost anything that's written is likely to be obsolete upon publication. Thus, following the current scene through financial newspapers and magazines is especially critical.

PART THREE

CENTRAL BANKING

The Federal Reserve System: Structure, Service Functions, and Current Organizational Issues

An act to provide for the establishment of Federal Reserve banks, to furnish an elastic currency, to afford means of rediscounting commercial paper, to establish more effective supervision of banking in the United States, and for other purposes.

The Federal Reserve Act (1913)

CONTENTS

CHAPTER HIGHLIGHTS

1. The rather complex structure of the Federal Reserve System, combining private and public elements.

2. The services that Federal Reserve banks provide to the nation's banks, to foreign central banks, and to the federal government.

3. How the Federal Reserve System was designed to increase the elasticity of U.S. currency and to enhance the liquidity of the banking system's assets.

4. The major components of the balance sheet of the Federal Reserve banks.

5. The relationship of the central bank to the legislative and executive branches of the federal government.

6. The issues of Reserve System membership and bank supervision.

The **service functions** of a central bank are the tasks performed by it on behalf of other banks, the government, and foreign central banks.

The **monetary control functions** of a central bank refer to all actions taken by it to shape the course of the monetary economy to conform to national economic goals.

A famous English economist once defined economics as "what economists do." A definition of a central bank, which, of course, is what the Federal Reserve is, may be derived similarly: A central bank is what a central bank does. In other words, study a central bank's functions and you will discover precisely what a central bank is.

A modern central bank is active in three major areas. First, it is the banker of the banking system, servicing the nation's banks as the banks themselves serve their clients. Second, it acts as the government's banker. Finally, it is the guardian of the national monetary system and hence is responsible for monetary policy.

That the Federal Reserve is involved with the nation's bankers is obvious from Chapters 8 and 9. You read that the Federal Reserve, among other things, regulates the formation of bank holding companies and the activities and operation of foreign bank offices in the United States. The Federal Reserve was authorized by Congress to fix maximum interest rates on savings deposits in commercial banks. This chapter and the next one deal with a broader group of central bank activities than those discussed previously. Chapter 12 outlines the **service functions** of the Federal Reserve, while Chapter 13 discusses the **monetary control functions** of this nation's central bank.

This chapter has other purposes as well. The service functions of the Federal Reserve are the key to understanding how the framers of the Federal Reserve Act sought to remedy the basic weaknesses of the banking system of the United States. We pick up the story from Chapter 4, where banking instability during the late nineteenth and very early twentieth centuries was attributed to the legacy of the National Bank Act.

Knowledge of Federal Reserve service functions also is a prerequisite for examining the financial position of the Federal Reserve; the consolidated balance sheet of all the Federal Reserve banks for 1980 is presented in this chapter. Finally, a number of contemporary issues dealing with Federal Reserve relationships with the government and the banking system are outlined in the present chapter. What is the proper role of the central bank vis-á-vis the President and Congress? Why has Reserve System membership been declining, and what has been done to mitigate its impact? Is the multiplicity of bank supervisory authorities really necessary? These questions are addressed here.

The chapter opens with a survey of the structure of the Federal Reserve System; you've got to learn the players and their roles before you can master the intricacies of the game.

☐ The Structure of the Federal Reserve System

The catalyst of legislative action often is crisis. The Panic of 1907 provided the impetus that culminated in the Federal Reserve Act of 1913. The Panic of 1907 differed little from the periodic banking crisis that had been a common, if not frequent, occurrence on the American financial scene. Fearing bank failure, large numbers of depositors demanded gold coin. These demands could not be met because of the very nature of fractional-reserve banking. The result was suspension of payments and bank closings. Of course, this not only justified the public's initial decision to demand coin but further fueled its fears. A vicious cycle of bank failures followed, causing losses not only to bank stockholders but, in the absence of deposit insurance, to the many depositors who had relied on the banks to safeguard their money.

The diagnosis of the ailment was discussed in Chapter 4—the inelasticity issue (the inability of the money supply to expand when more money was needed and to contract when the demand for money fell) as well as the problem of bank illiquidity (the banking system's inability to obtain additional reserves in order to prevent a deposit drain from snowballing into a panic). This analysis came from the National Monetary Commission, a bipartisan congressional body established in 1908 to examine the monetary and banking system and recommend needed reforms. In 1912 the Commission reported, advocating a National Reserve Association, a voluntary, banker-dominated organization. But before any action could be taken, the Republican Congress was replaced by a Democratic one and Woodrow Wilson became President. Wilson suspected that a banker-controlled system would be more responsive to banker needs than to the public interest, a concern that struck a responsive chord in Congress. The result was a novel approach to central banking, a decentralized central bank with shared private and public control. Even today the Federal Reserve System's structure survives as an anomaly.

A three-tiered Federal Reserve System was established by the 1913 legislation. The base layer, the broadest one, is composed of the *member banks*; the second, much narrower middle layer consists of the *Federal Reserve banks*; and at the apex stands the *Federal Reserve Board*. Each layer merits some description.

Member banks

All national banks were required to join the Federal Reserve System. State-chartered commercial banks were given an option: They could—and, it was hoped, would—become members, but the federal legislation did not mandate their joining. A state bank that applied for membership normally would be approved, provided that its capitalization was sufficient or (after the passage of deposit insurance legislation in 1935) the bank had been accepted by the FDIC.

Membership entails, among other obligations, the requirement to purchase stock in the district's Reserve bank.[1] Stock ownership entitles each member bank to vote for the directors of the Federal Reserve bank of its district. In addition to this voting right, paid-in stock carries a 6 percent annual dividend. Far more important to bankers are the operating services provided by the Federal Reserve banks, to be discussed a bit later in this chapter. Member banks are also required to abide by the System's numerous regulations.

Federal Reserve banks

In fact, then, the operating arms of the Federal Reserve System, the Reserve banks, are owned by the member banks. But ownership does not imply control. True, the bankers elect the majority of the directors of their district Reserve banks. But you should realize, first, that the field of candidates in such elections is circumscribed, and second, that the directors have severely limited powers. Moreover, member banks cannot profit from Reserve bank earnings; a profitable year will not advance dividends beyond the statutory 6 percent. So, despite formal ownership of the System by the member banks, policy is not dominated by the commercial banking community.

The Federal Reserve Act divided the nation into twelve Federal Reserve districts (see Figure 12.1) and established a Federal Reserve bank in each district. Each of these Federal Reserve banks is formally controlled by a nine-person board of directors. The Federal Reserve Act calls for three classes of directors. The three class A directors are bankers representing member banks, while the three class B directors are people who are actively engaged in enterprises other than banking. Class B directors may not be directors or employees of banks. Thus, while class A directors represent banking interests, class B directors speak for the borrowing groups.

---

[1]The obligation is to purchase an amount equal to 6 percent of the member bank's net worth. Only 3 percent, half of the requirement, has in fact been paid in to the Federal Reserve; that sum has been deemed sufficient by the Federal Reserve Board.

FIGURE 12.1 The Federal Reserve System: boundaries of Federal Reserve districts and their branch territories.

Source: Board of Governors of the Federal Reserve System.

Both class A and class B directors are elected by the member banks through a procedure designed to give small as well as larger banks an equal voice in the selection.[2]

Class C directors are not elected but are appointed by the Federal Reserve Board. These directors, who represent the broad public interest, may not even own stock in a commercial bank. One of these directors is designated as the chairman of the district Reserve bank and another as the vice-chairman.

The directors, of course, are not involved in the day-to-day management of the Reserve banks. For this they employ a professional management team. Perhaps the directors' most important function is appointing

---

[2]The member banks of the district are divided into three groups on the basis of size. Each member bank can vote for only one class A and one class B director.

the president of the Reserve bank, although this appointment is subject to the approval of the Board of Governors of the Federal Reserve System. The president of the bank, in addition to being responsible for the operation of the bank, holds a special position in the Federal Reserve System through membership in the Federal Reserve Open Market Committee. (This will be discussed more fully later.)

A second formal function of the directors is setting the discount rate, a function that is covered in the next chapter. This activity was placed solely in the directors' hands in the 1913 legislation, but today it is controlled by the Federal Reserve Board, leaving the directors without much influence in this area.

The original conception of the Federal Reserve Act was to make the Reserve banks the sun around which the System would revolve. Member banks would relate to the Federal Reserve banks for their needs, and the Reserve banks, using their supervisory staffs and operating facilities, would both regulate and service member banks. It was felt that the Federal Reserve banks, each with its regional focus, could best respond to the local needs of the member banks. However, the national and even international scope of the financial markets today has undermined the regional idea of the Federal Reserve. The System itself has become more centralized as well, as you will see very soon.

The Federal Reserve Board

The Federal Reserve Board was conceived to have only general supervisory authority over the Reserve banks. The original Act ceded few controls to the Board. The Board's monetary powers were limited, and in the absence of such later legislation as the Bank Merger Act or the Bank Holding Company Act, the Board could not shape the structure of the banking industry. Essentially, the Board was to make sure that the Federal Reserve banks carried out their statutory functions properly.

Despite its limited duties, the original Board was viewed as a centralizing force that would unify the regional Reserve banks. The Board was initially composed of five presidential appointees, each hailing from a separate Federal Reserve district so that geographic diversity would be assured. Occupational diversity was to be achieved through the selection of individuals from different economic backgrounds, the only mandate being that two of the appointees must have banking or financial experience. Two government officials were placed on the board ex officio—the secretary of the Treasury and the comptroller of the currency. Since the government's deposits were to be placed in the Federal Reserve banks, Congress felt that some oversight should be exercised by the government's chief financial officer. The comptroller was seated on the Board as the official responsible for the supervision of the national banks, which were required to become members of the System.

The appointed members' terms, initially set at ten years, were staggered so that the Board could not normally be dominated by the incumbent President. Moreover, overlapping terms provided for continuity. Once appointed, the board members could not be removed except for "cause," that is, dereliction of duty.

Since 1913 the picture has been altered radically. The authority of the Board has grown considerably. Decentralization of power has virtually disappeared, to be replaced by a strong centralized authority. And the structure of the Board has also undergone substantial change, as may be seen from the change of its official title (by the Banking Act of 1935) from "The Federal Reserve Board" to "The Board of Governors of the Federal Reserve System." (Since the earlier title is still frequently heard, both titles will be used interchangeably in this book.)

The 1935 Act also mandated removal of the two ex officio members, although the seven-member board was retained.[3] Since 1922, when the requirement of a banking background for two of the board members was eliminated, the entire board has consisted of seven presidential appointees coming from any walk of life. The geographic limitation—that no more than one member may come from the same Federal Reserve district—still applies, however. (See Box 12.1 for the members and their backgrounds as of mid-1981.) The 1935 Act lengthened the term of office to fourteen years, and also established the offices of chairman and vice-chairman of the Board of Governors; these officers are appointed for four-year terms.[4] (The Banking Act of 1935 initiated new instruments of monetary control and formalized other arrangements, but these are taken up in the next chapter. A section of the Act also established the FDIC.)

☐ The Federal Advisory Council and the Federal Reserve Open Market Committee

Two other organs of the Federal Reserve System must be mentioned to round out the organizational structure. The first is the *Federal Advisory Council* (FAC), which was formed under the 1913 Act. The board of directors of each Reserve bank elects one member to the Federal Advisory Council, which meets at least four times a year in Washington, D.C. The FAC confers with the Board on whatever matters it or the Board wishes, but its powers are consultative and advisory only.

The second organ is the *Federal Reserve Open Market Committee*

---

[3]The reason for this reform is interesting. Senator Carter Glass, then chair of the Senate Banking Committee, felt that the secretary of the Treasury possessed inordinate power and could dominate the Board. Glass spoke with authority, for he had served as secretary of the Treasury during World War I and by his own admission had had a pervasive influence on the Board. As a senator, he now felt that such domination was not in the best interests of the country, and successfully advocated abolition of the ex officio posts.

[4]If there are no vacancies on the Board, the President must appoint two of the seven to these two offices.

BOX 12.1 The Board of Governors of the Federal Reserve System

Paul A. Volcker, chairman of the Board, was born September 5, 1927, at Cape May, New Jersey. He earned a B.A. at Princeton University in 1949 and an M.A. in political economy and government at the Harvard University Graduate School of Public Administration in 1951. He attended the London School of Economics in 1951–1952. Volcker's first association with the Federal Reserve System was as a summer employee at the Federal Reserve Bank of New York in 1949 and 1950. He returned to the New York bank in 1952 as a full-time economist, and remained with the Federal Reserve until 1957, when he became a financial economist at Chase Manhattan Bank. In 1962 Volcker joined the U.S. Treasury as director of financial analysis, and in 1963 he became deputy under secretary of the Treasury for monetary affairs. From 1965 to 1969 he was a vice president of Chase Manhattan Bank. In 1969 he was appointed under secretary of the Treasury for monetary affairs, where he remained until 1974. During this time Volcker was the principal U.S. negotiator in the development and installation of a new international monetary system departing from the fixed exchange rate system installed after World War II. He spent the 1974–1975 academic year at Princeton University as a senior fellow in the Woodrow Wilson School of Public and International Affairs. Volcker became president and chief executive officer of the Federal Reserve Bank of New York on August 1, 1975, and remained in that office until he became chairman of the Federal Reserve Board on August 6, 1979.

Preston Martin, vice-chairman of the Board, was born on December 5, 1923, at Los Angeles, California. He received a B.S. and M.B.A. from the University of Southern California, and in 1952, a Ph.D. in monetary economics from Indiana University. Martin's experience encompasses the educational, government, and business sectors. From 1950–1965, he taught finance and real estate and also served as a consultant for real estate and banking firms. In 1967, then Governor Reagan selected Martin as California's Saving and Loan Commissioner, a position he held until his appointment in 1969 by President Nixon as chairman of the Federal Home Loan Bank Board. Martin returned to California in 1972 and organized some private businesses that were acquired by Sears, Roebuck in 1979. Prior to joining the board in 1982, Martin headed Seraco, Sears' real estate and financial holding company.

Henry C. Wallich was born in Germany on June 10, 1914, and became a U.S. citizen in 1944. He was educated in Germany, at Oxford University in England, at New York University (M.A., economics), and at Harvard University (Ph.D., economics, 1944). Wallich was on the staff of the Federal Reserve Bank of New York from 1941 to 1951, and was chief of the bank's Foreign Research Division from 1946 to 1951. He then became a professor of economics at Yale University, and he was appointed to the Seymour H. Knox chair in 1968. During 1958–1959 he was on leave from Yale as assistant to the secretary of the Treasury, and from 1959 to January 1961 he served as a member of the President's Council of Economic Advisers.

Wallich served as a senior consultant to the Treasury from 1969 until his appointment to the Federal Reserve Board on March 8, 1974. He has also served with the Advisory Board of the Arms Control and Disarmament Agency (1972–1973), as the U.S. representative on the United Nations Experts Panel on Economic Consequences of the Arms Race (1971–1972), and as a member of the Research Advisory Board of the Committee for Economic Development. He is a former director of a number of business firms and has written as an editorialist or columnist for the *Washington Post* and *Newsweek* magazine. His published works include four books.

J. Charles Partee was born October 21, 1927, in Defiance, Ohio, and attended Indiana University, where he received a B.S. in business (with distinction) in 1948 and an M.B.A. in finance in 1949. Partee joined the Federal Reserve Bank of Chicago in 1949 as an economist specializing in consumer finance, mortgage markets, and savings. In 1956 he went to the Northern Trust Company of Chicago as associate economist, and in 1958 he became second vice president.

Partee joined the staff of the Board of Governors in 1962, where he served as chief of the Capital Markets Section, Division of Research (1962–1963); adviser in charge of financial sections, Division of Research (1964–1965); and associate director (1966–1969) and director of the Division of Research and Statistics and adviser to the Board (1969–1974). In November 1973 Partee was appointed managing director for research and economic policy, holding that office until he became a member of the Board on January 5, 1976. He was the second member of the Board's staff to be appointed to the Board.

Nancy Hays Teeters was born July 29, 1930, in Marion, Indiana. She attended public schools in Marion, and in 1952 she received a B.A. in economics from Oberlin College.

In 1954 Teeters received an M.A. in economics from the University of Michigan, where she was a teaching fellow and did further graduate work in economics in 1956 and 1957. In 1955 and 1956 she was an instructor at the University of Maryland's overseas division in Stuttgart, West Germany. She was a staff economist in the Government Finance Section of the Federal Reserve Board's Division of Research and Statistics from 1957 to early 1966. In 1962 and 1963 she was on leave from the Federal Reserve to serve as an economist for the President's Council of Economic Advisers.

Following her service on the staff of the Federal Reserve Board from 1966 to 1970, Teeters became a fiscal economist with the Planning and Analysis staff of the Bureau of the Budget (which became the Office of Management and Budget). She was a senior fellow at The Brookings Institution from 1970 to late 1973, when she became a senior specialist with the Congressional Research Service of the Library of Congress. From late 1974 to the time she joined the Federal Reserve Board on September 18, 1978, as its first woman member, Teeters was assistant staff director and chief economist for the Committee on the Budget of the House of Representatives.

(continued)

Emmett J. Rice was born in Florence, California, on December 21, 1919. He was educated at the City College of New York, where he received a B.A. in 1941 and an M.B.A. in 1942, and at the University of California at Berkeley, where he received a doctorate in economics in 1955.

Rice was in the U.S. Air Force from 1942 to 1946 and held the rank of captain at the time of his discharge. At the time of his appointment to the Federal Reserve Board on June 20, 1979, he was senior vice president of The National Bank of Washington, where he had worked since 1971. Prior to entering commercial banking he had an extensive career in public service and served in a broad range of civic and nonprofit organizations.

Rice first became associated with the Federal Reserve System in 1960–1962, when he was an economist at the Federal Reserve Bank of New York. In 1962 he went to Nigeria as a member of a group of advisers who assisted in establishing the Central Bank of Nigeria. During his stay in Nigeria he taught at the University of Lagos. Rice became deputy director of the U.S. Treasury's Office of Developing Nations in 1964, and in 1966 he became its acting director. During this period he was a U.S. delegate to a number of international conferences on trade, international finance, and development. In 1966 he was appointed by the President to be alternate executive director for the United States at the International Bank for Reconstruction and Development (World Bank), the International Development Association, and the International Finance Corporation. He served in these offices until 1970, and was a member of the U.S. negotiating team at a series of international conferences on replenishment of the lendable funds of the International Development Association. During 1971 Rice was executive director of the Mayor's Economic Development Committee, making long-range plans for urban development of the nation's capital.

Lyle E. Gramley was born January 14, 1927, in Aurora, Illinois. He was educated at Aurora College and at Beloit College, where he received a B.A. in 1951. In 1952 he received his M.A. from Indiana University, and in 1956 he was awarded a Ph.D. in economics by the same institution.

Gramley first became associated with the Federal Reserve System in 1955, when he joined the Federal Reserve Bank of Kansas City as a financial economist. He remained there until 1962, when he joined the faculty of the University of Maryland. In 1964, he became a senior economist at the Federal Reserve Board, and subsequently he was associate adviser, adviser, associate director, deputy director, and director of the Board's Division of Research and Statistics. In 1977 Gramley became a member of the President's Council of Economic Advisers, where he served until he was sworn in as a member of the Federal Reserve Board on May 28, 1980.

Source: Board of Governors of the Federal Reserve System.

(FOMC), which consists of the seven members of the Board of Governors and five of the twelve presidents of the Reserve banks. (Eleven of the twelve serve on a rotating basis, while the president of the Federal Reserve Bank of New York is always a member. This particular form of the

FOMC—which remains in effect today—also was established by the Banking Act of 1935.) Formally, the FOMC decides only the monetary policy known as "open market operations," which also will be discussed in the following chapter. Informally, at the monthly FOMC meetings in Washington, D.C., *all* the presidents of the Federal Reserve banks join the members of the Federal Reserve Board to discuss the entire range of monetary policy issues: What is the present state of the economy? Where is the economy heading? Should the Federal Reserve's present monetary policy be altered, and if so, how much and using which instruments? This forum has evolved into the major monetary-policy-making body of the Federal Reserve System, which explains, of course, the close attention paid to its actions by financial journalists, Wall Street analysts, and economists in general.

Today, in sum, the central monetary and banking authority in the United States is the Board of Governors of the Federal Reserve System. The Federal Reserve banks implement the policy decisions of the Board. And although the Reserve bank presidents share in the decision-making process by virtue of their presence on the FOMC, the Board itself constitutes the voting majority. The Board has delegated much of its authority to the Reserve banks, especially in the area of banking supervision and regulation. The Reserve banks clearly must represent the public interest in their decisions, and because of this, the presidents of the banks view their function as that of a public servant. Their outlook toward their responsibilities is not diminished by the fact that the banks are owned by the member banks and the staff is formally responsible to a board of directors most of whose members are elected by privately owned member banks.

☐ Service Functions of the Federal Reserve

Services to the banking community: the Federal Reserve as the "bankers' bank"

The services provided by the Federal Reserve to the private banks in the United States fall into two categories: normal operational services and extraordinary services.

Normal operational services. Banks turn to the Federal Reserve in the course of their day-to-day business for currency supplies, clearing, funds and securities transfers, and other purposes.

Currency supplies. Every day commercial banks require currency—bills or coin. Much of the currency supply is kept in their vaults, but frequently bankers estimate that they'll need additional funds. They can obtain the needed currency from their district Reserve bank. Since banks keep deposits—their reserves—with the Reserve bank, the currency is debited against their reserve account. Similarly, when commercial banks are flooded with currency, they can ship the surplus to the Reserve bank and receive credit on their reserve account. (Recall the discussion of cash leakages in Chapter 10.) Since most of the nation's currency consists of Federal Reserve notes and since the Federal Reserve supplies its notes by charging the banks' reserve accounts, the Federal Reserve clearly dominates the dispensation of American currency.

Check Clearing. Check clearing is a vital service provided by the Federal Reserve System. Clearing involves the settling of balances between banks by netting out obligations and credits rather than transfering gross amounts. Picture the following situation: Depositors of Alpha Bank have written $50 million in checks in payment for goods and services provided by companies that maintain deposits in Beta Bank, and $10 million in checks to depositors of Gamma Bank. The first row of Figure 12.2 lists Alpha's obligations to Beta and Gamma.

At the same time, Beta's depositors have written checks totaling $40 million and $25 million to depositors of Alpha and Gamma, respectively, while Gamma's depositors have written checks equalling $60 million and $30 million to Alpha and Beta depositors, respectively. (See the second and third lines of the figure.) In the absence of clearing arrangements, Alpha would have to deliver the checks that it has received as deposits to Beta and Gamma and collect $40 million from the former and $60 million from the latter. While this was going on, Beta's messenger would be visiting Alpha and Gamma, and Gamma's collector would be visiting Alpha and Beta. Not only is this process inefficient, involving a large amount of duplication of effort, but insofar as each bank has to have sufficient cash on hand to pay off the gross outflow—$215 million in this example—it reduces the banking system's ability to make credit available. And of course, as the number of banks increases, the process becomes ever more cumbersome and inefficient.

Owes \ Is Owed	Alpha Bank	Beta Bank	Gamma Bank	Sums Owed to All Banks	Net Owed to Each Bank
Alpha Bank	—	50	10	60	40
Beta Bank	40	—	25	65	15
Gamma Bank	60	30	—	90	−55
Sums Owed by All Banks	100	80	35	215	0

FIGURE 12.2 Interbank clearing. (Note: Amounts are in millions of dollars.)

The alternative is a clearing arrangement in which representatives of Alpha, Beta, and Gamma meet at a common site, each bringing the checks received for collection from the others. They exchange the checks and pay each other only the net amount due. Instead of $215 million exchanging hands, only $55 million is transfered. As the "Sum" row and column numbers in Figure 12.2 indicate, Alpha owes the others $60 million but is owed $100 million by them. The final "Net" column shows that Alpha is a creditor, being owed the $40 million difference. Similarly, Beta is owed $80 million and owes $65 million, so it should receive a credit of $15 million. Gamma brings checks totaling only $35 million but must pay out $90 million, so it is a net debtor in the amount of $55 million. In the clearing Gamma will pay $40 million to Alpha and $15 million to Beta, and all accounts will be cleared.

Interbank clearing like this is normally accomplished between banks located in the same city and need not actively involve the district Federal Reserve bank. Indeed, in many of the nation's large cities formation of local clearinghouses preceded the establishment of the Federal Reserve System. New York City's "big ten" banks, for example, formed the first clearinghouse in 1853. Nevertheless, the Federal Reserve is intimately involved in the clearing process.

The role of the Federal Reserve System is a dual one. First, the local balances owed by banks to each other are settled when the appropriate entries are made in the books of the district Federal Reserve bank. In the previous example, Alpha will be credited with $40 million on its Reserve bank account, as Beta will for $15 million. Gamma's reserve account, on the other hand, will be reduced by $55 million.

Second, a good share of intercity clearings—those that are not chan-neled through correspondent banks—are conducted by the Federal Reserve banks. Local banks may send their out-of-town checks to the district Reserve bank, which will credit their account. When the bank on which the check is drawn is a member of the same district, the Reserve bank will simultaneously debit the latter's account. In the event that the issuing bank is located in another district (when, for example, a check from an Oakland, California, bank is deposited in a Fort Worth, Texas, bank), the checks will be cleared through the appropriate Reserve banks. The Federal Reserve Bank of Dallas will credit the depositing bank, while the Federal Reserve Bank of San Francisco will debit the Oakland bank's account.[5] The two Reserve banks will then settle the accounts through an internal mechanism known as the Interdistrict Settlement Fund.

The volume of checks handled by the Federal Reserve System is

---

[5] In intercity and interdistrict clearing, the credit to the depositing bank might not be recorded on the day of deposit at the Federal Reserve bank. Since some time will elapse before the check is cleared, the Reserve bank credits the depositing bank according to a preordained schedule, but never more than two days after receipt of the check. Even if the actual collection takes place after two days, the Reserve bank nevertheless will credit the depositing bank on the third day. This gives rise to *float*, or the dollar amount credited to the banks in excess of the amount actually collected (see p. 294).

immense; in 1980 alone over 16½ billion checks, valued at $8.6 trillion, were cleared by the Reserve banks. (See Box 12.2.) In order to handle this ever-growing volume effectively, the Federal Reserve and the nation's commercial bankers have instituted two types of facilities in recent years: **regional check-processing centers** (RCPCs) and **automated clearing-houses** (ACHs). The RCPCs are located in areas that produce significant volumes of checks. Some were established outside the immediate site of a Federal Reserve bank or branch, while others are located within existing Federal Reserve facilities. By scheduling around-the-clock working hours, the RCPCs are able to collect checks throughout the day and night, and often reduce delays due to transportation. Checks that formerly took days to clear frequently can be cleared in a single day.

Automated clearinghouses are the response of the nation's commercial banks and the Federal Reserve System to the check-processing volume. ACHs are a critical link in a system of clearing without checks. Consider this case, which is likely to become ever more prevalent: An employer sends his bank a list containing the wages due each employee and the employee's identification number. The bank processes this list, which may already consist of a computer tape, debiting the employer by the full

Regional check processing centers are check collecting and processing offices operated by the Federal Reserve banks.
Automated clearinghouses perform clearing functions on a computer-to-computer basis, obviating the use of checks.

BOX 12.2 Those Flying Checks

It might be said that the nation's banking system depends on the strength of the economy, the soundness of the commercial banks and on Kyle Johnson and Jesse Bennett.

Just how these two make their valuable contribution could be seen in the early hours of a recent morning when their twin-engine, Cessna Citation jet touched down at the municipal airport here. No sooner had the plane braked to a stop than co-pilot Mr. Bennett flung open the hatch and began tossing bulky canvas bags to the driver of a waiting van. In the five minutes that elapsed before the plane roared off again, millions of dollars had changed hands. . . .

Consider the jet route that Mr. Johnson and Mr. Bennett fly. Shortly after 8 P.M. they take off from Charlotte, N.C. (where they live) and head up the Atlantic coast. They stop at Richmond, Baltimore, Philadelphia, and Teterboro, N.J., (which serves New York City), picking up checks bound for other parts of the country.

From Teterboro their Cessna heads west, arriving in Elyria just after 3 A.M.. Here, checks bound for points further west are unloaded and checks for Southern banks are taken on.

From Elyria the plane heads south, stopping in Atlanta and Birmingham. Finally, a weary 11 hours and 2,200 miles after leaving Charlotte, it lands at New Orleans. After a few hours of sleep at a New Orleans apartment and a meal, the two pilots are off again on the return trip, again picking up checks along the route.

Source: Adapted from *The Wall Street Journal*, Feb. 2, 1976.

---

amount of the wages due and crediting employees who maintain accounts with that particular bank. The computer tape is then passed on to the ACH, which is located at the Federal Reserve. There the tape is computer-read and each bank is credited with the earnings of the employees who bank with it. The banks are notified, and they in turn inform each employee who banks there of the amount credited to his or her account.

Funds and Securities Transfer. Member banks can transfer funds across the country using the Federal Reserve wire or computer networks. A bank may request its own district Reserve bank to transfer funds to a specific bank, or it may handle the transaction itself. The latter is likely only for the larger banks, which are directly on line on the Federal Reserve's communications system. But whether the bank is on line or not, in each case the Federal Reserve bank will debit the initiating bank's account and credit that of the recipient bank. The annual volume of funds transfered through the Reserve banks runs into trillions of dollars.

Government securities are also transfered by the Reserve banks for their members. This relatively new mechanism is predicated on the substitution of computer records for actual bond certificates. Banks now accept a credit with the Federal Reserve bank that specifies the particular bond it owns, rather than taking physical possession of a piece of paper that contains the same information. (An obvious advantage is the safety factor; there are no bonds in the bank's vaults to be misplaced or stolen.) When the bank sells some of these securities to others, the district Reserve bank will transmit the information to the buyer's Reserve bank, which will credit the recipient's security account.

Other. The Federal Reserve banks also supply other services to member banks. They include economic intelligence, publications, and various types of information used by the banking community.

Extraordinary services: loans. Aside from providing these routine services, the Reserve banks supply other services that are not daily, pro forma occurrences. For example, the Federal Reserve banks lend to banks that maintain reserves with them. In general, such borrowing is not automatic. The Federal Reserve views borrowing as a privilege subject to Reserve bank discretion, rather than a right of the depository banks. It will be best to defer to the next chapter further discussion of the discount window and how it works. Here it suffices to note one method that is an exception—the **seasonal borrowing privilege:** The Federal Reserve permits smaller banks that experience wide seasonal swings in their deposits to borrow for periods up to nine months.

The **seasonal borrowing privilege** permits banks to borrow from the Federal Reserve to meet seasonal needs for funds.

In short, the Federal Reserve banks are "bankers' banks," providing to the nation's banks a variety of services similar to those supplied by commercial banks to their customers. The Reserve banks provide cash; collect, store, and transfer funds; offer advice and information; and lend. At the same time, these bankers' banks expect the banks to meet certain obligations. First, *all* depository institutions must maintain non-interest-earning reserves at the regional Reserve banks. In addition, *member* banks are subject to the supervision of the Federal Reserve, and state member banks must obtain permission from the Federal Reserve to consummate mergers or open branches. (National banks obtain permission from the comptroller of the currency.) Finally, the banks must pay for the services they use.

A minor obligation for most banks—but a reason that some banks have never joined the System—is the requirement that all member banks remit checks at **par**. A member bank may not deduct a service charge for the collection of a check.

Par collection requires a bank to credit the depositor with the face value of a deposited check.

Services to foreign central banks

Since New York City is a world financial center, much of the trade in U.S. government securities, especially in highly liquid Treasury bills, is conducted there. In addition, the foreign-exchange market is concentrated in New York. Foreign central bankers, buying securities either for their own account, for their government, or for their nation's commercial banks, frequently trade through the Federal Reserve Bank of New York and maintain deposits with it for that purpose. The New York bank, acting for the Federal Reserve System, performs this function not only for the good will it brings the central banking system but, more importantly, for the information it provides about domestic and foreign financial markets. This enables the Federal Reserve officials charged with carrying out domestic and international monetary policy to keep close track of movements in the markets. It also facilitates intervention in these markets. (Part Six looks at international monetary economics.)

Services to the Treasury

In addition to acting as the bankers' bank and as an agent for foreign central banks, the Federal Reserve System was charged by the Federal Reserve Act to serve as a depository of the U.S. Treasury. As mentioned in Chapter 6, the Federal Reserve acts as an agent to pay the Treasury's bills and collect its debts and receipts. In addition, the Federal Reserve banks handle the operations end of the government's debt, performing the various clerical services connected with actual sales and redemption. And as you have seen, the Treasury maintains an account with the Federal Reserve banks through which its various transactions are conducted.

More than clerical services are involved in this intragovernmental relationship. The Federal Reserve System, primarily through the Federal Reserve Bank of New York, serves as the key financial adviser to the Treasury. When the Treasury borrows from the public, the type of debt and its timing will be discussed with Federal Reserve officials. The Federal Reserve is also authorized to lend directly to the Treasury. It can temporarily accommodate the Treasury's financial needs by purchasing special short-term securities, although Congress does not permit the Treasury to owe more than $5 billion to the Federal Reserve at any time.

Finally, the profits of the Federal Reserve System flow into the coffers of the federal government. Some $11.7 billion were channeled to the Treasury in this way in 1980.

☐ Inelasticity and Illiquidity Resolved

With the service functions of the Federal Reserve fresh in your mind, it is appropriate to return to the two problems that were to be remedied by the establishment of the system. How was the Federal Reserve System to overcome the inelasticity of the currency supply and the illiquidity of banking assets?

The inelasticity problem, you will recall, dealt with the inability of the financial system to increase the currency supply to meet seasonal or cyclical demands. The issuance of national bank notes by commercial banks had proved ineffective; the quantity of these notes simply did not increase when they were needed. The solution provided by the Federal Reserve Act was the introduction of another series of paper money— Federal Reserve notes. Federal Reserve notes were to circulate side by side with national bank notes, with the former to accommodate the swings in currency demand.[6]

The original legislation declared that Federal Reserve notes were to be backed by a 40 percent gold reserve. In addition, 100 percent of the note issue was to be collateralized by commercial loans, so that each Federal Reserve note was covered by 140 percent backing.[7] Until 1933, Federal Reserve notes were redeemable for gold coin; now they are redeemable for "lawful money." Consequently, your $10 Federal Reserve note is redeemable for two $5 notes, ten $1 notes, or assorted change.

Elasticity of the currency supply was achieved as follows: When business expanded, so, too, did both the supply of bank loans and the demand for currency. Banks could present the promissory notes of borrowers to the discount window of their district Reserve bank and, provided that the notes met conditions specified by the Federal Reserve Act as to type and maturity,[8] receive Federal Reserve notes in exchange. Thus, an increase in the demand for currency would automatically bring

---

[6]National banks retained their note-issuing capacity until 1935, when it was formally suspended.

[7]In time this provision was watered down. In 1917 the 140 percent coverage was reduced to 100 percent. Since 1968, when the gold-backing provision was dropped entirely, the collateral of Federal Reserve notes has been almost entirely in the form of U.S. government securities. Since a government security is essentially a promise to pay Federal Reserve notes, Federal Reserve notes are backed by themselves!

[8]Under the 1913 Act the underlying notes tendered by a bank for discount had to be for short-term, productive purposes, clearly reflecting the real-bills doctrine. The eligibility requirement was removed in 1980.

forth a corresponding increase in the supply of currency. Similarly, seasonal demands for currency could be met by presenting such commercial bills at the Reserve banks; there was no need to call upon funds held on deposit at correspondent banks. In this manner the seasonal stringency of funds encountered in the past, which occasionally caused panics, would be relieved.

The new system of bank reserves also worked to prevent banking crises. Instead of pyramiding reserves—as was the case under the National Banking System, in which country banks were permitted to maintain reserves with reserve city banks, which in turn could hold deposits with central reserve city banks—now all member banks were required to keep reserves only with their district Reserve bank. Regional shortages of funds would not lead to a drain of funds from other areas. New York and Chicago banks would be spared the tightness that had been caused by drains stemming from the cash needs of country banks.

The second major issue, the illiquidity problem, was resolved by enabling the Federal Reserve banks to provide liquidity. The basic problem is endemic to fractional-reserve banking, for no single bank can pay off its depositors should they all wish immediate payment. Banks' liquid liabilities, as you know, almost always total more than their liquid assets. For the banking system as a whole, liquidity is even more constrained, since a simultaneous attempt by many bankers to convert liquid assets into cash will cause the price of these assets to plummet. The Federal Reserve banks, through their ability to discount commercial bank paper, would reduce the dimensions of the problem. Banks that were short of liquidity could turn to their Federal Reserve bank and, by using the discount window, obtain funds to pay off the claimants. Not only would a single bank be helped out of its crisis, but the stability of the entire banking system could be preserved. Bank runs would be averted, for the banking system could now turn to the Federal Reserve for liquid assets. Moreover, the breakup of the pyramiding of reserves acted to limit the transmission of panic. A bank no longer would have to demand reserves from its correspondent; reserves held at the Federal Reserve bank could be mobilized instead.

In passing, it should be noted that the system did not always function as intended; the massive bank failures of the late 1920s and early 1930s are sufficient evidence of that. But we will have an opportunity to examine that period later on in Chapter 23.

A further problem to be overcome by the new organization of the banking system was the inefficiency of the money transfer system. Before the institution of the Federal Reserve System, checks were often sent on long journeys to avoid paying clearing charges. Each bank would send checks only to a bank with which it had a par collection agreement. The story is told of a check drawn on a bank in Birmingham, Alabama, that was received by a Rochester, New York, bank. The check was sent from Rochester to New York City to Jacksonville, Florida, to Philadelphia to

Baltimore to Cincinnati and finally to Birmingham for payment. Under the Federal Reserve's par collection arrangement, such circuitous routing was eliminated. Checks were sent to the Federal Reserve bank or could be cleared through a member bank, which was not permitted to impose a clearing charge. To be sure, the writer of the check could gain considerable time under the earlier arrangements. But the depositor had to wait an equally long time before drawing on the account.

In recent years some large corporations have found it profitable to take advantage of slow check-clearing arrangements. They draw checks on banks located in remote areas and calculate the number of days it will take before the check finds its way back. They take advantage of the delay to invest the funds for a few days. At a 15 percent annual interest rate, a day's delay in paying $50 million comes out to almost $2,100.

□ The Balance Sheet of the Federal Reserve System

The consolidated balance sheet of the Federal Reserve banks, whose main components are summarized in Table 12.1, reflects the service functions of the System. (A more detailed balance sheet is presented in the appendix to this chapter.)

Begin with the asset side of the table. Over three-quarters of the Federal Reserve banks' assets consist of various types of *government or government agency securities*. Acquisition of securities has replaced the discount process as the primary means of providing an elastic money supply, not only on a seasonal or cyclical basis but also to meet the long-run demands of a growing economy. The income from these

TABLE 12.1 Consolidated Balance Sheet of the Federal Reserve Banks, December 31, 1980 (millions of dollars)

Assets		Liabilities and net worth	
Gold certificates	$ 11,161	Federal Reserve notes	$124,241
Cash items in the process of collection	12,554	Deposits	31,546
U.S. government and agency securities	130,592	Banks	27,456
		U.S. Treasury	3,062
Loans to member banks	1,809	Foreign	411
Bank premises	457	Other	617
Other assets	11,972		
		Other liabilities	10,352
		Total liabilities	166,139
		Net worth	
		Paid-in capital	1,203
		Surplus	1,203
Total	$168,545	Total	$168,545

Source: Federal Reserve *Bulletin*.

government securities, both interest and capital gains, accounts for the bulk of the Federal Reserve's earnings, although Federal Reserve policy is not motivated by the quest for profits. These securities also provide backing for the Federal Reserve notes.

The $12.6 billion in *cash items in the process of collection* consists mainly of the checks deposited by banks in the various district Reserve banks or check-processing centers that have not yet been collected from the issuing bank. Here the Federal Reserve acts as the bank of the bankers, clearing checks for the banks the way commercial banks clear their customers' checks.

Because the Federal Reserve credits a depositing bank according to a preordained schedule, some of the checks in this category will be credited to the depositing bank prior to being collected by the Federal Reserve banks. (Some $4½ billion was involved on December 31, 1980.) This gives rise to **float,** a double-counting of banking system deposits: The depositing bank receives credit, but there is no simultaneous debit on the account of the bank from which the check came.

Gold certificates are basically bookkeeping entries reflecting obligations of the Treasury to the Federal Reserve banks, debts that are backed by gold. Most of this sum represents gold sales by various groups—mining corporations, foreign suppliers—to the Treasury, which paid for it by debiting its account at the Federal Reserve. The Treasury replenishes its deposits by selling gold certificates to the Federal Reserve banks. This is one of the ways in which the Federal Reserve acts as banker to the Treasury. It should be noted that a small percentage of these certificates is held to provide backing for the Federal Reserve notes, even though the gold backing provision has been removed.

Loans to commercial banks totaled $1,809 million at the end of 1980. With the discount rate set at 13 percent during December and the Federal funds rate averaging 18.9 percent, banks practicing discretionary funds management found it profitable to turn to the Federal Reserve for funds. (Contrast this with the mere $27 million in loans from the Federal Reserve at the end of 1976. Then, the discount rate was 5¼ percent while the Federal funds rate averaged 4.66 percent.)

Turn now to the liability side, where clearly the largest category is *Federal Reserve notes*, the paper money we handle daily. As mentioned earlier, this liability is no longer redeemable; Federal Reserve notes are fiat money. When banks require currency, the Reserve banks issue notes, increasing this liability category. Thus, the dollar amount recorded on the balance sheet is the actual amount of Federal Reserve paper money in the hands of the public and the banking system.

The Federal Reserve banks provide banking and transfer services for the depository banks, as is indicated by the *banks* deposit entry. This category contains the required reserves of the banks plus a small sum, $675 million in excess reserves. (Recall from Chapter 10 that the banking system can create a multiple quantity of money based on these reserves.)

The Federal Reserve's services to the *Treasury and foreign central banks* are reflected by the deposits that these institutions maintain with the Reserve banks. (In connection with the Treasury, you might want to refer to the discussion of Treasury Tax and Loan accounts on page 139.)

Finally, the Federal Reserve banks' consolidated balance sheet contains the *net worth* entry, which consists of *paid-in capital* plus an equal amount of *surplus*. This surplus was accumulated from retained earnings; additions to it tend to be rather small. The earnings of the Federal Reserve banks are used to cover their own expenses as well as that of the Board of Governors. Also, the revenue goes to pay the mandatory 6 percent dividend to member banks. The remainder is paid to the Treasury of the United States.

☐ Current Issues: Structure, Membership, and Bank Supervision and Examination

This chapter has described the structure of the Federal Reserve System with respect to both the federal government and the commercial banking system. It would be optimistic to conclude with a statement that these relationships have stood the test of time and all problems have been resolved. In fact, the relationship between the Federal Reserve and the government has been under strong attack in recent years. Some members of Congress contend that the Federal Reserve has become far too powerful and unresponsive to Congress itself. At the same time, paradox-

Drawing courtesy of Auth © 1976, The Philadelphia Inquirer, The Washington Post Writers Group.

ically, the Federal Reserve hierarchy has felt itself growing weaker as System membership has shrunk. Each of these issues will be examined in turn. Finally, the Federal Reserve shares supervisory responsibility with other U.S. government agencies. These relationships have also come under scrutiny.

The government and the Federal Reserve

The links between Congress and the Federal Reserve System that were included in the legislation forming the System were weak ones. True, the Federal Reserve System was a creature of Congress and was responsible to it. Moreover, the members of the Federal Reserve Board could be appointed only with Senate approval. But once they had been appointed, formal control by Congress disappeared; the long terms of Board members effectively isolated them from political pressures. Finally, the Board and the Reserve banks were to be, and still are, self-financing, so that the power of the purse, perhaps the most potent source of congressional authority, was nullified.

The connection between the Federal Reserve and the executive branch of the federal government has undergone significant changes, as outlined earlier in this chapter. No longer do high executive officials serve on the Federal Reserve Board. The Federal Reserve is "independent within government"; that is, it is formally responsible to Congress, not to the President.

The reason for separating the Federal Reserve from the government was to isolate the monetary authority from the ebbs and flows of political tides. An independent board would assure the public that the government would not print money to pay for its expenses, thereby producing massive inflation. In addition, against the background of early-twentieth-century banking theory and the objectives of the Act, the Board and the Reserve banks were not viewed as powerful forces in the economy; their functions were seen as primarily technical.

Both the evolution of monetary policy as a significant molder of economic activity and shifts in the perception of the government's role in the economy have modified the earlier attitude toward Federal Reserve independence. Today a government agency that is isolated from Congress is seen as undemocratic. Consequently, congressional demands for reform have taken the shape of bills mandating closer congressional review of Federal Reserve actions and requiring annual budgetary appropriations for the Reserve banks and the Board. Such acts have often been proposed but have never been passed.[9] Nevertheless, the Federal Reserve is frequently placed on the defensive.

In at least one area Congress has required the Federal Reserve to

---

[9]Under the Federal Banking Agency Audit Act of 1978, the Federal Reserve System became subject to audits by a congressional agency, the General Accounting Office. However, the Act specifically forbids GAO investigations of FOMC operations and monetary policy decisions.

engage in a practice that it had long resisted. The chairman of the Federal Reserve now regularly reports to Congress on the monetary targets set by the System for the following year and, at least implicitly, indicates to the public the actions the Federal Reserve is likely to take in the near future. From the standpoint of Reserve System officials, this is like showing your cards before the bets are in. Perhaps they are right.

The Federal Reserve's independence from the executive branch has also been attacked. Monetary policy is but one of a number of government actions that impinge on the economy. The general responsibility for other economic policies rests with the President of the United States, in the sense that he proposes actions to Congress and acts in line with laws passed by Congress. Accordingly, it appears anomalous that the President is given broad authority and discretion in many vital areas of national security and economic policy but is denied a say in monetary policy. In addition to this remarkable lack of confidence in the nation's constitutional leader, economists have pointed out that divided authority can lead to uncoordinated policies. It would be more efficient if all economic policies, monetary policy included, were to be centralized in the hands of the chief executive.

Few observers of economic policy have been willing to go that far. Coordination is recognized as a virtue, but whether the subordination of the Federal Reserve to the executive would prove the best means of achieving this end has been questioned. A consensus has evolved on this issue: It is generally agreed that the existing procedure of informal coordination, involving monthly meetings of such executive officials as the secretary of the Treasury and the chairman of the Council of Economic Advisers with the chairman of the Board of Governors of the Federal Reserve System, is not enough. Since the latter official reserves the option of pursuing a divergent course of action, such coordination must be of limited value.

A middle-of-the-road solution has been proposed by a number of commissions that have examined this situation. This recommendation, which has found its way into the halls of Congress but has not yet been passed, requires that the tenure of the chairman of the Board of Governors be coterminous with that of the President of the United States. As a result, soon after taking office the President would be able to appoint the key official in the Federal Reserve System. It is assumed, of course, that this appointee would reflect the President's views on economic policies in general and monetary policy in particular. Accordingly, a closer relationship between the President and the chief monetary official, one that would produce a more coordinated set of economic policies, is anticipated.

Membership in the Federal Reserve System

A second problem confronting the Federal Reserve System has to do with membership in the System. As Figure 12.3 shows, a noticeable

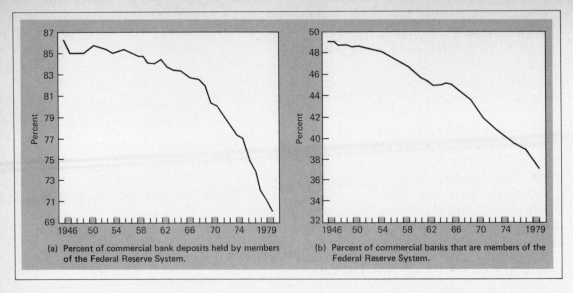

(a) Percent of commercial bank deposits held by members of the Federal Reserve System.

(b) Percent of commercial banks that are members of the Federal Reserve System.

FIGURE 12.3 Attrition in Federal Reserve membership. (Note: Total deposits and number of banks are as of December 31 each year.)

Source: Federal Reserve Bank of St. Louis, *Review*, August 1977; Federal Reserve *Bulletin*, 1977–1979.

decline has occurred in both the number of member banks and the percentage of total banking deposits in member banks. Federal Reserve officials have expressed concern; they view reduced membership as a dilution of monetary control. Fewer members mean that fewer banks are directly subject to changes in the reserve requirement ratio or discount rates. Moreover, the information that is fundamental to intelligent decision making becomes more difficult to acquire, since nonmember banks report to their supervisory authorities less frequently than member banks do to the Federal Reserve.

Why has this attrition in membership occurred? It appears that many of the newer banks decided not to join the System simply because the costs outweighed the benefits. Many of the services available to members, especially for smaller banks, could be obtained through correspondents. At the same time, the nonearning reserves required of members could be avoided. So, too, could the apparently more stringent supervision imposed by the Federal Reserve banks. And, for the same reasons, some of the more established banks had opted out of the System. However, the tradition of membership continued to keep many smaller banks in the System. The larger banks also maintained their membership, although there were some notable exceptions. For these giants, national charters offer some advantages. Moreover, because almost all are organized as holding companies, they fall under the aegis of the Federal Reserve anyway.

The Federal Reserve has long sought congressional action to halt the erosion of its monetary control. One section of the Depository Institutions Deregulation and Monetary Control Act of 1980 was designed to strengthen the central bank's control over the supply of money. The Act mandated that all banks that provide transaction account services to their customers keep reserves either in the form of deposits in the regional Federal Reserve bank or as vault cash. These reserves will not earn interest, and will apply to members and nonmembers alike, and to thrift institutions as well as commercial banks. The Act also provides that all depository institutions may borrow from the Federal Reserve, a logical extension of the imposition of the reserve requirement. (Since the money supply is now defined to include all transaction accounts and such accounts thus become subject to Federal Reserve control, they also fall under the Federal Reserve's responsibility as lender of last resort. Account-holding banks therefore should be entitled to borrow at the discount window.) It should be mentioned that the Act reversed a longstanding practice of the Federal Reserve: Services to banks were no longer to be free of charge. An appropriate fee must be levied.

In short, under the DIDAMCA banks and thrifts, whether or not they are members of the Federal Reserve, are placed on equal footing insofar as reserve requirements, discount privileges, and service charges are concerned. The Federal Reserve will not have to be concerned about the banks' reactions to its policies, nor will the banks' option of leaving the System have much meaning. The Act may well signal the beginning of the end of the dual banking system, since it eliminates the primary advantage of state charter, namely, lower and/or income-earning reserves. For the first time since the formation of the Federal Reserve in 1914, banking system reserves will be centralized. Moreover, again for the first time, the central banking authorities will exercise almost complete control over the reserves of the entire banking system. Only time will tell whether this concentration of reserves and total power will be used wisely by the monetary authorities.

Bank supervision and examination

This chapter has highlighted the service relationships between the Federal Reserve banks and the nation's commercial banks, the Treasury, and foreign banks. But the Federal Reserve supervises as well as provides services. Supervision entails both regulation and examination. Bank branching, holding-company formation, and expansion and mergers are among the activities regulated by the Federal Reserve; you encountered these functions in Chapter 8.

Supervision also entails examination of banks. Banks regularly report to the authorities, detailing both their balance sheets and their income statements. In addition, the authorities visit the banks to make on-site inspections. The examiners are interested in evaluating the "safety and soundness" of the bank. They evaluate the quality of its assets, the nature of its liabilities, and the adequacy of its capital. They inspect the bank's internal controls and procedures and evaluate the competence and policies of the bank's management. Occasionally the examiners uncover fraudulent practices, although this is not their primary function.

It is generally agreed that supervision of banks is necessary. Banks are granted special privileges, and abuse of those privileges, even innocent abuse, should be guarded against. This consensus breaks down, however, over the question of who should do the supervising. The first major schism has to do with federal versus state supervision. Since banking is limited by state boundaries and banking business is conducted within the state, state authorities are intimately involved. But banks also do business on a regional and national scale. The scope of state supervisors may be too limited; only the federal authorities have the national picture in view.

One result of the multiplicity of regulatory authorities is that banks can play one against the others. For instance, you know that banks are chartered on either the federal or the state level. In selecting a chartering authority, the banker chooses the supervisory agency to which the bank will be responsible. Moreover, the banker may switch from one charter to another. This dual banking system, a consequence of the development of banking discussed in Chapter 4, leads to a certain degree of competition in bank regulation—a "competition in laxity," according to some. Since banks presumably select the supervisory authority that promulgates the least onerous regulations, and since each regulatory authority is assumed to be subject to the bureaucratic imperative of empire building, each of the authorities has sufficient reason not to be too restrictive.

Nevertheless, total freedom from federal control is rare. True, state chartering avoids the supervisory attention of the comptroller of the currency. But it does not close other avenues of federal control. Since 97 percent of the nation's commercial banks are insured by the FDIC, they are subject to that agency's inspectors. And over a thousand state banks are members of the Federal Reserve. As a result, most state banks are subject to both federal and state regulation.

To reduce the extent of supervisory duplication, so that after one set of examiners has vacated a bank's premises it is not followed by a second set, the federal and state regulators coordinate their efforts. In fact, an experiment is under way to increase coordination still more: The reports of some state examiners are being accepted on a trial basis by the federal authorities.

Potential duplication of inspection exists even for federally chartered banks. A national bank, you will recall, must be a member of the Federal Reserve System and must be insured by the FDIC. The bank can then be supervised by three separate sets of authorities. Actually, a *modus vivendi* has been worked out in which national banks are subject to examination by the comptroller of the currency, state member banks by Federal Reserve officials, and state nonmember banks by FDIC examiners.

Similar cooperation, mandated by law, occurs when mergers are concerned; primary responsibility is ceded to one agency. The other federal regulators are required to submit opinions to the primary agency (which, however, is not required to heed their advice).

Unevenness in regulatory treatment is one consequence of variety in federal supervisory agencies. Studies have shown that the office of the comptroller of the currency tends to be the most lenient agency from the bankers' point of view while the Federal Reserve is the most difficult to contend with; the FDIC lies somewhere in between. This differentiation in the treatment of banks—and the occasional lack of cooperation between agencies—has led to frequent discussions of the possibility of consolidating federal supervisory powers. Why not have one instead of three, and do away with problems of coordination?

But which supervisory agency would remain? Naturally, each agency would prefer to have the consolidation take place under its own roof. The Federal Reserve may be in the strongest position, since it already has a number of regulatory functions independent of the other agencies. For example, approval of bank holding-company formation and expansion of permissible holding-company activities are solely in the hands of the Federal Reserve Board. It does not even have to seek the advice of the other agencies. In addition, the Federal Reserve's monetary responsibilities are supported by the information gathered through its supervisory activities.

But the FDIC also has a strong claim. Since most U.S. commercial banks are insured by the FDIC, if a bank fails it is the FDIC's responsibility to liquidate it in the least disturbing way. The authority that is ultimately required to pay off in the event of failure should also be the supervisor to make sure banks are sound.

An alternative proposal is the formation of a Federal Banking Commission. All present supervisory activities would be ceded to this new board. In effect, this would mean the end of the comptroller's office as well as the layoff of large numbers of employees who now perform similar duties in the three regulatory agencies. With banking becoming ever more complex as a result of new technology and the increasing internationalization of the banking system, it would seem plausible to develop a core of experts who would represent the public interest. An agency separate from the Federal Reserve Board would also permit the Board to pay more attention to monetary policy, an area that is also becoming more complex.

In 1978 Congress rejected all of these proposals and created a Federal Financial Institutions Examination Council instead. This board, consisting of representatives of all federal banking agencies, coordinates examination procedures among federal examiners and establishes uniform standards. It appears to be working out well.

☐ Summary

This chapter has surveyed a range of topics centering on Federal Reserve operations: the structure of the Federal Reserve; the functions the Reserve banks perform on behalf of the nation's commercial bankers, foreign central bankers, and the U.S. Treasury; and the manner in which the central bank's service functions contribute to an elastic and liquid banking system. The balance sheet of the Federal Reserve was outlined, and three current issues were discussed.

Structure. The Federal Reserve System comprises (1) member banks, subject to the direct supervision and control of the (2) Federal Reserve banks, which in turn are responsible to (3) the seven-member Board of Governors. The presidents of the Reserve banks participate with the Board in the deliberations and decisions of the (4) Federal Open Market Committee. A banker-composed (5) Federal Advisory Committee of minor importance completes the formal structure. For most banking and monetary issues, power resides with the Board of Governors, but the critical role of the FOMC should not be ignored.

Service functions. When the public comes to commercial banks for paper money, the banks turn to the Reserve banks, which supply Federal Reserve notes. The Reserve banks are also active in check clearing and in the transfer of funds and securities for banks. Information used by the banks is provided by the Federal Reserve. Finally, the Federal Reserve is a source of funds for the banking system, especially with respect to seasonal loans through the discount window. Services are also supplied to the central banks of foreign governments and to the Treasury of the United States.

Elasticity and liquidity. By providing for centralized reserves and for discounting, the framers of the Federal Reserve Act sought to increase the banking system's flexibility. Additional demands for cash from the public could be met by the Reserve banks, which would issue notes against the loans being offered for discount by member banks. Liquidity was provided by the discount operation, too, since banks that needed additional reserves could obtain them through a loan from the Federal Reserve. Theoretically, the banking crisis of the early 1930s should not have occurred.

The balance sheet. Securities issued by the government of the United States constitute the main asset of the Federal Reserve banks. Its major liabilities are Federal Reserve notes and deposits of commercial banks. These two liability items reflect the Federal Reserve Act's view of the central bank as an issuer of money and an institution that would centralize the reserves of the nation's banks.

The Federal Reserve and the government. Although Congress created the Federal Reserve, the legislators realized that they were ill equipped to manage a banking system. Thus, they ceded to the Federal Reserve an unusually large measure of independence. This independence was extended so that the Federal Reserve was only loosely linked to the executive branch of the government. While in most instances Federal Reserve and executive branch officials have coordinated economic policy, the fact that the Federal Reserve need not adhere to the economic proscriptions of the President has cheered some and angered others. Closer ties between the President and his cabinet and the Board of Governors of the Federal Reserve System have been recommended but not yet legislated.

Membership. On the other hand, the fears of adverse consequences stemming from attrition in Federal Reserve membership have been resolved. The Federal Reserve had been concerned about the erosion of its monetary powers as member banks accounted for an ever-decreasing share of the nation's deposits. Those powers have been strengthened by the provisions of the Depository Institutions Deregulation and Monetary Control Act (1980), which mandated all banks to maintain non-interest-bearing deposits at Federal Reserve banks or vault cash.

Bank supervision and examination. Coordination is also an important issue in this area. Most commercial banks in the United States are subject to at least one state banking authority and one or more federal banking regulators. The desirability of a set of coordinated rules and procedures is self-evident, but the matter of who should set the rules and who should do the inspecting is still controversial. While the federal agencies had been moving toward a more uniform policy, in 1978 Congress insisted that the comptroller of the currency, the Board of Governors of the Federal Reserve System, and the commissioners of the FDIC speed up the process.

This chapter has demonstrated that the goals set by the Federal Reserve Act—namely, providing an elastic currency, establishing a mechanism for increasing the liquidity of the banking system, and gaining greater control over the nation's banks—have been achieved. The Federal Reserve has been more successful than its originators could have imagined; it has become an integral component of the world financial scene. Indeed, it is impossible to contemplate a smoothly functioning domestic banking system in the absence of the Federal Reserve. The service functions alone, working outside of the public view, provide significant benefits to the population and to the banking system.

Monetary control, the third major area of Federal Reserve responsibility, is the subject of the next chapter. Precisely how does the central bank regulate the monetary system? How can the Federal Reserve slow down the banks' money-creating activity or, on the other hand, speed it up? These questions will be examined in Chapter 13.

☐ Questions and Exercises

1. What qualifications would you want an appointee to the Board of Governors of the Federal Reserve System to possess?

2. Examine the structure of a central bank in an industrial nation other than the United States. Compare it to the U.S. system with respect to ownership, responsibility for central bank policy, and central bank functions and services.

3. a. In 1981 President Reagan called for a tight monetary policy, and the Federal Reserve did pursue such a policy. Can this be taken to imply that the Federal Reserve's independence from the executive was being compromised?

   b. How would you interpret a newspaper headline in late 1980 that read, "Volcker [Chairman of the Board of Governors of the Federal Reserve System] Criticized by Carter on Rates/President Sees Peril in High Levels"?

4. The text conjectures that bank membership in the Federal Reserve System will increase. Do current membership data bear this forecast out?

5. While the Federal Reserve authorities have been trying to reduce float, bankers would prefer that float increase. How do you explain these divergent attitudes?

☐ For Further Study

Many early members of the Federal Reserve Board published their memoirs. Notable among them was a banker of substance, Paul M. Warburg, who wrote *The Federal Reserve System: Its Origin and Growth* (New York: Macmillan, 1930; reprinted by Arno Press, 1975). A more recent insider's survey is Sherman J. Maisel, *Managing the Dollar* (New York: W. W. Norton, 1973).

A. J. Clifford, *The Independence of the Federal Reserve System* (Philadelphia: University of Pennsylvania Press, 1965), looks in detail at an important issue, while the membership problem is carefully and thoroughly explored in George J. Benston, *Federal Reserve Membership: Consequences, Costs, Benefits, and Alternatives* (Chicago: Association of Reserve City Bankers, 1978).

An erudite article proposing a major structural overhaul of the entire Federal Reserve System is Thomas Mayer's "The Structure and Operation of the Federal Reserve System: Some Needed Reforms," in *FINE: Financial Institutions and the Nation's Economy: Compendium of Papers*, written for U.S. House of Representatives, Committee on Banking, Currency, and Housing (Washington, D.C. 1976), pp. 669–725.

The Federal Reserve's own view of its structure and operation is summarized in Board of Governors of the Federal Reserve System, *The Federal Reserve System: Purposes and Functions* (Washington, D.C., 1974). The Board's *Annual Report* contains a host of details about the myriad functions of the Board and its supervision of the banking system.

APPENDIX The Consolidated Statement
of Condition
of All Federal Reserve Banks

A skeletal Federal Reserve balance sheet was provided in Table 12.1 (p. 293); it highlighted the major features of the balance sheet. This appendix provides a more detailed explanation of the balance sheet, listing each category and its explanation.

Formally, the Federal Reserve banks are independently owned. Each publishes a weekly balance sheet and, of course, an annual statement as of December 31. These separate balance sheets are totaled to provide the "Consolidated Statement of Condition"; the 1980 statement is reproduced as Table 12A.1.

Assets

A1. Gold certificate account. When the U.S. Treasury purchases gold, the Treasury draws down its account with the Federal Reserve. To replenish its balance, the Treasury issues gold certificates—which, in fact, are in book entry form—and the Federal Reserve credits the Treasury's account.

A2. Special drawing rights (SDRs) certificate account. The International Monetary Fund has issued SDRs, or "paper gold," to each nation's

TABLE 12A.1 Consolidated Statement of Condition of All Federal Reserve Banks, December 31, 1980 (millions of dollars)

Assets		Liabilities and net worth	
A1 Gold certificate account	$ 11,161	L1 Federal Reserve notes	$124,241
A2 Special drawing rights certificate account	2,518	L2 Deposits	31,546
A3 Cash	397	L21 Member bank	
A4 Loans	1,809	reserves account	27,456
A5 Acceptances	776		
A51 Bought outright	0	L22 U.S. Treasury	
A52 Held under repurchase agreements	776	general account	3,062
A6 Federal agency obligations	9,264	L23 Foreign	411
A61 Bought outright	8,739	L24 Other	617
A62 Held under repurchase agreements	525	L3 Deferred availability	
A7 U.S. government securities	121,328	cash items	8,087
A71 Bought outright	119,299	L4 Other liabilities and	
A711 Bills	43,688	accrued dividends	2,265
A712 Notes	58,718	Total liabilities	166,139
A713 Bonds	16,893		
A72 Held under repurchase agreements	2,029	NW1 Capital paid in	1,203
A8 *Total loans and investments*	133,177	NW2 Surplus	1,203
A9 Cash items in the process of collection	12,554	Total net worth	2,406
A10 Bank premises	457		
A11 Other assets	8,181	Total liabilities and	
Total Assets	$168,545	net worth	$168,545

Source: Federal Reserve *Bulletin*.

treasury. The U.S. Treasury has monetized these SDRs by issuing SDR certificate credits to the Federal Reserve, receiving in exchange dollars credited to the Treasury's account with the Federal Reserve. (For additional information about SDRs, see pp. 615–616.)

A3. Cash. This consists mostly of coin held in the Federal Reserve banks.

A4. Loans. Credit granted primarily to member banks, both in the form of outright advances and as discounts.

A5. Acceptances. Bankers' acceptances are bills of exchange that have been "accepted" or guaranteed by commercial banks. These acceptances are either "Bought outright" (A51), in which case the Federal Reserve banks acquire unconditional title, or held under repurchase agreements (A52). In the latter case, the Federal Reserve bank acquires acceptances for a short period, usually no more than fifteen days, and requires that the seller buy back the asset on the specified date.

A6. Federal agency obligations. These are financial obligations of U.S. government agencies that are normally guaranteed by the federal government. These debts can be acquired outright (A61) or held under repurchase agreements (A62).

A7. U.S. government securities. The bulk of the Federal Reserve's assets consists of obligations of the U.S. Treasury. Most of those securities are bought by the Federal Reserve banks on the open market (A71). The table breaks down the total by the maturity of the obligation. Bills (A711) have an initial maturity of no more than one year; notes (A712) range in maturity from more than one to ten years; while bonds (A713) generally are issued with maturities exceeding ten years. Again, some securities are not purchased outright but are acquired under repurchase agreements (A72).

A8. Total loans and investments. This is the total of loans, acceptances, and federal agency and U.S. government securities.

A9. Cash items in the process of collection. This category consists of checks and other items being cleared by the Federal Reserve banks.

A10. Bank premises. This amount represents the value of land and buildings owned by Federal Reserve banks.

A11. Other assets. This miscellaneous category contains such items as computers and furniture.

Liabilities

L1. Federal Reserve notes. All notes in circulation—those in the hands of the public, the banks, and the Treasury—are included in this total. (Therefore, this sum exceeds the component of M-1, which counts only currency in the hands of the public and not the amount in the commercial banks or the Treasury.)

L2. Deposits. Included are the demand deposits of member banks, both required and excess (L21); the active Treasury account used to make government payments (L22); deposits of foreign central banks, some foreign governments, and the Bank of International Settlements (L23); and deposits of international organizations and reserves of certain types of international banking organizations (L24).

L3. Deferred availability cash items. This category consists of cash items received but not yet credited to member banks. When the Federal Reserve processes cash items, it credits member banks within two days, depending on the location of the bank on which the check is drawn.

The $4,467 million difference between cash items in the process of collection (A8) and deferred availability cash items (L3) is the float mentioned in the chapter (p. 294).

L4. Other liabilities and accrued dividends. These are miscellaneous items.

Net worth

NW1. Capital paid in. This is the amount paid by member banks when buying the mandatory Federal Reserve bank stock.

NW2. Surplus. This consists of the net earnings of Federal Reserve banks after paying dividends to member banks and making payments to the U.S. Treasury.

It will become evident in the next chapter that changes in the Federal Reserve balance sheet affect the money-creating ability of the banking system.

CHAPTER 13

Federal Reserve Policy: The "Hows" of Central Banking

As the Federal Reserve is continuously evolving, it is to be assumed that policy instruments will continue to be adapted to changing circumstances in the years ahead.

Ralph A. Young, former Federal Reserve official (1973)

CONTENTS

We should not underestimate the importance of the mundane, unheralded service functions of the Federal Reserve System that were surveyed in the previous chapter. The flow of financial instruments runs smoothly under the light touch of the central bank. Nevertheless, public attention is galvanized not by these service functions but by the actions taken by the central bank's officers to shape the economy. When the Federal Reserve modifies its monetary policy stance through one of its instruments, or even when it appears likely to do so, the press and the financial community spring to attention. The instruments of monetary control are the subject of this chapter.

What are these instruments? How are they used? What impact do they exert on the banking system and the public? Such questions are addressed in the next pages. First, it will be useful to distinguish between two types of control instruments: **general** and **selective.**

The general weapons of monetary action are four: (1) open-market operations, (2) variations in required reserve ratios, (3) discount rate changes, and, in the past, (4) modifications in Regulation Q. These instruments are directed at commercial banks' money creation and lending policies in general; they do not single out any specific area for distinct treatment. Selective weapons today include only changes in margin requirements, which are directed specifically at stock market credit. "Moral suasion"—preaching by Federal Reserve officials— straddles the fence; occasionally general exhortations are voiced, while at other times a particular phase of activity is singled out. Similarly, the panoply of credit controls provided by the Credit Control Act of 1969 can be used both generally and selectively.

Because they are most pervasive in terms of both impact and frequency of use, it is appropriate to commence with an analysis of the general credit controls.

A **general monetary instrument** is a broad, across-the-board tool that affects a wide variety of financial and economic activities, primarily by influencing the cost and/or availability of credit.

A **selective monetary instrument** is designed to affect a specific type of economic activity or a specific segment of the economy.

☐ Open Market Operations (OMO)

Almost daily the Federal Reserve intervenes in the U.S. government securities market as either a purchaser or a seller. As you will see shortly, such actions affect commercial bank reserves, either increasing them (in the case of OMO purchases) or decreasing them (in the case of sales).

Background

Open market operations were added to the monetary control arsenal by accident. The Federal Reserve Act had permitted the Federal Reserve banks to acquire U.S. government securities, the idea being to provide them with a source of revenue. During the early 1920s the Reserve banks, each acting on its own, traded in securities for their own accounts. It soon became evident that such transactions affected the securities markets and the reserves of the banking system. And it was realized that with each Reserve bank acting independently, the impact on the market was a hit-or-miss affair. A coordinated effort was called for, so in 1922 the presidents of the twelve Reserve banks formed the Open Market Investment Committee. Protests that this structure placed too much power in the hands of the bank presidents, who were not government officials, and none in the hands of the Federal Reserve Board led to a compromise structure, the present Federal Reserve Open Market Committee (FOMC). As mentioned in Chapter 12, the Banking Act of 1935 provided that the twelve-member FOMC was to consist of all seven members of the Federal Reserve Board, the president of the Federal Reserve Bank of New York, and four of the other eleven bank presidents, who would serve on a rotating basis. The decisions of the FOMC were to be binding on the Reserve banks, and the assets acquired and profits earned were to be shared by the banks.

Nowadays regular meetings of the FOMC are held in Washington, D.C., at least monthly. Its discussions encompass the entire range of monetary and macroeconomic issues, national and international. Decisions about the stance of monetary policy in general and open market operations in particular are made at those meetings. The participants in the FOMC's wide-ranging discussions include not only the twelve voting members but also the other Reserve bank presidents.

Before the FOMC meeting, the bank presidents and the board members study an analysis of the economy prepared by Federal Reserve staff economists, including an assessment of the direction of the economy and what alternative courses of action should be considered. Both longer-run and immediate policies are surveyed. A senior staff member normally opens the FOMC meeting by summarizing and evaluating the present economic situation, and a freewheeling discussion follows. Ultimately, the chairman of the Board of Governors, who presides over the meeting, summarizes the discussion. A formal vote is taken and a **policy**

directive composed. The policy directive informs the manager for domestic operations of the System Open Market Account (manager, for short), who is a vice-president of the Federal Reserve Bank of New York, what results the FOMC expects to see during the next month. (See Box 13.1) The manager is to translate this general statement into an operating program, buying or selling securities on a daily basis to achieve the goal of the FOMC directive.

A **policy directive** is a written order by the FOMC specifying the immediate objectives of open market operations.

Box 13.1. FOMC Directive Issued to the Federal Reserve Bank of New York, March 18, 1980

The information reviewed at this meeting suggests that real output of goods and services continued to grow in the first quarter of 1980 and that the rise in prices accelerated. In February retail sales declined moderately, but the decrease followed an exceptionally large increase in January. Industrial production expanded somewhat in both months, after a period of little change, and nonfarm payroll employment continued to rise. The unemployment rate edged down in February to 6.0 percent. Private housing starts declined further in January and were more than one-fifth below the rate in the third quarter of last year. The rise in producer prices of finished goods and in consumer prices was more rapid in the first month or two of 1980 than in 1979, despite some easing in prices of foods. Over the first two months of 1980 the rise in the index of average hourly earnings was somewhat below the rapid pace recorded in 1979. . . .

Growth of M-1A and M-1B, which had remained moderate in January, accelerated sharply in February, and growth of M-2 also quickened. In recent weeks, however, monetary growth has subsided. Expansion of commercial bank credit picked up in the first two months of this year from the reduced pace in the fourth quarter of 1979. Market interest rates have risen substantially in recent weeks. An increase in Federal Reserve discount rates from 12 to 13 percent was announced early on February 15, effective immediately.

On March 14 the President announced a broad program of fiscal, energy, credit, and other measures designed to moderate and reduce inflationary forces in a manner that can also lay the groundwork for a return to stable economic growth. Consistent with that objective and with the continuing intent of the Federal Reserve System to restrain growth in money and credit during 1980, the Board of Governors took the following actions to reinforce the effectiveness of the measures announced in October 1979: (1) a special credit restraint program; (2) a special deposit requirement for all lenders on increases in certain types of consumer credit; (3) an increase in the marginal reserve requirement on managed liabilities of large member banks; (4) a special deposit requirement on increases in managed liabilities of large nonmember banks; (5) a special deposit requirement on increases in total assets of money market mutual funds; (6) a surcharge of 3 percentage points on frequent borrowing of large member banks from Federal Reserve banks.

(continued)

Box 13.1 (continued)

Taking account of past and prospective economic developments, the Federal Open Market Committee seeks to foster monetary and financial conditions that will resist inflationary pressures while encouraging moderate economic expansion and contributing to a sustainable pattern of international transactions. At its meeting on February 4–5, 1980, the Committee agreed that these objectives would be furthered by growth of M-1A, M-1B, M-2, and M-3 from the fourth quarter of 1979 to the fourth quarter of 1980 within ranges of 3½ to 6, 4 to 6½, 6 to 9, and 6½ to 9½ percent respectively. The associated range for bank credit was 6 to 9 percent.

In the short run, the Committee seeks expansion of reserve aggregates consistent with growth over the first half of 1980 at an annual rate of 4½ percent for M-1A and 5 percent for M-1B, or somewhat less, provided that in the period before the next regular meeting the weekly average Federal funds rate remains within a range of 13 to 20 percent. The Committee believes that, consistent with this short-run policy, M-2 should grow at an annual rate of about 7¼ percent over the first half and expansion of bank credit should slow in the months ahead to a pace compatible with growth over the year as a whole within the range agreed upon.

If it appears during the period before the next meeting that the constraint on the Federal funds rate is inconsistent with the objective for the expansion of reserves, the Manager for Domestic Operations is promptly to notify the Chairman, who will then decide whether the situation calls for supplementary instructions from the Committee.

Votes for this action: Messrs. Volcker, Guffey, Morris, Partee, Rice, Roos, Schultz, Mrs. Teeters, Messrs. Winn and Timlen. Vote against this action: Mr. Wallich. (Mr. Timlen voted as alternate member.)

Mr. Wallich dissented from this action because he favored pursuit of a more restrictive policy for the period immediately ahead to assure maintenance of firm general credit restraint, especially as a means of buttressing the new anti-inflation program.

Method

How are open market transactions conducted? Assume that, on the basis of the directive and after the daily consultation with key members of the FOMC, the manager decides to acquire $250 million worth of government securities. Since the Federal Reserve is a not-for-profit organization, the manager need not be concerned with the price of this volume of securities. Nevertheless, the manager will attempt to obtain the $250 million at the lowest price possible. This is done by having the bank's staff of traders contact the thirty-six **dealers** in U.S. government securities that regularly transact with the New York Federal Reserve Bank. The dealers are asked to quote the selling prices of various quantities of securities, and the manager's staff will then purchase the

A U.S. government securities **dealer** is a firm that "makes a market" in this type of security. The firm is willing to buy or sell securities at prices determined by itself.

$250 million from the dealers offering the lowest prices. This procedure is followed for both outright purchases and repurchase agreements. (See Box 13.2.) The dealers will sell from their own portfolios but will normally replenish their security holdings by acquiring securities from the general public.

Box 13.2. Open Market Operations: Instruments and Techniques

The manager has a number of options in implementing FOMC decisions. A variety of instruments can be bought or sold, and the manager can choose among different sales/purchase techniques.

Instruments

The Federal Reserve is authorized to trade in direct obligations of the federal government as well as in the securities of agencies of the United States. The agencies (e.g., the Federal National Mortgage Association or "Fannie Mae") issue bonds, which are not U.S. Treasury obligations but are guaranteed by the Treasury. The central bank may also acquire or sell bankers' acceptances (commercial paper that is "accepted" or guaranteed by a commercial bank).

Since early 1977 open market trading has been almost entirely in U.S. government securities. In 1980, of the $20.2 million of gross purchases and sales of governments, three-quarters consisted of U.S. Treasury bills. U.S. Treasury notes and bonds accounted for most of the remaining quarter, while transactions in agency issues came to less than $1 billion.

Techniques

In the past the Federal Reserve commonly bought or sold "outright," that is, without any conditions attached. In recent years, however, the FOMC has preferred repurchase (RP) agreements over outright purchases, and reverse repurchases ("reverse RPs") or matched sales (MSPs) in lieu of outright sales. In an RP, the Federal Reserve buys securities for a specific number of days, with the seller (a government securities dealer) committing to repurchase the securities at an agreed-upon price at the end of the specified time. In a reverse RP, the manager agrees to sell, with a commitment to buy back at the end of the stated interval. Such agreements are made when the manager wants to supply or withhold funds for a relatively brief interval. Offsetting a decrease in float, for example, would be one reason for an RP; if it is timed right, float will be up to normal when the RP expires.

In 1980, outright purchase or sales accounted for only 1.3 percent of total open market transactions, while RP and reverse RPs accounted for the remaining 98.7 percent.

Source: Data from Board of Governors of the Federal Reserve System, *Annual Report, 1980.*

Open Market Operations and Deposit Creation

It will be useful to trace what happens to various accounts as a result of this transaction. (The dealers' accounts can be omitted, since their transactions are basically self-balancing. The dealers buy from the public and sell an equal amount to the Federal Reserve.)

When the Federal Reserve purchases the $250 million from Joel Q. Public and pays for it with a check drawn on itself, the initial reaction will appear on T-accounts as follows:

Federal Reserve Banks		Joel Q. Public	
U.S. government securities: +$250 million	Check to JQP: +$250 million	U.S. government securities: −$250 million	
		Check (drawn by FR): +$250 million	

When Joel Q. deposits his check into the First National Bank of Sharon, the result will be as follows:

First National Bank of Sharon		Joel Q. Public	
Cash item in process of collection: +$250 million	Demand deposit (JQP): +$250 million	U.S. government securities: −$250 million	
		Demand deposit: +$250 million	

And when the bank sends the check to its district Federal Reserve bank for collection, which completes the cycle, the three T-accounts can be portrayed as follows:

Federal Reserve Banks		First National Bank of Sharon		Joel Q. Public	
U.S. government securities: +$250 million	Deposits (bank reserve account), First National Bank of Sharon: +$250 million	Deposit at FRB (reserves): +$250 million	Demand deposit (JQP): +$250 million	U.S. government securities: −$250 million	
				Demand deposits: +$250 million	

Joel Q. Public has traded his securities for demand deposits, presumably at some gain to himself (which is omitted from the example to keep the numbers simple). The deposit is credited to his account at his commercial bank, which collected the check from the Federal Reserve. Note that *this $250 million deposit represents an increase in bank reserves*, a most important point. Finally, the Federal Reserve, which has acquired the government securities, pays for them by crediting the First

National Bank of Sharon's reserve account with $250 million. These reserves are *additions* to the total reserves available to the banking system; they were not present prior to the purchase. *Federal Reserve open market purchases create new banking system reserves.*

Of course, with new reserves available to the commercial banks, additional deposits can be created. Recall the analysis in Chapter 10. When banks operating under a fractional-reserve system acquire reserves, a multiple amount of deposits can be created. If the reserves required of First National are 10 percent of demand deposits, then the T-account of that bank can be rewritten as follows:

First National Bank of Sharon

Required reserves: +$ 25 million Excess reserves: +$225 million	Demand deposits: +$250 million

As you now know, a bank in a multibank system would create deposits in an amount no greater than its excess reserves; an adverse clearing flow has to be anticipated and sufficient cover must be at hand. Thus, First National could create an additional $225 million in demand deposits by either lending or investing that sum. For the banking system as a whole, however, the multiplier formula developed in Chapter 10 applies. The entire banking system can create $2,500 million, according to equation 10.1':

$$\Delta DD = \Delta R \ (1/r_{DD})$$

$$\$2,500 \text{ million} = \$250 \text{ million} \times \frac{1}{10\%}$$

The following T-accounts will be found:

Federal Reserve Banks		Commercial Banking System		Public	
U.S. government securities: +$250 million	Deposits (bank reserve accounts): +$250 million	Reserves: +$250 million Earning assets: +$2,250 million	Demand deposits: +$2,500 million	Demand deposits: +$2,500 million U.S. government securities: −$250 million	Borrowings from banks: +$2,250 million

(If the concepts contained in this paragraph are not crystal clear to you, you might want to reread Chapter 10.)

Thus, an open market purchase by the central bank will lead to a multiple creation of deposits; the acquisition of $250 million of securities leads to the creation of $2.5 billion in demand deposits. Open market purchases are therefore expansionary.

The reverse is true for open market sales by the Federal Reserve. The reduction of the Reserve banks' securities portfolio means an equivalent increase in the portfolios of other segments of the economy. The public, which acquires the securities, pays for them by writing checks. The process just described is run backward: The check received by the Reserve bank in payment for the sold securities is debited from the account of the bank on which it was drawn, Jean Q. Public's bank. This reduces reserves by an equivalent sum and, because of the deposit multiplier, drives deposits down even more. If the T-accounts presented earlier represented the standing of the three participants prior to an open market sale and the manager decided to sell $100 million worth of government securities, then, with a deposit multiplier of 10, deposits will fall by $1 billion. The balance sheets then will change as follows:

Federal Reserve Banks		Commercial Banking System		Public	
U.S. government securities: −$100 million	Deposits (bank reserve account): −$100 million	Reserves: −$100 million Earning assets: −$900 million	Demand deposits: −$1 billion	Demand deposits: −$1 billion U.S. government securities: +$100 million	Borrowings: −$900 million

Thus, by selling securities the Federal Reserve can contract the money supply, and by purchasing securities it can expand the supply of money. The extent of the increase or decrease is dependent on two factors: (1) the size of the central bank's purchase or sale, and (2) the value of the deposit multiplier.

"Defensive" and "Dynamic" open market operations and the Federal Reserve bank reserve statement

The Federal Reserve intervenes daily in the U.S. government securities market, acquiring or disposing of hundreds of millions of dollars' worth of issues. Most of these transactions are **defensive** in that they are meant to preserve the monetary status quo. Occasionally, open market operations are **dynamic**, and represent active intervention. They are meant to loosen or tighten the monetary reins.

Defensive open market actions are designed to prevent unwanted actions from disturbing the market.
Dynamic operations are engaged in changing the direction of the market.

You are aware that the flow of Treasury funds into the banking system leads to increases in banking system reserves. So, too, does an increase in Federal Reserve float. Or, as mentioned in the preceding chapter, foreign banks may be asking the Federal Reserve to buy securities for their own accounts. All of these actions by themselves lead to an increase in banking system reserves. Unless such a move is desired by the FOMC, the manager of the open market account will engage in offsetting transactions, selling, usually by means of a reverse RP, an equivalent value of U.S. government securities. This is a defensive response. If it is planned and executed precisely, the transactions offset each other, having a neutral impact on the securities markets, bank reserves, and the money supply.

When the FOMC has ordered a tighter monetary stance, the manager also will sell securities. The purpose of these sales, however, is to tighten market conditions and lead to the reduced money supply desired by the FOMC.

Each Friday the Federal Reserve Board publishes a statement, "Factors Affecting Reserves of Depository Institutions and Condition Statement of Federal Reserve Banks," that details the week's changes in bank reserves

---

BOX 13.3 Factors Affecting Reserves of Depository Institutions and Condition Statement of Federal Reserve Banks (adapted), week ended December 24, 1980

Reserves of depository institutions, Reserve Bank credit, and related items	Averages of daily figures (in millions of dollars)
Reserve Bank credit:	
U.S. government securities—	
Bought outright—System account	119,071
Held under repurchase agreements	266
Federal agency obligations—	
Bought outright	8,739
Held under repurchase agreements	10
Acceptances—	
Bought outright	—
Held under repurchase agreements	30
Loans—	
To depository institutions	1,649
Float	6,161
Other F.R. assets	8,361
Total Reserve Bank credit	144,288
Gold Stock	11,161
Special Drawing Rights certificate account	3,368
Treasury currency outstanding	13,410
	172,227
MINUS:	
Currency in circulation	135,952
Treasury cash holdings	449
Treasury deposits with F.R. Banks	2,287
Foreign deposits with F.R. Banks	395
Other deposits with F.R. Banks	392
Other F.R. liabilities and capital	4,975
	144,449
EQUALS:	
Reserve balances with F.R. Banks	27,778
PLUS:	
Total vault cash (estimated)	17,663
EQUALS:	45,441
OF WHICH:	
Reserve balances + total vault cash used to satisfy reserve requirements[a]	40,957
Required reserves (estimated)	40,029
Excess reserve balances at F.R. Banks[b]	928

[a] Reserve balances with Federal Reserve Banks plus vault cash at institutions with required reserve balances plus vault cash equal to required reserves at other institutions.
[b] During this week, banks borrowed $1,649 million from the Federal Reserve, J.P.

and their causes. In essence, this is a restatement of the Federal Reserve balance sheet, amended for the impact of U.S. Treasury monetary actions, and rearranged to show the impact on bank reserves. Box 13.3 reproduces the statement for the week ending December 24, 1980. In essence, the dollar sum of the activities that reduce banking system reserves is subtracted from the value of those that increase bank reserves. The net change, then, indicates an increase or a decrease in bank reserves. This can be most useful for economists who are trying to forecast the future of the money supply and the economy. Unfortunately, the statement does not indicate whether the actions taken by the Federal Reserve are defensive or dynamic in nature. Consequently, we cannot be sure whether any increase in bank reserves indicates a loosening of policy by the Federal Reserve or simply an error. Perhaps the manager had projected a smaller increase in reserves and took defensive actions that turned out to be too small. Obviously, the interpretation of the statements matters greatly: It is one of the activities that earn good economists handsome salaries.

The impact of a given open market operation depends crucially on the value of the deposit multiplier. In turn, the multiplier's value depends on the second instrument of monetary control: changes in the reserve requirement.

☐ Changes in the Reserve Requirement

Background

If open market operations were a child of the Roaring Twenties, reserve requirement changes were born in the Depression Thirties. The original Federal Reserve Act incorporated bank reserve requirements, which stemmed from the National Bank Act (see Chapter 4). While the Federal Reserve Act was a significant improvement in that it centralized reserves and eliminated reserve pyramiding, the Act nevertheless imposed rigid reserve requirements. It left no discretion to modify the stated ratios.

The Federal Reserve Act applied different reserve ratios to central reserve city, reserve city, and country banks, following the pattern that had evolved since the passage of the National Bank Act. Similarly, the Federal Reserve Act distinguished between demand and time deposit accounts. Consequently, between 1917 and 1935 the following reserve ratios were required of all member banks:

Reserve designation	Percentage required	
	Demand deposits	Time deposits
Central reserve city	13	3
Reserve city	10	3
Country	7	3

The inability of the central bank to function effectively during the early Depression years led to a reevaluation of these fixed reserve ratios. It was felt that the boom could have been slowed if credit had been made less available, and that the bust could have been alleviated by an enlarged money supply. The Federal Reserve's contribution to inhibiting either the boom or the bust was negligible; the Federal Reserve contended that it was powerless. It possessed only an ineffective discount rate weapon and a fledgling and not fully understood open market operation. Consequently, Congress amended the Federal Reserve Act to increase the flexibility of the Federal Reserve in dealing with adverse economic movements. The Banking Act of 1935 permitted the Federal Reserve Board to vary reserve requirement ratios within the following limits:

| Reserve designation | Required reserve ratio limits (percent) | |
	Demand deposits	Time deposits
Central reserve city	13–26	
Reserve city	10–20	3–6
Country	7–14	

The Federal Reserve Board utilized this new instrument soon after it was written into law. In 1937, in a move whose appropriateness has been a subject of considerable debate, the Board doubled the ratios. Since then the Board has modified the ratios in both directions. It imposed the maximum ratios during World War II, but since 1951 the trend has been a falling one.

Status in the 1970s

The system of reserve requirements as it evolved in the 1970s differed in numerous ways from the simpler setup of the past. Table 13.1 lists the requirements against deposits as of December 31, 1979. A number of distinctions are evident: First, since 1972 the tripartite reserve designation, which is based on geography and population, has been replaced by categories based on bank size. Smaller banks are required to maintain smaller ratios. Second, not only is there a distinction between demand and time deposits, but differences exist within each deposit type. Larger deposits must be covered by a larger *marginal* reserve ratio. As recently as December 1974 a third modification was introduced: The time deposit ratio was varied according to the maturity of the deposit. The longer the initial maturity date, the smaller the required reserve ratio[1].

---

[1]Another change involves the computation of the ratio. Until September 1968, a bank's daily totals of reserve deposits at the regional Reserve bank and (since 1959) its vault cash were averaged on a weekly basis and divided into the weekly average deposit. Since then, a more complicated scheme, which relates reserves held in any given week to the deposits of two weeks earlier, is used. Moreover, a bank is permitted to carry over excess or deficient reserves for a one- to two-week period. The Federal Reserve is considering restoring the contemporaneous accounting method.

TABLE 13.1 Federal Reserve Requirements, 1979

Type of Deposit, and Deposit Interval (Millions of Dollars)	Percent
Net demand:	
0–2	7
2–10	9½
10–100	11¾
100–400	12¾
Over 400	16¼
Time:	
Savings	3
Other time:	
0–5, maturing in	
30–179 days	3
180 days to 4 years	2½
4 years or more	1
Over 5, maturing in	
30–179 days	6
180 days to 4 years	2½
4 years or more	1

Source: Federal Reserve *Bulletin*.

Various motives underlie the increasing complexity of the required reserve ratio. First, it was felt that the size of a bank, as measured by its deposits, is more indicative of the nature of a bank's operation than the size of the city in which the bank is located. Large banks have much in common, and it matters little whether their home offices are in New York and Chicago or San Francisco and Dallas. Second, differentiated reserve requirement ratios encourage banks to foster and maintain specific types of deposits and specific maturities.

Liability categories and reserve requirements

For the most part, central bank reserve requirements were levied on banks' deposit liabilities. Mention was made in Chapter 7 of some exceptions; these, especially the ones imposed in October 1979, are dealt with here.

Historically, reserves were mandated against deposits. This worked well as long as deposits remained not only the banks' largest liability category but also a constant percentage of the total. To be sure, the reduction in the average reserve requirement ratio as the public shifted from demand to time deposits (pp. 134–135) did pose some problems for monetary control. Nevertheless, Federal Reserve officials did not feel that remedial action was needed. They were far more concerned with the erosion of their control as the proportion of bank deposits to total bank liabilities fell. As bankers managed their portfolios more aggressively, their reliance on borrowed funds increased at the expense of deposit funds. The zero reserve requirement on nondeposit liabilities meant that bankers could expand credit to the full extent of their borrowings. As you know from Chapters 6 and 7, bankers reduced their reliance on deposit sources, substituting borrowings instead. And, as already related, in the 1960s and 1970s the Federal Reserve Board imposed reserve requirements on various categories of borrowings.

In its most encompassing move, the Board of Governors acted in October 1979 to slow the growth in banks' nondeposit liabilities by imposing a marginal 8 percent reserve requirement on all managed liabilities. These were defined as

1. CDs in excess of $100,000 or more with an initial maturity of one year or less,
2. Eurodollar borrowings,
3. Repurchase agreements against U.S. government securities,
4. Federal funds borrowings from nonmember banks. (Borrowings from member banks were already subject to a reserve requirement.)

These requirements affected only banks with $100 million or more in the managed-liabilities category, and were imposed only on the growth of deposits beyond $100 million.

This policy move was directed at closing a loophole. By removing bankers' incentive to acquire nondeposit funds, the erosion of the reserve ratio would be halted. Table 13.2 traces the expected impact of the policy.

In the absence of borrowings and with an 8 percent reserve requirement imposed on deposits, Table 13.2(1a) shows that a representative

TABLE 13.2 The Impact of Nondeposit Liabilities on Excess Reserves

1. Reserve requirements on deposit liabilities only
a. *Before any adjustments* (required reserve ratio = 8%)

Assets			Liabilities	
Required reserves		$ 8 million	Deposits	$100 million
Excess reserves (available for use)		92 million		
	Total	$100 million	Total	$100 million

b. *After shift into nondeposit liabilities*

Assets			Liabilities	
Required reserves (8% of $75 million)		$ 6 million	Deposits	$ 75 million
Excess reserves (available for use)		94 million	Borrowings	25 million
	Total	$100 million	Total	$100 million

2. Reserve requirements on all liabilities

Assets			Liabilities	
Required reserves		$ 8 million	Deposits	$ 75 million
Excess reserves		92 million	Borrowings	25 million
	Total	$100 million	Total	$100 million

bank would hold $8 million (= 8 % of $100 million) in reserves, so that the remaining $92 million is in excess reserves. Should $92 million be lent or invested, these reserves would be transfered in payment (see Chapter 10). However, the banker could reduce the amount of required reserves and the ratio of reserves to total liabilities by inducing a shift in the liability mix. In Table 13.2(1b) the banker's balance sheet reflects a 75–25 percent distribution of deposit and nondeposit liabilities. Since borrowings are not subject to a reserve requirement, the banker must hold only 8 percent of the deposits of $75 million, or $6 million, in reserves. Required reserves have fallen by $2 million (and the ratio of reserves to total liabilities from 8% to 6%) and excess reserves have risen by the same amount, increasing the banker's ability to extend credit. To offset this liberalization, the monetary authority imposes an 8 percent reserve requirement on nondeposit liabilities, which removes this incentive to borrow, as the final T-account of the table shows. (Note: If the reserve requirements differ, the amount of excess reserves may increase or decrease following the imposition of the new policy. Calculate what would happen if the reserve requirement on deposits were 5 percent and that on nondeposit sources 8 percent.)

The Depository Institutions Deregulation and Monetary Control Act of 1980

Congress introduced a major reform in the reserve requirement structure with the Depository Institutions Deregulation and Monetary Control Act of 1980. As you know, all depository institutions were made subject to reserve requirements. But in addition, the Act modified the limits of the reserve ratio and the method of calculating it. A distinction is made between transaction (checking) and nonpersonal (i.e., corporate) time deposit accounts. The Federal Reserve must impose a reserve requirement ratio of 3 percent on transaction accounts of $25 million or less.[2] For sums exceeding that amount, the Board of Governors may set a ratio within the 8–14 percent range. For nonpersonal time deposit accounts, the range is from 0 to 9 percent. The requirements at the end of 1980 are listed in Table 13.3. Additional emergency and supplemental powers are also granted to the Board, permitting it to impose additional reserve requirements. However, these are to be allowed for limited periods only and in consultation with either Congress or the other regulatory authorities. The Act also sets up a transition period. Member banks' reserve requirements may, at the Board's discretion, be adjusted to their new levels over a four-year period. And nonmembers, which are now subject to Federal Reserve requirements, are given a seven-year adjustment period. In general, the new ratios lie below existing ones, and thus all member banks stand to benefit.

---

[2]This breakpoint will be adjusted annually by 80 percent of the growth in transaction accounts. Thus, if such accounts grew by 10 percent in 1980–1981, the 3 percent required reserve ratio would apply to the first $27 million [= $25 million + (0.10) (.8) ($25 million)].

TABLE 13.3 Depository Institutions Reserve Requirements, December 31, 1980

Type of deposit, and deposit interval	Depository institution requirements after implementation of the Monetary Control Act[a] (percent)
Net transaction accounts	
$0–$25 million	3
Over $25 million	12
Nonpersonal time deposits	
By original maturity	
Less than 4 years	3
4 years or more	0
Eurocurrency liabilities	
All types	3

[a]For existing nonmember banks and thrift institutions at the time of implementation of the Monetary Control Act, the phase-in period ends Sept. 3, 1987. For existing member banks the phase-in period is about three years, depending on whether their new reserve requirements are greater or less than the old requirements. For existing agencies and branches of foreign banks, the phase-in ends Aug. 12, 1982. All new institutions will have a two-year phase-in beginning with the date that they open for business.

Source: Federal Reserve *Bulletin*.

With all the changes introduced in recent years, the reserve ratio has become more complex to compute. This is not without negative consequences. First, however, it might be best to indicate how a change in the required reserve ratio (r_{DD}) affects the banking system and the money supply.

Changing the required reserve ratio

Assume that commercial banks maintain only demand deposits and the Federal Reserve Board imposes a uniform 10 percent required reserve ratio. The left-hand side of Table 13.4(a) then, represents a simplified balance sheet for the First National Bank of Sharon, while the right-hand side represents the balance sheet of the entire commercial banking system. This particular bank, as well as the entire banking system, cannot expand deposits further, since no excess reserves are available. All reserves are required reserves equal to the stated 10 percent of demand deposits.

Now the Federal Reserve Board takes an improbable step and cuts the required ratio (r_{DD}) in half, from 10 percent to 5 percent. The immediate impact is portrayed in Table 13.4(b). The reserve holdings of the First National Bank of Sharon still equal $10,000. However, only $5,000 is required $(r_{DD} = 5\%$ of DD $= \$100,000)$; the remaining reserves of $5,000 are now excess reserves. Of course, what is true for this particular bank is true for other banks as well, so the banking system is flooded with $5 million in excess reserves. Since these excess reserves are not earning assets, bankers will try to find borrowers or will invest the funds, creating new deposits in the process.

What dollar sum of new deposits can be created by the banking system?

TABLE 13.4 The Impact of a Decrease in the Reserve Requirement Ratio on Commercial Banks

a. Before the Decrease (r_{DD} = 10%)

First National Bank of Sharon				Banking System			
Required reserves	$10,000	Demand deposits	$100,000	Required reserves	$10,000,000	Demand deposits	$100,000,000
Earning assets	$90,000			Earning assets	$90,000,000		

b. Immediately After the Decrease (r_{DD} = 5%)

First National Bank of Sharon				Banking System			
Required reserves	$ 5,000	Demand deposits	$100,000	Required reserves	$ 5,000,000	Demand deposits	$100,000,000
Excess reserves	$ 5,000			Excess reserves	$ 5,000,000		
Earning assets	$90,000			Earning assets	$90,000,000		

c. After the Decrease Has Been Absorbed (r_{DD} = 5%)

First National Bank of Sharon				Banking System			
Required reserves	$ 10,000	Demand deposits	$200,000	Required reserves	$ 10,000,000	Demand deposits	$200,000,000
Earning assets	$190,000			Earning assets	$190,000,000		

One simple way to calculate this total is to use the multiplier formula (equation 10-1′):

$$\Delta DD = \Delta R \,(1/r_{DD})$$

Before the change, the equation yielded

$$\$10,000,000 \times 1/.10 = \$10,000,000 \times 10 = \$100,000,000$$

After the change, the value of the multiplier increased from 1/.10 to 1/.05, or from 10 to 20. The new deposit value is

$$\$10,000,000 \times 20 = \$200,000,000$$

The new totals calculated for the banking system when equilibrium is restored are found in Table 13.4 (c). Once again, no excess reserves exist and all available reserves are required reserves. A *decrease* in the required reserve ratio led to an *increase* in demand deposits.

It is important to stress that the increase in deposits is *not* accompanied by a rise in banking system reserves. The same volume of reserves, $10,000,000, appears both before and after. What has occurred is that, as a result of the decrease in the required reserve ratio, the existing quantity of reserves supports a larger volume of deposits. The deposit multiplier has increased. (In contrast, open market operations change the volume of reserves, leaving the multiplier unaffected.)

The reverse is true for an increase in the reserve ratio. If the Federal Reserve Board had raised the required ratio from 10 percent to 20 percent, the multiplier would have fallen from 10 to 5 (= 1/.20), and the deposits supported by the $100,000,000 in reserve holdings would have declined to $50,000,000. Each $1 of Banking system reserves would have been able to support only $5 of deposits instead of the previous $10.

How would this contraction have been accomplished? Essentially, as the public paid off its loans and thus reduced deposits (do you know why loan repayment goes hand in hand with reductions in deposits?), bankers would not issue additional loans or purchase new investments. Instead, they would sterilize these inflows in the form of required reserves.

Of course, the Federal Reserve never alters the ratio by the percentages used in these examples. Typically, the Board has changed the ratio by ¼ or ½ percentage point. With almost $40 billion in bank required reserves outstanding at the end of 1980, such changes are likely to modify banking system reserves by some $100–$200 million, and deposits by a multiple of those sums.

To summarize, the U.S. monetary authorities can use either or both of two instruments—open market operations and reserve requirement changes—to increase or decrease money supply. The impacts are outlined in Table 13.5.

Open market operations and changes in the required reserve ratio

As a matter of algebra, the desired impact can be obtained equally well by using open market operations or changing the required reserve ratio. (For example, if DD = $100 million, R = $10 million, the multiplier = 10, and the desired deposit total equals $200 million, the Federal Reserve can either buy an additional $10 million in securities or lower the reserve ratio to 5 percent. To be sure you understand this, it would be a good idea to work it through.) Nevertheless, changes in the required reserve ratio have been infrequent in recent years. Between 1965 and 1980 the ratio was changed only sixteen times, an average of just over once a year. There have been five increases and eleven decreases. Instead, the Federal Reserve has favored open market operations, deeming them more flexible and capable of being used with greater precision. At times those operations reinforce reserve requirement changes; at other times they are substituted for changes in the required reserve ratio.

Although not all economists agree that open market operations are more useful than changes in reserve requirements, it is quite clear that

TABLE 13.5 The Impact of Two Major Instruments of Monetary Policy

Instrument	Action	Affects	Impact on deposits
Open market operations	{ purchase } { sale }	bank reserves	{ increase } { decrease }
Changes in reserve requirements	{ decrease } { increase }	deposit multiplier	{ increase } { decrease }

commercial bankers prefer the asymmetric use of the reserve requirement. Reducing the ratio releases lendable funds and raises bank profits, while increasing it freezes more funds, thereby reducing returns and producing a skimpier bottom line. Thus, if expansion of the money supply is desired, bankers are happy if it is accomplished by reducing the required reserve ratio. On the other hand, if tight money is called for, then they would prefer open market sales over a higher reserve ratio. The Federal Reserve officials were not unaware of or unsympathetic to these preferences. As noted in the last chapter, the problem of Reserve System membership was a real concern to the central bankers. Further increases in the required reserve ratio would have stimulated member banks to withdraw from the System. And since the System could achieve the same result by using open market operations, why not solve two problems with one action? (Had mandatory reserve requirements on all depository banks been imposed in 1970 instead of 1980, might the reserve ratio have been altered more frequently?)

The complexity of the required reserve ratio causes problems, too. As noted earlier, the actual reserve ratio varies with the type of deposit, the size of the bank's deposit holdings, and, in the case of nonpersonal time deposits, with the maturity of the deposit. Now with DIDAMCA's transition phase-in of reserve requirements for all non-member depository institutions and a move to the new reserve requirement structure for those previously subject to the old regulations, the calculations become even more difficult. Consequently, writing the multiplier as $1/r_{DD}$ (or even the more complex formula of the appendix to Chapter 10) clearly is a major simplification. Surely this is appropriate when one is learning how the monetary system operates. But can the complexity of the real-world calculation be ignored by those charged with the smooth functioning of the economy? Ought they to make a tough job tougher still?

Actually, the multiplier has shifted about quite a bit, as Figure 13.1 shows. Of course, not all of this movement is due to planned modifications of the reserve requirement by the Federal Reserve. But the changes have not helped stabilize the pattern, either. Thus, many economists expect that the Federal Reserve Board is not likely to vary the required reserve ratio any more in the future than it has in the past.

Comparing then open market operations and changes in the reserve requirement ratio, it would be true to conclude that open market operations are more frequently used even though the reserve ratio is equal to the open market instrument in its ability to affect money supply. The open market weapon is easier to use, causes fewer side-effects, and especially when the alternative is to raise the required reserve ratio, receives the blessing of the banking fraternity.

The third general instrument of control, discount rate changes, is about to go on stage. It must be listed as inferior to the other two in terms of impact and in between them in terms of frequency of use.

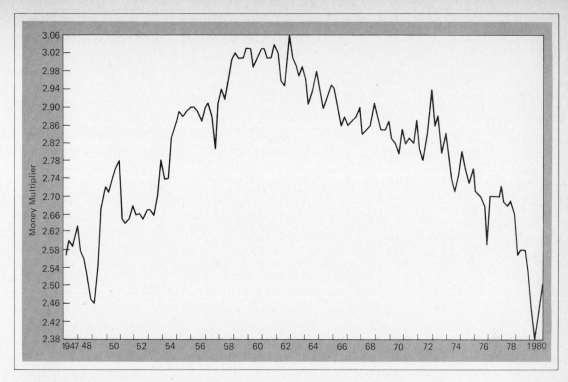

FIGURE 13.1 The money multiplier, 1947–1980. (Note: Derived from equation 13.2 on p. 336.)

☐ Changes in the Discount Rate

Background

One purpose of the Federal Reserve Act was to make the monetary system responsive to the "needs of trade." As business picked up and banks found that their ability to expand loans was limited, banks would be permitted to rediscount[3] commercial loans at their regional Federal Reserve bank, thereby obtaining reserves that could be used for new lending. Of course, this borrowing or **discounting** was not cost free. The Federal Reserve charged a **discount rate** for the loan. Control over the discount rate was initially placed in the hands of the directors of the

Discounting historically referred to a bank's sale of customer loans, endorsed by the member bank, to the Federal Reserve bank. Nowadays it is synonymous with borrowing from the Federal Reserve. The **discount rate** is the interest rate charged by the Federal Reserve for discounting.

[3]The term *rediscount* stems from the discount form of lending that was common at the time that the Federal Reserve was founded. A borrower who signed a three-month promissory note for $100,000 at an annual interest rate of 6 percent received only $98,500 from the bank; the $1,500 interest payment was discounted in advance (6% × ¼yr. × $100,000 = $1,500). If the bank then sold this note to a Federal Reserve bank, it had discounted the $100,000 note once again: hence "*rediscount*." Today the term has fallen into disuse, and *discount* and *discount rate* are used instead.

Federal Reserve banks, who could set the rate at whatever level they deemed consistent with credit conditions in their region.

The discount rate served a dual purpose. On the one hand, it provided revenue for the Reserve banks, which were to be self-supporting. On the other hand, the rate could encourage or discourage borrowing from the Reserve banks. It was believed that a low rate would induce commercial bankers to borrow; the funds would then be used to increase their lending. Conversely, a rise in the discount rate would discourage bankers from borrowing and thus restrain their lending policies. In other words, the discount rate was to be used as a countercyclical tool.

The nature of discounting and the role of the discount rate have changed drastically since 1913. First, as a national credit market replaced a regionally oriented one, regional rate setting became obsolete. As a consequence, the Reserve banks lost their ratesetting power. The directors of the Reserve banks still formally determine the rate, but the Board of Governors can veto the rate they set and, therefore, in effect has the decisive voice. In practice, discount rate changes are decided at FOMC meetings.

Second, few "discounts" are made nowadays. When banks wish to borrow from the Federal Reserve bank, they simply borrow against their own promissory notes, which are usually collateralized by U.S. government securities. This transaction is formally known as an **advance**; it is technically distinct from but conceptually and practically identical to a discount. (The terms are normally used synonymously.) The rate charged for advances is the discount rate.

An **advance** is a loan from the Federal Reserve to a bank.

Third, the original purposes of the discount rate—income and countercyclical influence—have become less important; open market operations have proven superior on both counts. Indeed, the relationship between open market operations and discount rate changes merits some discussion.

Discounting and open market operations

Place yourself in the seat of a Federal Reserve Board member. You and your colleagues have just voted to pursue a tighter monetary policy. Securities will be sold from the portfolio of the Reserve banks and interest rates will begin to rise as the additional supply of securities drives down their price. Simultaneously, commercial banks will find their reserves declining, and thus their ability to expand loans will be blocked, at least in part. In their attempt to escape the impact of monetary tightness, bankers will seek additional sources of funds and will turn to discounting to provide them with extra reserves. What would you do?

You realize, of course, that if the banks obtain reserves, they will nullify the open market action. You and your fellow policy makers have decided to reduce reserves, only to find the bankers coming through the back door of your own institution to acquire the reserves that have been taken away.

Indeed, some economists have argued that the discount procedure is not a policy tool but an escape hatch.

Obviously, you would like to dissuade the bankers from discounting. One means of persuasion is to raise the discount rate, thereby making it more expensive for the bankers to obtain the new reserves.

Take a look at Figure 13.2(a) which plots the discount rate and the Federal funds rate for 1966 to 1980. Is it at all surprising that, for the most part, interest rates (as represented by the Federal funds rate) rise first, followed by a change in the discount rate?

This observation gives rise to a number of others. First, it suggests that the level of the discount rate is not very important. Rather, it is the relationship of the discount rate to market interest rates that counts. In fact, this conclusion is supported by a number of empirical studies. Second, it implies that commercial bankers are profit-oriented individuals practicing discretionary funds management. Bankers will borrow from the Federal Reserve when it is profitable to do so, which is when the discount rate is relatively low.

This **profitability theory** of discounting is often contrasted to the **reluctance theory** of discounting. The latter hypothesis suggests that bankers prefer not to be indebted to the Reserve banks; it is either against the principles of good banking or bankers simply don't want to have Federal Reserve officials peeking over their shoulders. Figure 13.2(b) suggests that bankers are not terribly reluctant. As the difference between the Federal funds rate and the discount rate rises, increasing the incentive to borrow from the Federal Reserve, the volume of borrowing rises. And when the differential declines, so, too, does bank borrowing.

The **profitability theory** of discounting claims that bankers will borrow from the Federal Reserve when it is profitable to do so. In contrast, the **reluctance theory** believes that bankers will be reluctant to borrow from the Federal Reserve.

In 1980, recognizing profit-motivated bank behavior, the Federal Reserve imposed a surcharge on the discount rate. Banks with deposits of $500 million or more who had borrowed in two successive weeks or more than four times a quarter were required to pay an additional three percentage points.

A second way to dissuade bankers from borrowing is to impose quantitative limits on discounting. Borrowing is viewed by the Federal Reserve as a privilege, not a right, the implication being that it can and does say no. The Federal Reserve expects bankers to maintain sufficient reserves to comply with the reserve requirement. [The seasonal borrowing feature (p. 289) is the exception.] Moreover, should borrowing prove necessary and the Reserve bank officers comply with a discount request, speedy repayment is expected.

In fact, the discount operation is not run in a Draconian manner. Bankers' requests for borrowed funds are normally granted, and bankers are often dilatory in repaying. Thus, while borrowing from the Federal Reserve is not unlimited, bankers have sufficient room to maneuver and borrow when it is profitable to do so.

As a result, discount rate policy has become a supplementary instrument, reinforcing open market operations. By raising the discount rate

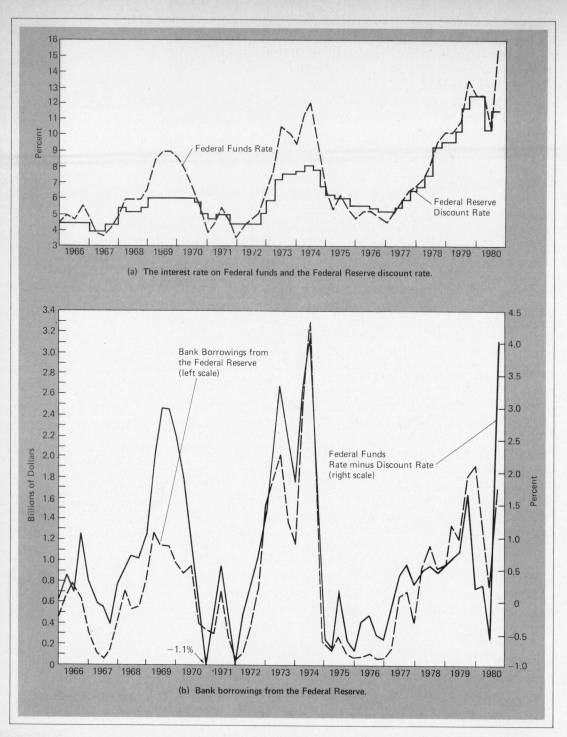

(a) The interest rate on Federal funds and the Federal Reserve discount rate.

(b) Bank borrowings from the Federal Reserve.

FIGURE 13.2 Money market interest rates and bank borrowings. (Note: The abnormally large volume of borrowing in 1974 is due to Federal Reserve support of the now-closed Franklin National Bank of New York.)

Source: Board of Governors of the Federal Reserve System, *Annual Statistical Digest 1970-1979* (Washington, D.C., 1980), p.5; Federal Reserve *Bulletin*, various issues.

relative to money market yields, the Federal Reserve makes it more difficult and expensive to offset tightening open market policy actions.

On occasion, however, discount rate policy may contribute to policy on its own. At times the Federal Reserve wishes to emphasize a particular policy stance. It wishes to inform the community that it is pursuing, say, a tight money policy. An increase in the discount rate, it is believed, is a signal that the Federal Reserve is serious about tightening money. This **announcement effect** works in the reverse when a decline in the discount rate heralds a period of monetary ease.

The **announcement effect** of a policy is the shock impact obtained by publicizing a given policy action.

Critics of this announcement effect have argued, Why not forthrightly inform the community what it is that you're doing? Moreover, the whole method is confusing. Sometimes the rate changes in order to "announce"; sometimes it is modified in order to make technical adjustments. How are observers to recognize which motive underlies a particular movement of the discount rate? Finally, nowadays alternative sources of information are readily available. A record of FOMC decisions is released one month after each meeting. Also, the chairman of the Federal Reserve Board periodically reports to Congress concerning actions that the Board is likely to take in the immediate future; that report specifies numerical targets. An interested, literate person can easily determine the objectives of Federal Reserve policy and can hazard a healthy guess at how closely its objectives are being achieved. Thus, the signal given by the discount rate is quite likely to have been anticipated, and will have no impact. It will already have been discounted (pardon the pun) by the market.

The discount window is still used to fulfill the "lender of last resort" function. When banks are in trouble, either because an individual bank is short of liquid assets or when the community is concerned about the financial health of the area's banks, the resources of the Federal Reserve can be marshaled through use of the discount mechanism. Thus, in 1974, when the giant Franklin National Bank, with over $5 billion in assets, was on the verge of bankruptcy, the Federal Reserve Bank of New York lent Franklin National almost $2 billion for a number of months. (Take another look at Figure 13.2[b].) This enabled the FDIC to arrange a smooth takeover by European-American Bank. Not only were Franklin National's depositors protected, but the financial system was spared a cataclysm that could have shaken the foundations of the banking structure.

In sum, the discount mechanism serves a number of functions: lending to banks in need, providing seasonal aid to smaller banks, and supplementing open market operations in controlling deposit growth.

☐ Regulation Q

In 1933 Congress authorized the Federal Reserve Board to set the maximum interest rates payable on time deposit accounts held at member banks, and in 1935 it authorized the FDIC to do the same for nonmember insured banks. (The Interest Rate Control Act of 1966 gave the Federal Home Loan Bank Board the same authority over savings and loan associations.) Like the ban on paying interest on checking accounts, this Great Depression legislation was aimed at holding down bank costs. It was thought that interest rates on deposits had been a cause of low-quality, high-risk bank loans. If interest costs were held down, loan quality and bank solvency would be enhanced.

Between 1936 and 1957 Regulation Q rates were not varied at all. They ranged from a 1 percent maximum on deposits with maturities between 30 and 89 days, 2 percent, for time deposits maturing between 90 and 180 days, and 2½ percent, for longer maturities and all savings deposits. This rigidity, of course, precludes discussion of Regulation Q as a control instrument. Ceiling interest rates were left unchanged, despite fluctuating economic conditions—the aftermath of the Great Depression, World War II, three postwar recessions, and three postwar expansions. Nor did the increase in 1954 foreshadow active use of this instrument, for the rates were left unchanged until 1962.

Actually, it is in the 1960s, with the advent of liability management (discussed in Chapter 7), that the Federal Reserve began to view Regulation Q as a tool of monetary control. Reserve System officials believed that Regulation Q could be used to restrain bank lending by reducing the attractiveness of CDs. As market interest rates rose above the Regulation Q ceiling, the competitive position of CDs would be undermined. Businesses with deposits in excess of their immediate needs would buy higher-yielding Treasury bills instead of the lower-yielding

TABLE 13.6 Interest Rate Ceilings for Commercial Banks in Effect on December 31, 1980

Type of deposit	Maximum interest rate (percent)
Savings	5¼
Negotiable orders of withdrawal	5¼
Other time deposits (less than $100,000), original maturity of	
14–89 days	5¼
90–365 days	5¾
1–2½ years	6
2½–4 years	6½
4–6 years	7¼
6–8 years	7½
8 years or more	7¾
Money market time deposits (26 weeks, minimum of $10,000)	rate on most recently issued 6-month U.S. Treasury bills + ¼ percent (as long as T-bill rate exceeds 8.75%)*
Small saver certificates (2½ years or more)	11.75% (as long as the average yield on 2½-year U.S. Treasury securities is 12% or more)*

*If the rate on the security is lower, other limits apply.
Source: Federal Reserve *Bulletin.*

CDs. And as banks found their deposit position eroded, their ability to lend would be constrained, too.

Again, as noted in Chapter 7, bankers devised means of circumventing the interest ceiling. Since 1970, when the ceiling on CDs worth $100,000 or more maturing between 30 and 89 days was suspended, and 1973, when the ceiling on other maturities of large-denomination CDs was lifted, Regulation Q has not been used as an instrument of monetary control. However, some interest rate ceilings still persist; those in effect on December 31, 1980, are listed in Table 13.6.

☐ Moral Suasion

Moral suasion involves using the persuasive powers of Federal Reserve officials to accomplish desired policy goals. The chairman of the Board of Governors, in public and in private, may suggest to bankers that inflation is the number-one problem today; that the banking community, because of its overly liberal lending criteria, is feeding the inflationary fires; and that it is in the best interests of the nation—and their own as well—to be more circumspect in their lending. The message will be repeated on the numerous occasions when Reserve Board members appear in public, before banking conferences, academic groups, consumer seminars, and so on. In this instance moral suasion is being used as a general instrument of monetary control. The objective is to influence deposit creation in general.

But moral suasion need not be limited to the general sphere; it can be used equally well as a selective instrument. Federal Reserve officials may suggest to bankers that too much credit is being granted for speculative activities rather than to finance productive investment. Since the direction of credit and not its total volume is involved, in this case moral suasion is being utilized selectively.

On one occasion in recent years, the former chairman of the Board, Arthur Burns, sent a letter to member banks that invited each banker's

personal cooperation in assuring that the rate of credit extension by your bank is appropriately disciplined.

The national interest calls for bankers to exercise financial statesmanship at this time. You and your colleagues can meet this need by intensifying your scrutiny of credit applications and by resisting excessive credit demands. A corollary requirement is the exercise of prudence in issuing large-denomination certificates of deposit and in borrowing from nondeposit sources. It is also appropriate that banks, while exercising this restraint, continue to give special consideration in using their limited supplies of lendable funds to the accommodation of credit needs originating within their local communities.[4]

---

[4]Letter from the Board to all member banks, May 21, 1973.

Here moral suasion is used both as an instrument of general credit control—to reduce loan volume—and for selective control—to accommodate local needs.

The effectiveness of moral suasion as a policy tool has been doubted by many observers. With over 14,000 commercial banks in the United States, such urgings tend to fall on deaf ears. Any one banker might remark, "Why, we're very careful how much (or for which purposes) we lend. That speech surely didn't refer to the policies of my bank." Moral suasion works far more effectively in places like Great Britain or Canada, where a few giant banks dominate the economy. When the governor of the Bank of England speaks to the heads of the few large banks, they are certain to pay careful attention.

Nevertheless, it is part of the duty of a central banker to admonish or urge when necessary. Moral suasion should be used not instead of, but in addition to, the other instruments of control.

□ Emergency Powers: The Credit Control Act of 1969

The Credit Control Act empowers the President of the United States to "authorize the [Federal Reserve] Board to regulate and control any or all extensions of credit."[5] In turn, the Board may "prohibit or limit any extensions of credit under any circumstances the Board deems appropriate."[6] This virtually dictatorial power over credit can be used either generally, selectively, or both. In fact, when President Carter invoked the Act for the first time in March 1980, the Board followed through with across-the-board measures to limit credit extension, as well as actions directed specifically at the consumer credit sector. A dose of moral suasion accompanied this "special credit restraint program" as the Board urged lenders to act with restraint and to favor "productive" loans over speculative ones.

Because it can be used generally or selectively, the Credit Control Act of 1969 serves as a useful bridge to the discussion of selective controls. Essentially, the only existing purely selective control, part of the normal arsenal of the Federal Reserve today, is the ability to vary the margin on stock market borrowing.

□ Stock Market Credit

Federal Reserve control over stock market credit also traces its heritage to the legislation of the 1930s. Stock market speculation had certainly been one of the features of the boom, and the stock market crash has been

---

[5]Credit Control Act, P.L. 9-151, Section 205(a).
[6]*Ibid.*, Section 206 (11).

blamed for the depth of the bust. (See Chapter 23.) This speculative fever had been fed by the rapid expansion of credit to acquire stocks. Shares could be purchased with small cash down payments; the remainder was borrowed. And in a rising market the increasing value of the shares served to collateralize still more loans. With the crash, the value of the stocks plummeted. The collateral securing many loans became worthless. Banks became insolvent, and bankruptcy ensued. In 1934 Congress passed the Securities and Exchange Act. Not only did the Act establish a framework for honesty when new securities were floated, establishing the Securities and Exchange Commission as the policing body, but it also charged the Federal Reserve Board with regulating stock market credit. Specifically, the Board was to set the **margin requirement** for securities purchases. The higher the margin requirement, the greater the down payment that must be made and the lower the percentage that may be borrowed.

The **margin requirement** is the percentage of nonborrowed funds that must be advanced when one is borrowing funds to acquire securities.

The rationale for the use of the margin requirement is simple: The larger the down payment and the lower the amount borrowed, the fewer stocks can be bought for a given amount of funds. (With $1,000 in cash and a 10 percent margin requirement, the purchaser could acquire $10,000 worth of stocks. But with a 50 percent margin the $1,000 buys only $2,000 worth.) The fewer stocks are bought, the less speculation there will be. With a 100 percent margin, as was the case in 1946–1947, borrowing for stock speculation is out altogether. Conversely, a lower margin requirement permits more stock market activity.

The Federal Reserve has varied the margin requirement infrequently. Since 1937, the requirement has been changed only twenty times; since 1970, only four times. At the end of 1980 the margin ratio stood at 50 percent.

How effective are margin controls? Or, to put it more broadly, how effective are selective controls in general? This question is not easy to answer. On the one hand, it would appear that tightening the control would restrict usage and hence lead to the desired results. Higher margin requirements should induce less stock market speculation. On the other hand, selective monetary controls tend to influence only one segment of the total picture, a part of the credit side. Circumvention appears easy and likely. Thus, if a speculator wants to play the market, what's to prevent him from taking a second mortgage on his home or borrowing for personal purposes and using the proceeds for stock dealings? Moreover, what's to stop a speculator from taking money she has saved for an automobile and using it for the market, borrowing an equivalent sum to finance the new car?

Because of these drawbacks, few economists have substantial faith in selective credit controls. In fact, controls that had been imposed on real estate and consumer credit during World War II were abandoned over thirty years ago. The margin requirement remains the only one that still regularly serves selective credit control purposes.

☐ Conclusion: Money Supply Movements

Deposits, according to the formula on page 315 as well as the discussion in Chapter 10, are determined by the reserves of the banking system and the deposit multiplier. The Federal Reserve, as you have now seen, exerts control over bank reserves through its open market operations, and over the multiplier through its ability to vary the required reserve ratio. An appropriate conclusion to this chapter is a brief survey of how deposits, reserves, and the multiplier have moved during recent periods. Instead of tracking deposits, however, the record of M-1, deposits plus currency in the hands of the public will be surveyed. In the place of reserves, a somewhat broader concept, the **monetary base** or **high-powered money,** will be followed. The monetary base measures the deposit expansion potential of the banking system by including the public's cash holdings in addition to bank reserves. If the public decides to hold less cash, it will deposit its surplus in the banking system. This newly obtained cash becomes reserves for the banks. In this sense currency in the hands of the public is deposit-creating potential. And in light of these changes, instead of the deposit multiplier, a **money multiplier** will be derived and followed here.

The relationship between money supply (M-1A), the monetary base (B), and the money multiplier is given by the following formula:

$$\text{M-1A} = \text{B} \times \mu^* \tag{13.1}$$

Data on M-1A and B are readily available from the Federal Reserve. μ^* is calculated from the other two variables:

$$\mu^* = \frac{\text{M-1A}}{\text{B}} \tag{13.2}$$

M-1A and the monetary base are plotted in Figure 13.3. (The money multiplier was charted in Figure 13.1.)

Look at the monetary base first. You'll notice that while in 1947 the base was less than $50 billion, by 1980 it had more than tripled, to exceed $150 billion. This growth can be attributed to changes in all of the variables appearing in the balance sheet of the Federal Reserve, as noted earlier in this chapter. Clearly, however, the major source of the increase in the base was the rise in the security holdings of the Reserve banks. In 1947, the Reserve banks held $22.6 billion in U.S. government securities; by 1980, the total (including securities of U.S. government agencies) had risen to $128 billion. This 568 percent increase in Federal Reserve holdings of U.S. government securities represents long-run open market operations designed to provide sufficient resources for the monetary expansion needed to accommodate economic growth.

The expansion of the monetary base enabled M-1A to grow. And grow it did, as Figure 13.3 illustrates. From $109.4 billion in 1947, M-1A expanded to a total of $397.7 billion by December, 1980, 3.6 times the earlier total.

> The **monetary base** or **high-powered money** equals bank reserves plus currency in the hands of the public.

> The number by which high-powered money is multiplied in order to calculate money supply is called the **money multiplier**.

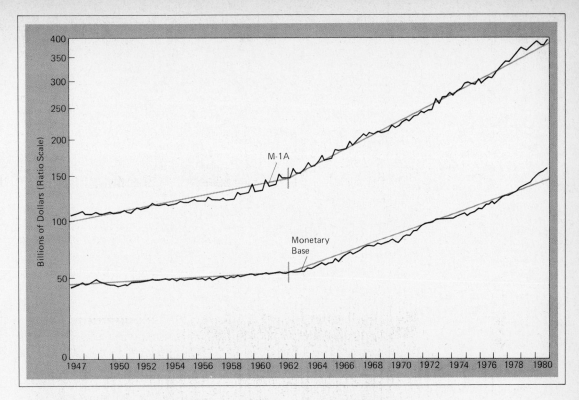

FIGURE 13.3 The money supply and the monetary base, 1947–1980. (Note: trend lines are fitted by eye.)

You'll have noticed that the growth in the base and the money supply did not proceed smoothly. The straight lines drawn into both series attempt to demonstrate the basic movements, abstracting from the temporary wiggles. In each case, a single line over the entire thirty-three years would be misleading, since the nature of growth in the late 1940s and 1950s differed markedly from its behavior in the last two decades. It was much slower in the earlier period—1.0 percent for the monetary base and 2.0 percent for M-1A; for the second half of the postwar period, the corresponding rates are 6.3 percent for the base and 5.4 percent for the money supply.

The difference in growth rate between the money supply and the monetary base represents the intensity of use of the base; in other words, the rate of growth of the money multiplier.[7] Thus, between 1947 and 1962 the multiplier rose at an annual rate of 1.1 percent, moving from 2.6 to 3.1. Between 1962 and 1980 the yearly growth rate was negative, −0.9 percent, as the multiplier fell from 3.1 to 2.5. (See Figure 13.1.)

---

[7]For those who recall logarithms, equation 13.1 (M-1A = B × μ*) can be transformed into log M-1A = log B + log μ*. Therefore, log μ* = log M-1A − log B. Logs approximate the percentage rate of change.

How can these movements in the multiplier be explained? As this chapter has indicated, one influence on the multiplier is the Federal Reserve, through its control over the reserve ratio. In fact, between 1945 and 1962, the Federal Reserve Board raised the required reserve ratio on demand deposits only four times (twice on time deposits), while reducing it fourteen times (five times on time deposits). The magnitude of the ratio declined by 17.5 percent over the period for the largest banks, from 20 percent in 1945 to 16½ percent in 1962.

The explanation of the fall in the money multiplier since 1962 is more complicated. First, recall the earlier mention of the fact that the trend of the required reserve ratio has been downward, which should have led to a larger multiplier. Offsetting this change has been the marked shift from demand to time deposits, a point noted in Chapter 6. As interest rates rose over recent periods and as time deposit liquidity increased through the development of the CD, the public decreased its relative holdings of demand deposit accounts. With fewer demand deposits and more time deposits held by the public, the multiplier was reduced. The net effect is portrayed by Figure 13.1.

You will have occasion to return to this analysis of how the central bank uses its instruments when monetary policy is discussed in Parts Four and Five. This chapter has shown that the Federal Reserve influences both the monetary base and the multiplier. But influencing is not the same as controlling; the Federal Reserve does not exert dictatorial power over M-1A. The various general instruments available—open market operations, modifications in reserve requirement ratios, discount rate changes, Regulation Q variations, and moral suasion—can help mold the trend of money supply, but other influences are at work simultaneously, and they may offset Federal Reserve actions.

Federal Reserve policy is not directed at the money supply as an ultimate goal. The money supply is important only because it is a critical variable in the economy, and through it such variables as inflation and unemployment can be influenced.

But how does money supply affect the economy? What impact do changes in the supply of money have on economic activity? This is the concern of the next part of this book.

☐ Summary

This chapter focused on the instruments of monetary control in the United States. Among the general weapons surveyed were open market operations, changes in reserve requirements, discount rate modifications, and adjustments in interest rate ceilings. Moral suasion and the emergency monetary powers were cited as instruments of both general and selective control, depending on how they are used, while the margin requirement remains the only regularly used tool of selective control.

Open market operations. The Federal Open Market Committee's decision to expand or contract bank credit and money supply leads to open market purchases or sales. When reserves are created by open market purchases, the money supply can expand by a multiple amount, and vice versa for open market sales. Although most open market transactions are for defensive purposes, policy changes are typically followed by dynamic open market operations. The impact of the open market operation depends on the size of the transactions as well as on the money multiplier, which is itself dependent on the required reserve ratio.

Changes in reserve requirements. Although reserve requirements were written into the Federal Reserve Act, they were made subject to Federal Reserve Board discretion only in the 1930s. Since then the Board has increased the complexity and the coverage of the required reserve ratios. Today after passage of DIDAMCA, reserve ratios differ according to (1) the type of deposit—transaction or time, (2) the volume of transaction deposits held by the individual bank, and (3) for nonpersonal time deposits, the maturity as well. Moreover, the ratios are imposed on Eurocurrency liabilities and on all depository institutions. The Act does reduce the average reserve requirement ratio of the banking system, since the upper range of permissible required ratios is significantly below the pre-Act maximum.

While the reserve ratio has been following a declining trend in the past thirty-five years, changes in the required ratios are infrequent. The Board has preferred to vary the money supply by using open market operations. Nevertheless, on the occasions when the required reserve ratio is amended, an increase works to reduce the money multiplier and, thus, the banking system's ability to create money. Conversely, a reduction in the ratio boosts the money multiplier and increases the banks' money-creating powers.

Discount rate modifications. The discount procedure was originally designed to increase the flexibility of the banking system in meeting the nation's financial needs. This positive aspect of discounting is partly offset by an undesired side effect: When money is tight, borrowing from Federal Reserve banks permits banks to evade, in part, the monetary stringency. Increases in the discount rate may dissuade some banks from borrowing, but evidence clearly indicates that the height of the discount rate is less important than its relationship to alternative borrowing rates. Today the discount rate is most often used to reinforce open market operations. Occasionally its announcement effect is sought.

Regulation Q. The ceiling interest rates permitted on time and savings deposits were used as a method of monetary control in the 1960s but were abandoned in the early 1970s. The Reserve authorities believed that by controlling the inflow of deposits—which it would do by forcing banks to offer their clients unattractively low interest rates—they could slow the expansion of bank credit. However, bankers were able to circumvent this restriction through a variety of innovative responses. Under the provisions of the Depository Institutions Deregulation and Monetary Control Act, Regulation Q will be abolished no later than 1986.

Moral suasion. At times the monetary authorities exhort the nation's bankers to pursue a given objective. They request bankers to restrain their granting credit in general or to divert credit from some uses to others. The large number of banks in the United States limits the effectiveness of persuasion, however.

Emergency monetary powers. Under the Credit Control Act the Board of Governors is granted total control over credit. This law must be activated by the President of the United States; it was used only once, in 1980.

Margin requirement. The Federal Reserve Board sets the margin requirement in order to restrain or encourage stock market activity. A lower margin requirement permits a larger percentage of any stock market transaction to be financed by credit. Changes in the margin ratio are infrequent; it has been 50 percent since January 1974.

The chapter concluded by relating the growth of the money supply since 1947 to its components—the monetary base and the money multiplier. Open market purchases by the Federal Reserve enabled the base to expand secularly. Until 1962, the rise in the base was fortified by falling reserve ratios, which meant larger money multipliers. Since 1962, however, the money multiplier has moved downward, restraining the growth in the money supply to some extent.

☐ Questions and Exercises

1. Where does the Federal Reserve obtain the funds to pay for its open market purchases?
2. Could the Federal Reserve authorities expand the money supply by acquiring private securities instead of government issues? If so, why do you think the FOMC has avoided such transactions?
3. Obtain a recent list of "Factors Affecting Bank Reserves." (You'll find it in the Federal Reserve *Bulletin*.) Analyze it to see if you can fathom FOMC policy.
4. Relate the profitability and reluctance theories of discounting to the portfolio management theories outlined in Chapter 7. Would you be surprised to learn that smaller banks rarely borrow from the Federal Reserve while larger ones borrow frequently?
5. List some of the reasons that complicate the monetary authorities' ability to achieve their targeted money supply growth rates.

☐ For Further Study

A good survey of the Federal Reserve's development and use of its control mechanism is R. A. Young, *Instruments of Monetary Policy in the United States: The Role of the Federal Reserve System* (Washington, D.C.: International Monetary Fund, 1973). Paul Meek's new *Monetary Policy and Financial Markets* (New York: Federal Reserve Bank of New York, 1982), an extension of his *Open Market Operations* (1973), is an invaluable aid to this important area of central banking activity. Another publication of the Federal Reserve Bank of New York, Arthur W. Samansky's *StatFacts: Understanding Federal Reserve Statistical Reports* (1982), provides a detailed description of a number of key Federal Reserve releases, including the weekly "Factors Affecting Reserves of Depository Institutions and Condition Statement of F. R. Banks" outlined in this chapter. Do not overlook its extensive glossary of technical terms.

"Reserve Requirements Under the Depository Institutions Deregulation and Monetary Control Act of 1980," by J. A. Cacy and S. Winningham, in Federal Reserve Bank of Kansas City, *Economic Review* (September-October 1980), contrasts the situation prior to passage of the DIDAMCA and the present transition period, and examines the expected impact of the Act. Much detail on the discount mechanism, including the views of academic observers, may be found in a three-volume Federal Reserve study, *Reappraisal of the Discount Mechanism* (Washington, D.C., Board of Governors of the Federal Reserve System, 1971).

PART FOUR

MONEY, PRICES, AND INCOME

CHAPTER 14

The Quantity Theory of Money: The More There Is, the Less It's Worth

The first panacea for a mismanaged nation is inflation of the currency; the second is war. Both bring a temporary prosperity; both bring a permanent ruin.

Ernest Hemingway, author (1935)

Inflation is unjust and deflation is inexpedient.

J. M. Keynes (1923)

CONTENTS

CHAPTER HIGHLIGHTS

1. The various kinds of price indexes, their uses, and their limitations.
2. The distinction between the equation of exchange and the quantity theory of money.
3. The galloping inflation of interwar Germany.

How much is an umbrella worth? In a barter economy the answer is readily ascertained by finding how many other goods and services will be traded for it. (Of course, more fundamentally, the amount traded for the umbrella will depend on the supply of umbrellas as well as the demand for them.) Perhaps the umbrella will trade for two haircuts or five pair of socks, or one-quarter of a sweater, and so on. The presence of a unit of account, a money, permits a simplified expression: 1 umbrella = $10. But of course, then 2 haircuts = 5 pairs of socks = ¼ sweater = $10.

Now rephrase the question and ask, How much is a dollar worth? The answer must be one-tenth of an umbrella or one sock or one-fortieth of a sweater, and so on. This example points out an elementary truth: The value of a unit of money can be measured in terms of the goods and services that it can purchase. Just as money serves as a means of measuring the value of goods and services, so, too, do goods and services serve to measure the value of money.

Why is anyone interested in ascertaining the value of money? The answer is that many decisions, private and public, hinge on the stability or lack of stability of the monetary unit. Inflation, which finds its complement in a decline in the value of money, affects different groups of people in diverse ways, and leads to modifications in their behavior. Inflation benefits debtors whose debts are expressed in money terms, while creditors lose. Five million dollars borrowed today will buy $5 million worth of goods and services today. But if inflation is endemic during the life of the loan, then the $5 million paid back by the debtor ten years hence will be worth less—conceivably far less—in terms of the goods and services that it will purchase then. The debtor's gain is the creditor's loss. Similarly, retired people living on government or private pensions find that the erosion of the dollar through inflation leaves them with diminished purchasing power.[1] If inflation is expected to prevail, those who may be affected adversely will act to protect their income or wealth; if they succeed, the cost of inflation will be shifted to those who fail to protect themselves adequately. Indeed, the major problem of inflation, provided that the inflation is not a "runaway" one, is the redistribution of income that results. This redistribution comes about in

---

[1]Since 1977 recipients of social security checks have been partially protected against inflation because Congress voted an automatic adjustment in their receipts.

an unplanned, random manner. Those who benefit are rewarded irrespective of merit; those who lose are blameless, but lose nevertheless.

Modern governments have resolved, at least verbally, to restrain if not halt inflation. Thus, public policy actions hinge on the presence or absence of inflation. Deflation, too (though far less common, since prices rarely seem to fall for prolonged periods and by substantial amounts), redistributes income unfairly and brings governmental responses. So, since private and public policy is determined by movements in prices, it is important to measure the value of money.

☐ Price Indexes

How is the value of money measured? As implied by the previous paragraphs, money's value is ascertained by computing its purchasing power: How much goods and services will a dollar purchase? Normally, money's worth is measured by calculating a **price index**, which enables the observer to compare changes in the value of money between two different dates. The basic idea behind a price index is to assemble a representative bundle of goods and services, obtain the prices charged for them in some base year—an arbitrarily selected year that becomes the reference point for further calculations—collect current prices, and compare the current prices to the past prices. The best known of all the U.S. price indexes is the carefully monitored consumer price index.

A **price index** measures the purchasing power of money by comparing prices in one period to prices in another period.

The consumer price index (CPI)

In 1972 and 1973 the Bureau of Labor Statistics (BLS), an office in the U.S. Department of Labor, and the Commerce Department's Bureau of the Census surveyed a large sample of Americans in a consumer expenditure survey. Almost 20,000 consumer units were interviewed in order to find out as precisely as possible how they spent their income during the year. Another 18,000 families were asked to provide detailed records of their total purchases for a two-week period.

The manner in which income was spent provided the basis for the weighting scheme used in the CPI. Table 14.1 lists the percentages spent on major categories.

Having calculated an average consumer budget, the next step is to obtain the prices paid by consumers. It would be highly impractical and immensely expensive to record every price for every item sold daily in

TABLE 14.1 Consumer Spending, by Major Categories, 1972–1973
(percentages)

Food	18.8	Medical care	4.6
Housing	42.9	Entertainment	4.5
Apparel	7.0	Personal care	1.7
Transportation	17.0	Other goods and services	2.8

Source: U.S. Department of Labor, Bureau of Labor Statistics, *The Consumer Price Index* (Washington, D.C.: 1977), p. 8.

the United States; the manpower needs alone would be truly staggering. Moreover, the immense amount of data collected could hardly be processed in a brief enough time to make the resulting statistics meaningful. Instead, the BLS relies on a sampling technique. A sample of the items that are deemed important in themselves or representative of important categories—some 400 goods and services—are priced in 85 urban areas in a variety of sales outlets. For many items, especially the food and fuel categories, BLS representatives make monthly visits, surveying shops in the designated communities and obtaining the retail prices of the selected commodities and services. For example, over 2000 food stores are visited personally each month, and some 25 items are sampled in each. The data for other items are collected less frequently, although in the five largest cities monthly surveys are conducted for most commodities.

The results are reported to the various BLS offices and then transmitted to the head office of the BLS in Washington. The calculations are made there and the index is released monthly.

Calculation of the CPI

The essence of the CPI involves comparing a weighted average of prices. Table 14.2 demonstrates, in a simplified way, how the CPI is computed. First the categories that are included in the index are listed (column 1). Their weights, which represent the importance of the items in the budget as derived from the expenditure survey, are listed in column 2, and two sets of prices, for the base period and the current month, appear in columns 3 and 4, respectively. Each price is then weighted by its appropriate weight; the products appear in columns 5 and 6. Columns 5 and 6 are then summed up, the result being an average price for that particular bundle or "market basket." Thus, in the base year the market basket cost 71¾ cents, while in the second period, the current month, the average price had risen to almost 86 cents for the same market basket of

TABLE 14.2 Computing the CPI: A Simplified Example

Category (1)	Weight (2)	Price, base year (3)	Price, current month (4)	Weight × Price, base year (5)(= 2 × 3)	Weight × Price, current month (6)(= 2 × 4)
Meat (lb.)	.22	$1.00	$1.25	$.2200	.2750
Eggs (dz.)	.33	.75	.80	.2475	.2640
Bus fare (trip)	.11	.50	.45	.0550	.0495
Newspaper (each)	.14	.25	.20	.0350	.0280
Cigarettes (pk.)	.20	.80	1.20	.1600	.2400
Totals	1.00			0.7175	0.8565

$$\text{CPI: } \frac{0.8565}{0.7175} \times 100 = 119.37$$

goods. To calculate the current value of the index, divide the new average by the base average and multiply the result by 100, as is done in the final line of the table. The result, 119.37, means that prices in the current month are about 20 percent higher than they were in the base year. The value of the dollar, as measured by the CPI, has declined by about 20 percent.[2]

The importance of the weighting process should be evident from this example. The prices of three goods (meat, eggs, and cigarettes) have risen, while those of two others (bus fare and newspapers) have fallen. Of the three that rose, two went up substantially and one by only a bit. If an unweighted average had been taken, so that each category was presumed to be equally important in the consumer's budget, the overall price rise would have been 10.4 percent $\left(\frac{+.25+.07-.10-.20+.50}{5}\right)$. But it is not true that each category weighs the same in the consumer's market basket. The 10 percent decline in bus fares had a small impact, affecting only 11 percent of the total budget, while the 25 percent increase in meat prices had twice the influence of fares, since it constituted 22 percent of consumer expenditures. And so it should be.

Figure 14.1 traces the CPI for 1965–1980. The following points can readily be made. First, the CPI rose throughout the period. In other words, the value of consumers' dollars has been declining. Indeed, this pattern has held ever since the Depression. Be aware, however, that this does not necessarily imply that the average consumer is worse off. Consumers' material well-being depends not only on the purchasing power of each dollar but also on how many dollars consumers have to spend. In general, the rise in consumers' income has more than compensated for the dollar's decline in value. Yet, as noted earlier, people living on fixed incomes lose out, while those whose incomes rose rapidly, and debtors, gain.

Second, the rate of the price increase has not been constant: From 1965 to 1970 prices rose at a rate of 4.2 percent each year, while in the following five years they rose at a more rapid annual rate of 6.7 percent. For the entire period between 1965 and 1980, prices rose an average of 6.6 percent each year. Does this mean that each of us lost out by the full extent of the cumulative price rise of 161 percent over that 15-year interval? An answer to this question hinges on an understanding of the limitations of the CPI.

Limitations of the CPI

Coverage. With the 1978 revision of the CPI, the coverage of the index was extended to all urban residents, or some 80 percent of the noninstitutional civilian population of the United States. The remaining 20 percent, primarily rural families, are excluded, as are military personnel.

---

[2]The actual decline is from a value of $1.00 in the base year to 1/1.1937 = $.84 in the current month.

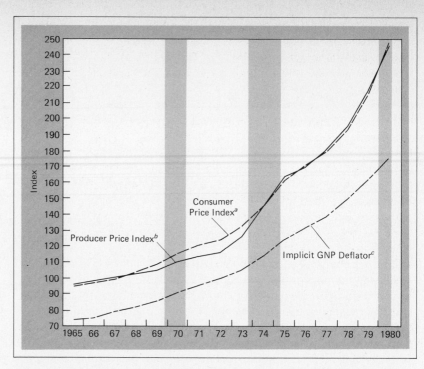

FIGURE 14.1 Measures of inflation, 1965–1980. (Note: Shaded areas represent business cycle contractions.)

[a]Urban consumers (1967 = 100).
[b]Finished goods (1967 = 100).
[c]1972 = 100

Source: Compiled from various issues of the *Economic Report of the President*, the *Survey of Current Business*, and the *Monthly Labor Review*.

The Relevance of the Average. Any average, by virtue of its being an average, is an artificial construction. Is someone standing with one foot in a pail of ice water at a temperature of 28.6° F and the other in a pail of near-boiling (168.6°F) water comfortable because the average temperature is 98.6° F? Any average covers a range of dispersion, and the average may be unsuitable to describe the impact on a specific individual. A sharp rise in the price of meat, which drives up the CPI, is meaningless to a vegetarian, as is a rise in the price of medical services to a person blessed with excellent health. To the homeowner, a fall in the price of houses or the rate of interest on mortgages bears little useful information, nor does a change in the price of cigarettes mean anything to a nonsmoker. Moreover, even for those who do consume meat, use doctors, buy homes, and smoke, the average price change need not and probably does not reflect the particular situation of a single individual. Prices of homes in San Francisco, California, may decline, but if one is in the market for a house in Salt Lake City, Utah, how relevant is the information? In short, if one were to calculate a price index that is relevant to a single individual, a personal price index, using that person's consumption pattern as weights and the prices of the commodities bought at the stores in which the person actually shops, would be required. And even then problems would arise.

Fixed Weights. In order to judge the change in prices, the market basket must remain constant. If the weights were changing, the resulting index would no longer be a price index but a combination price-quantity index. To maintain the purity of the CPI, the weights are adjusted relatively infrequently. Yet in measuring the impact of price changes on the consumer, constant weights cannot give a full picture of the impact of price changes. Price theory and our own experience confirms that price changes induce modifications in spending patterns.

Encountered here is a conflict between a price index and a **cost-of-living (c-o-l) index.** (The CPI is often mistakenly called a c-o-l index.)

A **cost-of-living (c-o-l) index** measures changes in the cost of maintaining a constant standard of material well-being.

Price indexes are designed to capture *price* changes, and to do so they must keep the market basket constant. C-o-l indexes, on the other hand, aim to measure changes in living standards, and since both price and quantity consumed affect the level of living, it is legitimate to vary both. The practical constraint on a c-o-l index is the primary reason that it has not been implemented. Continuous consumer expenditure surveys, certainly more often than once a decade, would be mandated. Only recently have funds been made available to finance this type of project; initial reports are due in 1982.

New Goods and Services. A related issue deals with the introduction of new products into the marketplace, ones that were not included in expenditure surveys. For example, snowmobiles were not included in the 1960–1961 consumer budget; today they are no longer insignificant. Similarly, while TV sets are found in the survey of consumer expenditures, video recorders are not. The CPI should not ignore new products, and in fact the BLS has the capacity to include new products by changing the weighting scheme. Both of the aforementioned items could be included in the "entertainment" group, and the weights of other products in that category could be reduced. However, this method does not permit changes in the broader category weights, a possibility that cannot be ruled out. Moreover, a new product is recognized as significant for inclusion in the CPI only after it has made an identifiable impact on the market. But in the nature of things this is always after the product should have been included; it has been growing in importance all along!

Quality Changes. Perhaps the thorniest problem of all involves the measurement of changes in quality. If hamburger rises from $1.00 per pound to $1.05 per pound, this is obviously a 5 percent rise in price. But is it? If the fat content of the more expensive burger was lower and the beef content higher, the 5¢ increase might well represent an improvement in quality that totally warranted a higher price. Indeed, when we think about a reduction in purchasing power, we conceive of paying more for the exact same item; purchasing an improved commodity at a higher price might not be considered inflationary at all.

But how does one distinguish a pure price increase from a pure quality increase? How much of the increase in the price of a TV set is due to the color innovation and how much is "inflationary"? Does the fact that "soft" contact lenses feel better and are safer than hard lenses warrant the price differential? (One should not imply from these examples that all quality changes are improvements. Obviously not. Most notably in the field of personal services, especially the employment of skilled labor, a good case can be made for the claim that quality has deteriorated. And the frequent recall of automobiles by their manufacturers hardly suggests improved quality.)

The problem remains, however. How does one measure quality? For most goods, and especially for services, no answer is yet at hand. Nevertheless, the recognition of this problem is important, and may well be critical when the CPI rises modestly. Consider the possibility that quality improvements range about 2 percent yearly, as some economists have contended. In that case a recorded 5 percent rise in the CPI really indicates a 3 percent rate of inflation. The actions taken to combat a 5 percent rate of inflation are likely to be significantly more severe than those taken to restrain a more modest 3 percent rate. Proper measurement is truly a prerequisite for proper policy.

The Treatment of Housing. Almost 43 percent of all consumer expenditures are devoted to housing, with half of these outlays representing the costs of home ownership. Home purchases account for 10 percent and financing costs for another 6½ percent of the CPI. Should the price of new homes and mortgage rates increase by 20 percent, the CPI will rise by 20 percent times the weight, 16½ percent, for a total of 3.3 percent. While this 3.3 percent boost reflects the price increases to the purchaser of a new home, it is clearly irrelevant to the typical homeowner, who bought a house years back and continues to remit the original mortgage payment. The BLS is cognizant of this anomaly, and has investigated alternative measures that would reflect housing costs and mortgage rates more correctly. (For 1979, the impact of the substitute measures would have ranged from insignificance to a substantial 18 percent reduction in the CPI.) A revised CPI, using a rental equivalency measure to replace new housing prices and mortgage interest rates, will be issued in 1983.

Breadth of Coverage. Finally, it must be realized that the CPI is limited to consumer prices. Thus, it does not record prices faced by businesses except insofar as they are reflected in retail prices. A rise in the price of a steel blast furnace or a petroleum-cracking plant is not reflected in the CPI. Neither are the freight costs incurred when coal is transported by train to an electricity-generating station. Nor are the costs of operating the government or the prices of exports, for they are not borne directly by consumers. A much broader index would be needed to encompass the economic activity of the entire nation.

The Usefulness of the CPI. Before turning to such an index, some concluding statements must be made in defense of the CPI. First, an educated user realizes the limitations of the CPI and hence will not try to derive unwarranted conclusions from it. The CPI, like most economic statistics, must be used judiciously. Second, the CPI is a timely statistic. It is released monthly, shortly after the end of the month in question. Even a less-than-perfect statistic is useful when it is readily available. Finally, the errors in the CPI are likely to remain relatively constant over short periods. True, comparing this month's CPI value to that of ten years ago is likely to be meaningless except in the most general terms. But compare the CPI values for the past few months to those for the same time last year, and a rather good approximation of reality is the likely result. Look again at the pattern of inflation traced out by the CPI in Figure 14.1. It coincides rather well with most people's impression of accelerating inflation during that period. The CPI is a most useful tool in the hands of someone who understands its limitations.

The producer price index (PPI)

A similar statement can be directed at another BLS aggregate, the producer price index (PPI). The PPI is also a quantity-weighted price index, but it is for large, bulk commodity sales rather than for retail sales. In general, prices are reported by the producers of manufactured and processed goods, but intracompany sales, individually priced items (e.g., works of art), and military goods purchased by the government are excluded. Most prices in the PPI are collected on a monthly basis, and the index, which is available for some 2,800 commodities and some thirty subgroups, is published monthly.

The PPI rose at a rate of 6.5 percent annually in the years between 1965 and 1980, confirming in general the indications of the CPI data (see Figure 14.1.) But in addition to the limitations that are common to all price indexes, the PPI suffers from the fact that it is restricted to commodities, so that services are entirely excluded. In an economy in which services account for approximately half of national output, such an omission cannot help but be significant. Thus, the PPI in itself is too narrow to measure the value of money.

The implicit GNP deflator (IGNPD)

The next chapter concentrates on the national income accounts, and especially on gross national product (GNP). This aggregate measures the entire output of the economy; all goods and services are included. Each product is recorded on the basis of its current value, its actual price at time of sale. The resulting statistic is recorded in **current** dollars, in that year's prices. It is also called **nominal** GNP, again to emphasize that its prices are current ones.

The Bureau of Economic Analysis (BEA) of the Department of Com-

Data listed in **current** values are presented in **nominal** units.

merce, which is responsible for gathering and publishing the national income accounts, also releases a figure called **real** GNP or GNP in **constant** dollars. This statistic is an attempt to measure the actual output of goods and services by keeping the price yardstick constant. It is designed to differentiate between movements in GNP that are a result of inflation (or, quite infrequently, deflation) and changes that increase the actual amount of products available to the various purchasers of GNP. The BEA now reports GNP in constant 1972 dollars, so that any change in this real GNP measure purports to indicate actual modifications in the economic output available to the economy, rather than price changes. Figure 14.2 charts U.S. GNP in current dollars against GNP in constant dollars for the years between 1965 and 1980.

The chart indicates clearly that real GNP has been rising; that U.S. residents have been receiving more goods and services over the sixteen-year period. But notice, too, that the rate of increase of real GNP is considerably lower than that of nominal GNP, and that in 1974 and 1980 real GNP actually fell while nominal GNP rose. For the entire period the former rose by only 3.2 percent annually against a 9.3 percent annual rate for the latter. Furthermore, in subperiods the rates diverge even more. For example, in the years between 1973 and 1976 real GNP rose by only 1 percent each year while nominal GNP increased by 9.2 percent, more than ninefold the real-GNP rate.

How can this discrepancy be explained? Since the difference between real and nominal GNP involves the action of prices, it is clear that prices

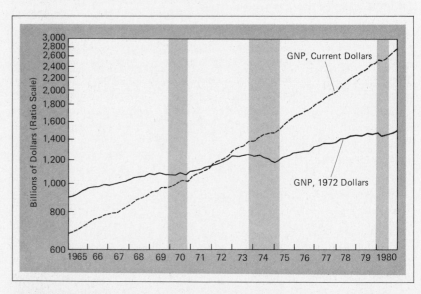

FIGURE 14.2 GNP in current and constant dollars, 1965–1980. (Note: Shaded areas represent business cycle contractions.)

Source: U.S. Department of Commerce, *Business Conditions Digest.*

Drawing by Joseph Farris; © 1974 The New Yorker Magazine, Inc.

were not stable. In fact, prices rose at an annual average of 6.1 percent for the entire period, and at an even faster 8.2 percent yearly rate for the 1973–1976 subperiod.

When one knows the relationship between nominal and real GNP, it becomes possible to compute the increase in prices that accounts for the lack of equivalence between the two. The process entails dividing real GNP into nominal GNP and, to put it into index number form, multiplying the quotient by 100. For example, in 1980 nominal GNP was $2,626.1 billion while GNP in constant 1972 dollars totaled $1,480.7 billion. Then,

$$\frac{2.626.1}{1,480.7} \times 100 = 177.4$$

In other words, GNP prices in 1980 were 77.4 percent higher than they were in the base year, in this instance 1972. This calculation derives the **implicit GNP deflator.**[3]

Because the implicit GNP deflator is the most broadly based measure of

The **implicit GNP deflator** measures the relative level of GNP prices, and is obtained by dividing nominal GNP by constant GNP and multiplying the quotient by 100.

[3]The reason for this measure's not being considered a price index is a result of the difference in computation techniques. A price index like the CPI is obtained from a collection of individual prices. In the case of the deflator, however, the prices are not observed directly but are "implicit" in the relationship between the two GNP series, constant and current. The term *deflator* reflects the fact that when it is divided into current GNP, the value of current GNP is reduced or deflated to a lower number, which is the real GNP value.

prices, it would appear that the deflator would best serve to record changes in the value of money. Indeed, many economists believe this to be true. Others, however, point out that the deflator suffers from a number of basic weaknesses. First, real GNP is obtained by deflating each of the many components of GNP. Thus, consumer expenditures in current dollars are deflated by the CPI (adjusted to include farm workers as well as urban residents), and business equipment outlays are deflated by using the appropriate portion of the PPI. Consequently, each component suffers from the limitations inherent in the price index used, and therefore the deflator itself must be faulty (see Box 14.1).

A second weakness of the deflator is that, for many components, any price change is arbitrarily defined as inflationary. Salaries of government employees, for example, are deflated by government salary rates, which implies that all government wage increases are inflationary. Yet this assertion cannot be accepted at face value, for it implies that the productivity of government workers never rises. (Only a cynic would accept this implication.) The same problem exists for the private service sector as well, and a similar issue arises in deflating the construction sector.

Third, since the deflator is a weighted average of the component deflators, a shift in the relative importance of any of the components will change the deflator even if prices had not changed at all. Thus, as the government sector grows in importance, the implicit GNP deflator will contain an inflationary bias.

Does this list of limitations mean that the deflator is useless? Again, the answer must be negative. But this statistic must be interpreted with care. Indeed, no single measure of price change is free from weakness; each has qualities that the others lack and limitations that are not found in the others. Yet the picture given by the various measures of the value of money does lead to a clear impression of what has happened to the dollar. Compare the movements of the CPI and the deflator as they appear in

---

BOX 14.1 The Personal Consumption Deflator

Some economists feel that the consumption component of the IGNPD, *the personal consumption deflator*, is a superior measure of inflation's impact on the consumer, preferring it to the CPI. Among their reasons are the replacement of housing prices and interest on mortgages (which are not considered consumption) with an index of rents, and the implicit inclusion of changes in consumer spending to mitigate the impact of price increases. (The CPI, for example, does not reflect the reduction in energy use following the substantial rise in fuel prices; the consumer component of the IGNPD does.) In fact, the IGNPD-consumption category is a cost-of-living index, while the CPI is, as noted earlier, a price index.*

*In case you're interested in the numbers, the consumption component of the IGNPD increased by 132 percent between 1965 and 1980, in contrast to the 161 percent increase in the CPI.

Figure 14.1 on page 350. Certainly the dollar was worth less in 1980 than it was in 1965. In fact, prices were higher in 1980 than they had ever been in the entire recorded history of the United States.

A more difficult question to answer is, By how much have prices risen? The data underlying the chart show modestly diverging answers, 6.6 percent annually for the CPI and 6.1 percent per annum for the deflator. (In 1980 the CPI rose by 13.5 percent while the IGNPD rose by only 9.0 percent). Moreover, there are differences in timing and in amplitude. Those who believe that economics is an exact science will perhaps be disappointed by this lack of accuracy. Those who are willing to settle for reasonable estimates will find the various measures of inflation useful even if imprecise.

Measuring the value of money, however, can be only the beginning. A changing price level invites the question "Why?" Why does the price level change, rising in inflationary times, falling or stable at other times? Economic theorists have long sought the answer.

☐ The Quantity Theory of Money

The equation of exchange

It is a truism that the value of purchases must equal the value of sales. If Claire buys a tire pump for $6.45, then she as purchaser spent $6.45, and the value of the sale must also and obviously be $6.45. This statement is true not only for individual transactions but for the entire economy. The entire economy's sales are but the arithmetic sum of each individual's sales, while all purchases are similarly the total of each individual's purchases. The **equation of exchange** expresses the relationship of sales and purchases for the entire economy.

The **equation of exchange** states that total purchases (MV) must equal total sales (PY_r).

The identity, $MV \equiv PY_r$, in the definition calls for further explanation. The meaning of each symbol is as follows:

M = the quantity of money
V = money's velocity
P = price
Y_r = real national production

M, the quantity of money, is the amount of money in the economy at a single point in time; in 1980 M-1A averaged $376.4 billion. *Velocity* refers to the turnover rate of money, or how many times M changed hands during the period. MV, then, measures the money spent by purchasers.

A picturesque example of velocity was given by Francis Edgeworth, an early twentieth-century British economist. It runs along these lines: Ned and Pete, partners in a barrel of beer, are on their way to the fair to sell it there. Pete, developing a thirst on the road, searches his pocket and finds a shilling. He asks Ned to sell him a stein of beer for the shilling. To Ned, of course, it matters not to whom he sells; it is important only that he sell and profit from the sale. So he draws a stein, and accepts the shilling in payment. But watching Pete rapidly downing his beer and smacking his lips in pleasure, Ned works up a thirst, too. Finding the shilling in his pocket, he buys a stein from Pete's half of the barrel. The trip is long, the weather humid, and Pete's thirst is reawakened. With the shilling he obtained from Ned (who got it from Pete), he purchases another stein from Ned's share of the barrel. To make a potentially long story short, the sixty steins in the barrel are consumed jointly by Pete and Ned. Their expenditures total 60 shillings, but the only money involved in all sixty transactions is a single shilling. In terms of M and V, M = 1 shilling and V = 60, for a total of 60 shillings purchased. How much was sold? 60 shillings' worth.

Money does not remain idle, lying quietly in a pocket or a checking account. Money is used, and each time it is used, it is as if more money were circulating. When you buy a theatre ticket for $5 and give a $5 bill to the cashier, for this transaction M = $5 and V = 1. If the cashier, absconding with the funds, spends that same $5 bill on a cab ride to the airport, M still equals $5 (since the same bill is being used), but V has now risen to 2. MV, or total purchases or total sales, is $10, even though only $5 is circulating. This result is identical to what would have happened if the cashier had put the $5 bill in his pants pocket and withdrawn a second $5 bill from his shirt pocket to pay the cabbie. Then M = $10—there are now two $5 bills in circulation—and the velocity of each bill equals 1. In this case, too, sales = purchases = MV = $10. Thus, a change in velocity has an impact analogous to that of a change in the quantity of money. Rising sales must be accompanied by either an increase in M, an increase in V, or some combination of the two. The opposite must be true for falling sales.

Turn now to the other side of the transaction, the sales receipts, or PY_r = $10: $5 for a single theatre ticket and $5 for the cab fare. In this case Y_r, real production, is the two services purchased—the ride and the ticket—while P = $5.

Table 14.3 shows an expanded tabulation of the equation of exchange. A million dollars' worth of goods have been sold. Each good is recorded in terms of its price and the physical quantities sold (columns 1 and 2). The sum, PY_r, is obtained by multiplying the price of each good (p) by its quantity sold (y_r), and adding down column 3. Hypothetical M and V values are given at the bottom of the table, and the equation of exchange is calculated.

The same procedure can be followed for the entire U.S. economy. Data on PY_r, or the value of total output of goods and services, are readily available. V, while not directly observable, can be derived as a residual. For if $MV \equiv PY_r$, then, by dividing both sides by M, the result is

$$V = \frac{PY_r}{M} \tag{14.1}$$

TABLE 14.3 The Equation of Exchange: A Hypothetical Example

Price (p)	Real product (y_r)	Value of sales (py_r)
(1)	(2)	(3)
$95.00	5,000 bicycles	$ 475,000
70.00	40 pairs of shoes	2,800
43.00	65 raincoats	2,795
0.25	75,000 ball point pens	18,750
0.10	3 million phone calls	300,000
0.65	300,000 one-pound loaves of bread	195,000
1.00	5,655 yoyos	5,655
	Sum of py_r = PY_r	$1,000,000

$$M = \$300,000; V = 3\tfrac{1}{3}$$
$$MV \equiv PY_r$$
$$\$300,000 \times 3\tfrac{1}{3} = \$1,000,000$$

In 1980 total national output for the U.S. economy was $2,626.1 billion. Since M-1A averaged $376.4 billion, then, using equation 14.1, V must have equaled $2,626.1 billion/$376.4 billion, or 6.977. In other words, each dollar held in cash and demand deposit accounts was used, on the average, almost seven times during 1980.

The equation of exchange can be manipulated arithmetically in a variety of ways. By itself, it has no meaning other than the obvious one mentioned earlier—that total sales equal total purchases. Thus, had M been double its 1980 average, $752.8 billion instead of $376.4 billion, any of the following could have been equally true:

Alternative A: V could have fallen to 3.4885 ($752.8 billion × 3.4885 = $2,626.1 billion).

Alternative B: P could have doubled, so that PY_r equalled $5,252.2 billion ($752.8 billion × 6.977 = $5,252.2 billion).

Alternative C: Y_r could have doubled, with P unchanged reaching $5,252.2 billion ($752.8 billion × 6.977 = $5,252.2 billion).

Alternative D: Any combination of A, B, and C could have occurred (e.g., $752.8 billion × 4.375 = $3,293.5 billion).

The equation of exchange has no explanatory or predictive value in and of itself and thus provides no method for singling out any of these four choices. Its usefulness lies in providing a framework for the quantity theory of money.

The quantity theory of money: Fisher's version

A number of assumptions must be made in order to convert the equation of exchange into the quantity theory as formulated by Irving Fisher, a twentieth-century American economist. (See Box 14.2.)

Assumption 1: Y_r *does not vary with changes in M.* Y_r is the real output, the physical amount of goods and services currently produced by business firms and other producers. Output is a result of input, namely, land, labor, and capital. With more or better land, labor, and capital, or more

Courtesy of Brown Brothers.

BOX 14.2 Irving Fisher (1867–1947)

Economist and businessman, statistician and reformer, Irving Fisher spent a long and active life equally comfortable and capable in numerous roles. Born to a Congregational minister who himself had been graduated from Yale College, Irving Fisher followed in his father's footsteps, entering Yale in 1884. He excelled in mathematics, continuing his studies at the Yale graduate school. But he also pursued a wide range of sciences and social sciences as a graduate student. His Ph.D. dissertation, which combined his loves of mathematics and economics, was the first one issued at Yale in pure economics; it is still considered a masterpiece today. Fisher taught mathematics at Yale for four years, but in 1895 he switched his priorities by joining the economics department there. He spent the rest of his academic life at Yale.

As an economist, Fisher is best remembered for two major works, the analysis of the quantity theory of money presented in this chapter and a theory of interest. "Why is interest paid?" inquired Fisher. His answer is twofold: First, lenders would not lend without receiving a return in excess of the principal lent, and second, borrowers are willing to pay. Lenders would prefer to spend their income currently, and to induce them to delay spending for a while—and, in the interim, lend the funds to others— borrowers pay a premium in the form of interest. Borrowers are able to pay this premium, for the investment that results from the borrowing has a productivity in excess of its costs. Consequently, the investor will earn a profit sufficient to cover all of his or her costs, including interest, and still have something left over.

This investment theory was picked up by Keynes; it played a major role in his own analysis (see pp. 459–462).

Another important insight of Fisher's was the distinction between the real rate of interest and the nominal rate, the latter including an inflation premium. One current admirer of Fisher has written: "The remarkable characteristic of Fisher's work is that it contains no *basic* error."*

As a businessman, Fisher was equally successful. He invented and marketed a card index system; in 1926 his corporation merged with others to form the giant Remington Rand, Inc. He served on its board of directors, and on the corporate boards of other companies as well, throughout his lifetime.

As a statistician, too, Fisher rates an important position as an innovator. His book on index numbers is an attempt to find an "ideal index number"; he felt that existing index numbers were biased and his ideal number tries to eliminate this bias. For practical reasons, however, his ideal index is less than ideal.

Fisher was involved in policy issues for a good part of his life; indeed, as he grew older he spent less time on theory and more on policy. His policy interests extended beyond economics, and unfortunately did little to enhance his professional standing. Among his economic policy proposals was the "compensated dollar," whose basic idea was to keep prices stable by varying the gold content of the dollar. In order to prevent hoarding during the Depression, he recommended "stamped money"—each dollar had to contain a stamp, to be obtained monthly, in order to retain its validity. Fisher's advocacy of "100 percent reserves" was not unique to him, but was nevertheless extreme; banks would hardly agree to maintain 100 percent reserve ratios against deposits.

Fisher suffered from an attack of tuberculosis in 1898, and after his recovery he became an ardent advocate of eugenics and public health. He collaborated with a doctor to write *How to Live: Rules for Healthful Living Based on Modern Science*, a book that has gone into over ninety editions since its publication in 1915 and has been translated into ten languages. Some of his ideas are perhaps bizarre to the modern mind: Good posture, appropriate shoe fit, and proper chewing are advocated as means of attaining longevity. But Fisher also objected to smoking and excess weight, and advocated exercise. He was also opposed to alcoholic beverages and wrote two books in favor of Prohibition.

Perhaps Fisher had more than his share of crackpot ideas, but his contributions to economics and statistics cannot be ignored. As Joseph Schumpeter has written, "His name will stand in history principally as the name of this country's greatest scientific economist."

*M. Allais, "Irving Fisher," *International Encyclopedia of the Social Sciences* (New York: Macmillan, 1968), 5, p. 476.

Source: J. A. Schumpeter, *Ten Great Economists: from Marx to Keynes* (New York: Oxford University Press, 1951), p. 223.

efficient combinations of the factors of production, output could be increased. Money, however, is not a factor of production, and an increase in the amount of money in the economy cannot, by itself, raise the level of economic output. (Many economists disagree with this contention for reasons to be discussed shortly. On the surface, however, the argument is appealing.)

Assumption 2: *Velocity does not vary with changes in M.* Fisher listed a number of determinants of velocity, which he classified as relating to (a) individual habits, (b) the community's payment system and (c) a category labeled "general causes."[4] The use of cash rather than credit cards is one example of "individual habits." Michael, the cash user, needs to hang onto a large stock of money to pay for his purchases; Rebecca, the credit card user, holds less money, since her purchases can be charged. Thus, if both spend $200 each Friday, but Michael has kept the required $200 on hand during the entire week, the velocity of his money will, by equation 14.1—sales (= purchases) divided by money balances—equal $200/$200, for a velocity of 1. Rebecca, who perhaps keeps an average of $50 on hand for purchases that cannot be made with a charge card, will find the velocity of her money to be 4, the result of her purchases of $200 divided by the cash balance of $50. Velocity, therefore, will vary with the habits of individuals and businesses.

[4] I. Fisher, *The Purchasing Power of Money* (New York: Macmillian, 1926), pp. 79f.

The payment system of the community also affects velocity. Consider the frequency of payment as an example. Helen, who earns $50 a day, is paid daily, and spends the entire $50 during the day, will achieve a velocity of infinity (= $50/$0 per day). For Joe, who is paid $250 a week but is paid only once a week, velocity will be less. To obtain the velocity of Joe's money holdings, first calculate the average daily money balance and then divide that result into total purchases. Assume that Joe gets paid on Monday morning and spends $50 during the day. By the end of Monday his balance will be $200. As Joe continues to spend $50 on each successive day, this balance declines by $50 daily until it reaches zero on Friday evening. The average money balance then is ($200 + $150 + $100 + $50 + 0) ÷ 5, or $100. Velocity then is $250/$100, or 2.5.

Transportation facilities are in the "general" category. The faster money can get around, argues Fisher, the higher its rate of turnover will be.

The fact that they are all basic structural features of the economy is the common element in all of these examples. Consequently, they are unlikely to change very rapidly. But even more important, an increase in the quantity of money will not affect these basic determinants of velocity. Employers are not going to pay their workers more or less frequently if the money stock increases or declines, nor will the transportation system work more speedily as the money supply changes.

Assumptions 1 and 2 are critical in converting the equation of exchange into the quantity theory of money. Because of these assumptions, the various alternatives listed previously (when examining the equation of exchange in the context of a change in the money supply) are reduced to one.

The quantity theory at work

As long as assumptions 1 and 2 are accepted, the equation of exchange can be rewritten as follows:

$$M\overline{V} = P\overline{Y}_r \tag{14.2}$$

The bars over V and Y_r indicate that these variables are invariant to changes in M. Now, if M is doubled to 2M, since V and Y_r cannot vary, the only way the equality can be maintained is by rewriting P as 2P; prices, too, must double. In general, *any change in the quantity of money will induce prices to change in the same direction and by the same proportion.* This is the **quantity theory of money.** In the 1980 arithmetic, had M doubled, the quantity theory requires that only alternative B would occur. M's rising from $376.4 billion to $752.8 billion would have led to a doubling in the price level.

The title of this chapter includes the statement that "the more there is,

The **quantity theory of money** states that changes in M will cause proportional changes in P.

the less it's worth." The quantity theory verifies that statement. For the more money is in circulation, the higher prices are. And the higher prices are, the lower is the purchasing power of each unit of money. A doubling of prices means that each dollar is worth only half as much as formerly.

The quantity theory is a theory of inflation. Why do prices rise? Because the money supply rose first! It is also a theory of deflation: If the money supply falls, prices will fall in its wake.

Most economists accept the quantity theory in certain circumstances. Few would disagree that very rapid increases in the quantity of money will cause inflation. History is replete with examples, as the next section, on interwar Germany, demonstrates. On the other hand, most contemporary economists feel that increases in the money supply are not necessarily inflationary in the short run. Indeed, even today's monetarists, the intellectual successors of the quantity theorists, reject the theory's short-run inevitability. The primary reason for this is the rejection of assumption 1, that M does not affect Y_r; that statement is too stringently formulated. True, money is not a factor of production; more money will not directly increase the supply of output. But without sufficient money, people might not demand enough goods, so that increasing the supply of money might lead to an increase in demand, which in turn would induce additional supply. This is more likely to be the case when productive facilities contain a large degree of slack and when a reservoir of unemployed labor can be drawn upon. A paint manufacturer who owns a plant that is working at only 75 percent of capacity and commands a force of underemployed workers will first utilize the existing plant and labor more fully and increase production when there is an increase in demand. It is unlikely that the producer's immediate reaction will be to raise prices. This is true for an underemployed economy as well: An injection of more money leads to increased demand and greater output, Y_r, rather than to higher prices (at least, not immediately.)

Where the monetarists and others part ways is over the relationship between the supply of money and its velocity. Although the differences have narrowed over the years, the monetarists basically accept the proposition that changes in M do not bring about significant changes in V, while the nonmonetarist school sees a close relationship between M and V. However, the debates between the Keynesians and the monetarists cannot be explored as yet; Keynesian macroeconomics, the subject of the next four chapters, must be examined first.

Just as monetarists agree with Keynesians that changes in M may affect the economy without leading to price changes, Keynesians in general accept the appropriateness of the quantity theory in **hyperinflationary** circumstances. When the money supply increases very rapidly in relatively brief periods, prices do the major part of the adjusting, rising rapidly in response to the money supply. Proceed onward to a classic example of hyperinflation.

Hyperinflation occurs when prices rise very rapidly. A working definition would be an inflation rate of over 50 percent monthly.

□ The German Hyperinflation, 1921–1923[5]

The Germans who lived through the inflation of the early 1920s have found this traumatic experience coloring their thoughts and actions to the present day. Much as the experience of the Great Depression strengthened America's resolve to avoid a replication of this tragic period of high unemployment and low production, so the German inflation firmed the German public's resolve not to see another inflation ravage their economy. And ravage it, it certainly did.

Some statistics on Germany's price experience will prove illuminating. Columns 2 and 3 of Table 14.4 reproduce the wholesale price index and cost-of-living index for 1921–1923. At the beginning of 1921, the c-o-l index was 1180 percent (or 11.8 times) higher than its prewar, 1913 base, while the wholesale price had mushroomed even further, by 1440 percent. Neither of these increases was negligible. During the early part of 1921, however, prices remained stable, and even declined a bit. By the end of 1921 consumer prices had risen by 64 percent and wholesale prices by almost 250 percent, a substantial increase, certainly, but slight in light of the German experience in 1922. In that year wholesale prices rose from 3,660 to 147,480, or more than fortyfold, just slightly less than for the entire period between 1913 and 1921. Retail prices rose even more rapidly than during the 1913–1921 period. Yet these numbers pale to insignificance in light of the inflation rate during 1923, when the hyperinflation reached its zenith. In the interval between June and July of 1923, consumer prices more than quintupled; between July and August, they increased over fifteen-fold; in the next month over twenty-five-fold; between September and October, by ten times the previous month's increase—246 times, to be exact. The rate slowed to a more modest 17,750 percent between October and November, and prices did not quite double between November and December.[6] The cost of living index records that the bundle of commodities that could be bought with 100 marks in 1913 cost 124,700,000,000,000 marks in December 1923. Kemmerer comments that if the wholesale price index were plotted on an arithmetic scale with an inch equaling 3,500 units and the 1913 index at 100, the chart plotting the index for December 1923 would be 560,000 *miles* high!

Column 4 of Table 14.4 looks at the same phenomenon from the viewpoint of the value of money, in this case, marks in terms of the U.S. dollar. An American visitor to Germany in January 1921 could acquire with one mark the equivalent of 1.6 cents' worth of goods and services. By the end of 1922, the single mark could buy only the value of one one-hundredth of a cent. By the middle of the next year, as the table

---

[5]Much of the detail in these paragraphs comes from Edwin W. Kemmerer, *Money* (New York: Macmillan, 1935), chap. 13.

[6]At the height of the hyperinflation, between October and November 1923, prices rose at a rate of 19.44 percent *daily*, or at an annual rate that exceeds 700,000 percent.

TABLE 14.4 Data on the German Inflation, 1921–1923

Month	Wholesale prices (1913= 100)	Cost of living (1913 = 100)	Average exchange rates Berlin-New York (cents per mark)	Paper money in circulation (billions of marks)
(1)	(2)	(3)	(4)	(5)
1921				
Jan.	1,440	1,180	1.60	78.5
Feb.	1,380	1,150	1.64	79.7
March	1,340	1,140	1.60	80.1
April	1,330	1,130	1.57	80.9
May	1,310	1,120	1.63	81.4
June	1,370	1,170	1.44	84.6
July	1,430	1,250	1.30	86.3
August	1,920	1,330	1.19	88.4
Sept.	2,070	1,370	0.96	94.5
Oct.	2,460	1,500	0.68	99.4
Nov.	3,420	1,770	0.39	108.8
Dec.	3,490	1,930	0.53	122.5
1922				
Jan.	3,660	2,040	0.52	123.9
Feb.	4,110	2,450	0.48	128.5
March	5,430	2,900	0.36	140.0
April	6,350	3,440	0.35	150.2
May	6,460	3,800	0.34	162.0
June	7,030	4,150	0.32	180.2
July	10,060	5,390	0.20	202.6
August	19,200	7,760	0.10	252.2
Sept.	28,700	13,320	0.07	331.9
Oct.	56,600	22,070	0.03	484.7
Nov.	115,100	44,610	0.01	769.5
Dec.	147,480	68,510	0.01	1,295.2
1923				
Jan.	278,500	112,000	0.007	1,999.6
Feb.	558,500	264,300	0.004	3,536.3
March	488,800	285,400	0.005	5,542.9
April	521,200	295,400	0.004	6,581.2
May	817,000	381,600	0.002	8,609.7
June	1,938,500	765,000	0.001	17,340.5
July	7,478,700	3,765,100	0.000,300	43,813.5
August	94,404,100	58,604,500	0.000,033,900	668,702.6
Sept.	2,300 million	1,500 million	0.000,001,880	28,244,405.8
Oct.	710 billion	370 billion	0.000,000,068	2,504,955,700.9
Nov.	72,570 billion	65,700 billion	0.000,000,000,143	400,338,326,400.0
Dec.	126,160 billion	124,700 billion	0.000,000,000,023	496,585,345,900.0

Source: Edwin W. Kemmerer, *Money* (New York: Macmillan, 1935), cols. 2 and 3 from Table 10, p. 291, cols. 4 and 5 from Table 9, p. 288.

indicates, the exchange rate of the mark had fallen to just about zero. In two short years the mark had moved from a position of being worth not quite 2 cents to that of a valueless currency.

A currency that becomes worthless loses its "money" features. Money is a unit of account, but if what has been legally declared to be money is changing in value on a daily basis, pricing goods and services in terms of the accepted monetary unit becomes exceedingly difficult. By 1922 many German merchants and industrialists had stopped quoting prices in terms of marks, listing them in dollars instead. To be sure, payments were typically made in marks, but price quotations were recorded in dollars. Some fortunate workers had their wages denominated in foreign currency or in physical goods, such as the leather salesman whose wage account was kept in terms of kilograms of leather. Actual payments were made in marks, but on the basis of the mark value of the physical amount of leather at the time when the payment was due.

Similarly, the mark ceased to serve as a store of value. With the purchasing power of the mark declining so rapidly, only the foolish would wish to hold on to it. Owners of marks switched out of "money" into goods, any good representing a better value than a deteriorating mark. Consequently, velocity rose drastically; people spent marks as rapidly as they acquired them.

Even the use of the mark as a medium of exchange was curtailed, although it was never eliminated entirely. Substitute moneys, issued by private corporations and local governments, and even foreign currency circulated throughout the country. What is surprising is that the mark maintained its medium-of-exchange function even during the last few months of rapid hyperinflation. This indicates that even a money that is rapidly becoming worthless is still more desirable for most people than complete reversion to a barter economy.

However, a money that maintains its value is still better. And as the inflation became ever more intense, substitute moneys, many of them illegal, circulated in ever-larger volume. Two thousand different kinds of emergency moneys were said to be in circulation in the fall of 1923. By that time the value of money substitutes actually exceeded that of legal tender money.

Dry statistics can never give as graphic a picture as concrete examples of what it was like to live in a hyperinflationary economy. A German visitor returning from a week's vacation in 1923 with what he thought was enough currency to take a cab home from the train station found that this sum would not even pay for a trolley ride. Businessmen traveling around the country discovered that they would have to borrow funds from their customers at each step of the way. The money they took to pay for the entire trip did not even suffice for moving on to the next customer. Kemmerer relates the story of a friend who was shopping for a pair of shoes. At 9:30 A.M. the price was quoted at 3¼ million marks; the same pair was priced at 7 million marks at 12 noon, and at 12:30 P.M. the price had risen to 14 million marks. Mailing a letter cost so much in the depreciated currency that the stamps virtually covered the entire face of the letter, leaving barely enough room for the address of the recipient. Stamps and money, too, were continuously overprinted as ever-larger denominations became necessary to pay for goods. Workers were often paid daily—and sometimes even more frequently, two or three times a day—so that they could buy goods in the morning before the inevitable afternoon price increase. Bankers were constantly on the phone, quoting the value of the mark in dollars as call after call came in from merchants who needed the exchange rate so that they could adjust their mark prices. This is hyperinflation, massive, snowballing inflation, with a vengeance.

What caused the hyperinflation? One can find both indirect and direct causes. Among the less direct forces underlying the German inflation were the reparations payments demanded after World War I by the victorious Allies, who were intent on both rebuilding their own war-dislocated economies and assuring the destruction of Germany's war-making capacity. More direct was the deficit-financing policy of the German government. Government debt, for example, expanded from 338 billion marks in April 1921 to 2,620,000,000,000 *billion* by April 1923. But the role of the money supply must be recognized as a direct cause. Column 5 of Table 14.4 follows the development of the official money supply. It increased by over 50 percent in 1921, by about 1000 percent in 1922, and by 25,000,000,000,000 percent in 1923. Velocity rose, too, as noted previously. And although Germany's industrial and agricultural production held up reasonably well until the middle of 1923, the rate of output growth was exceedingly modest when compared to the growth rate of MV. The inevitable outcome was hyperinflation, as predicted by the quantity theory of money.

The most blatant impact of the German inflation of 1921–1923 was the impoverishment of the middle class. Thrifty Germans who had saved and placed their money in corporate or government bonds found their lifetime efforts come to naught. Debtors ran after creditors to pay them with valueless currency. The debts of the German government and industry disappeared as their bondholders were paid off with worthless paper. On the other hand, many of the wealthy industrialists became wealthier still; being debtors, they gained from the fact that their debts were fixed in mark terms. Farmers, too, gained; like farmers elsewhere, German agriculturalists were, on the whole, debtors.

In its early stages the inflation actually encouraged production. Because real wages were lowered, labor costs fell, thereby increasing the profitability of production. Simultaneously, business management foresaw continued price increases and increased demand for productive inputs like machinery. We'd better buy now when prices are low, they reasoned, rather than later when prices rise to still higher levels. Nevertheless, as the hyperinflation progressed, this bubble burst; in the words of one investigator, by 1923 the hyperinflation had "disorganized all economic life." Workers soon realized that their real income was evaporating rapidly, and they began to spend considerable time negotiating pay adjustments. Insofar as they succeeded, they reduced the possibility of inflation-derived profits. Similarly, their work ethic suffered; they were more reluctant to work and less careful at work. Business decision-makers soon found that rational economic planning was impossible; they could not know what the prices of either inputs or outputs would be even in the near future. Speculation became the dominant activity. And as prices continued to skyrocket, German producers priced themselves out of foreign markets; exports fell. As a result of the decline in profitability, the inability to plan ahead, and the concern with speculation rather than production, unemployment rose by 600 percent, from 249,192 to 1,485,014. And as the hyperinflation got worse still, people found themselves unable to purchase; farmers refused to sell their crops for a worthless money, and merchants' inventory was rising so rapidly in money terms that it would have been foolish to reduce their stocks in exchange for the quickly depreciating currency. An economic crisis was at hand.

The inflation ended with the issuance of a new currency. The *Rentenmark* was valued at 1 trillion old marks and at 4.2 billion to the U.S. dollar. Success was assured when the public became convinced that the government would limit the volume of the new currency. A new administration in the central bank also served to inspire confidence. Indeed, since trust is so vital to the stability of a currency, once confidence had been restored, stability was a virtual certainty. Thus, velocity declined; people no longer felt compelled to spend their money as soon as it came into their hands. The mark once more became a desired medium of exchange and was again used as a unit of account and a store of value.

The German experience is not unique in the annals of hyperinflation. Such events have occurred in China, in Hungary, in the southern confederacy, in Brazil, and in other countries. Nor is hyperinflation limited to the past. In 1979, for example, Israel saw its prices rising at an annual rate of over 100 percent, while in the early 1970s Chile's rate of inflation reached 1 percent per day. Typically, these hyperinflations are the direct consequence of an unrestrained increase in the supply of money, and they can end only with the exercise of severe monetary restraint.

Accepting the quantity theory of money as an explanation of hyperinflation does not mandate its acceptance as the sole explanation of all inflations. Indeed, American economists of the Keynesian school do not accept the quantity theory as the single or even primary explanation of the inflation that has characterized the United States since the latter part of the 1960s. In general, more modest inflations are thought to come from other causes. A more complete examination of inflation must, however, await the development of the Keynesian theory of income determination in the coming chapters.

Aside from the rejection of the universality of the quantity theory, another reason for economists' coolness toward the theory has to do with its incompleteness. Essentially, Fisher's quantity theory postulates an increase in the quantity of money as causal, but it does not explain how prices actually increase. It describes a before-and-after situation, a shift from one equilibrium position to another, but not the mechanism by which the shift occurs. As noted in earlier chapters, the money supply is increased primarily by the workings of the banking system, by banks' willingness to lend and invest and by borrowers demanding funds. Thus, there ought to be a close relationship between money and spending, a point that is not dealt with by the quantity theory. Again, it is premature to explain the precise connection between increases in the supply of money and spending; that is done in Chapters 17 and 19. At this point it suffices to note that the inability to tie money creation to the spending mechanism limits the usefulness of the quantity theory. (Modern quantity theorists have grappled with this problem: The contributions of the monetarists are discussed in Chapter 20.)

□ Summary

This chapter opened with a discussion of how the value of money can be calculated. As with other questions of similar ilk, there is never a simple answer. Money's value is measured by its purchasing power, but the assessing of purchasing power is complicated. Is the CPI, the PPI, or the IGNPD the best measure? All have virtues that are missing from other indexes, but they all have deficiencies that are lacking in others. The CPI's coverage is limited, but the deflator is unable to accurately deflate the value of services. The PPI doesn't include services at all. None of the difficulties are so crippling as to suggest that the indexes are meaningless. Substantial movements of inflation are evident in all of the indexes, and as long as one is willing to settle for rough rather than precise averages, the indexes are a useful supplement to our economic data file. But they must be handled with care; small movements for brief periods are probably best ignored.

As an explanation of price changes, one popular theory is the quantity theory. Based on the identity known as the equation of exchange, the quantity theory argues that since neither real output nor velocity is dependent on the quantity of money, then any change in the quantity of money is reflected in changing price levels. In a hyperinflation this explanation is valid, but its validity for explaining less substantial movements in prices has been questioned by many economists. True, massive injections of money into the economy inevitably lead to inflation. But more modest increases in the money supply need not be inflationary in the short run. Moreover, inflation can occur without increases in the money supply. The quantity theory of money is an explanation of inflation, but it is not the only one. An alternative analytical apparatus is the Keynesian theory. It is more general than the quantity theory, for it seeks to explain not only price changes but movements in real output, too.

It is more complex, too, and Chapters 16 to 19 are devoted to it. But prior to examining the theory itself it will be helpful to explore the measures of national output, the so-called "family" of national income accounts. That is the purpose of the next chapter.

☐ Questions and Exercises

1. Try to calculate a personal or family price index, using your own or your family's budget expenditures for weights and then collecting price data for two consecutive months. Compare the impact of price changes on your budget with that of the CPI. (Your own city might be one of those for which the Bureau of Labor Statistics publishes a specific CPI. Check it out in the BLS's monthly, *The Consumer Price Index.*)
2. Calculate the components of the equation of exchange for a recent year. Can you infer anything about the impact of the money supply on inflation from these numbers?
3. Price freezes ordered by a government authority have often been used to restrain inflation. If obeyed, these freezes will be reflected in the price index. Does this fact contradict the quantity theory of money?
4. Examine a hyperinflation other than the German one to assure yourself of the relationship between growth of the money supply and price increases.
5. Complaints are often heard during a galloping inflation that there's not enough money around to pay for goods and services at the inflated prices. Yet the quantity theory asserts that the cause of the rising prices is continuous expansion of the money supply. Is this paradox explainable?

☐ For Further Study

The methodology of the CPI and its revision in 1978 is summarized in U.S. Department of Labor, Bureau of Labor Statistics, *The Consumer Price Index: Concepts and Content over the Years*, Report 517 (Washington, D.C., 1977). Its weaknesses over the last few years, especially with regard to housing expenditures, are discussed in Alan S. Blinder, "The Consumer Price Index and the Measurement of Recent Inflation," *Brookings Papers in Economic Activity* (1980): 539–570.

One of the most readable expositions of the quantity theory of money remains that of its American initiator, Irving Fisher, *The Purchasing Power of Money* (New York: Macmillan, 1926). A lucid contemporary treatment may be found in Chapters 2 and 3 of S. Rousseas, *Monetary Theory* (New York: Random House, 1972).

For a view of the German hyperinflation by the man who presided over its end, the autobiography of Hjalmar Horace Greeley Schacht, *Confessions of "The Old Wizard"* (Boston: Houghton Mifflin, 1956), makes for good reading. Max Shapiro, *The Penniless Billionaires* (New York: New York Times-Truman Talley, 1980), suggests that the inflation was planned in order to redistribute income. More technical is the intensive study of C. Bresciani-Turroni, *The Economics of Inflation* (London: Allen and Unwin, 1937). A number of papers that use modern econometric techniques to study highly inflationary economies are gathered in Milton Friedman, ed., *Studies in the Quantity Theory of Money* (Chicago: University of Chicago Press, 1956), and David Meiselman, ed., *Varieties of Monetary Experience* (Chicago: University of Chicago Press, 1970).

APPENDIX The Classical World and the Quantity Theory

This chapter has viewed the quantity theory of money in isolation, as a theory of price level determination. In fact, however, the quantity theory is but one component of a complete classical theory of income determination. This appendix is devoted to a schematic exposition of the classical theory. In addition, an alternative view of the quantity theory of money is presented.

The classical theory of income determination can best be understood by separating the components of the theory into isolated segments and then recombining them. Four such segments can be identified:

1. The labor market
2. The consumer goods market
3. The saving-investment market
4. The quantity theory

The labor market

The macroeconomic model of the labor market in the classical world is simply the aggregate of individual microeconomic labor markets. Thus, the mechanism that determines wages and employment on the microeconomic level is equally applicable to the macroeconomic level. A variety of influences induce a worker to offer his or her labor services to firms; the wage is thought to be a key variable. The higher the wage offered by employers, the greater the amount of labor that will be supplied. This expected labor supply curve is depicted as S_L in Figure 14A.1(a), with the normal positively sloped relationship. But it must be immediately noted that the wage that is relevant for work decisions is the *real* wage, not the nominal wage. For workers must of necessity be interested in the purchasing power of their income, not in the absolute wage level. A doubling of wages accompanied by a doubling of prices would not bring forth any additional labor supply.

The demand for labor, too, varies with the real wage rate. The lower the wage that employers are required to pay, the more labor they will be willing to hire. This aspect is portrayed by D_L, the demand-for-labor curve. The market wage, of course, is determined at the point where the demand and supply curves intersect, where the quantity of labor supplied equals the quantity demanded. In Figure 14A.1(a) the equilibrium annual wage is $15,000, and 80 million workers will be employed.

Total wages paid and total output produced can also be calculated from the diagram. Total wages are wages per worker times the number of workers employed, or $15,000 × 80 million, which equals $1.2 trillion. To compute total output, recall from your microeconomics course that the demand-for-labor curve equals the value-of-the-marginal-product-for-

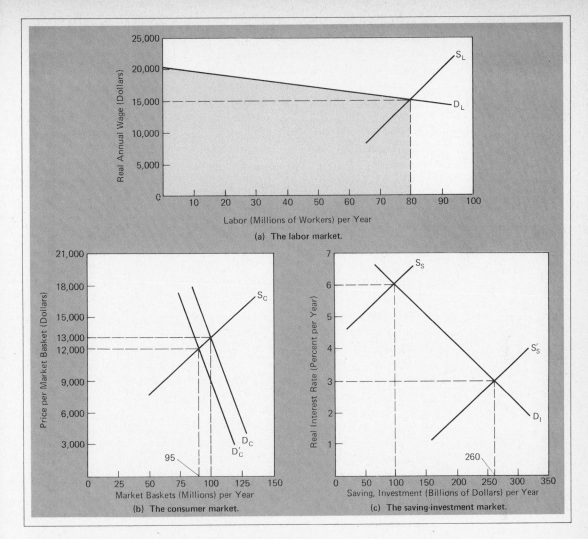

FIGURE 14A.1 The macroeconomics of the classical world.

labor curve (which itself equals the marginal physical product times marginal revenue). Furthermore, remember that the sum of the value of marginal products equals the value of total product. Thus, the value of total product or output equals the area below the demand-for-labor curve up to the equilibrium quantity of workers; it is the darkened area in Figure 14A.1(a). This value turns out to be $1.4 trillion, of which, as stated, $1.2 trillion goes to the workers and the remainder to owners of the other factors of production.

Note that this output level is a full-employment level. All workers who are willing to work at the equilibrium real wage of $15,000 find the employment they desire. True, those who are unwilling to settle for the going wage end up jobless, but this is voluntary unemployment; they are out of work because their own evaluation of the value of work differs from that of the impersonal market. Even more illuminating is the fact that in the classical system described here, involuntary unemployment can never occur. Should the demand for labor fall—demonstrated by a downward shift in the D_L curve—the equilibrium wage will fall. All workers who are unwilling to work at the new, lower wage voluntarily leave the market. The classical world, in theory, does not explain massive depressions. As long as people are willing to work for the going wage, jobs will be available.

The consumer market

The public has received an income of $1.4 trillion. How much of this sum will be spent? Microeconomic theory teaches that the lower the price of a particular good, the more of that good will be purchased by the public. Price here is *relative* price, meaning the price of one good in terms of another. Thus, a reduction in the price of wicker baskets from $4 per unit to $3 increases the quantity demanded only if other prices remain unchanged, for only then is there a reduction in the price of wicker baskets relative to the prices of all other goods. If all prices fall by 25 percent, then there is no reason why the consumer should purchase more of any one commodity or change his or her spending patterns. In what follows, prices of consumer goods are expressed in dollars, but in order to maintain the condition that the cause of changes in quantity demanded is relative price, the price of one commodity—say, earrings—will be kept constant. Thus, consumers buy a market basket that consists of all goods and services other than earrings; they buy more baskets if the price of a market basket relative to that of earrings falls and fewer baskets if the price rises relative to that of earrings.

Figure 14A.1(b) depicts the consumer market. The D_C curve is the consumers' demand curve, while S_C is the supply curve for consumer goods and services. In equilibrium the public spends $13,000 for each market basket, purchases 100 million such baskets, and spends $13,000 $\times$ 100 million, or $1.3 trillion.

The savings-investment market

Consumers may opt to save part of their income rather than spend it all. In the framework of classical theory, saving is responsive to the real interest rate: The greater the interest return that can be earned by the saver, the more income will be saved. Curve S_S in Figure 14A.1(c) is the supply-of-savings curve, rising with higher real interest rates.

Investors, too, are responsive to the real interest rate. At higher rates investors buy fewer capital goods in a manner similar to consumers spending less when prices rise. (A fuller statement of the relationship between interest rates and investment will be found in Chapter 17.) Lower real interest rates, on the other hand, induce more investment spending. The result is the demand for investment, the D_I curve in the diagram. In a simplified, direct-finance relationship, it is the savers who provide the funds that investors use to finance their spending. The desires of savers are brought together with the desires of investors. Equilibrium once again is at the supply-demand intersection, which in Figure 14A.1(c) is at 6 percent, and the volume of saving and investment equals $100 billion. This result must obtain; since the product produced is $1.4 trillion and $1.3 trillion is spent on consumption goods, the balance of $0.1 trillion must be spent by investors.

The real markets

These three markets—employment, consumption, and saving-investment—represent the basic production and consumption markets in the economy. They are "real" markets, for they deal with physical outputs. And with these markets the classical macroeconomic system is complete. Moreover, the system is a stable one. Full employment is maintained by the workings of the real wage rate, adjusting to equate workers seeking jobs with employers seeking workers. The goods market —consumer and investment goods—is also stable. For if consumers decide to spend less, stabilizing reactions will occur. First, decisions by consumers to spend less, to buy fewer market baskets at the going price, will bring about a reduction in the price of the market basket. Consequently, although fewer baskets will be purchased, the decline will be smaller than if prices had remained at their previous level. Second, a decision to spend less is simultaneously a decision to save more. If the supply of saving increases, the real interest rate will decline. In turn, the volume of capital investment will rise in response to the fall in the cost of borrowing funds. The net effect must be that investment will increase by precisely the amount by which consumption falls. It is as if consumption and investment were weights on the same side of a balance scale, as sketched out in Figure 14A.2. If the consumption weight is reduced, balance is still maintained by an appropriate increase in the weight of investment.

This can be portrayed diagramatically as well. Refer back to Figure 14A.1(b) and (c). In the former, D'_C represents a reduced level of demand; at the market price of $13,000, consumers wish to acquire only 87.5 million baskets. As the supply curve has remained unchanged, the equilibrium price drops to $12,000 per market basket, with a quantity purchased equal to 95 million units. In total, then, consumers spend only $1.14 trillion, down from the $1.3 trillion they spent previously.

Now turn your attention to the saving-investment market, as portrayed in Figure 14A.1(c). A decision to decrease consumption spending is also a decision to increase saving. A new saving curve, S'_S, replaces S_S. This

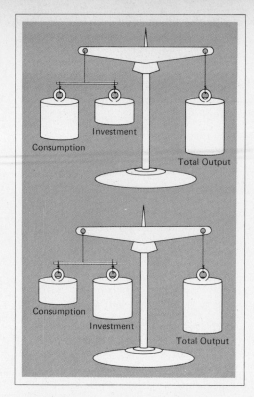

FIGURE 14A.2 The balance of consumption and investment. *Even when consumption falls, balance is maintained by an appropriate increase in investment.*

leads to a new real interest rate, 3 percent instead of the old 6 percent rate. At the lower interest rate investors spend more; the diagram indicates that their spending will rise from $100 billion to $260 billion. Note that this increase in investment spending is precisely equal to the decrease in consumer spending. The same total of $1.4 billion is being spent, but the distribution between investment and consumption has been modified. The balance, however, has not been tipped; all markets remain in a consistent set of equilibria.

The quantity theory of money

Enter the quantity theory. Up to this point the prices in the real markets have been relative prices. As noted earlier, relative prices are ratios of two prices, such as the price of umbrellas relative to that of watchbands or the price of cashew nuts relative to that of peanuts. And as stated previously, decisions in the real markets are based on these relative prices. Consumption decisions, for example, hinge on the price of one product in comparison to that of another product. If a pound of cashews were twice as expensive as a pound of peanuts, cashews would be purchased only by people whose marginal satisfaction from eating cashews was at least twice as great as the marginal satisfaction they derived from chewing peanuts. For someone whose marginal satisfaction was below that level, however, the relatively high price of cashews would lead to the substitution of peanuts. But if the price of cashews fell to 1½ times that of peanuts, some erstwhile peanut purchasers would switch and purchase the now (relatively) cheaper cashews.

If relative prices matter, it follows that any set of relative prices will give the same "real" results. Thus, if Julius is willing to purchase two pounds of cashews at a price of $2 per pound when peanuts sell for $1 per pound, he should be equally willing to purchase two pounds of cashews when they are priced at $4 per pound if peanuts are then priced at $2 per pound. And, if it does not seem absurd, conceptually the same result will occur if cashews are priced at $400 a pound and peanuts at $200 a pound. In each case the relative price is 2:1.

What, then, determines whether the price is $2, $4, or $400? The answer of classical theorists is the quantity theory of money. It is the quantity of money that determines whether prices in general will be high or low. A larger quantity of money means that everything will be priced high, while a smaller quantity of money means that all prices will be lower.

Perhaps this can be easily explained by learning an alternative formulation of the quantity theory, namely, the Cambridge version.

The Cambridge quantity theory

This version belongs to the academic tradition of Cambridge, the famous English college. Its present formulation can be attributed to the early master and founder of the particular brand of economics associated with Cambridge, Alfred Marshall. Following in Marshall's footsteps were such famous British economists as A. C. Pigou, Sir Denis Robertson, and the young John Maynard Keynes.

The Cambridge approach to money is to wonder why people hold onto money at all. Why not spend it? The answer given is basically related to transaction needs. True, one holds money in order to spend it, but prior to being spent it is being held. A person's spending takes place during some time span, say, a week. But income comes in at fixed intervals, say, once a week on Friday. The individual must of necessity hold onto money to bridge the gap between receipt of income and actual spending. If this is so, the amount of money people wish to hold depends on their income, and the following statement can be made:

$$L = kPY_r \qquad (14A.1)$$

where L is the demand for money (how much I wish to hold or how much money the public wishes to hold), k is the proportion of nominal income that the individual or public wishes to hold in money form, and PY_r, as before, stands for nominal income.

Equation 14A.1 states that the demand for money either by an individual or by the economy as a whole is some proportion of his or her or everyone's nominal income. So if $PY_r = \$1$ billion and $k = 1/10$, the demand for money to be held by people in anticipation of spending it will equal $\$1$ billion $\times 1/10$, or $\$100$ million.

In equilibrium, we know that the demand must equal the supply of money. If M is to stand for the supply of money available at any one moment, then

$$M = \text{constant} \qquad (14\text{A}.2)$$

and the equilibrium condition is

$$M = L \qquad (14\text{A}.3)$$

Substituting M for L in equation 14A.1, equilibrium is achieved when:

$$M = kPY_r \qquad (14\text{A}.4)$$

Where has this series of equations led? The answer is to a better understanding of what k is and how it is related to Fisher's version of the quantity theory as explained in this chapter. Now juxtapose equation 14A.4 with the equation of exchange:

$$MV = PY_r$$

$$M = kPY_r$$

Three of the terms in each equation are identical. Only k and V differ. Multiply both sides of the first equation by $1/V$ to derive the following:

$$MV(1/V) = (1/V)PY_r$$

Since $V(1/V) = 1$, the left side of the equation is simply M. Thus,

$$k = 1/V$$

This expression means that the proportion of income that people wish to hold in the form of money (k) is the reciprocal of velocity. If $k = 1/10$, then $V = 10$; if the public wishes to hold 10 percent of its income in the form of money, its average cash balance will turn over ten times. Or, to put it differently, if people decide to hold a greater proportion of their income in the form of money than previously (i.e., k increases), velocity will decline. Thus, both the Cambridge and Fisher versions come out to much the same formulation. Certainly they arrive at the same quantity theory conclusions.

This can be seen by analyzing the assertions of the Cambridge quantity theory. Begin by making the same assumptions that were made in connection with Fisher's version (pp. 359–361), namely, that Y_r and V (or k) are not dependent on M. Rewrite equation 14A.4 to reflect these assumptions by placing bars above the appropriate terms:

$$M = \bar{k}P\bar{Y}_r \qquad\qquad\qquad\qquad (14A.4')$$

Once again, if the supply of money, M, changes, then, by assumption, neither k nor Y_r will respond. The only variable left is P. Cambridge economists conclude that a change in money supply will bring about a proportional change in prices. Double the money supply and prices will double in its wake. This, of course, is the quantity theory conclusion.

Return now to the analysis of the classical system. It is the quantity of money that determines what the price level, P, will be. However, since a change in the money supply changes all prices, leaving relative prices unchanged, none of the real variables in the classical system will be modified. Employment will not be affected, for doubling wages will not induce more workers to enter the labor market if prices have also doubled, since the real wage remains constant. Doubling the prices of consumption goods will not decrease consumption, since nominal wages have increased and the public has the purchasing power to pay the doubled prices. Neither will consumption patterns be amended, relative prices having remained unchanged. Nor will saving or investment change; interest rates themselves are relative prices, and an increase in the supply of money does not bring about a change in the level of real interest rates.

This phenomenon, whereby the quantity of money determines the absolute level of prices while nonmonetary demand and supply forces determine the physical quantity of output, consumption, and investment, is known as the **classical dichotomy**. Money has no impact on the real world; it is a veil that covers up what is really going on. More money makes no difference except to raise prices. But that rise in prices makes no difference in terms of real economic behavior.

The **classical dichotomy** refers to the theory of classical economists that real forces determine production, employment, consumption, saving, investment, and relative prices, while the quantity of money determines the absolute price level.

A diagramatic analysis of the quantity theory

If you wish to complete the diagramatic exposition with a fourth diagram, read on.

It will be easiest to begin with a slight rephrasing of the quantity theory. Until now, the theory has been expressed by the relationship of the money supply to the price level, such that the greater the supply of money, the higher prices will be. But it is equally accurate to express the quantity theory in terms of the value of money. The more money is in circulation, the smaller the value of each unit of money. Saying that as the money supply increases, the price level rises, is equivalent to stating that less can be purchased with each dollar.

Recall now that the demand for money is related to the nominal income by the proportion factor, k (equation 14A.1). This equation states that the individual, and, by aggregation, the entire community, wishes to keep a certain proportion of income in money form. If the price level should rise (e.g., if P should double), then with k and Y_r remaining constant, the demand for money will rise in proportion (i.e., L will double). Check this out with equation 14A.1. The demand for money, then, varies directly with the price level and, by virtue of the previous statements, inversely with the value of money. This can be expressed by stating that the individual wishes to hold a constant "real" quantity of money, that is, a constant amount of purchasing power. See this by rewriting equation 14A.1, dividing both sides of the equation by P:

$$\frac{L}{P} = kY_r \qquad\qquad (14A.5)$$

According to equation 14A.5, if the price level doubles, the purchasing power of one's money holdings falls by half. In order to restore the relationship required by kY_r, the individual's money demand requires that cash balances must double, too.

Equation 14A.5 is expressed graphically in Figure 14A.3. The vertical axis, 1/P, measures the value of money, while the horizontal axis measures the quantity of money. The demand-for-money curve is represented by the rectangular hyperbole labeled L. Any point on this curve meets the qualification of equation 14A.5, for when the coordinates of the point are multiplied, the product equals kY_r. For example, when the value of money equals ½ (which means that the price level is twice as high as previously, so that the value of money is half the initial value) and the quantity of money demanded equals $200, then the product, ½ × $200, equals the real value of money or $100. Similarly, when the price level

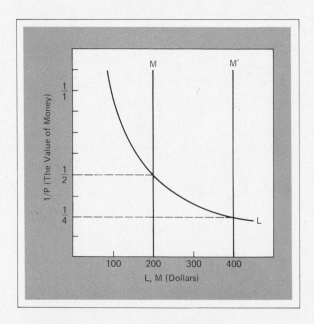

FIGURE 14A.3 The quantity theory of money.

doubles, so that the value of money equals ¼, the quantity of money demanded equals $400. Again, multiply ¼ × $400 to obtain the same constant $100 in real money obtained earlier.

Now consider the supply of money, represented by M. In the diagram M is set at $200. Equilibrium requires that L = M, the supply of money equals the demand for money, and thus the value of money will equal ½. Double the quantity of money to M' = $400. Equilibrium now occurs at a money value of ¼. A doubling of the quantity of money has led to a halving of the value of money.

The upshot of this diagram is that absolute prices and the value of money are determined by the supply of money. But this very conclusion minimizes the importance of money: Money determines the price level alone; it does not affect the volume of consumption, investment, or employment.

Summary

To sum up, the world of the mainstream classical economists is one of guaranteed full employment. Workers can always find jobs, as long as they are willing to work at the going wage. Decisions to reduce consumption in the classical scheme also have no adverse impact on the economy, for investment always compensates for the reduction in consumption. The primary mechanism for bringing about this balancing is the real interest rate. Decreased consumption means increased saving, which leads to a fall in the real interest rate. In response to the decline in the real interest rate, investment increases, and will increase enough to offset the reduction in consumption.

The determination of the price level is a wholly monetary phenomenon. The classical system can tolerate inflation. Its cause, according to the classical economists, is obvious: It is the increase in the quantity of money. Deflation, similarly, comes from a decrease in the quantity of money.

What about depression? Since the theory of the classics is a full-employment theory, it cannot explain a depression. But since depressions do occur, blame is placed on frictions in the economy that inhibit its smooth operation. Thus, if laborers are not willing to settle for lower wages, it is not surprising that unemployment will result. And if product prices do not fall because of monopolistic controls over prices, then again depressions can occur. It follows that the elimination of depressions involves simply the elimination of these frictions.

A further implication is that government intervention can do little good and immense harm; tax cuts won't help, nor will increased expenditures. It is not surprising that politicians of all parties rejected the concept of an unbalanced budget as a cure for the depression of the 1930s, for the prolonged downturn was not thought to be caused by inadequate spending. Nor could an increase in the money supply help. More money would only raise prices; it could not increase employment. Only with the theoretical apparatus proposed by Keynes would this classical theory be overturned. In the postwar world, the passive policy recommendations of the classical economists were replaced by the activist fiscal policies of the Keynesians. The next five chapters deal with the Keynesian revolution.

CHAPTER 15

The National Income Accounts, or The Numbers Game[1]

Even most widely accepted figures frequently have error components of unexpected magnitude, and consequently cast doubt on many currently accepted analyses in economics.

Oskar Morgenstern, professor (1963)

Income, n. The natural and rational gauge and measure of respectability, the commonly accepted standard being artificial, arbitrary, and fallacious.

Ambrose Bierce, satirist (1911)

CONTENTS

Measures of National Output and Income

Gross National Product (GNP)
Computation of GNP
Gross National Expenditure (GNE)
Net National Product (NNP)
National Income (NI)
Sources of Data
Personal Income (PI)
Disposable Personal Income (DPI)
Consumption and Saving

The National Income Family Since 1965

Summary

APPENDIX: A Closer Look at the National Income Accounts

Details of the Relationship of GNP to Disposable Personal Income, Consumption, and Saving
Problems in Computing GNP
Conceptual Issues in GNP Accounts

---

[1]This chapter may be skimmed by students who have already been exposed to the national income accounts. The end-of-chapter summary, however, might be reviewed.

Data are, in a way, the lifeblood of economics, useful not only for comprehending various economic relationships but for the practical application of economics as well. The price indexes examined in the last chapter, for example, inform us about the extent of inflation. They also send signals to policy makers, who, without knowing the degree of inflation, cannot make intelligent decisions.

The same statements apply with equal force to information about the economy in general. Economists are interested in ascertaining whether the national economy is growing rapidly or slowly, whether it is stagnating or declining. This information is useful for a number of purposes, including purely intellectual ones. Students of the well-being of the community follow closely the rise and ebb of the economic tide. Economic historians trace out how the American economy fared over the decades, knowledge of which can be used to identify the sources of economic growth. Economists who are interested in comparative economic systems compare American growth rates with those of other nations. But there are more practical reasons for gathering data about the economy: Policy designed to influence economic activity must be based on empirical knowledge.

Many organizations, public and private, gather information on economic activities. The Federal Reserve Board, for example, publishes each month an index of industrial production, which measures the physical output of goods-producing industries. The F. W. Dodge Corporation (no relation to the Dodge Division of the Chrysler Corporation) publishes a monthly series on housing contracts. And a horde of trade associations provide data on their industries. America is a rich country in terms of the volume of information it produces.

All such numbers, while useful for specific purposes, are too narrow in scope to be representative of the entire economy. A broader set of data is needed. Fortunately, such numbers are available. Known as the national income accounts, they provide an overview of economic activity for the entire national economy. The task of this chapter is to explain the nature of the national income data, their limitations, and their recent patterns.

Students often find the study of the national income accounts tedious. Admittedly, it is. It cannot be contended that you will become a better person by memorizing numerical interrelationships. Nevertheless, knowledge of what these accounts are and what they mean is terribly important in an age in which economic policy is headline news almost daily. And if you want to understand how economists believe the national economy operates—that is, the theory of income determination presented in the next few chapters—you cannot avoid mastering the building blocks and definitions in the present chapter.

The family of national income accounts includes five concepts: gross national product, net national product, national income, personal income, and disposable personal income. Each will be discussed in turn.

☐ Measures of National Output and Income

Gross National Product (GNP)

Gross national product (GNP) is a measure of the entire or aggregate national output. It includes all goods and services produced during the year or a quarter-year. The 7.5 million new automobiles that were sold at an average retail price of, say, $8000 contribute $60 billion to GNP, and the 2½ billion haircuts at $5 apiece add another $12½ billion to the aggregate product. Other amounts are added by all the food products and consumer durables, and all the homes and industrial plants built. Included also are the services of cabbies and bus drivers, street sweepers and police officers, accountants and lawyers, surgeons and opthalmologists, plumbers and masons, typists and file clerks. Indeed, all production is included. GNP is the most comprehensive statistic, encompassing the current production of the entire economic system.

If GNP includes everything produced, why is the definition so complex, including the terms *final* and *produced for the market?*

Final is included to eliminate **double-counting** of output. Outputs that are inputs at later stages in the production process should not be counted more than once. Otherwise, a false, inflated measure of national product will be inevitable. For example, galvanized iron, a product of the iron and steel industry, is made into pipes by the metal-fabricating industry. It is then fashioned into a sculpture by an artist. When the sculpture is sold, the retail price of $4,500 will be included in GNP. This $4,500 includes the value of the pipes and of the raw material that went into their manufacture. It would be exaggerating to add up the value of the **intermediate products**—the iron and the pipes—separately, in addition to the price of the art work. National output includes a piece of sculpture made out of iron pipes ($4,500), not a piece of sculpture plus pipes plus galvanized iron (i.e., not $4,500 + $200 + $50). Of course, output that does not enter into further current production—steel sheets that remain as inventory either at the steel mill or with steel processors, and the pipes that are still in the warehouse of the fabricator or in the studio of the sculptor—is itself a final product. As such, current production remaining in inventory is included in GNP.

Gross national product (GNP) is the value of final national output produced for the market during a specific period.

Double-counting is the error of including both final goods and services and their inputs in calculating GNP.

Any product that is processed further into a final good is known as an **intermediate product.**

The second exclusion is indicated by the limitation of GNP to production for the market. This qualifier serves to exclude (with a few exceptions, to be noted in the next paragraphs) goods and services that are not marketed. If a mechanic tunes up your car's engine, his services—the $50 paid him—are included. If you tune your own engine, even though the end product is the same (or better), your services are excluded. Similarly, when a homemaker cooks a meal at home, the cost of the food and utilities used is included in GNP, but the culinary talents—the services—of the cook are not part of GNP. But if the same meal is eaten in a restaurant, the services provided in preparing and serving it are counted. As one economist remarked years back, if you marry your housekeeper, GNP will decline.

There is a practical reason for limiting GNP to goods produced for sale: the inability to obtain reliable estimates of the value of these nonmarket products. And even if the omission is likely to be substantial—some have asserted that the United States' GNP would be increased by some 25 percent if just the nonmarket services of housewives were included—a useful belief is that the year-to-year changes are insignificant. Thus, even if the level of GNP is not truly accurate, annual changes do correctly reflect what is happening to the economy.[2]

The criteria of production for sale is not chiseled in stone; there are exceptions. Some nonmarket services for which data are difficult but not impossible to come by are included in GNP, while some market activities for which data are unobtainable are excluded. As an example of the latter, consider illegal activities. Surely gambling services, drugs, and similar products are marketed. But because of their very nature, reliable data cannot be obtained. The gross annual product of the underground economy, which includes legal activities that are not reported in order to avoid taxes, has been estimated by some to lie in the neighborhood of $600 billion.

On the other hand, the rental value of owner-occupied housing and the value of home-consumed agricultural produce, although neither is marketed, are included in GNP. It is possible to estimate the value of owner-occupied housing by comparing it to similar rental housing. (This implies that a landlord living in her own apartment is paying rent to herself. And to follow the logic through, it implies that the landlord's income is increased by the amount of the rent paid to herself, which suggests that she should pay income taxes on this rent. Indeed, some countries have accepted this logic, imposing income taxes on implicit rent.) Similarly, in the case of a farmer who sells part of his crop and retains a share for personal use, both portions can be valued at market prices.

In short, GNP basically includes all newly produced goods and services that are bought and sold in the market.

---

[2]The reliability of the GNP calculations is discussed in the appendix to this chapter.

The definition of GNP implicitly excludes two important types of economic transactions: asset transfers and transfer payments. Since GNP measures only current, newly produced output, it must not count exchanges of existing assets. If you buy ten shares of RCA common stock at $30 per share, the $300 payment is not included in GNP. The transaction simply involves an exchange of paper: You now own ten shares that you did not own before, but you have $300 less in your checking account. Your trading partner has $300 more and ten shares less. Ownership has changed hands, but nothing new has been created. (Note, however, that if you paid $10 to the stockbroker for arranging the trade, that $10 will be included. It is payment for newly produced services on the part of the broker.) Even if the seller bought the shares at $9 and now obtains a $21 profit on the exchange, this increase is not included in GNP; this capital gain does not represent increased production in the economy. Had the buyer purchased the stock from the original issuer itself, RCA, the transaction still would be no more than an exchange of assets. And if RCA used the funds so obtained to purchase new productive equipment, the value of the new machinery would be included in GNP, but not because of the stock sale. New machinery, being current production, is included in GNP on its own merits. Similarly, the purchase of an old house or a used car is but an exchange of existing assets and must be excluded from GNP computations.

An analogous line of reasoning applies to the exclusion of **transfer payments.** Take, for example, the receipts of a retired couple. Social security payments cannot be included in GNP, since the recipients have not produced any service currently. True, in their younger years they worked and paid into the social security insurance fund. Their contribution was included then, since they were producing goods and services. Currently, however, they are producing nothing; their payments are received for no service rendered in exchange, and therefore must be excluded from GNP. The same is true for people living on welfare and for anyone who receives income without providing current goods or services in exchange. Again, GNP includes only final current marketed production.

A **transfer payment** is a payment for which no current service has been rendered.

Computation of GNP

How is GNP computed? Conceptually, what is required is a production statement from each producing firm, stating its output and its production costs. By netting out intermediate goods and summing up the individual statements, one derives GNP. This method employs the **value added** concept.

Consider the example of the sculpture used earlier, and glance at Table 15.1. The first line details the value of the galvanized iron produced by the iron and steel industry. Since the processed iron is sold to the metal-fabricating industry at a price of $50, which is the price of the final product (column 3) and no intermediate goods were used (column 4), the

Value added is the net output of each producer. It equals the value of the firm's final production less its expenditures on intermediate goods.

TABLE 15.1 The Calculation of Value Added

Industry	Product	Value of final product	Value of intermediate product	Value added
(1)	(2)	(3)	(4)	(5)
Iron and steel	Galvanized iron	$50	$0	$50
Metal fabricating	Iron pipe	$200	$50	$150
Arts	Sculpture	$4500	$200	$4300
			Total	$4500

full amount of $50 is the value added, and it so appears in column 5. The next line details the value added in the metal-fabricating industry. The processor purchases the galvanized iron as an intermediate product for $50 (column 4) and sells it to the sculptor for $200 (column 3) in the form of pipes. The value added by the metal fabricating industry must be $150 (column 5), that is, $200 − $50. Finally, the sculptor sells the piece of work for $4500, the value of the final product. After subtracting the cost of the intermediate product—the $200 for the pipes—the value added is $4300. Add up the value-added entries of column 5, and the value of aggregate production must total $4500. If this procedure is followed throughout the economy, the result will be the value of all production, excluding all intermediate products and avoiding all double-counting. (To be precise, all goods produced and not sold—that is, inventories—must be added on.) In other words, the summation of value added by each industry for the entire economy equals gross national product.

Gross national expenditure (GNE)

A second method of calculating GNP is the **gross national expenditure (GNE)** approach. Its components provide the basic division of the economy into spending classifications that are the foundation of national income analysis.

Gross national expenditure (GNE) equals national spending on final economic output for a specific period.

Gross national expenditure views production not from the producers' side but from that of the ultimate user. The uses of output are divided into four categories:

Remember these categories for future use

1. *Personal consumption expenditures (C):* all consumer purchases during the year, except for new housing.
2. *Gross private domestic Investment (I),* which comprises four subcategories:
   a. residential construction
   b. business construction
   c. new business equipment
   d. change in business inventories

These subgroups are all-inclusive. The output of U.S. firms must have been sold either to consumers, to businesses as final goods, to the government, or to foreign purchasers. But since all that is sold (including inventories, which can be imagined as sold to oneself) must have been produced:

$$GNE \equiv GNP \qquad (15.1)$$

(How does this formulation differ from that of the equation of exchange, p. 357?)

One caveat is in order here; it has to do with the treatment of imports, which are subtracted in item 4. When computing GNE by summing up consumer, investment, and government expenditures, no distinction is made between the spending of these groups on domestic products and their outlays on foreign output. In other words, C, I, and G include expenditures on imported goods. But these goods were obviously not produced by domestic firms and must be excluded from GNE if it is to equal GNP. So the C, I, and G totals are left alone, but imports are subtracted from exports, leading to

$$GNP \equiv GNE \equiv C + I + G + X - M \qquad (15.2)$$

Net national product (NNP)

You may wonder why the national product and expenditure measures are described as "gross." The answer is that economists distinguish between a gross measure and a "net" measure of national product. The difference between the two lies in the treatment of what is technically termed *capital consumption allowances* but is essentially depreciation.[3] Each year some part of the existing business capital (productive facilities and equipment) wears out or becomes obsolete. Each year new capital goods are produced. Some of the new production simply replaces items that have depreciated. For example, when a business purchases a new machine worth $50,000 to replace another one that it has just junked, its productive capacity remains precisely the same. The purchase of the new equipment is called gross investment, but since this machine is only replacement, and since the firm's productive capacity is unimpaired, *net* investment, or addition to capacity, is zero.

The need to distinguish between additions to the nation's productive base and replacements of existing capital stock leads to the formulation of an account entitled **net national product** (NNP). The difference between

Net national product (NNP) (alias national income at market prices) equals GNP less capital consumption allowances.

---

[3]A more detailed definition is provided on page 405.

NNP and GNP lies in the subtraction of depreciation; GNP includes gross investment, while NNP includes only net investment. NNP is also called national income at market prices because the values of the goods and services included in NNP are based on their market prices, just as they are for GNP.

A brief digression on the meaning of depreciation is in order: it is one of those words that have multiple interpretations, and it is best to understand precisely what it means in the national income accounting context. First, depreciation is frequently used as a synonym for capital loss. When a new car is driven for its first run, right out of the showroom, its value is said to have "depreciated"; it is now a used car. This is definitely *not* what is meant here. A second meaning of depreciation is appropriate when one is talking about relative currency values: When the value of the dollar has fallen in relation to that of other currencies, economists say that the dollar has depreciated. While this concept is relevant to Part 6 it is also *not* appropriate here.

Third, accountants also use the term *depreciation*. Since machines and buildings do wear out or become obsolete, the Internal Revenue Service permits business accountants to deduct a certain percentage of the cost of business capital each year. A van purchased for $7,000 with a useful life of ten years may be depreciated, according to standard accounting procedures, at a rate of $700 each year. This definition of depreciation is time related; the shorter the useful life of the capital good, the greater the percentage that can be deducted each year. Accounting records are the source of the capital consumption allowance data used in compiling NNP, so this *is* the appropriate concept insofar as actual practice is concerned. Economists, however, prefer a fourth definition, one that is more closely related to actual usage rather than to time. Economists view depreciation as measuring actual wear and tear, which is related to how intensively the machine or other investment good is used. Again taking the van as an example, the economist's calculation of depreciation would depend on mileage: If the truck were driven 10,000 miles the first year and only 5,000 miles the second, an economist would apply twice as large a depreciation figure to the first year than to the second. Unfortunately, data on actual wear and tear are almost impossible to come by. Moreover, most firms depreciate on an original-cost basis (e.g.; the $7000 cost of the van). Inflation, however, will mean that the cost of replacing the van when it finally is discarded will be higher; the new van may well cost $10,000. Original-value depreciation will understate the actual value of replacement. Economists prefer depreciation data based on replacement cost, but these, too, are just not available.[4]

The result is a gap between what is conceptually best and what is most useful. Since NNP relates more clearly what is new in economic

---

[4]Accounting students will recognize an analogous issue when valuing inventory: LIFO (last in, first out) versus FIFO (first in, first out).

production, economists prefer NNP. NNP measures economic well-being better by subtracting depreciation. But as a practical matter lack of confidence in the depreciation adjustment has led most economists to prefer the GNP figures. Though both GNP and NNP reflect the movement of aggregate production and expenditures, the measurement problems of depreciation can be ignored when using the GNP figures.

National income (NI)

Spending by the various expenditure groups plays a key role in the analysis presented in the following chapters. This is especially true for consumers. Income is an important determinant of consumption. Unfortunately for the student, the income concept that is relevant is not GNP: You will have to learn some more terms. GNP is too all-encompassing in one sense, and too narrow in another, to yield the appropriate income concept. What follows is a set of adjustments in NNP that make it a more useful measure for this purpose.

The first of these adjustments involves the distinction between market prices and factor prices. As mentioned earlier, market prices are the values actually occurring on the market when goods and services are sold. **Factor prices,** on the other hand, refer to the returns received by the factors of production, that is, their income. The difference between the two is "nonincome charges," or payments other than those made to income recipients. The major nonincome charge is **indirect business taxes**, which are paid to the government rather than to production factors.

Market prices minus nonincome charges equals **factor prices.**

An **indirect business tax** is a tax levied on a good or service (e.g., a sales tax).

Take, for example, a van whose market price was $7000, which was the value recorded in GNP. If it was not a replacement item, the $7000 was included in NNP as well. But if an 8 percent sales tax had been imposed on the $6481.48 selling price, so that $518.52 went to the government, the factor price would have been $6481.48. Of course, this sum is what the dealer collects, net of the sales tax.

What happens to this factor income? Since it represents a return to the factors of production, it must be (or have been) paid out to those involved in producing the van. Say that $200 is the dealer's profit, $50 goes to rent, $20 goes to pay interest, and $272.50 is paid out in wages to sales and service employees. The remaining $5938.98 is the cost of the van to the dealer and is remitted to the manufacturer. But this $5938.98 can be broken down further into returns to the factors that contributed to the production of the van. Perhaps $100 goes to profit, $330 to wages and salaries, $40 to rent, and $30 to interest. The remaining $5438.98 goes to the firms that supplied the parts and raw materials. Of course, this sum can be decomposed further into wages and salaries (say, $3500), rents ($800), interest ($450), and profits ($688.99).

If you have followed this paragraph carefully, you should not be surprised to learn that if all the factor incomes are summed up, the total must equal $6481.48.

"We are gathered here today, gentlemen, to make money."

(Does the speaker mean "money" or "profit"? What's the difference?)
Drawing by Opie; © 1977 The New Yorker Magazine.

Wages and salaries:	$272.50	+ $330	+ $3500	=	$4102.50
Rents:	$ 50	+ $ 40	+ $ 800	=	$ 890
Interest:	$ 20	+ $ 30	+ $ 450	=	$ 500
Profits:	$200	+ $100	+ $ 688.98	=	$ 988.98
			Total:		$6481.48

National income at factor prices (or simply NI) is (a) the sum of all factor incomes in the nation for a specific period or (b) NNP less nonincome charges for the same period.

When nonincome charges are subtracted from NNP, the resulting concept is called **national income at factor prices,** or just plain national income (NI). But this aggregate can be derived equally well by summing up all the factor incomes throughout the economy—all wages, salaries, rents, profits, and interest.

Being able to calculate national income in two ways is extremely useful, for it implies that GNP, too, can be calculated in more than one way. On the one hand, the various final expenditures can be summed up: C + I + G + X − M. On the other hand, all income receipts can be added together to obtain NI. Add to NI all nonincome charges, first, to obtain NNI, and then add capital consumption allowances, and the resulting total is called **gross national income (GNI).** Consequently, there is a triple identity:

Gross national income (GNI) is GNP computed from the income side.

$$GNP \equiv GNE \equiv GNI \qquad (15.3)$$

Refer back to Table 15.1. The table shows that the retail price of a good equals the sum of the values added at each stage of the production process, being the difference between final prices and the cost of intermediate goods. But what is this difference between the final prices and intermediate product costs, if not the returns to the factors of production and some nonincome charges? The $150 value added of the metal fabricator, for example, must be the sum of the payments for wages and salaries, rent, interest, profits, and the nonincome charges: indirect business taxes and capital consumption allowances. This being so, the value added of any industry can be derived not only by subtracting the industry's costs of intermediate products from its final sales, but also by summing up all income payments and nonincome charges.

Table 15.2 (a) shows the identity of approaches for 1980, distinguishing between the product approach, which is the expenditure measure, and

TABLE 15.2 The Family of National Income Accounts, 1980 (billions of dollars)

a. The product and income measures of GNP

The expenditure approach		The income approach	
Personal consumption expenditures	$1672.8	Employees' compensation	$1596.5
Gross private domestic investment	395.3	Profits	313.3
		Rents	31.8
Residential construction	105.3		
Nonresidential structures	108.8	Interest	179.8
Nonresidential durable equipment	187.1	NATIONAL INCOME	2121.4
Changes in business inventories	−5.9		
		plus Nonincome charges	217.5
Government purchases of goods and services	534.7		
Net exports	23.3	equals NNI	2338.9
		plus capital consumption allowances	287.2
GNP	$2626.1	equals GNI	$2626.1

b. National income, personal income, disposable personal income, and their components[a]

	NATIONAL INCOME	$2121.4
less	Retained corporate earnings	128.3
less	Contributions to social insurance	203.7
plus	Transfer payments	370.8
equals	PERSONAL INCOME	2160.2
less	Personal income taxes	338.5
equals	DISPOSABLE PERSONAL INCOME	1821.7
of which:	Personal consumption expenditures	1672.8
	Consumer transfers	47.6
	Personal saving	101.3

[a]Greater detail is presented in the appendix to this chapter.

Source: U.S. Department of Commerce, Bureau of Economic Analysis, *Survey of Current Business,* June 1981.

the income side, the summation of income and nonincome charges. Assure yourself that nothing has been omitted and that the totals on both sides are in fact identical.

This equality of GNP (the product side) and GNI (the income side) is important for more than computational reasons. It becomes critical in the macroeconomic theory presented in the following chapter. Remember the principle that for every product produced, income is received, and for all income received, an equivalent amount of output must have been created. *In the aggregate, for the nation as a whole, the entire nation's production (GNP) must by definition equal the receipts for the production of that output (GNI). And, conversely, the entire nation's current income must have come from the production of new final goods and services.*

Sources of data

Before leaving GNP, a few parting words may be devoted to the sources of the data.[5] The identity of GNE and GNI permits national income accountants to use both approaches, checking one against the other to assure consistent fiures. To be sure, the results never come out precisely equal: A "statistical discrepancy" takes care of that. But considering that for 1980 the discrepancy was only $-0.7 million, or three-hundredths of a percent of GNP, the problem is hardly a major one. (The 1979 difference of $2.2 billion was 0.1 percent of GNP.)

The product side is derived by calculating each category separately. Data on government spending on goods and services is obtained from the budget reports of the various government entities, while export and import data are available from the Commerce Department's Balance of Payments Division. Data on consumption spending are calculated by a more indirect process. For expenditures on goods, the statisticians use a **commodity flow** approach. They trace out the flow of goods, beginning at the manufacturing level and following through the distribution network until the goods are sold at the retail level. Since only the value of goods is derived in this manner, expenditures for services have to be calculated separately. A variety of special census surveys are available for this purpose. Business equipment spending is also calculated by the commodity flow method, while data on the construction of residential and business structures are based on Census Bureau samples.

On the income side, the two major data sources are the reports of employers to the Social Security Administration on wages and salaries paid, and taxpayers' returns to the Internal Revenue Service. While employee compensation figures are derived primarily from the former, the wage and salary incomes of people who are not covered by social security, as well as rents, interest, and profit, come from income tax reports. (In light of the widespread aversion to honest reporting of income to the tax authorities, is it any surprise that in fact the income side of GNP will not be equal to the product side?)

Deriving the amounts spent by consumers on goods by tracing out the goods flow through their various production stages is known as the **commodity flow** method.

[5]See the appendix to this chapter for additional detail.

Personal Income (PI)

Not all of the income received by the factors of production is in fact available for consumer spending. Some of it is channeled into the pockets of other spenders. Moreover, consumers often are able to spend even though they have not earned income. Taking the diversions first, the major two categories are retained corporate earnings and contributions for social insurance. Corporate profits are included in NI. But since corporations retain some of their earnings for their own use, not all corporate profits are passed on to shareholders in the form of dividends. Consequently, retained corporate earnings must be deducted when calculating the income available for consumer expenditures. The same applies to payroll taxes, such as social security and unemployment insurance contributions. The social security contribution deducted from wage earners is siphoned off before they obtain their take-home pay; it is not available for their use.

On the other hand, transfer payments, which are paid primarily by government entities to the retired, the disabled, the unemployed, the poor, and the fraudulent, are sources of income to these consumers, although this income is omitted from the GNP calculation. It must be added to the income derived from supplying factor services to determine the extent of the consuming public's spendable income.

Personal income (PI) is the outcome of these additions and subtractions. Refer to Table 15.2(b) to see how the PI for 1980 is derived from NI.

Actually, this aggregate is not very useful; it is a sort of halfway house between NI and disposable personal income, the final account to be discussed here. Its primary virtue is a practical one: Data on PI are released on a monthly basis, the only member of the national income account family that is issued that frequently.

> **Personal income (PI)** is the income available to individuals from all sources, including transfer payments.

Disposable personal income (DPI)

Personal income measures the funds available to consumers from all sources. However, not all of these funds are subject to consumer discretion. The income tax authorities take their share first. Only after the public has paid its income tax liability to the government does it have full freedom to dispose of the remainder, **disposable personal income** (DPI), as it wishes (Box 15.1). Again, Table 15.2(b) shows the computation of DPI for 1980. (For greater detail, see Table 15A.1.)

> **Disposable personal income (DPI)** consists of the funds available to consumers to spend at their discretion. DPI equals PI minus personal income taxes.

Consumption and saving

What do consumers do with their disposable income? They either consume (i.e., spend) it, transfer it to others, or save it. For the economy as a whole, personal consumption expenditures were $1672.8 billion in 1980 [see Table 15.2 (b)], while saving was $101.3 billion.

Consumption expenditures and **saving** are key concepts in macroeco-

> **Consumption (C)** is spending by consumers on goods and services.
> **Saving (S)** is the part of DPI that is not spent.

nomic analysis, and they merit particular attention. If part of the nation's DPI is spent, the remainder (excluding transfers), or saving, must be the part of disposable personal income that is not spent. In the form of an equation, this is

$$S = DPI - C \tag{15.4}$$

Saving is passive; it is the act of not spending.

Is putting cash into a checking account saving? into a savings account? into common stock? The answer to all of these queries is no. Whatever such a transfer of financial assets may be called, it is not saving; it is not the act of refraining from consuming goods and services. Thus, when your paycheck of $350 is given to you by your employer and you pay $200 for a set of tickets to the Super Bowl, you will have consumed $200. By default, by not spending the remaining $150, you will have saved $150. It is immaterial in what form you hold that $150—in money, near-money, or whatever.

But what if you use the $200 to pay off a debt, spending the remaining $150 on food? Look carefully at the definition of consumption—have you spent the entire $350 on goods and services? The response must be negative; while $150 has been spent on goods, the other $200 has not. Equation 15.4 tells us that the $200 must be saving, for S = DPI ($350) − C ($150). Debt repayment is saving, for it is not spending on goods and services. This may appear strange, but that's the way it is. Learn the usage, and the next chapter will be that much easier to grasp.

The conceptual part of this chapter is now concluded; no further definitions. By way of review, you should be able to explain how GNP can be calculated by the value-added approach, GNE by the expenditure category method, and GNI by the income approach. Further, be sure that you understand why all these calculations must yield the same result. They are all measures of gross national output, but they attack it from different directions. Be especially sure that you can explain why the product total must equal the income total. You should also be more than familiar with the rest of the national income family—NNP, NI, PI, and DPI—knowing what they are measures of as well as how to derive them. Finally, be quite clear in your mind about the relationship among DPI, C, and S, and the meaning of each term.

☐ The National Income Family Since 1965

Figure 15.1 charts GNP, NNP, NI, PI, and DPI for the period since 1965. All of the curves move with a marked degree of consistency. They all rise for just about the entire period. All dip in 1970, 1974–1975, and 1980, reflecting the contractions in economic activity during these recessions. (Can you explain why the PI and DPI series are less responsive to recession than the other series? Relate it to your knowledge of the tax structure and the behavior of transfer payments during a contraction.) The annual rates of growth of all of the series differ by a maximum of 0.6 percent, being 9.3 percent for GNP, 9.1 percent for NNP, 9.2 percent for NI, 9.7 percent for PI, and 9.4 percent for DPI. (Note, however, that all these data are in current dollars. The annual increase, thus, reflects a combination of increased output and higher prices. See Figure 15.4 for GNP in constant dollars, for a much smaller rate of growth of real output, 3.2 percent to be precise.) This consonance is not really surprising; the definitions of the series are all closely related, with relatively minor adjustments distinguishing one from the other. When the economy is growing, all grow. And in a recession the rates of growth of all of the series will decline.

Turn now to Figure 15.2, which plots the expenditure components of GNP. The outstanding characteristic of these figures is the visible volatility of investment and net exports. Investment spending and net exports show definite wavelike movements, upturns and downturns; consumption and government spending rise steadily. Economists have often singled out investment as playing a major role in the business cycle because of these fluctuations. As investment rises, the economy is induced to expand, and vice versa as investment spending declines. To be sure, net exports show wide swings, too, but they are deemed unimportant in analyzing the U.S. economy, because of their small magnitude. The largest annual change in net exports between 1965 and 1980 was less than $20 billion, and the average absolute change (i.e., disregarding the

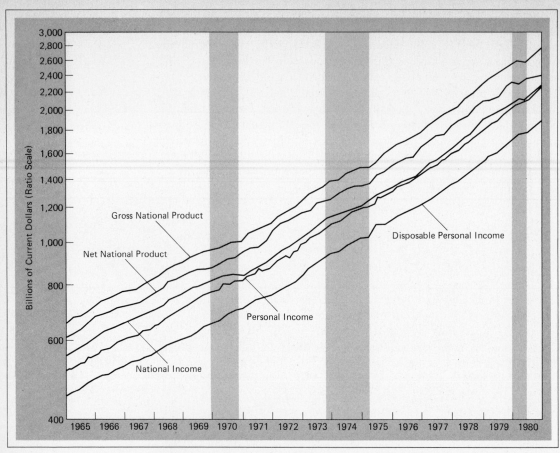

FIGURE 15.1 The national income accounts, 1965–1980. (Note: Shaded areas represent business cycle contractions.)

Source: U.S. Department of Commerce, *Business Conditions Digest*, June 1981; NNP data, Courtesy of U.S. Department of Commerce.

sign when averaging) was barely over $6 billion. On the other hand, the largest investment fluctuation was over $50 billion, and the average absolute change was $26.2 billion.

Nevertheless, the role of investment as a prime cause of economic fluctuations cannot be determined from the data alone. For on these grounds government spending was almost as volatile, averaging $24 billion a year. And consumption swings were even more influential, averaging $87.3 billion, though this is not apparent from glancing at the figure.

One can gain insight into the variability of the consumption data by examining the pattern of the saving ratio, which is saving divided by disposable personal income. Figure 15.3 plots the saving ratio; note that it

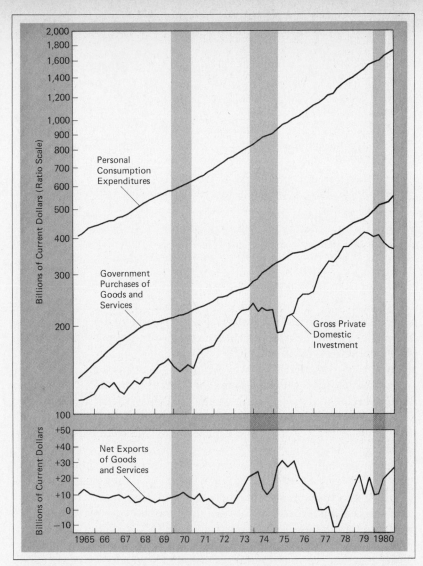

FIGURE 15.2 The components of gross national expenditure, 1965–1980. (Note: Shaded areas represent business cycle contractions.)

Source: U.S. Department of Commerce, *Business Conditions Digest,* June 1981.

varies mostly within a rather narrow range of around four percentage points. Nevertheless, because of the size of DPI, the absolute changes can be large. For example, between 1972 and 1973 saving rose by $26.4 billion.

In short, the data indicate a growing GNP in current dollars and concomitant growth in other national income data. At the same time, the

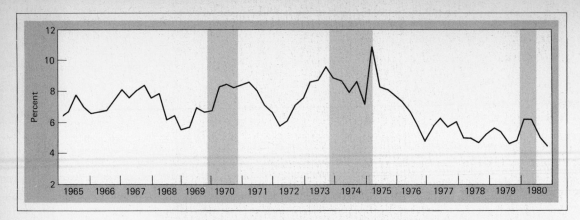

FIGURE 15.3 The personal saving ratio, 1965–1980. (Note: Shaded areas represent business cycle contractions.)

Source: U.S. Department of Commerce, *Business Conditions Digest*, June 1981.

components of GNP show a marked degree of fluctuation; their growth is not smooth at all. While the pattern of GNP movement must be related to the changes in its components, the data themselves cannot indicate which variables are causal and which are passive.

Turn now to Figure 15.4, which plots GNP in constant 1972 dollars against another series entitled **potential GNP**. Potential GNP is designed to answer the question, What would GNP have been in this period had the economy been producing at full capacity? Such GNP growth is a result of greater labor and capital inputs and their increased productivity.

Before turning to the use of this series, a word of caution must be included. Potential GNP is an estimate based on definitions and interpretations of data that are not universally accepted. Such numbers play a role in analyses of the economy, but they must be treated with care. Do not read into them more than they actually relate.

Notice the relationship between potential and actual GNP as portrayed in the diagram. In some periods actual GNP exceeded potential GNP; these were years of more than full employment and heavy use of production capacity. Such was the case for 1965 through the third quarter of 1969, and in 1972/1973. In other years, such as after 1974, potential GNP exceeded actual GNP; these were years of unemployment and low utilization of capacity.

In a very real sense, Figure 15.4 summarizes a policy problem and provides the rationale for measuring GNP. When potential GNP exceeds actual GNP, unemployment is present, business profits are reduced, and resources are being left idle despite willingness to employ them under sounder economic conditions. The magnitude of the gap tells the policy maker whether the economy's production problems are substantial or

Potential GNP measures the level of GNP that could be attained if the national economy were operating at full capacity.

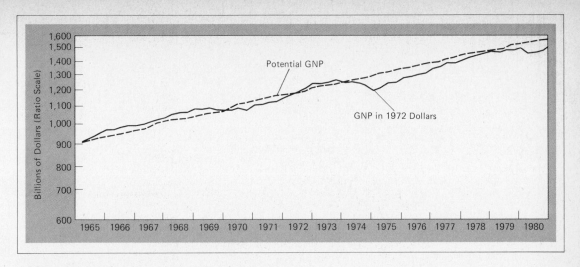

FIGURE 15.4 Actual and potential GNP, 1965–1980.

Source: Actual GNP, U.S. Department of Commerce; potential GNP, U.S. Council of Economic Advisers, unpublished data.

negligible. The movement of the gap—is it narrowing or widening?— indicates whether the problem is being resolved or intensifying. Is a strong policy mandated, or should the authorities leave well enough alone? The answer depends in part on the size and direction of the gap. Similarly, when actual GNP equals its potential, there is little call for radical measures to stimulate the economy. And when actual exceeds potential GNP, this must be understood as a temporary phenomenon. Over the long haul, actual production cannot exceed the economy's productive capacity.

☐ Summary

This chapter had a dual purpose: (1) to introduce the various measures of aggregate activity and thus set the stage for the theory of income determination coming up in the next chapters, and (2) to demonstrate the importance of the data for policy purposes.

The national income accounts consist of the following aggregates:

1. *Gross national product (GNP):* the value of the final economic national output produced during a given period. Excluded from this overall measure of aggregate economic activity are intermediate products (to avoid double-counting), most nonmarketed products (because it's virtually impossible to measure them accurately), transfers of assets (because they do not measure new production), and transfer payments (since no current service is rendered for such paynents).

2. *Gross national expenditure (GNE):* the combined spending of consumers, investors, and government (at all levels), and net exports (exports less imports).
3. *Gross national income (GNI):* the total of all factor and nonincome charges as well as capital consumption allowances. GNP, GNE, and GNI all measure national output from different perspectives. Consequently, GNP ≡ GNE ≡ GNI. It is critical to understand that all the income earned by the various economic units must equal the amount that has been produced.
4. *Net national product (NNP):* GNP less capital consumption allowances. NNP measures the net addition to the nation's aggregate output, ignoring investment that serves merely to replace depreciated capital goods.
5. *National income (NI):* the total income earned by the nation's factors of production, consisting of wages and salaries, rents, interest, and profit.

While these aggregates measure the nation's income and output in different ways, they must be adjusted in order to find the aggregate that is most useful for determining consumer spending and saving. In order to do this, the following concepts are calculated:

6. *Personal income (PI):* national income *less* (a) retained corporate earnings and (b) contributions to social insurance, neither of which are available for consumer spending, *plus* (c) transfer payments, which are included because consumers do obtain unearned payments that increase their spending power.
7. *Disposable personal income (DPI):* eliminates income taxes from personal income. It is DPI that can be spent or saved. (*Remember:* Saving is nonspending.)

In current-dollar terms, the entire national income accounts rose at a steady rate ranging between 9.1 and 9.7 percent during the period between 1965 and 1980. Yet the components of the aggregates did fluctuate. Consumption was especially volatile, but fluctuations in investment and government spending showed marked amplitude, too. One purpose of economic theory is to take these data and explain their causal interrelationships. The data are also useful for policy makers attempting to devise sound macroeconomic programs. The relationship of real GNP growth to potential GNP is an especially useful tool.

☐ Questions and Exercises

1. Does a rising GNP mean that a nation's population is becoming more prosperous?
2. Some economists have argued that the increasingly heavy tax burden imposed on U.S. income earners has led large numbers of them into the

underground economy. If this contention is both true and significant, how might the usefulness of the national income accounts be affected? And, to skip ahead a bit, would you care to comment about its impact on macroeconomic policy?

3. Would the following items be included in both GNP and DPI, neither, or just one of them?
   a Social security contributions paid by a wage earner.
   b Royalties received by a novelist.
   c An increase in the value of a painting while it is still in the hands of a collector.
   d An increase in the value of a painting that is realized upon sale.
   e Medicare payments to a retiree.
   f Dividends paid by IBM on its common stock.
   g The products of a forger of $20 bills whose printing press has just turned out 1,000 crisp, new notes.
   h Wages earned by a U.S. citizen on long-term assignment in Kuwait.
   i An inheritance sent by a Dutch uncle to his niece in Wichita, Kansas.

4. What is currently happening to the gap between potential and actual GNP? Do you believe that any policy measures are needed as a result?

5. How can potential GNP be increased?

□ For Further Study

William I. Abraham, *National Income and Economic Accounting* (Englewood Cliffs, N.J.: Prentice-Hall, 1969), and John W. Kendrick, *Economic Accounts and Their Uses* (New York: McGraw-Hill, 1972), are basic textbooks on the family of national income accounts.

Not only are data revised often, but the methodology is frequently changed. To keep current, consult the data and articles in *Survey of Current Business*, published monthly by the U.S. Department of Commerce's Bureau of Economic Analysis. Another useful publication of the Bureau of Economic Analysis, also monthly, is *Business Conditions Digest*. Its charts and tables on business cycle indicators and other major economic series are frequently consulted by forecasters.

The official guardian of the potential-GNP series is the President's Council of Economic Advisers, which reported its revisions of the method of calculating potential GNP in the *Economic Report of the President, 1977*. A more technical study is Peter K. Clark, "Potential GNP in the United States, 1948–80," *Review of Income and Wealth* 25 (June 1979): 141–165.

APPENDIX A Closer Look at the National Income Accounts

This appendix is designed to serve a number of purposes. First, for those who want to examine the relationships among the components of the national income family in greater detail, such detail is provided here. For those who would like to have a greater appreciation of the problems involved in computing GNP and related accounts, some of the difficulties are discussed in this appendix. Finally, there are a number of theoretical issues involved in the calculation of GNP. This topic, too, is included here.

The relationship of GNP to disposable personal income, consumption, and saving

Table 15A.1 presents the calculations involved in going from gross national product to personal saving.

Let us explore it line by line.

1. *Gross national product.* GNP is the total output of the economy, derived by summing up either expenditures or incomes.

TABLE 15A.1 From GNP to Consumption and Saving, 1980 (billions of dollars)

	1. *Gross national product*	$2626.1
less	2. Capital consumption allowances	287.3
equals	3. Net national product	2338.9
less	4. Indirect business tax and nontax liability	212.3
less	5. Business transfer payments	10.5
less	6. Statistical discrepancy	−0.7
plus	7. Subsidies less current surplus of government enterprises	4.6
equals	8. *National income*	2121.4
less	9. Corporate profits and inventory valuation adjustment	182.7
less	10. Contributions for social insurance	203.7
less	11. Excess of wage accruals over disbursements	0
plus	12. Government transfer payments	283.8
plus	13. Net interest paid by government and consumers	76.5
plus	14. Dividends	54.4
plus	15. Business transfer payments	10.5
equals	16. *Personal income*	2160.2
less	17. Personal tax and nontax payments	338.5
equals	18. *Disposable personal income*	1821.7
less	19. Personal outlays	1720.4
of which	20. Personal consumption expenditures	1672.8
	21. Consumer interest payments	46.4
	22. Personal transfer payments to foreigners	1.2
equals	23. Personal saving	101.3

2. *Capital consumption allowances.* The major part of this entry is depreciation, representing wear and tear as well as obsolesence of capital. One other item is included—accidental damage to fixed capital. Capital goods destroyed by fire, which accounts for the largest share of this subcategory, and losses due to similar accidental events are in fact equivalent to depreciation and are included here.

3. *Net national product.* NNP is GNP less capital consumption allowances. It is also called national income at market prices.

4. *Indirect business tax and nontax liability.* Indirect business taxes include all business taxes other than income taxes; for example, sales and excise taxes. Nontax liability items are business obligations to the government that are not taxes. They are payments to the government for specific services, such as license charges and franchise rights. Fines are also included. However, purchases from government enterprises are excluded.

5. *Business transfer payments.* These are payments by businesses to others for which no current services are received in exchange. Examples are corporate gifts to nonprofit institutions and consumer bad debts. The latter are, in a sense, involuntary gifts to consumers.

6. *Statistical discrepancy.* The product side of GNP is computed independently from the income side. Although conceptually the two sides must provide identical answers, they do not. The statistical discrepancy, which is the difference between GNP computed from the product side and GNP calculated from the income side, is introduced to assure statistical equality. Items 4 through 6 are subtracted when calculating national income; they are all considered to be charges against net national product, but not income received by the factors of production.

7. *Subsidies less current surplus of government enterprises.* Subsidies are considered to be payments to the factors of production, which are needed to induce the factors to supply their services. On the other hand, the surplus or profit (or loss) of government businesses like the Postal Service are excluded for technical reasons.

8. *National income.* NI is the income paid to the factors of production for producing current output.

9. *Corporate profits and inventory valuation adjustment.* Corporate profits less corporate dividend payments (14) equal retained corporate earnings. As they never reach the consuming public, they are removed when calculating personal income. Changes in inventory often reflect noncurrent prices and must be adjusted to bring the inventory account into consonance with the rest of the accounts. Most business firms use the FIFO (first in, first out) method of inventory valuation. Thus, if the year's beginning inventory held 100 units priced at $5 per unit, and during the current year 50 new units were produced and sold at $6 per unit, the accounting records would show sales of 50 units from inventory at $5 and 50 units added to inventory at $6. The first in, those already in inventory, are recorded

as sold (first out). The new inventory value will be 50 units remaining at $5 and 50 new units at $6, totaling $550. Thus, although the physical inventory remains the same, its value has risen by $50. At the same time, corporate profits are increased by $50, since the 50 units priced at $5 in inventory are sold at $6 per unit. These profits are more in the nature of capital gains than a return for factor supply, and are similar to an increase in the value of a share of common stock. Neither the increased value of the security nor the increased value of inventory should be included in income. Consequently, the inventory valuation adjustment rectifies this source of misstatement.

10. *Contributions for social insurance.* Payments by employers to employees in the form of fringe benefits are considered to be part of national income. However, as they are not paid to the worker they must be subtracted in determining personal income.

11. *Excess of wage accruals over disbursements.* NI is calculated on an accrual basis, which involves attributing income earned even though it has not been paid yet. PI is computed on a disbursement basis, that is, on the basis of actual payments. When payments are made to workers in the current period for earnings attributed to earlier periods (e.g., retroactive wage payments), adjustments are needed. If accruals were greater than disbursements, they must be subtracted to obtain PI.

12. *Government transfer payments.* Although these payments are not included in NI, since they are not payments to productive factors, they are sources of spending for the recipients.

13. *Net interest paid by government and consumers.* Such payments are also considered to be transfer payments, in contrast to interest paid by businesses. The latter is a payment to capital, one of the factors of production. However, neither the services of government nor consumer capital is reflected by the interest payments of government and consumer.

14. *Dividends.* See item 9.

15. *Business transfer payments.* These are subtracted in calculating NI, since they are payments without a *quid pro quo*, but they must be added here to obtain PI.

16. *Personal income.* PI is income available to all individuals from all sources.

17. *Personal tax and nontax payments.* Income and property taxes are considered to be part of gross earnings. So, too, are other payments to government entities (other than government enterprises). However, they must be subtracted in determining how much consumers have to spend or save.

18. *Disposable personal income.* DPI is the income available to consumers for discretionary spending.

19. *Personal outlays.* This is spending by consumers for goods, services, and transfers.

20. *Personal consumption.* This is the "C" category in the GNE account.
21. *Consumer interest payments.* These are transfers by consumers to others: they are not considered to be payments for services rendered. (See item 13.)
22. *Personal transfer payments to foreigners.* These, too, are payments for which no services are rendered in exchange.
23. *Personal saving.* This is DPI less personal outlays.

Problems in computing GNP

The basic difficulties that crop up in calculating GNP are due to the fact that no data are collected specifically for the purpose of deriving the national income accounts. Instead, the statisticians and economists of the Department of Commerce's Bureau of Economic Analysis must examine a variety of data gathered for other purposes, cull out the information useful to them, and adjust it appropriately. Moreover, the reporting is not complete, though it is as complete in the United States as it is anywhere else in the world, perhaps everywhere else in the world. So some items must be estimated. And when reports do exist, they are not always available annually, so that extrapolations and interpolations, fitting this year's data to last year's, are mandated. In what follows, a compilation of the methods used to compute the GNP through its components is supplemented by comments on the reliability of each estimate. An attempt is made to answer the question, How reliable are the GNP data?

GNP: The income approach. A good place to begin is on the income side of the GNP account, the major categories of which are employee compensation, profits, rents, and interest.

Employee Compensation. The data here are the most reliable of all the subgroups of GNP. The definition of compensation is clear and well understood; records are easy to keep and are maintained, if only for tax purposes; and the data base is comprehensive. The basic data sources are employer reports to the Social Security Administration and to state unemployment insurance offices. These reports are thought to be reasonably accurate.

Even here, however, gaps occur. Data for people who are not covered by either social security or unemployment insurance must be derived from other sources: payroll reports of government entities (government employees), agricultural census data (farm workers), the *Current Population Survey* (domestic service help), and so on. When there are no reports or the reports are of questionable accuracy (e.g., for tips), estimates based on limited samples are developed. In general, however, the problems are small and of insignificant magnitude; the accuracy of the reports on wages and salaries is not doubted. The same can be said for supplements to wages and salaries, which are mainly contributions to social insurance. Together, wages and salaries and their supplements make up the category of employee compensation.

Profits. The profits category combines corporate profits with those of unincorporated businesses. Corporate profit reporting ranks near employee compensation in terms of accuracy, since the basic data are derived from reports of the Internal Revenue Service. The knowledge that income tax reports are likely to be audited suggests that honesty is preserved. Nevertheless, actual audits do lead to data revision, so that there are inaccuracies that are rectified only after the fact. Such revisions, however, tend to be small. (This is not the case for quarterly estimates of GNP: the lag in reporting corporate profits is the primary source of errors in the quarterly GNP data.)

Income reporting by unincorporated enterprises is less satisfactory. Although income tax reports also provide the basic data, underreporting is thought to be extensive. Many of the businesses involved are small, and their record keeping is inaccurate, often intentionally so. Audits do repair some of the damage, but such audits are not extensive.

Also included in this category is the income of professional practitioners like lawyers and physicians. Here, too, income tax reports provide information on average income in each profession, which is then multiplied by the number of practitioners in each to obtain total income.

Rent. The rental income figure is believed to be the least reliable. Again, income tax records provide information on landlords, but not all landlords report, and there is no way of determining how many report accurately. But even this problem is insignificant when compared to the difficulty in ascertaining the rental income of owner-occupied housing, which is included in the GNP total. The procedure used requires first obtaining data on the extent of owner-occupied housing, which is derived from census sources, and then estimating its rental value. Rents are taken from the appropriate category of the consumer price index. Needless to say, inaccuracies exist in both these component parts. A rough idea of the magnitude of the error can be gleaned from the extensive revision undertaken for the 1964 national income accounts. The underestimate of rental income was found to be almost 50 percent.

Interest. The Internal Revenue Service provides the raw data for calculating interest earnings. While information on earnings from interest and payments of interest by corporations and financial institutions are easily obtained, this is not true for the interest income of unincorporated enterprises. Also, interest is imputed for financial intermediaries: Deposits are credited with interest receipts equal to the value of services rendered to depositors but not in fact paid to them. In general, the quality of the interest estimate is thought to lie between that of the estimates of rent and corporate profits, higher than the former but not as high as the latter.

Capital Consumption Allowances and Indirect Business Taxes. The two nonincome charges that are added to national income to obtain GNP are also based on a mixture of solid data and questionable estimates. The bulk of capital consumption allowances is depreciation, for which data come from the income tax authorities. While the reporting of corporate depreciation is thought to be reasonably accurate, the same cannot be said for the reports of unincorporated firms. And while accurate reports on federal exise and the indirect taxes of the states and larger cities can be obtained from the government entities concerned, this is not true for the indirect business tax receipts of small municipalities. Of course, errors in the latter group are unimportant; the bulk of such receipts are encountered in taxing authorities where the data base is accurate. However, reporting is done on a fiscal year basis, which does not correspond to the calendar year basis used by the national income statisticians, and adjustments are required. These adjustments reduce somewhat the reliability of the data.

In general, data provided by the Internal Revenue Service are the mainstay of all income figures other than employee compensation, which is derived from reports to the social insurance agencies. But while there is no reason to fault the accuracy of reporting for social security purposes, the coverage of all wage and salary earners is not complete. Coverage by the income tax authorities is quite comprehensive, but the accuracy of the taxpaying reporters is certainly open to question. Fortunately, the ability to calculate GNP by the product account provides a check of general accuracy.

GNP: The product approach. The problem of data collection is more complex on the product side than on the income side, for it involves tracing out the pattern of production through its various stages until final output at market prices is derived.

Consumer Spending. As mentioned in the chapter, the calculation of consumer expenditures on goods is based on the "commodity flow" method. While retail store sales data would also provide estimates of consumption, such data are not available by commodity groups, which are useful for other purposes. So the accountants begin with the Census of Manufacturers' commodity groups, segregating within each category goods that are sold directly to consumers without further processing from those that require additional manufacture. Nonmanufactured goods, such as agricultural commodities, are treated similarly. For commodities that require processing, transportation charges are added and the segregation process is repeated at the second production stage. Those that are sold to consumers are final consumer goods; those that are sold to wholesalers are treated by adding wholesale markups and other charges. These products are then followed through the retail stages, until in the end a figure is arrived at that is the sum of producer, wholesaler, and retail sales to consumers, each at the prices paid by consumers. (Incidentally, imports are included while exports are excluded.)

There are a few exceptions to the commodity flow method; separate calculations are made for passenger car, fuel, and tobacco sales.

Consumer services, too, are estimated independently. The rental value of housing services is calculated by the procedure previously described under rental income. Census data are used for some business services, such as entertainment and repairs, while personal services are estimated largely from income tax reports.

The reliability of the consumer expenditure component is thought to be high, in general; for the most part, the data are available, and while they require extensive processing, the errors appear to be fairly small. It remains true, however, that there are some notable gaps in the data, especially in the personal-services component.

Gross Private Domestic Investment. Each subgroup of investment is estimated separately. Business equipment expenditures are derived by the commodity flow method, and are as reliable as the consumer goods data. Census Bureau samples provide data on new construction, both for business and for residential housing. The major category insofar as questionable reliability is concerned is the inventory investment group. Because of a multiplicity of accounting methods and because of different treatment of price changes, the national income statisticians must revise the raw data extensively. Moreover, reporting inaccuracies are not infrequent. A 30 percent error in inventory investment was discovered as a result of the 1964 revision. And the inaccuracies that occur in preliminary GNP data are primarily in the area of inventory investment.

Government Purchases of Goods and Services. These figures are the most reliable ones on the product side, for they are based on reports by various government units on their expenditures. Reliability declines as one proceeds from the federal to the state level and then to the local level. Also, as remarked earlier, government budgets are recorded in fiscal years and the national income accounts on a calendar year basis, so that the government accounts have to be adjusted.

Net Exports. Based on reports filed by exporters and importers with the Customs Bureau, the data on merchandise transactions are thought to be highly accurate. Less reliable is the service component of net exports. At one extreme, American travelers returning from abroad provide information on their expenditures, a questionable source of accurate data. At the other extreme, federal government agencies report on their foreign outlays, and there is no reason to doubt their accuracy. In between lie a variety of firms doing business abroad, as well as foreign businesses selling in the United States—travel agencies, transport companies, foreign branches of American firms, and so on. The underlying series are thought to be relatively free from error.

In summary, accurate GNP data, based on data that run the gamut from highly reliable to questionable, are too much to expect. And if this is true for annual GNP figures, how much more so is it true for quarterly estimates of GNP? Moreover, the error is not eliminated by the statistical discrepancy (Table 15A.1, item 6). This discrepancy only indicates how much GNP on the product side differs from GNP on the income side. But since the two sides are not calculated entirely independently, errors that crop up in certain components are included on both the product and the income side. For example, the income of professionals is included on the income side as part of national income. But the same figure is entered on the product side as a measure of the value of professional services. An understatement on one side is an identical understatement on the other. These errors arise from inadequate or incorrect reporting; the statistical discrepancy item does not correct for such deficiencies.

How large is the error? One way of measuring the error is by comparing the earliest estimates of GNP with the data obtained after final revisions. The BEA recalculated the national income accounts in an extensive study done during the early 1960s. For the 1964 GNP figures, the statisticians found a 3 percent error when comparing old data with revised figures. While this $18 billion error appears large, it is relatively small when one considers the vast array of difficulties mentioned earlier. More important, the error over time was modest indeed. The understatement of the trend of GNP over the years between 1948 and 1964 was only one-tenth of one percent a year. Component errors, however, are larger; they partly cancel each other out in the aggregation process. Also, the magnitude of postwar recessions has been overstated by preliminary quarterly estimates. However, as far as the annual data go, the revisions have not mandated marked reinterpretations of the economic fluctuations during the 1950s and 1960s.

In short, because of the later revisions, some care must be taken in using preliminary estimates, especially quarterly ones. Nevertheless, the GNP aggregate remains a good estimator of basic macroeconomic tendencies.

Conceptual issues in GNP accounts

Not all of the problems surrounding GNP have to do with gathering and preparing the data for inclusion in the national income accounts. Conceptual issues abound, and while many of them have been settled, others remain unresolved. The few listed here will give the reader a taste of these problems.

The treatment of consumption. The objective of the national income accounts is to provide data that are useful for analysis and policy purposes. The distinction between consumption and investment is based on the belief that the economic forces that influence investment differ from those that determine consumer spending. Moreover, the categories are markedly dissimilar: Investment involves output that yields a flow of services over time—which is why residential construction is included in the investment category rather than being listed with consumer purchases—while consumption goods are here today and gone tomorrow.

Unfortunately, this distinction is clouded by the existence of consumer durables. Refrigerators and air conditioners, kitchen cutlery and dining-room furniture, fishing rods and Ping-Pong paddles all last for years with normal use, thereby providing consumers with a flow of services over time. Why, then, treat a house as a capital good yielding rental services while a new automobile purchased this year is considered to be a consumption good that provides its entire service in the year of purchase and no services over its remaining lifetime? Moreover, it is quite plausible to assume that the motives that induce consumers to purchase durable goods are not unlike those that induce investors to acquire new capital goods. Thus, the distinction between durable consumer goods and investment goods is difficult to justify theoretically. Indeed, in analyzing the national economy many economists do not treat the consumption expenditure category as homogeneous but distinguish between the behavior of durable and nondurable consumer goods.

The treatment of government. Government expenditures for goods and services are treated as a separate entity in the national income accounts. Yet a closer examination will reveal that the government purchases some goods and services, such as fuel and janitorial services, for current consumption. Other goods are acquired for the services they provide over the long haul; highways and aircraft carriers are examples. The latter expenditures, of course, are akin to private investment.

So why treat government as a distinct category? In fact, the reporting system advocated by the United Nations recommends that government investment be combined with private investment, and that a separate listing be maintained only for government consumption.

The treatment of taxes. As you know, indirect business taxes are subtracted from GNP in the process of computing NI. The underlying assumption that legitimizes this procedure is that such taxes are passed on by producers to consumers. Thus, the factor earnings that make up national income are not affected by the existence of indirect business taxes. And if this type of tax were increased, factor income would not be changed at all; since the tax is passed on, the price of final goods would rise by the full amount of the new taxes. On the other hand, direct taxes, such as corporate profits taxes, are assumed not to be shifted to others at all. Corporations, it is implicitly assumed, calculate their prices, receive income for selling their output, and then reduce their income by the amount of the income tax. Consequently, if corporate income taxes were increased, the assumption forces the conclusion that corporate profits would decline while output prices would remain unchanged.

Need it be asked how realistic these assumptions are? Are indirect business taxes always fully passed on, and are corporate income taxes never shifted to consumers through higher product prices? The theory of tax incidence suggests otherwise. Economists continue to debate the extent of shifting that occurs, but no one is willing to make the extreme assumptions that are implicit in the treatment of taxes in the national income accounts. In the absence of a consensus as to the degree of shifting, however, the present unrealistic method continues to be used.

Summary

This appendix has supplemented the chapter in diverse ways. It has detailed the calculation of DPI, C, and S from GNP, and explained in depth why GNP is difficult to compute. However, do not overemphasize the complexities. Basically, the GNP accounts are helpful for both analytic and policy purposes. Finally, some conceptual issues concerning the national income accounting system that were not mentioned in the chapter—the treatment of consumer durables, the distinction between government consumption and investment goods, and the treatment of taxes in the national income accounts—were raised here.

CHAPTER 16

What Makes the Economy Tick: The Elementary Theory of Income Determination

Friends and enemies of Keynesian economics tend to agree that The General Theory of Employment, Interest and Money *is one of a very small number of really influential twentieth century books. . . . Keynes rewrote the contents of economics and transformed its vocabulary.*

Robert Lekachman, economics professor (1966)

The General Theory of Employment *is a very difficult, disorganized, and complicated book, written in a very tricky special terminology.*

David McCord Wright, economics professor (1961)

CONTENTS

CHAPTER HIGHLIGHTS

1. The critical role played by business expectations in production and income decisions.

2. How equilibrium is established when aggregate demand equals anticipated sales.

3. The forces behind consumer spending.

4. The marginal propensities to consume and save, and the income multiplier.

5. The impact of saving on GNP.

6. Aggregate demand as the sum of consumption, investment, and government spending plans.

7. The government's budget as an instrument of macroeconomic control.

The United States passed its bicentennial year in mixed economic health. On the one hand, GNP had again achieved a new maximum, the number of people working continued to rise, and Americans still led the world in per capita electricity consumption, telephones, and bathtubs. On the other hand, unemployment remained a serious problem, with over 7.3 million people—over 7.7 percent of the labor force—unemployed. And, while inflation had declined from its double-digit peak of 1974, it had yet to be brought under control. In the years between 1976 and 1980 the unemployment rate fell gradually but the inflation rate rose dramatically.

In the preceding chapter the calculation of GNP, that broad measure of economic well-being, was described. This was essentially an exercise in arithmetic, numbers without explanation. Yet we need to do more than just count and sum up GNP. We would truly like to understand what makes an economy tick. Why does GNP rise by 6 percent in one year and by only 2 percent in another, while in the third year it actually declines by 1½ percent? Why does the economy weaken, leading to jobless workers and loss of production? Why does everything seem fine at other times, with job seekers readily finding employment and workers quitting because opportunities elsewhere appear so inviting rather than losing their jobs because there's not enough work to go around? Why do prices rise so rapidly that although take-home pay is higher than ever before, it doesn't buy as much? These are the kinds of questions that modern economists are concerned with, both to understand the whys and to try to ameliorate undesirable economic consequences.

The modern economy obviously is a complex mechanism, with myriad interrelationships that weave their pattern through the fabric of the system. Complexity can be handled by the finite human mind by simplifying, by abstracting, by theorizing. Theory seeks to find the central thread, or perhaps the few central threads, that, when unraveled, would reveal the basic structure of the economic cloth. Fortunately, the genius of John Maynard Keynes (pronounced Kaynes; see Box 16.1)

Courtesy of Brown Brothers.

BOX 16.1 John Maynard Keynes (1883–1946)

"We are all Keynesians now" is a tribute to the total victory of the Keynesian Revolution. No other twentieth-century economist since Karl Marx, has left such an imprint on modern civilization. And while Marx predicted the eventual dissolution of Western capitalism, the macroeconomic analysis of Keynes and his advocacy of stabilization policy have helped preserve the capitalist system.

John Maynard Keynes was born in Cambridge, England, to John Neville Keynes, a noted economist, and Florence Keynes, who later became the mayor of that university town. The senior Keynes became the chief administrative officer at Cambridge University, and it is not surprising that Keynes the son entered there upon graduating from Eton. He excelled at Cambridge, where he became the protégé of the two giants of the British economics establishment, Alfred Marshall and then Arthur Cecil Pigou. Nevertheless, he was not convinced that he wanted to become an economist, so he took the examinations for the British Civil Service, a path that had led many a young man to a respectable and often powerful and prestigious career. Although he spent the next two years as a civil servant, Keynes chafed at the lack of challenge and opted for an academic career, returning to Cambridge in 1909. Six years later, soon after the outbreak of World War I, he returned to government service, this time to the most important of the British government ministries, the Treasury. By the war's end Keynes had risen to third in the command structure of the Treasury, a remarkable feat for a man of only 34.

This combination of academic life and government service characterized much of Keynes' later life. Keynes served on numerous blue-ribbon government commissions: the Royal Commission on Indian Currency and Finance (1913): the British delegation to the Paris Peace Conference (1919)—from which he resigned in protest against the impossible economic terms levied on defeated Germany; the Macmillan Committee on Finance and Industry (1929): and the Bretton Woods Conference (1944), out of which came the World Bank and the International Monetary Fund. He served as one of Churchill's two economic advisers during World War II, and in 1942, in recognition of his services, he was knighted as Lord Keynes of Tilton.

Keynes was a highly original theoretical economist with a knack for finding practical solutions to pressing contemporary problems. He was also a gifted investor, speculating successfully not only for his own account but also for his college, a mutual insurance company of which he was chairperson, and some cultural institutions. Certainly he is best remembered for, and his preeminence in modern economic life derives from, his analysis of the workings of a modern capitalist economy, the Keynesian economics that we study as students of elementary economics. Keynes was a great believer in the power of ideas, and his concluding paragraph of the *General Theory* contains the following sentences:

The ideas of economists, both when they are right and when they are wrong, are more powerful than is commonly understood. Indeed, the world is ruled by little else. Practical men, who believe themselves to be quite exempt from any intellectual influences, are usually the slaves of some defunct economist. Madmen in authority, who hear voices in the air, are distilling their frenzy from some academic scribbler of a few years back. . . . Soon or late, it is ideas, not vested interests, which are dangerous for good or evil.

provided the insight into the modern macroeconomy that has enabled economists to comprehend how a market economy functions. The next few chapters outline Keynesian macroeconomics.

☐ The Simple Theory: The Role of Expectations

Like most ideas of genius that revolutionize thought—Newton's law of gravity and Einstein's theory of relativity come readily to mind—the basic Keynesian concept is a rather simple one. To switch metaphors, the skeleton of Keynesian theory is that businesspeople will produce as long as they expect to sell their output at levels of profit that are satisfactory to them. In a single phrase, then, *production equals expected sales*. Consequently, if sales are expected to increase, the output of the nation, or GNP, can be expected to do likewise. Conversely, if sales are expected to be weak, producers will cut back on their production plans. Of course, if business firms start cutting back, GNP will decline,[1] while if businesses raise their output, GNP will rise.

This is the basic theory: Production varies directly with business decisions, which are based on sales expectations. The remainder of this chapter and the next one are nothing more than an amplification of this basic concept. (Some people have claimed that the function of economists is to make the obvious incomprehensible. It is hoped that this cynical view will be disproved here.)

Production and income

Recall the argument in the preceding chapter that GNP is identical when calculated from both the production and income sides. A backpack that sold for $25 would be included in the product computation at the $25 selling price. But this commodity also returns incomes to the producers[2] —wages and salaries, rent, interest, and profit—of $25, so the $25 must also appear on the income side. It follows from this identity that if

---

[1]Actually, GNP rarely declines; a slowdown normally involves a reduction in the rate of growth of GNP (look again at Figure 15.1). However, it is far less cumbersome to write and read "decline" than to continually refer to a "reduction in the rate of growth."
[2]For simplicity in exposition, nonincome charges are omitted.

businesspeople in the aggregate expect to sell, say, $2½ trillion worth of goods and services and therefore produce $2½ trillion worth, then they must also have paid out $2½ trillion to the suppliers of the factors of production (including themselves as profit earners). Thus, *expected sales induce production that generates an identical amount of income.*

Income and spending

Income is a major determinant of spending. Most of us receive (or anticipate receiving) the bulk of our income by providing labor services. The reward, our pay, enables us to buy the goods and services we want. (Some wag once noted the presence of a vicious cycle here: We work in order to eat in order to gain strength to work. Fortunately, for most of us this is not quite the whole truth.) Similarly, business income enables firms to pay dividends and to retain part of their earnings for further investment. Governments at all levels, federal, state, and local, obtain receipts that finance their spending. Thus, if private businesses and government entities pay out incomes, these incomes provide the wherewithal with which goods and services are purchased. The result is a circular flow of output and income, as sketched in Figure 16.1. The public uses the income it earns from production to buy the output of firms; the

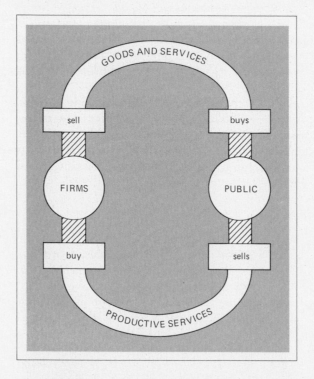

FIGURE 16.1 The circular flow of production and income.

firms pay for the services of productive factors on the basis of those sales. It is clear, however, that this circular flow can occur at any volume of sales, be it $1.05 billion, $2.36 trillion, or $3.87 trillion. While the sketch is useful in demonstrating the interrelationship between sellers and buyers, between production and income, it is too unsophisticated to explain the level at which production will take place.

A simple arithmetic example

To flesh out this descriptive skeleton, suppose aggregate sales or GNP is anticipated to reach $2.5 trillion in a particular production period. In order to achieve these sales (and assuming that no inventory of unsold merchandise remains), factors of production will be employed and will be paid $2.5 trillion. (Remember that profits, too, are considered income, and hence are included in the sum.) Now, if the income recipients spend the entire $2.5 trillion, business expectations will have been realized: Businesspeople had expected to sell $2.5 trillion, and sell it they did. If expectations for the next period are based on present actual sales, an equilibrium will have been attained—henceforth production will continue at $2.5 trillion.

Of course, there's bound to be a fly in the ointment. Who can guarantee that equilibrium will be attained? Perhaps the public does not spend all of its income; perhaps some people want to save. Follow through the impact of the decision of some income earners not to spend all of their income, say, $200 billion. Then aggregate spending will reach only $2.3 trillion of the $2.5 trillion earned. Producers expecting to sell $2.5 trillion now find themselves with sales totaling only $2.3 trillion. Their merchandise will move more slowly than anticipated, and sellers will have to offer inducements—price cuts, rebates, or giveaways—to move their stock. Business profits, of course, have been squeezed. Would you expect businesses to produce $2.5 trillion again in the next period? If you believe that they would not, and that firms will reduce output, the inevitable consequence is a reduction in incomes. GNP moves downward.

This example draws attention to a very critical fact: *Saving represents a drain on the spending stream.* Keynesian theory contradicts Benjamin Franklin's well-known epigram, "A penny saved is a penny earned." Modern economists say that a penny saved is a penny removed from a producer's pocket!

The famous bathtub analogy drives home this point. (This is one of the few economic experiments that can be conducted in a laboratory or even in the home. The only equipment required is a working bathtub.) The tub in Figure 16.2 is filled with a multicolored fluid called GNP. (In the home, water or beer will do.) As long as the drain is closed, the fluid level remains constant. But open the drain—conveniently labeled "saving"—and the fluid level, GNP, declines.

Of course, the converse is equally true. If the public, having earned

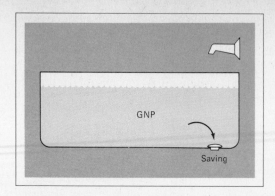

FIGURE 16.2 The GNP "bathtub."

$2.5 trillion, decides to spend $2.7 trillion—perhaps by running down a previously accumulated stock of savings or by obtaining credit—the demand for output will be brisk, stronger than anticipated. The rules of the competitive pricing system ensure that a rising demand working on a limited supply drives prices up, so that the $2.5 trillion produced will sell for $2.7 trillion. The existence of this excess demand will lead to a subsequent increase in supply if extra resources can be brought into production, but in any case GNP will rise.

In short:

Aggregate demand is the total value of goods and services desired by all spending groups in the economy.
The value of all goods and services supplied by the nation's producers is called **aggregate supply**.

1. If **aggregate demand** equals anticipated sales or **aggregate supply**, equilibrium is achieved.
2. If aggregate demand is less than anticipated sales, GNP will decline.
3. If aggregate demand exceeds aggregate supply, GNP will increase.

(Before proceeding further, be sure you understand the basic principles underlying these conclusions. Also, can you explain why saving represents a drain on GNP?)

☐ The Components of Aggregate Demand

In the short run, supply responses tend to be limited. Business firms cannot expand their plant quickly; investment takes time. Typically, firms can increase the output they obtain from their present equipment by lengthening the workweek and employing more labor, thereby using their capital more intensively. Over time, of course, new plant and equipment can be brought on line and production capacity increased. The analysis that follows is restricted to the short run; in other words, the economy's supply capacity is assumed to be fixed. In general, in basic Keynesian theory supply plays a passive role, responding to the lead of aggregate demand. (This should not be taken to imply that supply forces, such as the inflationary impact of higher oil prices, do not have short-run effects. Rather, these impacts are superimposed on or act in addition to demand effects. But because supply-side economics is not directly influenced by monetary forces, it is not discussed in this book.)

What, then, constitutes aggregate demand? As noted in the preceding chapter, the product side of GNP can be decomposed into consumption spending (C), investment spending (I), government spending (G), and net exports. Since the remainder of this part of the book deals with a "closed" economy—that is, one without an international sector—further discussion of exports and imports can be deferred to Part Six. The analysis, however, will not suffer from this omission. The plan of this chapter is to begin with a discussion of consumption, followed by an examination of a consumption-only economy. Then investment and government sectors are introduced to complete the simple model.

Determinants of consumer spending

It would be naive to ask why consumers spend. It is more difficult to identify the major determinants of consumer spending, and complex indeed to ascertain quantitatively the relative importance of the variables underlying aggregate consumption decisions.

The major influences of consumer outlays are thought to be income and wealth, but other influences are likely to be important, either in general (e.g., people's expectations of inflation) or in specific instances, such as widespread shortages of consumer goods. Economists have devoted considerable time and intellectual effort to the study of consumer spending, and have attempted to measure the relative importance of each factor. The consensus among contemporary economists views income as the most critical influence.

Income. While a consumer's income is the dominant force in his expenditure decision, one question that must be asked in assessing its importance involves the time horizon of consumption planning. Do people spend primarily on the basis of this week's income, this month's, this year's, or perhaps a whole series of incomes, past, present, and future? It is this question that underlies much of the research on aggregate consumption.

It is possible that most people use a somewhat longer time horizon than a year in planning their annual spending decisions. They consider not only their present income but also their past income. Thus, a family earning $25,000 a year will try to maintain its usual, past standard of living even if the primary income earner joins the ranks of the unemployed, thereby reducing the family's current income. Spending may well depend on this year's income relative to past income levels, so that a temporary fall in income may hardly affect consumption. Not surprisingly, this concept is known as the **relative income hypothesis.**

Other economists contend that future income should be considered as well. At the extreme lies the **permanent income hypothesis,** which views

The **relative income hypothesis** claims that aggregate consumer spending depends on the relationship of present income to the highest income earned in past years.

A lifelong horizon of income flows (past, present, and future) determines aggregate consumption decisions, according to the **permanent income hypothesis.**

CARMICHAEL

IMAGINE THE PANIC IF IT EVER GETS OUT THAT THESE ARE MY PEAK EARNING YEARS---
3-15

PAST DUE

BILL

BILL

BILL

© 1976 Los Angeles Times

Drawing by Eastman; © 1976 Los Angeles Times.

people as forecasting their lifetime income. People consider how much they expect to earn in their lifetime and, of course, how long they expect to live. While these forecasts cannot be accurate, consumers may act as if they carried out such calculations. Thus, a college student may spend all of his income and then some on the supposition that during his lifetime he will earn more than enough to pay off his debts and save enough to see him through his later years.

Similar to the theory of permanent income is the **life cycle theory.** Figure 16.3 sketches the lifetime income pattern of most people. Until people reach their teens, earnings are negligible. Only after high school or, for many, college do young Americans enter the labor force and begin to bring home income. Most workers can expect increasing incomes as they gain experience and seniority in their occupations; they will peak out sometime in middle age. As they age further and approach their 60s, people become more subject to physical impairments, accompanied by a greater frequency of illness and a higher likelihood of being laid off. Finally, they retire and live off social security, private pensions, and whatever they have managed to accumulate over their lifetime. If it can be assumed that people wish to improve their standard of living each year

The **life-cycle theory** views consumption spending influenced by age as well as by past, present, and prospective income.

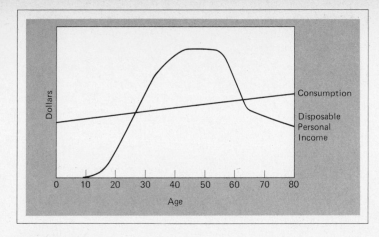

FIGURE 16.3 The life cycle theory.

and further assume—like the man whose last will and testament read, "Being of sound mind and body, I spent every last cent I had!"—leave nothing to their heirs, then the Consumption line in the figure represents their lifetime consumption pattern. Thus, until they reach the age of 27 they *dis*save, spending more than they earn. From 27 to 63 they become net savers, spending less than their earnings. With their savings, they are able to pay accumulated debts and finance the dissaving anticipated during old age. When they reach 63 and income again falls below consumption, they again dissave, using stored-up funds to finance their consumption. You will not be surprised to learn that the sum of the saving—the total of the vertical distances between disposable personal income and consumption during the years between 27 and 63—must equal the sum of the dissaving—the differences between C and DPI between the age of 0 and 27 and 63 and 80.

The critical implication of both the life cycle and the permanent income hypotheses should be driven home. *Spending in any single year is not dependent on that year's disposable income.* Indeed, in Figure 16.3 spending rises continuously despite the fact that income fluctuates.

Thus, all theories agree that income is an important determinant of consumer spending. They further agree that a single year's income is insufficient to explain consumption during that year. Most agree, too, that income is the single most important determinant of consumer spending. One study computed that a dollar's increase in per capita real disposable income would increase per capita consumption by 67 cents. No other variable that explains consumption comes close to that percentage.[3]

Wealth. Two people have equal incomes, but one is twice as wealthy as

---

[3]The appendix to this chapter elaborates on these three theories of consumption and discusses the paradox that the theories set out to resolve.

the other. Would you expect the spending of the two to be equal? Certainly not. The wealthier individual can not only spend from current income but draw on her wealth as well. Moreover, being wealthy removes some of the motive for saving. The study mentioned in the last paragraph concludes that wealth is an important determinant of consumption, though not as significant as income. An extra dollar of wealth was computed to increase per capita real consumption by about 5 cents.

Prices. Spending on particular goods and services is affected by the price tags attached to the specific commodity. A higher price on raincoats will lead to reduced sales of raincoats and, perhaps, increased sales of umbrellas. It is less certain, however, that a general rise in prices, as occurs during an inflation, will reduce consumer spending. Indeed, inflation might well do the reverse, for to maintain the same standard of living people may increase their dollar expenditures on consumption goods to meet the higher prices.

Inflationary expectations are another matter. If the public expects prices to rise, people may decide to spend now rather than wait. The old car that was going to be given a decent burial next year will be traded in this year, before prices go up. So, too, with the vacation in Las Vegas; better do it now, while travel and hotel prices are still low. Conversely, if prices are expected to fall, purchases will be delayed until they do.

Availability of goods. At the height of World War II (1942–1944), almost one-quarter of disposable personal income was saved, an unusually high rate. The simplest, and still best, explanation is the shortage of consumer goods. War production was given priority, and materials were used to feed the war machine. So even though consumers were willing and able to spend, there was little to buy, especially when it came to big-ticket items like automobiles and similar consumer durables.

Interest rates and credit terms. The existence of cheap and easily available credit may also induce greater consumption spending than might otherwise occur. Newspapers sometimes report on people who run up bills of thousands of dollars on bank credit cards, only to default on their obligations. While such occurrences are abnormal—that's why it's newsworthy—the existence of credit cards and other borrowing opportunities does allow a family to alter its pattern of spending, spending now and saving later rather than saving now and spending later. It is also possible that a rise in interest rates may stimulate saving, although there is little evidence to back this assertion. (In Chapter 19 another impact is mentioned: the relationship of interest rates to the wealth variable.)

The purpose of this examination of consumption motivations is to indicate its complexity. Many factors influence the amounts consumers spend yearly, with some more important than others. But having learned that the **consumption function** is complex, we can proceed with a simplification that permits us to ignore these complications for now. Just

The **consumption function** is the relationship between consumption and its determinants.

as in price theory, when one is investigating the impact of price on quantity demanded or supplied other variables are held constant, so, too, in the simple theory of income determination influences on consumption other than income will be held constant, so that they are out of sight, if not out of mind, for the moment.

Income determination: The consumption-only model (Model I)

For the immediate analysis, an additional simplification will be made, namely, that consumer demand is the only source of demand in the economy. Investment and government demand are ignored, though they will be introduced before the end of the chapter. One implication of this model is that GNP and disposable personal income are equal, for without the two sectors in the economy other than the household or consumer sector, all income that is earned is passed on directly to the consumer.

The arithmetic of Model I. Table 16.1 portrays a hypothetical consumption schedule. Prior to analyzing the equilibrium GNP, however, it will pay to spend a moment examining the table itself.

The first two columns are the **propensity to consume** schedule. For every level of disposable personal income (= GNP in this example), the schedule relates planned consumption expenditures to GNP. Thus, line 1 indicates that if the public received $3,000 billion in income, it would spend $2,500 billion of it on consumer goods and services. Similarly, the last line indicates that if consumers earned $1,500 billion, spending would be $1,750 billion. Skipping now to columns 5 and 6, two derived statistics are listed, the **average propensity to consume (apc)** and the **marginal propensity to consume (mpc)**.

The average propensity to consume answers the question, What proportion of its income does the public spend on consumer goods? The question is answered by computing the average, dividing consumption by disposable personal income. The result is the values listed in column 5.

The marginal propensity to consume answers a slightly different question: How much of each *additional* dollar's worth of income will the public spend on consumption as its income increases (or how much less, if its income decreases)? To put it differently, if one finds one's income increased (or reduced) by a dollar, how much more (or less) will one

The **propensity to consume** schedule is the relationship between consumption and income, all other influences being held constant.

The **average propensity to consume (apc)** equals aggregate consumption divided by disposable personal income.

The **marginal propensity to consume (mpc)** equals the change in aggregate consumption divided by the change in disposable personal income.

TABLE 16.1 Income Determination in a Consumption-Only Economy (all absolute numbers in billions of dollars)

GNP (paid out to income recipients)	Consumption demand	GNP (received back by producers)	Direction of GNP movement	Average propensity to consume (C/DPI)	Marginal propensity to consume ($\Delta C/\Delta DPI$)	Saving (DPI−C)	Average propensity to save (S/DPI)	Marginal propensity to save ($\Delta S/\Delta DPI$)
(1)	(2)	(3)	(4)	(5) (=2÷1)	(6)	(7) (=1−2)	(8)(=7÷1)	(9)
$3,000	$2,500	$2,500	downward	0.83		$500	0.17	
2,500	2,250	2,250	downward	0.90	0.50	250	0.10	0.50
2,000	2,000	2,000	equilibrium	1.00	0.50	0	0	0.50
1,500	1,750	1,750	upward	1.17	0.50	−250	−0.17	0.50

spend? To calculate the answer, which involves a change in income and spending, two sets of numbers are required: a set of consumption figures and a set of DPI data.[4] Note that all the *mpc*'s in column 6 are identical at 0.5. This is to be interpreted as follows: If the public's income increased by $100 billion, consumption would rise by $50 billion, or one-half of the change in income. The table shows the *mpc* to be constant (0.5) no matter what the income level at which the calculations are begun.

While this constant *mpc* might appear strange, especially since it suggests that a wealthy individual spends as much of his or her *additional* income as a poorer person does, empirical studies on the consumption function bear out the constancy assertion. Moreover, the facts are not as strange as they first appear. While it is true that a higher-income person spends more on consumption than a low-income individual and it is equally true that, on the average, the latter spends a larger proportion of income than the former (the *apc* of the latter is larger), these two statements do not contradict the equality of the marginal propensities. It is quite possible that as income *rises*, the same proportion of the *increase* is spent, even though the averages differ. Contrast columns 5 and 6; though the *mpc* is constant, total consumption rises and the *apc* falls as disposable income rises.

Recall now the relationship of consumption and saving to disposable personal income, or the definition of saving as the difference between income and consumption. The remaining columns of Table 16.1 can then be derived. Column 7, saving, is the difference between GNP (= DPI) and C. As long as DPI exceeds C, as it does in the first two rows of the table, S is positive. When C exceeds DPI, however, as it does in the last line, then S is negative; dissaving occurs. This is simply a technical way of stating that the public spends more than it earns. When all earnings are spent, as on the third line, S must be zero.

The average propensity to save (*aps*) is analogous to the *apc*, referring to the proportion of each income level that is saved, and is computed in column 8 as saving divided by disposable personal income. Similarly, to ascertain how much additional income will be saved (in percentage terms), the marginal propensity to save (*mps*) is calculated in column 9. The *mps* is computed by dividing the change in saving by the change in disposable personal income. Perceptive students might already have noticed that the $aps = 1 - apc$ and the $mps = 1 - mpc$. Can you explain why? (Basically, since all that is not spent must be saved, the fraction of income that is saved must be 100 percent minus the fraction of income that is consumed. Similarly with the *mps*.)

Now that the table has been mastered and the terminology is clear—

---

[4]To compute, take any two adjacent lines in Table 16.1 and obtain the change in both C and DPI, for example, C at $2,500 billion and $2,250 billion, for a change of $250 billion. The corresponding DPI figures are $3,000 and $2,500 billion, for a change of $500 billion. Divide the second figure, $500 billion into the first, $250 billion, for a quotient of 0.5 or ½, as in column 6.

and it must be clear and at your fingertips; it is part of the jargon of economics, and you will be coming across it not only in the remainder of this book but in your other studies of economics—the analysis can be developed.

The working of Model I. To begin with, note that consumption is positively related to GNP. That is, the higher GNP is, the more is spent on consumer goods. Note, too, that the *mpc* is 50 percent; it is critical for the following analysis that the *mpc* be less than 100 percent.

Proceed now to the first row of Table 16.1. Begin by assuming that businesspeople anticipate sales of $3,000 billion. Consequently, they will pay $3,000 billion to the factors of production (column 1). (Recall that GNP on the product side must equal GNP on the income side.) Consumers plan to spend only $2,500 billion, in accordance with their propensity to consume (column 2). But if they carry out their plans, sales will be less than anticipated; producers receive back in receipts only $2,500 billion, as indicated in column 3. Producers are disappointed, so they cut back on production, and therefore GNP declines (column 4). Say producers cut back to the actual sales of $2,500 billion. How much will firms then pay out to income recipients? Of course, the answer is $2,500 (row 2, column 1). What happens to consumption as a result? That, too, must decline. By how much? We know that the *mpc* is 0.5, so if income has fallen by $500 billion, consumption must fall by half of that, or $250 billion, to $2,250 billion, as is shown in column 2. Yet if that occurs, producers will be disappointed once again; sales will still be lower than expected, and once again GNP will decline (columns 3 and 4).

How far will this process proceed? Table 16.1 indicates that equilibrium GNP is $2,000 billion. At that level production is $2,000 billion, which equals income of $2,000 billion. According to the *apc* of 1.0 (column 5), all that is earned is spent, so the entire $2,000 billion goes to consumption. Producers' receipts (column 3) equal the amount they had expected to receive, so they have no reason to cut production further. In short, at a GNP of $2,000 aggregate demand equals aggregate supply.

Analogously, the entire process of GNP determination can also be viewed from the perspective of the saving process. Recall that saving is a drain, leaking out GNP. When GNP is $3,000 billion (row 1 again), $500 billion is drained out of the spending stream through the decision to save (column 7). This forces producers to cut back. But as production is cut back and income declines, saving, too, falls. When the GNP of $2,000 billion is reached, saving falls to zero, the drain ceases, all that is earned is spent, and equilibrium is attained.

To test your comprehension, explain why when GNP equals $1,500 billion the direction of GNP movement will be upward. See if you can explain it from both the consumption side and the saving side.

The geometry of Model I. As the epigram has it, a picture is worth a thousand words. The ease with which a diagram can be manipulated,

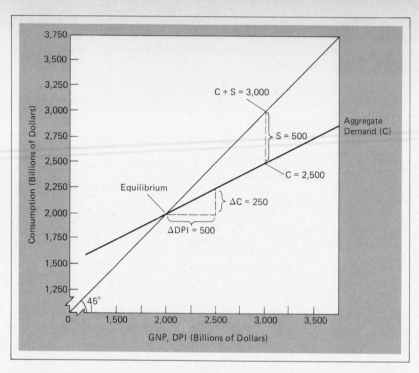

FIGURE 16.4 Income determination, Model I: the geometry of the consumption-only model.

combined with the fact that a single glance reveals much if not all, explains why students of economics are plagued with diagrams. A little investment of time now will reap great rewards in terms of comprehension later.

The axes of Figure 16.4 are both valued in billions of dollars. GNP is recorded along the horizontal or x axis, while along the vertical or y axis the components of GNP—in this simple case, C only—are measured. The 45° line emanating from the origin is a useful geometric construct with the property that it is everywhere equidistant from both the x and y axes. It permits measuring all horizontal values on the vertical scale. Thus, at equilibrium the $2,000 billion earned is spent entirely on consumer goods, while at an income of $3,000 billion, indicated by "C + S = 3,000," consumers spend only $2,500 billion (C = 2,500). The $500 billion distance between C + S and C is, of course, saving.

Aggregate demand for this case is consumption demand only. This is represented by the line labeled Aggregate Demand (C), which is derived from the propensity-to-consume schedule of Table 16.1. Thus, when GNP is $1,500 billion (on the horizontal, but also on the 45° line directly over that point), consumers demand $1,750 billion; the point on the

Aggregate Demand (C) line vertically above GNP = $1,500 billion is at a height of $1,750 billion.

How is equilibrium found? We know already that equilibrium requires equality of aggregate demand and aggregate supply. A glance at the diagram shows that this occurs where the GNP is $2,000 billion. At that point producers expect to sell $2,000 billion worth of goods, as represented by the equilibrium point on the 45° line, while demanders, represented by the equilibrium point on the Aggregate Demand (C) line, want to purchase $2,000 billion. Prove this to yourself. Assume that firms had expected to sell $3,000 billion and therefore produced and paid out in income that sum. The diagram shows that when GNP is $3,000 billion, C is only $2,500 billion. Firms will receive less in receipts than anticipated, and they will reduce production in consequence. Can you demonstrate that they will cease cutting back when GNP = $2 trillion? Of course, this is where expected sales equal actual sales. (You should also be able to show that at a GNP of $1,500 billion, the level of income will be driven up to $2 trillion. Try it.)

Two additional observations deserve mention. First, in the diagram saving is the vertical difference between the 45° line and Aggregate Demand (C) for any given GNP level. Thus, when GNP = $3 trillion and C = $2.5 trillion, then S must equal the difference, or $500 billion, which is exactly the distance between the value taken by the 45° line above GNP = $3 trillion and the value of Aggregate Demand (C) for that GNP. Saving is positive everywhere to the right of equilibrium and negative everywhere to the left. At equilibrium, saving equals zero. Again, note how a positive value of saving will, in this model, drive GNP downward. (Be careful, however, not to overgeneralize. Positive values of S may be consistent with equilibrium, as we will see shortly.)

A second point to be noted is that the slope, the steepness of the consumption line, equals the marginal propensity to consume, for it measures the change in consumption for a given change in GNP. Since the diagram is based on Table 16.1, the *mpc* will equal 0.5. This can be verified by measuring the change in DPI, say, from $2,000 billion to $2,500 billion, and measuring how much consumption changes. Consumption must rise by $250 billion, from $2,000 billion to $2,250 billion.

Compare the results of this diagramatic exposition with those obtained from the earlier arithmetic example. The answers must and do coincide; the diagram contains no information that is not contained in the table; it is simply a more picturesque (pardon the pun) way of presenting the data.

The lessons of the consumption-only model are basically two:

1. Equilibrium occurs when aggregate demand equals aggregate supply or, alternatively, when actual sales equal expected sales.
2. Any drain from the spending stream, such as saving, reduces GNP. These truths will not be modified when the model's complexity and conformance to reality increase.

Income determination: the C + I model (Model II)

Investment. Investment is the change in the stock of capital and includes new residential housing, new plant and equipment, and new inventory. Investment exerts a dual impact on the economic life of the nation. On the one hand, greater productive facilities increase the economy's productive capacity. However, as mentioned earlier in this chapter, the short-run nature of the model allows us to ignore the capacity-generating effect of investment.[5] Instead, your attention should be centered on the other impact of investment, namely, its influence on aggregate demand. Building new homes, plant, equipment, and inventories adds to the demand for economic output, just as consumption demand does. The theory of investment demand—what induces businesspeople to invest—is deferred to the following chapter. At this juncture all that is necessary is the assertion that investors demand output for their own purposes. From the producer's point of view, it really doesn't matter whether output is sold to an investor or to a consumer. Does it matter to the Chrysler Corporation whether a Dodge station wagon is bought by a painter who uses it to transport paints, ladders, and equipment, or by a family of seven that needs the extra room offered by a spacious vehicle? Demand is demand, whatever its source.

The arithmetic of Model II. Assume that investors have decided to spend $250 billion, and that they place orders for new capital goods. For ease of analysis, make the further assumption that investors will spend the $250 billion no matter what the level of GNP is. This **autonomous investment** can be introduced into both Table 16.1 and Figure 16.4, producing Table 16.2 and Figure 16.5.

Autonomous investment does not vary with the level of GNP (i.e., is not a function of GNP).

Consider now the equilibrium of Table 16.1 at a GNP of $2,000 billion. This position can no longer be one of balance when investment spending is added. While producers have paid out $2 trillion, the aggregate demand for their goods, as indicated by column 4 of Table 16.2, is $2,250 billion, consisting of the previous $2,000 billion of consumption *plus* $250 billion of investment spending. Producers have underestimated demand,

TABLE 16.2 Income Determination in a Consumption-Plus-Investment Economy
(billions of dollars)

GNP (Paid out to income recipients)	C	I	GNP (Received back by producers, C + I)	Direction of GNP movement	S
(1)	(2)	(3)	(4)(= 2 + 3)	(5)	(6)(= 1 − 2)
$3,500	$2,750	$250	$3,000	downward	$750
3,000	2,500	250	2,750	downward	500
2,500	2,250	250	2,500	equilibrium	250
2,000	2,000	250	2,250	upward	0

---

[5]As a matter of fact, the capacity-generating effect can be introduced without modifying the conclusions, as long as the rate of growth of demand exceeds the rate of growth of capacity. This refinement need not trouble you, however.

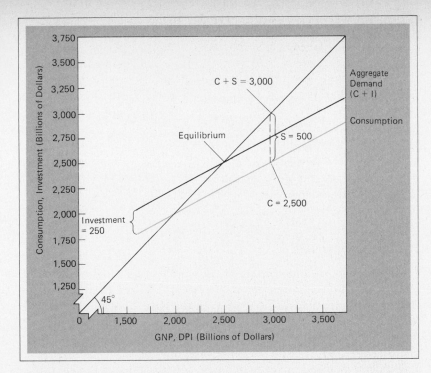

FIGURE 16.5 Income determination, Model I: C + I.

and in consequence will increase production and GNP. At a GNP of $2.5 trillion, consumers want to spend $2,250 billion while investors demand an additional $250 billion. Thus, aggregate demand sums to $2.5 trillion, which equals the amount producers had expected to sell. The result is equilibrium. (Show that if GNP had been $3 trillion, economic forces would have brought it back down to $2.5 trillion.)

The geometry of Model II. The same situation is portrayed in Figure 16.5. Investment, being a constant $250 billion, is added onto the consumption line, so that aggregate demand is precisely $250 billion higher at each level of GNP. The new aggregate demand, "Aggregate Demand (C + I)," crosses the 45° line at a GNP of $2.5 trillion. Businesses expect to sell $2,500 billion, and so they do—$2,250 billion to consumers and $250 billion to investors.

This situation can be viewed from the standpoint of drains also. Saving is a drain because it represents income paid out by producers that is not returned to the spending stream. Now that investment has been introduced, however, a source of new spending in addition to consumer expenditures is brought into play. The bathtub of Figure 16.2 is now provided with a faucet and a running fluid called investment. How can the level of fluid in the tub remain constant despite the open drain of saving? Experiment! Of course, the answer is by turning on the faucet so that the inflow is exactly equal to the drain. In this model, investment will have to equal saving to obtain equilibrium. Check that this is so in Figure 16.5 (and in Table 16.2 columns 3 and 6). Notice that only at a GNP of $2.5 trillion does the saving drain equal the investment addition. At no other point is this so. Thus, when GNP = $3 trillion, the drain equals $500 billion, the difference between the 45° line and the consumption curve vertically above $3 trillion, while the addition, Investment, the difference between the Aggregate Demand (C + I) and Consumption lines, is only $250 billion. Investors are putting back into the spending stream less than savers are draining out. Consequently, GNP must decline. (This is a good place to pause and make certain that you understand exactly how an equilibrium position is achieved. The chapter is going to be a bit more complex after this point.)

The income multiplier

A rather interesting contrast will come to light when the GNP equilibrium in the consumption-only model is compared with that in the consumption-plus-investment model. In the former, GNP was found to settle at $2 trillion: in the latter, at $2.5 trillion. To be sure, it is hardly surprising that with the addition of new demand—in this case, investment—GNP rises. What is not at all obvious is why an increase of *$250* billion in spending leads to a new equilibrium that is *$500* billion higher than the old equilibrium. The explanation of this puzzle lies in the **theory of the income multiplier.** Multiplier theory claims that new spending (diagramatically, an upward shift of the aggregate demand line) initiates a chain reaction of spending. New demand for, say, business inventories means new production. But as production increases, additional income is paid out to the workers and other contributors to the production process, so income earners have more to spend. And if they have more to spend, they spend more. But as these consumers spend more they increase someone else's income. In turn, the second group of earners increase their spending, and so on.

In the present example, investors spend $250 billion more. So initial spending and GNP rise by $250 billion. But, by definition, income rises by $250 billion, so income recipients have $250 billion more to spend. How much more will they spend? That will depend on their *mpc.* Since, by assumption, the *mpc* is 0.5, this first group will spend $250 billion × 0.5 = $125 billion. The second group of earners receive this eighth of a trillion dollars as their new income, so that their additional consumption expenditures will be $125 billion × 0.5 = $62.5 billion. And the next group's spending will be $62.5 billion × 0.5 = $31.25 billion. And so on ad infinitum, for a total of $500 billion.

The general formula to ascertain how much new GNP is generated by new spending involves simply multiplying the new spending times the income multiplier:

The **theory of the income multiplier** asserts that a change in spending leads to a many-fold change in GNP.

$$\Delta GNP = \Delta Sp \times k \qquad\qquad (16.1)$$

where ΔGNP is the change in GNP that results from the Δ Sp, the change in spending, and k, the income multiplier. Note that this formula works equally well for a decrease in spending, when the value of ΔSp becomes negative ($- \Delta GNP = - \Delta Sp \times k$).

The income multiplier is clearly related to the *mpc*. The higher the *mpc*, the larger the amount spent in each round, and therefore the greater the amount of income available to each new group of spenders. Indeed, there is a mathematical relationship between the *mpc* and k:

$$k = \frac{1}{1 - mpc} \qquad\qquad (16.2)$$

Since $1 - mpc = mps$ (see page 426), the equation can also be written as follows:

$$k = \frac{1}{mps} \qquad\qquad (16.3)$$

The multiplier is inversely related to the *mps*: The higher the *mps*, the lower the multiplier.

In the example used earlier, $mpc = mps = \frac{1}{2}$. By either equation 16.2 or equation 16.3, this works out to $1/\frac{1}{2}$, which equals 2. (What would the multiplier be if $mpc = \frac{2}{3}$? $\frac{4}{5}$? 1? To understand the need for the hypothesis on page 427 that the *mpc* must be less than 1, draw in a propensity to consume line with an *mpc* of 1.)

Now plug $k = 2$ into equation 16.1 and also insert the new investment spending of $250 billion.

$$\Delta GNP = \$250 \text{ billion} \times 2 = \$500 \text{ billion}$$

When this sum is added onto the old equilibrium of $2,000 billion, the new equilibrium of $2,500 is reached.

A word of warning: Do not confuse the income multiplier with the money multiplier discussed in Chapter 10. In formulation, the two multipliers are similar; the former is $1/mps$ and the latter is $1/r_{DD}$. But they refer to two distinct phenomena. The income multiplier relates to the new GNP created by additional spending, while the money multiplier demonstrates how much money can be created from a given reserve base.

Adding the government sector (Model III)

The multiplier operates not only when investment spending is introduced but whenever new spending of any sort, C or I or G or a combination of the three, occurs. As this juncture, then, it is appropriate to introduce the third component of GNP, government spending on goods and services, or G.

The existence of the government sector, like the introduction of investment, does not modify any of the basic principles expounded earlier, but it does introduce certain complications. This is so because the government not only spends, and thus is a demander of goods and services, but also collects income through taxes. The helpful assumption that GNP = DPI employed heretofore can no longer be considered valid or workable. Taxes must be subtracted from GNP in order to arrive at DPI, which is the foundation for consumption expenditures. However, a helpful assumption that can make life a bit easier is that the government collects a fixed sum of taxes—imagine a national property tax rather than an income tax. This assumption simplifies the arithmetic without damaging the principles.

Taxes will be set at $500 billion, and to keep the budget in balance—though this is not necessarily a virtue, nor is it a heinous crime—government spending on goods and services will also be maintained at $500 billion. Table 16.3 revises Tables 16.1 and 16.2 to include the government sector, while the updated diagram is presented in Figure 16.6.

As has been the case throughout this chapter, the first column, GNP (Paid out to income recipients), lists the amount that producers expect to sell and, thus, pay out to the factors of production. This sum now includes the taxes that will have to be paid. Taxes, listed in column 2, are assumed to be $500 billion, and disposable personal income, in column 3, will always be earnings less the half-trillion paid in taxes. Disposable personal income determines consumption in accordance to the propensity-to-consume schedule; columns 3 and 4 are still identical to columns 1 and 2 of Table 16.1, the basic propensity-to-consume schedule of this chapter. The next two columns, 5 and 6, list, respectively, investment and government spending, each of which is assumed not to be a function of GNP.

To determine equilibrium, aggregate demand must be computed. Aggregate demand now consists of the demand of all three sectors—consumer, investor, and government—and is found in column 7, which is the sum of the immediately preceding three columns. Equilibrium occurs in the middle row, when GNP equals $3 trillion paid out and $3 trillion received back by producers. The firms earn $2,250 billion from consumer spending, $250 billion from investment spending, and the remaining $500 billion from government expenditures.

Again, note what would have occurred had producers paid out $3,500 billion on the basis of a $3.5 trillion expected sales volume. Sales would

TABLE 16.3 Income Determination in a Closed Economy (C, I, and G Sectors) (billions of dollars)

GNP (Paid out to income recipients)	Taxes	Disposable personal income	C	I	G	GNP (Received back by producers, C + I + G)	Direction of GNP movement	S	Drains (S + T)	Additions (I + G)
(1)	(2)	(3)(=1−2)	(4)	(5)	(6)	(7)(=4+5+6)	(8)	(9)(=3−4)	(10)(=9+2)	(11)(=5+6)
$3,500	$500	$3,000	$2,500	$250	$500	$3,250	downward	$500	$1,000	$750
3,000	500	2,500	2,250	250	500	3,000	equilibrium	250	750	750
2,500	500	2,000	2,000	250	500	2,750	upward	0	500	750

have totaled only $3,250 billion: $2.5 trillion from C and another $750 billion from I + G. With sales lower than anticipated, GNP is driven downward. (By now you should be able to explain with ease why anticipated sales of $2.5 trillion drive GNP upward.)

The alternate approach of drains equaling additions must certainly lead to the same conclusion. Equilibrium is achieved when the drains are precisely offset by additions to the spending stream. The only modification in the now-complete model is to introduce a new drain—taxes—and a new addition—government spending. Taxes are considered drains because they reduce consumers' ability to spend. True, taxes differ from saving in that they are collected without individual consent while saving is a voluntary action. Nevertheless, their macroeconomic impact is identical. In and of themselves, taxes and saving reduce sales below the volume of income paid out, and lead to a reduction in GNP. On the other hand, just as investment spending replenishes the spending stream, so, too, does government spending. Both drive GNP upward. When the tax and saving drains are exactly offset by investment and government spending, the GNP level will neither rise nor fall but will remain stable. This is demonstrated in the middle row, columns 10 and 11, of Table 16.3.

However, if the drains exceed the additions—if S + T is greater than I + G—the net effect will be a reduction in GNP, as is indicated by the first row of the table. Conversely, when S + T is less than I + G, the excess of additions over drains boosts the GNP level upward.

The geometry of Model III. Figure 16.6 reproduces Figure 16.5, with two important modifications. First, the horizontal axis no longer measures both GNP and DPI, but only GNP. The result is to reduce the propensity-to-consume or C curve, moving it downward but not changing the slope. This schedule is based on the first and fourth columns of Table 16.3, which directly relate C to GNP. Second, government spending has been included, raising aggregate demand by a constant value of $500 billion. Again, because this number is assumed to be constant, the slope of the aggregate demand curve, now "Aggregate Demand (C + I + G)," remains unchanged.

The intersection of the 45° line and aggregate demand occurs at a GNP level of $3 trillion, as Table 16.3 has led us to expect. If producers had anticipated sales of $3.5 trillion, then aggregate demand would have proven insufficient. As the diagram indicates, C would have been $2.5 trillion, I, $250 billion, and G another $500 billion. Cutbacks would be in order, and would prevail until the equilibrium level was attained. An analogous process, the reverse of this one, would have occurred had aggregate supply been $2.5 trillion.

The drains = additions method can also be seen in the diagram. The additions are constant at $750 billion, being the difference between the Aggregate Demand (C + I + G) line and the C line. Drains vary (why?), and are calculated by the distance between the 45° line and the C line. Only at the $3 trillion GNP equilibrium are drains equal to additions.

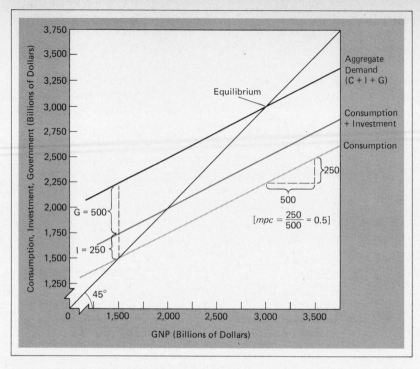

FIGURE 16.6 Income determination, Model III: C + I + G.

Must saving equal investment? The answer is clearly no.[6] Drains must equal additions, but the component sets of drains and additions—namely, S and I and T and G—need not. I might be greater than S—investors may well plan to spend more than savers plan to save—but if the government surplus—T being greater than G—is sufficiently large, S + T can still equal I + G.

Fiscal policy and aggregate demand

The government sector of the national income accounts contains not only the federal government's budget but those of other political subdivisions—states, counties, cities, and so on—as well. Government spending and income depend heavily on the political process and relatively little—in most cases, not at all—on macroeconomic considerations. Past budgetary decisions play a continuous and major role in any current budgetary plan. Indeed, the flexibility of most expenditure budgets is limited. It has been estimated that three-quarters of the annual

---

[6]Some textbooks define investment to equal I + (G − T), the former being private and the latter being government investment. Others define saving to equal S + (T − G), the former being private and the latter being government saving. These definitions appear strained, and the basic concepts of drains and additions not only seem easier to handle but also portray more clearly the forces involved in the determination of GNP.

federal budgetary expenditures are fixed as a result of earlier appropriations or long-term commitments. Many expenditures of government entities are closely circumscribed by the extent of their collected incomes, for their access to sources of borrowed funds is restricted. And income, too, is relatively inflexible for most local governments; state and local income taxes are not nearly as important to these public bodies as property and sales taxes, which are much less responsive to fluctuations in the income of their tax base.

The federal budget, on the other hand, is a more flexible document than local budgets. This is true for a variety of reasons. First, the federal budget relies heavily on the personal and corporate income taxes, which accounted for 61 percent of the federal government's receipts in 1980 (compared to 12 percent of state and local income). Collections of taxes from these sources vary with fluctuations in income, rising in times of prosperity and falling in poorer times. (Indeed, because of this quality the income tax is a mechanism that automatically corrects, to some extent, for destabilizing economic movements.) Second, the credit rating of the federal government is very sound, superior to that of all other borrowers in the United States. Finally, a significant constraint on local budgetary policies exists because the benefits of local expenditures often accrue to nonresidents even though they are paid by residents. (Better city roads benefit commuters who use them.) Similarly, in the area of taxes, higher taxes might well lead to reduced revenue if they induce a flight from the taxing locality. This type of escape hardly exists with respect to the impact of the federal budget. (Relatively few people set up residence outside of the United States in order to escape the federal tax burden.)

The inevitable consequence is that the federal government is the only government body with enough flexibility to use its budget to foster or retard GNP growth. Although practical problems of both an economic and a political nature frequently demonstrate the wide gap between theory and reality, it is no less true that, conceptually at least, the exercise of macroeconomic-oriented federal budgetary policy is rather uncomplicated.

The analysis of Model III demonstrated that government **fiscal policy** enters the GNP determination process in two ways: (1) By taxing, government reduces disposable personal income and, therefore, consumption; and (2) through its own spending, it increases demand directly. What would happen if the federal government decided to increase its expenditures without simultaneously modifying tax rates? The analysis forces the conclusion that aggregate demand would have to rise, and, in consequence, so would GNP. Moreover, because of the income multiplier, GNP would rise by more than the change in government expenditures. Refer back to Table 16.3 or Figure 16.6 and add, say, $250 billion in *new* government spending. Equilibrium can no longer be found at the $3 trillion level, since the new demand would total $3¼ trillion, and producers would have expected to sell only $3 trillion. With a multiplier of 2 and referring back to equation 16.1, the extra $250 billion in G will

Fiscal policy refers to a government's decisions to utilize its budget to achieve specific goals, especially with respect to macroeconomic objectives.

raise GNP by $500 billion, for an aggregate gross national product of $3½ trillion.

Additional government spending leads to an expansion of GNP. The new demand by government is added onto the demand of other sectors, bringing aggregate income upward. But the converse is equally true: A reduction in government demand will lead to a fall in GNP, and because of the income multiplier, the fall will exceed the value of the reduction in G.

The government's budget will, of course, reflect the new expenditures. When $250 billion in spending is added and tax collections remain unchanged, the budgetary deficit will increase by $250 billion. In reality, however, the deficit will be less than the full extent of government expenditures. This is so because of the income-oriented nature of the federal tax system. As GNP grows, the tax base also grows, so that tax revenues rise even though tax rates are not changed. (See Appendix B at the end of this chapter for further treatment of this case.)

What is true for changes in government expenditures is also true for changes in the government's taxation policy. If tax rates are increased, as in the case of the income tax surcharge imposed in 1969, consumption will tend to fall; the reduced consumer income will induce smaller consumption expenditures, other things remaining constant. (Of course, other things may not remain constant, so that the expected result may not materialize. But that's another issue entirely.) On the other hand, the tax rebate of 1973 may well have stimulated consumer spending, for taxpayers now found an unexpected windfall coming in the mail.

Active use of fiscal policy for stabilization purposes—stimulating the economy when it is weak and restraining it when it begins to forge ahead too strongly—is perhaps the major implication of the Keynesian model. Indeed, the practical side of the Keynesian revolution lay in convincing the molders of public opinion that the government's budget was more than a vehicle for providing the public with social consumption goods financed by tax revenues. The budget could and should be used as an instrument for controlling the ups and downs of a modern capitalist economy.

☐ Summary

This chapter has outlined the basic Keynesian macroeconomic theory of income determination. When aggregate demand equals aggregate supply, equilibrium is achieved. Aggregate supply is based on producers' willingness to produce, which is based on their expected sales. However, by the very act of producing, firms pay out the income that forms one of the cornerstones of aggregate demand. While consumer spending depends on a variety of influences, economists agree that income is the major force. Of course, consumer spending is only one component of aggregate demand. Government spending and expenditures by investors are the other two sources of demand that shape economic activity. The combination of all demand components is aggregate demand. When aggregate demand is precisely equal to aggregate supply, then equilibrium is achieved. When there is a discrepancy between what producers expect to sell and what demanders in total want to purchase, forces are set into motion to restore equilibrium. Greater-than-expected demand leads to a rise in GNP; inadequate demand leads to a reduction in GNP.

A second formulation of the equilibrium condition is presented in terms of drains from and additions to the spending stream. Saving and taxes are drains; investment and government spending are additions. Only when the drains are exactly offset by the additions is equilibrium attained. Excessive drains force GNP downward; excessive additions bring it up.

Another important concept introduced in the chapter is that of the income multiplier. An initial boost in spending, either C, I, or G, pushes the economy upward by a greater magnitude than the initial shock. Similarly, a reduction in spending brings the GNP downward by a magnified amount. The exact value of the multiplier is related to the marginal propensity to consume, which, by virtue of the formula $k = 1/1 - mpc$, determines the size of the income multiplier. To anticipate a bit, the impact of a given monetary policy varies directly with the value of the multiplier. Thus, if the value of the multiplier is large, a little stimulus can have a substantial effect, and vice versa if the value of the multiplier is small.

In a sense this theory is incomplete. While consumer spending motivations were investigated, the same cannot be said for investment expenditures. Moreover, the role of money and interest rates is noticeable only by its absence; no mention was made of either of these concepts in the chapter. To remedy the gap, a further expansion of the model is required. That is the purpose of the next chapter.

□ Questions and Exercises

1. You are given the following table (values in $ billions):

GNP (Paid out to income recipients)	Consumption demand	Investment demand	Government demand
700	600	50	25
600	525	50	25
500	450	50	25
400	375	50	25
300	300	50	25

    a. Calculate (i) the saving schedule, (ii) the marginal propensities to consume and to save, and (iii) the income multiplier.

    b. Find the equilibrium GNP. Explain why this is the equilibrium, using both the aggregate demand = aggregate supply approach and the drains = additions method.

    c.   What would have happened if businesspeople had expected to sell $700 billion worth of goods and services?

    d.   Assume that investors react to proposed legislation by cutting their planned spending in half. How is equilibrium GNP affected? What role does the income multiplier play in this process?

2.   Theories of the income-consumption relationship have practical implications. Explain how the various theories outlined in the chapter will predict consumers' reactions to an announced one-year income tax cut.

3.   Since financial institutions collect consumer savings and pass them on to borrowers who spend the funds, how can there be a discrepancy between drains from the spending stream and additions thereto?

4.   How can a government budget deficit stimulate economic activity?

☐ For Further Study

Keynes' *The General Theory of Employment, Interest and Money* (London: Macmillan, 1936) is tough going, but it is carefully expounded in Dudley Dillard, *The Economics of John Maynard Keynes: The Theory of a Monetary Economy* (Englewood Cliffs, N.J.: Prentice-Hall, 1948). All macroeconomics textbooks deal with the basic Keynesian structure at a level that is more accessible to the student.

The General Theory proved to be a fertile source for further research. Consumption theory has been developed extensively since Keynes' time, and a brief but thorough review may be found in Robert Ferber, "Consumer Economics: A Survey," *Journal of Economic Literature* 11 (December 1973): 1303–1342. Thomas Mayer, *Permanent Income, Wealth, and Consumption: A Critique of the Permanent Income Theory, the Life-Cycle Hypothesis, and Related Theories* (Berkeley: University of California Press, 1972), is a more comprehensive survey of the major theories of the income-consumption linkage.

APPENDIX A   Cross-Section and Time Series Consumption Studies

The close relationship between consumer spending and income has been verified by a number of statistical studies. Curiously, however, these very data have presented economists with a puzzle that remains to be resolved conclusively. The sources of income-consumption patterns are basically of two types: cross-section studies and time series propensity-to-consume series. In the cross-section studies, data is supplied by households that were interviewed during a specific year; the raw data are each family's income and consumption. The results of these data compilations show that the higher the family's income, the lower the marginal propensity to consume. In other words, as income rises, *mpc* declines. (See Figure 16A.1.) One implication of this pattern is the expectation that as the nation's income rises and more people move into higher income groups, the community's *mpc* should decline. (The curve reproduced here is visibly, yet not substantially, nonlinear, with *mpc*'s ranging from .88 between the $500–1,000 and $1,000–1,500 groups and .68 between the $4,000–5,000 group. The assumption of a constant *mpc* as used in the text of the chapter is not altogether appropriate.)

On the other hand, time series studies, which usually obtain their data from quarterly or annual national data on consumption and income, show an entirely different value for the marginal propensity to consume. Moreover, the data do not demonstrate the expected declining *mpc* as

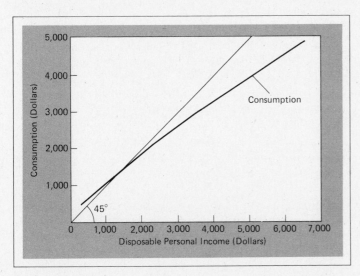

FIGURE 16A.1 The cross-section consumption function (1935–1936 family budget data).

Source: Raymond W. Goldsmith et al., *A Study of Saving in the United States* (Princeton, N.J.: Princeton University Press, 1965), 3, p. 183.

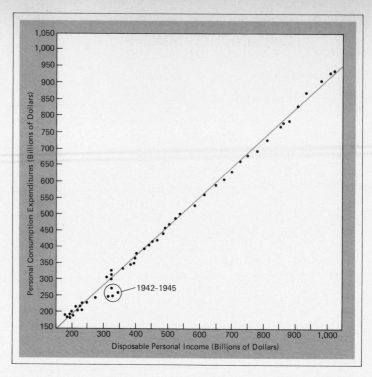

FIGURE 16A.2 The time series consumption function (billions of 1972 dollars).
Sources: 1929–1939, U.S. Department of Commerce, Bureau of Economic Analysis, *The National Income and Product Accounts of the United States: 1929–1974 Statistical Tables* 1940–1980, *Economic Report of the President* (1981).

aggregate income grows, the result predicted by the cross-section statistics. Figure 16A.2 plots the annual relationship between consumption and disposable personal income for the years between 1929 and 1980; the *mpc* equals 0.91 (excluding the abnormal years of World War II).

How can one reconcile the lower and declining *mpc* obtained from the cross-section data with the higher and constant *mpc* that results from the time series relationship?

Economists have attempted to reconcile the paradox in a variety of ways, which basically boil down to two responses. One group of scholars accepts the cross-section results as true, and the time series conclusions are explained away. For a second group of researchers, the validity of the time series data is accepted and the cross-section data are shown to be misleading. Three theories that deal with the paradox will be outlined here; the first two belong to group one and the third is classified in group two.

The absolute-income hypothesis

Recall the assumption made earlier (p. 425) that although the consumption function relates many causes to consumption, variables other than income are constant and are not included in the analysis. In actuality other influences do affect consumption spending and the statistical propensity-to-consume schedule. Consider the hypothetical cross-series data in Table 16A.1.

The four families listed in the table all have different incomes and different amounts of annual consumption expenditures. Two representative years for each family are chosen, year 1 and year 11. Looking first at columns 2 and 3 for year 1, notice that the first family spends more than it earns and the second spends all that it earns, while the other two save. This pattern is not atypical of families in a cross-section survey. Column 4 lists the *mpc*, which declines as income increases. The exact same calculation can be made for year 11, the only difference being the fact that each family's income and consumption have risen. Why this happened is not revealed by the data, but it could well be a consequence of an increase in wealth. The *mpc*'s in year 11 are also identical with those of year 1.

Compute now the time series *mpc*, which is found in the final line of the table. To obtain this fraction, add up consumption for all families, and similarly for income, for each of the two years. Then divide the change in aggregate family consumption by the change in aggregate family income. The result is an *mpc* of 1.0. But this *mpc* is not the true *mpc*, which is given by the budget surveys. It is a statistical artifact, derived by comparing consumption-income patterns without considering the impact of wealth or other explanatory variables. Had the appropriate statistical adjustment been made, the long-run or time series propensity to consume would have also demonstrated a declining *mpc* as income rose.

The relative-income hypothesis

The relative-income hypothesis (p. 421) provides another explanation for the discrepancy between the time series and cross-section *mpc*. According to this theory, consumption depends not on the absolute level of income earned by each household, but on relative levels. Relative income encompasses not only past income but also one's income in

TABLE 16A.1 A Hypothetical Cross-Section Survey and the Absolute-Income Hypothesis

	Year 1			Year 11		
Family no.	Disposable Personal Income	Consumption	*mpc*	Disposable Personal Income	Consumption	*mpc*
(1)	(2)	(3)	(4)	(5)	(6)	(7)
1	$ 7,000	$ 8,000		$ 8,000	$ 9,000	
2	10,000	10,000	0.67	11,000	11,000	0.67
3	13,000	11,500	0.50	14,000	12,500	0.50
4	16,000	12,500	0.33	17,000	13,500	0.33
Totals	$46,000	$42,000		$50,000	$46,000	

Time series *mpc*: $\dfrac{\$46,000 - 42,000}{\$50,000 - 46,000} = \dfrac{\$4,000}{\$4,000} = 1.0$

comparison to that of others. The expression "keeping up with the Joneses" contains more than a kernel of truth in explaining the consumption-income relationship. Glance at Table 16A.1 and note that though all family income increased in year 11 compared to year 1, the relative standing of each family has not changed at all. The relative-income theory argues that if relative income has not changed, then consumption patterns will not change either. Thus, the *mpc* also remains the same. Nevertheless, as the table demonstrates, a time series produces a constant *mpc* equal to 1.0.

Common to both the absolute-income and relative-income theories is the belief that the cross-section studies are valid and the time series results incorrect. The opposite tack is taken by the permanent-income hypothesis.

The permanent-income hypothesis

The response given by the permanent-income hypothesis to the paradox is to assert that the true *mpc* is rendered by the time series approach. The cross-section study misleads because the data are based on a year's income and consumption and ignore the longer planning horizon of consumers. As noted earlier (p. 421), people's spending plans are based on their permanent or lifetime expected income. Consequently, some people who now earn low incomes spend more than their present income would warrant; their present income does not reflect their permanent income. Since their present spending depends on their permanent income, these families spend more than they would if their present income were indeed their permanent income. For other house-holds the reverse is true. Consider the hypothetical data of Table 16A.2. When one compares current disposable personal income (column 3) to consumption (column 4) and computes the *mpc* out of DPI (column 5), the *mpc* declines as income rises. However, if one instead calculated the relationship among the "true" income measure, permanent income, and consumption, as is done in column 6, the "true" *mpc* of 1.0 would become apparent. The small and declining *mpc* is due purely to measuring the wrong concept—current income rather than permanent income. Thus, both the time series and the correctly calculated cross-section lead to an *mpc* of 1.0.

TABLE 16A.2 A Hypothetical Cross-Section Survey and the Permanent-Income Hypothesis

Family no.	Permanent income	Current DPI	Consumption	*mpc* out of DPI	*mpc* out of permanent income
(1)	(2)	(3)	(4)	(5)	(6)
1	$ 8,000	$ 7,000	$ 8,000		
2	10,000	10,000	10,000	0.67	1.0
3	11,500	13,000	11,500	0.50	1.0

Conclusion

The examples in this chapter have gone along with the convention that *mpc* is substantially less than one. For convenience, the assumption of a constant *mpc* was adopted. The analytic conclusions reached in the chapter will not differ if the *mpc* is 0.9 or if it is variable with respect to disposable personal income. The difference, however, has critical implications for policy. Remember that the income multiplier is dependent on the value of the *mpc*, and as the chapter has shown, the strength of fiscal policy depends on the multiplier. The same is true for the strength of monetary policy. Thus, the correct value of *mpc* makes a substantial difference. An *mpc* of 0.67 means a multiplier of 3; an *mpc* of 0.9 leads to an income multiplier of 10! Obviously, the amount by which government expenditures should rise to stimulate expansion of GNP will differ if the multiplier differs. Perhaps the truth is somewhere in between. Measuring income on an annual basis probably does underestimate *mpc*. Nevertheless, to accept the time series results and thereby reject all influences on consumption other than permanent income seems extreme.

APPENDIX B The Algebraic Treatment of the Simple Keynesian Model and Some Additional Complications

The two dimensions of the diagramatic treatment prohibit examination and development of more complex models, a problem that is resolved by treating the analysis through algebraic formulation. Even when the model is two-dimensional, algebraic treatment often is simpler. The essential role of setting up and solving a system of simultaneous equations is to make sure that the number of variables to be solved equals the number of equations. The purposes of the appendix are two: In addition to setting up the final model of the chapter in its algebraic terms, the model itself is developed further.

The algebra of Model III

The complete model, using C, I, and G, with S and T acting as drains, can be expressed by a system of five equations (all whole numbers in billions of dollars):

$$DPI = GNP - T = GNP - 500 \tag{16A.1}$$

$$C = 1000 + 0.5 \; DPI \tag{16A.2}$$

$$I = constant = 250 \tag{16A.3}$$

$$G = constant = 500 \tag{16A.4}$$

$$GNP = C + I + G \tag{16A.5}$$

To solve, substitute equation 16A.1 into equation 16A.2 and then 16A.2–16A.4 into 16A.5:

$$GNP = 1,000 + 0.5 \, (GNP - 500) + 250 + 500 \tag{16A.6}$$

Multiply out the terms in the parentheses:

$$GNP = 1,000 + 0.5 \; GNP - 250 + 250 + 500 \tag{16A.7}$$

Consolidate terms:

$$GNP = 1,500 + 0.5 \; GNP \tag{16A.8}$$

Subtract 0.5 GNP from both sides:

$$GNP - 0.5 \; GNP = 1,500 \tag{16A.9}$$

Factor out GNP:

$$GNP \, (1 - 0.5) = 1,500 \tag{16A.10}$$

Divide both sides by $(1 - 0.5)$:

$$GNP = \frac{1,500}{1 - 0.5} = 1,500 \, (1/\tfrac{1}{2}) = 1,500 \times 2 = 3,000 \tag{16A.11}$$

The equilibrium value, then, is $3,000 billion, and in equation 16A.11 the term 1/½ is the income multiplier.

If C, I, or G were increased by $250 billion, the multiplier would lead to an increase in GNP of $500 billion. To see this, add an additional 250 to the constant term in equation 16A.6 and solve as before. The result is an increase in GNP equal to the change in, say, G, government spending on goods and services, times the income multiplier, $1/1 - mpc$ or $1/mps$.

Tax cuts and the balanced-budget multiplier

What is the impact of a tax cut on GNP? What would happen if the $500 billion tax receipt in the model just presented were reduced to $250 billion? Following along the equations, we would derive a new equation for 16A.1:

$$DPI = GNP - 250 \tag{16A.1$'$}$$

Then equation 16A.6 becomes

$$GNP = 1,000 + 0.5 \, (GNP - 250) + 250 + 500 \tag{16A.6$'$}$$

Following along:

$$GNP = 1,625 + 0.5 \, GNP \tag{16A.8$'$}$$

$$GNP \, (1 - 0.5) = 1,625 \tag{16A.10$'$}$$

$$GNP = 1,625 \, (1/0.5) = 3,250 \tag{16A.11$'$}$$

Thus, a tax cut of $250 billion has half the impact on GNP of a rise in government expenditures of $250 billion. The former brings GNP up by $250 billion, while the latter raises it by $500 billion. Why this asymmetric impact?

The answer hinges on the distinction between the **government expenditure multiplier** and the **tax multiplier.** When the government spends $250 billion and the *mpc* is ½, then, as indicated earlier (p. 432), the multiplier process is begun. The first round is the initial government spending of $250 billion; a second round of $125 billion occurs as income earners spend half of the $250 billion earned; then there is a third round of $62.50 billion; and so on. The result is $250 billion × $1/mps$ (= 2), or $500 billion.

On the other hand, if taxes are cut so that government receipts fall by $250 billion, the initial $250 billion is added to the payrolls of income earners, whose disposable personal income is now increased. But consumers will not spend the entire $250 billion; with an *mpc* of ½, only $125 billion will be spent. Thus, the spending rounds will be $125 billion, $62.50 billion, $31.25 billion, and so forth, and the sum will be $250 billion. In terms of the multiplier formula, the tax multiplier will always be one absolute number less than the government expenditure multiplier. Since the government expenditure multiplier is $1/mps = 2$, the tax multiplier is $(1/mps) - 1 = 1$. Consequently, for a tax cut of $250 billion,

The **government expenditure multiplier** ($1/mps$) is the multiplier impact on GNP of a change in government spending for goods and services. The

tax multiplier $\left[\dfrac{1}{mps} - 1\right]$

refers to the multiplier impact on GNP of a change in government tax collections.

the impact of GNP equals $250 billion × 1 = $250 billion. (If the expenditure multiplier is 3, what will the tax multiplier be?)

An interesting implication of the distinction between the tax and government expenditure multipliers should be pointed out. If taxes are raised to collect, say, $100 billion and the budget is balanced by an expenditure of an identical amount, the effect on GNP will not be neutral but will be expansionary. Calculate the impact:

Tax multiplier: − $100 billion × 1 = − $100 billion

Government expenditure multiplier: + $100 billion × 2 = $200 billion

Net effect: an increase in GNP of $100 billion

The **balanced-budget multiplier** demonstrates that a change in government spending that is precisely offset by a change in government revenues does not have a neutral impact on the economy.

The **balanced-budget multiplier** is the government expenditure minus the tax multiplier.

Induced investment and the supermultiplier

The model set forth in this chapter assumed that investment spending is a constant amount and is not related to GNP. This unrealistic assumption can now be dropped, and I can be made a function of GNP[7]. Equation 16A.3 then becomes

$$I = a + dGNP \text{ (e.g., } I = 50 + 0.25 \text{ GNP)} \tag{16A.3*}$$

Substituting equation 16A.3* in equation 16A.6 and proceeding as before,

$$GNP = 1,000 + .5 (GNP − 500) + 50 + 0.25 \text{ GNP} + 500 \tag{16A.6*}$$

$$GNP = 1,300 + 0.75 \text{ GNP} \tag{16A.8*}$$

$$GNP = \frac{1,300}{1 − 0.75} = 1,300/\tfrac{1}{4} = 5,200 \tag{16A.11*}$$

The reason for the difference between equilibrium GNP in this formulation and that of model III is obviously a result of the new investment function. Note that the new multiplier is not the 2 of earlier examples but 4. This is the **supermultiplier.** The supermultiplier has two components, *mpc* and *mpi*, the latter being the marginal propensity to invest (the change in investment divided by the change in GNP), denoting how much investment will change for a given change in GNP. The reasoning underlying the supermultiplier is analogous to that of the simple multiplier: the chain reaction of spending. However, in the case of the supermultiplier the additional income generates not only new consumption spending but also new investment spending. Thus, if G increased by $100 billion, the second round would consist of $50 billion of additional consumption spending (*mpc* = 0.5) *plus* an additional $25

Supermultiplier

$$\left[\frac{1}{1 − (mpc + mpi)} \right]$$

is the name given to the income multiplier when investment is made a function of GNP.

---

[7]This formulation is not the accelerator discussed in Chapter 19. That relationship takes the form: $I = f(\Delta GNP)$, whereas the present form is: $I = f(GNP)$.

billion in investment spending ($mpi = 0.25$). The next round of income recipients earn $75 billion, and so on.

Proportional income taxes

An additional assumption made earlier was that tax receipts are a fixed amount. Assume instead that taxes vary with income, the simplest assumption being that they are proportional to income. Thus, equation 16A.1 becomes

$$DPI = GNP - T = GNP - tGNP = GNP - 0.2 \ GNP \qquad (16A.1^{**})$$

Consequently, equation 16A.2 is modified to

$$C = 1,000 + 0.5 \ (GNP - 0.2 \ GNP) \qquad (16A.2^{**})$$

Then, substituting as usual

$$GNP = 1,000 + 0.5 \ (GNP - 0.2 \ GNP) + 250 + 500 \qquad (16A.6^{**})$$

$$GNP = 1,750 + 0.4 \ GNP \qquad (16A.8^{**})$$

$$GNP = 1,750/0.6 = 2,916.67 \qquad (16A.11^{**})$$

Notice that the GNP equilibrium is lower here than in the original equation (16A.11). This is so because at the old equilibrium, taxes would be $600 billion (0.2 × $3,000 billion), which, when added to saving of $250 billion, would lead to a drain of $850 billion. But additions equal $750 billion, so GNP would fall. At the equilibrium GNP of $2,916.67, T = $583.33 and S = $166.67 total to $750 = I + G. Of course, had the tax rate been lower, GNP might well have been higher than in model III. Try it with $t = 0.1$.

A tax cut, in this model, leads to a deficit in the government's budget that is less than the initial revenue loss. Consider the present tax collections of $583.33 billion at GNP equilibrium. Cut taxes to 10 percent. This will reduce collections by 50 percent, to $296.67 billion; the budgetary deficit immediately rises by the same amount. However, the increase in disposable personal income induced by the tax cut leads to higher consumer spending (the consumption curve shifts upward; in the algebraic formulation, $t = 0.1$ instead of 0.2). Solving for the new equilibrium GNP, aggregate demand will equal aggregate supply at a GNP of $3,181.82 billion. But at a higher GNP level and with a larger DPI, the tax base increases. Tax collections become $318.18 billion, over $20 billion higher than the anticipated revenue of $296.67 billion.

Pulling the strands together

Examine now what happens in a model that combines the simple model III with an investment function and a tax function, both of which are directly related to GNP. Then

$$DPI = GNP - t \ GNP \qquad (16A.12)$$

$$C = c + b \text{ DPI} = c + b \text{ GNP } (1 - t) \tag{16A.13}$$

$$I = a + d \text{ GNP} \tag{16A.14}$$

$$G = \text{constant} \tag{16A.15}$$

$$\text{GNP} = C + I + G \tag{16A.16}$$

$$\text{GNP} = c + b \text{ GNP } (1 - t) + a + d \text{ GNP} + G \tag{16A.17}$$

$$\text{GNP} = c + a + G + \text{GNP } (b + d - bt) \tag{16A.18}$$

$$\text{GNP} = \frac{c + a + G}{1 - (b + d - bt)} = \frac{c + a + G}{1 - d - b(1 - t)}$$

The resulting income multiplier for changes in C, I, or G is

$$\frac{1}{1 - d - b(1 - t)}$$

and the tax multiplier is

$$\frac{1}{1 - d - b(1 - t)} - 1$$

These multipliers are certainly more complex than the income multiplier set forth in the body of the chapter. Yet even this formulation and model cannot approximate the real world. The tax structure is far too simple: other determinants of C, I, and G have been ignored: and the assumption of constant mpc's and mpi's has been retained. It is possible to formulate and solve more complex models, and such models have been not only designed but also tested empirically. Some of the results are discussed in Chapter 19.

CHAPTER 17

Money Enters the Illusion, Version I

Monetary theory is less abstract than most economic theory; it cannot avoid a relation to reality.
Sir John Hicks, British economist (1967)

There are some kinds of business and some capital expenditures that aren't profitable at 20 percent interest rates.
Treasurer of a large U.S. manufacturing firm (1981)

CONTENTS

The critical point made in the last chapter concerns the role of business expectations: When businesses are able to sell all they want so that their profits reach anticipated levels, then (barring other disturbances) that level of GNP will be maintained in subsequent periods. Alternatively, when the demands by the various components of aggregate spending —consumers, investors, and governments—just equal the supply offered by the nation's producers, GNP is in equilibrium. As noted in Chapter 16, consumer demand depends on a number of causative elements, of which the most important is income. Government spending, too, hinges on a number of key variables, both political and economic. And investment spending similarly is affected by a multiplicity of forces, a fact that was ignored in the elementary model of the previous chapter. There, the desire of investors to spend $250 billion on new capital goods served as a simplifying hypothesis. But it is surely right to wonder, What are the factors that determine how much businesses will spend on investment goods? One of the many purposes of this chapter is to answer that question. It will be shown that investment spending depends in part on the interest rate.[1] (Note: Interest rates here are in real terms.) So it will be necessary first to understand how the Keynesian paradigm depicts the determination of interest rates. For this purpose the chapter opens with a discussion of the demand for money.

☐ Determination of Interest Rates

The demand for money

Any market-determined price results from the interactions of supply and demand. Since the interest rate, too, is a price, its determination can best be understood by considering the supply and demand elements involved. But rather than discussing the supply and demand for bonds,

---

[1]"The" interest rate is obviously a simplification in light of the discussion of the multiplicity of interest rates in Chapter 3.

Keynes focused on the supply and demand for money. The interest rate then becomes the price of money. In fact, the two views are really identical, for if the alternative to holding onto money is buying bonds and the alternative to buying bonds is holding money, a 7 percent rate of interest means (a) the percentage to be earned if a bond is purchased or (b) the earnings rate foregone (the opportunity cost) if money is held instead of being used to buy the security. Indeed, anyone who holds onto cash or a demand deposit account (M-lA, which pays nothing) is losing some income. (If the M-1B definition of money is used, so that money includes some interest-earning deposits, the analysis has to be interpreted in terms of the higher interest earned from alternative assets.) Earning assets, no matter how little they pay, can always be held instead.

If such is the case, why hold money at all? After all, positive earnings are always better than zero returns. The answer, of course, is that money provides a variety of services, and for that reason, notwithstanding the cost, individuals and business do demand money. At any one time, the public wishes to hold a certain portion of its total income in the form of money. (Note the stress here on the demand for holding money, rather than on spending.) That is, people wish to have a certain amount of money on hand at all times.

The motives for holding onto money fall into three categories:

1. the transactions motive
2. the precautionary motive
3. the speculative motive

The transactions motive. Imagine the following situation. Frank gets paid $1000 once a month, in the form of a check deposited to his account at the Utopian Commercial Bank on the first day of each month. During the course of the month Frank pays all of his bills using credit cards, the bill for which is due on the first of the month. Frank, being a typical American consumer, spends all of his income. But because he wishes to avoid high finance charges, he pays his bills on time. In this instance Frank's demand for money is zero, since on the same day that his salary is credited to his account his credit card payment is debited from the account.

How unreal is this episode? Aside from the fact that credit cards cannot be used for all payments—parking meters or vending machines do not yet take credit cards—the typical consumer does not receive income at the same time that bills come due. Wages and salaries are paid at specified intervals (weekly, biweekly, or monthly), while expenditures take place daily. Since incomes and outlays are not synchronized, some money will be held to meet current expenses. (In a way this is reminiscent of a bank's holding onto reserves, as discussed in Chapter 7.) Frank, who demands no money holdings for his normal transactions needs, truly represents a hypothetical case.

On the other hand, consider Eleanor, Frank's wife. She is paid $210 at the beginning of each week and also manages to spend it all by the week's end. Since Eleanor has an aversion to debt and will not use credit cards, she needs money to finance her transactions. Assume that Eleanor spends her salary evenly throughout the week: She spends, say, $15 in the morning and $15 in the afternoon. Assuming that she receives her $210 salary on Monday morning, her balance after the Monday lunch hour is $195, since she has spent $15 that morning. By tomorrow morning she'll have spent $15 more, and so on through the rest of the week. Meanwhile, as long as she maintains cash or a checking account balance for the week's purchases, Eleanor is said to demand money for transactions purposes. Indeed, her average demand for money during the week can be calculated by adding up her midday balances and dividing the sum by the seven days of the week. Thus,

M	T	W	Th	F	S	S	Total balances	Total balances ÷ days of week
$195	$165	$135	$105	$75	$45	$15	$735	$105

Eleanor's average demand for money is $105. (An obvious method of arriving at this result is by simply glancing at the midweek or Thursday holding. Take a look.)

What is true for Eleanor is equally true for General Motors, IBM, or Sylvania. Businesses, too, receive payments and must settle accounts due their suppliers and workers, and rarely if ever are the payment inflows and outflows synchronized. So businesses also demand money for transactions purposes.

In passing, it might be noted that it is possible to reduce the demand for M-1A balances by holding onto money substitutes instead. Eleanor could certainly deposit her salary in her savings account and each day withdraw the $30 she needs for that day's purchases. Similarly, large firms or individuals might hold onto short-term securities in lieu of money. That such actions will reduce transactions demand for money is undeniable. (Can you calculate Eleanor's average balances under this assumption?) But we would not expect to drive the transactions demand to zero, if only because of the inconvenience, not to speak of the cost of going to the bank daily. Continuous switching into and out of short-term securities also has a limit, since the transactions costs—staff, brokerage fees, telephone calls—might exceed the gain in interest.

It can be expected that as income rises, the demand for money for transactions purposes increases too. If Eleanor's employer, realizing her true value, raises her salary to $280 a week, and she maintains her spending pattern but now spends more, her average money demand rises to $140 a week. (Can you show why?) For businesses, too, a larger volume of payments will increase the transactions demand for money. In short, the transactions demand for money is positively related to income.

The precautionary motive. People and firms hold money for another reason as well: to protect themselves against adverse happenings or to take advantage of favorable opportunities. When the Dipsy Doodle Noodle Company fails and its inventory of flour is up for grabs, Doughboy Donuts, with readily available funds, buys it up, while the Krinkle-Krisp Kracker Company, whose funds are held in less liquid forms, misses out. Similarly, consider the plight of the Dakota Egg Company, which, because of Dipsy Doodle's bankruptcy, finds itself writing off a substantial expected payment. Yet Dakota must pay its creditors, and will do so by relying on its precautionary balances, which were waiting in the wings for just such an occasion.

"Mad money"—the cash a cautious person takes along on a date just in case he or she is abandoned in the course of the evening—is another example of a precautionary balance.

Precautionary balances, too, are likely to be increased as income rises. Opportunities may well be more available to upper-income families and more profitable firms. It is also likely that an individual or business with larger asset holdings has a higher total liability and thus needs a larger precautionary balance to provide the same protection.

In sum, both transactions and precautionary balances are positive functions of income. Symbolically, $L_1 = f(Y)$, where L_1 stands for these two kinds of money demand and Y stands for income.

The speculative motive. Money, as noted earlier, is one of many assets that an individual may hold. A bond, which yields interest, is a money substitute, and the speculative motive refers to the decision to hold money rather than bonds.[2]

Since bond prices fluctuate, the decision to buy or sell bonds hinges heavily on expected future bond prices. If bond prices are expected to fall in the future, people will hesitate to buy now. Waiting to acquire the bonds after the prices have fallen is surely the wiser option. The purchaser not only pays less then, but is protected against a capital loss should the bonds have to be resold. Rather than buy, the public will prefer to hold money.

When are bond prices likely to fall? No one really knows. But if security prices are, in some historical sense, abnormally high, it's likely that they'll fall rather than rise. In fact, the higher bond prices are, the greater the probability that they will come down.

Remember now that when bond prices are high, interest rates are low (p. 55). And *when bond prices are high and interest rates are low,*

---

[2]The Keynesian analysis posits a two-asset world limited to money and long-term bonds. This restrictive assumption is maintained here even though the same basic outcome can be derived with less stringent conditions.

people would prefer to hold money rather than bonds. Conversely, when interest rates are high, not only can the bond buyer earn a high yield, but because the bonds were bought at low prices, the purchaser stands to obtain a capital gain. Thus, bond buyers will prefer to hold onto fixed-income securities, reducing the amount of money demanded.

The quantity of money demanded for speculative purposes, then, varies inversely with the interest rate. The higher the rate, the less money the public will want to hold; the lower the rate, the greater the quantity demanded. Symbolically, $L_2 = f(i)$, where L_2 is the speculative demand for money and i is the interest rate.

The total demand for money. The public's demand for money at any interest rate is the sum of each individual's and firm's transactions, precautionary, and speculative demands for money. Figure 17.1 sketches out the demand-for-money curve, L. L is composed of two subsidiary curves, L_1 and L_2. L_1 is a straight, vertical, interest-inelastic line that takes that shape by hypothesis: Transactions and precautionary demands are assumed to be independent of the interest rate, being determined solely by the income level. The curve indicates that no matter what the interest rate is, the public's L_1 demand is for $200 billion. The L_2 curve is

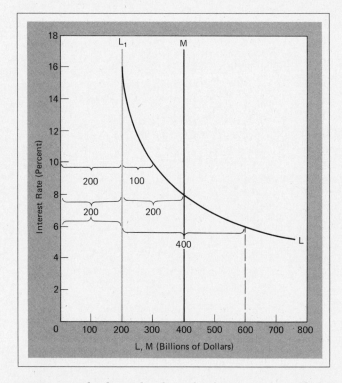

FIGURE 17.1 The demand and supply of money and equilibrium in the money market.

added onto the L_1 curve.[3] Thus, when the interest rate is 16 percent, the public wishes to place all of its non-L_1 balances in bonds, leaving its demand for L_2 equal to zero. However, if the interest rate were 8 percent, the public would want L_2 balances of \$200 billion, which, together with the L_1 demand of \$200 billion, sums to a total money demand, L, of \$400 billion. At 6 percent, a lower rate, the public wants to hold more speculative balances—\$400 billion—and, in addition to the \$200 billion L_1 demand, an L equal to \$600 billion.

Alternative explanations of the demand for money. Some economists have felt that the distinction among transactions, precautionary, and speculative balances is too artificial. After all, one doesn't say that the \$10 bill in my right pocket is for transactions purposes while the \$10 bill in my left pocket is being held for speculative reasons. The important element in the theory is the relationship between the demand for money on the one hand and the level of income and the interest rate on the other. This connection can also be established through (1) inventory theory and (2) the theory of portfolio balance.

Inventory theory and the demand for money.[4] In essence, the theory argues that just as a business maintains material inventories for rather obvious reasons, so, too, people hold inventories of money. When business improves, firms carry larger inventories. So, too, as GNP rises, the public demands more money. Furthermore, when interest rates rise, thereby increasing the cost of carrying inventories, businesses try to economize on their goods in stock. Analogously, businesses and consumers reduce their demand for money balances as interest rates rise, since higher interest rates increase the opportunity cost of holding money. Considering money, then, as an inventory item, the demand for money is positively related to GNP and negatively related to interest rates.

The theory of portfolio balance.[5] Another way of interpreting the demand for money relates to uncertainty and portfolio balance. Since future returns on assets—say, stocks and bonds—are uncertain, a portfolio manager will diversify her assets in order to minimize the risk of loss. In diversifying, the manager will hold a bit of this and some of that, including some money. Money differs from other assets in that a dollar of money today is certain to be worth a dollar of money tomorrow, whereas a dollar put into stocks or bonds may be worth more, but also may be worth

---

[3]The L_2 curve itself is not labeled in Figure 17.1. It is there nonetheless. If the L_1 curve were eliminated by moving the origin of the figure to \$200 billion, so that the line labeled L_1 became the ordinate, the curve that is now labeled L would become the L_2 curve. This follows from the derivation of L, which equals $L_1 + L_2$. Consequently, $L_2 = L - L_1$.

[4]This formulation was devised by W. J. Baumol, "The Transaction Demand for Cash: An Inventory Theoretic Approach," *Quarterly Journal of Economics* 66 (November 1952): 545–556.

[5]This originated with J. Tobin, "Liquidity Preference as Behavior Toward Risk," *Review of Economic Studies* 25 (February 1958): 65–86. (Calculus needed.)

less by tomorrow. Now, as income rises, the value of the total portfolio is likely to increase as well, raising the demand for all assets, money included. If interest rates rise, the rules of asset portfolio balance developed in connection with the economic theory of asset management (pp. 157–161) force a shift in the portfolio, leading to less money held and more of the portfolio devoted to earning assets. So here as well, higher GNP raises money demand, while higher interest rates reduce the demand for money. Figure 17.1 stands unchanged without having to rely on the distinction among transactions, precautionary, and speculative motives.

The supply of money

A good part of this book has been devoted to explaining the role of the commercial banks and the Federal Reserve System in determining the supply of money. It is superfluous to repeat it here, although it is sufficiently important so that you should be reminded of its critical role. The crux of the past discussion is that at any one time there is a specific quantity of money in the economy, jointly determined by the commercial banking system and the central bank. Assume that that quantity is $400 billion, which in Figure 17.1 is portrayed by a vertical line labeled M.

Equilibrium in the money market

Equilibrium is achieved when the quantity demanded equals the quantity supplied. Since all the money in the economy must be held—it's always in someone's possession—equilibrium implies that those who are holding money do so voluntarily; they respond to market conditions that make holding money worthwhile. In Figure 17.1 equilibrium occurs at an interest rate of 8 percent, when the $400 billion money supply is held—voluntarily—with $200 billion each in L_1 and L_2 balances.

Had interest rates been higher—say, 10 percent—only $300 billion in money would have been demanded. The extra $100 billion would have been withdrawn from speculative balances and placed in the bond market. This shift would put pressure on the bond market, raising bond prices and lowering interest rates, until the rate fell back down to 8 percent. Conversely, had interest rates fallen somehow to 6 percent, the public would have wanted to hold $600 billion, an impossibility when only $400 billion is available. Attempting the impossible, the public would have sold bonds for money. This action would lower bond prices and raise yields until the higher interest rates induced the public to reduce the quantity of money demanded to the available supply.

Shifts in supply and demand

Like that of any other commodity, the price of money will respond to changes in supply and demand. For example, if the money supply falls to $300 billion, the interest rate will rise to 10 percent. Similarly, if the demand for money shifts upward by $100 billion, the interest rate will rise to 10 percent. (You might sketch these in on Figure 17.1 to convince yourself.) The economic meaning of these changes may be evident. At this juncture, however, such explanations would divert us from our main task; we will return to them before the end of the chapter. Instead, a brief review of the salient points discussed in this portion of the chapter will prove useful.

Summary

While Keynes viewed the demand for money as a product of a tripartite division of money-holding motives (transactions, precautionary, and speculative), the essential point is that monetary demand depends on income levels and interest rates. At any given interest rate, the demand for money is the sum of the L_1 and L_2 demands, and is inversely related to the interest rate; as interest rates fall, the quantity of money demanded rises. When this negatively sloped demand curve for money, L, is juxtaposed with the vertical supply curve for money, M, an equilibrium interest rate, which equates the quantity of money demanded with the amount available, is determined. The next step is to demonstrate the linkage between the money market and investment in capital goods.

☐ Interest and Investment

Determinants of investment

In all economies some resources are diverted from the production of consumer goods and devoted instead to the production of producer goods or capital, goods that will be used to produce other goods. Business plant and equipment (the buildings and tools) are surely prime examples of capital. Conventionally, residential housing and business inventories are also included in the definition of capital. Investment, the national income definition familiar from Chapter 15, is the change in capital or an increase or decrease in:

a. residential housing,
b. business plant,
c. business equipment, or
d. business inventories.

(Although the term *investment* is used for both real and financial investment, the context will usually indicate which meaning is appropriate. In these chapters the meaning is real investment.)

What induces businesses to invest? As with most questions asked by economists, there is both a simple and a complex answer. The most obvious response is profitability—if the payoff from the investment exceeds the costs, investment will be undertaken; if not, the investment will be rejected. But what determines the profitability of an investment? Surely, no one element can explain profitability; many factors share the stage. You might consider just a few.

Since the basic nature of an investment is its durability, an investment decision involves forecasting the future situation. And, as some anonymous soul remarked: "To prophesy is extremely difficult, especially with respect to the future." Gasoline manufacturers who are contemplating building a new refining plant must consider the demand for gasoline when the plant will begin production as well as for years thereafter. This involves estimating not only the probable demands for gasoline based on the number of vehicles likely to be on the roads and how intensively they will be used, but also the price that can be charged. As we know from microeconomic theory, prices depend on the structure of the market (in the case of the oil industry, this might involve future government intervention) and on the availability and price of substitutes (will the electric automobile be the reality of the future?), as well as on income, tastes, and other variables. Moreover, the tax policies of the federal and local governments, along with a host of possible regulations—for example, pollution controls—must be taken into account. The present existence of excess capacity or, alternatively, a heavy backlog of orders will color the investment decision.

So, too, will the general psychological framework of the present. An optimistic business environment will lead to more positive feelings toward future payoffs, and vice versa when the business community is suffused with gloom. Finally, estimates of input costs—raw materials, labor, and so on—must be made. (What will happen to the price of oil in light of a producer's monopoly? What kinds of demands will be set forth by the unions?) In short, predicting the future is likely to be a complex, not to say hazardous, process surrounded with a large measure of uncertainty.

Nevertheless, investment decisions must be and are made. Businesspeople somehow arrive at an estimate of the profitability of a new investment. In fact, businesspeople face a series of investment decisions: Should a new plant be constructed? If so, how shall it be equipped? If not, how about remodeling an old plant? What about just buying some new equipment, or perhaps muddling along for awhile? And so on. Within some margin of error, it is true that the profitability of each choice can be calculated.

Many decisions, however, are not of the "either-or" but of the "more or less" type. How large shall the new plant be? How many machines shall be bought? Under these circumstances it is possible to array choices in terms of profitability. Consider the case of a moving company that is contemplating purchasing new moving vans. (See Table 17.1).

In light of the company's present backlog of orders, management estimates that the first van costing $8,000 will bring in a 50 percent profit. But if two vans are bought, the second $8,000 investment will return only

TABLE 17.1 Investment Opportunities for a Moving Company

New moving vans	Cost	Profitability
First	$8,000	50%
Second	8,000	40
Third	8,000	20
Fourth	8,000	20
Fifth	8,000	10
Sixth	8,000	0

a 40 percent profit, for it will be idle some of the time. As Table 17.1 indicates, additional vans—up to the sixth—will yield a positive profit. More vans permit greater flexibility; if five families want to move at the same time, the firm will have the equipment to accommodate them all. But on the other hand, when fewer moves are made, more trucks will stay idle and some movers will have to be paid nonetheless. Costs remain roughly the same while revenues fall, so that marginal profitability declines as investment increases (always assuming no modification of underlying circumstances). The relationship between profitability and investment is known as the **marginal efficiency of investment.**[6]

The **marginal efficiency of investment** is the rate of profit earned on additional investments.

Of course, should there be a change in conditions—for example, an increase in population mobility with a rise in the demand for moves—the profitability of *each* investment will increase. Thus, the first truck may now yield 75 percent, the second 65 percent, and so on. Still, the basic principle that the greater the amount invested, the lower the profit rate, holds true.

Our moving company is only one of the millions of businesses making investment decisions in the economy. For each of these investors, an analogous decision-making process can be assumed, so that the Table 17.1 can be replicated many times. Each investor's list of potential investments can be aggregated (in the same manner in which individual demand curves are added to arrive at a market demand for a particular commodity), which will lead to a relationship between potential investment by business and its expected profitability, or a marginal efficiency schedule for the entire economy. Table 17.2 presents such a schedule for a hypothetical economy, while Figure 17.2 plots the data. Both the figure and the table indicate that if $125 billion in new capital goods is put into the production process, business people expect to earn a profit of 10 percent. If an additional $125 billion is invested, bringing total invest-

---

[6]The appendix to this chapter calculates and defines this term more carefully.

TABLE 17.2 A Marginal Efficiency of Investment Schedule

Profitability (percent)	Investment (billions of dollars)
10%	$125
8	250
6	375
4	500
2	625

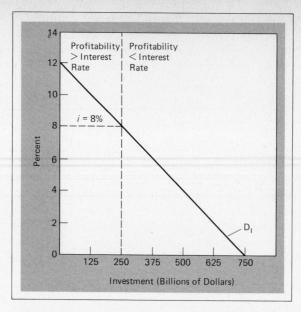

FIGURE 17.2 The demand for investment and the interest rate.

ment to $250 billion, this extra investment will yield only an 8 percent rate of return. Similarly, for a total investment of $375 billion the marginal $125 billion will return only 6 percent. This schedule is, in fact, a demand-for-investment schedule, and the corresponding curve, labeled D_I in Figure 17.2, is the Investment Demand Curve.[7] It is read as follows: If businesspeople want to invest $x billion, they can expect to earn a rate of profit on the marginal dollar equal to y percent. (This is similar to looking at a demand curve for, say, pens and asking, If the public wanted to purchase 9 million pens, how much would the marginal buyer be willing to pay? Granted, this is not the typical way of reading a demand curve, since normally we ask, How much will be bought at a price of P? However, it is equally legitimate.)

The actual volume of investment

This curve of potential investment levels and their respective profit rates is only half the story, since only one level of investment demand can be realized at any moment. We need additional information to determine which of these possible levels will be achieved in practice.

The additional information is the cost of finance. As a first approximation, we can inquire, How much will it cost to borrow the funds needed to finance the investment? To simplify, assume that each firm has access to the bond market and, moreover, that the volume of new financing is small

---

[7]The investment demand curve is derived less intuitively in this chapter's appendix.

relative to that of outstanding bonds. Also ignore self or internal finance. Thus, firms will issue bonds and pay the going yield for them.

What is the going rate of interest? Hasn't that been determined already by the demand and supply of money? Figure 17.1 indicates it to be 8 percent. Consequently, any investment that returns at least 8 percent—which will cover borrowing costs and leave something over for profits—will be undertaken. Conversely, any investment that pays back less than 8 percent will be rejected; such investments will not even recoup the cost of the borrowed funds. In terms of Figure 17.2, the horizontal line drawn in at 8 percent indicates the cost of borrowed funds; where it intersects the investment demand curve, D_I, is the cut-off point between profitable and unprofitable investment opportunities. (Ignore the riskiness of investment for the moment.) Thus, the first $250 billion of investments yield at least 8 percent and should be undertaken, but the next $1 billion and additional amounts will yield less than 8 percent and so should be rejected.

☐ Money, Investment, and GNP

Equilibrium

It is appropriate to weave together the several strands that have been kept separate until now. In the first section of this chapter we established the proposition that

1. The supply and demand for money determine the interest rate.

In the section just completed, you saw that

2. The marginal efficiency of investment and the interest rate jointly determine the level of investment for the entire economy.

Finally, in the preceding chapter you learned that

3. Investment (I), in cooperation with other spending flows, C and G, determines the level of GNP.

Figure 17.3 puts these three relationships together, with (a) reproducing Figure 17.1, (b), Figure 17.2, and (c) Figure 16.5. With the given demand curve for money, L, and the supply, M, equal to $400 billion (a), the interest rate will be 8 percent. At an 8 percent interest rate and investment demand of D_I (b), actual investment will be $250 billion. Moving now to (c), the I of $250 billion is added onto the consumption demand (to simplify, government demand is omitted here), leading to an equilibrium GNP of $2,500 billion.

Shifts of the schedules

Perhaps the operation of the entire aggregate economic system can best be understood by following through the impact of a change in one or

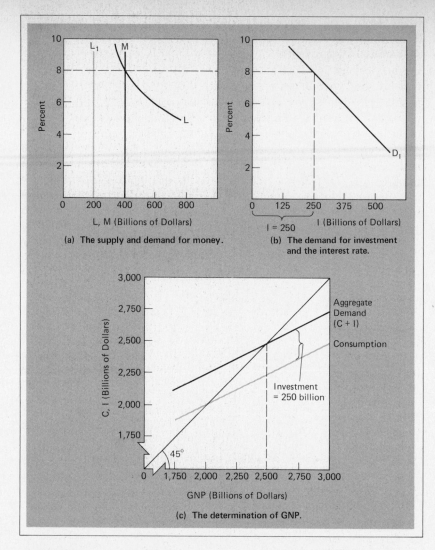

FIGURE 17.3 The interrelationship among money, investment, and gross national product.

another of the key variables. Two such modifications among the many possibilities that might be used as illustrations are (1) an increase in the money supply and (2) an increase in taxes.

An increase in the money supply. The money supply may increase as a result of either an active or a passive stance on the part of the monetary authorities. In the former case the central bankers may buy up government securities or lower the reserve requirement, while in the latter instance they may accommodate commercial bank discount requests or not offset greater deposit creation by the banks from the existing reserve base. No matter how or why, however, the result is a greater amount of money available to the public. But if the public is holding as much money as it wants to, consistent with the prevailing level of interest rates, it will not want to hold the additional money created. It will increase the demand for bonds, which, of course, will drive bond prices up and interest rates down. Interest rates will continue to fall until a level is reached at which the now-increased quantity of money demanded equals the enlarged supply. Figure 17.4(a) shows this graphically: As the money supply rises from $400 billion at M to $600 billion at M′, the interest rate

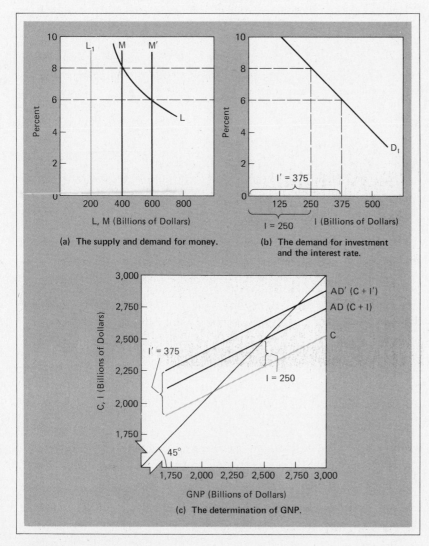

(a) The supply and demand for money.

(b) The demand for investment and the interest rate.

(c) The determination of GNP.

FIGURE 17.4 The impact of an increase in the money supply on interest rates, investment, and gross national product.

drops from 8 percent to 6 percent, where the $600 billion demanded equals the $600 billion supplied.

Repercussions in the investment market follow, for a lower interest rate makes some formerly unprofitable investments profitable. In fact, $125 billion more of investment will be undertaken, so that investment rises from $250 billion to $375 billion, [See Figure 17.4(b).] Finally, the additional investment leads to a larger GNP, moving it upward by a total equal to the increase in spending times the income multiplier. Recalling that the appropriate multiplier in Chapter 16 was 2, the rise in GNP equals $125 billion × 2, or $250 billion. [See Figure 17.4 (c).]

The net result of an increase in the money supply by $200 billion has been to increase GNP by $250 billion. The main point to be understood here is not the quantitative outcome but the direction of the change—*more money means lower interest rates, which result in more investment and a higher level of GNP.* (You should be able to demonstrate that the converse is equally true.)

An increase in taxes

Among the determinants of the profitability of investment mentioned earlier in this chapter was the rate of taxes levied on profits. If tax rates rise, the profitability of investments will, by and large, fall. The reverse will be true for a fall in tax rates on investment. Thus, it is no coincidence that the investment tax credit granted to businesses in 1962 stimulated investment and that its suspension from October 1, 1966, to March 9, 1967, acted to restrain it. Permitting more rapid depreciation write-offs, as the Revenue Act of 1981 did, will also speed up capital spending.

What happens if the government increases corporate income taxes by two percentage points. Clearly this means that in order to obtain an after-tax profit of 4 percent, any investment undertaken will have to pay a before-tax profit of 6 percent. And investments that now yield 1 percent before taxes will earn a return of −1 percent after taxes. Negative-yielding investments will not be undertaken even if borrowed funds are available as free as manna from heaven. In fact, if the interest rate is 8 percent, no investment that returns less than 10 percent will be profitable. In Figure 17.5(b), the demand-for-investment curve has shifted downward by two percentage points, the amount of the tax increase, with D'_I replacing D_I. At the cut-off point only $125 billion will be invested, since at that point the after-tax rate of return will equal the market interest rate. Less investment, however, leads to a reduced GNP; taking the income multiplier into account, a $125 billion fall in I reduces GNP by $250 billion. [See Figure 17.5 (c).] *Higher taxes induce less investment and therefore reduce GNP.* (You should be able to show that a tax cut will raise the GNP level. Try it.)

The role of money and its impact on GNP as discussed in this chapter are in the Keynesian tradition. Money affects interest rates, which in turn influence investment and thereby stimulate or retard GNP. More money

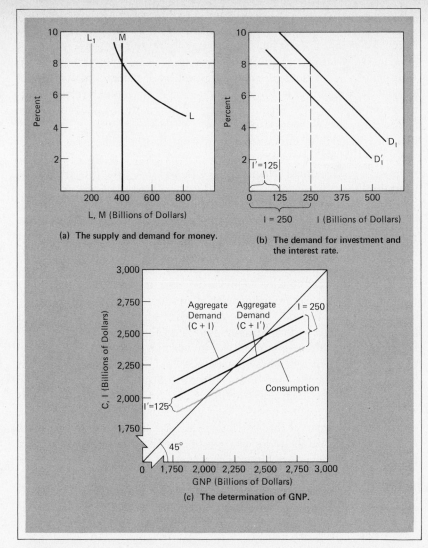

FIGURE 17.5 The impact of a tax increase on investment and gross national product.

lowers interest rates and increases investment and GNP, while a reduced money supply reverses the process—higher interest rates, less investment, and a lower level of GNP. Thus, by appropriately twisting the monetary handles, the Federal Reserve can raise or lower the nation's GNP.

Caveats

A number of caveats are in order. First, the simple theory outlined in this chapter fails to consider feedbacks or interrelationships. Such feedbacks not only complicate the theory but create difficulties for the monetary policy makers as well. A more sophisticated Keynesian theory, which handles some of the interconnections, is considered in the next chapter. Second, the channel from money to interest rates to investment need not be the only path through which money affects economic activity. Alternative explanations of money's impact on economic activity are the subject of Chapter 19. Finally, even if the conceptual relationships between money and economic activity are clearly understood, the complexities of life suggest that even a sophisticated theory cannot be blindly transplanted into a real-world context. The difficulties encountered when monetary policy makers practice their art are related in a number of subsequent chapters, beginning with the second half of Chapter 19.

A brief digression here will serve not only to conclude this chapter but also to bring a degree of realism to the analysis. Up to this point we have made assumptions that require ignoring self-finance as well as the riskiness inherent in any investment. Introducing both of these elements into the analysis fortunately will not modify the essential conclusions. First, consider self-finance. Obviously, not all capital expenditures depend on borrowing from financial institutions or from the money or capital market. Indeed, most companies finance the bulk of their investment outlays with internally generated funds. Nevertheless, self-finance is not costless; opportunity costs must be considered. Is it logical to suppose that a firm that has excess funds will invest in a project that will return 5 percent if the same firm could earn 18 percent by placing these funds in securities? The presumption is that internally generated funds will be valued in market terms and so will fluctuate with market interest rates. A rise in market interest rates will raise the opportunity costs of internal finance and therefore will induce investment restraint even if the firm has all the necessary funds at hand.

Investments are risky, and the longer the term of the investment, the greater the uncertainty connected with it. Thus, acquiring raw-materials inventories that will be used up in the next month's production is relatively riskless, certainly compared to purchasing a jet airliner whose useful life can exceed a decade. In order to reduce risk, many firms require their investments to be paid off in at least three to four years. This implies a minimum net return of 25–33⅓ percent, well above normal real market yields. Will a rise in interest rates from 8 percent to 9 percent affect investments whose payoff is so substantial? The logical answer must be yes. If interest rates rise, the cost of the investment rises, thereby reducing the profit per year obtained from the project. For example, a contemplated plant is expected to cost $4 million and anticipated returns, excluding interest charges, are calculated at $1,320,000 a year. At an annual interest rate of 8 percent, the net return will be $1 million and the investment will pay for itself in four years. It meets a four-year payback criterion. But if interest rates rise to 9 percent the net return will be only $960,000, falling short of the required 25 percent expected rate of return. The investment should be rejected.

In short, while dropping some restrictive assumptions may lead to greater realism, the basic outlines and conclusions of the analysis will not be modified. Other things remaining constant, a rise in interest rates will lead to a reduction in investment and GNP. The converse is true for a fall in interest rates.

☐ Summary

This chapter focused on three relationships:

1. The supply and demand for money as determinants of the interest rate.
2. The interest rate as a contributing element in establishing the volume of investment.
3. The connection between investment and GNP.

While the supply of money is jointly determined by the banking system and the central bank, the demand for money is a result of decisions by individuals and firms. Greater income or lower interest rates will increase the demand for money, while a reduced GNP or higher interest rates will lower it. (In the Keynesian analysis the transactions and precautionary demands for money are sensitive to income while the speculative demand is dependent on the interest rate.) The interaction between the money supply and demand schedules will determine the interest rate in much the same way that any set of supply and demand curves will set the equilibrium price of a commodity. Similarly, an increase in the money supply or a decrease in the demand for money will lower market yields.

Investment demand is predicated on its profitability, itself the outcome of a complex set of economic forces. Nevertheless, a definite connection can be established between the demand for investment and its expected marginal return: the more businesspeople wish to spend on investment, the lower the marginal profit rate that they will be forced to accept. This proposition permits the derivation of an investment demand schedule, representing the array of potential investment expenditures at their respective marginal rates of efficiency. This schedule can be juxtaposed with the interest rate, representing the cost of investing, resulting in the amount of actual investment spending that will be undertaken. That will occur at the point where the yield and the marginal profit are equal. For unless the profit rate on investment is at least as high as the cost of investment funds, investors will lose out.

The following sequence can then be outlined:

1. The demand and supply of money determine the interest rate.
2. The interest rate, in conjunction with the investment demand schedule, determines the actual demand by investors.
3. Investment demand, joined by the demands of consumers (and government units), determines GNP.

When the supply of money increases, the pattern can be traced out by following the three steps just listed: More money leads to lower interest rates, to greater investment spending, and thus to a larger GNP. The opposite will be true for a tax boost, which decreases the profitability of investment, or for a reduction in the money supply, which raises interest rates.

The Keynesian model presented in this chapter, while more complex than the simple paradigm of the last chapter, is still relatively unsophisticated. Introducing self-finance and the riskiness of investment does not really alter the simplicity of the model. Elements that expand and complicate the model while retaining its basic Keynesian thrust are the subject of the next two chapters.

☐ Questions and Exercises

1. Suppose an increase in bond prices led people to anticipate further bond price hikes. How would such beliefs affect the demand for money?
2. a. An increase in the demand for money would lead to changes in interest rates and investment. How could the Federal Reserve offset the impact of this modification in monetary demand?
   b. As businesspeople become more optimistic about the future, the investment demand curve will shift. Again, how can the Federal Reserve nullify this change?
3. You might play around with the slopes of the curves in Figure 17.3.
   a. What will happen to interest rate for a given rightward shift in the money supply if the demand-for-money curve is steeper?
   b. What will happen to investment for a given change in the interest rate if the demand-for-investment curve is flatter?
4. What is likely to happen if the government decides on a loose fiscal policy while the Federal Reserve simultaneously pursues a tight monetary policy? Discuss the impact of this policy mix on interest rates, investment, and GNP. Compare your answer with actual fiscal and monetary policy in 1981.
5. Assume that monetary actions of the central bank affect business expectations so that when interest rates rise, the demand for investment falls. Would the monetary authorities welcome such behavior? Why?

☐ For Further Study

D. E. W. Laidler, *The Demand for Money: Theory and Evidence* (New York: Dun-Donnelley, 1977), provides comprehensive yet succinct coverage of money demand. While knowledge of the IS–LM analysis discussed in the next chapter would facilitate understanding, even a student who has not mastered this tool can profit from the book.

Why businesspeople invest is a subject for a semester in itself. A good many of the theories are covered in D. W. Jorgenson, "Econometric Studies of Investment Behavior: A Survey," *Journal of Economic Literature* 9 (December 1971):

1111–1147. Robert Eisner, *Factors in Business Investment* (Cambridge, Mass.: National Bureau of Economic Research, 1978), offers an alternative to the Jorgenson model. A test of some econometric models of investment behavior presented at a level that is comprehensible to the average student is R. W. Kopcke, "The Behavior of Investment Spending During the Recession and Recovery, 1973–76," Federal Reserve Bank of Boston, *New England Economic Review*, November–December 1977, pp. 5–41. R. E. Hall, "Investment, Interest Rates, and the Effects of Stabilization Policies," *Brookings Papers in Economic Activity* 1 (1977): 61–103, is a difficult but significant article that touches on the Jorgenson model, Tobin's "q theory" of investment, and the importance of the putty-putty versus putty-clay hypotheses.

APPENDIX Financial Mathematics and the Investment Decision

This chapter has asserted that investment decisions depend on the expected profitability of investment and the interest rate. For a given expected investment demand schedule, a higher interest rate chokes off investment by reducing its net return. Conversely, lower interest rates encourage additional investment spending. The purpose of this appendix is to expand on this basic line of thought.

The role of time in investment decisions

Business investment in plant and equipment involves the acquisition of a durable good. The building or machine to be purchased lasts for a certain period, normally some years. As a result, the returns expected from the investment are also received over time.

One consequence of the durability of investment is the need to consider time explicitly in investment decisions. A return of $10,000 today is not the same as a return of $10,000 to be received ten years hence. Ask yourself: Would I be willing to give up $10,000 today in order to be paid $10,000 at some later date? Even if this return were certain, and even if prices and, hence, the purchasing power of the principal, remained stable, it is highly unlikely that you would accept the proposition. Why should you? The $10,000 in your possession today can grow to a larger sum in the future; interest can be earned, and interest accumulates over time. So time and interest are intimately related. Indeed, the reasoning behind the present-value calculation of financial investments (Appendix to Chapter 3) applies equally well to real capital investment.

The marginal efficiency of investment

The discounting formula developed in Chapter 3's appendix can be used to compute the present value of any flow of receipts. However, instead of calculating present value, it will be useful to compute the rate of return or the profit rate of the investment.

Assume that installing a new machine that costs $20,000 nets the investing firm the following profits, which are to be paid at the end of the year:

Year	Annual profits
1	$5,500
2	8,470
3	7,986
4	2,928.20 (includes salvage value)
	$24,884.20

What is the profit rate? It would be incorrect to simply subtract the cost of the machine from the sum of the annual profits ($24,884.20 − $20,000 = $4,884.20) and divide this into the initial cost. The resulting rate ($4,884.20 ÷ $20,000 = 24.42%) ignores the fact that profits in later years are worth less currently than profits in earlier years; time has not been taken into account in the calculation. Instead, a variation of the discounting formula can be used:

$$C = \frac{R_1}{1 + r} + \frac{R_2}{(1 + r)^2} + \frac{R_3}{(1 + r)^3} + \cdots + \frac{R_n}{(1 + r)^n} + \frac{S_n}{(1 + r)^n} \quad (17A.1)$$

C stands for the initial cost of the investment; the R's are annual profits, with the subscripts identifying the year; and S is the salvage value. All of these values are, for the purpose of the calculation, known, but r is unknown and must be solved for. It is the **marginal efficiency of investment** (*mei*).

To calculate the *mei*, which is also the profit rate, for the example given in the last paragraph, solve for r in the following equation:

$$\$20,000 = \frac{\$5,500}{1 + r} + \frac{\$8,470}{(1 + r)^2} + \frac{\$7,986}{(1 + r)^3} + \frac{\$2,928.20}{(1 + r)^4}$$

This solution can be obtained rather easily by using logarithms, but more easily still with an appropriately programmed calculator. The profit rate, r, turns out to be 10 percent, which will discount the annual values to $5,000, $7,000, $6,000, and $2,000, respectively, for a total of $20,000. In other words, an investment that pays the stated income stream and costs the given price will yield the investor a 10 percent return on the investment.

Of course, if any of the variables change—if profits are different from what was planned or if the time pattern is different or if the cost of the investment is modified—the rate of profit will change as well.

The **marginal efficiency of investment (mei)** is the percentage that equates the flow of profits derived from an investment and the cost of that investment.

The investment demand schedule

Each possible investment that a firm could undertake yields an expected profit and involves an outlay. For each of these possible investments, an expected profit rate can be calculated, and the profit rates can be arrayed in order. Some investments yield high rates of return; others yield more modest rates; and still others bring their investors only low returns.

There are two reasons for the decline in profit rates. First, consider the principle of diminishing returns. This principle asserts that if one factor of production is increased while other cooperating factors are not, then although total output will increase, the rate of output will increase at a diminishing rate. Twice as much of the variable inputs will lead to less than twice as much output. In the present context, as capital goods usage increases through new investment, the marginal product of capital, the rate of output increase, will decline. This means that each additional unit of capital will yield a lower absolute return than the previous unit, so the profit rate falls.

Second, if the supply curve of investment goods is a normal, upward-sloping one, an increase in the demand for investment goods (which shifts the demand curve to the right) leads to increased production only at an increased price. Thus, the cost of investment goods rises, again leading to reduced profit rates. For both of these reasons—diminishing returns and the increased cost of investment goods—the profit rate of investment declines as the volume of investment rises.

If the preceding is true for each individual firm, then, by aggregation, it is true for all firms. That is, if each firm can array investment opportunities, ranking them on the basis of their expected return, it is possible to add up the investment opportunities of *each* firm to derive the investment opportunities of *all* firms. The result will be a negative relationship between the rate of profit and the volume of investment for the entire economy. This is the investment demand curve portrayed in Figure 17.2.

Thus, the investment demand curve can be derived with a more solid theoretical basis than the one offered in the body of the chapter. Investment decisions depend on explicit consideration of time relationships. Since all investment opportunities can be ranked on the basis of a common denominator—the profit rate or the marginal efficiency of investment—the conclusion of a negatively sloped investment demand curve is certainly acceptable.

A final note about the cost of investment finance should be added. The interest rate serves to measure the cost of capital throughout the entire analysis. In fact, for a modern corporation the cost of capital is a far more complex phenomenon than finding the interest rate for borrowed funds. Firms have a variety of options, involving both internal and external finance. The costs of debt financing are not independent of the type of debt incurred: corporate debentures or bank loans. Similarly, the cost of finance through issues of common stock is not the same as it would be if preferred stock were sold, and both of these costs are different from those associated with debt finance. And in addition to the market evaluation of the diverse types of financing methods, the tax treatment of different methods is not homogeneous. (Interest paid on bonds is deductible in computing income taxes, but dividend payments are not.) Our earlier discussion made the simplifying assumption of a single interest rate indicating the cost of financing investment. The legitimacy of this assumption hinges on the general consistency of all costs of finance: When one goes up, the others tend to move in tandem. Nevertheless, it is a simplification and as such ought to be kept in mind.

CHAPTER 18

IS–LM Analysis[1]

When Hicks looked back on his "Mr. Keynes and the 'Classics'" piece with the benefit of a good deal of hindsight, he came to the conclusion that . . . his IS-LM apparatus was a useful one for the exposition of Keynes's central ideas in the General Theory.

Alan Coddington, British economist (1979)

CONTENTS

[1]This chapter may be eliminated without damage to continuity.

When the money supply increases, interest rates fall, investment rises, and the level of GNP rises in turn. This is a key lesson of the last chapter. Nonetheless, the lesson is incomplete for the simple reason that a higher level of GNP feeds back to the money market. It was noted in connection with the demand for money that transactions and precautionary demands are determined by GNP [$L_1 = f(Y)$], so that as Y rises, so also will L. But if L increases, so, too, will interest rates. In fact, the linear sequence suggested by the chapter—$\Delta M \rightarrow \Delta i \rightarrow \Delta I \rightarrow \Delta Y$—is best understood as circular:

If that is the case, the analysis must be revised to include the feedback.

One method of solving for equilibrium GNP is the IS–LM apparatus developed by Sir John R. Hicks in 1937.[2] This technique involves distinguishing two separate markets—the financial and the real—solving for equilibrium conditions in each market and then juxtaposing the set of equilibriums to find a unique equilibrium that is common to both markets. Developing that apparatus and exploring some of its implications is the task of this chapter.

☐ The Financial Market: The LM Curve

Recall now the demand for money outlined in the previous chapter. L_1, the transactions and precautionary demand, was declared to hinge on the level of income, Y, so that $L_1 = f(Y)$. On the other hand, speculative

[2]J. R. Hicks, "Mr. Keynes and the 'Classics', A Suggested Interpretation," *Econometrica* 5 (1937): 147–159; reprinted in American Economic Association, *Readings in the Theory of Income Distribution* (Philadelphia: Blakiston, 1951), pp. 461–476.

balances, L_2, were found to be related to the interest rate, so that $L_2 = f(i)$. The demand for money, L, equaled $L_1 + L_2$, and in equilibrium also equaled the supply of money, M. Let us dress up this skeleton by giving the functional relations some specific values. Assume that

$L_1 = .3Y$
$L_2 = 300 - 25i$
$M = 400$

(All absolute numbers are in billions of dollars and all interest rates are expressed in whole numbers.) For L_2, we can derive the following set of values:

i	L_2
4	200
6	150
8	100
10	50

These numbers are independent of the GNP level; that is, they will remain unchanged whether GNP is high or low. This being the case, and remembering that L_1 is dependent on Y (= GNP), we can generate the following:

	Case I (when Y = 500, L_1 = 150)			Case II (Y = 750, L_1 = 225)			Case III (Y = 1,000, L_1 = 300)		
	i	L_2	L_1	L	i	L_2	L_1	L	i	L_2	L_1	L
(1)	4	200	150	350	7	125	225	350	10	50	300	350
(2)	3	225	150	375	6	150	225	375	9	75	300	375
(3)	2	250	150	400	5	175	225	400	8	100	300	400
(4)	1	275	150	425	4	200	225	425	7	125	300	425

For equilibrium in the financial markets, L must equal M. But L = M = 400 in the third row in each of the just presented cases. In case I, equilibrium occurs when GNP = $500 and i = 2%; in case II, when GNP = $750 and i = 5%; and in case III, when GNP = $1,000 and i = 8%. Indeed, each of these—and additional unspecified positions as well—is an equilibrium point. If these equilibrium points were plotted as in quadrant III of Figure 18.1, an **LM curve** would result.

Note the positive slope of the curve. The economic rationale for this positive relationship between interest and GNP is as follows: As GNP increases, more L_1 will be demanded. The demand for money by people and businesses, L, therefore rises and, given a fixed money supply, the equilibrium interest rate will rise. Conversely, a fall in GNP means a reduction in L_1 as, with less business activity, the public holds less money for transactions and precautionary purposes. As L falls and M remains constant, equilibrium requires a drop in interest rates.

The **LM curve** is the locus of equilibrium points in the financial market. It portrays the relationship between interest rates and GNP, where for each combination of interest and income the supply of money equals the demand for money.

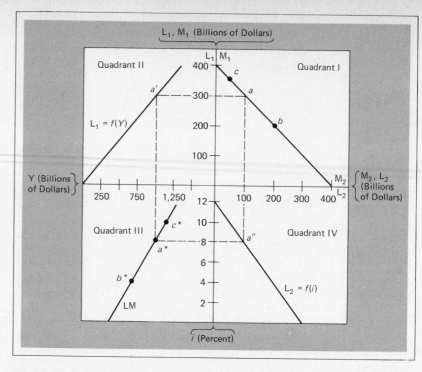

FIGURE 18.1 The LM curve—a geometric derivation.

A geometric generalization of the LM curve

While it is possible to solve for the LM curve arithmetically, it is far easier (although it may not seem so at first) to determine the LM curve geometrically. The technique portrayed by Figure 18.1 builds on material that you've already mastered. Quadrant IV is an almost exact reproduction of Figure 17.1, the demand for money. The only difference is that the demand plotted here is for L_2, not L. So no vertical L_1 segment appears in this quadrant. Instead, the demand for L_1 is shown in quadrant II; the demand for L_1 rises as income, Y, rises, as the earlier analysis noted. Quadrant I portrays M, money supply, divided into two categories—M_1, the supply of money available for meeting L_1 demand, and M_2, the supply used to satisfy L_2 demand. Any point on the negatively sloped line in quadrant I represents a different distribution of the total money supply to its M_1 and M_2 uses. Thus, point *a* indicates $300 (billion; we'll omit this word henceforth) available for M_1 balances and $100 for M_2 balances, for a total money supply of $400. On the other hand, *b* shows an alternative combination of the $400: $200 is allocated to M_1 and $200 to M_2. An infinite number of distributions is possible, all represented by the points on the line. Although no one point is in any way preferred over another, once a distribution has been selected, certain consequences inevitably follow.

Take point a, for example, and follow it leftward until it meets the L_1 line at point a'. By drawing the line parallel to the horizontal axis, you will reach a level of $L_1 = \$300$. It can be said that the demand for L_1 balances at that point equals the supply of money available for it; $L_1 = M_1 = \$300$.

At what income level will the public want to hold $300 in L_1 balances? Drop a perpendicular line from a' to the horizontal axis, Y, and you'll note that the income level is \$1,000. Or, to trace it backwards, if Y = \$1,000, the public's demand for L_1 balances equals \$300. Keep this conclusion in mind for a few moments.

Move back now to point a. Since \$300 of the \$400 money supply has been put into M_1 balances, only \$100 is available for M_2 purposes. Drop a perpendicular line to the M_2 axis from a, and continue past the M_2 axis (it meets the axis at \$100, as expected) until it reaches the L_2 curve in quadrant IV at a''. At this point the demand for L_2 balances equals the M_2 supply available for them; $L_2 = M_2 = \$100$. You can see from the point on the vertical axis level with a'' that the interest rate, consistent with an L_2 demand of \$100, is 8 percent.

Now put the statements together.

1. When the interest rate is 8 percent, the demand for $L_2 = \$100$.
2. When the income level is \$1,000, the demand for $L_1 = \$300$.
3. But the money supply = \$400.
4. Therefore, the demand for and supply of money will be equal when Y = \$1,000 and i = 8%. (Not surprisingly, this precisely matches the earlier arithmetic example.)

This conclusion can be visualized in quadrant III. Drop point a' down into the third quadrant and bring a'' leftward on the same horizontal plane until the two join at a^*. a^* has as its coordinates 8% and \$1,000 and is a point on the LM curve. In this diagram point b^* and c^* are similarly derived, beginning with b and c and working first leftward and downward and then downward and leftward. (The order doesn't really matter.) Since this exercise can be performed for every point on the M line, every point of the LM curve can be derived. Note again that this curve simply indicates the Y,i coordinates of every point at which the demand for and supply of money are equal.

The LM curve is but half the picture. We need a vehicle for choosing among the infinite number of equilibrium points on the LM curve. Will the actual equilibrium please stand up?

☐ The Real Market: The IS Curve

The basic equilibrium condition for GNP, the central point of Chapter 16, is the equality of the aggregate demand and supply for goods and services. This is achieved when businesses receive in sales income all they had anticipated. In the symbols to which you have become accustomed, this is when C + I + G = GNP. Alternatively, equilibrium occurs when outflows from the spending stream are precisely offset by inflows, or when S = I. In Chapter 16, investment was assumed to be constant and the GNP level was adjusted to bring S into equality with the given I. In Chapter 17, investment was made dependent on interest rates, although, of course, investment is influenced by many other variables. Now it becomes possible to posit a number of equilibriums for S and I, depending on GNP (= Y) and the interest rate (*i*).

To be more specific, assume the following:

$$S = -50 + \frac{1}{4}Y$$

$$I = 600 - 50i$$

(Again, the numbers are in billions of dollars while the interest rates are in whole numbers.)

The following table lists some results generated with the two equations.

Case I (Y = 800, S = 150)			Case II (Y = 1,000, S = 200)			Case III (Y = 1,200, S = 250)		
i	I	S	*i*	I	S	*i*	I	S
11	50	150	10	100	200	9	150	250
10	100	150	9	150	200	8	200	250
9	150	150	8	200	200	7	250	250
8	200	150	7	250	200	6	300	250

The **IS curve** is the locus of equilibrium points in the real market. It portrays the relationship between interest rates and GNP, where for each combination of interest and income, saving equals investment.

Note that for each income level there is a unique interest rate that equates S to I (third row). Plotting these in the first quadrant of Figure 18.2, the **IS curve** is generated.

Here also a logical explanation for the negative slope of the IS curve can be advanced. When GNP rises, saving rises. For I to equal a higher S, the equilibrium condition, investment must rise. But a precondition for that is a decline in the interest rate. So equilibrium of saving and investment requires an inverse relationship between income and interest.

A geometric generalization of the IS curve

Once again, the geometry can serve to generalize the derivation of the IS curve. The procedure is analogous to that used in sketching out the LM curve.

Quadrant II reproduces Figure 17.2 in mirror image, going from right to left instead of from left to right. But aside from this shift, which is for diagramatic convenience alone, the meaning is the same: As interest rates fall, investment demand rises.

Quadrant III relates saving to income. As Y rises (toward the bottom of the page), S rises, too. Note that the I and the S scales are identical. Thus, at any point on the scale, such as $200, both I and S equal $200.

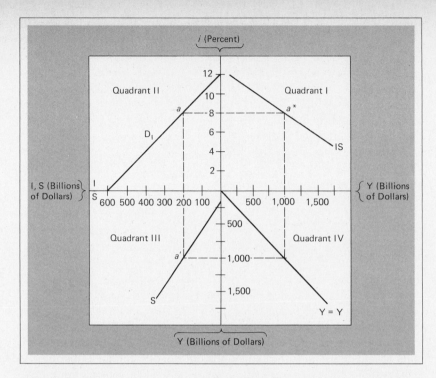

FIGURE 18.2 The IS curve—a geometric derivation.

What are the conditions under which both I and S actually equal $200? Draw a line perpendicular to the I = S axis at $200, until the upper part reaches D_I at *a* and the lower part hits S at *a'*. Then turn this vertical line perpendicular to itself until it touches the *i* axis in quadrant II and the Y axis in quadrant III. You can then see that

1. the interest rate is 8 percent for an investment demand equal to $200.
2. GNP equals $1,000 for S to equal $200.

Thus, an equilibrium I = S is achieved when Y = $1,000 and i = 8 percent. Again, this conclusion is precisely the same as in the arithmetic example.

Completing the geometry requires two more simple steps. First, continue rightward with the line from *a* to 8%, moving into the first quadrant. Do the same with the line from *a'* to $1,000, into the fourth quadrant. The diagonal in the fourth quadrant, Y = Y, is purely a geometric aid, permitting movement around the graph into quadrant I; it has no economic meaning. Once the horizontal line hits the Y = Y diagonal, turn 90° and proceed upward into quadrant I, reaching the *aa** horizontal. The two lines will converge at *a**, whose coordinates are Y = $1,000 and *i* = 8%. This is one point on the IS curve. Of course, an infinite number of points can be similarly derived, starting with a different I = S value. The process will generate a downward-sloping IS curve.

The second blade of the scissors has now been developed and you can proceed to assemble the sections.

☐ IS–LM Equilibrium

Figure 18.3 simply takes the LM curve of Figure 18.1 and places it on diagram together with the IS curve of Figure 18.2. It should not be difficult to find the equilibrium point.

To review: LM represents all the points at which L = M. IS plots all the points at which I = S. Equilibrium requires (1) I = S *and* (2) L = M. In Figure 18.3 that occurs at E, when the GNP level is $1,000 billion and the interest rate equals 8 percent. No other point can make that claim.

Indeed, any other point is a disequilibrium point and will set up a movement leading back to the equilibrium. Consider point F on the IS curve, with an interest rate of 7 percent and a GNP level of $1,200 billion. To be sure, the demand for goods and services equals the amount businesses wish to supply: It is on the IS curve. But it is not on the LM curve. For an income level of $1,200 the demand for L_1 balances is $400 billion, and at an interest rate of 7 percent the demand for L_2 balances is $125 billion. But the supply of money is only $400, so something must give. Either interest rates must rise or GNP must fall, or both. Whatever the reaction, however, the direction is back toward the equilibrium point, E. (To test your understanding, explain why G cannot be the equilibrium point.)

At this point you have seen how a complete GNP equilibrium is obtained. By dividing the economy into two separate markets—the financial market, where decisions are made with respect to holding money or bonds, and the real market, where the spending-saving decisions are made—we can solve separately for equilibrium in each market. In the financial market, the demand for money must be equated with the supply of money. In the real market, savings or the drains from the spending stream must be equaled by investment or additions to the spending stream. When an interest rate and an income level are such that they meet both conditions, then equilibrium in financial and real markets will have been achieved.

How can the IS–LM apparatus be used? The next sections proceed to apply the IS–LM scheme.

☐ Policy and the IS–LM Analysis

In the preceding chapter two policy decisions were evaluated. The same two decisions can be reviewed here. But because the IS–LM

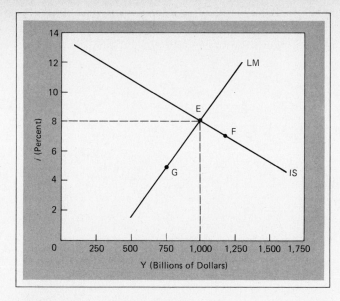

FIGURE 18.3 IS–LM equilibrium.

analytic scheme is more complete, some interesting distinctions can be pointed out. None of the general conclusions will be reversed, however.

An increase in the money supply

When the money supply increases, the M line shifts outward, becoming M'. (See Figure 18.4.) This suggests that with the given allocation of money to M_1 purposes, more would be available to M_2. If so, interest rates would have to fall, since at the existing interest rate L_2 equals the initial M_2; the public would move down the L_2 curve to willingly hold the greater M_2 only if i fell. Alternatively, if M_2 remains unaltered, more funds are available for M_1 purposes. But for L_1 demand to rise, GNP would have to increase. Of course, a third alternative suggests that more of the increased M could be devoted to both M_1 and M_2, which would lead to lower interest rates and higher income. In short, the LM curve shifts rightward, becoming LM', as can be seen in Figure 18.4 (In this diagram the dashed lines running from the M's to the L's are omitted. It would be useful to sketch them in to assure yourself that you know how LM' was derived.)

A rightward shift of the LM curve means that it crosses the IS curve to the southeast and a new equilibrium is achieved. GNP equilibrium now is attained at $1,250, and interest rates decline to 7 percent.

The explanation for this shift is straightforward. The new money supply initially drives interest rates down. But lower interest rates mean more investment (a movement along the D_I curve), which raises income. The

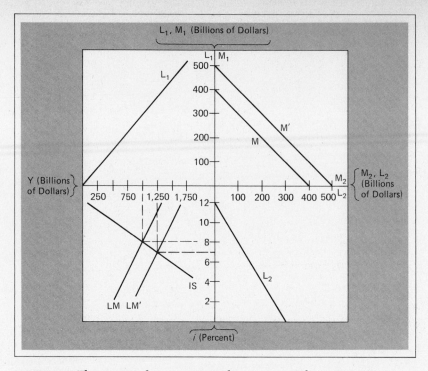

FIGURE 18.4 The impact of an increase in the money supply on IS–LM equilibrium.

increase in GNP has two ramifications: First, saving rises to achieve a new equality with the increased investment level, and second, the demand for L_1 balances increases (a movement along the L_1 curve). In the new equilibrium, the higher income level is consistent with more investment, higher saving, increased money holdings (both L_1 and L_2), and lower interest rates.

Contrast this to the result in Chapter 17. An increase in M led to lower interest rates, higher investment, greater income, and greater saving. However, L_1 demand remained the same, whereas in the more realistic model L_1 demand rose in conjunction with the increased GNP.

An increase in taxes

As you saw in Chapter 17, a rise in income taxes reduces the profitability of investment and thus lowers investment demand. In terms of the IS–LM analysis shown in Figure 18.5, D_I falls to D_I'; the old interest rate is now compatible only with a lower level of investment. For saving to be equal to the reduced investment level, it, too, must decline, and for that to happen, GNP must be smaller. In other words, I = S at the previous interest rate only if GNP is smaller. Alternatively, the old level

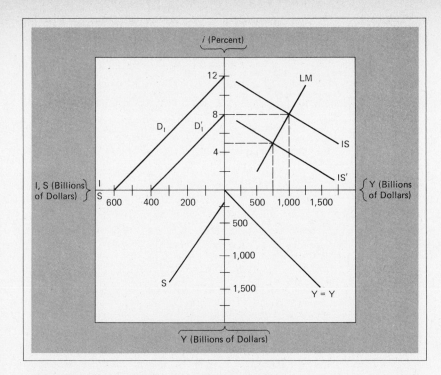

FIGURE 18.5 The impact of a tax on IS–LM equilibrium.

of income can be maintained only if the interest rate is reduced to bring investment on the lowered D_I' curve into equality with the old saving. Thus, either interest rates fall or income levels decline, or both. In all cases, the IS curve shifts inward to IS'. (Again, IS' is portrayed, but its derivation is left to you.)

With the same LM curve but a lower IS curve, overall equilibrium occurs at GNP = $750, $i = 5\%$, both values reduced from the original level. Thus, a tax hike lowers aggregate demand and brings GNP down.

Again, the reasoning is straightforward. Reduced investment leads to reduced GNP. Two consequences follow. First, less income means less saving. Second, less income means a reduced demand for L_1 balances. Since M_1 remains unchanged, however, more of it is available for M_2 purposes. To induce the public to hold the additional M_2 (to move down L_2), interest rates must fall.

Again, the basic conclusions are consistent with those derived in Chapter 17. Reduced investment leads to lower GNP, which leads to lower saving. But in the preceding chapter feedbacks to the financial markets were avoided. In the IS–LM analysis the feedback is intrinsic to the analysis. The conclusion that interest rates fall as the demand for money declines must be noted.

Indeed, because interest rates fall in this version, investment will not fall as much as in the simple Keynesian scheme. For further elucidation, glance at Box 18.1.

☐ IS–LM, Economic Fluctuations, and Anticyclical Policies

It is the nature of a modern mixed economy to undergo fluctuations. At times the economy grows strongly, at other times it moves forward only weakly, while at still other times it turns downward. The IS–LM apparatus can be used to explain what happens.

Slowdowns in economic activity are often related to lack of vigor in investment. When investment demand is low—the theories that explain this are too numerous to detail here—the D_I curve shifts leftward. When

---

BOX 18.1 The Income Multiplier in the IS–LM Analysis

In the preceding chapter's discussion of the income multiplier, you learned the formula for the income multiplier, $k = \dfrac{1}{1 - mpc}$. There, a decrease of investment spending of $100 caused GNP to fall by $200, since $mpc = 0.50$. Here, the $mpc = 0.75$ and the multiplier should be 4.

An alternative way of calculating the multiplier follows from solving the basic equation $\triangle GNP = \triangle Sp\,(k)$, where $\triangle Sp$ is the change in spending

and therefore, $k = \dfrac{\triangle GNP}{\triangle Sp}$. Thus, in Chapter 16, $\dfrac{-250}{-125} = 2$.

Now check the multiplier for the decrease in investment in the present case. The tax boost reduced investment initially by $200, and in its wake GNP fell by $250. Thus,

$$k = \frac{-\triangle GNP}{-\triangle Sp} = \frac{\$250}{\$200} = 1.25$$

Why?

The explanation hinges on the LM curve. As noted in the text, the decline in income reduces the interest rate. But at a lower interest rate investment increases. Thus, although the D_I curve shifted downward, the lower interest rate induced a movement *along* the D_I curve, from $0 (at 8%) to $140 (at 5%). True, the initial decline in investment was $200, but it was offset to a degree by the $140 investment generated by the lower interest rate. The negative action of the multiplier was attenuated.

This discussion suggests that there is no cut-and-dried method for calculating the multiplier, except after the fact. Policy makers who are deciding the extent of a tax change—or, for that matter, a modification in monetary policy—may well be facing uncertain results. Humility should surely be a characteristic of a policymaker.

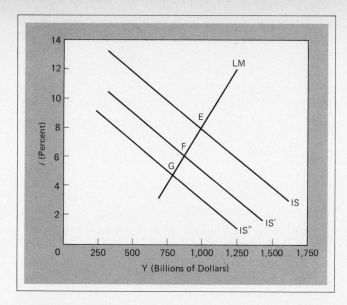

FIGURE 18.6 Shifting IS curves during an economic contraction.

this happens, the IS curve shifts leftward, too. In Figure 18.6 the original equilibrium is at E, the intersection of IS and LM, with an income of $1,000 billion and an interest rate of 8 percent. With the backward shift of the IS curves, a new intersection of IS′ at F, where Y = $875 and $i = 6\%$, results. If consumers respond by changing the propensity-to-consume schedule, fear of unemployment leading them to save more of their current income, the downturn will be intensified as decreasing consumer demand joins a falling investment demand. The IS curve shifts even farther leftward, to IS″, reducing income and interest rates further, until G is reached. Indeed, falling income and interest rates are both character-istic of economic contraction. (If the assumption of a fixed money supply is dropped, recognizing that banks create money in response to loan demand, the economic slowdown will be accompanied by reduced loan demand and less money. This will cause the LM curve to shift leftward, too.)

It is rather obvious that a reversal of the shift in the IS curve or an offsetting shift of the LM curve is needed to bring the economy back to its original position. Both monetary and fiscal policy can assist in bringing about such a remedy.

Monetary policy can, by increasing the money supply, shift the LM curve rightward. The fiscal authorities can work to reverse the movement of the IS curve by reducing taxes on consumers or investors. In an expanded model the government sector can be included in the system, and then a rise in government spending will also shift the IS curve upward. (You might sketch out the needed shifts.)

Two interesting points can be included here. First, some economists argue that expansionary fiscal policy can never work in the absence of expansionary monetary policy. These economists insist that increased government expenditures would drive interest rates upward, which would result in a **crowding out** of private expenditures by an equivalent amount. One way to validate this argument is to construct an LM curve that is perfectly inelastic, a straight vertical line.

To demonstrate this assertion, first a government spending curve will have to be introduced. Assume that government spending is independent of either the interest rate or the level of GNP, an assumption that can be justified by conceiving of the government's budget as determined by long-term national needs. The vertical line at $100 in quadrant II of Figure 18.7 represents the assumed volume of government spending. The I line is now relabeled "I + G," and the D_{I+G} curve is shifted leftward by $100 billion. Since the S curve is assumed to be unchanged, the IS curve in quadrant I shifts rightward by $400. (Remember the multiplier.) Figure 18.7 can now be used to demonstrate total crowding out, using the old and new IS curves and the postulated vertical LM curve. Let government spending increase from $0 to $100, which, as you've just seen, shifts the IS curve from IS to IS'. To be sure, interest rates rise, but

Crowding out refers to the reduction in private investment that is caused by an increase in government spending.

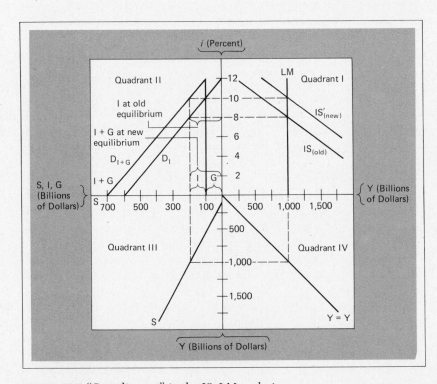

FIGURE 18.7 "Crowding out" in the IS–LM analysis.

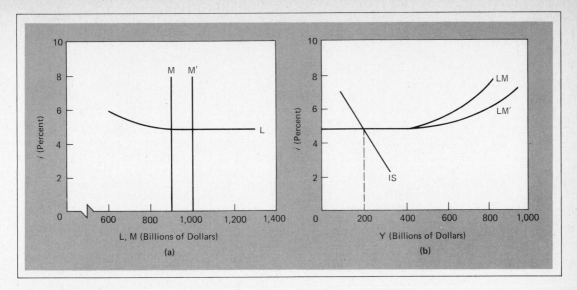

FIGURE 18.8 The liquidity trap and monetary policy.

the GNP level remains unchanged at $1,000. This is possible only if I falls by as much as G has increased. You can see this from quadrant II of Figure 18.7; while G has risen from $0 to $100, I has fallen from $200 to $100, a consequence of the higher interest rate. Thus, an increase in government spending unaccompanied by an increased money supply cannot increase GNP.[3] Total crowding out requires some highly implausible assumptions and is perhaps one of the reasons that this view has not gained much support.

At the other extreme lies the sterility of monetary policy. Keynes claimed that at some high level of bond prices all will agree that further increases are unlikely. Of course, this means that interest rates will have fallen as low as possible. Under such circumstances the demand for money becomes perfectly elastic, as shown in Figure 18.8(a) and the corresponding LM curve in Figure 18.8(b). In the **liquidity trap,** as this position is called, increases in the money supply from M (= $900 billion) to M′ ($1 trillion) in Figure 18.8(a) do not lower interest rates and therefore cannot induce added investment and higher income levels. Similarly, in Figure 18.8(b) the increased money supply leads to a new LM curve, LM′. Unfortunately, the segment of the LM′ curve that is intersected by the IS curve remains unaffected, and therefore the equilibrium GNP stays unchanged at $200 billion.

While few people believe the liquidity trap to be more than a

In the **liquidity trap,** any increase in the money supply is hoarded by the public; none of it is used to acquire bonds.

---

[3] Alternative paths to obtain the same crowding-out result may be found in Keith M. Carlson and Roger W. Spencer, "Crowding Out and Its Critics," *Federal Reserve Bank of St. Louis, Review* 57 (December 1975): 2–17.

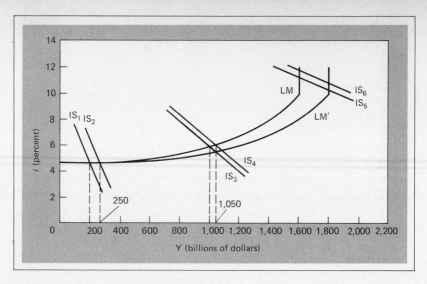

FIGURE 18.9 A generalized IS–LM diagram.

theoretical curiosity, the concepts of the liquidity trap and the crowding-out effect suggest that the shape of the LM curve—and, by extension, the IS curve—is likely to be important in applying policy. Figure 18.9 generalizes the theoretical possibilities and suggests the relative strengths of monetary versus fiscal policy. The LM curve has three segments: (1) the perfectly elastic liquidity trap, running from an income of 0 to $400 billion; (2) a segment of varying elasticity, from income levels of $400 to $1,600 billion; and (3) the perfectly inelastic, "crowding-out" segment at a GNP level of $1,600 billion.

Segment 1 is a reproduction of Figure 18.8; it is clear that an expansionary monetary policy will be ineffective—a change from LM to LM' does not increase income. On the other hand, an expansionary fiscal policy, a shift from IS_1 to IS_2, will increase GNP from $200 billion to $250 billion.

In the second segment IS_3 intersects LM at an income level of $1,000 billion. Both monetary and fiscal policy can bring GNP up to $1,050 billion, the former by a shift from LM to LM' and the latter by a shift from IS_3 to IS_4. Theoretically at least, both policies are equally effective.

Finally, in the third segment an increase from IS_5 to IS_6 will not affect income; there is just not enough money to sustain a higher level of income than $1,600 billion. Fiscal policy will prove futile. But since the constraint is an inadequate money supply, an increase in M will alleviate the difficulty and permit a further expansion of GNP. (Test yourself by working out the effectiveness of a decision to reduce spending.)

☐ IS–LM and Monetary Indicators

One of the issues to be discussed in Chapter 20 is that of how one can identify movements in economic activity that call for a response by the policy makers. The IS–LM framework serves beautifully to pose the problem.

Consider first a situation in which interest rates fall but the money supply remains unchanged. This fall in interest rates can occur for one of two reasons—the LM curve shifted outward or the IS curve shifted inward. For the LM curve to shift in the absence of a change in M, the demand for money balances—either L_1 or L_2—must decrease (the curves must shift, L_1 rightward and/or L_2 leftward). If the monetary authorities were satisfied with the condition of the economy prior to the shift, the appropriate reaction would be to decrease M consistent with the public's desire for less money. With the removal of some money, the LM curve would be moved back to its initial position.

Consider the example portrayed by Figure 18.10. Say that, because of electronic funds transfers, businesses are able to economize on their money holdings. As a result, the transactions balance demand curve shifts

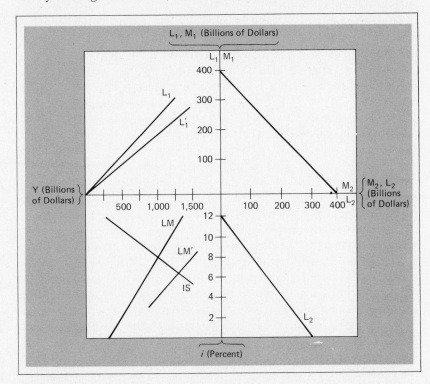

FIGURE 18.10 The impact of a decrease in the demand for money on IS–LM equilibrium.

from L_1 to L_1'. LM shifts to LM', intersects IS at a lower point, and reduces equilibrium interest rates from 8 percent to 6.5 percent. However, the reduced rate of interest induces greater investment spending and GNP, a consequence that is not desired by the authorities (by hypothesis). So the central bankers will employ their instruments to reduce M and thereby return LM to its previous position. (An interesting exercise would be to calculate the precise decrease in M. It can be done by using Figure 18.10. Try it by working from the desired equilibrium to the monetary conditions needed to justify it.)

But what if the decline in interest rates were due to a downward shift in the IS curve perhaps because investors foresaw a reduced demand for their products. Figure 18.5 showed a downward shift of D_I to D_I', a corresponding decline of IS to IS', and the obvious drop in the interest rate. The appropriate response of the monetary authorities to restore the original equilibrium GNP *should* be to increase money supply, shifting the LM curve rightward. (Take another look at Figure 18.9. If IS_4 had shifted downward to IS_3, a rightward shift of LM to LM' would bring GNP back to its former equilibrium position.) Would the authorities react in this way? Would they not decrease M in order to raise interest rates back to their initial level?

The indicator issue should be quite clear by now. If the monetary authorities pursue *interest rate indicators*, their actions will be appropriate if the root cause is a shifting LM curve. But if the interest rate change is due to an IS shift, not only will the interest rate target lead to a misdiagnosis but the implied remedy will exacerbate the problem. On the other hand, *money supply indicators* present problems of their own. True, in the case of the IS shift, the authorities would have avoided the error that would have been caused by pursuing an interest rate target. However, a money supply indicator would have misled them if the LM curve had shifted. For example, a decline in the demand for money would not have altered the money supply. The authorities would not have received a signal calling for action. Yet an offsetting policy to contract the economy surely should have been considered.

This conflict between those who favor interest rate targets and those who advocate monetary targets can be reduced to a question of fact: which is more likely to shift, the IS curve or the LM curve? While the controversy has not yet been settled, the pendulum has definitely swung away from full reliance on interest rate indicators. A great deal of attention is being paid to movements in the money supply.

This swing is due partly to the elements in the analysis just presented. But there is another reason that should be noted: the distinction between nominal and real interest rates. The inflation of the past decade has made the nominal interest rate an unreliable target. When prices are relatively stable, high interest rates signal monetary tightness and low interest rates indicate monetary ease. But when prices rise at double-digit annual rates, even a 20 percent interest rate may not be considered high. Real interest rates, of course, and not nominal interest rates are the appropriate indicators. In Chapter 3 you learned that real interest rates are not easily calculated, since they depend on expected rates of inflation. (Business managers contemplating new investment must consider future costs and therefore must program future inflation rates into their calculations.) There is as yet no precise method for projecting the inflation rate, and hence the real rate cannot be computed. Money supply data, on the other hand, require no adjustment for inflation.

Nevertheless, most economists favor eclecticism—they watch both the money supply and interest rates.

☐ Inflation: An Exercise

This chapter closes with a problem: How will inflationary expectations affect the IS–LM equilibrium? You will be able to answer this most easily by breaking the general issue into the more basic subissues.

1. How will the anticipated inflation affect consumer spending and saving decisions?
2. How will investors modify their investment plans if they expect prices to rise?
3. Will the public want to hold more or less money for transactions and precautionary balances if inflation is believed to be imminent?
4. How will speculative activity be affected—will the market participant want to hold more money or buy more fixed-income bonds—when the public anticipates that goods and services prices will move upward?

A good way to check the accuracy of your analysis is to ask whether your calculated outcome sounds right. Does it make sense in light of your own experience?

☐ Summary

While the analysis and conclusions of the past few chapters are not invalidated, the IS–LM technique does broaden the basic Keynesian theory of macroeconomic equilibrium. The IS–LM method requires the construction of separate equilibrium conditions for the real market, comprising the demand for investment and the supply of saving, and for the financial market, consisting of the supply and demand for money. The values of GNP and interest that are simultaneously equilibriums for the real and financial markets become the ultimate equilibrium values.

An increase in the money supply shifts the LM curve rightward and drives interest rates down and GNP up. On the other hand, an increase in taxes moves the IS curve leftward, reducing both interest rates and GNP.

Should the economy undergo contraction as the IS curve shifts leftward, a rightward shift of the IS curve induced by fiscal policy and/or a rightward shift of the LM curve encouraged by monetary policy constitute appropriate discretionary responses by the public authorities.

How effective these monetary and fiscal actions will be depends on the slopes of the IS and LM curves. If the LM curve is vertical, fiscal policy will prove impotent. Increased government expenditures will simply "crowd out" an equivalent dollar total of private spending. Monetary policy, however, will be very effective. On the other hand, a flat LM curve will lead to the reverse results—potent fiscal policy and sterile monetary policy. Of course, between these extremes lies a rising LM curve, which provides a setting for utilizing both types of macroeconomic policy tactics.

The IS–LM apparatus is also useful in understanding the monetary indicator problem. Whether the LM curve is more stable than the IS curve, so that the money supply is a better indicator, or more unstable, so that interest rates provide better indications, can be understood by playing with the IS and LM curves. In practice, however, interest rate indicators have been shunted aside, largely because of the unknown impact of expected inflation on real interest rates.

☐ Questions and Exercises

1. What will be the outcome for a given change in the money supply if (a) investment demand is extremely responsive to interest rates and if (b) investment demand responds only weakly to changes in interest rates? Work out the two cases separately and see how each affects GNP and interest rates.
2. Explain and sketch out what happens to the IS and LM curves and their underlying components when (a) the monetary authorities decrease the supply of money and when (b) the fiscal authorities rebate a given amount to each taxpayer.
3. The following relationships can be used to determine an IS–LM equilibrium (all values are in dollars except for interest rates, which are given in whole numbers):

$C = 750 + 0.75\ Y$ (Can you use it in this form?)
$I = 250 - 10\ i$
$L_1 = 0.15\ Y$
$L_2 = 400 - 20\ i$
$M = 500$

   a. Explain the meaning of each equation.
   b. Use them to find the IS and LM curves, and solve for equilibrium Y.
   c. Calculate and explain what happens to Y when M falls to 400.
   d. Calculate the new equilibrium when I rises to 350.
   e. Assume that at each income level people want to spend 100 more on consumption. Calculate the new equilibrium Y and compare your result to that obtained in (d). Comment on the two outcomes.
4. Draw an IS–LM diagram. Indicate in the diagram a point that is not on either

the IS or the LM curve. Explain how equilibrium would be achieved when starting from this nonequilibrium position.

5. When will interest rate movements serve as a better indicator for the monetary authorities than the supply of money? Why?

□ For Further Study

Additional information on the IS–LM technique and its applications may be found in any intermediate-level macroeconomics textbook. An interesting geometric extension of IS–LM analysis to three dimensions can be seen in J. W. Conard, *An Introduction to the Theory of Interest* (Berkeley: University of California Press, 1966), chap. 11. Robert H. Scott provides a simple empirical model in "Elements of Hicksian IS and LM Curves for the United States," *Journal of Finance* 21 (September 1966): 479–488. The Hall article mentioned at the end of the last chapter also presents some empirical estimates of the IS and LM curves.

"Crowding Out and Its Critics," by K. M. Carlson and R. W. Spencer, Federal Reserve Bank of St. Louis, *Review* 57 (December 1975), uses IS–LM techniques to examine the conditions for the crowding out of investment by government deficit spending. The possibility that government deficits might crowd in or induce investment expenditures is discussed in V. V. Roley, "The Financing of Federal Deficits: An Analysis of Crowding Out," Federal Reserve Bank of Kansas City, *Economic Review*, July-August 1981, pp. 16–29.

Interest rate versus money supply targets are examined using the IS–LM analysis in W. Poole, "Optimal Choice of Monetary Policy Instruments in a Simple Stochastic Macro Model," *Quarterly Journal of Economics* 84 (May 1970): 197–216.

CHAPTER 19

Money and the Economy: Variations on a Keynesian Theme

If . . . we are tempted to assert that money is the drink which stimulates the system to activity, we must remind ourselves that there may be several slips between the cup and the lip.

Lord Keynes (1936)

Remember that time is money.

Benjamin Franklin (1748)

CONTENTS

The Impact of Monetary Changes on Investment, Consumption, and Government Spending

Lags and the Money Supply

Summary

Money affects interest rates and, thus, investment and GNP. This statement sums up the central theme of Chapter 17. But this impact on investment, and specifically on plant and equipment investment, is not the only path by which money influences the economy. Its effect on economic activity is far more pervasive, extending to other forms of investment spending, especially housing, as well as consumer and government expenditures. Consequently, the first purpose of this chapter is to broaden the analysis of past chapters to include these other elements.

Increasing the realism of the analysis by introducing a more complete exposition adds an additional dimension to the Keynesian model. It also enables the reader to proceed to an important issue, that of lags in effect. The question to be explored is simply, How quickly does economic activity respond to monetary actions? For policy purposes it really is not enough to know the direction of influence—that, for example, an increased money supply induces economic expansion. We must also know how quickly or slowly such actions work. The second purpose of this chapter, then, is to investigate the length of time it takes for changes in the money supply to exert their impact on the economy. Essentially, this chapter follows the Keynesian tradition, leaving a discussion of monetarism to the next chapter.

☐ The Impact of Monetary Changes on Investment, Consumption, and Government Spending

In Chapter 17 it was shown that lower interest rates increase the demand for capital goods: Businesses decide to spend more as the lower interest charges increase the profitability of new capital spending. The rise in investment spending leads to a larger GNP. (Note that this process is symmetrical: Higher interest rates choke off investment and reduce GNP.)

This demand aspect is but one of the possible channels through which monetary changes may influence spending. Supply, too, must be considered. Indeed, the impact of money and interest rates on the supply of credit is extremely important in the housing market as well as in government spending.

Housing

Few people own sufficient assets to finance their homes from their own wealth. Instead, most purchases of residential housing rely on borrowed funds. How do higher interest rates affect the *demand* for housing? Will fewer houses be bought if interest rates on mortgages move upward?

At first blush, one would expect that higher interest rates would reduce the amount of housing the public desires. After all, higher interest charges lead to more expensive housing, and as the price rises, the quantity demanded should decline. Thus, if mortgage rates rise from 13 percent annually to 13½ percent, the repayment of principal plus interest on a 25-year, $25,000 mortgage will rise from $84,585 to $87,453, an increase of $2,868 in the outlay for the structure.

However, the issue appears less clear-cut than these calculations suggest. First, when one is computing the monthly carrying charges on this mortgage, the difference between the two annual rates is not substantial. It costs $281.95 a month at 13 percent, but only $9.56 more per month at the 13½ percent annual rate. Is this small monthly difference likely to deter a family that is intent on finding and financing a house? Moreover, even this small extra monthly cost can be absorbed by stretching out the mortgage. A 35-year, $25,000 mortgage debt carries a monthly carrying charge of only $283.83. To be sure, the total outlay by the mortgagee over time is significantly larger—$119,208.60 instead of $87,453.00—but the monthly effort is not. And there is good reason to believe that it is the monthly carrying charge, not the total financing bill, that is crucial in the decision to acquire a house. (Note, too, that the larger interest payment of the extended mortgage is deductible from income taxes, so that the net cost of the higher interest burden is lower, possibly substantially lower, than the gross cost.) In short, higher interest rates may not deter demand for residential housing very much, either because the higher charges are not significant or because they can be offset by varying other contract terms.

Does that mean that housing escapes the restrictive effect of high interest rates? The opposite would certainly appear to be true from Figure 19.1, which plots interest rates against residential construction. The supply of housing certainly appears to have varied with the cost of finance.

If the demand for housing is not much affected by interest rates, perhaps the supply of financing is. It is necessary first to make a few comments about the nature of mortgage loans. The initial point is that virtually all states have passed usury legislation that limits the interest rates lenders can charge. Of course, these usury laws vary widely both in terms of the maximum rate permissible—from Pennsylvania's 6 percent to Rhode Island's 21 percent—and in the extent of the exemptions and exceptions they permit.[1] Nevertheless, their existence was a fact of life

---

[1] For a summary of the usury laws of all states prior to passage of DIDAMCA see *Mortgage Banker Magazine*, October, 1978. For post-DIDAMCA legislation, see *Issues in Bank Regulation*, Summer, 1982.

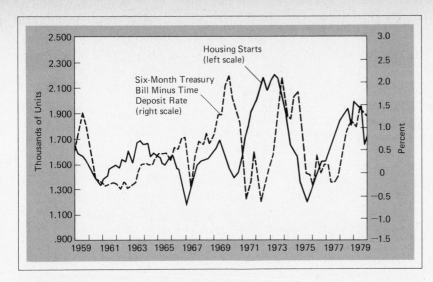

FIGURE 19.1 Housing starts and interest rates.

Source: Federal Reserve Bank of Boston, *New England Economic Review*, September-October 1979, p. 61.

prior to passage of the Depository Institutions Deregulation and Monetary Control Act of 1980. These maximums usually apply to loans on owner-occupied residential housing.

Second, 20 percent of all new housing is financed with insurance provided by the Federal Housing Administration (FHA) or a guarantee of the Veterans Authority (VA). While the latter is limited to veterans, FHA eligibility is not restricted to any specific group of purchasers. However, in both cases the mortgage must meet VA or FHA terms. One of these conditions is a maximum rate that the lender may charge; in 1980, this maximum averaged about 12 percent per annum.

Now try a little role playing. You are a commercial bank lending officer charged with making profitable loans in the pre-1980 period. You have been generous in providing mortgage loans all along, since the interest rate you charged was both high enough to meet your profit target and superior to that available on alternative lending opportunities. However, in the past few months the money supply has declined and interest rates have risen. Indications are that this trend will continue for some time. High-grade corporate borrowers are willing to pay 16 percent, but because of the ceilings on mortgage rates you may not charge private mortgage borrowers more than 10 percent. To whom would you lend?

Surely you would lend more to the higher-paying corporate borrowers than to the potential homeowners seeking financing. You would tighten mortgage terms by raising your rates to the maximum levels permissible when such ceilings exist, but the amount of mortgage funds sought even at that rate may well exceed the amount you want to make available. You would then dissuade borrowers by means of outright refusal or, in a less obvious manner, by increasing other mortgage terms, such as the percentage to be paid down. Whereas a 10 percent down payment might have been acceptable last year, with the bank willing to lend the remaining 90 percent, now you may insist on one-quarter or one-third down. Since relatively few people will be able to come up with this large a down payment, fewer mortgages will be issued.

Interest rate ceilings on deposits have also reduced the availability of mortgage funds. Commercial banks and thrift institutions have had to contend with the more attractive interest rates offered to depositors by alternative investments. The resulting outflow of funds, which was moderated but not halted by permitting depository intermediaries to issue money market certificates after 1978, meant that bankers had fewer funds available for mortgage lending.

The gradual ending of interest rate restrictions on deposits and the overriding of state usury laws by the Depository Institutions Deregulation and Monetary Control Act may cause additional funds to flow to the housing sector. Yet another influence may continue to limit mortgage supply, namely, the impact of inflation. In recent years housing prices have shot upward (64 percent between 1976 and 1979), forcing home purchasers to seek ever-larger mortgages. This is compounded by rising mortgage interest rates. (In 1976 the average rate was 8.99 percent; by the end of 1980 it stood at 12.65 percent, 41 percent more.) The combined result is a larger monthly outlay required of the borrower, which leads to additional loan rejections. This stems from bankers' concern about borrowers' ability to carry loans. To determine whether a potential borrower can finance a loan of a given size, bankers calculate the monthly mortgage payment as a fraction of the borrower's income. They turn down loan applicants whose carrying ability does not meet their preestablished rules of thumb. Since mortgage financing costs have risen more than income, more and more potential homeowners find themselves on the reject list.

In short, whether the weakness in the housing market stems from demand or supply, higher interest rates have reduced the amount of mortgage financing and, thus, had a negative impact on housing construction. On the other hand, when interest rates have declined, the housing sector has been revitalized.

Inventory investment

Business investment in inventories is closely related to sales.[2] As sales rise, inventories decline, leading sellers to restock their shelves and bins. Indeed, the fluctuations in inventory as sales rise and decline are often

[2]While this analysis deals only with inventory investment, there is evidence that supports the theoretical framework described here as applicable to investment in plant and equipment, too.

JAWS

The killer-shark interest rate policy of the Federal Reserve System has again chewed up the housing industry for this year, and will soon attack next year's housing.

Millions of building workers are laid off, while millions of would-be home-owners are frustrated by exorbitant mortgage rates.

Why must housing always be the victim of the Fed's yo-yo theories of money manipulation?

Maybe they should hear more from all of us. Write your views to The Honorable Paul A. Volcker, Chairman, Board of Governors, Federal Reserve System, Washington, D.C. 20551.

James E. Stewart

James E. Stewart, Chairman of the Board and Chief Executive Officer
Lone Star Industries, Inc., One Greenwich Plaza, Greenwich, Connecticut 06830
Reprints on request to Dept. C. Permission granted to reproduce.

LONESTAR

Number One in Cement . . . Serving America's Great Builders.

No more yo-yo interest rates!

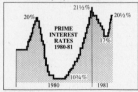

PRIME INTEREST RATES 1980-81

20% 21½% 20½% 17% 10¾% 1980 1981

Wide fluctuations cause instability

An advertisement sponsored by Lone Star Industries, that appeared in a number of national newspapers to protest the impact of Federal Reserve interest rate policies on the housing industry.
Courtesy of Lone Star Industries.

cited in explaining minor dips and upturns in the economy. The mechanism that relates investment to sales is the **theory of the accelerator.**

Table 19.1 may clarify the accelerator relationship. Assume that the typical businessperson keeps $2 in inventory for each dollar's worth of sales. In 1982 sales are $100,000, and the required inventory of $200,000 is held. Thus, investment in inventory is zero. During 1983 the firm's sales double to $200,000, requiring an investment in inventory of $200,000 (column 5) to bring the required inventory to $400,000 (column 4). The percentage change in sales is 100 percent (column 3), but the percentage change in inventory investment is infinite (200/0, column 6). In 1984 sales double again, requiring an inventory twice as large as formerly and a 100 percent inventory investment. Sales keep rising, and in 1985 they reach $600,000. However, this 50 percent sales increase, leading to a required inventory of $1,200,000, means that investment in new inventory is the same as in the last year, $400,000, which is a zero percentage change from 1984. Finally, as sales stabilize at the $600,000 level and inventories are maintained at the new, higher level of $1,200,000, inventory investment falls to zero, a 100 percent decline. Contrast the entries in column 3 with those in column 6; inventory investment reacts in a magnified or accelerated fashion to changes in sales. Unless sales rise by constant *percentages*, inventory investment will fail to keep pace.

The accelerator theory has been made more complex by introducing variables that destroy the fixed relationship between sales and inventory investment. For example, pressure on capacity during periods of strong business activity may well intensify the accelerator effect, while available capacity during recessions might weaken the accelerator.

Interest rates, too, may play a role. Interest rates reflect the costs of maintaining inventory; they represent the opportunity cost of keeping funds tied up in holding stocks of goods. Higher interest rates would induce businesspeople to cut back on inventory, while the reverse would be true of lower interest rates.

TABLE 19.1 An Example of the Accelerator: Inventory Investment (thousands of dollars)

Year	Sales	Change in sales	Required inventory	Inventory investment	Change in inventory investment
(1)	(2)	(3)	(4)	(5)	(6)
1982	100		200	0	
1983	200	100%	400	200	infinite
1984	400	100%	800	400	100%
1985	600	50%	1200	400	0%
1986	600	0%	1200	0	-100%

Consumption

How do consumers respond to increases or decreases in the money supply or to the lower or higher interest rates that result? On the analogy of business investment, it could be anticipated that changes in interest rates affect the costs of consumer borrowing. Higher interest rates should reduce consumer borrowing, especially to finance such postponable consumer durables as automobiles, furniture, and appliances. Of course, this assumes that consumers are aware of changing interest rates. Indeed, since the Truth-in-Lending Act of 1969, all consumers must be informed of the percentage rate and the dollar amount of any finance charges involved in their borrowing or installment plan purchases.

Despite this Act, many consumers appear to be unaware of the interest rates they pay. In a study comparing consumer perception of interest rates before and after the Truth-in-Lending Act, Lewis Mandell found that prior to the law's passage, only 14 percent of his sample families were able to state the true interest rate within a range of 20 percent. (If the actual interest rate was 10 percent, only 14 percent of the respondents identified the rate to be within 9–11 percent.) A year after the Act's passage, the percentage of correct respondents rose to 21 percent.[3] This, of course, means that in 1970, 79 percent of Mandell's sample families were unable to state the true interest rate by an error of 20 percent or less. True, with the passage of time and the increase in rates, perceptions of interest charges may have sharpened. Nevertheless, it is still clear that large numbers of consumers do not realize the actual interest rates they are paying. (Very few students appear to know that purchases made through a bank credit card, such as MasterCharge or Visa, if not paid within the grace period, carry a monthly rate of 1½ percent, which comes to an annual rate of 18 percent.) It follows that such consumers are not likely to be deterred by higher interest charges. Moreover, as mentioned in the earlier discussion of housing finance, higher interest rates can be diffused by extending payments rather than making larger monthly payments. Consumers are less likely to be dissuaded by stretched-out maturities than by higher monthly budgetary drains. Indeed, most studies indicate that consumers do not cut back purchases when interest rates rise.

There is, however, another channel, already alluded to in Chapter 16 (p. 424), by which higher interest rates might affect consumer spending. And recent studies show that this channel can hardly be ignored. As stated there, consumption is affected by wealth holdings; consumption outlays rise as wealth increases. Recall, too, the inverse relationship between interest rates and bond prices (pp. 54–55)—the lower bond yields, the higher bond prices.

---

[3]"Consumer Perceptions of Incurred Interest Rates: An Empirical Test of the Efficacy of the Truth-in-Lending Law," *Journal of Finance* 6 (December 1971): 1143–1153.

When a reduced quantity of money drives interest rates upward, it simultaneously reduces the value of bond holdings. Perceived wealth falls; a bondholder whose $10,000 bond is now worth only $9,000 feels poorer. And while the loss is only on paper (unless the bond is sold at the reduced price), the bondholder's spending is understandably affected by the balance sheet decline in his or her net worth. Since stock market prices tend to move in sympathy with bond market prices, shareholders also feel poorer. These paper losses adversely affect consumer spending, so that consumers will spend less as interest rates rise.

The converse is equally true. If interest rates decline, bond and stock prices rise. People feel richer; their perceived asset positions have improved. As a result, they'll spend more.

Government spending

The government sector of the economy includes the federal, state, and local governments. The impact of higher interest rates on federal government spending is rather indirect. The U.S. Treasury is judged by the financial markets to be a prime credit risk. Consequently, interest rates for any given maturity are always lowest for those issued by the U.S. government. One cannot imagine the federal government going broke. In the end, the national treasury can be replenished with tax money or by printing money. (The entire federal debt held outside of federal agencies was $616.4 billion in 1980; it could have been repaid by a one-time tax of 29 percent on that year's disposable personal income.) This is not meant to advocate either of these alternatives. Rather, it is meant to indicate that the possibilities exist and are reflected in the market's judgment of the inherent absence of risk of default on U.S. government securities.

Higher interest rates will not deter borrowing by the Treasury. If, as a result of congressionally budgeted expenditures and tax policies, a budgetary deficit occurs, the Treasury is bound to find the funds needed to finance this shortfall. Interest rate increases in the market cannot slow the Treasury's quest for funds or prevent the government's attaining its implicit financial objectives.

Nevertheless, the indirect effect alluded to earlier does exist. Higher interest rates raise the government's budgetary outlays. If a lid is placed on government spending, an increase in interest expenditures—a transfer payment—means reduced outlays on other budgetary categories, including expenditures for goods and services. Such a cap, albeit one that is not quite vacuum tight, comes about through the actions of the budget committees of the House of Representatives and the Senate. These committees are charged with recommending an annual federal budget figure to be binding in Congress each fiscal year. The annual expenditure total is bound to be firmer than the income total, for while Congress can decide how much to appropriate for spending, its control over income is more tenuous. Although Congress can set tax rates, the federal government's income is determined by a combination of tax rates and the economy's GNP, the tax base, the latter being beyond the direct control of the legislature. Thus, if increased interest costs are anticipated, Congress may be forced to reduce its other spending plans in order to maintain the budget within desired targets. In short, higher interest rates can mean reduced federal government expenditures on goods and services. But the impact is not likely to be strong, nor can it be expected to become effective in the current fiscal period.

A stronger impact can be anticipated on the state and local levels as well. Indeed, in states like Montana and Arizona, the state constitution mandates a balanced state budget. Higher interest rates paid by the state government will lead to diversion of funds away from construction projects or other types of spending and into interest payments.

An additional impact occurs in states whose legislature subjects them to an interest ceiling. Alabama, for example, may not pay an interest rate in excess of 6 percent annually on its borrowings. When market interest rates rise sufficiently to compensate for the tax-free quality of state and local bonds, the securities of these states lose their attractiveness. The effect is analogous to that of maximum interest rates on mortgage lending: Funds are diverted to more profitable opportunities.

Summary

The expanded Keynesian model has been developed well beyond the confines of Chapter 17. Changes in the money supply affect more than the demand for business investment. The housing market is responsive to variations in the money stock; higher interest rates reduce the demand for housing and, by diverting funds that would go for mortgages to other uses, reduce the supply of housing. Similarly, as perceived economic wealth is dependent on interest rates, consumption spending, too, varies (directly) with money supply changes. Other types of spending—inventory investment and government spending on capital projects—also are affected by increases or decreases in the stock of money.

A Keynesian model has been developed along these lines; the results are enlightening because they yield quantitative estimates of the magnitudes involved. To be sure, these estimates are just that; they are not to be taken as precise but, rather, as ballpark figures. For a $1 billion decrease in the money supply (sustained for three years), the model estimates that real GNP will fall by $1.4 billion in the first year and $3.3 billion by the end of three years. The major source of the decline in GNP is the fall in investment, moving from −$0.7 billion at the end of the first year to −$2.6 billion at the conclusion of the third. Of this, residential construction is estimated to fall by $1.0 billion, while business investment in plant and equipment will decline by $1.4 billion in the third year. Consumption is expected to fall by $900 billion. The sectors that are least affected by the monetary decline are state and local expenditures and business inventories, each of which falls by $300 million by the third year.[4]

The contentions of the complex Keynesian model are borne out by these estimates. Decreases in the money supply affect all sectors of the economy, and the same is true for increases. Note, however, that the impact of the monetary change is not spread evenly through the economic system. Some sectors are more sensitive than others; some are hardly affected at all.

The detailed exposition presented here is important not only for understanding how the macroeconomic system functions and for the role that money plays in the economy. Ultimately, clearer understanding leads to more effective policy, to actions designed to shape the economy to meet the goals we, the public, wish to achieve. There is one gap, however, that must be filled before our comprehension of money's impact on the economy is complete: the question of time. This gap is remedied in the next section.

☐ Lags and the Money Supply

Comparative statics is the method of analysis that considers "before" and "after" states. Chapters 16, 17, and 18 presented comparative static models: A "before" situation in the economy with given variables, such as money stock and investment demand, was contrasted with an "after" state in which the money supply was larger and, as a result, investment was greater and the level of GNP was higher. This type of analysis is extremely fruitful for explaining how variations in some key economic forces lead to modifications in the economic climate. Moreover, such models suggest how economic activity can be molded along socially desirable lines. In another aspect, however, comparative statics conceals rather than reveals. It does not describe the path by which the economy finds its way from one equilibrium position to another. More important for our present purposes, comparative statics is silent on the time dimension—how much time must elapse between the initial change and the ultimate impact. Yet both the Keynesian monetary theory discussed in past chapters and the theory of the monetarists explored in Chapter 20 suggest that the impact of time cannot be ignored.

When you thought about modern macroeconomic theory, you probably realized that the effect of, say, an increase in interest rates would not immediately drive investment spending down. Investment decisions cannot be turned on and off like a water spigot. Certainly, investment decisions that have already been made and financial commitments that have been agreed to by the borrower and lender will not be disturbed by

---

[4]I am indebted to Jared Enzler of the research staff of the Board of Governors of the Federal Reserve System for supplying these estimates, which were based on data beginning with 1976.

higher interest rates. And investment projects already in progress—housing under construction, equipment on the assembly line—will not be canceled when interest rates rise and monetary conditions become more stringent. At best, new investment programs that have not yet been firmly decided on will be discouraged by the tighter money conditions, so investment will slow in the future. In the interim, however, investments that have already been committed and those in the pipelines will still be moving forward. The demand they represent will continue to be felt, at least for some time.

In short, practical reasons dictate the belief that monetary actions influence economic activity over time. Economists today do not deny the existence of this lagged effect. They are critically concerned with precisely measuring it. It will be best to begin considering the question of how long the lag is, on the average, by defining some terms.

Economists have found it useful to distinguish between the **inside lag** and the **outside lag.**

Assume that the economy began a downturn in early April and the monetary authorities took the appropriate countercyclical action at the beginning of June. The inside lag is two months, the time it took the policy makers to react. But after the authorities have used one or more of the instruments subject to their discretion, further time will elapse before the economy responds. This reaction takes place, say, in early December. The outside lag is the six-month interval between June and December. The total lag, obtained by combining the inside and outside lags, is eight months. Figure 19.2 sketches this example out. But it goes slightly further by breaking the inside and outside lags each into two component lags.

Actually, the outside lag is the center of the present discussion, since the essential issue involves the time it takes for monetary changes to affect the economy. Nevertheless, this is an appropriate place to consider the inside lag as well. The inside lag is divided into a **recognition lag** and a **policy inauguration lag.** The recognition lag occurs for a variety of reasons associated with data collection and interpretation. The data needed to analyze the state of the economy are never fully contemporaneous, and

The **inside lag** refers to the interval between the need for remedial policy and the date on which such actions are implemented. The **outside lag** refers to the interval between a change in policy and the time at which the new policy affects the economy.

The **recognition lag** refers to the time it takes for policy makers to recognize that a modification in their policy stance is required.
The **policy inauguration lag** measures the time it takes to make a policy decision.

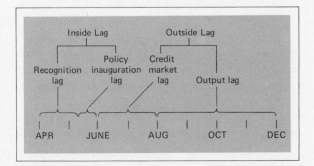

FIGURE 19.2 Lags in monetary actions: a schematic diagram.

"There's no cause for panic, Mrs. Munson, but, frankly, there are certain indicators that cannot be ignored."

Drawing by Chas Addams; © 1979 The New Yorker Magazine, Inc.

interpretation requires some assurance that the movements reflected in the data are not just random occurrences. Once the need for policy action has been recognized, action can be undertaken. But decisions might not follow immediately. Hence the policy inauguration lag.

After the monetary instruments have been brought into play by the Federal Reserve authorities—for example, they decide to tighten reserves by means of open market sales—participants in the credit markets must be induced to vary their behavior, to tighten the credit they issue. Since higher interest rates are apt to result from temporary, random movements, bank policies will not be revised unless bankers are convinced that a basic shift in the economic scene is imminent. This requires accumulated evidence, which, of course, takes time. Thus, credit markets, too, react with a delay, the **credit market lag**.

Finally, as noted earlier, when credit conditions turn either more or less favorable, the reaction of spenders is not immediate. This **output lag** leads investors to continue with their investment plans. Only after a while will they revise their plans and bring them in line with the modified credit market behavior. The same is true for other spending groups— namely, governments and consumers—as well.

How long have these various lags been?

Mark Willes, formerly an economist with the Federal Reserve Bank of Philadelphia (he later became president of the Federal Reserve Bank of Minneapolis), examined Open Market Committee minutes for the years from 1952 to 1960 in order to estimate the inside lag. By comparing business cycle turning points with indications in the FOMC minutes that the members realized that a turning point had indeed occurred, Willes discovered that the recognition lag averaged three months. That is, it took three months for the policy makers to realize that the economy had moved in a direction that called for a revision of their policies. Willes further found that there was no policy inauguration lag. Once the economic intelligence had been processed and interpreted, action followed immediately. This fact should not be surprising; remember that Federal Reserve policy makers can make decisions on the spot without applying to any other government official or agency for approval. As noted in Chapter 13, the monthly meetings of the FOMC are basic to the formulation and deciding of policy. Once a majority of the committee members have become convinced that a new policy is appropriate, they need only to vote for such a policy at the monthly meeting to install a new policy directive consistent with their conclusions. Thus, Willes found the inside lag of monetary policy to average three months. Other economists, however, disagree. Their computations lead them to believe that the inside lag is on the order of six months, not three.

Measurement of the outside lag is a more difficult proposition. In fact, it is not altogether clear how such measurement can be undertaken. One method would be to ascertain when interest rates or credit market conditions have varied in response to a shift in monetary policy. The result would be an estimate of the credit market lag. Studies along this line have been reported in the literature; they suggest that the credit market does react rapidly, within a month or two.

The next step is to measure the output lag, using as a starting point the date when the credit market reacted. The terminal point will be when output has changed in response to the new credit market conditions. Again, such research has been published, with output broken down into component types, such as residential construction, plant and equipment

The **credit market lag** refers to the interval between the policy decision and the time at which it is felt by the credit markets.

The time between a change in credit market conditions and the reaction of producers to those conditions is known as the **output lag.**

investment, and inventories. The computed output lags have varied from one month for inventory investment to two years for spending on plant and equipment. Using this method of computing lags by calculating the sublags, estimates of the outside lag run from three to four months to over two years, depending on the type of activity being surveyed.

A second method of computing the outside lag is to compare changes in money supply to changes in economic activity. The theoretical foundation for this method is the belief that changes in the money supply reflect decisions of the monetary authorities, and that such actions do impinge on economic activity. But even without a conceptual foundation, if one is interested in money's impact on the economy it might be perfectly appropriate to begin with a change in the supply of money and see what impact such a change has had. Again, estimates differ, ranging from three months or less at one extreme to a year and a half at the other.

Simulation involves tracing the quantitative impact of a change in one variable on other variables using econometric models.

Still a third method of estimating the outside lag is **simulation.** Simulation is normally performed on an econometric model, which is a mathematical-statistical description of some theoretical relationship. (See Box 19.1.) By varying the money supply and tracing out the impact of this modification on GNP or its components in subsequent time periods, an estimate of the lag can be derived.

BOX 19.1 Econometric Models

The consumption schedule of Chapter 16 (pp. 425–426) can easily serve as an example of an equation in an econometric model. Symbolically, the relationship between consumption and disposable personal income specified there can be written as follows:

$$C_t = a + b \text{ DPI}_t + u$$

where C_t is consumer spending in time period t, a and b are constants, and u is a random variable. The equation states that (1) consumption in any time period (e.g., year or quarter) depends on some constant, a, which is independent of other influences; (2) consumption spending varies with the level of disposable personal income of the contemporaneous time period, the relationship between C and DPI being specified by the constant b; and (3) consumption further depends on a purely random element, u. Theory, however, cannot tell us the precise values of a and b. The result is that while this equation relates the direction of influence (namely, that as DPI grows, so, too, will C), this statement is weak because it is qualitative. A more useful statement would be a quantitative relationship linking DPI more precisely to C. Such a relationship can be calculated by statistical methods, using past data on consumption and DPI. The econometrician takes the theoretical model, plugs it, with the appropriate data, into a computer containing the needed program, and obtains a solution. The result will be of the order

$$C_t = \$1,000 \text{ billion} + \tfrac{1}{2} \text{ DPI}_t$$

The meaning of this quantitative relationship is that consumption spending each period will equal half of that period's DPI plus $1,000 billion. Thus, if DPI_t equals $1,400 billion, then $C_t = \frac{1}{2}(\$1,400 \text{ billion}) + \$1,000 \text{ billion}$, or $1,700 billion. The econometrician has found that a equals $1,000 billion, while b equals $\frac{1}{2}$. (Incidentally, b is the marginal propensity to consume. Can you explain why?)

Actual econometric models are more complex, both in terms of the number of variables used to explain any single variable, such as consumption, and in terms of the number of equations. Moreover, many of the variables to be explained depend not only on present values of the explanatory variables but also on past values of these or other variables. (Thus, C_t may depend also on C_{t-1}, C_{t-2}, etc.) But all the models are similar in that they begin with a theoretical relationship or set of relationships, which are then fitted to past data on the basis of statistical methods. A large model can have hundreds of variables, which seek to explain some key objective such as GNP and its components.

Econometric models can be used for forecasting. Some economists use them to predict movements in the entire economy, while others have a narrower focus, such as predicting sales in a particular industry. Another use is less practical in the immediate sense; it is more research oriented. Often it is interesting to determine what will happen to the value of some specific variable if the value of a different variable is changed. How, for example, will GNP change if a variable like the money supply is increased? That is the essence of simulation: introducing a new value and finding its impact on the model's outcome. Indeed, this is how the estimates of the effects of a change in the money supply on GNP and its components (given on p. 505) were derived. The Federal Reserve regularly simulates in order to trace out the impact of alternative growth rates of money supply.

Unfortunately, simulations also prove inconclusive. Different econometric models yield different lag estimates. Some show a brief, one-quarter outside lag while others find the average lag to exceed a year.

The results of all the studies are confusing, not only to the student but to the trained economist as well. Is the lag short or is it long? Is it sustained or does it fizzle out in a short time? To be told that the outside lag ranges from three months to three years is not comforting, even though in the scope of human experience three years is brief. Economists have not been happy with this result, either, and many articles have been written to reconcile or at least explain the differences. Most of the articles are technical, dealing with issues of econometrics. But questions of formulation and definition are also discussed. Unfortunately, the results are ambivalent, and no conclusion that is generally acceptable has surfaced, at least not yet. Nevertheless, hope springs eternal, and perhaps by the time you read these pages a major breakthrough will have been made.

To continue on this optimistic road, perhaps another controversy will be settled, too. The orthodoxy of Keynesian economics that you've now mastered has been challenged by the monetarists. The contribution that this school of economists has been making to monetary theory, empirical work, and policy merits that its position be examined. That, and how monetarism differs from Keynesian macroeconomics, is the task of the next chapter.

□ Summary

This chapter extended and deepened the basic Keynesian model of previous chapters. Two issues were considered: (1) the impact of monetary changes on the various spending sectors and (2) the time it takes for variations in money supply to affect the economy.

Sectoral impacts

Housing responds to interest rate changes on both the demand and supply sides. Higher interest rates raise the costs of home ownership, thus reducing demand for new homes. However, mortgage arrangements often can accommodate these increased costs, for example, by extending the length of the mortgage. Supply constraints appear to have been a more important element in the financing of housing. Insofar as interest rate ceilings make mortgage lending less profitable, funds will be diverted away from the housing sector. Moreover, inflation, which has raised financing needs, has also made bankers more tight fisted. Bankers are reluctant to lend to borrowers whose ability to carry the high monthly payments has become more questionable. The softening of interest rate ceilings mandated by the Depository Institutions Deregulation and Monetary Control Act will remove one of the impediments to mortgage financing.

Inventory investment can be explained by the theory of the accelerator, which relates the demand for inventory to sales. Although interest rates affect neither sales nor inventory directly, higher rates do make storing goods more costly, thereby reducing investment in inventory.

Consumption is affected by interest rates mostly indirectly. Higher financing costs do not appear to switch off demand for consumer durables. But higher interest rates do mean lower bond and stock prices, reducing the net worth position of consumers. Consequently, they spend less.

Government spending at the federal level has not been much affected by either higher or lower interest rates. The Treasury must finance any budgetary deficit. This, however, is not true on the local level. Statutes limiting the interest rates payable by states or provisions mandating balanced budgets mean that when interest expenses rise, other outlays, especially for capital improvements, fall.

One estimate of the impact of a reduced money supply and higher interest rates on GNP and its components suggests that if M-1A were to fall by $1 billion, GNP would fall by $3.3 billion within three years. Similar results would occur for a rise in the money supply and reduced interest rates.

Lags

Any change in the money supply influences GNP and its components over time, a fact of life for both the theoretician and the policy maker. Proper policy diagnosis takes time; this is the *recognition lag*. Some time (which, in the case of monetary policy, is normally brief) elapses just to implement policy, the *policy inauguration lag*. These two lags make up the *inside lag*, which has been estimated to be in the three-to-six-month range.

The *outside lag* consists of the *credit market* and *output lags*. The former measures the interval between a policy action and its impact on credit markets, while the latter considers the time lapse between an alteration in credit market conditions and its effect on output.

It is not at all clear how best to measure the outside lag. The various methods used have produced estimates ranging from as little as three months to as much as over a year. Yet this information is crucial to policy makers. They must know with some degree of precision when the impact of a decision made now will be felt.

☐ Questions and Exercises

1. a. Determine the dollar impact of an increase in the mortgage rate from 9 percent to 13 percent annually on an $80,000, 30-year mortgage. (Your friendly banker should have a book of tables that will permit you to calculate the numbers. Alternatively, your library should have a book of financial tables.)
    b. Might these increases (which correspond roughly to mortgage terms on new homes in December 1980) have significantly deterred people from buying homes?
    c. Would your answer be different if the public expected inflation to proceed at a 10 percent pace for the foreseeable future?
2. Study President Reagan's budget-cutting policies in 1981 after his initial budgetary projections were upset by the high interest rates paid by the U.S. Treasury on the federal debt.
3. Does the extension of interest rate impacts to variables other than investment strengthen or weaken the hand of the monetary authority? Why?
4. How do the floating interest rates on commercial and business loans discussed in Chapter 5 and the variable rate mortgages mentioned in Chapter 11 affect the lag of monetary policy?
5. You might try to estimate the inside lag of recent monetary policy by comparing a recent business cycle turning point to the recognition of that turning point as revealed by the "Record of Policy Actions of the FOMC" (published monthly in the Federal Reserve *Bulletin*).

☐ For Further Study

Neil G. Berkman, "Mortgage Finance and the Housing Cycle," Federal Reserve Bank of Boston, *New England Economic Review*, September-October 1979, discusses the effects of financing and interest rates on home construction, while an earlier conference of the Boston Federal Reserve Bank, *Housing and Monetary Policy* (Boston, 1970) provides some useful background.

The impact of interest rates on consumption is explored in a wide-ranging article by F. Modigliani, "Monetary Policy and Consumption: Linkages via Interest Rates and Wealth Effects in the FMP Model," in Federal Reserve Bank of Boston, *Consumer Spending and Monetary Policy: The Linkages* (Boston, 1971). This piece has been reprinted in A. Abel, ed., *The Collected Papers of Franco Modigliani* (Cambridge, Mass.: M.I.T. Press, 1980), vol. 2.

The lag issue is another seminal contribution of Milton Friedman, whose "The Lag in Effect of Monetary Policy," *Journal of Political Economy*, 69 (October 1961): 447–466, started a major controversy. A good deal of that controversy is excerpted as selections 38–42 of J. Prager, *Monetary Economics: Controversies in Theory and Policy* (New York: Random House, 1971). Recent literature has examined the lag in the structure of econometric models, such as the FMP model mentioned in this chapter and the St. Louis model considered in the next chapter.

CHAPTER 20

Monetarism: An Updated, Controversial Doctrine

We are all Keynesians now.
Milton Friedman, economics professor (1963)

We are all monetarists now.
Franco Modigliani, economics professor (1976)

We are all confused now.
Anonymous economics student (1981)

CONTENTS

Monetarism

Monetarism is a doctrine that blossomed in the early 1960s and ripened in the late 1960s and the 1970s. The theory then was refined and scrutinized and, in the process, gained a substantial degree of public acceptance. Monetarist enclaves can be found in academic circles, in government offices, in the research departments of major American banks, and in the media. Moreover, monetarism has been exported; its concepts and proscriptions have been examined and put into practice in the United Kingdom and on the European continent. Monetarism has become a serious rival to the Keynesian orthodoxy that has dominated macroeconomics since the 1940s.

One objective of this chapter is to outline the basic tenets of monetarism and to consider some of its implications. Later chapters on monetary policy and history also touch on some aspects of this doctrine. A further objective is to contrast monetarism with the Keynesian theory developed in the last few chapters, so that the differences as well as the similarities become clear.

A prefatory warning is needed. There is a tendency for journalists, popularizers, and even textbook writers to exaggerate the positions of both the monetarists and the Keynesians. Because there are divisions within each camp, it is possible to focus on the views of the extremists; glaring contrasts often do facilitate comprehension. It is far more difficult, and certainly less controversial, to contrast the more moderate consensus positions of the two groups. Often the differences will consist of nuances in concept or esoteric technical issues; the policy prescriptions may well be similar. A student of money and banking should strive for a level of sophistication that transcends conventional wisdom, and a textbook should facilitate this quest.

☐ Monetarism

While monetarism may mean different things to different people, most will agree on a number of propositions. Keynesians for the most part will not accept these monetarist assertions. Both monetarist thought and the contrasting Keynesian attitudes are outlined in the next few paragraphs. The points to be discussed are: the role of money, how money affects the economy, whether the economy is basically stable or unstable, whether economists should be interested only in the economy as a whole or in its component sectors as well, velocity, empirical support, lags, the role of fiscal policy, monetary indicators, monetary rules, and money's impact in an international setting.

Money matters most

The essence of monetarism is the primacy of money. Contemporary monetarists, tracing their intellectual heritage to the quantity theory of money, believe not only that money matters but that it matters more than any other single influence on overall economic activity and price levels. Indeed, some monetarists would argue that "only money matters."

Keynesians do not dispute the fact that money matters. Indeed, modern Keynesians as well as monetarists believe that in the short run the money supply changes affect aggregate output, and that in the long run variations in money supply lead to price level modifications. The difference between the two views lies in the emphasis placed on monetary variables. Monetarists believe that money supply matters most of all, while Keynesians relegate monetary influences to a lower rung on the ladder of causality.

The transmission process

The last few chapters sketched out in some detail the mechanism by which a change in money supply influences economic activity. Keynesians believe, for example, that an increase in money supply drives interest rates down. This in turn raises the *profitability* of investment; some previously unprofitable investment projects, whose rates of return were inadequate given the previous high interest rate, now become profitable.

Monetarism denies this approach. Its adherents favor alternative views of money's impact on the economy, one of which was proposed by Milton Friedman.

Assume that at the present moment all people hold their desired quantity of money, other financial assets, and real assets. This equilibrium means that currently the public does not want to alter the proportions of its portfolio holdings of money, bonds, common stocks, real estate, antiques, automobiles, and so forth. (However unrealistic this assumption is, it is quite useful for expository purposes, so bear with it.) What would you expect to happen if suddenly the amount of money in the economy increased? Of course, the previous equilibrium would be disturbed; some people would be holding onto more money than they desired. They would rid themselves of this excess quantity by converting it into other types of assets, both financial and real. The same reasoning would apply to business firms: Their asset portfolios would also be upset by the increase in the money supply, and they too would react by increasing their spending on both financial and nonfinancial goods.[1] In short, a larger money supply will lead to increased spending by upsetting asset equilibrium rather than by modifying the profitability of investment, as the

[1]The appendix to this chapter expands on Friedman's version of the transmission mechanism.

Keynesians assert. To be sure, both theories predict that spending will rise. They also predict that interest rates will fall. (You should be able to explain why this will be so in Keynesian theory.) According to monetarism, interest rates decline because the increased demand for financial assets subsequent to the monetary increment bids asset prices up, driving their yields down.

Thus, a subtle theoretical difference that distinguishes Keynesians from monetarists lies in the way changes in the money supply impinge on the economy: Does it work by affecting the profitability of investment (Keynesians) or by modifying asset equilibriums (monetarists)? Both theories agree, however, that the impact of a monetary change is broad based. Monetarism suggests that consumption as well as investment spending is affected by the mechanism outlined in the previous paragraph. And though the simple Keynesian analysis views investment spending as the primary vehicle for relating monetary variations to GNP, recall the neo-Keynesian version in the previous chapter which concluded that the money supply affects consumption as well.

The stability of the economy

An implication of the monetarist proposition that monetary changes exert a major impact on the economy and that other forces are far less significant is that the economic system is basically stable. True, GNP does not always move ahead at a steady pace; it has its ups and downs. Monetarists assert that these fluctuations around the trend would be relatively mild were it not for government intervention in the economy. Intervention by public authorities to stabilize the economy and damp its fluctuations in fact destabilizes the economy and intensifies these cycles. A more stable monetary growth rate, contend the monetarists, would be highly beneficial, since then monetary swings caused by well-intentioned but incompetent central bankers would be eliminated as a cause of cyclical instability (see the next section).

Keynesians reject this contention, believing instead that the private economy is inherently unstable. Left to itself, the economy would move in cycles, with occasionally sharp and prolonged downturns followed by heady upturns. Government intervention is needed to stabilize the economy. (Keynesians view the economy as a rocking chair, while monetarists see it as a four-legger.)

Rules versus discretion

Monetarists view a good deal of the economy's ills as stemming from poorly executed central banking policies. Moreover, many believe that such policies are endemic to discretion; these monetarists have little faith that a different group of central bankers, even if they were better versed in economics, could have improved the record substantially. So their prescription is to find a **monetary rule** and stick faithfully to it.

Of course, advocates of the rule do not believe that the money supply should be fixed at a constant dollar level forever. They realize that

Under a **monetary rule** money supply is increased according to a predetermined formula.

economic growth might be harmed by too little of the monetary "grease" that keeps the economy's wheels rolling. Instead of a constant stock of money, monetarists have proposed a rule embodying a constant rate of monetary growth. "Increase the money supply by x percent a year" is their recommendation.

But what is x?

Here we must return to the equation of exchange as explained in Chapter 14. As you recall, by definition

$$MV \equiv PY_r \qquad (20.1)$$

where M stands for the supply of money, V is its velocity, P is prices and Y_r is real output. This equation can be transformed into logarithmic form as follows:

$$\log M + \log V = \log P + \log Y_r \qquad (20.2)$$

With but a touch of imprecision, this equation may be interpreted as "The *percentage change* in M plus the *percentage change* in V equals the *percentage changes* in P and Y_r." In lieu of absolute values of the four key variables, we can now deal with percentage changes or percentage rates of growth. Now subtract $\log V$ from both sides to arrive at

$$\log M = \log P + \log Y_r - \log V \qquad (20.3)$$

This form of the equation allows us to move from definition to analysis. One can now say that $\log M$, the rate of monetary growth (the policy goal), should be set equal to the sum of the three terms on the right side of equation 20.3.

Milton Friedman, who initially formulated the rule, also gave it empirical content.[2] The rate of growth of real output between 1872 and 1955 was 3.5 percent, while velocity over the same period fell by 1 percent a year. Since price stability is an ultimate goal of policy, $\log P$ should be set equal to zero. Substituting these values into equation 20.3 leads to a target rate of monetary growth equal to 4.5 percent annually.[3]

So all the central banking authorities need to do is make sure that the rate of monetary growth is on target. A daily increase in M-2 by 0.00011798 would do the job. (A more sophisticated rule mechanism is described in Box 20.1.)

Criticisms of the rule. To begin, the rule is not as easy to implement as its simplicity suggests. Definitional problems must be dealt with; the period selected is not obvious; changing structure must be accommodated; and the rule itself must be capable of implementation.

Definitional problems. The monetary rule recommends expansion of the money supply by a given percent per year. But what is the money supply that is to be increased? Remember the search for an appropriate definition of money (Chapter 2). Moreover, the problem is an ever-

---

[2] *A Program for Monetary Stability* (New York: Fordham University Press, 1960), chap. 4.
[3] 4.5% = 0 + 3.5% + 1.0%. These numbers conform to Friedman's preferred definition of money, M-2, and to his own calculations mentioned in *ibid.*, p. 91.

BOX 20.1 The Rule Refined

While the simplicity of a constant-growth money supply rule appeals to some economists, others have contended that a more sophisticated rule could be devised, one that would achieve monetary goals more accurately. The basic idea is to engineer a "feedback" mechanism, that is, automatic signals that would trigger a shift in policy. The concept is analogous to the thermostat that directs a heating system. Once the thermostatic target has been set at, say, 20°C (68°F), the automatic mechanism is in full control. Should the temperature in the room fall below 20° as recorded by the thermometer that is part of the device, an electrical connection closes and the heating system starts. When the temperature reaches 20°, the switch automatically cuts off, breaking the connection and shutting off the furnace.

How divine it would be if a similar device could be designed for economic policy purposes. Once the targets had been set, the job of the policy makers would terminate. If the economy moved ahead on target, money would trickle in at the predetermined rate. Should the economy falter, however, signals would automatically be fed back to the monitoring mechanism, which would direct the appropriate faster-growing money supply to be released and do so until the economy was back on target. The reverse would happen should the economy race ahead too rapidly. The mechanism would automatically lead to a reduction in the rate at which money was pumped into the economic system.

Some econometric experiments have been performed with feedback rules. In one such study, using the major econometric model described in Chapter 19, Cooper and Fischer concluded that "a monetary rule using . . . a systematic policy of leaning against the wind would have reduced the variability of the rates of inflation and unemployment over the period 1956.I to 1968.IV, as compared with a constant growth rate rule."[*]

However, this feedback mechanism turns out to perform less well than a simpler rule during a period of major shocks to the economy like the period from 1973 to 1975.[**] (In 1973–1974 rising inflation was a serious problem, and in 1974–1975 an extremely sharp recession occurred.)

Thus, it is not clear whether greater sophistication in devising rules does lead to more accurate controls. But of even more significance is another point. However sophisticated these models are, their usefulness depends on the validity of the rule itself. If a simple rule has serious and perhaps fatal flaws, more complex rules surely cannot be contemplated.

[*]J. Phillip Cooper and Stanley Fischer, "Simulations of Monetary Rules on the FRB-MIT-Penn Model," *Journal of Money, Credit and Banking* 4 (May 1972): 384–396.
[**]Roger Craine, Arthur Havenner, and James Berry, "Fixed Rules vs. Activism in the Conduct of Monetary Policy," *American Economic Review* 68 (December 1978): 769–783. This study uses the same model, but in its updated version.

evolving one. We do not know precisely what is to be included in "money" today. We can be sure, however, that the money of the future will be different from present-day money. Certainly the evolution of money has taught us this lesson. We can predict that if the rule-defined money supply grows too slowly to meet the public's demand for it, new forms of money will be discovered. Will the rule then have to be revised? If so, what happens to its automaticity? Will someone have to decide when or how to redraft the rule? Is that not discretion?

Selection of an appropriate period. The proper monetary definition is related to another problem—the appropriate time horizon for calculating the rule. Earlier in this chapter the rule was computed by applying historical data on Y_r and V to equation 20.3. This procedure may be correct, but we must ask, What historical period is appropriate? Should a long period, encompassing many decades, be selected, or would a more recent interval, limited to a single decade, be better? Table 20.1 lists a number of possible quantitative monetary targets, using different periods and two definitions of money, to point out the variety of growth rates that are all equally legitimate. Note that one alternative calls for a negative rate of monetary growth, while the positive values range from a paltry 0.45 percent to 3.09 percent. Which target would you choose?

Problems of changing structure. The demand for money depends on a number of variables, including interest rates and GNP. A lower GNP reduces the demand for money and should be accompanied by a reduced money supply in order to keep prices constant. This certainly is the implication of the monetarist transmission process outlined earlier. Now, GNP growth depends on many causes, such as productivity, technological progress, and labor force growth, not only on the money supply. Consequently, when structural change occurs in the economy, leading to a new trend of GNP growth, the money supply must be adjusted if inflation or deflation is to be avoided. The rule, by locking in the old historical pattern, may well cause the problems it was designed to avoid.

Implementation. Let the money supply grow by x percent, says the rule. But how does one achieve that? The Federal Reserve has no direct control over the deposit component of M-1. As you know from Chapter 13, the Board of Governors of the Federal Reserve System can modify reserve requirements and thereby change the deposit multiplier. Similarly, the Federal Open Market Committee, by modifying the security portfolio of the Federal Reserve banks, can control high-powered money. But in either case the control is exerted on an underlying element in the money creation process, not on the money supply itself. In the absence of major reform of the Federal Reserve's powers, and as long as the banks and the public play a role in the money supply process, the grip of the

TABLE 20.1 Monetary Rules Under Various Definitions and Periods

Period	Definition of money	Annual percent growth rate of real income (Y_r)	Velocity (V)	Monetary rule (percent per year)
(1)	(2)	(3)	(4)	(5) (= 4 − 3)
1914–1980	M-1	3.16	1.04	2.12
1914–1980	M-2	3.16	0.07	3.09
1947–1980	M-1	3.37	3.56	−0.19
1947–1980	M-2	3.37	1.93	1.44
1958–1980	M-1	3.36	2.91	0.45
1958–1980	M-2	3.36	1.17	1.19

authorities on the money supply will never be absolute. How, then, can the money supply be increased at the rate that the rule propounds?

The rule—an evaluation. In light of all of the questions just raised, many monetarists, as well as Keynesians, reject the idea of a rule. It is not a panacea for all of the nation's economic, or at least monetary, problems. The policy choice obviously is not between a rigid rule and extremely flexible discretion, but a question of how to use discretion wisely. One lesson has been learned: Economists no longer believe in **fine tuning.** But it is equally undesirable to leave the dial fixed at one setting. The realm of the possible lies between the two extremes.

Contemporary economists, both in and out of the Federal Reserve System, feel that discretion is needed, but it must be handled gingerly (one is tempted to write "with discretion"). The authorities need not and should not respond to every minor aberration in the economy. They must realize that it is not possible to keep the economic system absolutely stable and that any attempt to achieve this unrealistic goal is likely to intensify, not moderate, fluctuations. What can and should be done is to make the economy less unstable—when the economy is clearly erupting, the damper must be clapped down. By proposing a policy of self-restraint, advocates of the rule have made their point. But self-restraint should not mean impotence.

Aggregate analysis versus sectoral examination

Since monetarists believe that it is the imbalance between the demand for and the supply of money that upsets equilibrium, it is unimportant, and in fact irrelevant, to search for the source of the disequilibrium. All that we need to know is that there is too much or too little money in the economy in comparison to consumer and business demands for money. We can then be certain that the public will maneuver to remedy this imbalance, thereby creating an increase or a decrease in nominal GNP, depending, of course, on whether the supply of money exceeds demand or demand is greater than supply.

Keynesians are more interested in sectoral detail. First of all, Keynesian theory, presented in the past few chapters, requires distinguishing the various economic sectors and analyzing the causal relationships within each sector. Keynesians feel that it is important to know what determines consumer spending, investment, and so on. Second, because Keynesians believe the economy is unstable, it is useful and even important to ascertain the sources of the instability. A business cycle expansion may have its origins in one of the basic economic sectors, and so, too, for a contraction in economic activity. Knowledge of the source may be crucial in fostering the appropriate policy response.

Velocity

How will a change in the money supply affect its velocity? Keynes

Fine tuning involves careful adjustment of the policy dials to moderate both over- and under-expansion of the economy.

argued that since money supply variations modify interest rates, velocity will respond. You know that if the supply of money declines, interest rates will rise, inducing people to hold less money. But if they hold less money relative to GNP, then, according to the equation of exchange, V will rise.[4] The decline in GNP induced by the higher interest rates will be offset in part by the rise in velocity. The opposite will happen when interest rates fall. Keynesians believe that the effect of interest rates on velocity is too strong to be ignored.

Most monetarists agree that velocity and interest rates are linked. However, they believe that the impact of velocity is weak, so that monetary variations will affect primarily GNP and be only modestly offset by variations in velocity.[5]

Empirical support: the St. Louis model

Chapter 19 recorded the results of a large-scale econometric model that was fundamentally Keynesian. Contemporary followers of Keynes have not been alone in developing econometric models to test their theories. Over the last decade economists at the Federal Reserve Bank of St. Louis have been in the vanguard of monetarist model building, and have constructed an extremely simple but highly controversial model. It contains only one equation in which GNP growth is made dependent upon monetary and fiscal forces.[6] When the data are fed into the

---

[4]For those who read the appendix to Chapter 14, recall that the proportion of money held relative to GNP, i.e., M/GNP, was shown to equal the inverse of velocity. If you did not read that appendix, it suffices to note that since V = GNP/M (from the equation of exchange), its inverse, 1/V = M/GNP. Thus, if the public wishes to hold less money relative to GNP, 1/V falls and V rises.

[5]The contrast between the extreme views of both schools is especially glaring in this context. During the 1940s and 1950s some Keynesians denied that money affects GNP at all. They claimed that an increased money supply will so depress interest rates and so diminish velocity that it will fully offset the increase in the money supply. A 10 percent increase in the money supply will induce a 10 percent decrease in velocity, leaving GNP unaltered.

Extreme monetarists deny the impact of monetary changes on interest rates. Increasing the money supply will not drive interest rates down and hence will not affect velocity, so that any change in M is reflected completely in GNP. Thus, a 10 percent rise in M means that GNP rises by 10 percent.

[6]K. M. Carlson, "Does the St. Louis Equation Now Believe in Fiscal Policy?" Federal Reserve Bank of St. Louis, *Review* 60 (February 1978): 13–19. The specific formulation is

$$\dot{Y}_t = a + \sum_{i=0}^{4} m_i \dot{M}_{t-i} + \sum_{i=0}^{4} e_i \dot{E}_{t-i} + u$$

This equation asserts that $\dot{Y}_t$, the rate of change in income in period t, is determined by four explanatory variables: (1) a constant, a; (2) the rate of change in the money supply, $\dot{M}$ (where over the course of four quarters each quarter's monetary rate of change, $\dot{M}_{t-i}$ is multiplied by the appropriate coefficient, m_i, itself calculated by the statistical process); (3) the rate of change of government fiscal policy, symbolized by $\dot{E}$ (the e_i is analogous to m_i), and (4) a random variable, u. [E is defined as "high-employment expenditures," which calculates the government's budgetary situation if actual GNP were equal to potential GNP (see Chapter 15). The random variable, u, disappears; a random variable cannot have a systematic influence on the independent variable.]

computer and the results analyzed, the monetary variable turns out to be far more important than the fiscal variable. Thus, these monetarists conclude that the data support the contention that money matters most.

Will you be surprised to learn that contemporary Keynesians reject these conclusions? They fault the methodology and find the monetarist interpretation to be meaningless. While simplification is often a virtue in scientific thinking, it can be carried to the point of absurdity, they claim. [7]

Lags

The previous chapter's discussion of lags pointed out the reasons that monetary changes possess a time dimension. Empirical estimates of Keynesian models suggest that it will take three years for an increase in the money supply to be absorbed by the economy, with less than half of its impact occurring during the first year.

The monetarist equation developed in St. Louis reports otherwise. The lag is short, so brief that 40 percent of the impact of a monetary variation is achieved in the quarter in which it occurs and the entire impact is felt within the same year. Monetary actions are not only potent, as was pointed out earlier, but give quick, fast-acting relief.

Fiscal policy

Monetarists and Keynesians differ in their views on the efficacy of fiscal policy, their positions reflecting their attitudes toward monetary policy. Monetarists believe that the money supply is of primary importance, and consequently relegate fiscal policy to a lesser role. Keynesians are less confident about the overwhelming importance of monetary variables and believe fiscal policy to be at least as crucial, perhaps more so, than monetary actions. (Can you see why some economists refer to Keynesians as "fiscalists"?)

Monetary indicators

To explain the differences between monetarists and Keynesians concerning how best to track the economy, it is necessary to devote some paragraphs to a discussion of **indicators** and **targets**.

A monetary **indicator** is a source of information that responds to changes in monetary policy and signals the impact of policy actions.
A monetary **target** is an objective to be achieved by setting an appropriate policy.

Somehow Federal Reserve decision makers must receive feedback from the economic system in order to evaluate the effectiveness of their actions. Moreover, they must forecast future economic conditions if they wish to consider appropriate countermeasures. Given policy targets, the central bankers need indicators.

[7]The debates on this point are highly technical. Among the easier articles that the interested student might read is the report that started the controversy: L. C. Andersen and J. L. Jordon, "Monetary and Fiscal Actions: A Test of Their Relative Importance in Economic Stabilization," Federal Reserve Bank of St. Louis, *Review* 50 (November 1968): 11–23. Also accessible is an updating by B. M. Friedman, "Even the St. Louis Model Now Believes in Fiscal Policy" *Journal of Money, Credit, and Banking* 9 (May 1977): 365–367

The ultimate macroeconomic targets of modern market economies are high employment levels and price stability. To be sure, there are other objectives, nor can the employment and price level targets always be achieved simultaneously. Although further elucidation of these points must be deferred to later chapters, here it suffices to note that these societal objectives are also the ultimate targets of the monetary authorities.

Operational decisions, however, cannot be based on these ultimate objectives; they are just too far removed from the actions of Federal Reserve policy makers. Surely inflation is undesirable, but if inflation is caused partly by forces other than monetary ones, the presence of rising prices alone may not be significant to the central bankers. Consider the impact of the 1973–1974 fuel crisis: The skyrocketing energy prices boosted production costs, which were passed on to consumers in the form of higher prices. Whether monetary actions could have—or, if they could, should have—wiped out the price hikes is debatable. The point is that rising prices, in and of themselves, may not send the kind of signals that the monetary authorities need.

This is where the indicators come in. These indicators bear a predictable relationship to the monetary targets but are themselves more closely related to variables that are subject to control by the monetary authorities. Thus, a rise in real interest rates or a decline in the growth rate of the money supply would suggest that monetary policy is acting to restrain spending and thus reduce pressure on prices. Indeed, the growth rate of the money supply has become a key indicator, watched carefully not only by the monetary authorities but by all who observe the current economic scene. The Federal Open Market Committee uses money supply growth rates in its directives to the manager for domestic operations (see p. 312).[8]

You realize that expansion of the money supply is not determined only by the monetary authorities; the banking system and the public are also involved, as the multiplier analysis of Chapter 10 demonstrated. Thus, though the money supply can be used as an indicator, it cannot be controlled directly by the Federal Reserve. This is equally true for interest rates; the central bank can influence interest rates, but it cannot determine them. The manager for domestic operations directly controls only the securities portfolio of the Federal Reserve banks. When the Federal Reserve buys or sells securities on the open market, its immediate impact is on the unborrowed reserves of the banking system and on the Federal funds rate. These variables, which are fully controllable by

---

[8]Actually, money supply growth can serve as both an indicator and a target. When the FOMC calculates the rate of growth it wishes to achieve and it does so because monetary growth and the ultimate macroeconomic goals are related, then money supply growth is a target. (Some have called this an "intermediate target.") The track record of the actual growth of the money supply is the indicator.

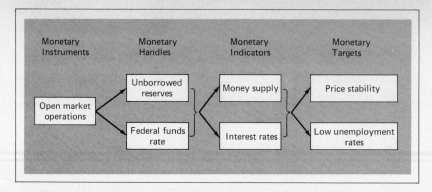

FIGURE 20.1 The pattern of Federal Reserve policy.

A **monetary handle** is an economic variable that is directly and fully controllable by the monetary authorities.

the Federal Reserve in a direct way, are called **monetary handles.** Figure 20.1 is a schematic diagram that outlines these relationships. Federal Reserve officials observe overall movements in the monetary targets, but focus most carefully on monetary indicators. They respond, if need be, by altering the setting of one of their instruments (usually open market operations), thus modifying the monetary handles. The objective of this action is to influence the indicators and, hence, ultimately the targets. (You may want to reread the directive on pp. 311–312).

While Keynesians and monetarists differed in their preferred choice of indicators and, to some extent, of monetary handles, these differences have narrowed in recent years. Monetarists obviously select the money supply as the appropriate indicator, while Keynesians have been more eclectic, tracking interest rates and supplementing this information by observing money supply movements as well. But as inflation intensified and interest rates reflected inflation, too, the difficulty of calculating real interest rates led to a reduced emphasis on their role. The FOMC gives more attention than ever to money supply growth, with a corresponding reduction in reliance on interest rates. Even the monetary authorities in the United Kingdom, where the Keynesian tradition is much stronger, have done the same.

International aspects

Not only do the monetarists claim that monetary factors bear the primary responsibility for happenings in the domestic economy, but they believe such elements are responsible for developments in the international economy as well. When the money supply increases in one country, creating imbalances there, the excess supply spills beyond the country's boundaries, affecting exchange rates and domestic developments in other nations. Higher prices at home following an increase in the money supply will raise foreign prices. Inflation in one country leads to inflation throughout the world.

*"With your permission, gentlemen, I'd like to offer a kind
word on behalf of John Maynard Keynes."*

Drawing by Lorenz; © 1981 The New Yorker Magazine, Inc.

While Keynesians do not deny that domestic circumstances have
international repercussions, they emphasize an alternative transmission
mechanism, focusing on the impact on various spending sectors. An
increase in the money supply will lead to increases in spending by
consumers, investors, and government entities. Some of the increased
spending will be for imports, affecting exchange rates and incomes
abroad. Ultimately, the higher rate of spending abroad will lead to higher
prices.

In short, the difference in the transmission mechanism described
earlier lies at the center of the way each school looks at international
macroeconomics.[9]

☐ Summary

Table 20.2 summarizes in simplified form the key attitudes of most
Keynesians and monetarists. While the table is neither exhaustive nor
detailed, it should give you more than the flavor of the division. But take
care. Often the differences consist of nuances or are finer technical points;
the gross distinctions that reach the popular economic press are not truly
representative of the mainstream of each school.

---

[9]This rather brief discussion of the international economy is expanded in the final chapters of
this book.

TABLE 20.2 Monetarism versus Keynesianism

Topic	Monetarists	Keynesians
The importance of money in determining prices and economic activity	the most crucial variable	important, but other factors are equally, if not more, critical
How monetary changes affect the economy	upsets portfolio balance of both financial and nonfinancial assets	the profitability of investment goods is changed, as is the wealth of consumers
Stability of the economy	basically stable	fundamentally unstable
Discretion or the monetary rule	more prone to favor the rule	prefer discretionary controls
Aggregate analysis versus sectoral scrutiny	no need to be concerned with the various sectors of the economy	study of the basic sectors is important
Velocity	velocity is not very responsive to interest rate changes	interest rates and velocity vary with each other
Empirical evidence	small econometric models are used to support basic monetarist contentions	large-scale models question the results of the small-scale models
Lags	monetary actions work quickly (as well as powerfully)	monetary actions work neither as quickly (nor as powerfully) as monetarists contend
Fiscal policy	a much weaker impact than monetary actions, possibly negligible	a strong effect on the economy
Monetary indicators	the money supply is the best indicator	a more eclectic approach, using a variety of indicators, is preferred
International aspects	monetary changes upset asset equilibrium at home and abroad	monetary changes affect spending flows and thus affect both domestic and international economies

☐ Questions and Exercises

1. Contrast the impact of an open market sale of securities from the vantage points of the monetarists and the neo-Keynesians.
2. What are the likely impacts of a monetary growth rule on interest rates? Would this influence be important?

3. Some economists believe that increased government spending will be fully offset by decreased private spending. What would the role of fiscal policy be if this "crowding out" exists? Would your answer differ if private spending were only partially crowded out?

4. Test the monetary rule by contrasting the actual rate of growth of M-1A to the one that would have prevailed had M-1A grown by 3.5 percent a year since 1958. Evaluate the relative performance. [A more sophisticated version can be found in F. Modigliani, "Some Empirical Tests of Monetary Management and of Rules Versus Discretion," *Journal of Political Economy* 72 (June, 1964): 211–245.]

5. The velocity of M-1A has more than doubled over the past two decades. Can you suggest some reasons? Why has the velocity of M-2 grown more slowly? (Think about the many changes that have occurred over this period, as mentioned in Chapters 2 and 6.)

☐ For Further Study

Thomas Mayer, *The Structure of Monetarism* (New York: Norton, 1978), provides an excellent survey of the monetarist-Keynesian literature, and was a major source of the material in this chapter. In addition to an extensive bibliography, the volume contains comments by a number of prominent economists. W. Poole, *Money and the Economy: A Monetarist View* (Reading, Mass.: Addison-Wesley, 1978), is another useful book on monetarism.

Milton Friedman's "Money: Quantity Theory," in *International Encyclopedia of the Social Sciences* (New York: Crowell Collier and Macmillan, 1968), 20: 439–446, presents one version of modern monetarism. Other versions may be found in R. W. Spencer, "Channels of Monetary Influence: A Survey," Federal Reserve Bank of St. Louis, *Review* 56 (November 1974): 8–26.

Friedman's monetary rule was first expounded in *A Program for Monetary Stability* (New York: Fordham University Press, 1960). Among the rule's critics are Daniel Ahearn, *Federal Reserve Policy Reappraised, 1951–1959* (New York: Columbia University Press, 1963), especially pp. 225–231, and Franco Modigliani, "Some Empirical Tests of Monetary Management and of Rules Versus Discretion," *Journal of Political Economy* 72 (June 1964): 211-245. You might also read through Modigliani, "The Monetarist Controversy or, Should We Forsake Stabilization Policies," *American Economic Review* 67 (March 1977): 1–19.

APPENDIX The Neo-Quantity Theory of Milton Friedman

In the Keynesian speculative demand for money, the money demander was offered a choice between money and fixed-interest bonds. The portfolio choice was limited to two assets, and increases or decreases in the money supply could affect only the bond market or, what is virtually the same thing, the money market. This appendix expands on the two-asset choice. In doing so, it reaches a conclusion that differs from that advanced by Keynes.

In a sophisticated economy with highly developed financial markets, a choice between only two assets appears highly artificial. The possible choices include not only money and bonds but also equities—common and preferred stocks—and real assets—houses, paintings, wine—as well. This wider range of choice leads to a theoretical development of major consequence. It can best be understood by reconsidering the demand for money.

The demand for money can be treated analogously to the demand for any commodity. When economists think about the demand for, say, plane travel, they list among the causal variables income, tastes, the price of air fare, and the prices of alternative modes of transportation. High income, a strong preference for flying, low air fares, and high bus and train fares all will induce a strong demand for air travel.

Similarly for money. Money offers a certain convenience in effecting transactions. Moreover, the transaction costs involved in converting other assets into money are not incurred when money itself is held. Thus, other things being equal, people do prefer to hold some amount of money. Other elements, too, influence the demand for money. Just as the public's income helps determine the demand for travel, so will wealth condition the amount of money that different people will prefer to hold. It is not really startling that a Rockefeller or a Kennedy will maintain larger balances than the average American worker. Moreover, as the nation's wealth increases, so, too, will the population's demand for money. However, measures of national wealth are rather imperfect, so it is difficult to relate wealth to the demand for money. Fortunately GNP can serve as a useful proxy, so that on practical grounds monetary demand can be declared to be dependent on GNP. Money (M-1A), of course, carries no return, since the payment of interest on demand deposits is illegal. (However, when we consider the fact that in the United States banks often absorb service charges on checking accounts, or that in other countries banks do pay interest on such deposits, we should qualify this statement to read that banks pay nominal returns on demand deposits.) Other assets, which are substitutes in one sense or another, do offer a variety of returns. Bonds offer a fixed interest return but also a chance of capital gain or loss. Equities, especially common stocks, give the owner a varying rate of return, depending on the profit position of the firm, as well as an opportunity for capital gains and losses. Real assets not only offer services but also act as a hedge against inflation, since their prices rise with general increases in prices.

Thus, the demand for money, according to Friedman, depends on the following:

1. Public preferences for money holdings.
2. National wealth, represented by GNP as a proxy.[10]
3. The return on money, which is close to, if not equal to, zero.
4. The return on money substitutes, consisting of
   a. the interest return on bonds plus potential capital gain or loss.
   b. the dividend rate on common stocks plus potential capital gain or loss.
   c. the rate of price change.

The transmission mechanism

Assume that the public is in an equilibrium position, holding precisely the quantities of the various assets it wants to hold at prevailing prices. Suppose that the quantity of money is increased, say, by an open market purchase of government securities by the Federal Reserve. The increased quantity of money now held puts the holders into disequilibrium and, much as in the Keynesian case, induces them to seek alternatives. The closest alternative to money is some fixed-interest security, so the demand for bonds increases, raising their prices and lowering their yields. (Considering the variety of bonds in terms of maturities and qualities, you realize that it is necessary to simplify and think in terms of very general categories.) But whereas the Keynesian analysis now suggests that real capital investment is affected, the Friedman analysis diverges. Friedman contends that the financial impact has not yet ceased. Higher bond prices—and lower yields—lead to an outflow of funds from the bond market as well as a slowing of funds coming into the bond market. Instead, money begins to flow into the stock market, which is the closest substitute for bonds. But this will force an increase in stock market prices and a reduction in the yield on common stocks. So the next link in the chain is affected: Markets in existing real assets—land, houses, bulldozers, automobiles, and refrigerators, indeed, any durable good— feel the increased demand and this leads to a rise in their prices.

Until now the chain has consisted of existing assets, which are being exchanged at higher prices. But asset transfers are not reflected in GNP,

---

[10]Because Friedman includes human capital—the value of a person, which takes into account acquired skills and potential earnings—he also includes a variable that permits one to distinguish the monetary demand of someone whose wealth is primarily in the form of tangible capital, including financial assets, from that of another whose wealth is heavily concentrated in human capital. Whose monetary demand would you expect to be higher?

and to this point the level of economic activity remains unchanged. The final link in the chain must now be forged. Higher prices on used assets shifts demand to new assets. With the new and higher prices, suppliers are willing to respond to the greater demand. Greater demand for new goods and services, accompanied by suppliers' willingness to respond, causes GNP to rise.

The conclusions of the Friedman and Keynesian analyses are generally identical—more money means more GNP. But as mentioned in the body of the chapter, the channel through which the effect is realized differs markedly. In the monetarist analysis, the final change in output follows a shift in the prices of a variety of assets—financial and real—which itself is a result of a modification of the portfolios of assetholders. Financial market impacts spread out in a ripple effect until real markets are affected. The Friedman analysis denies that the lower interest rate leads to more investment by changing the relative profitability of investment.

PART FIVE

MONETARY POLICY

CHAPTER 21

Macroeconomic Goals: The Objectives of Policy

To translate into practical reality the right of all Americans who are able, willing, and seeking to work to full opportunity for useful paid employment at fair rates of compensation; to assert the responsibility of the Federal Government to use all practicable programs and policies to promote full employment, production, and real income, balanced growth, adequate productivity growth, proper attention to national priorities, and reasonable price stability; to require the President each year to set forth explicit short-term and medium-term economic goals; to achieve a better integration of general and structural economic policies; and to improve the coordination of economic policymaking within the Federal Government.

The Full Employment and Balanced Growth Act (1978)

Adam Smith (pseudonym for George J. W. Goodman), economic journalist:
   What is an acceptable rate of inflation?

Dr. Arthur F. Burns, former chairman of the Federal Reserve Board:
   An acceptable rate of inflation: An acceptable rate? Why, zero. Zero!
(1973)

CONTENTS

By now you have learned, with varying degrees of pleasure and pain, some monetary and banking history, absorbed a good deal of information about the U.S. banking system, and discovered how the commercial banks and the Federal Reserve jointly create money. In the past few chapters you mastered the role of money in the economy as viewed both by Keynesian and monetarist economists. The next three chapters build on that foundation and examine monetary policy: how the monetary authorities influence the economy by using the various instruments at their command. The time has come to put it all together.

Helping the economy implies some vision about where the economy should be. If the Federal Reserve policy makers can be thought of as marksmen, then this chapter deals with the macroeconomic policy targets on which they must set their sights. (The plural here is used purposely, since policy targets are many.) In the present chapter these goals are discussed and analyzed. Possible conflicts between the targets are considered in the next chapter, where the question posed is, Are all macroeconomic goals achievable simultaneously?

The setting for all macroeconomic policy—fiscal and monetary—is the Employment Act of 1946. As World War II was winding down, many political leaders and economists, both inside and outside of the government, began to look at the problems of converting to a peacetime economy. Memories of the termination of World War I, which resulted in a sharp economic contraction in 1920–1921, were reinforced by the conclusions of Keynesian analysis. The latter suggested that a severe cutback in government military spending would lead to a reduction in aggregate demand and a decline in employment. The employment situation would be exacerbated as the millions of discharged soldiers began to seek civilian employment. The result of these concerns was the Employment Act of 1946, which spelled out for the first time the federal government's responsibility for maintaining high levels of employment. It is worthwhile to cite in full the key paragraph of this Act:

The Congress hereby declares that it is the continuing policy and responsibility of the Federal Government to use all practicable means consistent with its needs and obligations and other essential considerations of national policy, with the assistance and cooperation of industry, agriculture, labor, and state and local governments, to coordinate and utilize all its plans, functions, and resources for the purpose of creating and maintaining, in a manner calculated to foster and promote free competitive enterprise and the general welfare, conditions under which there will be afforded useful employment opportunities, including self-employment, for those able, willing, and seeking to work, and *to promote maximum employment, production, and purchasing power. (Italics added)*

The italicized words indicate the thrust of the new governmental responsibility—to assure high, though not "full,"[1] employment.

But how does one translate this generalized statement into an operational one? How are those charged with influencing macroeconomic policy expected to interpret the low-unemployment goal?

☐ Unemployment

The causes of unemployment

In order to understand what can and cannot be achieved by macroeconomic policy, it is best to understand the causes of unemployment. The following categories can be singled out: frictional, seasonal, structural, induced, and cyclical.

Frictional unemployment is the unavoidable outcome of normal movements in the labor market. Workers quit to search for better jobs or because they do not get along with their employers. Similarly, they may be fired for poor performance or a myriad of other reasons related to themselves and their firms rather than to national economic conditions. Workers who are entering or reentering the market may find it takes a while to find the right job. Strikes and lockouts are included in this category, too. Even in a "full-employment" economy, some frictional unemployment would exist simply because of the workings of a free labor market. (In the USSR, where unemployment may be considered "parasitism," a crime against the state that is punishable by a prolonged visit to a labor site in Siberia, frictional unemployment, understandably, is minimal.)

Seasonal unemployment, as the name implies, is derived from seasonal swings in business. The construction and agricultural sectors of the economy are characterized by seasonal movements due to the weather. Other industries experience seasonal patterns for reasons of custom. Baseball is a spring-and-summer activity; automobile sales are strong when the new models are introduced in the fall. Workers in seasonal industries are laid off during slack periods but return to their jobs when

---

[1]The original bill used the term "full employment," but Congress affirmed a toned-down, less extreme title. It was reinstated in The Full Employment and Balanced Growth Act of 1978, to be discussed later in this chapter.

business picks up. Various programs—both private (e.g., union payments) and public (e.g., unemployment insurance)—ease the financial burden of workers caught in seasonal lows. Economists agree that such programs are a more effective means of combating seasonal unemployment than strategies, such as monetary policy, designed to stimulate the economy in general.

Structural unemployment arises from numerous causes related to changes in the structure of the economy. Losses of jobs in the steel industry because countries with more modern plants are able to undercut domestic prices is one recent example. So, too, is regional unemployment; as the Sunbelt gains jobs and the older industrial Northeast loses positions, people who are unable or unwilling to migrate may find themselves without jobs for substantial amounts of time. If it is true that the United States is becoming a more technologically oriented society, with greater demands for educated and skilled labor, then the uneducated and the unskilled will be structurally unemployed.

In this case, too, those who advocate government action prefer specific policies designed to cure specific problems. Retraining programs, relocation loans, training and educational programs, and services that provide information about job opportunities are all means of reducing structural unemployment. Monetary policy, working on economic activity in general, would be inefficient in addressing itself to alleviating structural unemployment.

Induced unemployment occurs when unemployment results from government policies rather than being reduced by such programs. With the government transfer payments accounting for 15 cents of each dollar's worth of disposable income, it is not surprising that conflicts in objectives arise. Thus, the fact that unemployment compensation is not taxable for most recipients is highly beneficial; the family's entire income can be spent. On the other hand, the nontaxable aspect of the payment may well induce the recipient to stay unemployed a bit longer than if the subsidy were taxed as regular income. Similarly, the extension of unemployment benefits from 26 weeks to 52, and in some cases 78, weeks has made prolonged unemployment more attractive. And welfare payments, which for some workers virtually equal the wage income they would receive in the labor market, has undoubtedly induced unemployment. Precisely how to remedy these conflicts lies beyond the scope of this book. However, again economists agree that monetary policy would be a poor means of solving the problem of induced unemployment.

The percentage of the labor force that is unemployed because of frictional, seasonal, structural, and induced causes is called the **natural rate of unemployment.**

Cyclical unemployment may be viewed as the unemployment arising from a lack of adequate aggregate demand in the national economy.

The term **natural rate of unemployment** is used to refer to the types of joblessness just described. **Cyclical unemployment** is the unemployment remaining after frictional, seasonal, structural, and induced unemployment have been accounted for. More precisely, it arises from insufficient spending by the various spending groups—consumers, investors, and governments.

Translating these concepts into numbers is hardly a simply exercise, and it is not surprising that economists differ as to what the correct numbers are. During the 1960s a loose consensus viewed a 4 percent unemployment rate as caused by forces other than aggregate demand; 4 percent unemployment was the natural rate. This rate would be reduced by policies designed to remedy the specific causes. Only unemployment in excess of 4 percent would be attacked by macroeconomic policies.

Figure 21.1 shows the unemployment rate for all unemployed people as well as for males aged 20 and older, and teenagers. The total unemployment rate has fluctuated from below 3 percent in 1953 to almost 9 percent in 1975. Periods of "overfull" employment—in which the rate fell below 4 percent—have been more than compensated for by periods in which the rate exceeded 4 percent. The decade of the 1960s is instructive: The high rate of unemployment in 1961, coming during the 1960–1961 recession, fell throughout the decade, corresponding to the rise in economic activity that continued until 1969–1970.

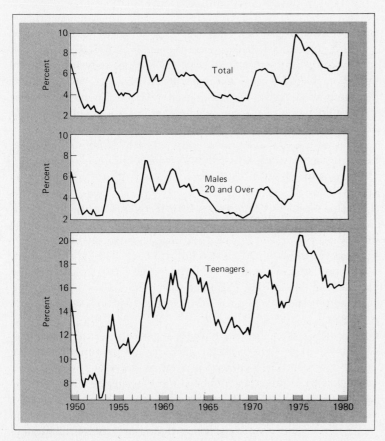

FIGURE 21.1 Quarterly unemployment rates, 1950–1980 (seasonally adjusted).
Source: Board of Governors of the Federal Reserve System.

What has disturbed many economists, as well as the general public, has been the rise in the unemployment rate in the 1970s. Consequently, while a 4 percent rate was achieved during the 1960s, it apparently was not a realizable goal for the 1970s. The continued higher rate of unemployment led to a reexamination of the 4 percent standard. Perhaps that standard, though appropriate for the 1960s, was no longer relevant.

Is the natural rate of unemployment greater than 4 percent?

The natural unemployment rate may have risen for two distinct reasons. First, the composition of the labor force has changed, leading to higher average unemployment rates. Second, the amount of induced unemployment has probably grown.

Compositional shifts. An example will illustrate the impact of changes in the labor force on unemployment rates. Consider two groups, M and T. M constitutes 75 percent of the population and had an unemployment rate of 4 percent in 1960. T, accounting for the remaining 25 percent, had an unemployment rate of 6 percent. The average unemployment rate, which must be computed as a weighted average, equals $(.04 \times .75) + (.06 \times .25)$, or 4.5 percent. In 1970 we find the unemployment rate of each group unchanged. But the M group now accounts for only 50 percent of the population, the T group having grown to 50 percent. The new unemployment rate equals $(.50 \times .04) + (.50 \times .06) = 5$ percent. The rise in the unemployment rate from 4.5 percent to 5 percent is, in this example, entirely an outcome of the increased importance of the T group. But in terms of the unemployment rate of each group, nothing has changed. In a sense, then, this increase in the unemployment rate is misleading; it indicates a rise when, in truth, within each group no increase has occurred.

How can this misleading implication be corrected? One way to do so is to maintain the old weights, thereby removing any changes resulting from shifting components. (You may recall that this principle underlies the calculation of the consumer price index; see p. 348.) If we do that, then in 1970 both M and T will be weighted at their 1960 weights and the unemployment rate in 1970 will again be 4.5 percent. In other words, a 5 percent unemployment rate in 1970 is really identical with the 4.5 percent rate in 1960.

While the numbers in this example are hypothetical, the principle is correct. Two types of changes affected the overall unemployment rate between the 1960s and the 1970s. First of all, as is evident in both lower panels of Figure 21.1, unemployment declined during the 1960s both for males aged 20 and over and for teenagers, and trended upward during the 1970s for both groups. These movements were basically cyclical, and hence are not relevant when considering the natural rate of unemployment. But a second change is relevant, namely, the increase in the proportion of teenagers (and women) in the labor force. While the chart does not indicate the weights of the two groups, it does provide important information about the unemployment rates of each category. For every year recorded, the unemployment rate of teenagers exceeded that of older workers. Thus, had there been no cyclical component in the total unemployment rate, it still would have increased during the 1970s because of the heavier weight of teenagers in the labor force.

To correct for such shifts in the composition of the labor force, a fixed-weight average can be computed. One such calculation has been made by the Department of Commerce, which publishes a measure called the **high-employment unemployment rate.** On the basis of the composition of the labor force and the relative unemployment rates among age and sex groups in 1955, which, at 4 percent, was assumed to be a high-employment year, the corresponding number for the 1960 average would be 4.35 percent; for the 1970s, 4.9 percent; and for 1975–1980, 5.1 percent.[2] In other words, compositional shifts alone would have raised the natural rate of unemployment from 4 percent in 1955 to over 5 percent two decades later.

The cyclical component of unemployment, then, is likely to be equal to the difference between the unemployment rate and approximately 5 percent.

A simpler alternative way to track unemployment and avoid the problem of compositional shifts is to focus on a critical subgroup. Thus, some economists monitor closely the behavior of the prime-age unemployment rate, the rate for males between 25 and 54. On that basis, maximum noncyclical unemployment would be based on the behavior of that group alone. A 3 percent natural rate in the 1960s would be appropriate for the 1970s as well. Consequently, the fact that the actual unemployment rate for this group averaged 5.7 percent in 1975 would indicate substantial cyclical unemployment.

Induced unemployment. A second explanation for the rise in the employment rate in the 1970s is related to induced unemployment and the official definition of unemployed. In its monthly sample survey of the population, the Census Bureau obtains information on respondents' employment status—working or not working, part time or full time, and so forth—and if they are not working, finds out whether they're seeking employment, how long they've been unemployed, and so on. Someone who is not working but is actively seeking a job is defined as unemployed. Those who are not working and not looking are not considered unemployed but, rather, are excluded from the labor force. In recent years a change in welfare laws has made it more difficult for people on the public aid rolls who are capable of working to declare that they're not seeking employment. An unknown number of respondents who formerly stated that they were not looking for jobs, and therefore were not in the labor

The **high-employment unemployment rate** adjusts the unemployment rate only for changes in the composition of the labor force and for trends in unemployment rate differentials among groups, but not for cyclical changes.

[2]Frank de Leeuw et al., "The High-Employment Budget: New Estimates, 1955–80," *Survey of Current Business* 60 (November 1980): 16–17.

force, now claim to be job seekers and thus enter the ranks of the measured unemployed. In fact, their actual status has not changed. The outcome is that the higher unemployment rate in the 1970s represents an unknown degree of overstatement, perhaps as much as 0.4 percentage points.

Nevertheless, even with these adjustments, it is clear from Figure 21.1 that for most of the 1970s the unemployment rate exceeded the target implied by the Employment Act of 1946.

The Humphrey-Hawkins Act

Not all observers agree with the preceding analysis or its conclusions. Accepting a 5 percent unemployment rate in a labor force of 105 million people means tolerating more than 5 million unemployed. Can this be in the best interests of the economy or the social fabric of the nation? Obviously in the belief that the answer was a strong negative, a bill was introduced into Congress by the late Senator Hubert H. Humphrey of Minnesota and Representative Augustus F. Hawkins of California. The original bill would have set a 3 percent target rate of unemployment to be reached by the early 1980s; in the final Act discretion was ceded the President if the goal could not be achieved on time. "The Full Employment and Balanced Growth Act of 1978" is now law; it shows that employment goals continue to rank high among public policy objectives.

☐ Inflation

In Chapter 14 you read about the great German hyperinflation. In your own time, inflation in the United States has not even come near that level. At its highest point in the past quarter-century, the implicit GNP deflator recorded a rise of 9.3 percent (1975), while the consumer price index rose by 11.3 percent (1979). Nevertheless, these rates were not insignificant; if maintained, a 10 percent rate of inflation leads to a doubling of prices in around seven years. Americans who had been accustomed to near price stability in the late 1950s and early 1960s saw themselves threatened by the rising prices of the late 1960s and 1970s.

Figure 21.2 charts the quarterly rate of inflation using the GNP deflator and the CPI. Note that in both sets of data there is a discernible difference between 1958–1964 on the one hand and 1971–1980 on the other. This has led many political leaders to decry inflation as the number-one enemy of the United States.

What precisely is inflation?

A simple definition might be "a sustained rise in prices." In other words, prices keep on rising, never to fall. By that definition, a glance at Figure 21.2 will show that inflation has been endemic in the United States since 1960. (On the chart, any point above the zero line indicates inflation. An upward movement means that inflation is intensifying, while

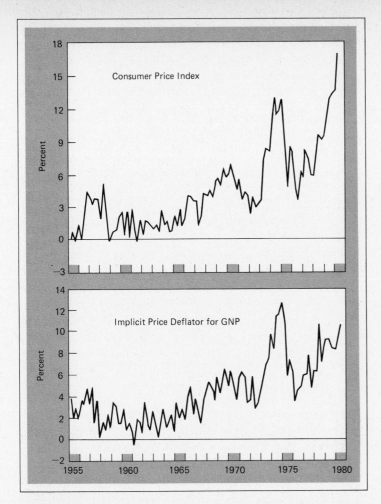

FIGURE 21.2 The consumer price index and the implicit GNP deflator,
1955–1980 (quarterly changes at annual rates, seasonally adjusted).
Source: Board of Governors of the Federal Reserve System.

a downward change means that prices are rising less rapidly than before.
Only a fall below zero shows that prices are actually falling.) Yet most
Americans were not concerned about inflation in the early 1960s. Indeed,
most of us would distinguish between mild and rapid price increases, and
though we would be hard pressed to define these terms with any degree
of precision, we would normally reserve the term *inflation* for the more
rapid, less tolerated price hike. We could live with an annual price rise of
1–2 percent; we would be decidedly unhappy with a 10–15 percent yearly
increase in prices.

Figure 21.2 portrays a second source of concern: the rising rate of
inflation. While the rate of inflation fluctuated in the years between 1955

and 1967, it did so within a relatively narrow range and averaged around 3 percent. Since that time, however, the range has widened and the trend has been clearly upward. In other words, inflation has been accelerating. In the next few pages we focus on these two aspects of inflation: (1) its intensity and (2) its trend.

The intensity of inflation

Most people are not disturbed by moderate increases in the overall price level for a very simple reason: Their incomes rise more rapidly than prices. With real income up, they are better off even after inflation. The converse is also true: When prices increase faster than incomes, as has occurred only infrequently in the last thirty years, public dissatisfaction grows. (It happened in 1980. Could that have been a factor in the Reagan landslide?) And while people like pensioners and bondholders, who live on fixed incomes, lose even when inflation is mild, they feel it most painfully when it intensifies.

Of course, not everyone loses from inflation. Debtors gain as they pay off their fixed interest and principal charges with cheaper dollars. The

"We have to overcome your obsession with
inflation . . . and by the way, my fee has gone
up from $75 to $100 a session."

Drawing by Bernhardt from The Wall Street Journal, permission by Cartoon Features Syndicate.

public purse, too, is filled more rapidly, for with progressive income taxes, taxpayers move into higher liability categories and pay a larger share of their income to the government.

Inflation is unfair, and it is this inequitable redistribution of income that troubles most people. Why should some groups be deprived of purchasing power through no fault of their own? Why should other groups be permitted to gain, having done nothing to merit the benefit? And the higher the rate of inflation, the more we experience its injustice.

A recent Brookings Institution study by economist Joseph Minarik comes to some interesting, indeed startling, conclusions concerning the distributional impact of inflation.[3] Taking data on a cross-section of families from the Census Bureau and the Internal Revenue Service, Minarik calculated the impact of a 2 percent increase in prices on the range of family income. When he used current cash income as the measure of family income, he found that in the first year lower-income families lost a bit; middle-income families (in the $6,000–13,000 real-income range) broke even; and upper-income recipients gained a bit. But when the inflation has been around for six years, the picture changes. While income recipients earning less than $10,000 a year average an insignificant loss of approximately 0.6 percent, those with incomes over $25,000 *lose* from inflation. Dividend income appears not to rise sufficiently to offset price increases for the rich.

Even more revealing is Minarik's more comprehensive income measure, which includes such benefits as health care paid by employers, such balance sheet changes as the value of homes, and charges like taxes. Using this measure, both the middle- and upper-income classes suffer from inflation even in the first year. By the sixth year, the lower-income classes actually benefit, while for real incomes above $12,000, the greater the income, the greater the loss from inflation. This is most easily explained by the fall in the value of fixed-income securities as interest rates rise (remember the inverse relationship between the two) during inflation, combined with the fact that the upper-income classes hold a proportionally larger share of their assets in security portfolios.

These conclusions appear to contradict conventional wisdom, which suggests that the poor suffer more than the wealthy. Inflation, according to the Brookings results, appears to be a progressive tax.

Nevertheless, inflation is a tax that is imposed unintentionally. And there is a qualitative difference between a mild, 2 percent inflation rate and the double-digit rates that have threatened the American public in recent years.

Accelerating prices

In the long run a stable rate of inflation, even one that is not moderate, may not impose significant costs on the economy. This is so because

[3]"Who Wins, Who Loses from Inflation?" *The Brookings Bulletin* 15 (Summer 1978): 6–10.

people and policies can be expected to adjust when the rate is stable and, therefore, predictable. Indexing of contracts is one adjustment method, as is the simpler expedient of including the known inflation premium in all calculations. Thus, if both workers and employers are convinced that prices will rise by 13 percent next year, employees will demand a 13 percent inflation increment and their firms will cover the increased cost by raising their prices by 13 percent. Similarly, lenders will charge 13 percent more per year and borrowers will pay it, leaving the financing process unaffected.[4]

The scenario differs markedly for an unstable, inflation-prone economy, especially one in which inflation is intensifying. When prices rise more rapidly each year, redistribution of income and wealth becomes inevitable. Even automatic indexing plans normally do not compensate fully; they operate with a lag, so that the recipient is always struggling to catch up. (Social security benefits, for example, are adjusted in July to reflect the increase in the CPI between the first quarter of the preceding and the first quarter of the current year.) Conflicts between labor and management intensify, with each side seeking maximum protection against the unknown.

But more than income redistribution is at stake during a period of accelerating inflation. Uncertainty about inflation undermines business planning. Long-term investment, always rooted in the unknown future, becomes even riskier, so that investment projects are deferred, if not canceled. Short-term profit targets take priority over future returns. Speculation aimed at protecting oneself and one's business against the ravages of intensifying inflation is encouraged, while productive investment is discouraged. All this reduces productivity, which in turn exacerbates inflation. Inflation becomes self-generating and self-justifying, for as everyone expects prices to rise ever more rapidly, people's very actions guarantee the realization of their expectations.

These concerns underlie the real fear of inflation that has gripped the American public, irrespective of their social or economic status, in recent years. Figure 21.3, which plots changes in the consumer price index from 1913 to 1980, may put the issue in historical perspective. The basically stable trend of prices until 1960 is disturbed by occasional large bulges, all of which are related to wartime episodes (World War I: 1914–1918; World War II: 1941–1945, with price decontrol accounting for the 1946 spike; the Korean War: 1951–1953). But you'll notice that after each inflationary surge the rate drops back to acceptable levels. The 1960s and 1970s,

---

[4]Of course, this paragraph is not to be taken as a description of reality. In the real world inflation is never perfectly stable, nor can adjustments be made without frictions that impede the smooth functioning depicted here. Moreover, even on the analytic level some economic theorists have argued that anticipated inflation does have real impacts. For example, the demand for money holdings will decline, leading to portfolio readjustments and changes in the demand for investment.

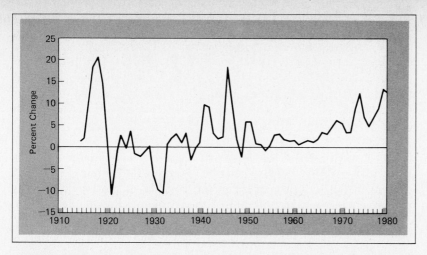

FIGURE 21.3 Changes in consumer prices 1913–1980. (Note: December to December changes except for 1980 which is from December 1979 to November 1980. All are given at a seasonally adjusted annual rate.)
Source: *Economic Report of the President*, 1981.

however, differ in two respects. First, the rising rate of inflation is not attributable to a major outbreak of war (the Vietnam conflict notwithstanding). Second, after prices rose, they didn't fall back as far as they'd risen. Consequently, each new inflationary bout started at a higher rate of growth than the previous one. The resulting upward trend reflects accelerating inflation.

In light of these inflationary circumstances and in response to increasing public concern, Congress has shifted its priorities. The Employment Act of 1946 did not mention inflation. The 1978 Humphrey-Hawkins Act specifically amends the Employment Act to include "reasonable price stability" as a national economic goal, having found that "inflation is a major national problem." While the Full Employment and Balanced Growth Act certainly did not neglect the employment goals of the U.S. government, its inclusion of price stability as a policy target makes explicit what has long been controversial.

☐ Other Important Macroeconomic Goals

In addition to the two primary goals, a number of other objectives are sought by the American public. Among the most important are a healthy rate of economic growth and currency that is stable abroad as well as at home.

Economic growth

The "balanced growth" of the Humphrey-Hawkins Act refers to the attainment of a satisfactory rate of economic growth. In the context of economic development, growth in general is taken to mean increasing GNP per capita. To most of us, this implies an ever-improving standard of living, which, with but minor interruptions, has been the historical legacy of the United States.

Recently, some observers have expressed the fear that our historical rate of growth is slowing. The data do not bear out this claim. In the nineteenth century, per capita annual economic growth averaged 2.12 percent; it fell to 1.69 percent in the first half of the twentieth. The growth rate increased significantly in the prosperous decade of the 1960s, reaching 3.0 percent, but then fell back to 2.26 percent in the period between 1970 and 1979. Even this growth rate is high by historical standards.

Nevertheless, an argument can be made for faster economic growth and for policy measures aimed at achieving this goal. A faster rate of growth means more than just a more rapid increase in living standards. With a growing population, speedier growth reduces economic and social tensions. In a fast-growing economy, more jobs are available and fewer hands are left idle. Teenagers are more quickly absorbed into the labor force, and thus have less difficulty finding a place in the community's economic life. When the size of the economic pie is growing more rapidly, people are less committed to protecting their slice, leading to diminished intergroup tensions. The same is true when labor and management negotiate, and when skilled laborers face new methods of production that would replace them with machines and unskilled workers. In a more rapidly growing economy, where there's additional room for everyone, economic and personal relations are more generous and tolerant.

In recent years, especially in view of the public's concern about environmental quality, the appropriateness of faster economic growth as a national goal has been questioned. Is faster growth worth the price of destroying the quality of the air we breathe and the water we drink, natural resources that are irreplaceable, and the quality of life in general? This question must be answered by each of us personally, by weighing the gains from faster growth against its costs. Care must be taken, however, to assess correctly the benefits and costs; too much glib talk has replaced the careful analysis that the issue deserves.

Exchange rate stability

Another important policy target is the international value of the dollar. Since 1973 the price of the dollar on international markets has been determined largely by the forces of supply and demand. When the demand for dollars by foreigners who want to purchase U.S. goods and services, buy U.S. securities, or acquire direct ownership over American farms and factories increases, the value of the dollar compared to foreign currencies like the West German mark or the Swiss franc rises. Conversely, when foreigners are more interested in acquiring currencies other than the dollar, the value of the dollar declines. As will become evident in Chapter 25, the consequences of a falling dollar are not always undesirable. Indeed, fluctuating foreign exchange rates can provide substantial benefits to U.S. residents. However, at times the dollar may be depressed for reasons that have little to do with basic economic trends; speculation, which becomes self-justifying, takes over. For if speculators believe the dollar is going to decline they sell dollars, and sure enough the value of the dollar declines. Speculators' actions now confirm their beliefs, and a new round begins.

Halting excessive swings of the dollar has become a policy goal of U.S. monetary and fiscal authorities. On occasion the nation's economic leaders have even gone so far as to subsume domestic employment goals to this exchange rate target. Thus, in November 1978 a series of moves by the Treasury and the Federal Reserve to protect the dollar was designed to raise U.S. interest rates and thereby increase the demand for dollars. With many economists predicting a recession in 1979, it seemed clear to many analysts that the unemployment goal had become subsidiary, at least for the moment, to the international-value-of-the-dollar goal.

In these paragraphs you have implicitly been introduced to the concept of the **trade-off**. More rapid economic growth may have to be traded off to preserve environmental quality. Similarly, lower employment may be the sacrifice resulting from measures taken to prop up the dollar. However, the trade-off that has been a prime concern of both economists and the public is that between employment and inflation, the subject of the next chapter.

A **trade-off** involves the sacrifice of one objective in order to attain an alternative objective.

☐ Summary

The chapter's focus on national macroeconomic goals has highlighted the battle against unemployment and inflation. Unemployment can be classified as frictional, seasonal, structural, induced, and cyclical. Only cyclical unemployment is caused primarily by shifts in aggregate demand and responds significantly to policies designed to stimulate or retard overall economic activity. The other types of unemployment, which together are designated as "the natural rate of unemployment," are mostly microeconomic in origin.

Measuring the cyclical component of the unemployment rate requires removing the natural unemployment rate from the overall rate. While 4 percent was long considered the natural unemployment rate, shifts in the composition of the labor force since the mid-1950s have led to a reconsideration of that number. Now the natural rate is calculated to exceed 5 percent.

The Full Employment and Balanced Growth Act (the Humphrey-

Hawkins Act) of 1978 finds even 4 percent unacceptable and mandates its reduction to 3 percent. In terms of practical politics, this goal is viewed more as an expression of intent than as an operational target to be achieved in the near future.

Inflation, defined as a rapid and sustained rise in prices, has been troublesome lately both because the rate of inflation is higher than it has been in the recent past and because it is rising ever more rapidly. While even a mild inflation is inequitable, benefiting some economic groups at the expense of others, the greater the rate of inflation, the greater the inequity. Creditors lose unfairly, while debtors gain undeservedly. People with fixed incomes lose, while those who can overcompensate for inflation gain. Surprisingly, those in the upper strata of the income and wealth scale lose considerably more than those lower on the scale, primarily because the former experience capital losses on their fixed-income securities.

Accelerating prices cause more than redistributive injustice. Labor peace and business planning suffer; productivity declines; and ultimately inflation gains a self-sustaining momentum. The Full Employment and Balanced Growth Act formally introduces "reasonable price stability" as a national macroeconomic goal.

Other macroeconomic objectives discussed in this chapter are increased economic growth and exchange rate stability. Although the rise in per capita GNP in recent decades has been high by historical standards, more rapid growth rates mean faster improvements in living standards and corresponding reductions in both economic and social tensions. However, the costs of faster growth, especially in terms of environmental pollution, cannot be ignored.

Greater stability in the international sphere is also desired. In a world of fluctuating exchange rates, extreme instability caused by speculative excesses can be destructive to national economic progress. Minimizing such speculation has become a goal of governments around the world.

However, not always can all desired objectives be achieved simultaneously. The trade-off between unemployment and inflation is the main topic of the next chapter.

□ Questions and Exercises

1. Give some examples of frictional, seasonal, structural, and induced unemployment. Why would monetary ease be an inefficient means of resolving these kinds of joblessness?
2. After 1985 income tax payments will be indexed to reduce the impact of inflation. Who is likely to benefit most from this reform, and who stands to lose? What impact is this new tax policy likely to have on government income and expenditures?
3. A number of countries, such as Brazil and Israel, have adopted extensive indexing of contracts and wage income. Might this be a solution to the

redistributive impact of inflation in the United States? Might there be disadvantages, too?

4. Unemployment insurance is an example of an automatic stabilizer that buoys up the economy as it turns downward. How does this work? Can you think of other such stabilizers?

5. What do you suppose will happen to the economy if the authorities attempt to achieve the Humphrey-Hawkins unemployment target in the current year?

☐ For Further Study

Chapter 3 of the 1975 *Economic Report of the President* (Washington, D.C., 1975) contains an extensive discussion of unemployment, including its measurement, its differential effect on various components of the labor force, and income maintenance programs designed to mitigate its impact. An entirely new approach to explaining unemployment has been developed in the last decade. It is available (to students who are willing to exert themselves) in Arthur M. Okun, *Prices and Quantities: A Macroeconomic Analysis* (Washington, D.C.: Brookings 1981), chap. 2, or E. S. Phelps, *Inflation Policy and Unemployment Theory: The Cost-Benefit Approach to Monetary Planning* (New York: Norton, 1972).

A good survey of the causes, consequences, and cures of inflation is provided by British economist Brian Griffiths, *Inflation: The Price of Prosperity* (New York: Holmes and Meier, 1976), while R. Lekachman's most literate pen has contributed *Inflation: The Permanent Problem of Boom and Bust* (New York: Vintage, 1973).

CHAPTER 22

The Inflation-Unemployment Trade-off: It May Be as Bad as It Seems

In the years ahead, our country will be wrestling with two central domestic issues. The first is economic in nature: How can we reduce inflation while maintaining the economic growth that keeps our people employed?

Jimmy Carter (1981)

CONTENTS

The preceding chapter described the national macroeconomic goals that represent the consensus view among contemporary Americans, a view that is shared by people in many other countries as well. While an optimist might believe that all of these goals could be achieved simultaneously, evidence from the United States over the last decade or two indicates otherwise. This somewhat depressing conclusion was alluded to at the end of the last chapter and will be explored here.

The trade-off between inflation and unemployment is represented by the Phillips curve. After the Phillips curve has been developed in the early part of the chapter, its policy implications will be examined. Finally, the views of those who question the value of Phillips curve analysis will be analyzed.

Since economic policy depends to a large extent on properly defining

The inflation-recession (= unemployment) trade-off.
Drawing by Auth © 1978 Philadelphia Inquirer.

the issue, the existence or nonexistence of the Phillips curve is of more than academic interest. Whether government authorities should act and, if they should, what the impact and side-effects of their decisions will be, are questions that can hinge on the outcome of the Phillips curve controversy.

□ The Unemployment-Inflation Trade-off: The Phillips Curve

In the Keynesian theory outlined in earlier chapters, the distinction between GNP in current dollars and GNP in constant dollars was not emphasized. Chapter 17, for example, demonstrated that as the money supply increased, GNP rose, but whether this was in real or nominal terms was not important at that point. Nevertheless, you surely realize that the increase in aggregate demand caused by a rise in M need not express itself only as an increase in output. Part of the expansion may well reflect an increase in prices.

Figure 22.1 distinguishes among three possible reactions to demand shifts. When the supply curve is flat (elasticity is infinite), as it is in region I, and the demand curve also lies within that region, then as demand increases—AD_1 shifts to AD_2—prices remain unchanged. Real GNP increases by the full amount of the increase in demand. The reason for this—and for the flat segment of the supply curve—is the assumption that the costs of production remain stable. This is most likely to occur in a slack economy with abnormally large segments of the labor force unemployed and a good deal of idle capacity. However, as the economy expands it becomes more expensive to employ labor; wages are driven up. Similarly, pressure on capacity begins to be felt. The result is operating in region II. A shift in the AD line leads to output increases

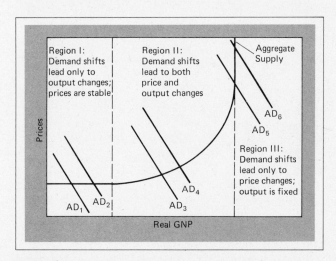

FIGURE 22.1 The impact of shifts in aggregate demand on prices and real GNP.

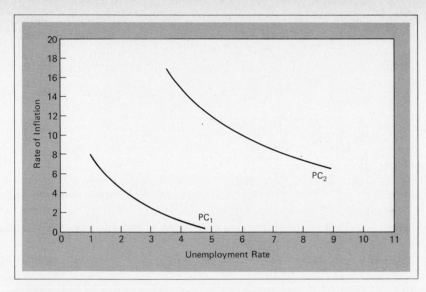

FIGURE 22.2 Benevolent and malevolent Phillips curves.

accompanied by price increases. As the economy continues to expand, ultimately full capacity is reached, the physical limit of GNP cannot be expanded further, and any increases in demand, as from AD_5 to AD_6 will result only in price hikes.

The central conclusion, then, is that, except in extreme cases, output and prices move in tandem, as demonstrated by region II. Greater demand leads to higher output and prices, while reduced demand results in reduced output and prices.

An alternative way of expressing the same thought was first advanced by A. W. Phillips.[1] When Phillips plotted the change in the wage rate of English workers against their unemployment rate, he discovered that the lower the unemployment rate (indicating strong demand for labor), the higher the rate of growth of wages. But since prices and wages are interrelated—prices tend to rise by the rate of growth of wages less the growth in labor productivity[2]—it is just a small step further to relate the rate of inflation to the unemployment rate. Figure 22.2 does just that. The negatively sloped curves are called **Phillips curves.** As the lowest curve indicates, an inflation rate of 1 percent is consistent with an unemployment rate of 4 percent. This is a **benevolent Phillips curve** in that both targets—reasonable price stability and tolerably low levels of unemployment—are achievable at the same time. However, should an attempt be made to reduce inflation further, unemployment is bound to rise. Conversely, an attempt by, say, the monetary authorities to loosen

Phillips curves demonstrate the inverse relationship between the rate of inflation and the unemployment rate.
At some point on a **benevolent Phillips curve,** the goals of price stability and low unemployment can be achieved simultaneously.

[1]A. W. Phillips, "The Relation Between Unemployment and the Rate of Change in Money Wage Rates in the United Kingdom, 1861–1957," *Economica* 25 (November 1958): 283–299.
[2]If wages in the nation rise by 11 percent and worker productivity rises by 2 percent, prices are going to increase, on average, by 9 percent.

the money supply in order to decrease unemployment below the 4 percent rate will result in an ever-sharper rise in the rate of price increase.

Phillips curves, however, need not be benevolent. The uppermost curve in Figure 22.2 represents a **malevolent Phillips curve.** In this situation an inflation rate of 10 percent is consistent with an unemployment rate of 6 percent. Neither of these numbers is satisfactory from the point of view of the national interest. The economy finds itself in a **dilemma.** Indeed, this was the situation faced by the nation's policy makers during the late 1970s and 1980. In 1980, for example, the unemployment rate had hovered around 7½ percent for most of the year, and the rate of inflation, which at the end of 1977 stood at 6 percent, had reached 10½ percent by the final three months of 1980.

Figure 22.3 plots data for both price increases and unemployment for the 1966–1980 period and draws in three Phillips curves that correspond to the numbers. PC_1, which describes the 1966–1969 years, is a reasonably benevolent curve, with the 4 percent unemployment rate accompanied by a 3 percent inflation rate and a 5 percent unemployment rate consistent with 2 percent inflation. In the early 1970s the picture gets gloomier; on PC_2, 5 percent unemployment is achieved with a 6 percent inflation rate, which would move higher quite rapidly should attempts be made to reduce unemployment further. A very malevolent Phillips curve, PC_3, portrays the years between 1974 and 1980. Living with a high, 7 percent unemployment rate would also mean tolerating a 7–8 percent inflation rate; attempting to reduce inflation to the 5–6 percent annual rate of increase would imply acceptance of unemployment in the 8 percent range. At this rate, over 8 million workers would be jobless.

What could the Federal Reserve—and, for that matter, the executive and Congress—do? If they tried to bring the inflation under control by reducing aggregate demand, they risked raising an already high unemployment rate still further. If they manipulated the economy to reduce unemployment to the 5 percent natural rate, what would the inflationary consequences be? (The increasing intensity of the problem is expressed by the *discomfort index*—see Box 22.1.)

Clearly, then, when the goals conflict and the alternative policies are equally unpalatable, demand management cannot do the job. An additional policy tool is needed.

BOX 22.1 The Discomfort Index

Arthur Okun had a way of coining apt terms to summarize economic phenomena. Best known for Okun's law, which states that for every 3 percent decline in GNP below its potential, the unemployment rate rises by 1 percent, this former chairman of the Council of Economic Advisers (1968–1969; member, 1964–1968) also gave us the discomfort index. Okun suggested adding the rate of inflation to the rate of unemployment as a

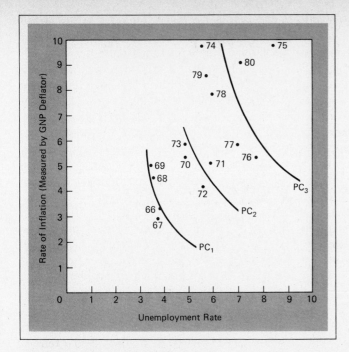

FIGURE 22.3 Empirical Phillips curves.

simple device to indicate the harm being done the economy by these twin evils. To be sure, this measure arbitarily assigns equal weight to 1 percent unemployment and a percent rise in prices. Nevertheless, the trend of the index, as depicted here, is certainly discomforting.

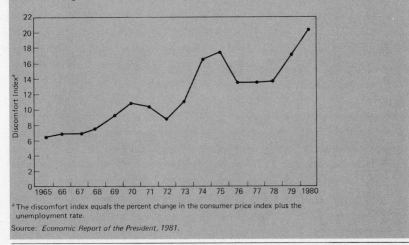

[a] The discomfort index equals the percent change in the consumer price index plus the unemployment rate.

Source: *Economic Report of the President, 1981*.

☐ Incomes Policy

Many experts believe that the way out of the dilemma is through control directed at prices and wages, or **incomes policy.** In the United

An **incomes policy** aims to control prices and wages directly, rather than through the indirect methods of demand management.

States, extensive price and wage controls were imposed during World War II. Employment was not a problem in those years; labor was in short supply. The major macroeconomic problem was inflation—in a demand-strong but goods-deficient economy, prices could skyrocket. So in 1942 virtually all prices, including rents, interest rates, and wage rates, were frozen. Short supplies were allocated by a rationing process. Each family received coupons that gave them rights to purchase certain commodities. In many cases raw materials were physically allocated to manufacturers. In general, the system worked well, not least because the public was united in its support of U.S. involvement in the war. A smaller-scale control system was instituted during the Korean War period in the early 1950s.

But in peacetime wage and price controls are inconsistent with the free-market economy of the United States. Rigid prices inhibit the adjustments needed for efficient operation, and cannot reflect new technologies and changes in relative scarcities. Nevertheless, in August 1971 President Nixon instituted his "new economic policy" by freezing wages and prices for a ninety-day period. The background was a slow rate of economic growth, with the unemployment rate hovering around 6 percent and the inflation rate, which was in the 4–5 percent range, not expected to decline. Indeed, the chances were good that it might increase. The Phillips curve analysis implied, of course, that measures taken to reduce unemployment would exacerbate inflation.

The Phase I freeze was followed by Phase II, during which wages and prices were allowed to thaw. However, the thaw was a controlled one, with two presidentially appointed boards established to supervise the adjustments. Approval for price changes would come from a Price Commission, while wage increases were subject to the guidance of a Pay Board consisting of representatives of business, labor, and the public. The Price Commission operated with a target of a 2½ percent annual price rise maximum, while the Pay Board adhered to a 5½ percent annual maximum wage increase. (With productivity expected to rise by 3 percent, the two guidelines are consistent. See footnote 2 on p. 555 if you're not sure why.)

By the end of 1972 the President and his advisers felt that the goals of the controls had been achieved—the rate of price increases had decelerated and the unemployment rate had declined by almost a full percentage point—so in January 1973 Phase III was introduced. Essentially, Phase III replaced mandatory price and wage controls with voluntary ones that proved to be highly ineffective. In the first half of 1973 the CPI rose at an annual rate of 8 percent, and there were indications that the end was not in sight. A new freeze, a sixty-day Phase IIIB, was announced in June, followed by Phase IV, actually a tougher Phase II, in August. In anticipation of the expiration of legislation authorizing the controls in April 1974, the controls were gradually phased out.

Did the controls work? In the half-year prior to the beginning of Phase I in 1971, prices rose at an annual rate of 4 percent and average weekly earnings rose by 6 percent. By the end of the year, the recorded increases (again at an annual rate) were 2.4 percent and 3.5 percent, respectively. Realize, however, that these numbers are hardly surprising, and cannot be used to evaluate the success of the policy. If prices and wages are controlled, then of course inflation will be slowed. But only the symptoms are being controlled; the fundamental causes are not being treated. As a consequence, demand is delayed, not dissipated, so that when the controls are removed, prices rise again. This was certainly the case with the "new economic policy."

President Nixon's economists, armed with hindsight, evaluated the experience as follows:

> The final judgment on the effects of price and wage controls . . . will long be debated. . . . However, the evidence of the controls period . . . does support a partial but important judgment: . . . whatever contribution it may have made was probably concentrated in its first 16 months, when the economy was operating well below its potential. [3]

In other words, when aggregate demand is not strong, as in the beginning of Figure 22.1's region II, controls may help. But if AD^1 lies near the right side of region II, an incomes policy may not prove effective at all.

President Carter faced an even more serious problem in 1978, as PC_3 in Figure 22.3 indicates. He, too, turned to an incomes policy designed to restrain wages and prices. Abjuring compulsion, Carter requested voluntary action by both corporate management and labor officials. This voluntarism was supervised by a Council on Wage and Price Stability with little staff and minimal muscle. (The "voluntary" rules became rather complex, as can be seen from the brief case study in Box 22.2.) In addition, government policies that had an inflationary impact were to be reviewed and revised.

The way out of a policy dilemma thus appears to be to use additional controls on prices and wages to supplement aggregate-demand tools. However, there is little agreement on whether these means are or ever can be effective.

☐ But Is There Really a Phillips Curve? A Monetarist Response

Does the Phillips curve really exist, or is it only an illusion? Monetarists claim that the inverse relationship between unemployment and inflation is only a temporary phenomenon, and that in the long run the negatively sloped Phillips curve is only an illusion. Milton Friedman's seminal argument runs as follows:

Assume that businesses experience rising prices but workers are not yet aware of them. Without any pressure to raise wages, then, and with an increase in profit margins (the difference between the higher prices and the constant wage), firms are induced to increase employment. The data

[3] *The Economic Report of the President, 1975*, p. 228.

Box 22.2 U.S. Says Hershey Meets Price Rule

WASHINGTON, Nov. 20—In the first public test of compliance with President Carter's price guideline, the Government said today a 5-cent rise in the price of the Hershey chocolate bar that now sells for 20 cents would not be a violation.

But the logic by which this conclusion was reached seemed to preclude any shrinkage in the size of the Hershey bar before Oct. 1, 1979.

The verdict was rendered by the Council on Wage and Price Stability. Normally, it would not be expected to issue statements about individual price changes. But the Hershey price rise was questioned by a reporter during a televised Carter press conference on Nov. 9, bringing it to national attention.

On its face, the nickel price rise amounts to a 25 percent increase.

But, explained the wage-price council, the Hershey company said it was also making the bar bigger, to 1.2 ounces from 1.05 ounces, an increase of almost 15 percent. Taking that into account, the council said, the price increase "came to 9.4 percent."

That, too, on its face might still look like a violation because Mr. Carter had said his initial goal was to confine price rises for the entire economy to 6 to 6½ percent. But the guideline permits a good deal more flexibility for individual prices.

The formula says a company should raise prices for all its products by no more than a half a percentage point less than average price increases in 1976–1977. For the Hershey company, that average was 13.75 percent, the council said.

But that would not let the Hershey company raise prices by 13.25 percent. The reason is that the guideline sets an upper limit of 9.5 percent for companies with price rises of more than 10 percent in 1976–1977.

Against that standard, 9.4 percent for the Hershey bar just gets by. Taking account of other Hershey chocolate products, the average price rise is 8.9 percent, according to Hershey data, and the company is comfortably under the wire.

However, the guideline also asks that in the first six months of the program companies take no more than half of the price rises they are entitled to. "Hershey met the requirements for an exception," the council said, "because the company traditionally announces its prices for the entire year about this time every year."

Source: *The New York Times*, November 21, 1978. © 1978 by The New York Times Company. Reprinted by permission.

will then show rising prices and reduced unemployment, as predicted by the Phillips curve. But wage earners will not long remain oblivious to the rise in prices and will adjust their wage demands accordingly. They do not want to suffer from the effects of inflation. Soon the rate of wage increase will equal the rate of inflation. When that occurs, profit margins will shrink back to their earlier level, leading to dismissal of the extra workers hired previously. The outcome is a series of steps portrayed in Figure

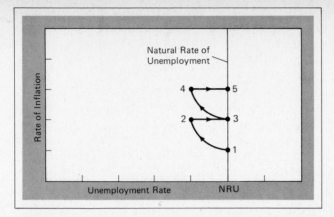

FIGURE 22.4 The monetarist version of the Phillips curve. Begin at (1). When prices rise and wage earners have not caught on, the economy moves to (2), with higher prices but fewer people unemployed. However, once the workers catch on, prices and wages rise at the higher rate, so that employment falls back to the original level (3). This process can be repeated again and again (3 → 4 → 5), but the end result will lie somewhere on the vertical line.

22.4. The end result of this sequence, which can be repeated any number of times, is a return to the initial unemployment position, but at an ever-greater inflation rate. The locus of the initial points will be a vertical line at NRU, the natural rate of unemployment, which will be the long-run equilibrium for the economy. (To be sure, the natural rate can be shifted leftward by reducing frictional, seasonal, structural, or induced unemployment. However, aggregate-demand methods will not move the curve.)

A reconciliation

Actually, those who accept the Phillips curve do not necessarily reject the conclusions of the monetarists. Perhaps in the long run the Phillips curve does lose its downward slope. Similarly, the monetarists concede that in the short run unemployment and inflation do move in opposite directions. So in truth, both views may be correct, depending on the time horizon under consideration.

☐ The Rational-Expectations Hypothesis (REH)

This conclusion is rejected by the proponents of a new theory that has gained a good deal of support in academic circles in recent years. And if importance is to be measured by recognition outside the groves of academe, it must be taken seriously by nonacademics as well. Indeed, some of President Reagan's prominent advisers have used the REH to buttress their claims that unemployment and inflation can be reduced simultaneously if the President's programs are adopted.

The basic assumption of the REH is that people are rational in the sense that they act on the basis of all available information to attain their individual goals. Thus, if businesspeople know that an increase in the money supply leads to an increase in prices, they will not remain passive. Expecting their costs to rise, they will maintain their profits by raising prices. And they'll do it as soon as it becomes evident that the money supply has increased. More than that, if price setters know, on the basis of past experience, that in any given circumstance (such as a recession) the authorities pursue an established policy (such as increasing the money supply), they will anticipate the move and act in advance of the central bankers.

This statement denies the Phillips curve trade-off even in the short run. Increases in the money supply can never lead to a decline in unemployment, according to the REH, for even before the Open Market Committee decides to raise the monetary stock, the public will have anticipated the action. Businesses will raise prices and workers will demand higher wages. But if the costs of doing business—the prices of raw materials, intermediate products, and labor—rise, no incentive to employ additional workers will have been created. So unemployment will remain where it is, at its natural rate.

Objections to the REH

Despite the current interest in the REH, the majority of economists have not been persuaded by its advocates. Objections are raised on both theoretical and practical grounds. It can safely be granted that people are basically rational, as the theory postulates. They do act in accordance with their interests, and they do make the most of available information. Nevertheless, the conclusions of the REH do not have to follow. Consider the fact that information is not costless, an element that is omitted by the REH. Certainly time, and frequently money, must be spent to obtain information; search costs are not zero. Individuals and corporate officers will have to make decisions on the basis of incomplete knowledge and revise them as more information is amassed. They may find waiting a cheaper alternative than spending time and money on the search for information. Consequently, their reaction to an increase in the money supply may not be to raise prices or wages immediately; they may wait to see how their competitors react. If sufficient time elapses during this waiting period, output may well be affected in the short run.

Multiperiod labor contracts also cast doubt on the practical validity of the REH's implications. It may well be that labor unions would demand higher wages to compensate for expected inflation as soon as the money supply increased. But wage contracts span at least a year, and three-year contracts are not uncommon. During the contract period, wage rates are specified and simply cannot be increased just because one party wants to raise them. The effect, of course, is once again to leave scope for an inflation-unemployment trade-off. For if an increased money supply leads to greater demand at constant wages (held down by the labor contract), businesses may well lengthen work hours and hire more employees.

An evaluation of the REH

Despite these criticisms, the REH has made an important contribution to policy analysis. By focusing on the learning process, it forces policy makers to realize that the public does modify its habits and actions as a result of the activities of the authorities. True, it may take time to understand precisely what the authorities' objectives are and to ascertain how the policy makers will react in any given circumstance. Ultimately, however, the public will become aware and may so modify the economic structure that the policy will be nullified.

For example, indexed wage contracts have now been written for some 10 percent of the labor force. (Indexing is a way of life in many countries where inflation is endemic.) As prices rise, such contracts call for automatic increases in hourly wage rates, thereby offsetting inflation's impact on the worker. This cost-of-living increase clearly reduces the lag between price and wage increases; wage boosts are no longer dependent on the contract's expiration date. But then increasing the money supply, which leads, sooner or later, to higher prices, quickly will lead to higher wages and will correspondingly reduce the incentive of businesses to increase employment.

Thus, even if one need not accept the extreme implications of the REH—that macroeconomic policy actions do not affect real variables like employment—neither ought we to reject its emphasis on learning through experience. Clearly, the authorities and the public interact, and in setting policy, government decision makers must be prepared to integrate the expected reactions of the public when devising and implementing their policies.

The REH's denial of a trade-off between inflation and unemployment, even in the short run, cannot be reconciled with the mainstream view that the Phillips curve is vertical in the long run but negatively sloped in the short run. For some time at least, unemployment can be reduced at the expense of higher inflation, and lower inflation can be achieved at the cost of higher employment.

What about a positively sloped Phillips curve, in which unemployment and inflation increase together? Impossible, you say? Milton Friedman doesn't think so.

☐ A Positive Phillips Curve?

In his Nobel prize address in 1976,[4] Friedman suggested that in recent years the Phillips curve has taken on a positive slope—*higher* inflation is accompanied by *higher* unemployment. He reasoned as follows: The higher the average rate of inflation, the more variable the rate. This implies that the higher the rate of inflation, the more uncertain it is, too. While it is relatively easy to plan ahead if the inflation rate is constant—if you know that prices will increase by 5 percent a year, you adjust your prices accordingly—it becomes more difficult to do so as variability increases: You're not sure whether the rate will be 7 percent or 10 percent or 13 percent. This may lead to more friction in the decision-making process and, thus, higher unemployment. Also, increasing government intervention in an attempt to control the higher inflation rates lead to still further friction, to disturbances in the functioning of the price system, and to higher unemployment.

It is obvious that the nation's economic goals are many, with the most important being high employment levels and low, if not zero, rates of inflation. Given the proper circumstances, these goals can be achieved simultaneously. But conditions are not always appropriate, and at times— and certainly this has been the case in the past decade—hard decisions must be made in deciding which of the two goals receives priority. Alternatively, an equally tough decision must be initiated: to attempt an incomes policy, sacrificing the benefits of the price system, in order to control inflation without raising unemployment.

These are very sticky questions, ones that no country in the West has grappled with successfully. The next chapter pulls together some of the implications of the theory section of this book to indicate how monetary policy can deal with some simpler problems. But it would be presumptuous to claim that economists are united in their solution to the issues of the 1970s. Certainly, unanimity does not prevail in anticipating and resolving the problems of the 1980s.

☐ Summary

Phillips curves set the tone of this chapter, for they represent the trade-off between inflation and unemployment. When the economy is neither at full employment nor operating with significant unemployed labor and capital resources, additional aggregate demand will lead to both higher prices and greater output. Conversely, a drop in aggregate demand will be accompanied by less inflation and more unemployment.

---

[4]M. Friedman, "Nobel Lecture: Inflation and Unemployment," *Journal of Political Economy* 85 (June 1977): 451–472.

This trade-off may pose a vexing policy dilemma, for if the two national macroeconomic goals of full employment and reasonable price stability cannot be achieved simultaneously (as was the case during the 1970s), which target is a responsible authority to stress? Incomes policy, designed to control prices directly, may work in some circumstances, but it has not proven very effective in controlling inflation in recent years. Neither President Nixon's nor President Carter's attempt in this direction had more than marginal significance. If an increased money supply to stimulate employment also initiates a new round of inflation, serious questions about macroeconomic policy targeting are raised.

One way out of this dilemma is to deny it. If the Phillips curve does not exist, then, of course, an inflationary policy will not increase employment. Nor will an antiinflationary policy reduce employment. At least two arguments were presented—the monetarist contention and the rational-expectations hypothesis—that deny a negatively sloped Phillips curve. The monetarist argument accepts a short-run trade-off, but claims that it disappears in the long run. Wages may be slow to rise initially and, by lagging prices, stimulate employment. But ultimately wages will catch up, dissipating the inducement to hire new workers. The end result is no additional employment accompanied by higher prices and wages.

The rational-expectations hypothesis denies even the short-run Phillips curve. The public short-circuits a lengthy adjustment process by quickly responding to signals from policy makers and the economy. Because wage earners know that an increase in the money supply will increase prices, they will demand higher wages right away. If so (and this is a crucial and questionable "if"), prices will rise immediately, too, so that no inducement to employ new workers will have been created. Thus, nothing happens on the employment front, but prices rise. This, of course, creates a vertical Phillips curve.

The role of monetary policy as a means of controlling inflation is implicit in all of these theories. All believe that inflation can be restrained by slowing monetary expansion. The crucial question is, At what cost? According to the REH, the cost in terms of unemployment is zero. Most mainstream economists disagree. They believe that in the short run higher unemployment, perhaps significantly more joblessness, will follow slower monetary growth. This is as much a political as it is an economic issue, and it will not be resolved by economists alone.

Unemployment affects the lower strata of society. As W. Allen has cogently noted, "The government is unresponsive to the needs of the little man. Under five-seven, it is impossible to get your Congressman on the phone."[5] Inflation affects different groups. Ultimately, the decisive voice will be political consensus.

---

[5] Woody Allen, *Side Effects* (New York: Random House, 1980), p. 60.

☐ Questions and Exercises

1. How will changes in the supply of goods (e.g., the oil shortage) affect inflation and the Phillips curve trade-off?
2. How would the advocates of a monetary rule (see Chapter 20) respond to the choice implied by the Phillips curve?
3. Tax-based incomes policy (TIP) involves using the tax system to reward those who abide by noninflationary wage and price guidelines and/or penalize those who fail to adhere to the guidelines. Evaluate TIP as a device to shift the Phillips curve downward.
4. Examine British incomes policies over the past decade and comment on their successes and failures.
5. The Federal Reserve's weekly announcements of increases in the money supply have brought an immediate response of higher money market interest rates. How would the rational expectations hypothesis interpret this?

☐ For Further Study

The Phillips curve has given rise to an enormous outpouring of articles, most of which are beyond the grasp of the beginning student. One exception is R. W. Spencer, "The Relation Between Prices and Employment: Two Views," *Federal Reserve Bank of St. Louis, Review*, 51 (March 1968). Chapter 4 of the 1978 *Economic Report of the President* (Washington, D.C., 1978) is another. Somewhat more difficult is F. Modigliani and L. Papademas, "Targets for Monetary Policy in the Coming Year," *Brookings Papers in Economic Activity*, 1 (1975). For a thorough survey of the professional literature, see Robert J. Gordon, "Recent Developments in the Theory of Inflation and Unemployment," *Journal of Monetary Economics*, 2 (April 1976). His *Macroeconomics* (Boston: Little, Brown, 1981) also devotes a number of chapters to this topic. You might also read through a brief textbook: S. A. Morley, *Inflation and Unemployment* (Hinsdale, Ill.: Dryden, 1979).

CHAPTER 23

Monetary Policy: Theory and History

The Federal Reserve System today is taking actions as if it were being run by either fools or knaves. If. . . they cannot do anything about the money supply, then they should resign for incompetence. If, on the other hand, they are administering policy in view of the election events, then they are guilty of violating a trust and should not hold office.

Jesse Helms, Senator, R., North Carolina (1981)

We have enough wisdom to take some prudent actions. But we do not have enough wisdom to fix our course forevermore; we must keep recharting it in light of our errors.

Arthur M. Okun, American economist

The major goals of macroeconomic policy were formulated two chapters ago. The national consensus is to keep employment high and inflation low. Showing how monetary policy can help achieve these possibly inconsistent goals is one purpose of this chapter. In fact, this segment of the chapter is brief, for it merely involves pulling together ideas expressed in previous chapters, especially Chapters 16, 17, and 19. A second purpose of the present chapter is to examine how monetary policy has performed in the past. Instead of surveying the entire history of twentieth-century monetary policy, however, a number of specific periods will be singled out and evaluated. In particular, we examine the Great Depression (1929–1939), the years encompassing the Vietnam War (1964–1969), and the period between 1975 and 1979. To anticipate a conclusion that will hardly be surprising by now, no consensus will be reached. Economists subscribing to dissimilar schools of thought reach different and often contradictory conclusions. This is true even though they all have access to the same information.

☐ Monetary Policy

When the problem facing the economy is an excess or a deficiency of aggregate demand, monetary policy can be used to retard or stimulate the economy. In the former case, demand by consumers, investors, and government authorities strain the economy's productive capabilities. The result is rising prices—an **excess-demand inflation.**

Excess-demand inflation results from strong aggregate demand pressing on the economy's limited capacity to supply.

The remedy for excess-demand inflation is a reduction in aggregate demand. The spending proclivities of one or more groups must be restrained. If the plausible assumption is made that spenders will not reduce their spending voluntarily—if prices were rising and you thought they would continue to do so, would you cut back on your own expenditures?—some form of compulsion, either direct or indirect, will be needed. Traditional fiscal policy calls for a tighter budgetary stance: lower government spending and/or higher taxes to cut business or consumer expenditures.

The appropriate monetary policy is "tight money" or monetary restraint. The money supply must be cut back.[1] This, of course, is the responsibility of the monetary authorities, the men and women who lead the Federal Reserve System. The decision by the Federal Open Market Committee to sell securities, which reduces the monetary base, or by the Federal Reserve Board to boost the reserve requirements on deposits, which lowers the value of the money multiplier, will lead to a smaller money supply. Both the neo-Keynesians and the monetarists agree that this, in turn, will cause reduced aggregate demand. Precisely how that will occur is still being debated. Will the higher interest rates choke investment spending by affecting the profitability of borrowed funds and reduce consumer spending through their impact on wealth, and will certain borrowers be unable to raise funds and thus be effectively barred from spending, as the neo-Keynesians contend (Chapter 19)? Or is the transmission mechanism different, such that a change in the money supply upsets a portfolio equilibrium and leads to attempts to restore it, as the monetarists claim (Chapter 20)?[2] Or are both groups right? In any case, less money in the economy leads to a lower level of aggregate demand.

Figure 23.1 presents this explanation in diagramatic form using the apparatus built up in earlier chapters. GNP is now $GNP, indicating nominal values, so that a movement along the horizontal axis can represent an increase in both real output and prices. Further, let the equilibrium value of real GNP, established at $3,000 billion in Chapter 16, be considered the noninflationary, full-employment (NIFE) level. In other words, when the actual aggregate demand curve is given by AD, which crosses the 45° line at a GNP of $3,000 billion, the equilibrium of the economy not only is a position of stability but also represents a level of full employment with stable prices.

The actual equilibrium of the economy, however, need not be at the NIFE level. Indeed, it would be fortuitous if that happened. Equilibrium requires only that actual sales equal expected sales or that aggregate demand equal the amount businesses had expected to sell, and this can happen anywhere along the 45° line. Consider a situation in which aggregate demand is described by AD'. Demand at the NIFE level exceeds the amount businesses expected to sell by $100 billion. Consumers, investors, and government want to acquire goods and services worth

---

[1] In actual fact, in a growing economy what will be reduced is not the absolute stock of money but, rather, its rate of growth. So whenever a reduction in the money supply is mentioned, the appropriate term would be "a decrease in the growth rate of money supply." Here, less precision is traded off for reduced awkwardness.

[2] In the case of a decrease in the money supply, people and firms will be holding onto less money than they want to, whereupon they'll sell securities of various sorts—bonds, equities, etc.—to restore their money balances. However, the security sales bring about lower prices for these financial assets, or higher interest rates. Real assets will also be sold, and their prices will decline, too. The buying public will respond by reducing its demand for *new* goods and services—aggregate demand will drop.

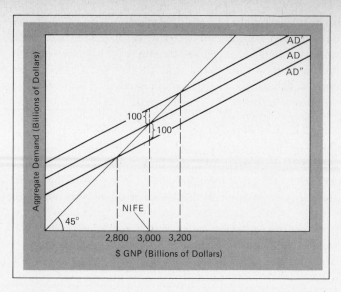

FIGURE 23.1 Excess-demand inflation, noninflationary full-employment equilibrium, and unemployment equilibrium.

$3.1 trillion when the nation's productive capacity is assumed to limit output at current prices to $3.0 trillion. Something must give. With suppliers faced with excess demand, they are able to raise prices, so inflation is the outcome. In the comparative statics of this example, a new equilibrium will be achieved at a nominal GNP of $3.2 trillion. The $200 billion increase in this case is pure excess-demand inflation. Buyers are simply paying 6⅔ percent more for the same quantity of goods and services.

The remedy for this excess-demand inflation is simplicity itself: Shift AD′ down to AD. Reduce the money supply and you'll reduce spending. Whatever the transmission mechanism may be, less money means less aggregate demand. Alternatively, fiscal policy in the form of budgetary surpluses could achieve the same result.

The converse is true for a situation in which aggregate demand is insufficient. Such a case is characterized by high levels of unemployment and generally by stable prices. The various spending groups—consumers, investors, and governments—are not spending enough to keep the business community operating at or near capacity. The labor requirements of business are correspondingly weak. The solution prescribed by an activist monetary policy is monetary stimulus. Increase the money supply so that aggregate demand will expand.

One simple way to do that would be for the Federal Reserve to print more money and distribute it directly to the American public. This gift would hardly be repulsed. It may be assumed that those who received the bonus would spend a good part if not all of it. Unfortunately, monetary policy doesn't work this way. Instead, the Federal Reserve will buy securities and thereby expand the monetary base and/or reduce reserve requirements and thus raise the money multiplier. The money supply will increase and interest rates will fall. Again, the neo-Keynesians and monetarists differ in explaining how these new circumstances will lead to stronger demand, but both schools of thought ultimately reach the same conclusion: GNP will rise. Indeed, there even appears to be a consensus that in the short run the primary impact will be to stimulate output growth, while in the long run prices will rise.

Again, a deficiency in aggregate demand can be portrayed by Figure 23.1. The AD'' line implies a $GNP equilibrium of $2,800 billion, $200 billion less than the NIFE level. Should the business community be tempted to expand output to the NIFE level, disappointment will follow. At NIFE, AD'' indicates that demanders will want to purchase only $2.9 trillion, less than expected sales, so that ultimately the economy will find its equilibrium position at $2.8 trillion. Of course, this represents underemployed or unemployed resources, since by definition full employment was set at $3.0 trillion.

An activist policy calls for raising AD'' to AD, using a stimulative or "easy" monetary and/or fiscal policy. The expected outcome of this policy will be greater production but not higher prices, given the presence of slack.

The analysis of excess-demand inflation and unemployment caused by inadequate demand can be recast in terms of Figure 23.2. When the AD line crosses the supply curve to the left of the NIFE edge, shifts in AD

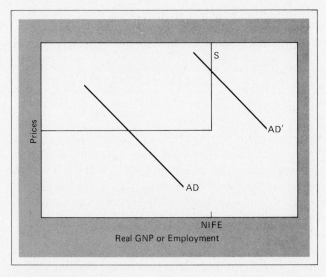

FIGURE 23.2 Aggregate demand, prices, real GNP, and employment: a simplified relationship.

affect only real GNP and employment. Prices remain stable along the horizontal segment of the supply curve. On the other hand, when the economy's capacity, given by NIFE, is reached, changes in aggregate demand affect only prices.

Contrast this diagram to Figure 22.1 (p. 554). Which do you think better describes the actual economy? If you chose the latter, you're in good company, for it is highly unlikely to expect the dichotomy described by the right-angled figure. Indeed, the Phillips curve is an explicit rejection of the view that prices remain stable while unemployment falls and vice versa.

This being the case, the policy-maker is in a far more ambiguous situation, since policy decisions now involve trade-offs. This is only one of the practical issues faced by the monetary authorities.

The length of the lag is another mundane but critical area, with neo-Keynesians and monetarists offering different viewpoints. In both the restraint and stimulus cases, the monetarists tend to find relatively short lags; the impact is significant within the first year. The neo-Keynesian empirical work suggests a longer time frame.

Moreover, the neo-Keynesians suggest that the impact is not symmetrical—monetary policy does not exert the same degree of force over a recessed economy as it does over an inflated economic system. In the latter case the strong demands for funding can be inhibited by reducing the availability of finance. If less money is available, obviously less can be spent. On the other hand, in a recession the Federal Reserve can supply the banks with funds but cannot force them to lend. You'll recall the old adage: You can lead a horse to water, but you cannot make him drink. The monetarists, on the other hand, find symmetry plausible. In either case—whether one is contracting or expanding the money supply—portfolio balance is upset, and the changes that follow thereon should occur independently of the present state of the economy.

☐ Some Practical Policy Issues

Theory can only go so far. By its very nature, it deals on an abstract level and avoids the complexities of the "real" world. A student can well understand how theory could be applied. But should that student be placed in a position where the theory must be applied, he or she is likely to be overwhelmed by the practical problems faced in translating theoretical lessons into actual policy prescriptions.

Before addressing yourselves to specific historical cases, it will be useful to discuss some general issues that are likely to arise. They can be summarized by a number of key queries: Whether to act? Overkill? When to act? This case? Shocks? Relevance?

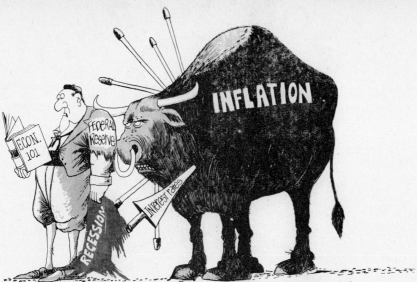

"ACCORDING TO THE BOOK... HE SHOULD BE GIVING GROUND AT ANY MINUTE!"

Drawing courtesy of Gamble; © 1980 Nashville Banner, The Register and Tribune Syndicate.

Whether to act or not

You'll recall the recognition lag of Chapter 19. At any point in time, the policy makers must know where the economy stands and, more important, where it is heading. Thus, if the economy is in the doldrums but is recovering, perhaps inaction is the wisest course. On the other hand, a stimulus could prove helpful. Accurate economic forecasts provide the foundation for appropriate policy action. In today's state of knowledge, forecasting is still an art, not a science. So the initial question facing the policy makers is, How much reliance do we place on our staff's forecasts?

Overkill

Assuming that the forecasts are reasonably correct and the policy makers have decided to intervene, a further decision concerning the actual degree of stimulus or restraint must be made. Too much action can push the economy out of a slump and into an inflation, or wring the inflation out so substantially as to pull the economy into a severe contraction, while too little may prove insufficient to achieve the policy goal. (The fear that the tight-money policy adopted by the Federal Reserve in early 1981 was going to overkill is evident in an advertisement

POISON · WARNING

The interest rate policy of the Federal Reserve System
is driving the economy of the United States into <u>self-destruction</u>.

You can help!

Write or wire your feelings to:

The Honorable Paul A. Volcker
Chairman
Board of Governors
Federal Reserve System
Washington, D.C. 20551

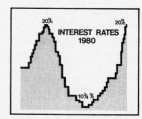

And to your Congressman. Send us a copy if you can.

<u>Speak up</u>—if you don't, nobody else will.

You're not too big or small to count!

James E. Stewart

James E. Stewart, Chairman of the Board and Chief Executive Officer
Lone Star Industries, Inc., One Greenwich Plaza, Greenwich, Connecticut 06830.

Number One in Cement... Serving America's Great Builders

One firm's attitude toward the Federal Reserve's interest rate policy in 1981.
Courtesy of Lone Star Industries.

that was placed in a number of prominent newspapers; see illustration on page 574.)

When to act

Again, recall the discussion of the outside lag in Chapter 19—how long does it take for policy, once implemented, to affect the economy? Significant differences exist among economists in their estimation of the average lag. But while academic economists can luxuriate in theoretical discussions, policy makers must act. So they implement despite an incomplete understanding of the timing of their actions.

This case?

Theory, being general, abstracts from the specific case and focuses on the typical. But a policy maker must deal with each individual situation as it crops up. For example, knowledge that in the years since 1960 the average recession has lasted 12⅓ months is of only background help to the policy maker. What the policy maker needs to know is the length of this particular recession.

Shocks

Not only is each particular situation unique, but each is subject to unknown random influences. In the long run these disturbances may well cancel each other out. But the policy maker lives in the short run. Thus, if a major strike occurs during the period under discussion, it must be programmed into the specific case. And it is not enough to do this in qualitative terms; the policy maker must have a quantitative measure of impact.

Relevance

How relevant is the general theory to the specific case? This, too, is a critical question. Perhaps the rules that frequently work do not work any longer. Then again, maybe they do. Theory, for example, predicts that an increase in interest rates should lead to a decline in investment spending. But what if investors, watching the Federal Reserve tighten interest rates, are led to anticipate still further increases. Then the higher interest rates might *induce* rather than inhibit investment. A tight policy will have led to more instead of less investment spending! Only in recent years have monetary theorists begun to explore the whole issue of expectations, their formation and impact. Yet the policy maker cannot wait for the theorists to reach a definitive conclusion (if they ever do).

In short, theory translated into policy in a specific case is fraught with complexities. Keep this in mind when evaluating how successful monetary policy has been.

Drawing courtesy of Auth; © 1979 The Philadelphia Inquirer, the Washington Post Writers Group.

☐ Historical Episodes

The Great Depression

Most of you did not experience the Depression of the 1930s, and surely not the Roaring Twenties that preceded it. But the chances are that your parents lived through those times. The experience colored a generation of thinking about the U.S. economy. Ask them to tell you about it; statistics alone are too unemotional to indicate the impact the Depression had on the economics, psychology, sociology, and political life of the nation. Does it mean much to you that 25 percent of the labor force was unemployed in 1933? Almost 13 million people faced a future of poverty—there was no unemployment insurance (that came in 1935) or social security (also in 1935), and job prospects were dim at best. How about the fact that 10,590 banks closed their doors between 1929 and 1933, virtually wiping out their depositors' savings? The FDIC, founded in 1935, came too late for those depositors. Novelists like Dos Passos (*U.S.A.*) and Steinbeck (*The Grapes of Wrath*) portray the plight of the American worker far more graphically than raw numbers can. (See Box 23.1 for a personal account of the Depression.)

The picture appears even bleaker when the decade of the 1930s is contrasted to the previous decade. Figure 23.3 records some important patterns for the 1920s and 1930s. Between 1920 and 1929, real GNP rose

BOX 23.1 Ben Isaacs [Reminisces]

It is a house, with garden and patio, in a middle-class suburb on the outskirts of Chicago.

I was in business for myself, selling clothing on credit, house to house. And collecting by the week. Up to that time, people were buying very good and paying very good. But they start to speculate, and I felt it. My business was dropping from the beginning of 1928. They were mostly middle-class people. They weren't too rich, and they weren't too poor.

All of a sudden, in the afternoon, October, 1929 . . . I was going on my business and I heard the newspaper boys calling, running all around the streets and giving news and news: stock market crashed, stock market crashed. It came out just like lightning.

I remember vividly. I was on my route, going to see my customer. It didn't affect me much at the time. I wasn't speculating in the market. Of course, I had invested some money in some property and some gold bonds, they used to call it. Because I have more confidence in the gold bonds than the stock market. Because I know the stock market goes up and down. But the gold bond, I was told from the banks, is just like gold. Never lose its value. Later we found to our sorrow that was fake.

They turned out to be nothing. Those banks, they'd take the people's money that they were saving, they would loan it out a mortgage on the property. The property was worth $100,000, they would sell $200,000 gold bonds on that property. The banks.

I have suspicions the bankers knew. They were doing it for their own personal gain. If it wasn't for the Crash, this fake would probably keep going on. Lotta these banks closed down overnight.

We lost everything. It was the time I would collect four, five hundred dollars a week. After that, I couldn't collect fifteen, ten dollars a week. I was going around trying to collect enough money to keep my family going. It was impossible. Very few people could pay you. Maybe a dollar if they would feel sorry for you or what.

We tried to struggle along living day by day. Then I couldn't pay the rent. I had a little car, but I couldn't pay no license for it. I left it parked against the court. I sold it for $15 in order to buy some food for the family. I had three little children. It was a time when I didn't even have money to buy a pack of cigarettes, and I was a smoker. I didn't have a nickel in my pocket.

Finally people started to talk me into going into the relief. They had open soup kitchens. Al Capone, he had open soup kitchens somewhere downtown, where people were standing in line. And you had to go two blocks, stand there, around the corner, to get a bowl of soup.

Lotta people committed suicide, pushed themselves out of buildings and killed themselves, 'cause they couldn't face the disgrace. Finally, the same thing with me.

I was so downcasted that I couldn't think of anything. Where can I go? What to face? Age that I can't get no job. I have no trade, except selling is my trade, that's all. I went around trying to find a job as a salesman. They

(continued)

BOX 23.1 (continued)

wouldn't hire me on account of my age. I was just like dried up. Every door was closed on me, every avenue. Even when I was putting my hand on gold, it would turn into dust. It looked like bad luck had set its hand on my shoulder. Whatever I tried, I would fail. Even my money.

I had two hundred dollar in my pocket. I was going to buy a taxi. You had to have your own car to drive a taxi, those days. The man said: You have to buy your car from us. Checker Cab Company. So I took the two hundred dollar to the office, to make a down payment on the taxi. I took the money out—he said the kind of car we haven't got, maybe next week. So I left the office, I don't know what happened. The two hundred dollar went away, just like that. I called back: Did you find any money on the table? He said no, no money.

Things were going so bad with me, I couldn't think straight. Ordinarily, I won't lose any money. But that time, I was worrying about my family, about this and that. I was walking the street just like the easy person, but I didn't know whether I was coming or going.

I didn't want to go on relief. Believe me, when I was forced to go to the office of the relief, the tears were running out of my eyes. I couldn't bear myself to take money from anybody for nothing. If it wasn't for those kids—I tell you the truth—many a time it came to my mind to go commit suicide. Than go ask for relief. But somebody has to take care of those kids. . . .

I went to the relief and they, after a lotta red tape and investigation, they gave me $45 a month. Out of that $45 we had to pay rent, we had to buy food and clothing for the children. So how long can that $45 go? I was paying $30 on the rent. I went and find another a cheaper flat, stove heat, for $15 a month. I'm telling you, today a dog wouldn't live in that type of a place. Such a dirty, filthy, dark place.

I couldn't buy maybe once a week a couple of pounds of meat that was for Saturday. The rest of the days, we had to live on a half a pound of baloney. I would spend a quarter for half a pound of baloney. It was too cold for the kids, too unhealthy. I found a six-room apartment for $25 a month. It was supposed to be steam heat and hot water. Right after we move in there, they couldn't find no hot water. It wasn't warm enough for anybody to take a bath. We had to heat water on the stove. Maybe the landlord was having trouble with the boiler. But it was nothing like that. The landlord had abandoned the building. About two months later, all of a sudden—no water. The city closed it for the nonpayment of the water bill.

My wife used to carry two pails of water from the next-door neighbors and bring it up for us to wash the kids and to flush the toilet with it, and then wash our hands and face with it, or make tea or something, with that two pails of water. We lived without water for almost two months.

Wherever I went to get a job, I couldn't get no job. I went around selling razor blades and shoe laces. There was a day I would go over all the streets and come home with fifty cents, making a sale. That kept going until 1940, practically. 1939 the war started. Things start to get a little better. My wife found a job in a restaurant for $20 a week. Right away, I sent a letter to the relief people: I don't think I would need their help any more. I was disgusted with relief, so ashamed. I couldn't face it any more. *So for you the hard times were—*

1928 to 1944. I was realizing that many and many other people are in the same boat. That gave me a little encouragement. I was looking at these people, waiting in line to get their relief, and I said, My God, I am not the only one. And those were wealthy people . . . They had failed. But still my heart won't tick. Because I always prayed in my heart that I should never depend on anybody for support. When that time came, it hurted me. I couldn't take it.

Shame? You tellin' me? I would go stand on that relief line, I would look this way and that way and see if there's nobody around that knows me. I would bend my head low so nobody would recognize me. The only scar it left on me is my pride, my pride.

Source: *Hard Times: An Oral History of the Great Depression*, by Studs Terkel. © 1970 by Studs Terkel. Reprinted by permission of Pantheon Books, a division of Random House, Inc.

---

by 45.4 percent and real GNP per capita by 27 percent; the corresponding numbers for 1930–1939 show an increase only one-third as great— 14.1 percent—for GNP and a rise of only 15.4 percent for per capita GNP. The data show an average rate of unemployment of 4⅔ percent for the former years and 18.2 percent for the latter.

Understandably, the desire to invest was weakened; investment fell from 16.9 percent of GNP in the earlier period to 8.4 percent in the Depression decade. About the only positive gain that came out of the Depression was the continued decline in prices. The CPI fell from 60.0 (1967 = 100) to 51.3 between 1920 and 1929, and it fell further, from 50.0 to 41.6, between 1930 to 1939. (Some would argue that the repeal of Prohibition in 1932 should also be included as a benefit.)

The monetary statistics for the period are interesting. The money supply rose by 10.5 percent during the earlier period and by 33 percent in the later one. But between 1929 and 1933, the end of the boom and the worst of the bust, the money supply fell by 24.8 percent. Interest rates, too, declined. Commercial paper rates averaged 5.09 percent and were 5.08 percent for long-term, Aaa bonds in the 1920s; the respective numbers for the 1930s are 1.6 percent and 3.9 percent.

What was national macroeconomic policy during these years? When you recall that these were the pre-Keynesian years, you will understand that neither were surplus budgets called for during the 1920s to restrain the economy's exuberance, nor were deficits even thought of in the early Depression years. Planned deficits were heresy. Both the Republicans, who controlled the presidency and Congress before 1929–1932, or the Democrats who unseated their opponents in the 1932 elections, solidly backed a balanced budget and recommended reduced government

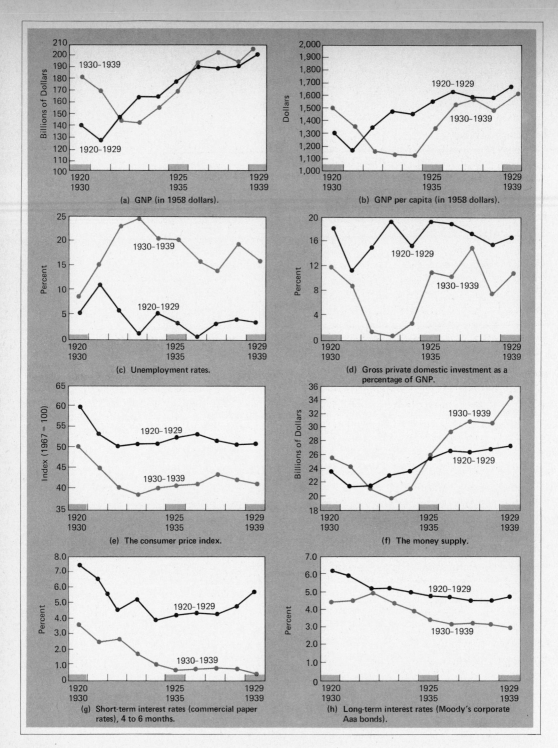

FIGURE 23.3 Economic indicators, 1920–1929 and 1930–1939.

Sources: *a–c:* U.S. Department of Commerce, *Historical Statistics of the United States: Colonial Times to 1970* (Washington, D.C., 1975), pp. 224, 135; *d:* U.S. Department of Commerce, Bureau of Economic Analysis. *Long Term Economic Growth, 1860–1970* (Washington, D.C., 1973), pp. 187, 183; *e–h:* U.S. Department of Commerce, *Historical Statistics of the United States; Colonial Times to 1970* (Washington, D.C., 1975), pp. 210–211, 992, 1001, 1003.

spending to bring about the desired balance. Countercyclical fiscal policy had not yet achieved recognition. Indeed, to balance the federal budget, taxes were *increased* in June 1932. So the full burden of stabilization policy fell on the shoulders of the nation's central bankers.

The Federal Reserve itself possessed only limited powers. The authority to vary reserve requirements was first enacted into law in 1933. Open market operations were still in their fledgling stage but were being used. The discount rate was truly the only instrument with a track record of more than a decade. And it was not used effectively, primarily because of intra-System policy disagreements.

Return to the 1927–1929 period.

Of the events that preceded the Depression, the most dramatic and conspicuous was the stock market boom. The 1920s were characterized by confidence, and the stock market speculation subsequent to the recession of 1927 seemed to many observers to be warranted by America's glowing prospects. The Standard and Poor index of stock prices, which stood at 14.6 in December 1927, rose almost uninterruptedly to reach 254 in September 1929. Volume on the New York Stock Exchange doubled, from 582 million to 1,125 million shares, over the same interval. At least for its first three quarters, 1929 was a year of unrivaled prosperity, with business profits reaching record highs.

Indeed, the confluence of a strong economic expansion and speculative fever that gripped America posed a problem of its own. To those who were worried about the excessive stock market activity, of which a good share was financed on margin, the resolve to temper the speculation clashed with the desire to do nothing to upset the basically sound underlying economy. The monetary authorities were frozen into inactivity. On the one hand, the presidents of a number of Federal Reserve banks, notably the New York bank, repeatedly proposed increasing the discount rate to curb bank financing of stock market speculation. The Federal Reserve Board, however, felt that such measures would not directly affect stock market credit. Instead, higher interest rates would slow business activity, a move that certainly was not justified under the existing circumstances. Insofar as open market operations were concerned, the security portfolio of the Federal Reserve was not large enough to undertake substantial sales. Indeed, the portfolio had declined by almost two-thirds in an attempt to inhibit bank lending in the early part of 1928. Moreover, open market sales faced the same dilemma—curtailing lending in order to slow speculation would also constrain the general financing of business activity.

It is easy, and not altogether unjustified, to blame the Federal Reserve authorities for doing nothing. (When they finally raised the discount rate in August 1929, it was a move in the wrong direction.) They have also been blamed for following an overly easy monetary policy in 1927. To accommodate Great Britain's return to the gold standard with what turned out to be an overvalued pound—the pound was declared to be worth more in relation to the dollar than was justified by the evaluation of the market—the Federal Reserve lowered the discount rate and bought securities. The overvaluation had made British goods more expensive, so England became a good place to sell to but a poor place to buy from. The resulting rise in imports and fall in exports led to an outflow of gold from Britain into the United States. Lower interest rates were designed to reverse this capital outflow; lower interest rates would reduce the incentive for keeping funds in the United States. But this low-interest-rate policy also stimulated domestic investment and made available funds that fueled speculative fires.

Black Tuesday came on October 29, 1929. The market crashed. Within a month the index of stock prices fell by 53.4 points, wiping out fully one-third of paper values. What followed was a two-year period of sharp collapse. Actually, the economy had begun to turn down in August of that year, but the snowball turned into an avalanche after the Crash. Unemployment rose from 3.2 percent to 24.9 percent, and the industrial production index dropped from 38.4 to 26.5 (1957–1959 = 100). GNP in 1958 prices, which stood at $203.6 billion in 1929, fell to $169.3 billion in 1931. Business failures rose from 22,909 in 1929 to 26,355 in 1930 and 28,285 in 1931. Banks shared in the general business collapse, their numbers falling from 24,000 in 1929 to approximately 20,000 by 1931.

The Depression did not stop there. Real GNP continued to fall throughout 1932 and 1933, reaching $141.5 billion in the latter year. Industrial production fell by 48 percent, to its low point of 20.7 in 1932. Prices, too, continued to fall, bottoming out in 1933.

The financial marketplace echoed these movements. The money supply (M-1A), which stood at $26.4 billion in 1929, fell to $19.8 billion by the end of 1933, and interest rates, both long and short term, declined. The rates on long-term government bonds, which averaged 3.60 percent in 1929, fell to 3.31 percent by 1933. Interest rates on commercial paper declined from 5.85 percent in 1929 to 1.73 percent in 1933.

In this pre-Keynesian world, fiscal policy was procyclical. To be sure, the government's budget went into deficit as a result of the decline in tax revenue, itself a direct consequence of falling worker income and business profits. But the conventional wisdom of the day was to restore budgetary balance. Even the Democratic party's 1932 platform proclaimed the sanctity of the balanced budget, not realizing that reducing government expenditures would weaken aggregate demand and thus intensify the downturn. And, as mentioned earlier, taxes were actually increased in 1932. Indeed, it was not until later, with the reality of the Depression starkly evident to the nation's political leaders, that positive steps were taken to augment government spending.

Monetary policy responded to the downturn in a more positive way. The discount rate was progressively lowered during the second half of 1929, 1930, and early 1931, moving from 6 percent to 1½ percent. However, in the fall of 1931 the monetary authorities *raised* the discount rate and ended their loose-money policy. This move, which was unfortunate from the point of view of domestic concerns, once again came as a response to an international crisis. Dollars were leaving American shores, and so, too, was gold. The monetary theory of the time called for stemming gold outflows by raising interest rates just as, in 1927, the gold inflow had been slowed by lowering interest rates. Open market sales were undertaken simultaneously. Moreover, at that time Federal Reserve notes and deposits had to be backed by a gold reserve held by the Reserve banks. The loss of gold potentially threatened the money supply. The policy had its effect, but at the cost of prolonging the Depression. By April 1932 this tight-money policy was reversed, and between 1932 and 1936 the authorities pursued an expansionary course.

But before recovery could get under way, the famous bank holiday was declared. Between 1931 and 1932, 3,700 banks had failed. In the absence of deposit insurance, the public's fear of bank failures was expressed by runs on the banks. Unfortunately, under the fractional-deposit banking system, many inherently sound banks were unable to meet their depositors' demands for cash and were forced to close. The vicious cycle then was intensified. By March 1933 thirty states had placed some form of restriction on the ability of the public to exchange their deposits for cash, and on March 6 President Roosevelt declared a four-day bank holiday during which all banks were closed. Emergency legislation provided for the banks to reopen, depending on their financial situation, and in fact, more than half of the banks opened on the 10th to do business as usual.

The period between 1932 and 1936 saw the enactment of significant new monetary legislation. The Federal Reserve System was reorganized, with the locus of power swinging clearly to the now-reorganized Board of Governors. (See Chapter 12 for details.) Reserve requirements were made variable, subject to Federal Reserve Board discretion, as was control over margin ratios for security loans (see Chapter 13); deposit insurance was introduced; interest payments on demand deposits were eliminated; and commercial bankers were barred from acting as investment bankers. At the same time, the whole array of New Deal legislation pumped spending power into the economy; farmers, businesses, the unemployed, the old, the infirm, even poets were subsidized in one way or another. Thus, both monetary and fiscal actions were pointed toward stimulus.

The bottom of the Depression is dated at March 1933. From that time on, the economy moved slowly forward. As Figures 23.3(a) and (c) show, real GNP rose and unemployment fell. However, not until near the end of the decade did real GNP reach its pre-Depression peak. In all, the decade of the Depression was a depressing experience.

What caused the Depression, and what role did or could monetary policy play in that period? The two main schools of economic thought, the Keynesian and the monetarist, interpret the issue quite differently. On the Keynesian side, the emphasis is placed on a decline in aggregate demand. Some Keynesians blame the severity of the Depression on the decline in investment demand and, in a recent study, on consumption demand.[3] Peter Temin, in this neo-Keynesian analysis, finds that part of the decline in consumption was caused by the stock market crash. The fall in stock prices reduced the wealth of American consumers and, in turn, brought consumption spending down. Temin notes, however, that this wealth effect accounts for only a minor portion of the decline in consumption; the bulk of the decline remains unexplained. Nonetheless, it is the fall in aggregate demand that bears the responsibility both for causing the downturn and for the seriousness of the decline. And once the Depression was under way, its momentum became self-reinforcing. Moreover, Europe was simultaneously undergoing a depression, and the depression here reinforced and was stimulated by the depression there.

If you wonder why the low interest rates did not stimulate investment, since this is one key conclusion of Chapters 17 and 19, the answer is that the prospect for future profits looked rather bleak. And if potential profit is anticipated to be low, even low interest rates will not encourage investors.[4]

The money supply and the monetary authorities play a secondary role in this scenario. True, the monetary authorities could have acted more firmly in 1928 and 1929; they could have held down interest rates in 1931 instead of raising them; and they could have played a more active role in stimulating demand. But even if they had performed perfectly, at best they could have slowed the downturn somewhat or provided the conditions for encouraging an upturn. Monetary forces were not the cause of the Great Depression, nor could they, by themselves, bring about a recovery.

Not so, rejoin the monetarists. Take a look at what happened to the money supply. [See Figure 23.3(f).] The money supply declined by 11.3

---

[3]See Thomas Wilson, *Fluctuations in Income and Employment* (London: Pitman, 1942), for the former view, and Peter Temin, *Did Monetary Forces Cause the Great Depression?* (New York: W. W. Norton, 1976), for the latter.

[4]Begin with an investment demand represented by D_I and an interest rate of 6 percent. Then $50 million will be invested. If investment opportunities shrink because future profits are less likely, D'_I replaces D_I. On D'_I, even a lower interest rate of 2 percent leads to investment of only $40 million.

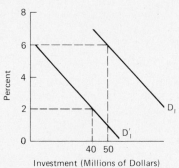

Investment (Millions of Dollars)

percent between 1929 and 1931. Milton Friedman and Anna J. Schwartz, in their monumental *A Monetary History of the United States, 1867–1960*,[5] write, "Prevention or moderation of the stock of money . . . would have reduced the contraction's severity and almost as certainly its duration." Further,

> The monetary collapse was not the inescapable consequence of other forces, but rather a largely independent factor which exerted a powerful influence on the course of events. The failure of the Federal Reserve System to prevent the collapse reflected not the impotence of monetary policy but rather the particular policies followed by the monetary authorities, and, in smaller degree, the particular monetary arrangements in existence. (p. 300)

The lines between the two schools are sharply drawn. Did a fall in aggregate demand cause the Depression, or was it a consequence of the decline in the money supply? The former view not only partially exonerates the monetary authorities but also suggests that monetary forces, by themselves, are incapable of causing the damage wreaked by the Great Depression. The latter belief clearly condemns the monetary authorities—one of the Friedman-Schwartz subheadings is "Why Was Monetary Policy So Inept?"—and equally surely places great emphasis on the force of monetary changes.

Certain policy conclusions hinge on these views. The relative role of monetary versus fiscal policy, discussed in Chapter 20, is one. Neo-Keynesians feel that fiscal policy is a useful tool for controlling aggregate demand, as is monetary policy. Moreover, in a deep contraction monetary policy cannot by itself stimulate expansion, so government expenditure and tax policy must be utilized. Monetarists find monetary policy alone to be sufficiently strong to prevent a contraction as well as to stimulate the economy out of it.

A second conclusion is implicit in the preceding analysis. Was the failure of the monetary authorities to take the appropriate action endemic to any discretionary authority, or was it an exception? If you believe that the performance was inept but was a consequence of improper understanding or inadequate tools, there is hope for an activist monetary policy. Next time will be different; the failures of the past need not be repeated. But if the authorities, when faced with a challenge, are unlikely to cope, or are just as likely to pursue the wrong policy as the right one, the proper counsel is to remove the power from the monetary authorities. (Recall the monetary rule discussed in Chapter 20.)

One concluding thought about the Great Depression is worth noting. While the cause of the Depression is still being debated, it is generally agreed that another Great Depression is unlikely to occur. The structure of the economy itself is more stable; for example, bank runs are far less

---

[5]Princeton, N.J.: Princeton University Press, 1963, p. 301. The chapters on the Depression have been published separately as *The Great Contraction, 1929–1933* (Princeton, N.J.: Princeton University Press, 1965).

likely now that deposits are insured. Also, unemployment insurance and welfare payments provide for income maintenance when jobs are lost. Moreover, our understanding of how the economy can be stimulated, combined with the willingness to pursue expansionary policies when unemployment reaches abnormal levels (remember the Employment Act of 1946 and the Full Employment and Balanced Growth Act of 1978), means that positive actions will be taken in response to contractionary threats. In fact, it is not accidental that no sharp, prolonged depression has occurred for over half a century.

The soaring sixties and Vietnam

In sharp contrast to the gloom of the Depression stands the decade of the 1960s. The period from 1961 to 1969 represents the longest economic expansion on record. These were years of prolonged prosperity, with all economic groups sharing the fruits of economic advance. GNP in real terms grew annually by 4.5 percent, while the unemployment rate reached and then fell below its minimum target rate of 4 percent in each of five years. The staid President Eisenhower was replaced in 1961 by a youthful President Kennedy, whose theme became "Ask not what your country can do for you—ask what you can do for your country."[6] The shock and despair that swept the nation with the news of the President's assassination was slowly dissipated when it was realized that his successor, President Johnson, meant to use his copious energies to further the Kennedy ideals. The Great Society was launched, and in 1964 a War on Poverty was declared.

But while harmony and prosperity characterized the domestic scene, a small-scale military action in southeast Asia escalated into a major conflict, with severe repercussions on political life and on tranquillity at home. The Vietnam War marred an otherwise optimistic future, led President Johnson to decide against seeking reelection, and brought to the office of chief executive Richard M. Nixon, the man who promised to, and did, end the war.

But it is not the politics or the ethics of the Vietnam episode that concerns us here. Rather, it is on the economy that our attention must be focused. What impact did the war have on the national economy, and what policies—fiscal and monetary—were or should have been undertaken?

The period between 1965 and the end of the decade must be put into historical perspective. A brief recession in 1960–1961 gave way to a slow recovery in the early 1960s. Real GNP rose 5.8 percent in 1962 and 4.0 percent in 1963. Unemployment, which averaged 6.7 percent in 1961, fell slowly to 5.7 percent by 1963. This increase in production and employment was accomplished without pressure on prices—both the CPI and

---

[6]Inaugural Address, January 20, 1961.

the GNP deflator rose at a rate of slightly less than 1.5 percent per year.[7] [See Figure 23.4(a, b, c)].

Two problems were viewed as particularly vexing. One, which will not concern us here, was the balance-of-payments situation; America was continuing to experience a substantial dollar and gold outflow. On the domestic side, the still-high level of unemployment, over 42 percent above the full-employment target, was hardly satisfactory. In a period of stable prices and still-unused industrial capacity, unemployment could be reduced by means of fiscal stimulus and an accommodative monetary policy. Thus, the stage was set for the tax cut of 1964. Both individual and corporate taxes were reduced by a total of $8.4 billion, for an impact on GNP of at least double that. (Recall the income multiplier of Chapter 16.) Monetary policy, which was much concerned about the international problem, was receptive to the fiscal stimulus. Short-term interest rates had risen from 2.4 percent in 1961 to 3.2 percent in 1963, while long-term bond rates had fallen somewhat. But 1964 saw only a slight rise in both short- and long-term interest rates. The money supply rose 5.3 percent between 1961 and 1963; it increased further, by a modest 4.0 percent, in 1964, as can be seen in Figure 23.4(d, e). Continuation of the expansion seemed likely, with prices again rising moderately, only 1.5 percent, during the year. To be sure, concern about potential inflation was expressed, and noninflationary "guideposts" for wage and price behavior had been devised. But these suggestions hardly constituted an incomes policy; they were not even in the category of voluntary controls.

Thus, by virtually all measures the early 1960s were years of promise and, for the most part, promises kept. Demand management, consisting of both stimulative fiscal policy and a loose monetary policy, prodded the economy forward. Real income rose; standards of living moved ever upward; inflation was negligible; and if unemployment had not yet reached its natural rate, it was moving in that direction. The dramatic narrowing of the gap between potential and actual GNP [Figure 23.4(f)][8] illustrated the momentum of the economy.

And then Vietnam exploded. Actually, the initial impact of defense spending that was directly related to the conflict was not large. In 1966 defense spending rose by $7.2 billion, only 5.4 percent of federal government expenditures and less than 1 percent of GNP. But coming in an economy with little slack, as Figure 23.4(f) demonstrates, and with full employment,[9] the increase had disruptive effects. The Phillips curve discussed in the last chapter (Figure 22.3, page 557) showed the consequences of excessive aggregate demand—an inflation rate that progressed

---

[7]Given the problems raised in Chapter 14 in connection with price indexes, it is quite likely that there was no inflation at all in this period.

[8]If you're unclear about these terms, take a look at pp. 400–401.

[9]Unemployment fell to 4.5 percent in 1965, to 3.8 percent in 1966 and again in 1967, and still lower, to 3.6 percent, in 1968. Thus, actual GNP exceeds potential GNP for these years.

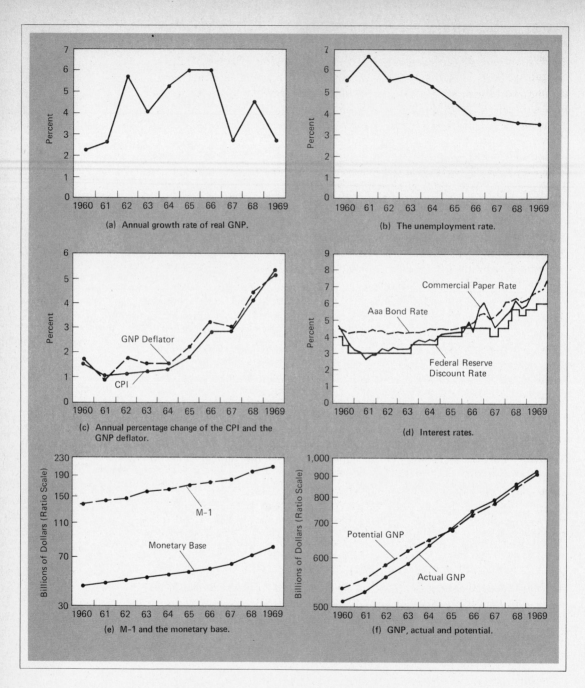

FIGURE 23.4 Economic Indicators, 1960–1969.

Source: *a–c, e: Economic Report of the President,* 1981, pp. 269, 293, 237, 301, 307; *d:* Board of Governors of the Federal Reserve System, *Banking and Monetary Statistics 1941–1970* (Washington, D.C., 1976), pp. 726–727; *f: Survey of Current Business,* November 1980, p. 17.

from 2.2 percent in 1965 to 3.3 percent in 1966, paused briefly by rising only 2.9 percent in 1967, and shot up to 4.5 percent in 1968 and 5 percent in 1969, even as unemployment declined. In a denial of the classic conflict of "guns versus butter," President Johnson pursued simultaneously both his increased defense budget and his expensive Great Society programs. And although already in 1966 the President's economists were recommending fiscal restraint in the form of tax increases, the President decided that the time was inopportune. Only in 1967 did he propose raising taxes, a move that gained congressional assent a year and a half later. (Recall the "policy inauguration lag" of Chapter 19.) By then the tax surcharge of 10 percent was too small and too late to slow inflation. Nor could the wage-price guidelines be effective, and they were quietly abandoned.

What role did the monetary authorities play in the second half of the decade? One way of interpreting their actions is to look again at the movement of interest rates shown in Figure 23.4(d). The sharp increases in interest rates after 1965 suggest that monetary policy was tightening. Indeed, use of the instruments of monetary control reinforce that impression. Reserve requirements on time deposits were raised twice in 1966, and those on demand deposits were raised twice in 1968. The directives of the Federal Open Market Committee were almost continuously aimed at tightening up on money and credit conditions, implying frequent sales of government securities. Discount rates were increased, primarily in 1968 and 1969, and as a result of Regulation Q, severe monetary crunches were experienced in 1966 and 1969. (See pp. 331–333 for a discussion of Regulation Q, and pp. 164–168 for the methods used by the banks to circumvent its impact.) At best, however, these policies prevented inflation from moving ahead even more rapidly; they obviously did not prevent it from accelerating.

But the role of monetary actions in the late 1960s, as in the 1930s, is subject to diverging interpretations. It can be claimed that the cause of the accelerating inflation lay in the actions of the fiscal authorities. By failing to prevent the rise in aggregate demand and by not reducing the government's budgetary deficit, they placed the entire responsibility for inflation control in the lap of the Federal Reserve. Monetary policy should not be expected to carry the entire burden. Only by 1968, when the tax hike came into effect, did fiscal policy move in the right direction and become a partner in inflation control. The monetary authorities acted appropriately on the whole, but when heavy artillery is needed, a few rifle shots cannot halt the enemy's advance.

The monetarists feel otherwise. The fact is that monetary policy is powerful. And the actions of the monetary authorities do explain economic changes during the second half of the 1960s.

Take a closer look at the movement of M-1[10] and the monetary base as

[10]You understand that each time M-1 appears in this chapter it refers to M-1A, since M-1B did not come into being until 1980.

they are plotted in Figure 23.4(e). It is obvious that the rate of growth of both these indicators was slower in the first half of the decade than in the second half. (For M-1 it was 2.9 percent annually compared to 3.9 percent, while for the monetary base the respective numbers were 3.6 percent and 4.8 percent.) These numbers certainly do not indicate a policy of monetary tightening, and the Federal Reserve should not shirk its responsibility for the accelerating inflation of those years.

Figure 23.5 can be used to buttress the claims of the monetarists. In this diagram the rate of growth of M-1 is plotted and is juxtaposed with changes in nominal and real GNP and prices. Note first the sharp decline in M-1 during 1966. After averaging 4.6 percent in 1965 and 4.7 percent during the first half of 1966, it ground to a halt during the second half of the year. This sharp reversal touched off the "credit crunch" of 1966 and nearly brought on a **recession** as real-GNP growth slowed to a fractional rate in the first quarter of 1967. By the beginning of 1967, M-1 growth had rebounded; it averaged 6.5 percent for the year and 7.7 percent for 1968. The corresponding growth rates of real GNP were 2.7 percent and 4.6 percent, while prices rose by 3.0 percent and 4.4 percent. The recession of 1969–1970 is evident in Figure 23.6. That was the final year of the longest economic expansion. Note, too, what happened to the growth rate of the money supply during 1969.

A **recession** is often said to exist when the growth rate of real GNP is negative for two consecutive quarter-years.

If you study Figure 23.5 carefully, you'll notice a recurring pattern: Money supply changes, real-GNP changes, and the rate of inflation move in tandem for many of the quarters. Higher money supply growth is frequently accompanied by higher inflation rates, and vice versa.

The monetarist analysis is straightforward: It is the changes in the money supply that *caused* real GNP and prices to behave the way they did. More money means more spending, ultimately resulting in higher prices.

Neo-Keynesians are less ready to accept this type of evidence. That some variables move together does not prove causation. A chicken-egg debate cannot be resolved merely by demonstrating close relationships. In fact, it can be and has been argued that the shifts in the growth rate of GNP *caused* the changes in M-1 growth. As GNP expands, the demand for money increases, too.

A further question that must be examined is, Why did the money supply follow this pattern? Again the monetarists and neo-Keynesians differ. The monetarists place responsibility firmly at the doorstep of the Federal Reserve authorities. Federal Reserve policy is characterized by a stop-and-go pattern, one of continual late guessing followed by overreaction. Fears of an overheated economy in 1965 led to a policy of overkill in 1966; the reaction to the slowdown in 1966 led to an overexpansion the next year. And in 1968, when the tax increase was finally passed by Congress, the Federal Reserve eased off too much. The monetary authorities believed that the restraining impact of the new fiscal action might choke off the expansion; a looser monetary policy would be appropriate. But again they were wrong. The money supply rose too

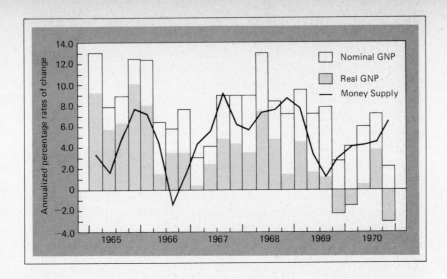

FIGURE 23.5 Growth of nominal GNP, real GNP, prices, and the money supply, 1965–1970.
How to read this chart: The height of a column indicates the growth rate of nominal GNP; the darkened in portion of a column represents the growth rate of real GNP; and the blank distance, which is the difference between nominal and real GNP, represents the rate of inflation.

Sources: GNP: U.S. Department of Commerce, Bureau of Economic Analysis, *The National Income and Product Accounts of the United States, 1929–76* (Washington, D.C., 1981), pp. 387, 389; Money supply: Board of Governors of The Federal Reserve System, *Money Stock Measures and Liquid Assets: Historical Data* (mimeograph), October 2, 1981.

much; prices continued to rise; and again the authorities overreacted, their tight-money policy putting an end to the decade-long expansion. Clearly, believe the monetarists, the years between 1965 and 1969 demonstrate both the potency of monetary actions and the inability of the monetary authorities to control the economy effectively.

Many neo-Keynesians, and even some members of the Federal Reserve, are sympathetic to the monetarist critique of Federal Reserve behavior in this period. However, the conclusions they draw are not as drastic as those reached by the monetarists. Mistakes were made; but if we learn from our mistakes we won't repeat them. The problems of predicting, coordinating with the fiscal authorities, and executing policy exist, but they can be overcome.

Perhaps the expansion of 1975–1979 can shed further light on the role of monetary policy in the economy.

1975–1979

As noted in the preceding chapter, the 1970s posed a new challenge to economic policy makers. The coexistence of high inflation rates and high levels of unemployment were difficult to explain and even more complex to control. The incomes policy of the Nixon years had been largely forgotten, and a sharp recession beginning in mid-1974 had brought down considerably the skyrocketing price level. But what was disturbing to economists, and the public as well, was the fact that, even in this sharpest of postwar recessions—real GNP had declined by 6.7 percent between the cycle's peak in the second quarter of 1974 and the cycle's trough in the first quarter of 1975 and the unemployment rate had increased in the same interval from 5.1 percent to 9.1 percent—in early 1975 prices continued to rise at an annual rate of 7½ percent.

Fiscal policy was expansionary: Taxes were cut in the first half of 1975. Consumers were given a rebate on 1974 taxes, and the withholding rates for 1975 personal tax collections were reduced. Corporations were aided by an increased tax credit on new investment as well as a reduction in the corporate tax rate.

Between the end of 1974 and well into 1975, monetary policy was stimulative. The Federal Reserve's portfolio of securities increased by $5.2 billion between December 1974 and May 1975, in line with an expansionary open market policy. Reserve requirements were reduced in a series of steps, and the discount rate was cut a number of times, so that it was brought down from 8 percent in December 1974 to 6 percent in May 1975.

The impact of these policies, together with the natural upswing of the business cycle, led to a resurgence in economic activity during the second half of 1975. This continued throughout 1976, as Figure 23.6(a, b) shows. Economic recovery was especially strong during the early part of 1976; it began to falter as the year progressed. Unemployment declined at a despairingly slow pace; by the year's end 7.3 million workers, 7.7 percent of the civilian labor force, were out of work. Because of slack in the labor market and substantial unused capacity, as well as temporary factors, inflation moderated, averaging about 5 percent for 1976. [See Figure 23.6(c).]

Fiscal policy was not stimulative during 1976. The budget deficit, which had reached an annual rate of $100 billion in mid-1975, fell to $55 billion in 1976. Monetary policy for the most part facilitated expansion. The monetary authorities watched the slow progress of recovery with concern, and the relatively low rate of inflation gave them some leeway to further ease the monetary reins. Thus, in January 1976 reserve requirements on some time deposits were reduced and the discount rate was lowered by one-half of a percent, to 5½ percent. The discount rate was cut again in November, to 5¼ percent, and in December reserve requirements on demand deposits were further reduced. For banks with demand deposits of less than $10 million, the ratio was reduced by one-half of a percentage point. Marginal ratios on deposits in excess of $10 million were decreased by only one-quarter of a percentage point. [Can this differential, favoring the smaller banks, be related to the membership problem of the Federal Reserve? (See pp. 297–299.)]

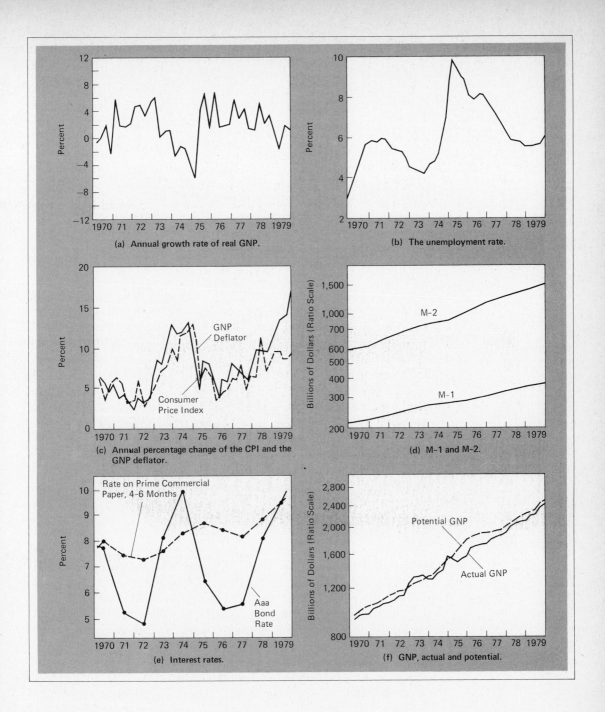

FIGURE 23.6 Economic indicators, 1970–1979.

Sources: *a–e:* Board of Governors of the Federal Reserve System, *Historical Chart Book* (1980); *f: Survey of Current Business*, November 1980, p. 17.

These monetary actions, which saw M-1 grow by 5.7 percent and M-2 by 10.9 percent, contributed to the continued decline in both short- and long-term interest rates. [See Figure 23.6(d, e).] Other factors, too, must share responsibility for the falling rates. Among them are the substantial buildup in corporate liquidity, which reduced the demand for funds, and the decline in the rate of inflation, which reduced the desired nominal rate of interest.

In many ways 1977 was a replay of 1976. The recovery remained strong as real GNP rose by 5½ percent. Unemployment continued to decline, falling by over a percentage point, to 6½ percent, by year's end. Again, the recovery was strong in the first part of the year; economic activity slackened as the year progressed. Inflation, however, moved further ahead; for the year, the consumer price index recorded a 6.8 percent increase. The Phillips curve trade-off functioned predictably as the lower unemployment rate was accompanied by an acceleration of inflation.

Both fiscal and monetary policy were forced to cope with this dilemma. In the early part of 1977 President Carter introduced an expansionary fiscal policy designed to reduce the unemployment rate. The Tax Reduction and Simplification Act that Congress legislated and the President signed in May was less stimulative than initially proposed. Economists and the nation's political leaders recognized that the economy was forging ahead more strongly than anticipated. The tax law extended a variety of tax credits for individuals and corporations, enacted in 1975 and 1976, that would have expired. It also increased the personal standard deduction, introduced an employment tax credit specifically aimed at increasing employment in the private sector, and provided additional funds to the states to bolster public employment. Other stimulus-providing legislation was enacted, and the Council of Economic Advisers estimated that the total fiscal injection would increase the federal government's budget deficit by $6.1 billion in 1977 and almost $17 billion in 1978.

Presidential attempts to slow inflation were of two kinds—structural change and voluntary exhortation. Proposing less government regulation of the economy, President Carter hoped that the spur of competition would hold prices down. Similarly, he requested Congress to lower excise taxes, which are reflected in higher consumer prices. In addition, the President asked that businesses and workers voluntarily restrain their wage and price demands.

The monetary authorities, too, were concerned with enabling the expansion to proceed. But at the same time they were afraid of the increasing inflation. The Federal Open Market Committee began the year with the view that an M-1 growth rate of 4½–6½ percent was consistent with its goals. However, actual monetary growth overshot its target in the early months of 1977, and failed to decelerate as the year proceeded. The central bankers moved to restrain monetary growth, but they did so cautiously. At first they were unclear about whether they had set an unrealistically low target and about whether the rapidly expanding money supply was responding appropriately to the needs of the economy. If so, restraint was not called for. On the other hand, perhaps their targets were correct, the increase in M-1 was too strong, and a firming policy was timely. By April the Fed decided in favor of the second alternative and began to close the monetary spigot. Over the remainder of the year monetary targets were lowered, and bank reserves were supplied less readily as open market policy tightened. (However, banks were able to acquire additional reserves by substantially increasing their borrowing from the discount window. Member bank borrowing rose from its 1976 average of $62 million to $558 million in 1977.) The discount rate was boosted a number of times, moving from 5¼ percent to 6 percent by the end of the year. One consequence was visible in the money and capital markets—interest rates rose, reversing their decline over the past two years, as Figure 23.6(e) shows.

Yet, despite all of these moves designed to slow the money supply growth rate, despite higher interest rates, despite a target range of 4½–6½ percent, M-1 rose by 7.8 percent during 1977.

Thus, a prognosis for moderating inflation in 1978 would have been highly optimistic. The economic expansion was entering its fourth year after two years of high and accelerating price increases. The annual growth rate of real GNP, measuring the actual output of the economy, was 4.2 percent; real GNP thus rose much more rapidly than potential GNP, as Figure 23.6(f) implies. True, unemployment at year's end was still a high 6.3 percent, implying slack in the economy and room to expand output without exerting severe pressure on demand. However, against this mitigating force stood the inflation psychology, the "buy now, for it'll be more expensive tomorrow" attitude. This led to increased consumption and less saving out of personal income, putting pressure on prices. Simultaneously, workers found their real income being eroded by a combination of inflation and higher tax rates. They responded by pushing harder for wage increases that would at least compensate them for their losses.

In fact, 1978 turned out to be a year of rising inflation accompanied by somewhat lower unemployment. Consumer prices rose by 9.0 percent, while the implicit GNP deflator showed a 7.3 percent rise. Unemployment fell from 6.3 percent at the beginning of the year to 5.9 percent at the year's end, hovering between 5.9 and 5.8 percent from August on. Fiscal policy switched from a highly stimulative stance to a less expansive one, with proposed income tax cuts pared down and their implementation delayed. Moreover, a more formal "voluntary" price and wage program was introduced in October 1978 to supplement the firmer fiscal policy. Wages were to rise by no more than 7 percent, while price increases were to be held below their average rate of increase during 1976–1977.[11]

Monetary policy continued to tighten, primarily through open market operations. At the regular FOMC meetings target Federal funds rates were continuously raised. They moved from 6¾ percent in January to over 10 percent in December. The discount rate was raised seven times, reaching a historic high of 9½ percent in November. To a large extent, the increase in the discount rate reflected the Federal Reserve's response to an international problem, the continually falling exchange rate of the dollar. However, this policy was not inconsistent with domestic monetary policy goals. A special reserve requirement on large time deposits was also imposed in November of 1978.

Despite all of these actions, M-1 grew by more than 7 percent, again in excess of the monetary target. Moreover, the recorded increase in the money supply may underestimate the true increase. According to some economists, the high market interests rates that could be earned led to legal subterfuges that reduced the official M-1 data. To mention one example, consider overnight "repos" or repurchase agreements, which the Federal Reserve does not include in M-1 but may well belong there. (See p. 42.) Gillian Garcia and Simon Pak have argued that the spreading use of such instruments has biased money supply data significantly.[12]

In sum, neither fiscal, monetary, nor voluntary wage and price policies were able to halt the accelerating inflation of 1978. The same was true for 1979. Inflation continued to accelerate, and the varied policies of the government, including the central bank, appeared to be stymied. Fears of a recession in 1979 complicated the problem, for while the authorities desired to cool off the sizzling economy, no one wanted to plunge it into a recessionary deep-freeze. As the decade ended, the feared downturn did not materialize. But 1980 turned out both to be more inflationary and to carry more unemployment.

The economic history of the past few years has been interesting for a number of reasons. As in other episodes discussed in this chapter, had the Federal Reserve kept a firmer grip on money supply, the inflation would have been contained—or so the monetarists contend. Moreover, the monetarists have emphasized the distinction between real and nominal interest rates, a point that is of considerable importance. The monetarists,

[11]In 1979 the President also proposed a "real wage insurance" program. Under this plan, workers who complied with the wage standard would receive a tax credit equal to the difference between the 7 percent wage increase and the actual rate of inflation. Thus, if the actual inflation rate was 10 percent, the complying worker would get a 3 percent reduction in taxes. This would lead to an after-tax pay increase of 10 percent. The objective was to alleviate demands for higher pay, thereby reducing pressure on businesses to raise prices. Congress, however, never approved the plan.

[12]"The Ratio of Currency to Demand Deposits in the United States," *The Journal of Finance* 34 (July 1979): 703–715.

Curiosa

Inflation and the Tooth Fairy

Rosemary Wells of the Northwestern University School of Dentistry surveyed over 400 dental patients. She found that for 1981, the average amount left by the tooth fairy for a baby tooth was 66¢. This compared to 30¢ in 1966 and 19¢ in 1956.

Source: Reported in *The New York Times*, June 23, 1981.

Inflation and the Runner

James Fixx, author of the *Complete Book of Running*, puts in at least 10 miles a day, keeping his eye on the road and incidentally, picking up the cash he spots lying loose. He reports the following found treasure:

1970	$0.66
1971	$0.43
1972	$0.51
1973	$0.74
1974	$0.33
1975	$0.21
1976	$0.55
1977	$0.38
1978	$2.27
1979	$4.91

Fixx postulates that the sudden increase in his serendipitous finds are due to the decline in the value of the dollar, making it no longer worthwhile for people to bend down for the dropped dime or quarter.

Source: Reported in *The New York Times*, April 16, 1980.

Recession and the Bank Robbers

The Associated Press reported that a group of anarchists robbed a Berlin bank of $43,000, leaving chocolate cream puffs for the people in the bank. They described their motive as a "modest contribution" to bringing the recession to a halt by increasing the supply of money in circulation.

Source: Reported in *The New York Daily News*, August 1, 1975.

---

and other economists, too, note that, far from pursuing a tight monetary policy, the Federal Reserve's behavior was moderate indeed. The fact that short-term interest rates exceeded 13 percent by the end of 1979, the fact that the discount rate reached its highest point to that time at 12 percent, the fact that the prime rate stood at 15.3 percent—these facts do not mean much; these rates are nominal. Adjust the prime rate by an annual rate of inflation of 8½ percent and you obtain the real pretax cost to the corporation borrowing at the prime rate: only 6.8 percent. And if it was borrowing through commercial paper issues, the real interest rate was a low 4¾ percent.

This brief history of the late 1970s should reinforce concepts and questions raised earlier. Realize how critical forecasting is—as long as the authorities are unsure of the future, they are limited in their decision-making ability. They tend, therefore, to act cautiously. But caution has its price; it leads to failure when decisive moves must be made. Consider, too, the problem of lags—both fiscal and monetary actions were taken over the period. How much of the apparent failure to control inflation is a consequence of the slow-acting nature of fiscal and monetary policy, and how much is due to caution? This question is more easily raised than resolved.

Realize that a general conceptual understanding of monetary policy impacts has limited usefulness when dealing with a particular episode. And in recent years the problems of the central bankers have been compounded by the public's heightened sensitivity to inflation. Inflationary expectations have become important, but the authorities have only limited knowledge about those expectations, how they are formed both independently of and in response to public policy actions, and how they are modified.

The past years have also been extremely trying for the monetary authorities because of a number of changes in the deposit structure of the public. With thrift institutions permitted to offer checking accounts, money market funds offering short-term, highly liquid time-deposit-type accounts, and commercial banks and thrifts selling large volumes of money market certificates, it has been difficult to interpret movements in the monetary aggregates. In fact, the current period has left a good share of the nation's economists feeling rather frustrated.

☐ Some Concluding Thoughts

This chapter has reviewed three major episodes in the history of the United States. The first, the Great Depression, left its mark on the nation's economic and political structure; it also influenced economic thought and political choices. Only recently have we been able to say that our political leaders are not children of the Depression; no longer can they remember personally the misery and dislocation of the 1930s. Yet their thinking has been conditioned by the fact that their professors lived through that horrible period. The capture of the economics profession by Keynesian economics, which is still the mainstream of economic thought if not universally accepted, is a legacy of the immediate prewar period. The lasting concern with unemployment and the faith in government policy to alleviate it are other obvious baggage from that era. Many experts believe that if the Keynesian remedies had been tried, the Depression would have been shallower and shorter.

What about inflation? Keynesian remedies are symmetrical: Stimulate during a recession; restrain to halt inflation. Why, then, did the U.S. economy suffer from inflation in the late 1960s and again in the late 1970s?

One answer is simple—the Keynesian prescriptions were not followed. The political leaders lacked the courage or the ability, or did not see the necessity for taking the appropriate counter measures. Yet this is not the entire answer. You realize that the problem is a more complex one. When should the countervailing action be taken? What precisely is the appropriate countermove? What combination of monetary and fiscal policy should be used? What changes are taking place in the nature of the economy? What is the trade-off between inflation and unemployment?

These questions loom large, however, only if discretionary policy is advised. For only if the authorities are expected to act must they correctly filter information, think through the consequences of their action, and then move. Whether the policy makers are neo-Keynesians or monetarists, whether they have faith in a combination of instruments or in monetary policy alone, whether they believe the lags are long or short, action ultimately lies in the hands of the policy makers.

But perhaps discretion itself is the problem. Perhaps the economy could be made to run better without the meddling of the authorities, no matter how well intentioned.

Most economists today reject blind adherence to a monetary rule. But they also reject fine-tuning. The consensus argues in favor of a steadier hand on the monetary wheel than was shown in the past. Just as a good driver doesn't jerk the wheel this way and that to avoid every pothole, no matter how small, so, too, must the monetary authorities refrain from trying to moderate every fluctuation in economic activity, no matter how slight. But just as the driver who wants to avoid costly axle and wheel alignment jobs had better turn the wheel to avoid those big ones, so, too, should the monetary authorities anticipate and react to major obstacles to economic progress. No, the economy will not move along a sharply defined growth path, never deviating from it. But neither will substantial divergencies be encountered. Modulated fluctuations are the best that can be hoped for, given our present state of knowledge.

☐ Summary

The creed of contemporary monetary activists runs as follows: An excess-demand inflation can be cured by removing the excess demand that was the source of the rising prices. A tight monetary policy, consisting of open market operations and/or increases in the required reserve ratio, will slow down monetary growth and reduce spending. Many will agree that fiscal policy, in the form of a budgetary surplus, will also reduce aggregate demand. Conversely, unemployment caused by deficient aggregate demand can be reversed by a loose monetary and/or fiscal policy.

Applying these theoretical prescriptions to a faltering economy takes a bit of doing. Leaving aside the thorny issue of the trade-off between unemployment and inflation discussed in the preceding chapter, the authorities must make a number of decisions before implementing any given policy. Among the questions that must be addressed are these:

1. Is action preferred over inaction? Should the economic system be left alone to use its own recuperative powers?
2. If a decision to intervene is made, how powerful is the action to be? Will it be strong enough to achieve its goal without being too powerful to cause undesired side effects?
3. Should action be taken now or delayed? What lag can be expected between the time a decision is made and the time its impact is felt?
4. How relevant is past experience? Is the present situation unique?
5. Is the conceptual framework underlying the contemplated action appropriate, or are the economy and its numerous participants operating under a significantly modified environment?

There are no rules that can provide the monetary authorities with a guaranteed set of answers. As a result, they learn by doing.

The complexities of policy making were examined in three different episodes: the Depression of the 1930s, the Soaring Sixties, and the second half of the 1970s. The Great Depression, with its masses of unemployed, abysmally low production, and generally pessimistic view of the future, brought radical changes in economic policy. New attitudes toward government intervention and new institutions designed to implement these concepts sprang forth during those years. The role of the monetary authorities in causing or failing to prevent the Depression, as well as their inability or unwillingness to foster conditions for economic renaissance, is still being debated. Monetarists fault the Federal Reserve with misfeasance, if not malfeasance. Neo-Keynesians, while not sympathetic to the actions of the Federal Reserve during those critical years, nevertheless are less severe in their condemnation. Monetary actions alone would have proven inadequate in any case. Most economists agree today that the structural features created during the 1930s, such as deposit insurance and social security programs, as well as the new consciousness of the government's macroeconomic responsibility, make a recurrence of the Great Depression most unlikely.

The 1960s posed a different sort of problem. While the early years of the decade saw inflation low and unemployment falling, by the second half of the decade inflation started accelerating even as unemployment continued to decline. Fiscal policy responses were slow in coming, and the monetary authorities carried most of the burden of an antiinflation policy. Could they have done more? Again, it's a matter of interpretation. The monetarists condemn the central bankers for delayed reactions followed by policies that overcompensated. Apologists for the Federal Reserve admit the truth of some of the charges, but argue that the authorities acted with wisdom and conscience in an imperfect world. They did the best they could.

The final period, between 1975 and 1979, was in a way the most frustrating one, featuring the coexistence of high unemployment rates and high rates of inflation. While the monetary authorities became ever more concerned with the inflationary spiral, their cautious moves saw monetary growth exceed the targets they had hoped to achieve. As the period neared its end, worries about weakness in the economy and the possibility of severe monetary restraint causing a recession left the leaders of the Federal Reserve on the horns of a dilemma, with no easy way off.

These historical episodes should give you some feeling for the difficulties encountered in translating concepts into practice. For this reason, some economists have advocated putting an end to discretion and replacing it with a monetary rule. But rules have weaknesses, too, and the choice is not between the perfect and the imperfect but between various imperfect methods.

Two lessons may be gleaned from this chapter—indeed, from the whole book:

1. Monetary theory, monetary policy, and monetary history can give us a better understanding of how the macroeconomic system functions and how it can be manipulated for society's desired ends.
2. Perfection in policy choices is not easily achieved; it may not even be attainable. But monetary actions can be used to enhance the performance of the economy. The proper institutions are needed. So, too, is a clear understanding of the concepts that underlie policy actions and their limitations. In addition, the right people in the right place at the right time, combined with a good measure of luck, can improve the conduct of the monetary system and help the nation achieve its macroeconomic goals.

☐ Questions and Exercises

1. Analyze a recent monetary policy decision in light of the practical issues outlined on pages 573–575. How was each one resolved? In retrospect, were the decisions correct?
2. Assume that you were a member of the Federal Reserve Board during the 1930s. With the benefit of hindsight, outline a monetary policy that could have led to an earlier and more substantial recovery. Explain why your suggestions would have proven effective.
3. Examine monetary policy during the 1960s and/or 1970s to see how various sectors of the economy (e.g., housing, automobiles, inventory investment) fared as a consequence of monetary policy actions.
4. Has anything changed in the 1980s with respect to the conduct of monetary and fiscal policy?
5. Compare the first half of 1980 with the first half of 1981 in terms of economic conditions and the Federal Reserve's response to those conditions.

☐ For Further Study

Monetary policy can be surveyed by consulting the annual reports of the Board of Governors of the Federal Reserve System. However, these tend to portray the Federal Reserve in a more favorable light than neutral observers might feel is warranted. As a counterpoint to these reports, read the comments on monetary policy that appear at least annually in the *Review* of that bastion of monetarism, the Federal Reserve Bank of St. Louis.

Fiscal policy from the Hoover presidency in the 1920s to the Johnson tenure in the 1960s is skillfully examined in Herbert Stein, *The Fiscal Revolution in America* (Chicago: University of Chicago Press, 1969). Robert A. Gordon, *Economic Instability and Growth: The American Record* (New York: Harper & Row, 1974), examines macroeconomic history and policy for a longer period, covering the early 1920s through the Nixon years. His son, Robert J. Gordon, overlaps the later period, reviewing the years between 1947 and 1979 in "Postwar Macroeconomics: The Evolution of Events and Ideas," in M. Feldstein, ed., *The American Economy in Transition* (Chicago: University of Chicago Press, 1980). A monetarist interpretation of the period from 1965 to 1975 may be found in Phillip Cagan, *Persistent Inflation: Historical and Policy Essays* (New York: Columbia University Press, 1979).

Two think tanks regularly comment on recent economic events, and their contrasting views often make interesting reading. The Brookings Institution, a liberal organization, regularly publishes the *Brookings Papers in Economic Activity* and an annual review of the government budget entitled *Setting National Priorities: The 19— Budget*. The conservative American Enterprise Institute issues its *AEI Studies on Contemporary Economic Problems* annually. And, of course, the president's Council of Economic Advisers publishes a survey of the year gone by in its report, which is issued together with the *Economic Report of the President* at the start of each calendar year.

Don't miss the fascinating autobiography of a Utah banker who weathered the Great Depression and headed the Federal Reserve System from 1935 until 1948: Marriner S. Eccles, *Beckoning Frontiers* (New York: Knopf, 1951).

PART SIX

MONEY AND MONETARY POLICY IN AN INTERNATIONAL SETTING

CHAPTER 24

The International Scene

The Caterpillar was the first to speak.
"What size do you want to be?" it asked.
"Oh, I'm not particular to size," Alice hastily replied;
"only one doesn't like changing so often, you know."
"I don't know," said the Caterpillar.

Lewis Carroll (1865)

For more than a decade now, we have been besieged by problem after problem in the working of international financial mechanisms. Strain and turbulence have, in fact, been so constant a feature of the international financial scene in recent years that I suspect they are coming to be widely regarded as the normal state of affairs.

Arthur F. Burns, former chairman of the Board of Governors of the
Federal Reserve System (1977)

CONTENTS

Summary

CHAPTER HIGHLIGHTS

1. How exchange rates are determined by the forces of supply and demand.
2. The effect of government intervention in the supply-demand process.
3. The impact on the U.S. dollar of the substitution of managed floating for a fixed exchange rate system.
4. The structure and meaning of the balance of payments.
5. The reasons underlying the deterioration of the U.S. balance of payments.

On August 15, 1971, the President of the United States announced the suspension of dollar convertibility; the government would no longer permit the conversion of dollars into Treasury-owned gold. With that announcement, the world's financial system changed suddenly. Within the next two years a system that had been based on exchange rates whose stability was maintained by government intervention turned into one in which exchange rates were determined predominantly by market forces. By 1973 the anchor that had held the exchange rate system stable—the fixed gold value of the dollar—had been jettisoned, and the ship of exchange rate values was permitted to drift. The result was a voyage into unchartered waters whose waves govern both international trade and finance, and whose currents have repurcussions in the domestic arena as well.

The purpose of this chapter is twofold: (1) to explain how exchange rates are determined today and contrast this with the pre-1973 situation, as well as to outline the sources of this major modification in the international economy, and (2) to introduce you to the fundamental international accounting device—the balance of payments. The next chapter will focus on the monetary aspects of the international economy and their impact on the domestic economy.

☐ Determination of Exchange Rates

An **exchange rate** is the value of one country's money in terms of that of another country.

The typical American comes into direct contact with the **exchange rate** only when traveling abroad. Honeymooners visiting Osaka, Japan, normally pay for their food and lodging in Japanese yen. Those yen will most likely be obtained at a foreign bank, where the visitor exchanges American dollars for a given value of the foreign currency. (In 1980 the American tourist would have received, on the average, 221½ yen for each U.S. dollar.) In a less direct way, each of us is exposed to the exchange rate without even leaving the country. When we buy a Japanese TV set, an Italian car, or a bottle of French perfume, pour paprika on a pot roast, enjoy a glass of authentic Spanish sherry, or nibble on a Greek fig or a chunk of real Swiss cheese, somewhere in the chain of transactions leading from the producer to the consumer—us—an exchange rate was involved. The first question addressed in this chapter is, How is the exchange rate, the price of one foreign currency in terms of another, determined?

Supply and demand analysis

Economists analyze the forces that determine exchange rates in terms of supply and demand. Americans who want to buy foreign goods, use foreign services, or invest abroad must buy foreign currency with U.S. dollars. In other words, Americans *supply* dollars. Of course, if the dollar buys more units of foreign currency, Americans will be stimulated to buy more goods from abroad. Thus, if a native brass ornament sold in India for 80 rupees, the importer would be more prone to purchase it if the rupee could be acquired for 10¢ than if it cost 25¢. In the former case, the importer would get 10 rupees for the dollar and pay $8 for the item; in the latter, only 4 rupees would be obtained per dollar and the ornament would cost $20. Thus, the quantity of dollars supplied by domestic purchasers of foreign goods and services rises as the value of the dollar (in terms of its ability to purchase foreign currency) rises. This statement is given graphic form in Figure 24.1. In that diagram the horizontal axis measures the number of U.S. dollars (whether demanded or supplied), while the vertical axis indicates the value of the dollar in terms of foreign currency, in this example the Japanese yen.

The supply curve then relates that when the price of the dollar is 150 yen, Americans will want to sell $10 billion (and will be able to acquire 1,500 billion yen—$10 billion × 150 yen—to buy Japanese goods and services). When the price of the dollar rises to 250 yen, Japanese products will be cheaper for Americans—since each dollar now buys 100 more yen—and U.S. importers and travelers will now want to sell $20 billion (assuming that prices in Japan remain unchanged, at least initially).

Consider now the demand for dollars, that is, the demand by Japanese individuals and firms who want to buy dollars in order to acquire goods and services in the United States. Just as the foreign exporter wants to be paid in his or her domestic currency, so, too, the American producer desires to be paid in U.S. dollars. (After all, U.S. firms need dollars to pay American workers, landlords, interest recipients, and raw-materials suppliers.) For the foreign importer of U.S. products, the lower the price of dollars, the cheaper the goods are to him; the importer is able to obtain more dollars for each unit of foreign currency. Thus, in Figure 24.1 the demand curve shows that at 250 yen per dollar, Japanese want only $10 billion, but as the exchange rate of the dollar falls to 150, they will demand $20 billion.

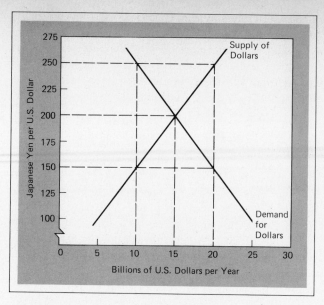

FIGURE 24.1 The determination of exchange rates.

As you know, in a competitive market that is not subject to governmental control, price and quantity will be set at the intersection of the supply and demand curves; at that point the quantity that buyers want to acquire matches the quantity that sellers want to supply. And so it is in the foreign-exchange market, which, with exceptions to be noted later, operates basically as a free, competitive market. In Figure 24.1 the yen price of the dollar will be 200, and at that exchange rate Japanese will buy, and Americans sell, $15 billion.

Intervention and the exchange rate

What would happen if the freedom of the market were curtailed by governmental intervention? Assume that the Japanese government wants to establish a low yen price[1]—to insist that the dollar is worth 250 yen, not 200 as the market dictates. Of course, the desire to fix an exchange rate at a specific level is not tantamount to doing so. For the diagram demonstrates that at a 250 yen per dollar rate, the market supply of dollars to acquire Japanese products and services exceeds the quantity demanded by Japanese, who are dissuaded from acquiring as many dollar goods as they otherwise would. This excess supply of $10 billion would normally lead to a decline in the yen/dollar exchange rate. Japan, however, could intervene to maintain an artificially high yen/dollar rate. The central bank of Japan would have to absorb the excess supply of dollars; it would have

---

[1]Perhaps it does so in order to discourage imports and encourage exports.

to buy those $10 billion, paying for it 250×10 billion yen.[2] (You should be able to work out independently what actions would be necessary to maintain a 150 yen/dollar exchange rate.)

Shifts in supply and demand

Demand and supply could shift for any number of reasons, and to analyze their impact on the exchange rate, take a look at Figure 24.2. Begin with the 200 yen/$ rate at equilibrium (at the intersection of S and D) and assume that the demand for dollars rises to D'. This might have occurred because Japanese prices are rising more rapidly than U.S. prices, so that American products have become bargains, or because Japanese incomes have risen, leading to a stronger demand for imports, or because new investment opportunities abroad or political instability has led Japanese to seek a foreign haven for their funds, or because a marvelous new American tourist attraction has opened up, or for any of a great many other reasons. Given the same American supply curve, the new demand curve, D', cuts S at a higher exchange rate: The rise in the demand for dollars leads to an increase in the dollar's foreign-exchange value (and a corresponding fall in the value of the yen). At the new equilibrium rate of 250 yen to the dollar, supply and demand are once again equated, but at a higher value of trade—$20 billion instead of $15 billion.

On the other hand, had the exchange rate been pegged or fixed at 250 yen per dollar, the shift in demand obviously would not have changed the exchange rate. However, the excess supply would have disappeared, ending dollar purchases by the central bank of Japan.

Of course, if demand had fallen, the exchange rate would have fallen in the case of free-market rates, or, in the case of fixed exchange rates, an increase in excess supply at the pegged rate would have resulted. Similarly, supply changes, leading dollar holders to offer more or fewer dollars, will lead to either exchange rate changes or changes in excess supply. (To test your understanding, work through Figure 24.2 when supply shifts. Show what happens to the exchange rate when it is permitted to fluctuate. Also indicate the impact on excess demand when the exchange rate is pegged.)

The two instances portrayed in Figure 24.2 conform, respectively, to a regime of **freely floating** or **flexible exchange rates,** the system that in principle has been operating since 1973, and one of **fixed exchange rates,** which existed in the post-World War period until 1973.

Freely floating (or **flexible**) **exchange rates** respond only to market forces, which determine the relative value of any two currencies.
Fixed exchange rates are relative foreign-currency prices established by governments and maintained through active intervention.

---

[2]Again, an analogy from simple supply and demand analysis may prove helpful. If the government fixes the price of apples above the market price, the excess supply will drive the price back down to equilibrium unless the government purchases the excess supply. This is the idea underlying the famous farm price support programs, which buy agricultural products in order to buoy their prices.

The impact of a country's acquisition of foreign exchange on its domestic economy is discussed in the next chapter.

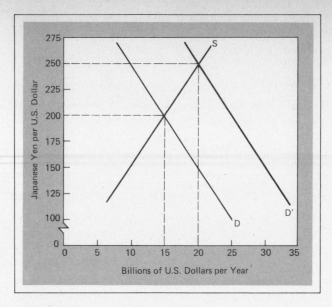

FIGURE 24.2 Demand shifts and exchange rate equilibrium.

Today most major free-world currency rates are primarily determined by the interplay of market forces. In the course of any day, exchange rates fluctuate as the demand and supply of the various currencies shift. If the latest inflation rates indicate an unexpected rise in Japanese inflation, the foreign-exchange market will react. Traders will expect a decline in the supply of dollars and other currencies to acquire yen, while the demand for foreign currencies by Japanese yen holders will rise.

A rise in the price of foreign currencies (= a fall in the price of yen) will follow. With the latest economic and political happenings being reported continually, exchange rates rise and fall throughout the day. Similarly, as days become months and years, and as more basic forces work themselves out in the international economy, the various exchange rates will undergo adjustments. Fluctuation, not stability, is the key word in foreign exchange. (For an alternate theory of exchange rate determination, see Box 24.1)

The value of the dollar, 1967–1980

Figure 24.3 shows how the foreign-currency value of the dollar has varied between 1967 and 1980. Two comments are in order before you proceed to this diagram. First, until now the discussion has been in terms of the yen/dollar exchange rate. But there is also a mark/dollar and a Canadian/U.S. dollar exchange rate; indeed, for every country there are as many possible exchange rates as there are foreign currencies. In order to better comprehend the overall picture, one can amalgamate the

BOX 24.1 The Monetary Theory of Exchange Rates

A growing number of economists find fault with the theory of exchange rate determination as described on these pages. They view its reliance on the relative demand and supply of goods, services, and capital investments as indirect at best, and theoretically misleading at worst. Instead, these economists believe that foreign money must be incorporated into the portfolio theory of money demand as described in Chapter 20.

In simplified form, the theory runs as follows: Firms and individuals at any one time wish to hold a certain value of financial and real assets. The former consists of domestic money, bonds, equities, and other financial instruments, while the latter consists of various kinds of durable goods. How much the public will demand of each asset will depend upon their utility functions, measuring the satisfaction obtained from each asset type, the demanders' income or wealth, and the return available from each asset. The demand of the public will be matched with the supply to yield a set of equilibrium values.

Assume that the supply of domestic money increases. If you followed the chain reaction described on page 531, you'll recall that initially this increased supply of money, being greater than the amount demanded, leads the public to dispose of it by buying various financial assets. But, in doing so, the demand for each asset rises, causing its price to rise and it yield to fall. Equilibrium ultimately will be restored when the price level rises sufficiently to bring the amount of money supplied back into equilibrium with the amount demanded.

The international sector can be introduced into the analysis with only modest extension: Let one of the financial assets be foreign money, and its price, of course, is the exchange rate. Then, as the excess supply of money of the previous paragraph flows through the financial system, upsetting equilibrium in domestic asset markets, it also upsets balance in the foreign exchange market. The public, who now acquires more domestic assets, also demands more foreign money. As a result, the exchange rate of the domestic money is driven down. The impact of increased money supply on the economy is a combination of inflation and decline in the exchange rate. (To test your understanding, describe what happens when the supply of domestic money is reduced. Why will prices fall? Why will the exchange rate rise?)

In short, exchange rates are determined by movements of money supply relative to the demand for money in each country. Do you want to predict what will happen to the exchange rate of the dollar relative to the French franc? Study money supply growth rates relative to demand in each country or more simply relative rates of inflation, and the answer will be evident.

(A word of caution: Don't risk your own money playing the foreign exchange market on the basis of this simplified analysis.)

The monetary theory of the exchange rate has enriched our understanding of exchange rate determination by stressing the demand for foreign exchange as an asset. Few international economists today, however, are willing to stop tracking alternative channels by which the exchange rate is determined (such as GNP movements in the various economies).

numerous exchange rates into an average exchange rate showing the relationship between the domestic currency and all (at least, all important) foreign currencies. When averaging, care must be taken to give greater weight to important trading partners and lesser weight to currencies in which little trade is conducted. This gives rise to the statistic known as **trade-weighted dollar,** whose value is measured on the vertical axis. Note that it is given in index form, so that what is shown are the changes from the base month of March 1973, which has the index value of 100.

A second comment is directed at the floating rate itself. While the discussion in these pages has focused on two extremes—freely floating exchange rates and fixed exchange rates—compromises do exist. Some countries, such as the members of the European Economic Community (EEC), combine fixed and floating exchanges. Most of the nations that constitute the EEC keep exchange rates between themselves fixed, but allow their rates to fluctuate against non-EEC nations. Many nations intervene in foreign-exchange markets to prevent speculators from upsetting the foreign value of the home currency or, in general, to reduce excess volatility. In this way they give rise to the **managed float.**

Consequently, the movement of the dollar over the years since 1973 reflects not the history of a freely floating exchange rate system but that of a system that is substantially more responsive to market forces.

Turn now to Figure 24.3. Clearly, a major readjustment of the dollar's value occurred between 1971 and 1973 as the value of the dollar fell compared to that of other currencies. The magnitude of this decline in the exchange rate is significant. It means, of course, that foreign goods and

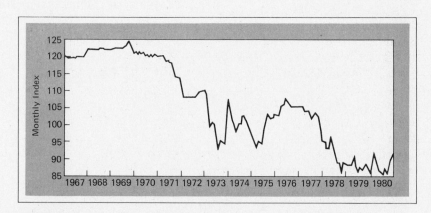

FIGURE 24.3 Trade-Weighted average value of U.S. dollar (March 1973 = 100).
Source: Board of Governors of the Federal Reserve System.

services cost more to Americans. (But as will be seen in the next chapter, the falling dollar has its advantages, too.) Note, too, that the trend since 1973 has been relatively stable. Fluctuations exist, but they center on the 90–100 range.

The movement in the value of the dollar compared to that of other currencies raises a number of questions:

1. What happened in the early 1970s to reduce the exchange rate of the dollar so significantly, and what has happened since then to maintain its stability?
2. What impact does a lower exchange rate have on the economy?
3. What role has monetary policy played in causing or stemming the decline of the dollar?
4. Does the floating exchange rate system pose special problems or offer unusual opportunities for control of the domestic economy by monetary policy?

The next chapter will deal with the last three issues. The remainder of this chapter will be concerned with analyzing the causes for the dollar's initial decline and subsequent stability. Of course, the obvious answer to the question about the falling exchange rate is that the supply of dollars expanded more rapidly than the demand for dollars; this certainly is the solution implied by the discussion of Figure 24.2. Nevertheless, this answer does not suffice; we need to penetrate behind the supply and demand curves to ask, What forces caused the shifts in supply and demand? One way to get a handle on these forces is to examine the **balance of payments**.

The **balance of payments** is a record of a nation's complete international transactions over a specific period.

☐ The Balance of Payments

The U.S. balance of payments is an accounting device for listing all trade and money flows between U.S. residents and foreigners. As such, it includes trade in goods and services as well as investment flows. Table 24.1 presents an abridged balance of payments, using data for 1980.

A word about the method of recording **credits** and **debits** is in order. While the idea of double-entry bookkeeping underlies the balance-of-payments account, one need not be an accountant to understand the basic rules. For example, an export of U.S. wheat would be recorded as a credit because of the obligation of the foreign importer to pay for the wheat. Similarly, when a U.S. resident purchases common stocks in British Rolls Royce, a debit is recorded to show that the American is obliged to pay for the securities. (Credits can be called exports and debits imports.) One consequence of double-entry bookkeeping is that, if the recording is accurate, the balance of payments must always be in balance. Every plus must be offset by an equal minus.

A **credit** ("export") is recorded for any transaction that results in a receipt from a foreigner. A **debit** ("import") entry denotes any transaction that induces a payment to a foreigner.

TABLE 24.1 The U.S. Balance of Payments, 1980 (billions of dollars)

1. Exports of goods and services	(+)259.9
1*a*. Merchandise	(+)224.0
1*b*. Investment income (net)	(+) 32.5
1*c*. Military transactions (net)	(−) 2.5
1*d*. Other services (net)	(+) 5.9
2. Imports of goods and services	(−)249.3
2*a*. Merchandise	(−)249.3
3. Balance of trade	(−) 25.3
4. Balance on goods and services	(+) 10.8
5. Unilateral transfers	(−) 7.1
6. Balance on current account	(+) 3.7
7. Change in U.S. private assets abroad	(−) 71.5
8. Change in foreign private assets in the United States	(+) 34.8
9. Balance on current account and private capital account	(−) 33.0
10. Change in U.S. government assets	(−) 13.4
10*a*. Reserve assets	(−) 8.2
10*b*. Other government assets	(−) 5.2
11. Change in foreign official assets in the United States	(+) 15.5
12. Balance on current and capital accounts	(−) 30.8
13. Discrepancy	(+) 29.6
14. Allocation of SDRs	(+) 1.2
15. Final balance	0

Source: Adapted from U.S. Department of Commerce, Bureau of Economic Analysis, *Survey of Current Business*, June, 1981, p. S-1.

The meaning of the entries

Line 1 lists all exports of goods and services, and includes both goods sold abroad (1*a*) as well as a variety of services (1*b, c,* and *d*). The services include income earned by Americans on their foreign investments (1*b*), which is listed net of returns on investments paid by American companies to foreigners. Military sales to foreigners are also listed net of purchases (1*c*), as are all other services, such as travel and tourism (1*d*). In 1980 total exports of goods and services reached $259.9 billion. Line 2 records purchases of foreign goods by Americans, which came to $249.3 billion. Line 3 records the sum of lines 1*a* and 2*a*, the merchandise accounts, which is called the **balance of trade.** The sum of lines 1 and 2 is recorded on line 4 and is called **the balance on goods and services.** In 1980, while Americans bought $25.3 billion more goods from abroad than foreigners bought in the United States, service income more than compensated for these outlays, leaving a positive balance on goods and services of $10.8 billion. When unilateral transfers (line 5)—payments made to others for which nothing is expected in return, such as gifts—are added to the balance on goods and services, another sum, the **balance on current account** (line 6), results, current account being items 1, 2, and 5. For 1980, the balance on current account was in surplus by almost four billion dollars.

The **balance of trade** equals the difference between merchandise exports and imports, while the **balance on goods and services** adds service receipts and outlays to the balance of trade.

The **balance on current account** equals the sum of goods and services exports plus unilateral transfers less goods and services imports.

In contrast to the goods and services listed in the current account, the capital account deals with asset transactions. This encompasses both short- and long-term, private as well as government activities. Some of the transactions recorded in the capital account are the balancing items for current-account activities. For example, the payments made for exports and imports are found here. But the capital account also lists the financial flows coming from independent decisions, such as commercial bank lending to foreign governments. Lines 7 and 8 refer to private asset changes—bank accounts, bonds and equities; line 7 lists changes in the ownership of foreign assets by American residents and businesses, and line 8 to similar transactions representing the stake of foreigners in U.S. assets. Private activities led to a net dollar outflow of $36.7 billion, which, when added to line 6, yields line 9, the balance on current and private capital account.

Lines 10 and 11 deal with the international financial transactions of government, line 10 to U.S. government changes and line 11 to changes in foreign-government ownership of U.S. assets. Note that U.S. government assets are subdivided into reserve assets (10a) and other (10b). Reserve assets include gold, foreign currency, and special drawing rights (which are explained in connection with line 14). These assets represent the **official reserves** of the U.S. government and can be used to buy dollars from foreign governments that no longer want to hold them (although since 1971 gold has no longer been automatically transfered to foreign governments). Again, combining the $2.1 billion surplus of lines 10 and 11 with line 9 yields the balance on both current and capital accounts (line 12). Line 12 shows a $30.8 billion negative sum.

Official reserves consist of government-owned gold, foreign exchange, SDRs, and some assets related to membership in the International Monetary Fund.

In fact, line 12 should be zero, owing to the nature of the double-entry recording method. Each plus must have a corresponding minus; each debit, a corresponding credit. Two reasons for the imbalance may exist. Inaccuracies, due both to errors and to unrecorded transactions, creep in to unbalance the account. In 1980 these errors and omissions, listed in line 13 as a "discrepancy" with a sign opposite from that of line 12, almost balance the account. Normally, the discrepancy does the entire job; the exception is on the infrequent occasions when **special drawing rights (SDRs)**, which are listed on line 14, are issued.

Special drawing rights (SDRs) are created international reserves, or so-called paper gold.

What are SDRs? The members of the International Monetary Fund, (IMF) an organization that includes most of the nations of the world and is charged with maintaining world financial order (see Box 24.2), have agreed to create this international asset at irregular intervals. These created SDRs are then allocated to the member nations on a predetermined basis. When a nation wants to reduce a foreign debt or obtain foreign currency to finance its exports, a procedure exists to transfer SDRs from its account at the IMF to the creditor country. The creditor nation accepts SDRs not only because of the international agreement to accept them but also because it knows that it can pass them on to others to pay for its own international purchases or settle its own debts. These

SDRs are international money—once created, they are generally accepted and used as an international medium of exchange and store of value.[3]

SDRs are free money. When SDRs are created, no country loses anything; indeed, all who acquire SDRs gain. Since the SDRs accrue to the nation through the international economy, they must be recorded in the balance of payments. Thus, line 14. And when these last two categories are taken into account, the final balance must be zero, as it is in Table 24.1.

BOX 24.2 The International Monetary Fund

At the close of World War II, the thoughts of the Allies turned to reconstructing the world economy. They identified two key issues—rebuilding a physically devastated world and reviving the world's financial system. The first was resolved in part by the establishment of the World Bank, officially titled the International Bank for Reconstruction and Development. Still functioning today, the World Bank and its affiliates are the major international lending agencies working to develop the poorer nations of the world.

Repairing the disarray of the international financial system was high on the list of priorities of the Allied officials meeting in Bretton Woods, New Hampshire, in 1944. Order was to be achieved by the establishment of the International Monetary Fund, which would be a supranational agency headquartered in Washington, D.C., and would supervise the Articles of Agreement. The five major points of these Articles were as follows:

1. Each of the original member nations would establish a par value for its currency, that par value fixing its domestic currency unit to gold or to the dollar. (Thus, the U.S. dollar's par value was $1/35$ ounce of gold.) Each nation committed itself to maintain the value of its currency on foreign exchange markets within 1 percent of the par value on either side.
2. Par values would be changed only with the approval of the IMF and only for reasons of fundamental disequilibrium (see p. 631).
3. Member nations agreed to the principle of currency convertibility, so that any member owning the currency of another member could sell it back to the latter.
4. Restrictions were not to be placed on current-account transactions, although they would temporarily be allowed for capital transactions.
5. Each member would pay into the IMF a certain quota of gold and foreign currency, but would also be allowed to borrow funds from the IMF for balance-of-payments purposes.

The IMF has run into its share of problems and critics. Any evaluation of its success would be colored by the bias of the analyst. There are those who argue that the IMF has been the voice of the financially strong against the weak, that the measures called for by the IMF hierarchy have often caused

---

[3]The SDR is also a unit of account and a standard of deferred payments (see pp. 10–18).

more harm than good, that its evolution has been too slow, and that the IMF no longer serves a useful purpose. While the justice of some of these complaints can be recognized, the fact remains that the IMF has enabled the international financial system to evolve in an orderly way. Nations have had a forum in which to discuss joint international action rather than unilaterally implementing potentially disruptive moves. Such cooperation led to the creation of the SDR and is currently being applied to the development of a constructive method of recycling the billions of dollars flowing into the coffers of the OPEC nations. The IMF has 143 members today, the glaring exceptions being a number of Soviet bloc nations, including the USSR, and fiercly independent Switzerland.

As the table stands, it is a record, a combination balance sheet and income statement. As such, it has accounting validity but tells us very little about cause and effect, about impacts on the domestic economy. To do this, a more careful glance at the various "balances" is necessary.

The balances of the balance of payments

The accounting balances must always be zero, yet frequently we read about "deficits" in the balance of payments. These deficits refer to the various "balance" components, especially those listed in lines 3, 4, and 6. Each balance has its own meaning and special implications.

The *balance of trade* (line 3) reflects the basic strength or weakness of the production sector of the economy, since it encompasses only transactions in goods. Changes in a nation's relative costs of production or the quality of its products will be reflected in the balance of trade. So, too, will the stage of the business cycle. If one nation's economy expands while those of its trading partners slacken, the balance of trade will be affected. The expanding nation's imports of consumer and producer goods will rise, but its own exports, which are the imports of its partners, will lag.

The *balance on goods and services* (line 4) is a more comprehensive measure, including not only goods transactions but also the services exported and imported. This balance is especially informative, for it indicates something about the impact of international transactions on domestic production, employment, and prices. Exports represent domestic production, using domestic physical resources and workers, sold abroad. Demand for exports not only encourages domestic production but can exert pressure on domestic prices, especially when the economy nears full employment. Imports, on the other hand, represent domestic demand transfered to foreign shores. As such, it replaces domestic demand for output and for the factors of production. Unemployment may follow, but pressure on domestic prices is also relieved. Imports can be most welcome when the domestic economy is overheated, but they can add recessionary momentum when domestic demand is weak. Line 4 shows that in 1980 the foreign sector intensified inflationary pressure, since Americans sold $10.8 billion more to foreigners than foreigners purchased from U.S. residents. In the inflationary circumstances of that year, net exports clearly were not beneficial to the economy.

The *balance on current account* (line 6) spells out the supply of dollars by Americans, who used the dollars not only to buy foreign goods and services but also to send abroad as gifts, as well as the demand by foreigners for U.S. money to use for purchases and for gifts in the United States. In 1980 the foreign demand for U.S. dollars slightly exceeded the supply of dollars.

All of these balances refer to current-account transactions. In addition, the balance of payments records capital transactions or changes in the ownership of assets. Because the sum of capital account transactions (except for the statistical discrepancy and occasional SDR allocations) equals the negative of the balance on current account, it provides no additional information. Some economists, however, do pay attention to the composition of the capital account, distinguishing between short- and long-term capital flows and between private and government transactions.

When economists, political leaders, or journalists converse about deficits or surpluses in the balance of payments, their discussion centers on one or more of the definitions just presented. No one is better than the others, but each is used for different purposes.

The balances, 1960–1980

Table 24.2 lists the balances, showing their movements over the past two decades and providing a sense of the trend in U.S. international financial relations.

A general pattern is evident in the first three columns, which deal with the current account. They all show growth during the early 1960s, but then the five-year pattern reverses and the three accounts fall for the remainder of the decade, but remain positive. All of the balances fluctuated sharply during the 1970s, often turning negative. During the 1970s American demands for imports of goods exceeded foreign demands for products made in the United States, and this difference was substantial by the decade's end. (Could you relate this to skyrocketing petroleum prices?) But foreign demand for American services, primarily the income earned by Americans on their foreign investments, kept the balance on goods and services positive for most of the years between 1970 and 1980.

Unilateral transfers have been negative for a long time, reflecting American affluence. But whereas during the 1960s the other components of the balance on current account were sufficiently positive to offset these outflows, the weakening of the goods and services balance meant a smaller and often negative current-account balance.

Despite the strength of the current-account balance during the 1960s,

TABLE 24.2 International Payments Balances of the United States, 1960–1980 (millions of dollars)

Year	Balance of trade	Balance on goods and services	Balance on current account	Balance on current and long-term capital account[a]
1960	4,892	5,132	2,824	−1,155
1961	5,571	6,345	3,821	20
1962	4,521	6,026	3,388	−979
1963	5,224	7,167	4,414	−1,262
1964	6,801	9,603	6,822	28
1965	4,951	8,284	5,431	−1,814
1966	3,817	5,961	3,029	−1,614
1967	3,800	5,709	2,584	−3,196
1968	635	3,563	611	−1,349
1969	607	3,393	399	−2,879
1970	2,603	5,624	2,330	−3,039
1971	−2,260	2,268	−1,434	
1972	−6,416	−1,941	−5,795	
1973	911	11,021	7,140	
1974	−5,343	9,309	2,124	
1975	9,047	22,893	18,280	
1976	−9,306	9,382	4,384	
1977	−30,873	−9,464	−14,068	
1978	−33,759	−9,008	−14,075	
1979	−27,346	7,008	1,414	
1980	−25,342	10,779	3,723	

[a]Series discontinued after 1970.

Sources: 1960–1977—*Economic Report of the President, 1981;* 1978–80—*Survey of Current Business,* June, 1981.

heavy American investment abroad led to dollar outflows, a situation that is evident from the final column of Table 24.2. Adding long-term capital outflows onto the current-account balance leaves one with an overall picture of a negative balance and the corresponding strong demand for foreign currencies by Americans.

In the pre-1973 world of fixed exchange rates, this stronger demand for foreign currencies did not cause a decline in the dollar's international value. Instead, it led to a buildup of short-term liabilities against U.S. banks, corporate and noncorporate businesses, and the federal government. Not only did foreign nationals hold vast amounts of dollar debt, but foreign governments, too, were amassing substantial holdings of dollars. Until 1971 these governments had the right to obtain gold from the United States government in exchange for these dollar claims.

The lessons of the balances

The balance-of-payment trends just outlined point to a dollar whose real market value (as opposed to its artificially maintained rate) increasingly came to depend on the willingness of foreign holders to acquire and maintain large dollar balances. In 1971 and again in 1973, this desire was tested and found wanting; a loss of confidence led to substantial pressure on the United States, and when the dollar was cut loose from its artificial mooring, marked declines in the exchange rate of the dollar followed. A chronic problem, slowly gathering momentum, had finally erupted.

Three interrelated fundamental problems underlay the decline in the exchange rate: (1) the eclipse of American supremacy in world markets; (2) the decline in the role of the dollar as the major international reserve currency; and (3) the perception of a dollar glut. Each of these points merits a brief explanation.

The competitive decline of the United States. The United States was the preeminent world economic power in the years immediately after World War II. The dollar was the world's strongest currency, more sought than gold. But as the world economy recovered from the ravages of the 1939–1945 war—and this took decades—and as other economies gained strength, their competitive position was restored and the demand for dollars was reduced correspondingly.

The dollar as a reserve currency. Most of the theoretical material in this chapter on the determination of exchange rates is equally applicable to currencies other than the dollar. The exchange rates of the British pound, the Norwegian krone, the Brazilian cruzeiro, and other world currencies—even the Soviet ruble—are subject to the same forces of world supply and demand. But in one sense the dollar is different. For many decades the dollar has been the world's money, fulfilling in the international arena the four functions that characterize money (recall Chapter 1). Many international contracts utilize the dollar as a unit of account and a standard of deferred payments. And the dollar remains unsurpassed as the international medium of exchange. For this reason, the dollar has also become a store of value for citizens, banks, and governments the world around. Central banks, for example, hold dollar assets in their international reserve portfolios for use when necessary.

A **reserve currency** is any currency held by governments for use as an international medium of exchange and a store of value for their international transactions.

This demand for the dollar as a **reserve currency** takes on an added role in determining the exchange rate of the dollar. In the postwar period the nations of the world not only needed dollars to pay for their current imports but also hoarded them to be used at a later date, reacting no differently than any of us who save dollars for future needs. When the demand for the dollar as a reserve currency was combined with the demand for dollar goods and services, the demand for the dollar remained strong. But once again, as other economies, especially those of Western Germany and Japan, gained vitality, their currencies, too, began to fulfill the reserve function. The uniqueness of the dollar as a reserve currency disappeared. Although it is still preeminent as an international reserve, the dollar is no longer the only currency used by the world's nations as a store of value. Consequently, the demand for dollars as an asset held for future use has weakened as well. This, too, must be included in the list of causes for the dollar's decline.

The dollar glut. Gold has played the role of international money for centuries. In this century (until very recently), in practice, gold played a secondary role to reserve currencies. For most of the 1900s, the dollar was at least as good as gold, basically because of the readiness of the U.S. monetary authorities to exchange dollars for gold at a fixed price.[4] From 1900 to 1933, the Treasury sold or bought gold at $22.67 per ounce, 90 percent pure. From 1934 to 1971, the price was fixed at $35.00 per ounce. Although the public could not buy gold directly from the Treasury, central banks could acquire the metal. In essence, the United States fixed the price of gold not only by setting its price but by being willing to buy or sell whatever amounts of gold were necessary to maintain this price. Thus, gold (to a lesser extent) and dollars (to a greater extent) were international money.

Now, just as more domestic currency is needed as the domestic economy grows, so, too, is more international money needed as world exports and imports increase. And world trade has increased significantly in the past thirty years. In 1949, total international trade amounted to $59.3 billion; by 1980, that number had risen to over $1,900 billion.

Where does the international money come from to finance this trade? Gold proved to be a poor source. At the fixed price of $35 per ounce, gold mining was profitable only in a few countries, notably the Union of South Africa and the Soviet Union. From 1949 to 1969 only $6.1 billion worth of gold found its way into the monetary reserves of the world. The dollar, of course, was the other source, and the dollar holdings of foreign nations expanded by three times that amount in the same period.

But the very success of the dollar led to concern. The international community began to ask, Is the supply of dollars increasing too rapidly? Will the dollar be able to maintain its value? Can the United States maintain its commitment to sell gold for dollars when its dollar liabilities far exceed its gold holdings? This doubt led to nervousness, which meant a reduced willingness to hold dollars. (See Box 24.3.)

The cumulative impact of these various pressures began to be felt in the late 1960s. A watershed was reached in 1971, the year in which these fears crystallized into a panic. During the first seven months of 1971, U.S. international reserves fell by 8.3 percent. By early August, the dimensions of the dollar outflow were such that if the outflow had continued at that rate, the entire stock of U.S. reserves would have been depleted in less than a year. Policy makers began to pay attention to the lessons of history that showed convincingly how panics are self-reinforcing.

The outflow came to an abrupt halt in August, when the President of the United States announced his decision to cease dollar convertibility. No longer could individuals or official institutions automatically obtain gold from the United States in exchange for dollars. Multilateral negotia-

---

[4]Actually, dollars were better than gold, for dollar assets earned interest whereas gold not only provided no current return but created storage and insurance expenses.

BOX 24.3 SDRs and Dollars

The international community was certainly aware of the changing climate and the increasing fragility of the dollar. The SDR was a novel way to expand world liquidity, one that would not rely on extracting scarce metals* and yet would win international confidence. In 1967, the IMF created the special drawing right (SDR). The members agreed, in essence, to accept entries of SDRs on their accounts at the IMF as payment for obligations due them. By this consent, the world community turned SDRs into international money. And by creating this "paper gold" as needed, it could expand its money supply without having to rely on gold or the U.S. dollar.

Initially, the value of the SDR was set at par with the dollar and with gold. Thus, a unit of SDR was worth $1, and 35 SDRs equaled an ounce of gold. But after the gold-dollar connection was dropped in 1971, the IMF had to reconsider the way in which the SDR was calculated. An international money should be stable, and with both gold and the dollar likely to fluctuate, neither was optimal as a means of valuing the SDR. In 1974 the decision was made to link the SDR to a "market basket" of currencies, including the dollar.** The basic idea is that while the component currencies will fluctuate, many of these movements will be offsetting; when some go up, others go down. Consequently, the average value of the basket will remain relatively stable, certainly more so than that of any individual currency. Since then the SDR not only has been an international reserve asset but it has increasingly found a role as an international unit of account.

These developments in international finance further reduce the demand for the dollar, since a substitute that is more stable than the dollar has been devised. Some international bond issues are all denominated in SDRs. Surely, it is natural to use one money as a unit of account, medium of exchange, store of value and standard of deferred payment, and the SDR can do the job.

---

*The absurdity of metallic reserves should be evident. Does it make sense for the U.S. government to pay South Africa to remove gold from the earth, refine it, and ship it to Fort Knox, Kentucky, and then bury it in an underground vault?
**The basket consists of the following currencies and their respective weights: U.S. dollar (42%), West German mark (19%), and the British pound, the Japanese yen, and the French franc (each 13%). Before 1981 the basket consisted of sixteen currencies.

---

tions were held at the Smithsonian Institution in Washington, D.C., in December 1971, and the resulting "Smithsonian Agreement" saw an official realignment of exchange rates, a greater willingness to let currencies float against each other (although within stated limits), and a new dollar price of gold. Gold, which had sold for $35 per ounce since 1934, was revalued upward by 8½ percent, and the value of the dollar was correspondingly reduced to $38 per ounce of gold by congressional action in March 1972. Figure 24.3 (p. 612) clearly depicts this drop in the dollar's exchange rate.

The market reaction to the new price of the dollar was not encouraging, and forced foreign central banks to support the dollar's price by intervening in the foreign-exchange market. Speculative purchases of Swiss francs, West German marks, and Japanese yen, financed by sales of U.S. dollars, led to suspension of the limits on floating in March 1973. And with this freedom from government intervention, which had aimed to preserve exchange rates within narrow limits, the market's judgment that the dollar had been artificially overvalued prevailed and the dollar's value fell.

Since 1973 the exchange rate of the dollar has been relatively stable, responding to basic supply and demand forces. To be sure, the exchange rate has moved up and down. Market confidence in the dollar—perhaps because U.S. exports are likely to grow more than U.S. imports, perhaps because investment opportunities are exceptionally strong, perhaps because interest rates are higher in the United States than elsewhere—leads to dollar strength. Declining confidence, related to basic economic forces, leads to a fall in the dollar's exchange value.

There are a number of lessons to be drawn from this survey. The obvious ones concern the theoretical, accounting, and historical information conveyed—how exchange rates are determined, what the balance of payments is, what has happened to the exchange value of the dollar, and why these patterns have occurred. But there is another lesson, albeit not as evident: Change is an inescapable fact of history. The preeminence of the United States in economic affairs, which seemed so assured and everlasting in the 1950s, was eroded in the 1960s and severely tested in the 1970s. A structured international economy, predicated on fixed exchange rates between nations, has given way to a new system based on floating exchange rates and responsive to market forces. But a watchful eye and an occasional interventionist arm is exercised by the monetary authorities of the world's economies.

A corollary lesson has to do with the inability to manage change. While it is not possible to review here the various attempts made by well-meaning and well-informed leaders of the international financial community to preserve the fixed exchange rate system during the 1950s and 1960s, events proved stronger than imposed policies. The market remains a strong force in the international monetary sphere. While it is possible to influence and shape market forces at some times and to some extent, neither economists nor politicians have devised a coercion-free method of dominating the market.

In a sense, these remarks set the stage for the next chapter. The United States has become a more open economy subject to many of the constraints and problems that other nations have been facing for decades. The dollar no longer finds as warm a welcome abroad. Consequently, the U.S. monetary authorities, who were cognizant of the impact of their actions on the international economy, must now be concerned with how international developments impinge on their ability to manage domestic economy.

☐ Summary

The exchange rate, which is a price, can be determined by the demand of foreigners for a given currency—say, the dollar—and the supply of that currency by dollar holders who want to acquire foreign money. The demand for dollars is a demand both for U.S. goods and services and for U.S. assets, such as factories, real estate, or financial instruments. Similarly, the willingness of Americans to part with dollars reflects their demand for foreign goods, services, and assets. In a competitive market the intersection of the supply and demand curves sets the price. Shifts in either the supply of or the demand for dollars will alter the exchange rate. When governments intervene in foreign-exchange markets, their interference with the market process affects the exchange rate.

In a freely floating exchange rate system, market forces alone determine price, while in a fixed exchange rate system, the hand of the government predominates. The present international financial system can best be described as a compromise. Under managed floating, basic market forces determine the exchange rate, but government intervention may be occasioned when exchange rate fluctuations are extreme.

The exchange rate of the dollar fell sharply in the early 1970s but has remained stable since then. Fundamental to understanding this decline are developments in the U.S. balance of payments, which records all international transactions as either credits (exports) or debits (imports). While the balance of payments is always balanced by definition, components may either be net credit or debit items. Among the components traced by economists are the balance of trade, the balance on goods and services, and the balance on current account. All of these balances moved from a position of surplus in the 1960s to a more mixed picture, with not infrequent deficit positions, in the 1970s. The eclipse of U.S. supremacy in world markets since the 1940s and 1950s, the decline in the role of the dollar as an international reserve currency, and the perception that the world was being flooded with dollars were all reflected in the balance-of-payments position of the United States. The gradual erosion of confidence in the dollar reached its nadir in 1971, when substantial foreign demands for gold in exchange for dollar forced the United States unilaterally to cease such exchanges. Further pressure in foreign-exchange markets led to an end of the international effort to preserve the dollar within given bounds, and in 1973, as a consequence, the managed float began. Leaving the value of the dollar to the market meant a reduction in its value between 1971 and 1973.

Since 1973 the exchange rate of the dollar has been relatively stable, responding primarily to the forces of supply and demand.

☐ Questions and Exercises

1. Examine the U.S. balance of payments for 1981 or a more recent year. Also, study movements in the exchange rate of the dollar for the same period. Can you
   a. explain what happened to each? (You might want to compare them to figures for an earlier year).
   b. understand why the changes occurred?
2. In 1981 President Reagan announced a policy of nonintervention in the foreign-exchange market. The United States would neither buy nor sell dollars. How should such a policy affect the international value of the dollar if
   a. other nations adopt similar policies?
   b. other nations continue to pursue managed floating?
   What did happen?
3. The United States is less dependent on the international sector of its economy than most other nations. Examine the balance of payments and the exchange rate for a recent period for a developed nation like the United Kingdom or France and for a less developed one like Egypt or Jamaica and see if there are any significant differences.
4. What do you believe is the likely impact of the new-found strength of the OPEC nations on their own current accounts and the exchange rates of their currencies? What would you expect to happen to the current accounts and exchange rates of oil-importing nations? Examine your conclusions in the light of reality by inspecting the data in *International Financial Statistics*, a monthly of the International Monetary Fund.
5. The political victory of the socialists in France (1981) brought the exchange rate of the franc down. What is the connection between politics and the value of a nation's currency?

☐ For Further Study

All textbooks designed for a course in international economics deal extensively with how exchange rates are determined and with balance-of-payments accounting, and will expand on the material summarized in this chapter.

Two thoughtful and provocative essays by Fritz Machlup deal with the issue of precisely what the balance of payments means: "Three Concepts of the Balance of Payments and the So-Called Dollar Shortage" and "The Mysterious Numbers Game of Balance-of-Payments Statistics." Both are contained in his *International Payments, Debts, and Gold* (New York: Scribner's, 1964). Robert Solomon has written an authoritative account of the world's monetary troubles in the postwar period: *The International Monetary System, 1945–1976: An Insider's View* (New York: Harper & Row, 1977).

The annual report of the International Monetary Fund in Washington, D.C., is a useful source for recent developments in the international financial sphere.

CHAPTER 25

The International Economy and the Domestic Economy: Their Interrelationship and the Role of Monetary Policy

The central dilemma confronting policymakers in interdependent nations is the contrast, heightened by economic openness, between de jure sovereignty over policy instruments and de facto control of ultimate targets.

Ralph C. Bryant, U.S. economist (1980)

Just as generals prefer to fight the previous war, economists tend to solve the last crisis, or even the crises before that.

Brian Johnson, British economist (1970)

CONTENTS

The last chapter sketched out two alternative methods of exchange rate determination—fixed and flexible. This chapter will explore the advantages and disadvantages of these two systems. It is also devoted to the impact of international transactions, especially as they affect the monetary system and, thereby, the domestic economy. You may recall that in the last chapter four key questions were raised but only one was answered.

The task of this chapter is to understand the remaining three:

1. What impact does a lower exchange rate have on an economy?
2. What role has monetary policy played in causing or stemming the decline of the dollar?
3. Does the floating exchange rate system impose any special problems or offer any unusual opportunities for control of the domestic economy by monetary policy?

☐ The Balance of Payments and the Domestic Economy

We turn first to the impact of foreign transactions, and especially their monetary effects on the domestic economy. It will be simplest to deal with the fixed exchange rate system first, and then introduce the modifications needed to analyze a regime of flexible exchange rates.

For any international transaction involving goods and services, a distinction must be made between the direct, real impact of the action and the indirect, monetary effect. Employment, production, and prices are affected whenever a nation exports more than it imports or imports more than it exports. This is so for a very simple reason: Exports represent a demand for domestically produced goods. In fact, exports influence the domestic economy in the same way as any other component of aggregate demand—consumption, investment, or government spending. Imports, on the other hand, divert domestic income to foreign products, and in this way constitute a drain from the domestic spending stream analogous to the savings drain described in Chapter 16. So when the balance on goods and services is in surplus (exports exceed imports), the demand-stimulating impact exceeds the demand-depressing influence. The economy will surge forward, with increased production and employment and higher prices. Conversely, when the goods and services balance is in deficit, the demand-diverting effect predominates and the impact on the economy is depressing—less demand means less employment, production, and/or lower prices.[1]

This effect, the income-expanding or -retarding influence of international transactions on the domestic economy, is only part of the impact. You realize from the last chapter that any deficit in one account must have a compensating entry in another account. The acquisition of Ghanaian cocoa or an Icelandic wool sweater must be paid for; the import of the merchandise gives rise to a dollar obligation to the exporter. The financial side of the account also has repercussions on the domestic economy. To understand this impact, it is necessary to demonstrate the link between foreign financial flows and domestic bank reserves.

Foreign flows and bank reserves

Money flows coming into a country from external sources are expansionary, and, unless offset, induce domestic money supply growth. Conversely, money outflows reduce the domestic money supply. The next few paragraphs are devoted to demonstrating the truth of these statements and indicating some of their implications.

Follow a typical case. A U.S. importer of rioja wines buys $100,000 worth of the beverage from a Spanish firm. Figure 25.1 presents a series of T-charts (familiar to you from Chapter 10) to show one plausible way in which payment might be effected. (For simplicity, all payments are assumed to be made in dollars, even in Spain. The complications introduced by foreign-exchange conversions are irrelevant in this instance.)

Start at the lower left and note what happens to the balance sheet of the U.S. importer, whose inventories (assets) rise upon receipt of the merchandise, but who must also pay for them. Wine Importers, Inc., orders its banker to transfer funds, whereupon $100,000 is deducted from its account at the First National Bank. The U.S. banker can turn either to a foreign exchange dealer-bank to handle this transfer to Spain or, if the bank has foreign exchange facilities, handle the transaction itself. In the latter case, the bank deals directly with a foreign institution. Reconciliation of the accounts is done by the respective central banks as follows. The Federal Reserve Bank of New York, say, deducts the sum from the

---

[1]You might want to work out the impact of the foreign sector explicitly by adding net exports to the analysis in Chapters 16.

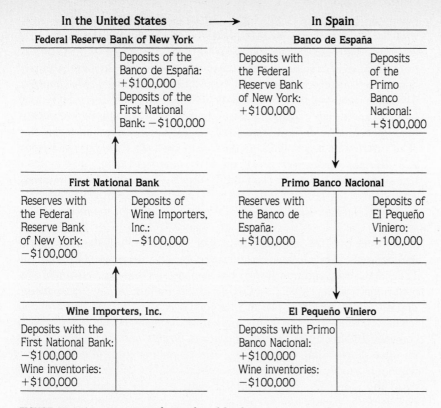

In the United States   ⟶   **In Spain**

Federal Reserve Bank of New York	
	Deposits of the Banco de España: +$100,000 Deposits of the First National Bank: −$100,000

Banco de España	
Deposits with the Federal Reserve Bank of New York: +$100,000	Deposits of the Primo Banco Nacional: +$100,000

First National Bank	
Reserves with the Federal Reserve Bank of New York: −$100,000	Deposits of Wine Importers, Inc.: −$100,000

Primo Banco Nacional	
Reserves with the Banco de España: +$100,000	Deposits of El Pequeño Viniero: +100,000

Wine Importers, Inc.	
Deposits with the First National Bank: −$100,000 Wine inventories: +$100,000	

El Pequeño Viniero	
Deposits with Primo Banco Nacional: +$100,000 Wine inventories: −$100,000	

FIGURE 25.1 An international transfer of funds.

account of the First National Bank (middle left panel), so that the latter's balance sheet shows both a decrease in liabilities (its obligation to Wine Importers) and an equivalent decrease in assets (the obligations of the Federal Reserve to the bank.)

The next step involves the Federal Reserve Bank and the Banco de España, the Spanish central bank. Since many foreign central banks maintain accounts with the Federal Reserve, payment can be made by adding $100,000 to the account of the Banco de España. In this instance the U.S. end of the transaction, as shown in the upper left-hand panel, is completed: First National's account with the Federal Reserve Bank of New York is reduced and a corresponding increase is recorded in the American central bank's obligation to its Spanish counterpart.

Turn now to the Spanish side.

The assets of the Banco de España have been increased by $100,000, which it must transfer to the account of the Primo Banco Nacional. Corresponding to the Banco de España's rise in assets is the $100,000 rise in liabilities, which is also reflected in the increase in assets of the Spanish commercial bank, as seen in the middle right panel. The transaction is completed when the Primo Banco Nacional adjusts the account of El

Pequeño Viniero, indicated by an increase in the bank's liabilities to the winery. The transfer is recorded in the balance sheet of the exporter in the lower right-hand T-account.[2]

This chain of transactions is not much more complex than a purely domestic transfer of funds. But one difference is vital. In domestic payments, reserves from one bank flow to another bank; the reserve total remains unaltered. (If you're not sure that this statement is correct, check the explanation of deposit creation on pages 228–235.) Not so in the case of an international payment. *An outflow of funds to a foreign bank leads to a decrease in the reserves of the U.S. banking system.* As is evident from Figure 25.1, the U.S. banking system has lost $100,000 in reserves. Analogously, as is evident from the T-charts on the Spanish side, *an inflow of foreign currency causes an expansion of banking system reserves.*

Consider now the monetary impact of a deficit in the balance on goods and services. The destruction of reserves—the deposits held with the Federal Reserve and now lost by the banking system—leads to a multiple contraction of deposits, its exact value depending on the value of the deposit multiplier described in Chapter 10. And with fewer reserves and fewer deposits—in other words, tighter money—the economy is forced to contract. In effect, *this outflow of funds to foreign nations is equivalent to an open market sale of securities.* The reverse is true, of course, for a payments surplus—the monetary impact will be stimulating. In both cases the monetary, indirect impact buttresses the direct, real impact. Net imports means less spending at home and less money to finance domestic borrowing demands.[3]

The capital account and bank reserves

The previous chain of events was predicated on a deficit in the balance on goods and services. But now that the linkage between foreign flows and bank reserves is clear, you can well understand that any set of transactions leading to an inflow or outflow of funds from the banking system has an expansionary or contractionary impact on the domestic economy. Thus, the desire of Americans to invest in oil wells abroad or buy foreign securities or acquire Swiss bank deposits involves a similar outflow of dollars and a constraining impact on the domestic economy. (Absent in these instances, however, are the direct effects on production, since domestic demand is not reduced by pure financial transactions.) Conversely, an inflow of funds from foreigners purchasing domestic financial assets leads to an increase in bank reserves and sets the stage for monetary expansion.

---

[2]Accounting students will realize that technical liberties have been taken in the handling of some of these transactions.

[3]Actually, the impact on the United States differs from that described in this illustration because of its status as a reserve currency nation. This is discussed on pages 645–646.

☐ Financial Flows and Fixed Exchange Rates

A deficit (however defined) in the balance of payments cannot continue unabated. When a nation's exchange rate is fixed, so that a given value of domestic currency units exchanges for a given value of foreign currency units (e.g., $1 = 250 yen), a deficit means that the demand of foreigners for the domestic currency is less than that of domestic demanders for foreign currency. Turn back to page 608 and take a look at the excess supply for dollars at the fixed exchange rate of 250 yen to the dollar. Americans had wanted more yen to buy Japanese goods, services, and investments than our Western neighbors had wanted dollars to acquire U.S. goods, services, and assets. You now should understand why dollars are amassed in the Japanese central bank. If this process were to continue for an extended period, the Bank of Japan would find itself with two problems on its hands. First, the continuing inflow of dollars to Japanese banks would expand that nation's bank reserves and money supply, with potentially inflationary consequences. Second, the Bank of Japan ultimately would find itself owning far more dollars than it may want to own.

The impact in America is quite the opposite. The continuous outflow of funds has contractionary consequences. Moreover, the overhang of obligations against the United States implies that at some future date foreign holders of dollars will be able to acquire dollar goods and services, possibly at moments that are not suitable from the standpoint of the national interest of the United States. Thus, instead of the balance of payments being in equilibrium, with inflows and outflows roughly equal, the persistent deficit represents a **fundamental disequilibrium.** Nations that have a fundamental disequilibrium are expected to take corrective measures.

A **fundamental disequilibrium** exists under a regime of fixed exchange rates whenever the balance of payments is persistently in surplus or deficit.

Deficit remedies

Remedies for a deficit in the payments balance run the gamut from letting the economic system reverse itself without government interference to instituting monetary and fiscal policies to devaluating its currency to placing direct controls on capital flows and/or trade. Each of them has been used, and each merits analysis.

Self-adjusting mechanisms. Under a fixed exchange rate system, a variety of automatic mechanisms function to reduce, if not eliminate, a deficit.

1. *Income effects.* The excess of imports over exports has a depressing effect on the economy, as was pointed out earlier. But as incomes fall, so, too, does the demand for imports. When people earn less income, they spend less not only on domestic products but on foreign goods and services as well. Moreover, as domestic demand eases, companies whose sales activities were directed toward the home market will have

a greater stimulus to search out foreign markets. Thus, imports fall and exports rise, and the deficit diminishes.

2. *Price effects.* Prices may play a role, too. The reduced pressure on demand slows the growth of domestic prices, giving the public further incentive to buy more at home and less abroad.

3. *Monetary effects.* The outflow of funds leads to tighter money at home. This also restricts domestic demand and works to restrict imports and encourage exports. In addition, a capital flow impact comes into play. Higher domestic interest rates lead to decreased capital outflows and additional capital inflows. With higher earnings available in the debt instruments of the deficit country, both domestic and foreign holders are less likely to send funds out of the economy that is experiencing the payments deficit.

4. *Foreign effects.* Each of these pressures at home is reinforced by opposite economic reactions abroad. In the surplus country (or countries), where exports exceed imports, (a) the increase in domestic income leads to greater import demand and a reduced export supply, (b) the possible pressure on prices induces greater import demand and less export supply, and (c) the increased money supply not only reinforces the expansion of domestic demand and higher prices, but, insofar as interest rates fall, induces capital outflows.

Indeed, if the system is left alone, the long-run impact must be restoration of equilibrium. The combination of expansion in one country and contraction in the other ultimately will remove the disequilibrium and validate the fixed exchange rate.

Patience, however, is not characteristic of most political and economic leaders. And the gap between exports and imports can be narrowed by appropriate fiscal and monetary policies.

Aggregate-demand policies. Self-adjustment requires constrained economic activity in the deficit country and expansion in the surplus country. It should be obvious that fiscal and monetary policies can be used to achieve these goals. Were a policy of tightness to be pursued in the deficit country, with some combination of tax hikes and reductions of government expenditures on the fiscal end and a mix of open market sales and increases in reserve requirement ratios, then domestic demand would be retarded and interest rates would be pushed up. A loose fiscal and monetary policy in the surplus country would speed up the adjustment process there.

In fact, if you studied the operation of the gold standard around the turn of the present century and looked at some contemporary money and banking textbooks, you would find that precisely such advice was offered and so, too, was policy conducted.[4] You need go no farther than the

---

[4]Of course, since Keynes' great work was not yet written, the income impacts and the use of fiscal policy were still undiscovered. However, monetary policy did play a key role in maintaining international financial stability.

discussion (in Chapter 23) of monetary policy before and during the Great Depression to discover how balance-of-payments considerations led to changes in monetary policy.

Were such remedies acceptable in the postwar international economy in light of a new understanding of policy options and consequences? In certain circumstances the answer is yes. When the deficit country is experiencing an overly buoyant, inflationary economy and the surplus country is in the doldrums, the prescriptions for domestic economic stability and payments balance are consistent. When the deficit country is combating inflation, tight monetary and fiscal policies are properly imposed to restrain the price rises. Tightness, too, will lead to a reduction in the payments deficit. Conversely, an expansionary policy is appropriate both for stimulating the domestic economy and for reducing a payments surplus; the impact of a loose policy is to encourage momentum in the domestic economy and simultaneously retard the surplus in the foreign account. These policy options are outlined in Figure 25.2: Domestic inflation and payments deficit call for restraint, while domestic contraction and payments surplus signal the appropriateness of an expansionary policy. But these circumstances constitute only two of the four possibilities outlined in Figure 25.2. Domestic contraction may also occur when the payments position is in deficit. Similarly, an inflationary economy may coexist with a payments surplus. [These latter cases are another example of the dilemmas discussed in connection with the Phillips curve (pp. 555–557).] What is the proper policy in these circumstances?

Consider the former case: Slackened aggregate demand is accompanied by high percentages of unemployed labor, and severe underutilization of capital capacity pervades an economy that is also experiencing a deficit in the balance of payments. Orthodox Keynesian remedies call for loose monetary and fiscal policies to stimulate the domestic economy. But the very success of these aggregate-demand policies will intensify the pay-

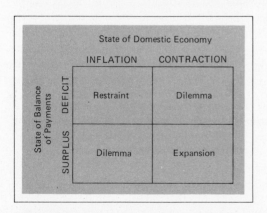

FIGURE 25.2 Policy options under varying domestic economic and balance-of-payments conditions.

ments deficit. Imports will increase; exports will decline; and, in reaction to the falling interest rates resulting from a loose monetary policy, capital will leave the country. On the other hand, policies designed to reverse the payments deficit—tight money and fiscal restraint—will intensify the weakness in employment and capacity utilization.

The country facing a payments surplus and a strong domestic economy similarly must choose. The antiinflationary policy that is beneficial to the domestic economy leads to a slower rate of price growth, increasing the competitiveness of domestic goods and services in the international marketplace and thus stimulating exports. This, of course, intensifies the surplus. Similarly, the higher interest rates that are a consequence of tight money lead to a capital inflow that reinforces the current-account surplus. Thus, policy makers in the surplus country, too, are in a dilemma.

Yet the two dilemma cases are not altogether symmetrical. The pressures on the deficit country are greater than those on the surplus nation. The reason is simple: A prolonged deficit leads to the exhaustion of foreign reserves and foreign credit. No nation can be an eternal borrower. True, the deficit countries can buy time by using their own or borrowed foreign-exchange reserves, but ultimately they must follow a policy that brings stability to the payments accounts.

The predicament in the surplus country is less intense. While it accumulates stocks of foreign currency, a lender never faces the pressure of a borrower. (Today one does not hear about the problems of the oil-exporting nations, whose surpluses have led to massive holdings of gold, dollars, and other currencies. The complaints and fears come from the oil-importing countries, which are running out of the means to pay their skyrocketing fuel bills.) The major problem comes from the monetary impact on the domestic economy; the inflow of the funds means increased bank reserves and money supply, and consequent inflation.

Sterilizing operations involve offsetting the impact of foreign money flows on the domestic monetary system.

Central banks, however, can cope with this problem by **sterilizing** the inflow. They can engage in domestic tightening. Reserve ratios can be raised (to over 100% if need be); securities can be sold on the open market; and direct controls can be (and have been) imposed to limit bank lending.

Thus, the pressure to adjust rests heavily on the deficit country. The typical method of adjustment under a fixed exchange rate system is the next option, devaluation.

Devaluation and revaluation. Figure 25.3 reproduces the supply and demand diagram of Figure 24.1, with the yen/dollar exchange rate pegged at 250 yen per dollar. As mentioned on page 630, when the supply of dollars exceeds the demand for them, dollar balances are being built up in Japan, corresponding to the U.S. loss of dollars.

In a **devaluation,** the official exchange rate of the currency with respect to other currencies is reduced, so that more domestic currency is required to obtain one unit of foreign exchange.

One way for the United States to stop this outflow is to **devalue.** If the amount of yen obtained per dollar is reduced, thereby reducing the

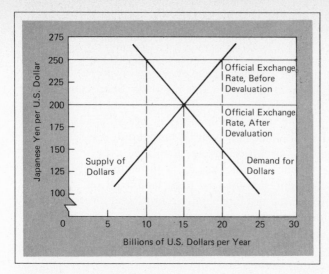

FIGURE 25.3 Devaluation.

dollar's purchasing power in Japan, Japanese exports become more expensive to Americans and U.S. exports are made cheaper to yen earners. If the new exchange rate is pegged at 200 yen per dollar—which, by the way, is not only a devaluation of the dollar but a **revaluation** of the yen—and the demand and supply curves do not shift permanently, the fundamental disequilibrium is replaced by an equilibrium. At this exchange rate the supply and demand for dollars is equal.

In a **revaluation,** the official exchange rate vis-à-vis other currencies is increased.

Exchange controls. An alternative to devaluation is the imposition of restraints, either on trade or on capital flows. Importers may find that foreign exchange can be obtained for specified purposes only, such as for needed investment goods but not for luxury consumption goods. Or, in order to buy foreign exchange from licensed banks demanders might have to pay a premium over the formally pegged exchange rate. Capital flows may be restrained by barring lending to foreign customers or to domestic borrowers who want to transfer the funds abroad. Alternatively, interest rate surcharges may be imposed by the authorities on anyone who ships capital out of the country. Thus, through either quantity or price rationing, scarce foreign exchange is husbanded in the deficit nation.

These measures of control, though frequently used, normally come as a last resort. IMF member nations have agreed that exchange controls limit the free interchange of goods, services, and capital, and thus reduce the benefits of international exchange. If alternative methods can do the job of stabilizing a nation's payments position, it is inappropriate to turn to exchange controls. In fact, over the past thirty years the nations of the world have made substantial progress in reducing the degree of exchange control, so that today few industrial nations impose such restraints on capital.

In short. In theory, then, a fixed exchange system works as follows. Exchange rates are set so that all countries are expected to achieve long-term equilibrium in their payments positions. Short-run deviations from the pegged rates are tolerated, with foreign-exchange reserves and international borrowing serving to finance temporary deficits.

Monetary and fiscal policy may be used to speed up the restoration of equilibrium. Because of unacceptable domestic trade-offs, however, aggregate demand policies cannot always be brought into play. Should the short-term disequilibrium turn out to be long-lived and irreversible, the rules under which the system operates require that the exchange rate be modified either upward or downward.

In fact, this mechanism worked tolerably for two decades following 1945. It was only in the late 1960s that the strains overwhelmed the fixed exchange rate system, leading to its dissolution in the early 1970s.

Problems of a fixed exchange rate system

Dissatisfaction with the fixed exchange rate arises on both theoretical and practical grounds. Among those to be surveyed here are the following:

1. The issue of policy dilemmas.
2. The short-run versus long-run impact of devaluation.
3. A related problem of devaluation-induced inflation.
4. The question of how exchange rates are determined.
5. The constraint imposed by the fixed exchange rate system on the conduct of discretionary policy.

Policy dilemmas. Under a fixed exchange rate regime, it may be necessary to implement domestic policy measures that are unpopular and may well be economically unsound if not for the need to eliminate the payments deficit. Neither political leaders nor economists, and certainly not the citizen, will be overjoyed to endorse a deflationary policy unless, of course, the economy is substantially overheated.

The short run. Nor is devaluation undertaken lightly. When the international value of a currency is reduced, imports become more expensive. A devaluation causes immediate harm to segments of the economy that are heavily reliant on imports, especially when domestic substitutes are not available.[5] The benefits of the devaluation, however, will take place over a longer interval.

Even in a nation as relatively independent of the foreign sector as the

---

[5] Japan imports 99 percent of its total consumption of oil. Because its industrial and transportation system is heavily dependent on oil, a devaluation of the yen immediately raises the price of fuel, which is priced in dollars, and increases the cost of virtually everything to Japanese producers and consumers.

United States—in 1980 only 2 percent of GNP was derived from net exports of goods and services—devaluation does not bring immediate relief. Look at what happened to the value of the dollar between 1970 and 1972; Figure 24.3 shows it to have fallen by about 10 percent. Look again at Table 24.2. Did the U.S. trade position improve? What happened to the current account? The reason is simple: In the short run, the quantity of imports and exports tends to be relatively inelastic (not terribly responsive to price changes). Thus, if imports do not decrease by much and exports do not increase by much, yet the foreign exchange received per unit of exports has fallen and the dollars paid for each unit of imports have risen, it is hardly surprising that the value of imports (price × quantity) rises and the value of exports falls. Thus, the immediate impact of a devaluation may well be a worsening of the deficit. This situation gives rise to the J-curve. (See Box 25.1).

Inflation. One direct consequence of the impact of the devaluation on import prices is its causal role in domestic inflation. Import prices are included directly in the consumer price index and, because imports are inputs in the production process, influence other prices as well. The more important imports are to the domestic economy and the greater the devaluation, the greater the inflationary impact will be. For example, with imports constituting 10 percent of the commodity bundle used to weight the price index, a devaluation of 20 percent will mean that the price index rises by $(.10)(.20) = 0.02$, or 2 percent. Obviously, if either component of this product is larger, the increase in the index will be proportionally greater.

Determining exchange rates. A further weakness of the fixed exchange rate system involves the establishment of the exchange rates themselves. It's fine for textbook writers to draw supply and demand curves and state that the point at which the curves intersect is the equilibrium exchange rate. But try doing that for a particular country. Moreover, should anyone successfully compute empirical supply and demand curves, what happens whenever basic supply and demand conditions change? Economists have spent countless hours devising methods to determine equilibrium exchange rate values, but all suffer from fatal flaws. Trial and error is the technique that is most often used, but that is hardly scientific. Surely a better way could be found to set exchange rates.

Policy constraints. Finally, constraints are imposed on economic policy by the fixed exchange rate system. Many experts view this infringement on the freedom of the authorities as a major weakness.

Posit the following situation: an open economy, subject to fixed exchange rates and capital-account flows, that is suffering from excess-demand inflation. The monetary authorities, by selling securities on the open market, decrease bank reserves and, through the money multiplier, cause a multiple contraction in deposits. Neo-Keynesian theory suggests

BOX 25.1 The J-Curve and the Balance on Goods and Services

A devaluation affects the balance on goods and service immediately and continues to exert its impact over a prolonged period. The immediate effect may well be in a direction opposite to the long-run impact, so that the balance on goods and services may worsen initially following a fall in the exchange rate. In the long run, however, the decline in the exchange rate is expected to lead to an improvement in the balance of goods and services. The accompanying table illustrates this phenomenon.

Period	Import volume (million units)	Price per dollar, Mexican pesos	Dollar price per unit	Dollar costs of imports (millions)	Export volume (million units)	Dollar price per unit	Dollar revenue from exports (millions)	Balance on goods and services (millions)
(1)	(2)	(3)	(4)	(5) (= 4 × 2)	(6)	(7)	(8) (= 6 × 7)	(9) (= 8 − 5)
1	100	30p	$1.00	$100	75	$1	$75	$−25
2	100	25p	1.20	120	75	1	75	−45
3	90	25p	1.20	108	80	1	80	−28
4	85	25p	1.20	102	85	1	85	−17
5	75	25p	1.20	90	90	1	90	0
6	70	25p	1.20	84	95	1	95	+11
7	60	25p	1.20	72	100	1	100	+28

In period 1, with the exchange rate at $1 = 30 pesos, the United States imports $100 million in Mexican goods and exports only $75 million, leaving the United States with a deficit in its goods and services balance. As the dollar is devalued to 25 pesos, we move to period 2. The decline of the dollar is immediate, as is evident from columns 3 and 4, but trading patterns lag. Neither Americans nor Mexicans will quickly adjust their buying plans, so that for a while the volume of imports and exports remain as they were prior to the devaluation of the dollar (period 2, columns 2 and 6). The result is a *decline* in the goods and services balance, not the anticipated increase.

In time, however, Americans will cut back on the more expensive Mexican imports, while American exporters will find it more profitable to sell in Mexico. Thus, from period 3 on, import volume declines and export volume rises. The net impact on the balance is to move it steadily upward, as is evident in column 9.

When the final column is plotted against time, the resulting diagram takes on the shape of a lopsided J.

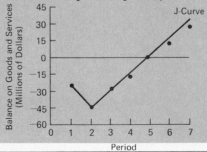

that, in turn, interest rates will rise and consumption and investment spending will fall, slowing aggregate demand and hence inflation. The monetarists might see a more direct effect—less money means lower prices—but the end result will be the same, provided that reserves and the money supply fall.

Need that happen in an open economy? Not necessarily. The higher interest rates may induce capital inflows, as foreigners and domestic holders of foreign currency ship in their funds. Purchases of stocks, bonds, time certificates of deposit, and other liquid and nonliquid assets swell the reserves of the banking system.[6] Thus, the decline in reserves originating with the open market sale is offset by the reserve-increasing impact of capital inflow. In the extreme, no domestic monetary action can be effective, since the slightest rise in interest rates triggers countervailing capital flows. (Work out the reverse to show why an expansionary policy cannot work either.)

Many of these problems disappear under a system of flexible or floating exchange rates. To this we now turn.

☐ Flexible Exchange Rates and Monetary Policy

Market-determined exchange rates do not suffer from the disadvantages of a fixed exchange rate system. No one has to know what the equilibrium rate is; at any given moment the functioning of the market ensures that an exchange rate at which international transactions take place exists. No one need be concerned about how to set the exchange rate when supply or demand shifts; the market does the job. No nation needs to hold foreign exchange reserves; in the absence of deficits, they are extraneous. (In terms of Figures 24.1 and 24.2, exchange rates are always at the intersection of the supply and demand curves; deficits or surpluses can occur only when the exchange rate is pegged at a rate other than the equilibrium one.)

The trade-off between payments balance and domestic stability also disappears. Obviously, if there's never a deficit or a surplus, domestic stability is the only relevant concern. Monetary policy regains its independence; it can be directed toward domestic goals and need be less concerned about capital offsets.

This last statement requires some elaboration. Take the situation outlined on page 637—an open economy undergoing inflation—but assume flexible exchange rates rather than fixed ones. The central bank sells securities on the open market, reducing bank reserves and driving interest rates up as it aims to slow down domestic expansion. Foreign

---

[6]When a British investor buys a Treasury bill from a U.S. bill dealer, the foreign currency leaving England ultimately will become domestic currency added to the account of the dealer at a domestic American bank. In the process the central bank in the selling country will have acquired foreign currency but will have credited the seller's bank with the domestic currency equivalent on the bank's *reserve* account.

capital begins to flow in response to the new, higher interest rates. But this increased demand for domestic money raises the exchange rate, which increases the cost of selling foreign money for domestic money and makes the higher interest rates less attractive. The capital inflow is choked off. Consequently, bank reserves are not replaced, and the tight-money policy succeeds.[7]

Disadvantages of flexible exchange rates

Floating rates, however, are not an unmixed blessing. Perhaps the most serious flaw lies in the complexity that floating adds to international transactions. Since all foreign transactions involve an exchange rate risk, someone may get stuck holding or having to be paid in a currency whose value has declined. In the postwar fixed exchange rate system, fluctuations were kept within narrow ranges—1 percent or less of their fixed value—by the intervention of the exchange rate authorities. True, devaluations did occur, but for the most part these happened infrequently. Moreover, while the exact timing of a devaluation was never known, it could be foreseen by market participants. With flexible exchange rates, instability is more prevalent, and therefore the risk of losing through a decline in the exchange rate is greater. To be sure, one can hedge in forward markets (see Box 25.2), but this form of insurance involves an added expense. In short, because the risk is greater, the costs are greater.

BOX 25.2 The Spot and Forward Foreign Exchange Markets

Every day the financial pages carry foreign-exchange values—yesterday's price of the dollar and many other currencies. Some of the prices are "spot" prices—how much a dollar traded for yesterday in immediately available British pounds. Thus, on Monday, March 3, 1980, the spot price of the pound was $2.2360. Future prices are also listed. Thus, someone who yesterday wanted to buy pounds three months from now could have acquired a forward contract requiring that $2.2257 per £ be paid upon delivery three months hence.

Prices in both the spot and the forward market are market determined. The market consists of two broad groups of individuals: speculators and hedgers. The former are the gamblers; the latter are in the market basically to protect themselves against foreign exchange risks.

Consider a U.S. importer who must pay £100,000 due three months from now. The importer may acquire sterling now (spot) and pay $223,600 at the spot price noted earlier. Of course, the firm would be wise to keep the pounds in its English bank account and earn interest for three months. Alternatively, the importer can hold the $223,600 in an interest-paying U.S. bank account for three months and buy pounds just before the debt

---

[7]Do not read this as a contrast in black and white, namely, failure under a fixed system and success under a flexible one. It is more correctly viewed as greater success for monetary policy under a flexible system.

comes due. You'll have noticed the risk—what happens if the pound becomes more expensive during those three months? This is where hedging via the forward market comes in. The importer can purchase £100,000 forward, paying the price of $222,570. Then, no matter what happens to the spot price three months hence, the importer is protected. Whether the pound's price rises or falls, the importer takes the pounds as per the contract. Of course, if the pound's price falls, the firm has lost the opportunity to profit from the decline; it could have bought the £100,000 for fewer dollars. But the reverse could also have happened. Essentially, the hedger is trading off security against exchange rate profit.

The speculator is on the other side of the trade. A speculator who believes that the price will decline will sell a forward contract short, that is, will promise to deliver pounds three months from now even though he or she owns no pounds today. Three months pass; if the speculator is right and the price of the pound has declined, spot pounds will be purchased for less than the contracted sales price. The difference constitutes the speculator's profit. Of course, if the price rises the result could be disaster; the speculator will have to pay the higher spot price in order to honor the forward contract.

Because the margin on forward contracts is low, a small investment will support a large speculative position. With a highly leveraged stance, small shifts in exchange rates can lead to spectacular profit rates but also to abysmal losses.

With a 3.5 percent margin, $1,000 can buy a futures contract worth $28,571.43 (= £12,837.05 at the forward rate of $2.2257). If in three months the spot rate falls 10¢ below the contracted rate, so that the speculator can buy pounds at $2.1257, the profit on the $1,000 investment will be $1,283.71—over 100 percent. But if the rate rises by 10¢ the loss will also be over 100 percent; the entire investment will have been dissipated by a 4½ percent change in the exchange rate. Foreign-exchange speculation is not for the fainthearted.

A second problem concerns destablilizing speculation. If traders gang up on a currency (an explicit or implicit conspiracy to drive down, say, the dollar), then, in the absence of official intervention, they can often achieve their goals. (Cornering a market in a particular stock or group of stocks was not unknown in the 1920s and was one reason that the Securities and Exchange Act was passed in 1933. In *Business Adventures*[8] John Brooks has included a marvelous account of one such attempt, "The Last Great Corner.") Thus, an exchange rate may not fluctuate because of basic forces of supply and demand, but because of profit-directed, speculative pressure.

A pragmatic compromise has been reached by the major central bankers of the world, one that permits exchange rates to find their own

---

[8]New York: Weybright and Talley, 1969.

levels but also accepts limited intervention. Under managed floating, when the authorities suspect that the rates are way out of line they step in to support the exchange rate.

☐ The Questions Answered

This long preamble should enable you to comprehend the greater complexity of the monetary aspects of an open economy. It also sets the stage for answering the questions posed at the beginning of the chapter.

1. *What impact does a lower exchange rate have on the economy?* You should now understand that a lower exchange rate provides opportunities in both the product and capital markets. A lower price for the dollar in terms of foreign currency means lower prices for American goods, and encourages exports. This implies greater domestic demand and, depending on the state of the economy, increased production, employment, and prices. Similarly, the lower dollar price discourages imports, again expanding domestic demand. These influences will be supplemented by financial flows; bank reserves will increase, and this, too, will have an expansionary effect. In the same vein, the lower exchange rate may increase the profitability of financial investment in the domestic currency, since it takes less foreign currency to buy dollar assets and, conversely, more dollars to purchase foreign assets. This also reinforces the expansionary direction of the economy.

However, these effects will not occur immediately. A deterioration in the trade balance may lead to a short-run contraction and an outflow of money. Both real and capital flows may exacerbate the current situation. Instead of reversing the falling trend, the initial impact may well be an intensification of the existing movement, the J-curve effect.

In the long run, however, exports pick up, imports fall, and the capital flow reverses itself. Thus, most economists feel that the decline in the international value of the dollar after 1970 increased the competitiveness of U.S. goods and services and induced additional investment in the United States throughout the decade.

Of course, whether the reduced exchange rate helped or hindered the economy depends on whether additional aggregate demand and more money was desired or not. The results here are not conclusive insofar as the experience of the United States is concerned, since much hinges on the speed of the reaction to the lower exchange rate. If the lags are relatively brief, the declining dollar gave a needed boost to the American economy during the 1974–1975 recession; it made purchases here more attractive and thus helped stimulate domestic demand. But during 1973–1974, as the rate of inflation moved into the double-digit zone, the same declining dollar was disruptive; it added fuel to the inflationary fire. Similarly, the dollar's decline between 1977 and 1979 was not helpful— again, the foreign sector's impact intensified rather than relieved the ongoing inflation.

2. *What role did monetary policy play in causing or stemming the decline of the dollar?* Our early theoretical survey suggests that it would be useful to examine not only monetary actions since 1971 but also those undertaken during earlier periods, when the dollar was the linchpin of the fixed exchange rate system.

Recall that under fixed exchange rates monetary actions affect both the international sector and the domestic economy through their influence on interest rates and bank reserves. An effective tight-money policy— leading to reduced banking system reserves and higher interest rates— reduces income and slows price increases. The dual outcome is a slowing of the domestic economy and a deficit-reducing impact on the balance of payments. However, as you are now well aware, when dilemmas occur, tight-money policies will not always be implemented.

The decade of the 1960s as described in Chapter 23 is divided into two subperiods: 1961–1965 and 1966–1969. The early period was one of noninflationary growth as the economy recovered from the 1960–1961 recession. Conventional domestic monetary policy argued against restraint. Yet the balance on current and long-term capital account was disturbingly negative, and implied tightness as a policy response. A way out of the dilemma had to be found.

A series of measures were instituted, both on the executive–legislative side and by the central bank. In 1961 President Kennedy announced a program designed to strengthen the American payments position, including reduction of the duty-free limit on imports by returning American tourists, a plan for promoting American exports, and perhaps most important, a decision to issue special high-interest bonds available only to foreign monetary authorities. These bonds, of course, were designed to induce foreign central bankers to maintain their dollar balances in the United States. In 1963 Congress, at President Johnson's request, imposed an interest equalization tax (IET). The IET was levied on American purchasers of foreign securities; it made foreign stocks and bonds more expensive and hence less attractive, and thus would slow the capital outflow. Further control measures followed in 1965 and 1968. The "voluntary" foreign credit restraint (VFCR) program on bank loans abroad was imposed in the former year and on corporate direct investment in the latter. The two best-known Federal Reserve actions were Operation Twist and implementation of the "swap network."

Operation Twist was an ingenious attempt to resolve the dilemma facing Federal Reserve decision makers in the early period. The underlying rationale was as follows: Domestic investment is (thought to be) dependent on the long-term rate of interest, while speculative foreign flows depend on short-term interest rates. Why, then, not keep short-term interest rates high, inducing foreign funds to remain in the United States, and simultaneously maintain low long-term interest rates, thereby stimulating domestic investment? Ingenious, yes, but unfortunately not effective. Operation Twist was abandoned after a short time.

The more lasting reform was the establishment of central bank

Operation Twist was designed to reshape the term structure of interest rates, raising short-term rates while reducing long-term rates.

A **swap** involves exchanges of
domestic money by central
banks.

cooperation on an international basis via the **swap** network. Again, the
fundamental idea was simple. While any central bank can create its own
domestic currency, no central bank can create foreign currency. Why not
trade domestic currency created by one central bank for domestic
currency created by another? Thus, the Federal Reserve could create
dollars and trade those dollars for pounds or marks, the latter currencies
being created by the Bank of England or the Deutsche Bundesbank.
When the Federal Reserve acquired marks, it was obtaining foreign
currency, as was the Bundesbank when it received dollars. Now either
country could use these foreign currencies to defend its position.

And so it was during the 1960s. A number of international crises
involving the pound and the franc, as well as lesser currencies, were
relieved by the use of swaps. The Federal Reserve, too, was able to sell
foreign exchange in order to protect the dollar. Downward pressure on
the dollar, as speculators and others sold dollars to buy foreign currencies, was offset by Federal Reserve purchases of these dollars by
concomitant sales of currencies acquired through swaps.

In short, the major effort of the U.S. monetary authorities was to isolate
the domestic sector from the foreign sector. Monetary actions were taken
to stimulate the domestic economy in the early 1960s, but monetary
policy turned restrictive as inflation took over. The growing seriousness of
the deficit in the balance of payments was not treated by classical
monetary measures in the early period. Instead of acting to reduce the
deficit, U.S. policy makers simply lived with it, borrowing internationally
to enable the United States to preserve the dollar's value. By the end of
the 1960s antiinflationary domestic policy measures and deficit-closing
actions were identical, so the dilemma was resolved.

Unfortunately, the buildup of dollar debts, already commented on in
the last chapter, carried the seeds of its own destruction. The fixed
exchange rate regime finally gave way in the early 1970s.

U.S. monetary policy since 1971 again has paid heed mostly to the
domestic arena. In the world of floating exchange rates, the attitude of
both Federal Reserve and U.S. Treasury officials has been primarily one
of benign neglect. They have adopted the creed of the exponents of
floating exchange rates—let the market determine the true exchange
rate. Only infrequently has the Federal Reserve intervened to protect the
dollar against obvious speculative threats.

With floating exchange rates came the dismantling of the no-longer-
needed controls over credit flows. The IET was abandoned, as was the
VCFR. The swap network remains, however.

The answer to question 2 is that monetary policy was aimed at
strengthening the dollar and stemming its decline. This was especially
true after 1965, when the monetary authorities' antiinflationary stance
and the consequent rise in interest rates made the dollar more attractive
to foreigners.

3. *Does a floating exchange rate system impose any special problems or*

offer any unusual opportunities for control of the domestic economy by monetary policy? In one sense monetary policy is an ineffective tool for some countries operating in a fixed exchange rate system. The theoretical basis of this argument is that, in a world of unregulated capital flows, any domestic policy that, say, drives interest rates up will induce a capital inflow, leading to an increase in bank reserves and the money supply. The initial monetary action is nullified by this foreign thrust.

A fall in the exchange rate makes a tight-money policy even more difficult to implement, for foreign purchasers of the domestic currency are able to buy it for fewer units of their own money. (This assumes that foreign buyers of domestic money do not expect the exchange rate to fall further. Otherwise, they'd wait to take advantage of the still-lower future price.) Thus, they will be even more eager to send money into the country whose exchange rate has declined.

This analysis is correct for a non-reserve-currency country. It must be modified for the United States, primarily because foreign official institutions and private organizations hold large amounts of their reserves in dollar-denominated assets. Thus, the following scenario can emerge: The Federal Reserve acts to tighten money and raise interest rates in the United States. Brazilians, attracted by the favorable rates, purchase dollars from the central bank of Brazil for their cruzeiros, and send the dollars to New York City, where they acquire Treasury bills from U.S. bill dealers. The bill dealers take their dollar receipts and deposit them in their commercial bank accounts, whereupon they become new reserves for the recipient bank. Do these reserves, however, constitute additions to the reserves of the banking system as a whole? The answer to this question hinges on the source of the dollars obtained by the Brazilian central bank to pay its nationals in exchange for the cruzeiros. It's quite likely that the central bank sold some of its holdings of U.S. Treasury bills, assets that were a segment of Brazil's foreign-exchange reserves. The sale of those Treasury bills in New York removed dollars from the United States, thereby reducing U.S. reserves. If you consider the entire transaction—the Treasury bill/cruziero exchange by the central bank and the cruziero/Treasury bill exchange by the Brazilian nationals—you must conclude that the net impact on the U.S. banking system's domestic reserves was zero. In effect, the Brazilian central bank sold its own U.S. Treasury bills to its Brazilian citizens without any involvement of the American banking system. (It must be emphasized, however, that this offset occurs only because the dollars and dollar securities are held by foreign central banks as reserves and are used to meet their residents' needs for foreign currency.)

Because of this consideration, the Federal Reserve authorities need be less concerned than most central bankers about foreign flows offsetting its policy actions when exchange rates are fixed. This is even more true in a world of floating exchange rates. In this instance movements of the exchange rate aid the central bank in achieving its goals. For countries other than those that supply international reserve currencies, clearly flows of foreign funds can be upsetting. Their domestic monetary policies can be conducted more effectively under a flexible exchange rate regime.

Does all this mean that the Federal Reserve can remain aloof from the consequences of a declining exchange rate? It would seem not, primarily because of the short-run J-curve impact of the fall. The falling value of the dollar raises the costs of imports and thus drives prices upward. The Federal Reserve is once again faced with a dilemma, a Phillips curve problem. In its simplest terms, the rise in import prices shifts the Phillips curve upward; the existing unemployment rate is now consistent with a higher, import-induced rate of inflation. (See Figure 25.4.) The monetary authorities can restore the old inflation rate by means of a restrictive policy, but only by increasing the unemployment rate beyond its present level, as the figure indicates. Alternatively, they can accept the prevailing unemployment rate, but then they must be resigned to the higher inflation rate, at least in the short run.

The fall in the dollar's external value between 1977 and 1979 was at least partially responsible for the higher rate of inflation in the United States.[9] The Federal Reserve has been criticized for not combating the inflation with sufficient vigor and for ignoring, for the most part, the causal role of the dollar. The monetary authorities have responded that they cannot singlehandedly tackle all of the economy's macroeconomic problems. Moreover, while the short-run consequences of a falling exchange rate are inflationary, the longer-run consequences are beneficial. The monetary authorities must not be shortsighted.

The response to the final question concerning the role of monetary authorities in a floating exchange rate regime can now be summarized. New opportunities are provided, but new problems arise. Floating exchange rates aid the authorities in bringing their monetary instruments to bear on the domestic economy. When monetary policy is tightened and interest rates rise, foreign funds are attracted to the country, posing a threat to the policy of monetary constraint. Yet this very demand for domestic currency by foreigners raises the exchange rate. The rise in the exchange rate increases the cost of foreign-exchange conversion, which reduces the currency inflow and thus limits the impact on domestic money creation. On the other hand, the greater volatility of exchange rates under a floating exchange rate system poses new problems. A decline in the exchange rate raises import prices, with short-run inflationary implications. This may intensify the Phillips curve dilemma. Conversely, a rise in the exchange rate may exert a deflationary impact on an economy that needs to be defended against further deflation.

---

[9]Prakken estimated that the 12 percent decline in the value of the dollar between 1977 and 1978 pushed up consumer prices by 1.7 to 2.4 percent over a two- to three-year interval. See Joel L. Prakken, "The Exchange Rate and Domestic Inflation," Federal Reserve Bank of New York, *Quarterly Review* (Summer 1979): 49–55.

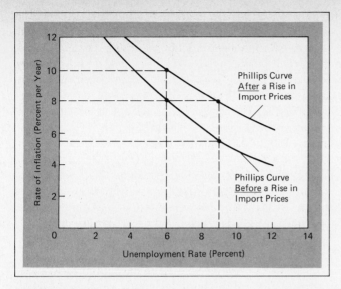

FIGURE 25.4 The impact of a rise in import prices on the Phillips curve.

☐ Summary

When exchange rates are fixed, both the monetary and real effects of a payments surplus or deficit reinforce each other. A deficit not only diverts production and employment from the domestic economy to foreign producers but also is accompanied by an outflow of funds. This outflow—indeed, any outflow that is not offset—reduces bank reserves and the supply of money, and has a contractionary impact on the domestic economy. Although monetary tightening may be desirable when the economy is overheated, it could prove unfortunate should fund outflows occur during a recession.

Persistant deficits can occur under a system of fixed exchange rates when the fixed rate maintained by the authorities is not the equilibrium rate. Equilibrium can be restored in a number of ways: (1) permitting the domestic economy to contract; (2) using monetary and/or fiscal instruments to force the economy to contract (in both of these instances the authorities attempt to shift the supply or demand curves to justify the original exchange rate); (3) devaluing the currency, which changes the fixed rate to a lower value in terms of foreign exchange; and (4) imposing exchange controls. However, each alternative suffers from its own flaws, which basically stem from the major weaknesses of the fixed exchange rate system. These encompass (1) the likelihood of having to choose between payments balance and domestic stability; (2) the inelastic short-run responses to exchange rate adjustments (the J-curve); (3)

devaluation-caused inflation; (4) the difficulty of finding the proper exchange rate, especially in a dynamically evolving world economy; and (5) the constraint imposed on monetary policy by foreign flows triggered by the policy actions themselves.

Flexible exchange rates resolve most of these disadvantages. This is especially meaningful for the conduct of monetary policy. Tight money, for example, may induce inflows of foreign funds, but this will lead to higher exchange rates. On the other hand, under a floating exchange rate system exchange rates are more volatile and subject to bursts of speculation.

A lower exchange rate does encourage exports and foreign investment, and discourage imports and domestic investment abroad. Thus, the lower value of the dollar on international markets since 1971 has increased the competitiveness of American goods abroad. However, in times of strong domestic demand (e.g., 1977–1979) this increased foreign demand may strengthen an already inflation-prone economy.

Monetary policy actions to preserve the dollar during the early 1960s consisted of Operation Twist and the implementation of a swap network among the major central banks. As inflation intensified, a policy of tight money was consistent with domestic and international policy objectives. These policies proved inadequate, and after floating was introduced the Federal Reserve was able to concentrate more heavily on domestic issues, intervening only infrequently in the foreign-exchange market. However, exchange rate fluctuations make the Federal Reserve's domestic problems more difficult in one respect: A falling exchange rate raises domestic prices and contributes to inflation. Floating exchange rates have not solved all monetary problems.

☐ Questions and Exercises

1. The Japanese yen appreciated by 22 percent between December 1979 and June 1981.
   a. Suggest some reasons that might explain this substantial increase.
   b. What impact could this appreciation have had on the Japanese economy?
   c. Japan's inflation rate rose during 1980. Did the rise in the yen's value aid or hinder the Japanese central bank in its pursuit of price stability?
2. Under the gold standard, each nation fixed the value of its currency in terms of gold and agreed to maintain that value.
   a. What kind of monetary policy was needed to preserve the currency's international value in each of two nations if gold was continually flowing out of one country and into the other?
   b. What impact would these monetary policies have had on the economy of each nation?
3. Examine Table 24.1 (p. 614) and discuss the impact of international transactions on U.S. bank reserves.

a. How would the Federal Reserve have reacted if it wished to sterilize this flow?

b. Would the monetary authorities of, say, Belgium have acted differently had they wanted to sterilize a similar flow?

4. The U.S. dollar rose sharply (in terms of its international value) in 1981. In the same year interest rates reached historic highs. Is this relationship fortuitous, or can you advance an economic rationale for it?

5. How will differing rates of inflation in two countries affect the exchange rate and/or the balance of payments between them under a regime of (a) fixed exchange rates and (b) flexible exchange rates?

☐ For Further Study

The advantages of freely floating exchange rates are convincingly argued in M. Friedman, "The Case for Flexible Rates," which is reprinted in his *Essays in Positive Economics* (Chicago: University of Chicago Press, 1953). The freedom given to domestic monetary policies by floating rates in recent years is discussed in the context of West Germany in L. O. Laney, "More Flexible Exchange Rates: Have They Insulated National Monetary Policies?" Federal Reserve Bank of Dallas, *Voice*, February 1980. A more theoretical discussion, covering both monetary and fiscal policies, is available in Robert A. Mundell, *International Economics* (New York: Macmillan, 1968), chaps. 11, 14–18, and, in slightly expanded form, in Bo Södersten, *International Economics* (New York: St. Martin's Press, 1980), chaps. 26–28.

Marina V. N. Whitman, "Global Monetarism and the Monetary Approach to the Balance of Payments," *Brookings Papers in Economic Activity*, 3 (1975), presents the monetarist interpretation of balance-of-payments deficits, while M. Mussa, "The Exchange Rate, the Balance of Payments, and Monetary and Fiscal Policy Under a Regime of Controlled Floating," in J. A. Frenkel and H. G. Johnson (eds.), *The Economics of Exchange Rates* (Reading, Mass.: Addison-Wesley, 1978), demonstrates the monetarist version of exchange rate determination. Rudiger Dornbusch criticizes the monetary approach in "Monetary Policy Under Exchange-Rate Flexibility," in Federal Reserve Bank of Boston, *Managed Exchange-Rate Flexibility: The Recent Experience* (Boston, 1978), but this is not an easy article to read. A work that is policy oriented but rather technical is Ralph C. Bryant, *Money and Monetary Policy in Interdependent Nations* (Washington, D.C.: Brookings, 1980).

The letter *n* after a page number indicates that the reference is in a footnote. Page references to illustrations are printed in **boldface** type.